PRODUCTION AND
OPERATIONS MANAGEMENT
A life cycle approach

The Irwin Series in
Quantitative Analysis for Business
Consulting Editor ROBERT B. FETTER *Yale University*

Richard B. Chase

Nicholas J. Aquilano

Both of the University of Arizona

Production and operations management

A LIFE CYCLE APPROACH

THIRD EDITION

1981

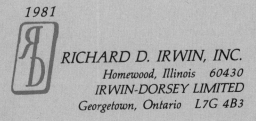

RICHARD D. IRWIN, INC.
Homewood, Illinois 60430
IRWIN-DORSEY LIMITED
Georgetown, Ontario L7G 4B3

ISBN 0-256-02525-8
Library of Congress Catalog Card No. 80–85123

Printed in the United States of America

1 2 3 4 5 6 7 8 9 0 H 8 7 6 5 4 3 2 1

To HARRIET and NINA

PREFACE

This book is designed to satisfy the American Assembly of Collegiate Schools of Business requirement that member schools provide production/operations management in their undergraduate and graduate core. It is also designed with the objective of providing the most up-to-date, teachable, and interesting book in the field.

The following material presented in this edition is not available in any other single introductory text in production and operations management:

CPM/MRP model for project management.

Contact approach to service operations.

Sandman system for job shop scheduling.

Japanese approach to quality control and productivity improvement.

Focused forecasting.

Learning curves in manufacturing strategy.

In-depth treatment of service level calculations for inventory management.

Production audits for manufacturing and service firms.

This edition also retains important subjects from the previous edition which are not found in other texts (or which we introduced):

The life cycle approach which provides a logical structure for the field.

Plant startup, steady state, and termination discussions.

Technical notes (formerly termed supplements) which provide in-depth coverage of quantitative topics at appropriate points in the text.

Treatment of COPICS and IMPACT computer systems for inventory control; and excerpts from packaged programs for scheduling, line balancing, and maintenance.

Further, we have added entire chapters on capacity planning and forecasting, a large number of new problems and a few carefully chosen case studies.

Finally, another first for the field, a student workbook (prepared by Professor Kalyan Singhal) is available to accompany the text.

ACKNOWLEDGMENTS

We would like to express our thanks to the following individuals who provided reviews at various stages of this revision: Robert B. Fetter, Yale University; Carter Franklin, III, Houston Baptist University; Frank L. Kaufman, California State University, Sacramento; Lee Krajewski, Ohio State University; Hugh V. Leach, Washburn University; John R. Matthews, University of Wisconsin; Brooke Saladin, University of Georgia; Ted Stafford, University of South Carolina.

We are also greatly indebted to our typist, Theresa Saunders, whose dedication to the project and cheerful attitude made our work much easier. Last, but certainly not least, we would like to thank our families who for the third time let the life cycle of the book disrupt theirs.

Richard B. Chase
Nicholas J. Aquilano

CONTENTS

xi

SECTION THREE   STARTUP OF THE SYSTEM

SECTION FOUR   THE SYSTEM IN STEADY STATE

SECTION FIVE   TERMINATION OF THE SYSTEM

APPENDIXES

INDEXES

PRODUCTION AND
OPERATIONS MANAGEMENT
A life cycle approach

Chapter 1

INTRODUCTION

It has been said that the objective of a business is "to make a product which costs a dime, sells for a dollar, and is habit-forming." If we analyze this statement, we obtain a quick insight into the two essential functions of any company—production and marketing. The marketing function deals with the selection of a perhaps "habit-forming" product and its "dollar" selling price; production deals with the creation of that product at the cost of "a dime." The purpose of this book is to present the concepts and techniques by which modern production and operations management goes about achieving this goal in manufacturing and service organizations.

More specifically, the objectives of this book are: (1) to explain how one manages the production function; (2) to introduce to the reader some standard tools and techniques used by production (or operations) managers; (3) to develop an appreciation for the interaction of this management activity with other management systems within the organization; and (4) to develop an understanding of the field as a totality. With respect to the last objective, we intend to show that production/operations management is not just a loosely knit aggregation of tools but rather a *synthesis* of concepts and techniques which relate directly to, and enhance the management of, productive systems. This point is important because operations management, like many other fields, is in a state of change which in some instances generates some confusion as to the boundaries and content of the subject matter. One of the sources of confusion is the name of the field itself. Because the field has its origins in the factory environment, the term *production management* has been, and still is, widely used to denote it.

Within the past few years, however, it has become more apparent that the value of production management concepts and techniques extends far beyond the shop floor—that it encompasses virtually all types of productive enterprises: hence the need for a broader and more appropriate title, such as *operations management,* to describe the discipline—a fact that has been recognized by a number of writers and practitioners. Nevertheless, we feel that at this time in the development of the subject, the transitional term *production and operations management* most readily conveys the nature of the material to the uninitiated reader. This term, therefore, is used in the title of this book. However, for ease of presentation, *operations management, production management,* and *production and operations management* will be used interchangeably throughout the text.

OPERATIONS MANAGEMENT DEFINED

Operations management may be defined as *the performance of the managerial activities entailed in selecting, designing, operating, controlling, and updating productive systems.* These activities are in turn defined as follows.

Selecting: the strategic decision of choosing the process by which some good or service is to be made or performed. In a steel mill producing railway wheels, the primary process decision might be whether the wheels will be forged or cast; in a restaurant, the decision might be between cafeteria or table service.

Designing: the tactical decisions involved in the creation of methods of carrying out a productive operation. In both the steel mill and the restaurant, tactical decisions would be made with regard to the form and content of jobs to be performed and to the type of service and control activities needed to assure smooth operation.

Operating: the decisions of planning long-term output levels in the light of forecast demand and the short-term decisions of scheduling jobs and allocating workers. In the railway wheel factory, this activity would range from forecasting the growth in rail cars for the next five years to determining which order to process first out of the array of orders on hand. In the cafeteria-style restaurant, this activity would range from monitoring community growth and competition to determine whether a new culinary specialty should be introduced to positioning busboys at various stations in the dining area.

Controlling: the procedures involved in taking corrective action as the product or service is created. In the steel company, control activities would range from monitoring and adjusting the metallurgical characteristics of heats of steel to the expediting of orders to meet delivery deadlines. In the restaurant, control would range from the inspection of incoming food and linen to ensuring speed and hospitality on the part of its staff and waiters.

Updating: the implementation of major revisions of the productive system in the light of changes in demand, organizational goals, technology, and

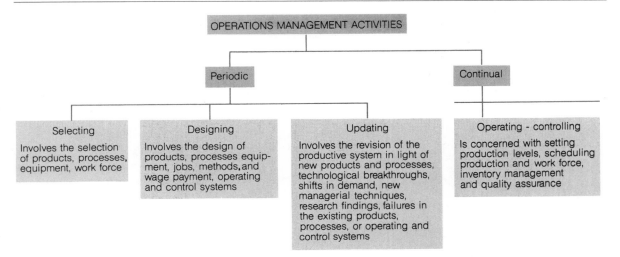

EXHIBIT 1.1
Organization of operations management activities

management. In the steel company, updating might take the form of installing new capital equipment to produce a new alloy or the introduction of a computer-based production control system. In the restaurant, updating might range from the addition of car-service facilities to offering complete home-service catering.

These five activities can be further differentiated on the basis of the relative frequency of their occurrence, and selecting, designing, and updating activities in general occur far less frequently than operating and controlling activities. Hence, we will refer to the former as *periodic* and to the latter as *continual.* This distinction is useful because it provides an insight into the rationale for both the production literature and for the practitioners' giving "subsystem" status to some activities and not to others. That is, periodic activities, while they may be performed according to a specific set of procedures, by their very nature do not present the daily time-pressure problems of information and action inherent in the continual activities. Partly for this reason, activities such as quality assurance, production planning, and output scheduling are generally viewed and constructed as "systems"[1] while such activities as product design, process selection, and job design are not. A listing of some of the major operations management activities following the periodic-continual dichotomy is presented in Exhibit 1.1.

THE PRODUCTION FUNCTION AND ITS ENVIRONMENT

In most organizations, production is an internal function which is buffered from the external environment by other organizational functions.

---

[1] "System" is used here to denote an ongoing series of interrelated activities or processes as distinct from one-shot or infrequent occurrences.

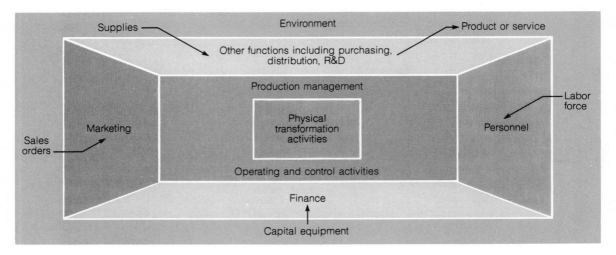

The diagram shows: Environment containing — Supplies, Product or service, Other functions including purchasing, distribution, R&D, Production management, Physical transformation activities, Operating and control activities, Marketing, Sales orders, Personnel, Labor force, Finance, Capital equipment.

EXHIBIT 1.2
Relationship between production function, other organization functions, and the environment

Consider the relationship between the production and other organization functions and the environment shown in Exhibit 1.2. Orders are received by the sales department, which is an arm of the marketing function; supplies and raw materials are obtained through the purchasing function; capital for equipment purchases comes from the finance function; the labor force is obtained through the personnel function; and the product is delivered by the distribution function. Thus while there may be a good deal of interaction between the firm and its environment, the production function is rarely involved in it directly:

Buffering the production function from direct environmental influence is desirable for several reasons:

1. Interaction with environmental elements (e.g., customers and salesmen on the production floor) can be a disturbing influence on the transformation process.
2. The technological transformation process is often more efficient than the processes required in obtaining inputs and disposing of finished goods.
3. In certain technologies (for example, assembly lines, petroleum), maximum productivity can be achieved only by operating as if the market could absorb all of the product being manufactured and at a continuous rate. This means that the transformation process must shift at least some of the input and output activities to other parts of the firm.
4. The managerial skills required for successful operation of the transformation process are often different from those required for successful operation of the boundary systems, for example, marketing and personnel.

Of course not all production functions are sealed off from their environment, nor do all those that are designed to be sealed off have impermeable boundaries. Custom-product industries, which must meet unique product specifications, often have customers who interact with production function personnel, and service organizations such as fire and police departments must carry out their production functions *in* the environment. Nevertheless, isolation of the technical core (or the transformation process) is the rule in manufacturing and process industries.

Formal organization of the production function

Formal organization of the production function involves placing the aforementioned operations management activities into departments and assigning the authority and responsibility for their performance to a manager or supervisor. Not surprisingly, the most direct translation of a production activity to a functional department is evidenced in manufacturing organizations where such specific activities as quality control, production control, product design, and process selection are typically given departmental status. And though the locus of production activities is more difficult to determine when we consider nonmanufacturing installations, these activities are performed in most organizations; and common sense usually, though not always, is sufficient to "crack the code" of a given organization chart, allowing us to discern just where they are performed.

We have identified the location of "production" activities in four different types of organizations in Exhibit 1.3.[2] Aside from differences in terminology, the nonmanufacturing organizations depicted in Charts a, b, and d also differ from the manufacturing example in that certain production activities are scattered throughout the organization's structure. This does not mean that the activity is any less a production one but only that it is deemed best performed under the aegis of a different department.

Jobs related to the production function

Exhibit 1.4 provides a listing of some line and staff jobs which are frequently viewed as relating to the production function. The focus on materials in manufacturing gives rise to more staff specializations under this manufacturing heading than for services.

For the reader contemplating a career in operations management (OM), the typical entry level jobs are as a foreman trainee, an "assistant to plant manager" or "materials management specialist I."

In terms of how well people in production and operations management fare financially, a survey of roughly 7,000 MBA's in 1978 indicates that they do quite well indeed. In the study, conducted by *MBA Magazine,* it was noted that "A major in production/manufacturing was the most lucrative." (Exhibit 1.5 provides the data.) While we have no similar survey data for undergraduate majors, a check of salaries (especially after a few years of experience) will show that compensation levels are more than competitive with other business disciplines.

---

[2] For examples of operations management responsibilities in hospitals and universities, see Russell Morey, "Operations Management in Selected Nonmanufacturing Organizations," *Academy of Management Journal,* vol. 19, no. 1 (March 1976), pp. 120–24.

EXHIBIT 1.3
Sample organization charts of four diverse firms

Chart (a) : Airline

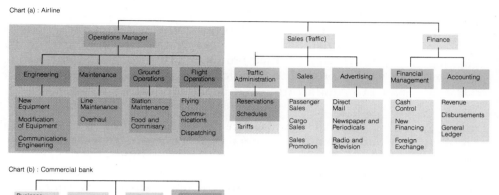

Operations Manager | Sales (Traffic) | Finance

- Engineering
  - New Equipment
  - Modification of Equipment
  - Communications Engineering
- Maintenance
  - Line Maintenance
  - Overhaul
- Ground Operations
  - Station Maintenance
  - Food and Commisary
- Flight Operations
  - Flying
  - Communications
  - Dispatching
- Traffic Administration
  - Reservations
  - Schedules
  - Tariffs
- Sales
  - Passenger Sales
  - Cargo Sales
  - Sales Promotion
- Advertising
  - Direct Mail
  - Newspaper and Periodicals
  - Radio and Television
- Financial Management
  - Cash Control
  - New Financing
  - Foreign Exchange
- Accounting
  - Revenue
  - Disbursements
  - General Ledger

Chart (b) : Commercial bank

- Business Development
  - Loans
    - Commercial
    - Industrial
    - Financial
    - Personal
  - Investments
    - Securites
    - Real Estate
    - Trusts
- Legal
- Personnel
  - Bank Operations Manager
    - Tellers
    - Check Clearing
    - Collections
    - Transaction Records
  - Building Operations
    - Vault
    - Guards
    - Maintenance
    - Cafeteria
- Auditor*

Chart (c) : Manufacturing firm

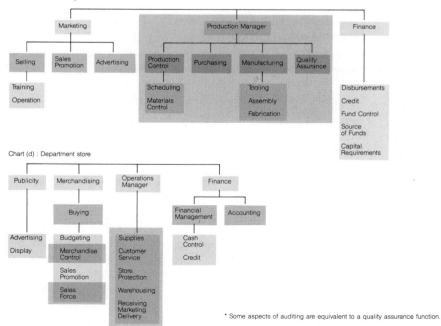

- Marketing
  - Selling
    - Training
    - Operation
  - Sales Promotion
  - Advertising
- Production Manager
  - Production Control
    - Scheduling
    - Materials Control
  - Purchasing
  - Manufacturing
    - Tooling
    - Assembly
    - Fabrication
  - Quality Assurance
- Finance
  - Disbursements
  - Credit
  - Fund Control
  - Source of Funds
  - Capital Requirements

Chart (d) : Department store

- Publicity
  - Advertising
  - Display
- Merchandising
  - Buying
    - Budgeting
    - Merchandise Control
    - Sales Promotion
    - Sales Force
- Operations Manager
  - Supplies
  - Customer Service
  - Store Protection
  - Warehousing
  - Receiving Marketing Delivery
- Finance
  - Financial Management
    - Cash Control
    - Credit
  - Accounting

* Some aspects of auditing are equivalent to a quality assurance function.

* Some aspects of auditing are equivalent to a quality assurance function.

EXHIBIT 1.4
Line and staff jobs in production/ operations management (POM)

Organizational level	Manufacturing	Services
Upper	Vice president of manufacturing	Vice president of operations (airline)
	Regional manager of manu- facturing	Chief administrator (hospital)
Middle	Plant manager	Store manager (department store)
	Department supervisor	Branch manager (bank)
Lower	Foreman	Department supervisor (insurance company)
	Crew chief	Assistant manager (hotel)
Staff	Production controller	Systems and procedures analyst
	Materials manager	Purchasing agent
	Quality controller	Inspector
	Purchasing agent	Dietician (hospital)
	Time study analyst	
	Maintenance manager	
	Process engineer	

EXHIBIT 1.5
Compensation of MBA's by individual variables

Variable and category	Number	Mean	Standard deviation	Median	First quartile	Third quartile
MBA major						
Accounting/auditing	442	$27,163	$18,721	$23,500	$19,200	$29,750
Behavioral science/In- dustrial relations/ Personnel	268	$31,672	$52,099	$25,100	$20,052	$32,015
Finance	1,469	$32,264	$21,896	$27,144	$21,500	$35,703
General management	1,857	$31,979	$30,553	$26,870	$21,509	$34,047
International business	126	$33,836	$24,703	$28,420	$24,000	$35,262
Marketing/Sales	780	$31,187	$17,882	$27,150	$21,272	$35,160
Production/Manufacturing . .	167	$37,603	$69,334	$28,500	$22,775	$36,600
Quantitative Methods	316	$29,521	$15,418	$26,000	$21,900	$31,635
Other	327	$28,396	$19,481	$24,735	$20,000	$30,987

Source: Steven Langer, "1978 MBA Salary," *MBA Magazine* (October–November 1978), p. 12.

Objectives of the production function

In a general sense, the objectives of the production function are (1) to produce the desired product, (2) to achieve the desired rate, and (3) to minimize the cost. However, for operational purposes, we must be more specific, and classifying objectives is useful in this regard. The classification scheme we propose (though there are others) is one that separates objective into "output" and "cost" categories. The output category is further broken down into "volume" and "performance" categories, wherein volume refers to how much must be produced, inventoried, and so forth, and performance refers to the extent to which the system meets the standards set for quality, time, and so forth. Similarly, cost objectives are broken down into "explicit costs" and "implicit costs" categories, wherein explicit costs refers to those

EXHIBIT 1.6
Classification of production function objectives

Output objectives		Cost objectives	
Volume objectives	*Performance objectives*	*Explicit costs*	*Implicit costs*
Production rate	Time schedules	Material input,	Stockouts
Inventory level	Quality	scrap, and rework	Grievances
	Efficiency of work	Direct and indirect	Late deliveries
	force, equip-	labor	Unused capacity
	ment,	Maintenance	Opportunity costs
	facilities		Equipment downtime

costs that are measured by standard cost accounting methods, such as costs of materials and wages; and implicit costs refers to those costs that cannot be measured by cost accounting methods, such as idle time and stockout costs. This classification is presented in Exhibit 1.6.

As in the case of the firm as a whole, these objectives are often in conflict, and to achieve a balance among them for many situations tests the mettle of any production manager. In this regard, the production literature habitually uses the term *optimal* to denote the end state desired from balancing these objectives, and this text maintains the tradition. Nevertheless, while useful in discussing production decisions, achievement of the optimal (i.e., the most desirable) solution is rarely possible, or even provable, for a variety of reasons, some of which follow.

1. Optimization requires that all possible alternatives be considered. Not only would this be a difficult task, the decision maker would likely not even be aware of many of them.

2. Optimization requires that the decision maker have all relevant data at his disposal. This is often a practical impossibility because of time, resources, and cost considerations.

3. Optimization is time dependent in that what constitutes an optimum at one point in time is not necessarily optimum at subsequent moments in time. Conditions change so rapidly in business organizations that it may be argued that for a decision to be truly optimal, the gathering and weighing of alternatives must be continued up to the moment of choice.

In the light of such limitations, most managers do not really optimize but, rather, attempt to achieve some satisfactory result. That is, they recognize, implicitly or explicitly, the imperfections and incompleteness of data and the complexity of the calculations required to achieve optimality. Hence they set themselves levels of achievement that, though not ideal, are feasible in terms of time and effort. This approach—setting feasible objectives (and pursuing them "within reason")—is commonly termed *satisficing.*

In summary, then, although we will be using *optimize* to describe the *goals* of various techniques used in production management, keep in mind that the person who employs such techniques is, more likely than not, *satisficing.*

PRODUCTIVE SYSTEMS

As previously defined, operations management is directly concerned with productive systems, and we shall now elaborate on this concept. For our purposes, a productive system may be thought of as *a set of components whose function is to transform a set of inputs into some desired output.* A component may be a machine, a person, a tool, or a management system. An input may be a raw material, a person, or a finished product emanating from another system, which is to be acted upon. Some transformations that take place are:

a. Physical, as in manufacturing.
b. Locational, as in transportation.
c. Exchange, as in retailing.
d. Storage, as in warehousing.

In addition, there are physiological transformations—making a sick person well—and attitudinal or gratificational transformations—entertainment or reading for pleasure. These phenomena, of course, are not mutually exclusive. For example, a department store is set up to enable shoppers to compare prices and quality (informational), and to hold items in inventory until needed (storage), as well as to sell goods (exchange). Exhibit 1.7 presents sample input–transformation–output relationships for some typical kinds of systems.

EXHIBIT 1.7
Input–transformation–output relationships for typical systems

System	Primary inputs	Components	Primary transformation function(s)	Desired output
Hospital	Patients	MDs, nurses, medical supplies, equipment	Health care (physical)	Healthy individuals
Restaurant	Hungry customers	Food, chef, waitress, environment	Well-prepared food, well served; agreeable environment (physical and exchange)	Satisfied customers
Automobile factory	Raw materials	Tools, equipment, workers	Fabrication and assembly of cars (physical)	Complete automobiles
College or university	High school graduates	Teachers, books, classrooms	Imparting knowledge and skills (informational)	Educated individuals
Department store	Shoppers	Displays, stock of goods, sales clerks	Attract shoppers, promote products, fill orders (exchange)	Sales to satisfied customers

It should be emphasized that the table lists only the direct production components of these systems; a complete system description would, of course, require inclusion of managerial and support functions as well. In addition, the desired outputs specified are merely indicative of the nature and specificity of actual outputs and are presented from the point of view of society in general, rather than that of management or labor.

THE LIFE CYCLE APPROACH

Two common complaints from students in beginning production and operations management courses are that (1) the presentation of the subject matter in most texts lacks continuity, jumping from topic to topic, and (2) it is difficult to visualize the "big picture" of the discipline. In consequence, students often walk away from such courses with the impression that production and operations management is merely a convenient way of denoting a set of tools, such as linear programming, time study, PERT, and economic lot size models, rather than a distinct discipline. The structure we have adopted in this book was developed specifically to overcome this misconception. This structure, which we have termed *the life cycle approach,* follows the progress of the productive system from its inception to its termination—a concept that we feel reflects the true breadth of the area. The following discussion illustrates how a productive system evolves through its life cycle.

At the onset, let us assume that some idea for a product or service is proposed. This product or service must be examined as to its marketability, its producibility, its capital requirements, and so on. If the decision is made to produce this good or service, then the final form of the product, the location of the producing facility, the building, and the floor layout all must be specified. The required equipment must be purchased and the production, inventory, and quality control systems designed. The particular tasks to be done must be designed, the functional groups staffed, and production initiated. Quite likely, there will be problems in this start-up phase requiring design changes, re-layout, and personnel adjustments. Once the facility is in operation, problems become more of the day-to-day type, requiring decisions on scheduling priorities, minor changes to remove inefficiencies, and maintenance to assure continued operation. We term this operation stage the *steady state* of the system.

This steady-state operating condition may be changed in a number of ways: new products may come into the system or a new service may be offered; new developments may cause significant changes in the present methods; markets may shift, or even cease to exist. If these changes are moderate, a slight revision may be all that is necessary to bring the system into line. At times, though, the needed revisions may be of such magnitude that certain phases of the life cycle must be repeated, probably calling for new designs, more or less extensive restaffing, and restarting the revised system. *If the system cannot adjust to the stimulus that has generated the need for revision, then, in the extreme case, the enterprise will die (through liquidation) or cease to exist as a separate entity (through sale or merger).*

In reality, most enterprises operate within this dynamic life cycle. A system, whether it is a manufacturing firm, service facility, or government agency, is born of an idea, passes through a growth stage, and continuously changes to meet new demands. And sometimes, of course, it is deliberately terminated.

Some of the key decision areas at the various stages in a system's life cycle are shown in Exhibit 1.8. It must be emphasized that this is a dynamic process, one in which a number of phases in the life cycle may be occurring concurrently. Indeed, many firms allocate a large portion of their resources to foster a continuous rebirth or rejuvenation program through the medium of research and development staffs. Further, no interconnections are shown in the illustration. In actuality, the introduction of a new product, for example, might cause the system to loop back to basic product design, followed by the activities of process selection, new system design, staffing, and start-up.

EXHIBIT 1.8
Key decisions in the life of a productive system

Stage	Key decisions
BIRTH of the system	What are the goals of the firm? What product or service will be offered?
PRODUCT DESIGN and PROCESS SELECTION	What is the form and appearance of the product? Technologically, how should the product be made?
DESIGN of the system	What capacity do you need? Where should the facility be located? What physical arrangement is best to use? How do you maintain desired quality? How do you determine demand for the product or service? What job is each worker to perform? How will the job be performed, measured; how will the workers be compensated?
STARTUP of the system	How do you get the system into operation? How long will it take to reach desired rate of output?
The system in STEADY STATE	How do you maintain the system? How can you improve the system? How do you revise the system in light of changes in corporate strategy?
TERMINATION of the system	How does a system die? What can be done to salvage resources?

It should also be emphasized that this text is not built around the life cycle of any one system. On the contrary, we have intentionally sought illustrations from a variety of products and services. By doing this, we hope to emphasize the fact that production and operations management is essential in such diverse systems as hospitals, supermarkets, banks, universities—and, of course, factories.[3]

OPERATIONS MANAGEMENT AND OTHER BUSINESS SPECIALTIES

Operations management (OM) is a required course in many business schools not only because it deals with the basic question of how products and services are created but because it impacts on every other field of business in the real world.

Accountants, be they internal or external to the firm, need to understand the basics of inventory management, capacity utilization, and labor standards in order to develop accurate cost data, perform audits, and prepare financial reports.

Financial managers can use inventory and capacity concepts in judging the need for capital investments and forecasts of cash flow and in the management of current assets. Further, there is a mutual concern between OM and finance in specific decisions such as make-or-buy and plant expansion.

Marketing specialists need an understanding of what the factory can do relative to meeting customer due dates, product customization, and new product introduction. In service industries, marketing and production often take place simultaneously, so a natural mutuality of interest should arise between service marketing and OM.

Personnel specialists need to be aware of how jobs are designed, the relationship of standards to incentive plans, and the skills required of the direct work force.

Computer specialists often install manufacturing information systems which they themselves design or off-the-shelf software developed by computer companies. Moreover, the major application of computers in management is in the area of production control.

BACKGROUND NOTE: HISTORICAL DEVELOPMENT OF THE FIELD

Operations management has existed as a function since man first organized to hunt and gather food and later to farm, trade, and build. His degree of sophistication in performing this function, however, has varied enormously. Clearly, the Egyptians must have had a high degree of coordi-

---

[3] It is worthy of note that weapons systems acquisitions by the U.S. Air Force follow a similar "life cycle" approach, which includes the following phases: Conception (examining such things as feasibility and risk), Validation (source selection and production planning), Full-scale development (producibility and methods), Production (with emphasis on improvement and control), and Transition and phase-down (essentially delivering the weapons system to the Air Force Logistics Command and ceasing production). (For further development of the parallelism between the two life cycle concepts, see W. K. Goss and L. W. Lockwood, "Acquisition Program Management Tasks: A Program Office/AFPRO Comparison of Relative Task Size and Priority," Department of Research and Communicative Studies, Air Force Institute of Technology, 1975.)

native ability to construct the pyramids, the Chinese to build the Great Wall, the Romans to build their aqueducts, the Incas to build their temples, and so forth. It seems fair to say that most of the great civilizations enjoyed a "golden age" of master works in which early project managers had to contend with such operations management questions as job design, quality control, materials handling, and inventory control. Indeed, archaeologists and historians have provided us with evidence of some of the concepts and techniques used by earlier societies, indicating that insight into work organization and management is not strictly a 20th-century phenomenon.

We may begin our history survey with the writings of Mencius (circa 372–289 B.C.). This Chinese philosopher not only dealt with the concepts of systems and models in an almost contemporary fashion, but pointed out the advantages to the individual and society of a division of labor. The ancient Greeks certainly were aware of the value of uniform work methods, as we find noted in an army manual that detailed how soldiers should arrange their clothes and weapons in encampments to enable dressing and arming at a moment's notice.[4] In attempting to make trying or monotonous jobs more palatable, the inventive Greeks also employed songs and standard motions to achieve a smooth work tempo—concepts basic to current-day industrial management. Plato (circa 427–347 B.C.), in *The Republic,* acknowledged the merits of division of labor, stating that "a man whose work is confined to such a limited task [e.g., shoe stitching] must necessarily excel at it."[5] Work specialization was in fact so extensive in Greece that stonemasons didn't even sharpen their own cutting tools, relying instead upon a specialist supporting staff.

The dominance of feudalism in the period between the fall of the Roman Empire and the Renaissance (roughly from the fourth into the 15th century) inhibited the development of new technological and managerial ideas. Only toward the end of the 14th century do we find a development of major significance: the mechanical clock (see Exhibit 1.9). This device, by enabling precise coordination of man's activities, led historian Lewis Mumford to state: "The clock, not the steam engine, is the key machine of the modern industrial age. For every phase of its development, the clock is both the outstanding fact and typical symbol of the machine: even today, no other machine is so ubiquitous."[6]

By the 15th century, the value of standardization of parts was fairly widely recognized. The Arsenal of Venice planning committee was now requiring that bows be made to accommodate all types of arrows, all stern-parts of ships be of identical design so that rudders would not have to be specially fitted, and all rigging and deck furnishings be uniform.

The ideas of Adam Smith and Eli Whitney dominate the historical devel-

---

[4] Claude S. George, Jr., *The History of Management Thought* (Englewood Cliffs, N.J.: Prentice-Hall, 1968), pp. 12–13.

[5] Ibid., p. 15.

[6] Lewis Mumford, *Technics and Civilization* (New York: Harcourt Brace Jovanovich, 1934), p. 13.

	Year	Concept or tool	Originator or developer
EXHIBIT 1.9 **Historical summary**	1370	Mechanical clock	Heinrich von Wyck (Paris)
	Circa 1430	Assembly line outfitting of ships at the Arsenal of Venice	Venetian shipbuilders
	1776	Economic benefits from division of labor	Adam Smith (England)
	1798	Interchangeable parts	Eli Whitney (U.S.)
	1832	Skill differentials in wage payment; general concepts of time study	Charles Babbage (England)
	1911	*Principles of Scientific Management;* formalized time study and work study concepts	Frederick W. Taylor (U.S.)
	1911	Motion study; basic concepts of industrial psychology	Frank and Lillian Gilbreth (U.S.)
	1913	Moving assembly line	Henry Ford (U.S.)
	1914	Activity scheduling chart	Henry L. Gantt (U.S.)
	1917	Application of economic lot size model for inventory control	F. W. Harris (U.S.)
	1931	Sampling inspection and statistical tables for quality control	Walter Shewhart, H.F. Dodge, and H. G. Romig (U.S.)
	1927–33	Hawthorne studies' new light on worker motivation	Elton Mayo (U.S.)
	1934	Activity sampling for work analysis	L. H. C. Tippett (England)
	1940	Team approaches to complex system problems	Operations research groups (England)
	1947	Simplex method of linear programming	George B. Dantzig (U.S.)
	Since 1950	Extensive development and application of simulation, queuing theory, decision theory, mathematical programming, computer hardware and software, project scheduling techniques of PERT and CPM	U.S. and Western Europe
	1970s	Development of a variety of computer software packages to deal with routine problems of shop scheduling, inventory, layout, forecasting, and project management; rapid growth of materials requirements planning (MRP),	Computer manufacturers, researchers, and users in the United States and Western Europe
		Quality management and productivity improvement concepts from Japan	Japanese firms with initial help from U.S. specialists

opments of the 1700s. In his classic *Wealth of Nations*, Smith noted with respect to pin manufacture that division of labor increases output for three reasons: (1) increased dexterity on the part of each worker, (2) avoidance of lost time due to handling, and (3) "the invention of a great number of machines which facilitate and abridge labor and enable one man to do the work of many."[7] These observations were of particular significance since they laid the groundwork for the subsequent development of modern work simplification, process analysis, and time study.[8] Eli Whitney's use of interchangeable parts in the making of guns paved the way for rapid production of other multicomponent assembled items. Whitney also employed cost accounting concepts and quality control procedures at his musket factory.[9]

A striking historical anomaly in the development of production and general management concepts is found in the application of highly advanced techniques by the Soho Engineering foundry in England at the beginning of the 1800s. According to Claude George, Jr., this remarkable firm left "concrete evidences of market research and forecasting, planned site location, machine layout study . . . , established production standards, production planning, standardized components, cost control applications, cost accounting, employee training, work study and incentives, and an employee welfare program." If these practices did in fact exist, it would be difficult to dispute Professor George's claim that the Soho foundry was "a century ahead of its time."[10]

In 1832, the gifted engineer, philosopher, and mathematician, Charles Babbage, published *On the Economy of Machines and Manufactures* in which he advocated the use of the scientific method in analyzing business problems, the use of time study, the performance of research and development activities, the location of factories on the basis of economic analysis, the use of bonus payment plans, and a number of other concepts that are standard practice today. As we shall see, much of what Babbage recommended was proposed and widely applied some 75 years later in the context of the scientific management movement headed by Frederick W. Taylor. Besides being an avant-gardist on matters of organization, Babbage was also the designer of the first digital computer. One could speculate that Taylor might have received his time study records on a computer printout if the British government had not withdrawn funds needed by Babbage to complete his final prototype.[11]

---

[7] Adam Smith, *An Inquiry into the Nature and Causes of the Wealth of Nations* (London: A. Strahan & T. Cadell, 1776), vol. 1, pp. 7–8.

[8] Not everybody waited for Adam Smith. By 1496, Leonardo da Vinci had developed a machine that could make 400 needles per hour—automatically!

[9] George, *History of Management Thought*, p. 63.

[10] Ibid., p. 60.

[11] The Chancellor of the Exchequer found Babbage's project "indefinitely expensive. . . . The ultimate success problematical. . . . The expenditure utterly incapable of being calculated." Edward C. Bursk, Donald T. Clark, and Ralph W. Hidy, *The World of Business* (New York: Simon & Schuster, 1962), vol. IV, p. 2310.

With the advent of scientific management around the turn of the century, the field of production and operations management began to assume the form it has today. As we have said, the concept of scientific management was developed by Taylor, who, like Babbage, was an imaginative engineer and insightful observer of organizational activities. Unlike Babbage, however, Taylor was a shrewd promotor of his own ideas and synthesizer of the ideas of others. Here, perhaps, his great talents shone most brilliantly. A good historical case can be made that Taylor did not *discover* any of the major concepts or tools that are associated with his development of scientific management. Time study, methods analysis, bonus payment plans, and the advisability of the scientific method in solving production problems were all known and applied—some, many centuries before—yet it remained for Taylor truly to amalgamate these concepts and tools into a philosophy that could be broadly applied throughout industry.[12]

The essence of Taylor's philosophy was that scientific laws govern how much a man could produce per day and that it is the function of management to discover and use these laws in the operation of productive systems (and the function of the worker to carry out management's wishes without question). This philosophy, however, was not greeted with approval by all his contemporaries. On the contrary, there were unions that resented or feared scientific management and with some justification. In too many instances, managers of the day were quick to embrace the "mechanisms" of Taylor's philosophy—time study, incentive plans, and so forth—but they ignored their responsibility to organize and standardize the work to be done. Hence, there were numerous cases of rate cutting (reducing the payment per piece if the production rate were deemed too high), overwork of labor, and poorly designed work methods. Such abuses resulted in overreaction—leading even to the introduction of a bill in Congress in 1913 to prohibit the use of time study and incentive plans in federal government operations. The unions advocating the legislation claimed that Taylor's subject in several of his time study experiments—a steelworker called "Schmidt"—had died from overwork as a result of following Taylor's methods (in evidence whereof they even distributed pictures of Schmidt's "grave"). It was later discovered that Schmidt (whose real name was Henry Nolle) was alive and well and working as a teamster.[13] Ultimately, the bill was defeated.

Notable contemporaries and co-workers of Taylor were Frank and Lillian Gilbreth (motion study, industrial psychology) and Henry L. Gantt (sched-

---

[12] There is strong evidence that Taylor's most famous book, *Principles of Scientific Management* was actually an ill-disguised rewrite of a manuscript entitled *Industrial Management* written by a close business associate, Morris L. Cooke. (See C. D. Wrege and A. M. Stotka, "Cooke Creates a Classic: The Story Behind F. W. Taylor's Principles of Scientific Management," *Academy of Management Review*, vol. 3, no. 4, October 1978), pp. 736–49.

[13] Milton J. Nadworny, "Schmidt and Stakhanov: Work Heroes in Two Systems," *California Management Review*, vol. 6, no. 4 (Summer 1964), pp. 69–76.

uling, wage payment plans). We will discuss their contributions in somewhat more detail later.

The year 1913 also saw the introduction of one of the machine age's greatest technological innovations—the moving assembly line for the manufacture of Ford automobiles.[14] Before the line was introduced, in August of that year, each auto chassis was assembled by one man in about 12½ hours. Eight months later, when the line was in its final form, with each worker performing a small unit of work and the chassis being moved mechanically, the average labor time per unit was 93 minutes. This technological breakthrough, coupled with the concepts of scientific management, signaled both the promise and the problems of the machine age. Workers were now able to achieve unheard-of levels of output. Moreover, they were now able to become consumers on a scale never before dreamed of. But unfortunately, thanks to this same technological advance, they were also to become de-skilled and made subservient to the machine. This issue is still far from resolved today, as we shall see in Chapter 11, "Job Design and Work Measurement."

Mathematical and statistical developments dominated the evolution of operations management from Taylor's time up to around the 1940s. An exception was the Hawthorne studies, conducted in the 1930s by a research team from the Harvard Graduate School of Business Administration and supervised by the sociologist, Elton Mayo. These experiments were designed to study the effects of certain environmental changes on the output of assembly workers at the Western Electric plant in Hawthorne, Illinois. The unexpected findings, reported in *Management and the Worker* (1939) by F. J. Roethlisberger and W. J. Dickson, intrigued sociologists and students of "traditional" scientific management alike. To the surprise of the researchers, changing the level of illumination (for example) had much less effect on output than the way in which the changes were introduced to the workers. That is, reductions in illumination in some instances led to increased output because workers felt an obligation to their group to keep output high. Discoveries such as these had tremendous implications for work design and motivation and ultimately led to the establishment of personnel management and human relations departments in most organizations. They also played a major part in the development of new academic disciplines in schools of business administration.

World War II, with its complex problems of logistics control and weapons-systems design, provided the impetus for the development of the interdisciplinary, mathematically oriented field of operations research. Operations research, or "OR" as it is often termed, brings together practitioners in such diverse fields as mathematics, psychology, and economics. Specialists in these disciplines customarily form a team to structure and

---

[14] Ford is said to have gotten the idea for an assembly line from observing a Swiss watch manufacturer's use of the technology.

analyze a problem in quantitative terms so that a mathematically optimal solution can be obtained. Operations research, or its approximate synonym, "management science," now provides many of the quantitative tools used in operations management as well as in such basic business functions as marketing, finance, and accounting.

In the late 1950s and early 1960s, scholars began to write texts dealing specifically with production management as opposed to industrial engineering or manufacturing management, which, as their names imply, are heavily oriented toward factory problems. Two books especially had significant impact on the coalescing of the field: E. H. Bowman's and R. B. Fetter's *Analysis for Production Management* (1957) and E. S. Buffa's *Modern Production Management* (1961). Although other texts on the topic had been published earlier, these two texts clearly noted the commonality of problems faced by all productive systems and emphasized the importance of viewing the production function as a system rather than as an agglomerate of vaguely related activities. In addition, they stressed the useful applications of waiting line theory, simulation, and linear programming, which are now standard topics in the field.

Undoubtedly the major development of the past 20 years is the application of the high-speed digital computer to the multidimensional problems encountered in production systems. Problems that, because of sheer size, had previously all but defied solution now are solved in moments by the computer. While virtually every aspect of operations management has been touched by this tool, the areas of scheduling and inventory management seem to have been most ardently subjected to computer programming. One of the more striking aspects of the growth in computers is the associated growth in commercial programming packages for use in these areas. A perusal of an IBM catalog, for example, will quickly indicate the tremendous variety of "canned" programs available, especially for manufacturing applications. (We will discuss several of these software packages in this book.)

In concluding our historical survey, we must highlight what some have referred to as a "productivity revolution" taking place in Japan. The Japanese, through continual technological innovation, participative management, and an unrelenting concern with product quality have become the leaders in productivity in almost every industry in which they compete. What they are doing, particularly with respect to quality control, is of great current interest to operations managers.

REVIEW AND DISCUSSION QUESTIONS

1. What is meant by the statement that "production is an internal function?" What are the effects of being "internal?"

2. Take a look at the want ads in *The Wall Street Journal* and evaluate the opportunities for an OM major with several years of experience.

3. How does your major area of the study compare with production/manufacturing salary levels in the *MBA Magazine* survey?

4. Why are objectives of the production function (Exhibit 1.6) limited to output and cost rather than, say, revenue or profit?

5. In what ways might volume objectives conflict with performance objectives? Be explicit.

6. Using Exhibit 1.7 as a model, describe the input–transformation–output relationships found in the following types of systems: (1) an airline, (2) a state penitentiary, (3) a branch bank, (4) a home office of a major banking firm.

7. What is the life cycle approach to production/operations management? Does it make sense to you? Could it be applied to any other fields you are studying?

8. Comment on the following comments:

   "I don't need to know anything about production management to be a loan officer in a bank."

   "Once an accountant knows how a company values its inventories—Fifo, Lifo, or Nifo (next in first out?), an understanding of inventory control is not really necessary."

   "I can't really see how the four P's of marketing have any significant production implication."

9. Suppose that *Variety*, the Hollywood trade paper noted for its colorful jargon, presented the following headlines related to the history of POM. What particular events, people, or issues would they be referring to?

   LABOR BOOGIE CLIMBS CHARTS IN ATHENS
   CLOCK-WISE HISTORIAN GOES GA GA OVER TICKERS
   BEAN COUNTERS AND QC FREAKS HELP ELI'S BANG BUSINESS BOOM
   BRITISH TAX HACK NIXES CHUCK'S NUMBER CRUNCHER
   SCHMIDT—R.I.P.
   "FOR YOU, 93 MINUTES," SAYS HENRY
   HAWTHORNE WORKERS DO IT FASTER IN THE DARK
   OPERATIONS RESEARCHERS ZAP HUNS
   THIS ISSUE PRINTED COMPLETELY BY CONFUTER
   YOU CAN CALL IT PM, OR YOU CAN CALL IT OM, OR YOU CAN CALL IT POM, OR . . .

RECOMMENDED PERIODICALS

The following periodicals are listed according to a rough estimate of the number of OM-related articles found in a typical issue. They, of course, vary in their emphasis and degree of technical sophistication.

*Journal of Operations Management**
*International Journal of Operations and Production Management**
Production and Inventory Management

---

* First issues in 1980.

Industrial Engineering

AIIE Transactions

International Journal of Production Research

Management Science

Interfaces

Decision Sciences

Harvard Business Review

SELECTED BIBLIOGRAPHY

Bowman, Edward H., and Fetter, Robert B. *Analysis for Production and Operations Management.* 3d ed. Homewood, Ill.: Richard D. Irwin, Inc., 1957.

Buffa, Elwood S. *Modern Production Management.* 3d ed. New York: John Wiley & Sons, 1961.

Bursk, Edward C.; Clark, Donald T.; and Hidy, Ralph W. *The World of Business.* vols. 3 and 4. New York: Simon & Schuster, 1962.

George, Claude S. *The History of Management Thought.* Englewood Cliffs, N.J.: Prentice-Hall, 1968.

Groff, Gene K., and Muth, John R. *Operations Management: Analysis for Decisions.* Homewood, Ill.: Richard D. Irwin, Inc., 1972.

Mumford, Lewis. *Technics and Civilization.* New York: Harcourt Brace Jovanovich, 1934.

Nadworny, Milton J. "Schmidt and Stakhanov: Work Heroes in Two Systems," *California Management Review,* vol. 6, no. 4 (Summer 1964), pp. 69–75.

Smith, Adam. *An Inquiry into the Nature and Causes of the Wealth of Nations.* London: A. Straham & T. Cadell, 1776.

Taylor, Frederick W. *The Principles of Scientific Management.* New York: Harper & Bros., 1911.

Timms, Howard L., and Pohlen, Michael F. *The Production Function in Business.* 3d ed. Homewood, Ill.: Richard D. Irwin, Inc., 1970.

Organizing for production

The first decision in creating a production system is determining what type of product is to be produced. This decision affects and is affected by available technology and the structure of the production function within the organization. This section considers these subjects relative to manufacturing and service organizations.

Chapter

2

PRODUCT DESIGN AND PROCESS SELECTION— MANUFACTURING

There are four broad areas of concern in operations management decision making. These areas are:

1. **Product.** That combination of goods and services provided by the productive system.
2. **Technology of transformation.** The physical steps by which a productive system creates those goods and services.
3. **Operating and control systems.** The management and support systems required to coordinate the transformation process (that is, organization structure, production control, quality control, and so forth).
4. **Workforce.** The employees who have the responsibility of carrying out the steps of the transformation process.

In this chapter we focus on areas 1 and 2, the product and the technology of transformation, with particular reference to manufacturing systems. All four areas will be brought into play in subsequent chapters.

PRODUCT DESIGN AND THE SYSTEM LIFE CYCLE

The growth stage of the organization determines how, in general, the product design process is carried out. For the company just starting into operation, the new product may be the only one or part of a small product line which the entrepreneur has presold or is making for stock. "Spin-off" engineering firms, for example, may enter into business by building a special-purpose machine to be used by the company for which the entre-

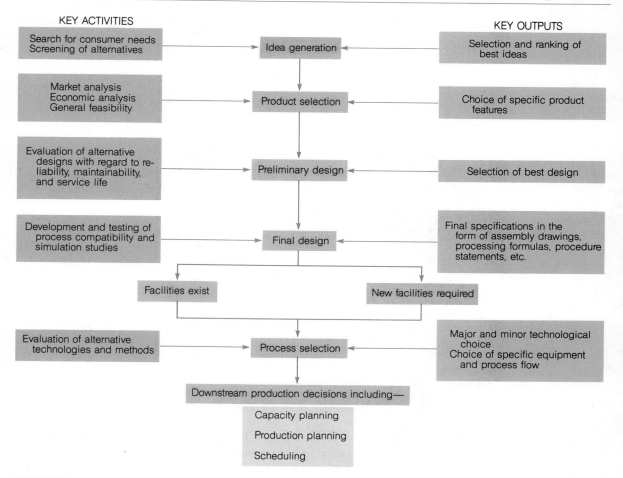

KEY ACTIVITIES

KEY OUTPUTS

Search for consumer needs
Screening of alternatives

Idea generation

Selection and ranking of
best ideas

Market analysis
Economic analysis
General feasibility

Product selection

Choice of specific product
features

Evaluation of alternative
designs with regard to reliability, maintainability,
and service life

Preliminary design

Selection of best design

Development and testing of
process compatibility and
simulation studies

Final design

Final specifications in the
form of assembly drawings,
processing formulas, procedure
statements, etc.

Facilities exist

New facilities required

Evaluation of alternative
technologies and methods

Process selection

Major and minor technological
choice
Choice of specific equipment
and process flow

Downstream production decisions including—

Capacity planning

Production planning

Scheduling

EXHIBIT 2.1
**Product design
and develop-
ment sequence**

preneur previously worked. A specific case in point is a Tucson design
engineer starting his own company to make peptide synthesizers to be
used in volume manufacturer of peptides by his former employer. In this
instance, the design process was a creative undertaking by one person.
In contrast, a firm which has been operating for several years may have
a staff of design personnel who are responsible for generating new products
on a fairly regular basis to fill a particular niche specifed by top management and/or market research specialists. In this chapter, we will assume
that the organization is large enough to have specialists in all of the relevant
functions to carry out a formal approach to product design (and process
selection) decisions.

PRODUCT DESIGN AND DEVELOPMENT SEQUENCE

Every new product starts with an idea. The steps leading from the
idea stage to production of a new product are outlined in Exhibit 2.1.

Idea generation and product selection involve the production function to some degree, but the operations manager's major activities generally begin when the engineering department (in manufacturing organizations) turns over the product specifications. Prior to this time, the operations manager's role is one of "consultant" with respect to the compatibility of the proposed product to his or her current manufacturing plan. Thus, while we will talk briefly about idea generation and product selection, our emphasis will be on design and process-selection decisions.

Origin of the product idea

Product ideas may originate from any number of sources, some of which are not obvious. Marketing textbooks and journals frequently cite unusual examples of sources for new-product ideas to emphasize that businesses must be keenly attuned to all possible sources to ensure that the "golden idea" is not missed or passed over without adequate consideration. A meat packing company once got the idea of developing an onion soup from a suggestion of one of its executive's wives. An appliance manufacturer developed a foot warmer on the basis of a customer inquiry. A maker of pottery designed a new vase after seeing a similar one at a museum exhibit. A producer of plastic products designed a film slide viewer after reading a list of needed inventions published by a bank.[1] While such examples constitute the exceptional rather than the more common sources of ideas for new products, they indicate that ideas are to be found almost anywhere and that aggressive firms cannot afford to discount an idea simply because it originates from an unusual source.

Choosing among alternative products

The idea-gathering process, if properly carried out, will often lead to more ideas than can be translated into producible products. Thus a screening procedure designed to eliminate those ideas which clearly are infeasible must be instituted. The screening procedure seeks to determine if the product is generally compatible with the company's objectives and resources. Regarding objectives, a product may be dropped if it is deficient in profit potential or in prospective growth or stability of sales or if it is deleterious to the company image. In terms of resources, a product may be dropped if it exceeds the company's capital availability or is incompatible with the company's managerial and technical skills or physical facilities.

Of the several techniques available to aid in the screening process, perhaps the most commonly used are rating checksheets. In one such sheet, a number of important considerations are enumerated—for example, sales volume, patent protection, competition—and the product is categorized from "very good" to "very poor" for each of these considerations. The product selected will show a rating pattern that meets the company's standard, from favorable to unfavorable ratings. More refined rating devices apply numerical weights to the important considerations and quantify

---

[1] Thomas L. Berg and Abe Shuchman (eds.), *Product Strategy and Management* (New York: Holt, Rinehart & Winston, 1963), pp. 421–22.

the "goodness" categories. An example of this type of checklist is illustrated in Exhibit 2.2, where the object is to obtain a total score by which the product can be compared to other product possibilities or to a predetermined cutoff score. For this list, the best score that could be obtained is 40 and the worst is 0. Note, however, that this approach attempts to quantify the unquantifiable and may create the illusion that a "very good" rating is, for example, four times as high as a "poor" rating.

If the product passes the screening procedure, more rigorous analysis of its cost and revenue characteristics is undertaken. Sometimes, this analysis consists of a comparison in which products are ranked according to an indexing formula such as the project value index:

$$PVI = \frac{CTS \times CCS \times AV \times P \times \sqrt{L}}{TPC}$$

where

PVI = project value index
CTS = chances for technical success on an arbitrary rating scale, say 0 to 10
CCS = chances for commercial success on an arbitrary rating scale, say 0 to 10
AV = annual volume (total sales of product in units)
P = profit in dollars per unit (i.e., price minus cost)
L = life of product in years
TPC = total project cost in dollars

Where a more detailed evaluation is deemed necessary, the tools of financial analysis—break-even charts and rate-of-return calculations—come into play. (These techniques are discussed in detail in Chapter 5.) The major problem associated with these tools is that their value is limited to short-run evaluation of the product alternatives, since long-term developments in costs, the competition, and the economy make the numerical inputs inaccurate (in many cases) within a year. Furthermore, even in the short run, where cost and revenue are known with relative certainty, the techniques may not give clear-cut answers.

EXHIBIT 2.2
Product evaluation sheet

Performance feature	(A) Relative weight	(B) Rating					Factor score (A) × (B)
		Very good 40	Good 30	Fair 20	Poor 10	Very poor 0	
Sales	0.20	✓					8
Competition (number and type)	0.05	✓					2
Patent protection	0.05	✓					2
Technical opportunity	0.10		✓				3
Materials availability	0.10		✓				3
Value added	0.10		✓				3
Similarity to major business	0.20		✓				6
Effect on present products	0.20				✓		2
	1.00						29

PRODUCT DESIGN

It should be understood that the product design process as depicted in flowchart form in Exhibit 2.1 in an idealized case synthesized from a number of approaches to product design. It should also be mentioned that product design and development rarely follow the discrete sequence suggested by the diagram. Typically, there are frequent loops to prior steps, and certain activities are often performed concurrently. Further, the extent to which these phases are formalized and specified varies from industry to industry. Generally, firms which require a good deal of research and tooling or lean heavily on innovation to compete adhere to a more formalized program than those that do not. Likewise, large companies with a broad product line would also tend to require a carefully prescribed development sequence simply to facilitate coordination.

From the production manager's point of view, the critical output of the product design activity is the product's specifications. These specifications provide the basis for a host of decisions he or she must make, including the purchase of materials, selection of equipment, assignments of workers, and often even the size and layout of the productive facility.

Product specifications, while commonly thought of as blueprints or engineering drawings, may take a variety of other forms, ranging from highly precise quantitative statements to rather fluid guidelines. A sampling of specifications along a continuum ranging from the exact to the general is provided in Exhibit 2.3.

Preliminary design

Whether or not it is a separate phase in the sequence of design activities, preliminary design is usually devoted to developing several alternative designs that meet the conceptual features of the selected product. If, for example, a refrigerator manufacturer decides to manufacture freezers, questions of style, storage capacity, size of motor, and so forth, will likely be encountered here. During preliminary design, it also is common to specify the key product attributes of reliability, maintainability, and service life. For a freezer, these would be manifested in decisions relative to frequency of breakdown of component parts (reliability), the ease of repair

EXHIBIT 2.3
Specification continuum

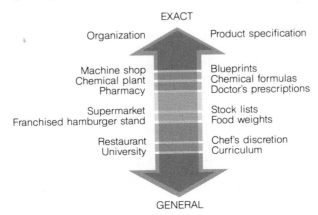

EXACT

Organization — Product specification

Machine shop — Blueprints
Chemical plant — Chemical formulas
Pharmacy — Doctor's prescriptions

Supermarket — Stock lists
Franchised hamburger stand — Food weights

Restaurant — Chef's discretion
University — Curriculum

GENERAL

and general maintenance (maintainability), and the anticipated useful performance period (service life).

Final design

During the final design phase, prototypes are developed and "bugs" are worked out of the design so that the product is sound from an engineering standpoint. Thus, ultimate output of the final design includes the complete specification of the product, its components, and assembly drawings, which provide the basis for its full-scale production.

At this point, too, the effectiveness of alternative designs must be balanced with cost considerations, and—inevitably—compromises must be made. This is especially true in selecting the configuration and material for manufactured items. The complexity of this tradeoff can be seen when we consider that even such a relatively unsophisticated product as a home freezer has roughly 500 components, each of which could conceivably be subjected to an alternative cost analysis. Typical considerations that must enter the analysis are component *compatiblility* and *simplification*.

Compatibility refers to the fitting together and proper articulation of parts during operation. Problems of compatibility arise not only with parts that must mesh, such as freezer door latches, but also with parts that must respond similarly to conditions of stress. Drawbridge components must be course fit together, but they must also have similar tensile strength so as to accommodate high winds and similar expansion coefficients so as to adjust equally to variations in heat and cold. *Simplification* refers to the exclusion of those features that raise production costs. Lack of simplification might be evident where such seemingly innocuous requirements as rounded edges or nonstandard hole sizes create production bottlenecks and subsequent repair problems when the item is in use.

In addition to the above design activities, some organizations engage in rather formalized product testing programs and redesign activities during the final design stage. Product testing may take the form of test marketing in the case of consumer products or test firing of a weapons system in the case of the military. In both instances, a good deal of planning would necessarily precede the tests. Product redesign generally takes place after the prototype has been tested and may be major or minor in scope. If the redesign is major, the product may be recycled through the preliminary design phase; if the change is minor, the product will probably be carried through to production. It should be noted, however, that there are "minor changes *and* minor changes;" in some instances an apparently slight modification to some component may greatly alter the integrity of the entire product.

Modular design

It is rare to find a firm that produces only a single type of product. In the United States especially, competition is so keen and the market so segmented that most manufacturers produce a variety of products. This of course affects the product design function, and therefore it is not surprising that production management is interested in finding ways in which combination products can be designed and produced with minimum cost.

EXHIBIT 2.4 **Advantages and disadvantages of standard subassemblies**	*Advantages*	*Example*
	Fewer types of standard designs must be inventoried in any one market.	Programming packages often contain several subroutines that can be combined to form a multitude of programs.
		Storage space for a few subroutines is much smaller than space for storing several complete programs.
	Fewer types of standard parts provide tighter quality control and standard testing procedures.	Producing bigger quantities of the same circuit board means that standard testing procedures can be created.
		The costs of developing these procedures are spread over a greater number of boards.
	Repair is simplified by ease of replacement.	Repairmen need carry only a few types of standard modules to quickly repair appliances.
	Cannibalization (the use of parts from one application to repair a second) is simplified.	Standard modules removed from an unrepairable aircraft can be used to repair a radar van.
	Additions to a product line can be simplified.	New-generation computers can be manufactured from standard subassemblies already designed and tested.
	Adaptation to market segments is simplified.	Use of options can alter an automobile's market segment.
	Disadvantages	*Example*
	More parts than required are used.	Excess nuts and bolts in an assembly kit are thrown away.
	Excess parts increase cost of transportation and handling.	Nuts and bolts which are not necessary are packaged and shipped at some cost.
	Interconnection of modules may be difficult.	"Backboard wiring" of modules in a computer is time consuming and costly in terms of reliability.

Source: Timothy L. Shaftel, "How Modular Design Reduces Production Costs," *Arizona Review,* vol. 21, nos. 6–7 (June–July 1972), p. 4.

An approach to this problem is *modular design.* The essence of this approach is to develop a number of standard designs or modules consisting of various parts or subassemblies that can be used over a wide range of product designs. (Some sample applications are given in Exhibit 2.4). From an analytical standpoint, the "modular design problem" consists of finding how many of each part or subassembly are to be included in each module and how many of each module are to be used in each application. The objective is to find the product design that minimizes the costs of production, inventory, consumer disutility, repair, and maintenance.[2]

---

[2] For a discussion of the mathematical complexities and models used in finding the optimum size and number of modules, see David P. Rutenberg and Timothy L. Shaftel, "Product Design: Subassemblies for Multiple Markets," *Management Science,* vol. 18, no. 4 (December 1971), pp. B220–31, and Martin K. Starr, "Modular Production—A New Concept," *Harvard Business Review* (November–December 1965), pp. 131–42.

PROCESS SELECTION

Technological decisions in process selection

Process selection entails a series of decisions encompassing the theoretical feasibility of making the product, the general nature of the processing system, the specific equipment to be employed, and the specific routing through which the product must flow. These decisions—major technological choice, minor technological choice, specific equipment choice, and specific process flow choice—are summarized in Exhibit 2.5.

Major technological choice. The basic issue is: Can the product be made—Does the technology exist for producing the product under consideration? This question has little to do with economic feasibility; it deals only with natural laws of science, and the question must be answered, even if only in probabilistic terms, before an organization can select a product. And it must be answered *conclusively* before it enters into production.

Because technological sophistication is increasing so rapidly, this issue is of more than academic interest. Indeed, the amount of current research

EXHIBIT 2.5
Technological decisions in process selection

General-process decision	Decision problem	Decision variables	Decision aids
Major technological choice	Transformation potential	Product choice Laws of physics, chemistry, etc. State of scientific knowledge	Technical specialists
Minor technological choice	Selecting among alternative transformation processes	State of the art in equipment and techniques Environmental factors such as ecological and legal constraints Primary task of organization General financial and market strength	R&D reports Technical specialists Organizational objectives Long-run market forecasts Mathematical programs
Specific component choice	Selecting specific equipment	Existing facilities Cost of equipment alternatives Desired output level	Industry reports Investment analysis, including make-or-buy, break-even, and present-value methods Medium-range forecasts
Process flow choice	Selecting production routings	Existing layout Homogeneity of products Equipment characteristics	Product specifications Assembly charts Route sheets Flow process charts Equipment manuals Engineering handbooks

underscores the importance of making this determination, and stories abound of the success of companies that made breakthroughs in technology amid cries that it couldn't be done. Still, it is often a long road from possibility to feasibility. Iron *can* be made into gold, water *can* be obtained from rock, and man *can* walk on Mars; but going into the *business* of doing these things is not yet profitable. Certainly, in the more exotic industries the production manager is pretty much dependent on technical specialists, and he or she must wait in the wings until the minor technological choice is made.

Minor technological choice. Manufacturing operations, in the general sense of transforming some material input into some material output, can be categorized into three types of processes, with the ultimate choice being pretty much determined by the foregoing technological choice decision. These processes are:

Continuous processes—those which must be carried out 24 hours a day to avoid expensive shutdown and startups. These are typified by *process industries* such as steel, plastics, chemicals, beer, and petroleum.

Repetitive processes—those in which items are produced in large lots following the same series of operations as the previous items. These are typified by *mass production* using production lines in such industries as automobiles, appliances, electronic components, ready-to-wear clothing, and toys.

Intermittent processes—those in which items are processed in small lots or *batches,* often to a customer's specifications. These are typified by *job shops,* which in turn are characterized by individual orders taking different work-flow patterns through the plant and requiring frequent starting and stopping. The majority of manufacturing firms are job shops. Common examples are repair facilities, capital-equipment manufacture, and custom clothing. Also under the heading of intermittent is *unit* production, referring to the manufacture of one-of-a-kind items or items made one by one. Unit production is typified by large turbine, airplane, and ship manufacture, and major *projects* such as found in construction.

While the decision as to which general type of process to use is often straightforward, choosing a specific method for manufacture can be quite involved. Consider the alternative processes for fabricating, joining, and finishing two pieces of metal. According to Exhibit 2.6, there are 11 possible casting and molding processes, 8 cutting processes, 10 forming processes, 7 assembly processes, and 8 finishing processes, or 44 processes in all. To evaluate all possible five-stage sequences would involve (5) $\times$ (11 $\times$ 8 $\times$ 10 $\times$ 7 $\times$ 8), or 246,400 decisions (assuming that the selection of a process in one stage does not eliminate a process in another)—clearly a large undertaking if we seek an optimum combination. In practice, of course, the assumption of no process dependence would be violated since some processes would not be performed on the same piece of metal— sand casting *and* forging, for example. Also, expert judgment, built upon technical training, substantially reduces the number of reasonable alternatives. Still, it can pose a tough problem, which can be more complex if

EXHIBIT 2.6
Basic processes in manufacture of hardware

Casting and molding	Cutting	Forming	Assembly	Finishing
Sand casting	Turning	Forging	Soldering	Cleaning
Shell casting	Drilling	Extrusion	Brazing	Blasting
Investment casting	Milling	Punching	Welding	Deburring
Die casting	Shaping	Trimming	Mechanical	Painting
Permanent mold	Cutoff	Drawing	fastening	Plating
casting	Broaching	Rolling	Cementing	Heat
Powdered metal	Grinding	Forming	Press fitting	treatment
molding	Honing	Coining	Shrink fitting	Buffing
Compression molding		Swaging		Polishing
Transfer		Spinning		
Extrusion				
Injection molding				
Laminating				

the metals themselves become decision variables. Similar problems of choice arise in many manufacturing situations.

Looking at the process-selection decision in a broader context, continuous process industries *generally* provide fewer options since the technology is often analogous to one big machine, rather than a linkage of several individual machines. Intermittent processes and to a lesser degree, repetitive processes often can be decoupled into discrete processing stages and as a result, present management with more production alternatives.

Specific equipment choice. This is a key comparison which must be made before specific equipment is selected. The choice not only involves a significant investment decision but may also set the limits of production system operation for a long time to come. Factors that should be considered in this comparison are given in Exhibit 2.7.

Firms may have both general-purpose equipment and special-purpose equipment. For example, a machine shop would have lathes and drill presses (general-purpose) and could have transfer machines (special-purpose). A hospital would have a spectrophotometer to perform only one blood test at a time (general-purpose) and may have a multiphasic screening unit to perform multiple tests at the same time (special-purpose). An auto repair shop would have test gauges (general-purpose) and may have a diagnostic center (special-purpose).

Automation. One of the significant developments in the "specific equipment choice" area in recent years is *automation*. This term, while familiar to most people, still eludes a commonly agreed upon definition. Some authorities view automation as a totally new set of concepts that relate to the automatic operation of a production process; others view it as simply an evolutionary development in technology wherein machinery performs some or all of the process-control function. The view of automation we prefer is first, that it replaces human supervision of machines and productive processes by automatic supervision and second, that this substitution requires a closed loop or feedback control to enable the machine or process to control its performance at any moment by means of data sup-

EXHIBIT 2.7
General versus special-purpose equipment choices

Decision variables	General-purpose equipment	Special-purpose equipment
Initial investment	Lower due to more suppliers and availability of used models	
Output rate		Higher due to less handling and rapid loading; not necessarily due to faster running speeds
Direct labor		Lower, but indirect may be higher
Flexibility	By definition they have a broader range of application	
Setup time	Less; problems are more predictable	
Maintenance	Less complex equipment requires less skill in repair; greater availability of parts	
Product quality		Greater consistency due to reduced relocation from one piece of equipment to another
Obsolescence	Less affected because of easier modification and easier use in other situations	
In-process inventory		Few breaks in production sequence and therefore less opportunity for inventory buildup
Amount of equipment required	Greater variety of operations can be performed on each piece of equipment, so redundant units are less likely to be required	
Operator skill requirements	Depends on equipment operation, monitoring, and setup	

plied to the "automatic" control unit that supervises the operation. By this conceptualization, automation is a new set of concepts (relating to control) and is also evolutionary in the sense that it is a logical and predictable step in the development of equipment and processes.

Some major recent developments in manufacturing automation lie in computer aided manufacturing (CAM), machining centers, and industrial robots.[3]

Computer aided manufacturing is a sophisticated extension of direct numerical control of machine tools. In CAM systems the computer not only directs machine movements but assists in data requisitions as well. In its ultimate application, once loaded, all of the machines in a factory are run automatically by the computer, which in addition generates status reports on run time, quality levels, inventory levels, and so forth.

Machining centers are an extension of CAM which in addition to automatic control of machinery processes have the capability of automatic

---

[3] For a thorough discussion of these new technologies, see Herber W. Yankee, *Manufacturing Processes* (Englewood Cliffs, N.J.: Prentice-Hall, 1979).

tooling changes. For example, a single machine may be equipped with a shuttle system of two work tables that can be rolled into and out of the machine. While this work is being done at one table, the next part can be mounted on the second table. Then when machining is complete, the first table is moved out of the way and the second part is moved into position.[4]

Industrial robots are essentially mechanized arms which can be fitted with a variety of hand-like fingers or grippers, vacuum cups, or a tool such as a wrench. They are capable of performing many factory operations ranging from machining processes to simple assembly. There are at present only about 8,000 robots used around the world (mostly in Japan), but their low cost and easy programmability suggests that they will become widely employed in the future. Exhibit 2.8 provides a sampling of their current application.

Process flow choice. Although this is the last phase to be discussed, process flow considerations generally enter into the earlier specific component choice and minor technological choice. Obviously, unless sufficient thought is given to the flow of the product through the factory, it is difficult to determine the type and number of machines required. One reason process flow is presented at this point is that, unlike the other choices, it recurs as output and product mix change. In job shops, for example, different products follow different routes through their manufacture, some even skipping entire operations for which equipment is available. In this type of production, therefore, the process flow can only be estimated at the time the equipment is selected and thus presents a rather challenging problem in layout design (see Chapter 8).

Several production management tools are used in dealing with the process flow; the most common are assembly drawings, assembly charts, route sheets, and flow process charts. It should be noted that each of these charts is a useful diagnostic tool and therefore is employed for improving operations during the steady state of the productive system.

An assembly drawing such as Exhibit 2.9 is simply an "exploded" view of the product in terms of its component parts. An assembly or Gozinto[5] chart as in Exhibit 2.10 utilizes the information presented in the assembly drawing and defines (among other things) how parts go together, their order of assembly, and often the overall material flow pattern. An operation and route sheet (as in Exhibit 2.11), as its name implies, specifies operations and process routing for a particular part. It conveys such information as the type of equipment, tooling, and operations required to complete the item.

A flow process chart such as Exhibit 2.12 typically uses standard ASME

[4] Ibid, p. 28.

[5] A. Vazsonyi credits the development of this type of chart to the "celebrated Italian mathematician Zepartzat Gozinto." (See A. Vazsonyi, *Scientific Programming in Business and Industry,* New York: John Wiley & Sons, 1958), p. 429.

EXHIBIT 2.8
**Automatons
are all around**

The future of industrial robots looks black—in terms of ink, that is. It took the robot business years to pass from prototype to profit, but the industrial robot's ability to, quite literally, lend a hand around the shop is gaining recognition. Here are just a few specific applications robots have received:

• International Harvester/Canada has applied robots to a heat-treating and forming line used in producing harrow disks. The robots have resulted in improved quality, increased production volume, and better production control. And the workers who were replaced are delighted, having been reassigned to work that is not so hot and heavy.

• Xerox uses robots in manufacturing a family of duplicator parts. Robots were chosen over single-purpose hard automation because their flexibility can accommodate the model changes and variable demand of this operation. The robots' manufacturer also notes that this soft automation "resulted in a high degree of unit machine independence, minimized control system complexity, and included the ability to support and maintain the equipment by plant maintenance personnel."

• Robot welding systems at several Chrysler assembly plants have reduced the time and cost required by model changeovers. "This, along with the flexibility of the system during operation, is important to us because we operate with fewer assembly lines than most of our competitors," said Richard A. Vining, vice-president of Chrysler's Stamping and Assembly Division, where the first system was planned. "When you've got fewer lines, you need more flexibility to handle your product mix."

• Labor costs are rising, but small-batch manufacturers may find hard automation too expensive for their low-volume needs. Do-ALL Co., a leading supplier of machine tools, cutting tools, and precision measuring equipment, increased productivity by incorporating robots in a small-batch system using conventional and NC equipment. The robot operation combines the programming convenience of computer numerically controlled equipment (CNC) with a simplified approach to parts classification, thus boosting efficiency without the expense of group technology using computer-aided design/computer aided manufacturing (CAD/CAM) techniques.

Source: Carl Remick, "Robots: New Faces on the Production Line," *Management Review*, vol, 68, no. 5 (May 1979), p. 27.

EXHIBIT 2.9
**Plug assembly
drawing**

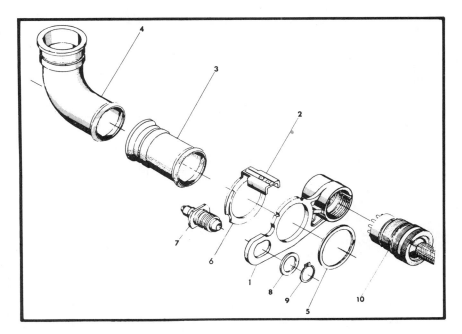

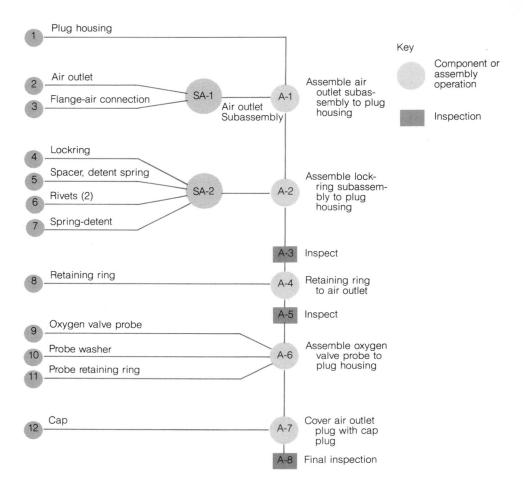

EXHIBIT 2.10
Assembly (or "Gozinto") chart for plug assembly

Key

○ Component or assembly operation

■ Inspection

1 — Plug housing

2 — Air outlet
3 — Flange-air connection
— SA-1 Air outlet Subassembly — A-1 Assemble air outlet subassembly to plug housing

4 — Lockring
5 — Spacer, detent spring
6 — Rivets (2)
7 — Spring-detent
— SA-2 — A-2 Assemble lockring subassembly to plug housing

A-3 Inspect

8 — Retaining ring — A-4 Retaining ring to air outlet

A-5 Inspect

9 — Oxygen valve probe
10 — Probe washer
11 — Probe retaining ring
— A-6 Assemble oxygen valve probe to plug housing

12 — Cap — A-7 Cover air outlet plug with cap plug

A-8 Final inspection

EXHIBIT 2.11
Operation and route sheet for plug assembly

Material Specs. _____	Part Name: Plug Housing	Part No. TA 1274
Purchased Stock Size _____	Usage: Plug Assembly	Date Issued _____
Pcs. Per Pur. Size _____	Assy. No. TA 1279	Date Sup'd. _____
Weight _____	Sub. Assy. No. _____	Issued By _____

Oper. No.	Operation Description	Dept.	Machine	Set Up Hr.	Rate Pc/Hr	Tools
20	Drill 1 hole .312 +.015 -.005	Drill	Mach 513 Deka 4	1.5	254	Drill Fixture L-76, Jig #10393
30	Deburr .312 +.015 -.005 Dia. Hole	Drill	Mach 510 Drill	.1	424	Multi-Tooth Burring Tool
40	Chamfer .900/.875, Bore .828/.875 dia. (2 Passes), Bore .7600/.7625 (1 Pass)	Lathe	Mach D109 Lathe	1.0	44	Ramet-1, TPG 221, Chamfer Tool
50	Tap Holes as designated - 1/4 Min. Full Thread	Tap	Mach 514 Drill Tap	2.0	180	Fixture #CR-353, Tap, 4 Flute Sp.
60	Bore Hole 1.133 to 1.138 Dia.	Lathe	H&H E107	3.0	158	L44 Turrett Fixture, Hartford
						Superspacer, pl. #45, Holder #L46,
						FDTW-100, Inser #21, Chk. Fixture
70	Deburr .005 to .010, Both Sides, Hand Feed To Hard Stop	Lathe	E162 Lathe	.5	176	Collet #CR179, 1327 RPM
80	Broach Keyway To Remove Thread Burrs	Drill	Mach. 507 Drill	.4	91	B87 Fixture, L59 Broach, Tap. .875120 G-H6
90	Hone Thread I.D. .822/.828	Grind	Grinder		120	
95	Hone .7600/.7625	Grind	Grinder		120	

Source: Arizona Gear & Manufacturing Company.

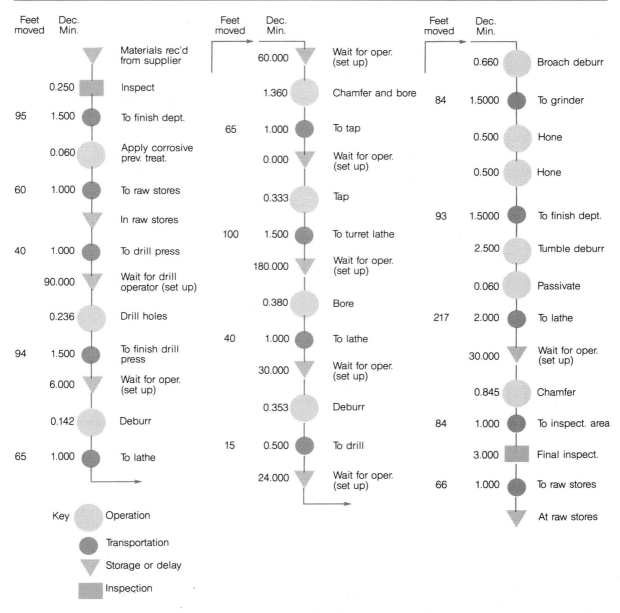

Feet moved	Dec. Min.			Feet moved	Dec. Min.			Feet moved	Dec. Min.		
		▽	Materials rec'd from supplier		60.000	▽	Wait for oper. (set up)		0.660	○	Broach deburr
	0.250	▢	Inspect		1.360	○	Chamfer and bore	84	1.5000	●	To grinder
95	1.500	●	To finish dept.	65	1.000	●	To tap		0.500	○	Hone
	0.060	○	Apply corrosive prev. treat.		0.000	▽	Wait for oper. (set up)		0.500	○	Hone
60	1.000	●	To raw stores		0.333	○	Tap	93	1.5000	●	To finish dept.
		▽	In raw stores	100	1.500	●	To turret lathe		2.500	○	Tumble deburr
40	1.000	●	To drill press		180.000	▽	Wait for oper. (set up)		0.060	○	Passivate
	90.000	▽	Wait for drill operator (set up)		0.380	○	Bore	217	2.000	●	To lathe
	0.236	○	Drill holes	40	1.000	●	To lathe		30.000	▽	Wait for oper. (set up)
94	1.500	●	To finish drill press		30.000	▽	Wait for oper. (set up)		0.845	○	Chamfer
	6.000	▽	Wait for oper. (set up)		0.353	○	Deburr	84	1.000	●	To inspect. area
	0.142	○	Deburr	15	0.500	●	To drill		3.000	▢	Final inspect.
65	1.000	●	To lathe		24.000	▽	Wait for oper. (set up)	66	1.000	●	To raw stores
										▽	At raw stores

Key
○ Operation
● Transportation
▽ Storage or delay
▢ Inspection

EXHIBIT 2.12
Flow process chart of plug housing from plug assembly

Note: These production times were based on a run of 500 items.
Source: Arizona Gear & Manufacturing Company.

(American Society of Mechanical Engineers) symbols to denote what happens to the product as it progresses through the productive facility. As a rule, the fewer the delays and storages in the process, the better the flow—although there are exceptions. For example, if there were no delays in processing for any product, it might signal that the system is not working to capacity since there is always free equipment and available personnel.

CONCLUSION

In this chapter, we have attempted to organize product design and process selection in terms of the decisions that must be made in undertaking these activities. It should be emphasized that while means exist for improving product design[6] after full-scale production is under way, a systematic, before-the-fact analysis of production considerations (for example, simplification and compatibility) is generally far less costly. Undoubtedly, an ounce of prevention is worth a pound of cure. Likewise, to look beyond initial costs and process alternatives to questions of adaptability and obsolescence in process selection is obvious good sense.

As a final comment, while a career in manufacturing may not be one's life goal, an appreciation of what's involved in it is warranted when we consider that the food we eat, the clothes we wear, and our living environment are all, to some extent, the result of manufacturing processes.

REVIEW AND DISCUSSION QUESTIONS

1. What is the primary production document derived from the product design process? What other types of documents does one require to make a product?

2. What is the "modular design problem?" Give an example of a product that uses this concept as a selling point.

3. What cost tradeoffs must be made in choosing standardized versus customized subassemblies?

4. What is the difference between automation and mechanization?

5. Why should a person trained in business administration be concerned with manufacturing processes?

6. With reference to Exhibit 2.3, what form does the product specification take for the following organizations: a wine company, a book publisher, a baseball-card manufacturer?

7. What type of manufacturing process (i.e., continuous, repetitive, or intermittent) would you expect to be dominant in the organizations listed in question 6 above?

8. You have just accepted a position as a robot salesman for the R2D2 Industrial Robot Company. Your first potential customer is a manufacturer of lawn mower blades who supplies blades of different sizes to a variety of end product manufacturers.

    What points would you emphasize to get the manufacturer to shift from its general purpose manually operated heat treating equipment to your robots?

PROBLEMS

1. The manager of Kosher Comida Food Company, Manuel Schwartz, is trying to decide which of two products should be developed by his firm. One of

---

[6] For example, *Value Analysis* programs. (See Chapter 19 "Maintaining and Improving the System.")

$C+S = 7.5$ | 9.5
$CCS = 5$ | 8.0
$AV = 500,000$ | $300,000$
$P = 45¢/lb$ | $35¢$
$L = 5 years$ | 5
$TPC = 20,000$ | 2000
2000 | $60,000$
$120,000$ | $120,000$
$750,000$ | $750,000$
$892,000$ | $93,$

$PVI = 21.15$

these is *huevos rapidos* (instant eggs), which would be made by flash freezing and drying chicken eggs and then mixing them with a combination of chili peppers specially grown for this purpose. The end result would be a Mexican omelet for use by campers and harried housewives. The other product is a chili bagel, which, according to a local delicatessen owner, "when topped with smoked salmon and cream cheese will become a new taste sensation that will displace both corned beef sandwiches and tamales as the standard lunch of the Southwest."

Schwartz figures that the probability of being able to produce *huevos rapidos* is 75 percent, the chances of it being a success in the market are 50–50, and annual sales should be about 400,000 pounds for the next five years. He figures he can sell the product at $0.75 a pound to retailers and that it will cost $0.30 a pound. He estimates that the cost of developing the process and the new chili will be about $20,000 and that modifications of existing equipment to produce *huevos rapidos* at full-scale production levels will cost about $2,000.

Schwartz estimates that the probability of producing a satisfactory chili bagel, or "chigel" as the boys in R&D refer to it, is 95 percent. He figures that the probability of its being a success in the market is 80 percent, with annual sales being about 300,000 pounds for the next five years. Chigels should cost about $0.50 a pound and sell for $0.85 a pound to retailers. The cost of developing the chigel process is $2,000, and a high-speed bagel press and special packaging line will have to be purchased at a total cost of $60,000.

The work force required for either product is projected as six full-time operators at $4 per hour, fifty weeks per year.

Schwartz estimates his cost of capital as 10 percent.

Given the above information, choose between the products using the project value index formula.

2. Bo Schwartz (Manuel's wife) is considering introducing a new novelty item for sale to summer visitors in the Catskill Mountains in upstate New York. This product is a wraparound sash which has pockets which vacationers to the area could carry their suntan lotion, playing cards (or Mah-Jongg tiles), and "noches" (e.g., chili bagels). The sash, which she will market as "Borscht Belts" was greeted with wild enthusiasm by members of her yoga club.

The prototype model consists of six identical naugahyde pockets which are sewn onto a terry cloth sash, and a metal buckle in the shape of different astrological signs. Once production begins, Bo will obtain naugahyde and terry cloth in bulk rolls, and buckles will be supplied by a local machine shop. Bo has available two heavy-duty sewing machines and a stud-riveting machine (left over from her Burt Reynolds Levi pants production) to attach the belt buckles. Prior to entering production, she would like to know:

a. What an assembly chart would look like for the belts.
b. What a flow process chart would look like for the entire operation from raw materials receipt to final inspection.

3. SYSTEM DESIGN EXERCISE.

The purpose of this exercise is to gain experience in setting up a manufacturing process. (We suggest that this be done as a team project.)
Assignment:
a. Get one ping pong paddle.
b. Specify the type of equipment and raw materials you would need to

manufacture that paddle from the receipt of seasoned wood to packaging for shipment.

c. Assume that one unit of each type of equipment is available to you and is already placed in, say, a rented hanger at your local airport. Further assume that you have a stock of seasoned wood and other materials needed to produce and box 100 paddles. Making reasonable assumptions about times and distances where necessary,

   (1) Develop an assembly drawing for the paddle.
   (2) Prepare an assembly chart for the paddle.
   (3) Develop a flow process chart for the paddle.
   (4) Develop a route sheet for the paddle.

SELECTED BIBLIOGRAPHY

Chaddock, D. H.   "Sparkling Ideas in the Design Process," *Engineering* (July 1974), pp. 550–52.

Gavett, J. William.   *Production and Operations Management.* New York: Harcourt, Brace and World, Inc., 1968.

Jacobson, R. A.   "Design with Manufacturing in Mind," *Machine Design* (November 14, 1974), pp. 144–49.

Niebel, B. W., and Draper, A. B.   *Product Design and Process Engineering.* New York: McGraw-Hill Book Company, 1974.

Remick, Carl.   "Robots: New Faces on the Production Line," *Management Review,* vol. 68, no. 5 (May 1979), p. 27.

Yankee, Herbert, W.   *Manufacturing Processes,* Englewood Cliffs, N. J.: Prentice-Hall, 1979.

Chapter 3

PRODUCT DESIGN AND PROCESS SELECTION— SERVICES

Service: adjective—the trades—from filling stations to universities.

Webster's New Collegiate
Dictionary, 1973.

The growth of service organizations in both the public and private sector has spurred interest in the subject on the part of practitioners, students, and teachers of operations management. In this chapter, we will lay the groundwork for subsequent discussions of services throughout the book by presenting our particular view of service systems. Procedurally, we will first discuss the nature and importance of service systems as they pertain to OM. Next we will present a classification scheme for services based upon the unique influence of the customer on service production. Then we will provide some observations about product design and process selection in general and conclude with a review of two current philosophies of service system design.

THE NATURE AND IMPORTANCE OF SERVICES

Looking at the importance question first, Exhibit 3.1, showing employment trends, illustrates the growth of services in the past twelve years. Not only is there remarkable growth in the category labeled "services, personal, professional, business" but in areas which contain a large number of service operations such as government, finance, and transportation. Similar trends exist for other developed countries, especially Canada and those of Western Europe. Clearly, the provision of services is big business and deserving of serious study by students of OM.

Regarding the nature of services, our work in the area leads to the four following generalizations about what must be considered a vast topic.

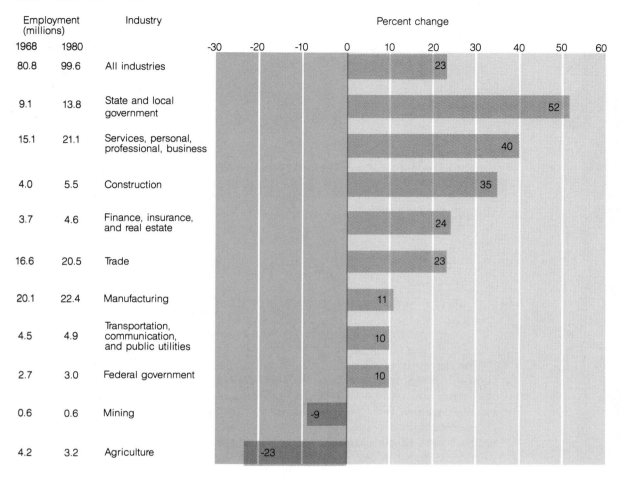

Employment (millions)		Industry	Percent change
1968	1980		
80.8	99.6	All industries	23
9.1	13.8	State and local government	52
15.1	21.1	Services, personal, professional, business	40
4.0	5.5	Construction	35
3.7	4.6	Finance, insurance, and real estate	24
16.6	20.5	Trade	23
20.1	22.4	Manufacturing	11
4.5	4.9	Transportation, communication, and public utilities	10
2.7	3.0	Federal government	10
0.6	0.6	Mining	-9
4.2	3.2	Agriculture	-23

Source: U.S. Department of Labor.

EXHIBIT 3.1

Employment trends in various industry sectors, 1968–1980

1. Everyone is an expert on services. That is, we all think we know what we want from a service organization and, by the very process of living, we have a good deal of experience with the service creation process.

2. Services are idiosyncratic—what works well in the provision of one kind of service may prove disastrous in the provision of another kind. For example, consuming a meal at a restaurant in less than half an hour may be exactly what you want at Jack-in-the-Box but be totally unacceptable at an expensive French restaurant.

3. Service quality is in the eye of the beholder. In this case people are idiosyncratic. Some people want to chat with the clerk at the supermarket checkout stand; others want to avoid any such delays (or amenities?).

4. Most services contain a mix of tangible and intangible attributes. This creates problems in defining what constitutes the critical elements

of the service product and hence, in effectively managing the service system.

A CLASSIFICATION OF SERVICES

The nature of services described above serves as a basis for our thinking about service-system classification. This classification and its implications for service-system design which follow are taken from a recent *Harvard Business Review* article written by one of the authors.[1] Service systems are generally classified according to the service they provide, as delineated in the Standard Industrial Classification (SIC) code. This classification, though useful in presenting aggregate economic data for comparative purposes, does not deal with the production activities through which the service is carried out. What the manager needs, it would seem, is a service classification system that indicates with greater precision the nature of the demands on his or her particular service system in terms of its operating requirements. In manufacturing, by contrast, there are fairly evocative terms to classify production activities (e.g., unit, batch, and mass production), which, when applied to a manufacturing setting, readily convey the essence of the process.

It is possible, of course, to describe certain service systems using manufacturing terms, but such terms, as in the case of the SIC code, are insufficient for diagnosing and thinking about how to improve the systems without one additional item of information. That item—which we believe operationally distinguishes one service system from another in terms of what they can and cannot achieve in the way of efficiency—is the extent of customer contact in the creation of the service.

To elaborate, *customer contact* refers to the physical presence of the customer in the system, and *creation of the service* refers to the work process that is entailed in providing the service itself. *Extent* of contact here may be roughly defined as the percentage of time the customer must be in the system relative to the total time it takes to serve him. Obviously, the greater the percentage of contact time between the service system and the customer, the greater the degree of interaction between the two during the production process.

From this conceptualization, it follows that service systems with high customer contact are more difficult to control and more difficult to rationalize than those with low customer contact. In high-contact systems, such as those listed in Exhibit 3.2, the customer can affect the time of demand, the exact nature of the service, and the quality of service since he tends to become involved in the process itself. In low-contact systems, by definition, customer interaction with the system is infrequent or of short duration and hence has little impact on the system during the production process.

---

[1] R. B. Chase, "Where Does the Customer Fit in a Service Operation?" *Harvard Business Review,* vol. 56, no. 6, (November–December 1978), pp. 137–42.

EXHIBIT 3.2
**Classification
of various
service systems
by extent of
required
customer
contact in the
creation of the
service product**

Pure services *(typically high contact)*	*Mixed services* *(typically medium contact)*	*Quasi-manufacturing* *(typically low contact)*
Entertainment centers	"Branch" offices of: financial institutions government computer firms law firms ad agencies real estate firms etc.	"Home" offices of: financial institutions government computer firms law firms ad agencies real estate firms etc.
Health centers		
Hotels		
Public transportation		
Retail establishments		
	Park service	Wholesale establishments
Schools	Police and fire departments	Postal service
Personal services	Janitoral services	Mail order services
Jails	Moving companies	News syndicates
	Repair shops	Research laboratories
	Funeral homes	

Increasing freedom in designing efficient production procedures →

Technical core

One way to conceive of high- versus low-contact business is that the low-contact system has the capability of decoupling operations and sealing off the "technical core" from the environment, while the high-contact system does not. As one researcher has pointed out, "The technical core must be able to operate as if the market will absorb the single kind of product at a continuous rate and as if inputs flowed continuously at a steady rate with specified quality."[2] Indeed, decoupling production from outside influences (for example, via inventory buffers) is a common objective in designing manufacturing systems.

Several industries provide examples of shifts in customer contact through two or more of the stages given in Exhibit 3.2:

1. Automatic banking tellers, with their 24-hour availability and their location for easy access, illustrate pure service; branch offices, with their provision of drive-in tellers, coordinated waiting lines, and often visible back offices, illustrate mixed service; and home offices, designed for efficient receipt, processing, and shipping of bank paper, illustrate quasi-manufacturing.

2. Airlines exhibit mixed service characteristics at their terminals (high-contact ticket counters and low-contact baggage handling), pure service characteristics within the planes, and quasi-manufacturing characteristics in their billing and airplane maintenance operations.

3. Blood collection stations provide an obvious example of pure service—they are (or should be) operated with the psychological and physiological needs of the donor in mind and, in fact, often take the "service"

[2] James D. Thompson, *Organizations in Action* (New York: McGraw-Hill Book Company, 1967), p. 20.

to the donor by using bloodmobiles. The blood itself is processed at specialized facilities (bloodbanks) following "manufacturing" procedures common to batch processing.

4. Many consulting firms switch back and forth between pure service and quasi-manufacturing. Pure service takes place when data are gathered at the client's facility, while quasi-manufacturing takes place when data are analyzed and reports are prepared at the firm's home offices. Other firms, of course, have facilities designed for mixed service operations; their client waiting areas are planned in detail to convey a particular image, and back offices are arranged for efficient noncontact work.

Effect on operations

Of course, the reason it is important to determine how much customer contact is required to provide a service is that it has an effect on every decision that production managers must make. Exhibit 3.3 is a list of some of the more interesting decisions relating to system design. The points made in this exhibit lead to four generalizations about the two classes of services systems.

First, high-contact systems have more uncertainty about their day-to-day operations since the customer can always make an input to (or cause a disruption in) the production process. Even in those high-contact systems that have relatively high specified products and processes, the customer can "have it his way." Burger King will fill special orders, TWA will (on occasion) delay a takeoff for a late arrival, a hospital operating-room schedule will be disrupted for emergency surgery, and so on.

Second, unless the system operates on an appointments-only basis, it is only by happenstance that the capacity of a high-contact system will match the demand on that system at any given time. The manager of a supermarket, branch bank, or entertainment facility can predict only statistically the number of people that will be in line demanding service at, say, two o'clock on Tuesday afternoon. Hence, employing the correct number of servers (neither too many nor too few) must also depend on probability.

Low-contact systems, on the other hand, have the potential to exactly match supply and demand for their services since the work to be done (e.g., forms to be completed, credit ratings analyzed, or household goods shipped) can be carried out following a resource-oriented schedule permitting a direct equivalency between producer and product.

Third, by definition, the required skills of the work force in high-contact systems are characterized by a significant public relations component. Any interaction with the customer makes the direct worker in fact part of the product and, therefore, his attitude can affect the customer's view of the service provided.

Finally, high-contact systems are at the mercy of time far more than low-contact systems. Batching of orders for purposes of efficient production scheduling is rarely possible in high-contact operations since a few minutes' delay or a violation of the law of the queue (first come,

Decision	High-contact system	Low-contact system
Facility location	Operations must be near the customer.	Operations may be placed near supply, transport, or labor.
Facility layout	Facility should accommodate the customer's physical and psychological needs and expectations.	Facility should enhance production.
Product design	Environment as well as the physical product define the nature of the service.	Customer is not in the service environment so the product can be defined by fewer attributes.
Process design	Stages of production process have a direct immediate effect on the customer.	Customer is not involved in the majority of processing steps.
Scheduling	Customer is in the production schedule and must be accommodated.	Customer is concerned mainly with completion dates.
Production planning	Orders cannot be stored, so smoothing production flow will result in loss of business.	Both backlogging and production smoothing are possible.
Worker skills	Direct work force comprises a major part of the service product and so must be able to interact well with the public.	Direct work force need only have technical skills.
Quality control	Quality standards are often in the eye of the beholder and hence variable.	Quality standards are generally measurable and hence fixed.
Time standards	Service time depends on customer needs, and therefore, time standards are inherently loose.	Work is performed on customer surrogates (e.g., forms), and time standards can be tight.
Wage payment	Variable output requires time-based wage systems.	"Fixable" output permits output-based wage systems.
Capacity planning	To avoid lost sales, capacity must be set to match peak demand.	Storable output permits setting capacity at some average demand level.
Forecasting	Forecasts are short-term, time-oriented.	Forecasts are long-term, output-oriented.

first served) has an immediate effect on the customer. Indeed, "unfair" preferential treatment in a line at a box office often gives rise to some of the darker human emotions, which are rarely evoked by the same unfair preferential treatment that is employed by a distant ticket agency whose machinations go unobserved by the customer.

Implications for management

Several implications may be drawn from the foregoing discussion of differences between high-contact and low-contact systems.

To start with, rationalizing the operations of a high-contact system can be carried only so far. While technological devices can be substituted for some jobs performed by direct-contact workers, the worker's attitude, the environment of the facility, and the attitude of the customer will determine the ultimate quality of the service experience.

Another point to keep in mind is that the often-drawn distinction between for-profit and not-for-profit services has little, if any, meaning from a production management standpoint. A not-for-profit home office can be operated as efficiently as a for-profit home office, and conversely, a high-contact, for-profit branch is subject to the same inherent limitations on its efficiency as its not-for-profit counterparts.

Clearly, wherever possible, a distinction should be made between the high-contact and low-contact elements of a service system. This can be done by a separation of functions: all high-contact activities should be performed by one group of people, all low-contact activities by another. Such an adjustment minimizes the influence of the customer on the production process and provides opportunities to achieve efficiency where it is actually possible to do so.

Finally, it follows that separation of functions enhances the development of two contrasting classes of worker skills and orientations—public relations and interpersonal attributes for high-contact purposes and technical and analytical attributes for low-contact purposes. While some writers have urged mixing of duties under the general rubric of job enrichment, a careful analysis before doing so seems warranted when one recognizes the considerable differences in the skills required between high- and low-contact systems.

SERVICE PRODUCT DESIGN AND DEVELOPMENT SEQUENCE

Although there are significant operating questions arising from whether management is concerned with the high- or low-contact portion of a given service system, the general service design and development sequence is analogous to that of manufacturing when the service organization is first starting out. That is:

1. Idea generation.
2. Product selection.
3. Preliminary design.
4. Final design.
5. Facility requirements.
6. Process selection.
7. Downstream decisions (capacity, layout, production planning, scheduling).

There are, however, some notable differences. First, the output of the final design step is a combination of tangible product and intangible service features. Secondly, the development sequence is less formalized, and there is less product testing in services. Further (in private industry), marketing enhancements are part of virtually every step of the sequence, in contrast to manufacturing where the details of design are turned over to engineering and production at the final design stage. Thirdly, services are often "designed" by the training individuals receive before they become part of the service organization. In particular, professional service organizations (or PSOs as they are often called) are usually severely limited in what changes they can make in the duties carried out by these members. Doctors, lawyers, teachers, and so forth bring a rigid discipline to the service system which is instilled by their professional backgrounds. (Customer service organizations (CSOs), such as clothing stores, restaurants, and grocery stores which provide relatively standardized services, are free from such restrictions).

Finally, while the sources of service ideas are often just as unpredictable as for manufactured items, the nature of the service idea is rarely just one thing, such as a calculator, a toy, or a food processor. Rather, new service ideas are concepts which embody many attributes. For example, in a discussion of the founding of Holiday Inns, Lundberg draws upon a range of customer needs in defining what Holiday Inn should try to provide:

> The traveler in the automobile wants to know ahead of time what he will find in the way of food, drink, and lodging. He wants to know what it will cost. He wants security and sanitation. He does not expect luxury but is pleasantly surprised when he gets it for a price within his budget. He expects a certain standard, and he wants it without undue effort or inconvenience on his part.[3]

PRODUCT DESIGN AND PROCESS SELECTION—
HIGH-CONTACT SYSTEMS

In the high-contact side of a service business, product design and process selection are often one and the same. In low-contact systems, they can be treated as separate though interrelated issues. In high-contact systems we have the following three-way interaction:

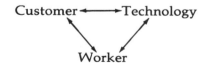

In low-contact systems we have just a two-way interaction:

Technology ←——→ Worker

Obviously, the inclusion of people-to-people interaction in the high-contact system adds complexity and uncertainty. In effect, the organization must account for the fact that the major throughput of the system can

---

[3] Donald E. Lundberg, *The Hotel and Restaurant Business*, 2d ed. (Boston, Mass.: CBI 1976), p. 289.

exert itself in a purposeful way and change the production process. Such is not the case in low-contact operations.

In view of this people-to-people interaction, a high-contact system's *product design* to a large extent boils down to the procedures by which direct workers carry out the process. Such procedures, in turn, must be developed for *information exchanges, material delivery* to and from the customer, *monitary exchanges,* and *physical contact.* Further, these procedures may follow a variable sequence, happen concurrently, and even differ in duration from one customer to the next. The extent to which there is variation is a function of what the product is perceived to be by the customer and the procedural options built into the process itself. In this respect, it is common to think of the service product as being either *standardized* or *customized* in nature. If it is standardized (the same procedural schedule for all customers), it is anticipated that there will be a limited amount of variability in procedures. If it is customized, it is presumed, naturally, that at least some degree of variability in procedures as well as the tangible components will exist. Unfortunately for the system manager, however, services designed to be standardized in fact permit (or cannot avoid) a variable procedure sequence. Some customers, as noted in the *Harvard Business Review* article can disrupt even the most rigidly prescribed process and customize it for their own purposes to some degree. You can, if you are persistent, "have it your way" in many standardized service systems.

PRODUCT DESIGN AND PROCESS SELECTION— LOW-CONTACT SYSTEMS

Product design and process selection in low-contact systems in many instances can be treated in the same way proposed for manufacturing organizations. The product output is often a tangible item (e.g., a document, a repaired item, a filled prescription) which has been created or added to in response to a customer order or initiated by a different function or unit of the organization. Process selection is likewise analogous to manufacturing in that there is often a range of options available with respect to equipment and procedures. For offices, common equipment alternatives are typewriters, calculators, and computers. For restaurants, hospitals, car dealerships, and so forth, the equipment and procedure choices can be made in the same way as for manufacturing. Moreover, even the processing steps can be specified as if the product were being made in a factory. (See the Big Mac assembly diagram in Exhibit 3.4).

EVALUATING SERVICE-SYSTEM DESIGN

Price/
attributes

A common means of evaluating a service is simply to relate its attributes to its price. Successful firms usually find the point where the customer is at least minimally satisfied with the service received relative to the price paid. In the process of seeking this balance, service firms are constantly surveying customers as to their satisfaction with the service. Some-

EXHIBIT 3.4
Assembly chart for a "Big Mac"-type hamburger

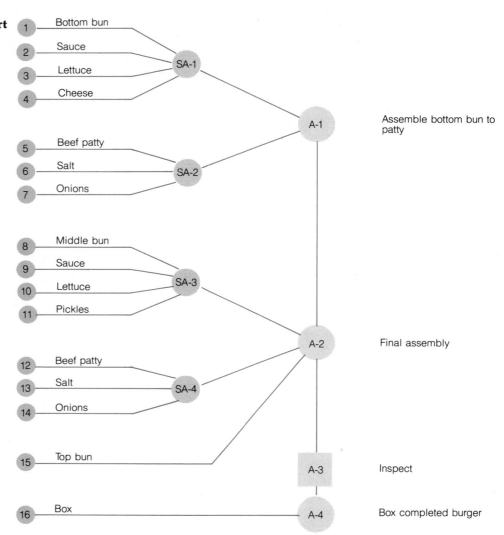

times these surveys are informal, such as asking a customer if everything was OK ("Was the meal good?" or "How was the flight?"). In other instances, it may entail a formal mail questionnaire survey ("Were you treated well at the clinic?" or "How satisfactory is our bank by phone procedure?").

Balance

Many service operations contain a series of steps which take varying amounts of time to complete. When designing or analyzing a service system an attempt should be made to assure that:

1. The steps are arranged in a logical sequence.
2. Capacities of each step are balanced to minimize bottlenecks.
3. Necessary steps are eliminated or the process shortened by paralleling steps.
4. Appropriate flexibility is available at each step.

EXHIBIT 3.5
Flow chart of car rental check-in and check-out process

The information/materials flow chart such as shown in Exhibit 3.5 is particularly useful in carrying out these steps.

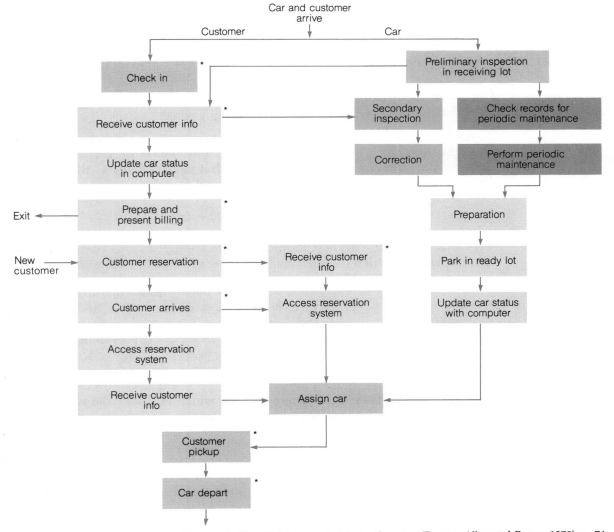

Source: Modified from Sasser, Olsen, and Wycoff, *Management of Service Operations* (Boston: Allyn and Bacon, 1978), p. 74.

Service coverage

Any service organization must decide on how much capacity it must maintain to meet variations in customer demand. This involves a tradeoff between having excess capacity available—too many resources (workers, equipment, inventory, and so forth) with inadequate capacity—(too little of these resources). Too many resources, of course, wastes money, and too few will result in losing customers. A method of approaching this trade-off analytically has been presented in Sasser, et al.[4] They propose the use of a classical marginal analysis formula which provides an optimum service percentage (or "critical fractile," in their words) taking into account cost stockout and cost of excess capacity. This formula is as follows:

$$CF = \frac{C_{so}}{C_{so} + C_o} \times 100$$

where

$CF =$ Critical fractile or desired coverage, %
$C_{so} =$ Cost of stockout, \$/unit of capacity
$C_o =$ Cost of overage, \$/unit of capacity

For example, suppose that the manager of a rental car agency estimates that the average cost of keeping a particular model of car in stock is \$20 per day and the cost of not having that car available is the average lost revenue of \$40 per day. Then the critical fractile is

$$CF = \frac{\$40}{\$40 + \$20} \times 100 = 66\%$$

This means that the agency should provide enough cars to cover demand up to a level of which the manager is 66 percent confident of experiencing.

Time

Time to provide the service is one of the major design features of high-contact systems. Obviously, it is important in marketing the service—for example, "fast foods" and "slow cruises." It is also important in the sense that delays have an instantaneous effect on the system which is magnified because of the customer's presence.

Juran provides the subdivisions of time frequently identified by service industries.[5]

Access time. This is the length of time which elapses from the client's first effort to gain the service company's attention until he has that attention. The standard for this "accessibility" is expressed, for example, in the form:

80% of the incoming telephone calls should be answered within 15 seconds after the first ring.

Measurement of telephone access time can usually be done by automated

---

[4] Earl Sasser, Paul Olson, and Daryl Wycoff, *Management of Service Operations* (Boston: Allyn and Bacon, 1978), p. 91.

[5] J. M. Juran, *Quality Control Handbook* (New York: McGraw-Hill Book Company, 1974), section 47, pp. 4–5.

recorders actuated by the telephone equipment. Other forms of access time require sampling studies by observers.

Queuing time. Some services involve a queuing of clients due to variable loads or to considerations of economy. In such cases the consumer is concerned with:

a. The length of the queue and, therefore, the waiting line. The service company is in a position to plan this based on past history and probability considerations ("queuing theory").

b. The integrity of the queue; that is, adherence to the principle of first come, first served.

Action time. This is commonly defined as the interval between taking the customer's order and providing him with the service requested.

Make-or-buy

We usually think of make-or-buy questions in the context of manufactured products. For example, should a manufacturer of high-quality tape recorders make their own screws and nuts or buy them from a supplier. If they make their own, they are able to match thread sizes exactly and keep quality high. (Kudelski, a Swiss tape-recorder company, does this.) On the other hand, if they buy, they free up their screw-machine capacity for other components and may be able to get a lower per-unit cost from an outside source.

Similarly, service firms have make-or-buy type decisions. For example, a travel agency may package its own tours or buy from a travel broker; a restaurant may make its own veal oscar or buy it frozen from a supplier; and the Dallas Cowboys get their football players through the college draft while the Redskins buy proven veterans from other teams.

In any case, factors which must be weighed in make-or-buy decisions for either services or manufacturing are:

1. Direct costs of items or skills being considered.
2. Opportunity costs related to use of facilities, work force, and capital.
3. Supplier reliability and number of alternative sources.
4. Quality control.
5. Patents and trade secrets.
6. Capacity utilization.
7. Leasing alternatives.

TWO PHILOSOPHIES OF SERVICE DESIGN

Two contrasting views on service-system design are offered by Levitt, on one hand, and Lovelock and Young, on the other.

Substitute technology for people

The product-design and selection process for retail service has been revolutionized by the McDonald's hamburger chain. In an insightful article, Theodore Levitt[6] suggests that an essential feature of McDonald's success is its treating the delivery of fast food as a manufacturing process rather

---

[6] Theodore Levitt, "Production-Line Approach to Service," *Harvard Business Review*, vol. 50, no. 5, (September–October 1972), pp. 41–52.

than a service process. The value of this philosophy is that it overcomes many of the problems that are inherent in the concept of service itself. That is, service implies subordination or subjugation of the server to the served; manufacturing, on the other hand, avoids this connotation because it focuses on things rather than people. Thus in manufacturing and in the case of McDonald's, "the orientation is toward the efficient production of results not on the attendance on others." Levitt notes that besides McDonald's marketing and financing skills, the company carefully controls "the execution of each outlet's central function—the rapid delivery of a uniform, a high-quality mix of prepared foods in an environment of obvious cleanliness, order, and cheerful courtesy. The systematic substitution of equipment for people, combined with the carefully planned use and positioning of technology, enables McDonald's to attract and hold patronage in proportions no predecessor or imitator has managed to duplicate."[7] Levitt cites several aspects of McDonald's operations to illustrate these concepts:

> The McDonald's french fryer allows cooking of the optimum number of french fries at one time.
>
> A wide-mouthed scoop is used to pick up the precise amount of french fries for each order size. (The employee never touches the product.)
>
> Storage space is expressly designed for a predetermined mix of prepackaged and premeasured products. There is no space for any foods that were not designed into the system at the outset.
>
> Cleanliness is pursued by providing ample trash cans in and outside each facility (and the larger outlets have motorized sweepers for the parking area).
>
> Hamburgers are wrapped in color-coded paper and boxes.
>
> Through painstaking attention to total design and facilities planning, everything is built integrally into the (McDonald's) machine itself, into the technology of the system. The only choice available to the attendant is to operate it exactly as the designers intended.[8]

Increase customer involvement

In contrast to Levitt's approach, Lovelock and Young[9] propose that the service process can be enhanced by having the customer take a greater role in the production of the service. Automatic-teller machines, self-service gas stations, direct long-distance dialing, and in-room coffee-making equipment in motels are approaches by which the service burden is shifted to the consumer. Obviously, this philosophy requires some selling on the part of the service organization to convince customers that this is beneficial to them. To this end, Lovelock and Young propose a number of steps including developing customer trust, promoting the benefits in terms of

---

[7] Ibid., p. 44.

[8] Ibid., p. 46.

[9] C. H. Lovelock and R. F. Young, "Look to Customers to Increase Productivity," *Harvard Business Review*, vol. 57, no. 2, 1979, pp. 168–78.

cost, speed, and convenience, and following up to make sure that the procedures are being effectively utilized.

CONCLUSION

Services represent one of the relatively unexplored areas in the field of operations management. And while we believe the contact view answers some questions as to how to deal with them, we fully expect to see other production-oriented theories emerge in the near future. In any event, we hope that the reader will have gained some insight about why services behave as they do and will be able to place in context the concepts and methods discussed in subsequent chapters to make production decisions in service organizations.

REVIEW AND DISCUSSION QUESTIONS

1. Exhibit 3.6 presents 12 propositions relating to *high-contact* services. For each of these propositions, give an example of a service system where it would apply. Choose a different service system example for each.

EXHIBIT 3.6
OM characteristics of high contact services—some propositions

1. The service product is multidimensional (time, place, atmosphere), and hence, its quality is in the eye of the beholder.
2. The direct worker is part of the service product.
3. Demand for the service usually cannot be stored.
4. Because production is generally customer initiated, an optimal balance between service system demand and resources is difficult to achieve.
5. Changes in the capacity of the system affect the nature of the service product.
6. The production schedule has a direct, personal effect on the customer.
7. Only part of the service can be kept in inventory.
8. Verbal skills and knowledge of policy are usually required of the service worker.
9. Wage payments must usually be related to labor hours spent rather than output.
10. It is assumed that service-system capacity is at its long-run level when the system first opens.
11. A service-system malfunction will have an immediate, direct effect on the customer.
12. The location of the service system modifies its value to the customer.

2. Who is the "customer" in a jail? a cemetery? a summer camp for children?

3. Critique the philosophies of service-system design offered by Levitt and Lovelock and Young.

4. Identify the "best restaurant in town." What production features make it the best? Do your classmates agree with your choice? For the same reasons?

5. Explain why, in the face of record prices for gasoline, most gas stations have become self-service.

6. Provide a definition of flexibility in the provision of services. Explain how you achieve "flexibility" in the following services.

   a. A dental office.
   b. An airline.

      c. An accounting office.

      d. An automobile agency.

7. What are the practical limitations of the critical fractile concept?

8. What makes a PSO different from a CSO?

PROBLEMS

SYSTEM DESCRIPTION EXERCISE

The first step in studying a productive system is the development of a description of that system. Once a system is described, we are better able to determine why the system works well or poorly and to recommend production-related improvements. Since we are all familiar with fast-food restaurants, try your hand at describing the production system employed at, say, a McDonald's or Wendy's. In so doing, please organize your description into the categories listed below. (These are the four areas of operations management listed on page 27.) Please don't bother the personnel, as they tend to be a little gun-shy about unidentified observers of their systems who ask questions about their operations.

1. Product:
   a. What is the "product" of the restaurant?
   b. Is it a broad or narrow product line?
   c. Can it be customized?

2. Technology of transformation:
   a. What are the steps in the production-distribution flow within the outlet? Present your answer in the form of a flow chart such as that shown in Exhibit 3.5.
   b. Identify where inventories are held and when quality inspections occur.
   c. Describe schematically the general layout of the system.

3. Operating-control system:
   a. How is on-site production control carried out? (You may wish to show this schematically.)
   b. What is the nature of the organization structure at the outlet? (Try to make an organization chart of the outlet.)

4. Workforce:
   a. What is the skill level of the work force?
   b. What are the critical skills required of the worker?

   General questions:
   1) What do you believe to be the critical production problems faced by the branch manager of the restaurant?
   2) What do you believe to be the critical variables in the success of such an outlet?

SELECTED BIBLIOGRAPHY

Bessom, R. M., and Jackson, D. W. "Service Retailing: A Strategic Marketing Approach," *Journal of Retailing*, vol. 51, no. 2 (1975), pp. 75–84.

Chase, R. B. "Where Does the Customer Fit in a Service Operation?," *Harvard Business Review,* vol. 56 (1978), pp. 137–42.

Levitt, T. "Production Line Approach to Service," *Harvard Business Review,* vol. 50 (1972), pp. 41–52.

Levitt, T. "The Industrialization of Services," *Harvard Business Review,* vol. 54 (1976), pp. 41–52.

Lovelock, C. H., and Young, R. F. "Look to Customers to Increase Productivity," *Harvard Business Review,* vol. 57 (1979), pp. 168–78.

Sasser, W. E.; Olsen, R. P.; and Wyckoff, D. D. *Management of Service Operations.* Boston: Allyn and Bacon, 1978.

Shostack, G. L. "Banks Sell Services—Not Things," *The Bankers Magazine* (1977), pp. 40–45.

Reed, J. "Sure Its a Bank but I think of It as a Factory," *Innovation,* vol. 23 (1971), pp. 19–27.

SECTION TWO

Design of the system

Designing a production system is in reality designing and fitting together subsystems. This section develops these subsystems and introduces technical notes on quantitative tools which can be used for these purposes.

The subsystems, following a typical sequence in the evolution of a production organization are:

Forecasting
Capacity planning
Layout
Quality control
Job design
Production planning
Scheduling
Inventory control

And the tools are:

Financial analysis
Linear programming
Waiting line theory
Simulation

Chapter

4

DESIGN OF THE
FORECASTING SYSTEM

"If I had only known that would happen I would have . . ."

Forecasting is crucial to every business organization. Indeed, virtually every significant management decision is predicated on some forecast of the future. At the corporate level, forecasting is the essence of long-run planning. Within the functional areas, finance and accounting rely on forecasts of demand for budgetary planning and cost control. Marketing relies on sales forecasting in planning new products, compensating sales persons, and so forth. Production and operations management uses forecasts in making periodic decisions involving process selection, capacity planning, and facility layout, and for continual decisions pertaining to production planning, scheduling, and inventory.

In this chapter, we will look at the general types of forecasting and then concentrate primarily on several time series techniques. We will cover moving averages (simple, weighted, exponential), linear regression analysis, trends and seasonal ratios, and "focused forecasting."

Before we begin, however, it is important to stress the fact that a perfect forecast for most companies is a practical impossibility. There are simply too many factors in the business environment that cannot be predicted with certainty. Therefore, rather than search for the perfect forecast, what is far more important is to establish the practice of continual review of forecasts and learning to live with inaccurate forecasts. A satisfactory forecast can be obtained by using two or three techniques and simply looking at them from the common sense view. Are there expected changes in the general economy that will affect the forecast? Are there changes in consumer behaviors? Will there be a shortage of essential complimentary items? And so on. Continual review and updating in light of new data is basic to successful forecasting. Learning to live with forecast inaccuracy is an unavoidable requirement of most production systems and is accomplished by having a flexible production-planning system and competent production managers.

DEMAND MANAGEMENT

"Passive response to demand" and "active influence on demand" are two planning strategies. The passive response states that in some situations a firm would simply accept demand for its products or services as a given factor without making any attempt to change demand. Active influence on demand states that firms, in most situations, can take an active role both in influencing the environment (price cuts, managerial pressure on the sales force, incentives and campaigns) and in adapting themselves to the environment (contracyclical product mix, or creation of order backlogs).

A great deal of coordination is required to "manage" this demand on the firm's productive facilities since these demands originate from a variety of functional areas. For example, replacement parts for repair of previously sold products originate from the product service department; new products are sold through the sales department; restocking standard items may be handled by the factory warehouse; and in-process inventories and partially completed subassemblies are determined by the manufacturing function. The challenge of *demand management* is to blend all of these demands so that the productive system can be utilized efficiently and the products or services delivered on time.

TYPES OF FORECASTING

Forecasting can be divided into four basic types—*qualitative, time series analysis, causal relationships,* and *simulation.*

Qualitative techniques are subjective or judgmental and are based on estimates and opinions. Time series analysis, the focus of this chapter, is based on the idea that data relating to past demand can be used to predict future demand. This past data may include several components, such as trend, seasonal, or cyclical influences, and will be described in the following section. Causal forecasting assumes that demand is related to some underlying factor or factors in the environment. Simulation models allow the forecastor to run through a range of assumptions about the condition of the forecast. Exhibit 4.17 in the conclusion of this chapter briefly describes a variety of the four basic types of forecasting models.

COMPONENTS OF DEMAND

In most cases, the observed demand for products or services can be broken down into six components: average demand for the period, a trend,

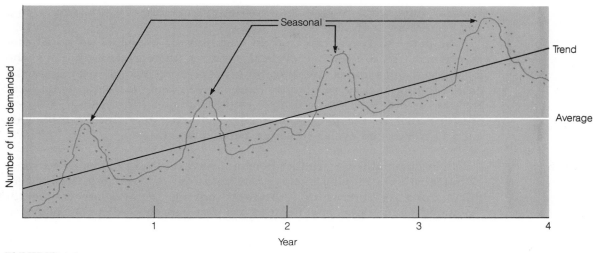

EXHIBIT 4.1
Historical product demand consisting of a growth trend and seasonal demand

seasonal influence, cyclical elements, random variation, and autocorrelation. Exhibit 4.1 illustrates a demand over a four-year period showing the average, trend, seasonal components, and randomness around the smoothed demand curve.

Cyclical factors are more difficult to determine since the time span may be unknown or the cause of the cycle may not be considered. Cyclical influence on demand may be due to such occurrences as political elections, war, economic conditions, or sociological pressures.

Random deviations are caused by natural chance variation. When all known causes for demand are removed from the total demand (average, trend, seasonal, cyclical, and autocorrelative), what remains is the unexplained portion of demand. If one is unable to attribute the cause of this demand to specific sources, it is attributed to natural chance randomness.

Autocorrelation denotes the persistence of occurrence—the value expected at any point in time is highly correlated with its own past values. In queuing theory, the length of a waiting line is highly autocorrelated. That is, if a line is relatively long at one point in time, then shortly after that time one would expect the line still to be long.

When the demand is random, the demand from one week to another may vary widely. Where high autocorrelation exists, the demand will not be expected to change very much from one week to the next.

TIME SERIES ANALYSIS

Time series forecasting models try to predict future occurrences based on a set of past data. For example, weekly sales figures collected for six weeks may be used as a basis to forecast the seventh-week sales. Several familiar time series models are moving average, exponential smoothing, and regression analysis.

Past data, however, can contain a variety of elements as previously mentioned (trend, seasonal, cyclical, random, autocorrelation). Thus, the managerial question is deciding how deeply one wants to analyze the data. Moving-average techniques (simple, weighted, and exponential) use the data as observed. More complicated techniques (Box Jenkins, Fourier, Shiskin) analyze the data statistically and separate it into components such as trends and cycles to gain a better prediction.

Simple moving average

When demand for a product does not have a rapid growth or seasonal characteristics, a moving average can be useful in removing the random fluctuations for forecasting. Although moving averages are frequently "centered," it is more convenient to use past data to predict the following period directly. To illustrate, a centered five-month average of January, February, March, April, and May gives an average centered on March. However, all five months of data must already exist. If our objective is to forecast for June, we must project our moving average—by some means—from March to June. If the average is not centered but is at the forward end, we can forecast more easily, though perhaps we will lose some accuracy. Thus if we want to forecast June with a five-month moving average, we can take the average of January, February, March, April, and May. When June passes, the forecast for July would be the average of February, March, April, May, and June. This is the way in which Exhibit 4.2 and Exhibit 4.3 were computed.

Although it is important to try to select the best period to use for the moving average, there are several conflicting effects of different period lengths: the longer the moving average period, the greater the random elements are smoothed—which may be desirable. However, if there is a trend in the data—either increasing the demand or decreasing it—the moving average has the adverse characteristic of lagging the trend. Therefore, while a shorter time span produces more oscillation, there is a closer "fol-

EXHIBIT 4.2
Forecast demand based on a three- and a nine-week simple moving average

Week	Demand	3 week	9 week	Week	Demand	3 week	9 week
1	800			16	1,700	2,000	1,800
2	1,400			17	1,800	1,833	1,811
3	1,000	1,067		18	2,200	1,900	1,911
4	1,500	1,300		19	1,900	1,967	1,933
5	1,500	1,333		20	2,400	2,167	2,011
6	1,300	1,433		21	2,400	2,233	2,111
7	1,800	1,533		22	2,600	2,467	2,144
8	1,700	1,600		23	2,000	2,333	2,111
9	1,300	1,600	1,367	24	2,500	2,367	2,167
10	1,700	1,567	1,467	25	2,600	2,367	2,267
11	1,700	1,567	1,500	26	2,200	2,433	2,311
12	1,500	1,633	1,556	27	2,200	2,333	2,311
13	2,300	1,833	1,644	28	2,500	2,300	2,378
14	2,300	2,033	1,733	29	2,400	2,367	2,378
15	2,000	2,200	1,811	30	2,100	2,333	2,344

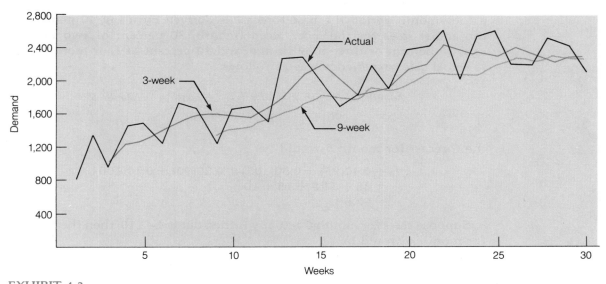

EXHIBIT 4.3
**Moving average
of three- and
nine-week peri-
ods versus actual
demand**

lowing" of the trend. Conversely, a longer time span gives a smoother response but lags the trend.

Exhibit 4.3, a plot of the data in Exhibit 4.2, illustrates the effects of various lengths of the period of a moving average. We see that the growth trend levels off at about the 23rd week. The three-week moving average responds better in following this change than the nine-week, although overall, the nine-week average is smoother.

The main disadvantage in calculating a moving average is that all individual elements must be carried as data since a new forecast period involves adding new data and dropping the earliest data in the moving average string. For a three- or six-period moving average, this is not too severe; however, for a long period, such as the 200-day moving average of the New York Stock Exchange, there is a costly amount of data to carry along.

**Weighted
moving
average**

Whereas the simple moving average gives equal weight to each component of the moving average data base, a weighted moving average allows any weights to be placed on each element, providing, of course, that the sum of all weights equals one. For example, a department store may find that from a four-week data source (28 days), the closest forecasts are made by using 40 percent of the sales experience for the same day in the four previous weeks and the remaining 60 percent as the average of the remaining 24 days. Mathematically, this could be stated as:

$$F_t = 0.40 \frac{(F_{t-7} + F_{t-14} + F_{t-21} + F_{t-28})}{4} + 0.60 \frac{\left(\sum_{t-1}^{t-6} F_t + \sum_{t-8}^{t-13} F_t + \sum_{t-15}^{t-20} F_t + \sum_{t-22}^{t-27} F_t \right)}{24}$$

A simpler example can be used for easier calculation. Suppose that in a four-month period the best forecast is derived by using 40 percent of the actual sales for the most recent month, 30 percent of two months ago, 20 percent of three months ago, and 10 percent of four months ago. If actual sales experience was as follows,

Month 1	Month 2	Month 3	Month 4	Month 5
100	90	105	95	?

the forecast for month 5 would be:

$$F_5 = 0.40(95) + 0.30(105) + 0.20(90) + 0.10(100)$$
$$= 38 + 31.5 + 18 + 10$$
$$= 97.5$$

Suppose sales for month 5 actually turned out to be 110; then the forecast for month 6 would be:

$$F_6 = 0.40(110) + 0.30(95) + 0.20(105) + 0.10(90)$$
$$= 44 + 28.5 + 21 + 9$$
$$= 102.5$$

The weighted moving average has a definite advantage over the simple moving average in being able to vary the effects of past data.

Exponential smoothing

In the previous methods of forecasting (simple moving average, weighted moving average) the major drawback is the need to continually carry a large amount of historical data. (This is also true for regression analysis techniques, which will be covered in the next section.) As each new piece of data is added in these methods, the oldest unit is dropped, and the new forecast is calculated. In many applications (perhaps in most), the most recent occurrences are more indicative of the future than those in the more distant past. If this premise is valid—that the importance of data diminishes as the past becomes more distant—then exponential smoothing may be the most logical and easiest method to use.

Exponential smoothing is the most used of all forecasting techniques. It is an integral part of virtually all computerized forecasting programs, and is widely used in ordering inventory in retail firms, wholesale companies and service agencies.

In using the exponential smoothing method, only three pieces of data are needed to forecast the future: the most recent forecast, the actual demand that occurred for that forecasted period, and a smoothing constant (α). This smoothing constant determines the level of smoothing and the speed of reaction to differences between forecasts and actual occurrences. The value for the constant is arbitrary and is determined both by the nature of the product and the feeling by managers of the firm as to what constitutes a good response rate. For example, if a firm produced a standard item with relatively stable demand, the reaction rate to differences between actual and forecasted demand would tend to be small—perhaps just a few percentage points. However, if the firm were experiencing growth, it would be desirable to have a higher reaction rate in order to give greater importance to recent growth experience. The more rapid the growth, the higher the reaction rate should be. Sometimes, users of simple moving average will switch to exponential smoothing but would like to keep the forecasts about the same as the simple moving average. In this case, alpha is approximated by $\dfrac{2}{(n+1)}$ where n was the number of time periods.

The equation for a single exponential smoothing forecast is simply

$$F_t = F_{t-1} + \alpha(A_{t-1} - F_{t-1})$$

where

F_t is the exponentially smoothed forecast for period t
F_{t-1} is the exponentially smoothed forecast made for the prior period
A_{t-1} is the actual demand in the prior period
α is the desired response rate, or smoothing constant

This equation states that the new forecast is equal to the old forecast plus an adjustment proportional to the difference between the previous forecast and the actual experience.[1]

To demonstrate the method, assume that the long-run demand for the product under study is relatively stable and a smoothing constant (α) of 0.05 is considered appropriate. If the exponential method were used as a continuing policy, a forecast would have been made for last month.[2] Assume that last month's forecast (F_{t-1}) was 1,050 units. If 1,000 actually were demanded, rather than 1,050, the forecast for this month would be

$$\begin{aligned}
F_t &= F_{t-1} + \alpha(A_{t-1} - F_{t-1})\\
&= 1050 + 0.05(1000 - 1050)\\
&= 1050 + 0.05(-50)\\
&= 1047.5 \text{ units}
\end{aligned}$$

Since the smoothing coefficient is small, the reaction of the new forecast to an "error" of 50 units is to decrease this next month's forecast by only 2½ units.

As can be shown, the equation applies exponential weighting since each increment in the past is decreased by $(1 - \alpha)$, or

		Weighing at $\alpha = 0.05$
Most recent weighting	$= \alpha(1 - \alpha)^0$	0.0500
Data 1 time period older	$= \alpha(1 - \alpha)^1$	0.0475
Data 2 time periods older	$= \alpha(1 - \alpha)^2$	0.0451
Data 3 time periods older	$= \alpha(1 - \alpha)^3$	0.0429

[1] Some writers on the topic prefer to call F_t a smoothed average.

[2] When exponential smoothing is first introduced, the initial forecast or starting point may be obtained by using a simple estimate or an average of preceding periods.

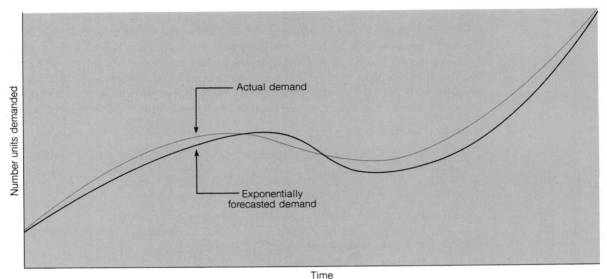

EXHIBIT 4.4
**Exponential
forecasts versus
actual demands
for units of a
product over
time showing the
forecast lag**

Single exponential smoothing has the shortcoming of lagging changes
in demand. Exhibit 4.4 shows a hypothetical demand curve for a product.
On an increase, the forecast lags the actual demand, and when a change
in direction occurs, the forecast "overshoots." To help in closer tracking
of actual demand, a trend factor may be added. What also will help is
to adjust the value of alpha. This is termed *adaptive forecasting.* Both
trend effects and adaptive forecasting are briefly explained in following
sections.

The simple exponential smoothing model has many applications in addition to inventory control. Berry, et al. have shown that simple exponential
smoothing can be valuable in scheduling services, such as bank tellers.[3]
Their study showed that the causes of customer demand can be identified
and used to improve forecasting (such as by banks located near large
employers using known payday schedules). While this had been done
intuitively, the study shows how such forecasting can be routinely used
as an ongoing, continually updated planning tool.

Trend effects in exponential smoothing. As noted above, an upward
or downward trend in data collected over a sequence of time periods will
cause the exponential forecast to always lag behind (be above or below)
the actual occurrence. Exponentially smoothed forecasts can be corrected
somewhat by calculating the differences between the two previous forecasts and adding this amount to the new forecast as:

Forecast including trend (FIT) $= F_t +$ Trend correction

[3] William L. Berry, Vincent A. Mabert, and Myles Marcus, "Forecasting Teller Window
Demand With Exponential Smoothing," *Journal of the Academy of Management,* vol. 22, no. 1
(March 1979), pp. 129–37.

In order to smooth the trend to prevent erratic responses due to stray or random causes, the trend equation uses a smoothing constant δ in the same way as the exponential equation; that is,

$$T_t = T_{t-1} + \delta(F_t - F_{t-1})$$

The value of delta determines how fast the trend responds to differences in the past two forecasts. In order to get this equation going, a trend must be put in the first time it is used (after that, it is computed). This initial trend value can be an educated guess or a computation based on observed past data.

Example. Assume an initial starting forecast of 100 units, a trend of 10 units, an alpha of .20, and a delta of .30. If actual demand turned out to be 115 rather than the forecasted 100, then the next forecast would be

$$F_t = F_{t-1} + \alpha(A_{t-1} - F_{t-1})$$
$$= 100 + .2(115 - 100) = 103$$

The trend is

$$T_t = T_{t-1} + \delta(F_t - F_{t-1})$$
$$= 10 + .3(103 - 100) = 10.9$$

And the forecast including trend (FIT) is

$$FIT_t = F_t + T_t = 103 + 10.9 = 113.9$$

Supposing the actual then turned out to be 120, the sequence would be repeated and the forecast for the next period would be

$$F_{t+1} = 103 + .2(120 - 103) = 106.4$$
$$T_{t+1} = 10.9 + .3(106.4 - 103) = 11.9$$
$$FIT_{t+1} = 106.4 + 11.9 = 118.3$$

Adaptive forecasting

Exponential smoothing requires that the smoothing constant alpha (α) be given a value between 0 and 1. If the real demand is stable (such as demand for electricity or food), we would like a small alpha to lessen the effects of short-term or random changes. If the real demand is rapidly increasing or decreasing (such as in fashion items or new small appliances), we would like a large alpha to try to keep up with the change. There are two approaches to try to control the value of alpha.

1. *Two or more predetermined values of alpha.* Wybark measures the amount of error between the forecast and the actual demand.[4] Depending on the degree of error, different values of alpha are used. Alpha values are not computed but are discrete values selected by Wybark. For example, if the error is large, alpha is .8; if the error is small, alpha is .2.

---

[4] D. Clay Wybark, "A Comparison of Adaptive Forecasting Techniques," *The Logistics Transportation Review*, vol. 9, no. 1 (1973), pp. 13–26.

2. Computed values for alpha. Trigg and Leach use a tracking signal which computes whether the forecast is keeping pace with genuine upward or downward changes in demand (as opposed to random changes).[5] The tracking signal is defined as the exponentially smoothed actual error divided by the exponentially smoothed absolute error. Alpha is set equal to this tracking signal and therefore changes from period to period within the possible range of 0 to 1.

In logic, computing alpha seems simple. In practice, however, it is very prone to error. There are three exponential equations—one for the single exponentially smoothed forecast as done in the previous section of this chapter, one to compute an exponentially smoothed actual error, and the third to compute the exponentially smoothed absolute error. Thus, the user must keep three equations running in sequence for each period. Further, assumptions must be made during the early periods until the technique has a chance to start computing values. For example, alpha must be given a value for the first two periods until actual data are available. Also, the user must select a smoothing constant in addition to alpha which is used in the actual and absolute error equations. Clearly, anyone using adaptive forecasting on a regular basis would be wise to use a programmable calculator or a computer.

In testing exponential models, Dancer and Gray found that adaptive forecasting (using either predetermined or computed alpha as in 1 and 2 above) has the distinct advantage over constant alpha exponential smoothing models when autocorrelation in the data exists.[6] That is, when current demand is related to past demand, then the adaptive model is better. When demand is highly variable but current demand is not highly correlated with past demand, then both the constant and adaptive models perform equally as well.

Finally, a recent paper by Gardner questioned the accuracy of the adaptive forecasting models.[7] A group of smoothing models were simulated under a variety of conditions over 9,000 time periods. Contrary to previous research published, the forecast errors showed that adaptive smoothing tended to generate unstable forecasts even when the average demand was stable. They suggested using single exponential smoothing or trend adjusting models.

Decomposition of a time series

A time series can be defined as chronologically ordered data which may contain one or more components of trend, seasonal, cyclical, autocorrelation, and random. Decomposition of a time series means identifying

[5] D. W. Trigg and D. H. Leach, "Exponential Smoothing With an Adaptive Response Rate," *Operational Research Quarterly,* vol. 18 (1967), pp. 53–59.

[6] Robert Dancer and Clifford Gray, "An Evaluation of Constant and Adaptive Computer Forecasting Models for Inventory Control," *Decision Sciences,* vol. 8, no. 1 (January 1977), pp. 228–38.

[7] Everette S. Gardner, Jr. and David G. Dannenbring, "Forecasting With Exponential Smoothing: Some Guidelines for Model Selection," *Decision Sciences,* vol. 11, no. 2 (April 1980), pp. 370–83.

and separating the time series data into the components. In practice, it is relatively easy to identify the trend (even without mathematical analysis, it is usually easy to plot and see the direction of movement) and the seasonal component (by comparing the same period year to year.) It is considerably more difficult to identify the cycles (these may be many months or years long), autocorrelation, and random components (the forecaster usually calls random anything left over which cannot be identified as another component).

When demand contains both trend and seasonal effects at the same time, the question is how do they relate to each other. In this section we will examine two types of seasonal variation: *additive* and *multiplicative.*

Additive seasonal variation. Additive seasonal variation simply assumes that the seasonal amount is a constant no matter what the trend or average amount is.

Forecast including trend and seasonal (FITS) = Trend + Seasonal

Exhibit 4.5A shows an example of increasing trend with constant seasonal amounts.

Multiplicative seasonal variation. In multiplicative seasonal variation, the trend is multiplied by the seasonal factors.

Forecast including trend and seasonal (FITS) = Trend × Seasonal factor

Exhibit 4.5B shows the seasonal variation increasing as the trend increases since its size depends on the trend.

The multiplicative seasonal variation is the more useful relationship and will be explained in more detail.

Seasonal factor. A *seasonal factor* is the amount of correction needed in a time series to adjust for the season of the year. For example, assume that a firm in past years sold 1,000 units of a particular product line, with an average of 200 units sold in the spring, 350 in the summer, 300 in the fall, and 150 in the winter. The seasonal factor is the ratio of the amount during the season divided by the amount without regard to the season (in this case, the yearly amount divided equally over all seasons, or $1,000/4 = 250$). The seasonal factors therefore are: spring, $200/250 = 0.80$; summer, $350/250 = 1.40$; fall $300/250 = 1.20$; winter $150/250 = 0.60$.

Since the seasonal factor is a constant (which periodically may be updated as new data is available), the higher the average or trend, the greater the effect of the seasonal factor.

To illustrate the seasonal factor and multiplicative variation, consider the following example:

Example. Company A sells outdoor recreational equipment. In analyzing its past sales by quarters, there has been a straight-line upward trend in sales of one of its product lines of the form,

$$\text{Trend}_t = 1,000 + 75t$$

EXHIBIT 4.5
Additive and multiplicative seasonal variation superimposed on changing trend

A. Additive seasonal

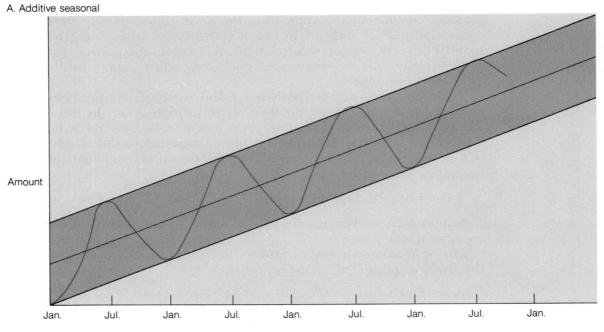

B. Multiplicative seasonal

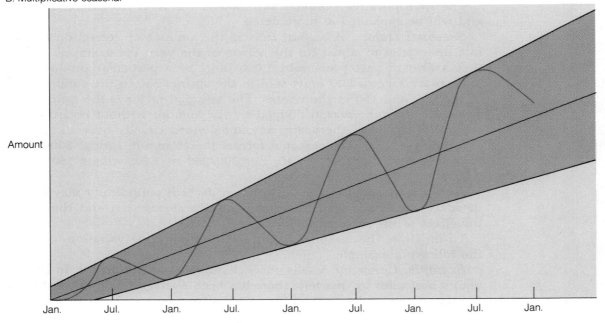

where t is the quarter of the year with the first or base quarter Jan–Mar 1978. Thus, forecasted sales for the four quarters of 1980 are:

$$\text{Trend}_9 = 1,000 + 75\ (9) = 1,675$$
$$\text{Trend}_{10} = 1,000 + 75(10) = 1,750$$
$$\text{Trend}_{11} = 1,000 + 75(11) = 1,825$$
$$\text{Trend}_{12} = 1,000 + 75(12) = 1,900$$

In analyzing past sales, the greatest sales were the summer months and the least were in the first quarter. Assume an analysis showed sales have the seasonal pattern of

$$S_1 = 0.3 \text{ January–March}$$
$$S_2 = 1.5 \text{ April–June}$$
$$S_3 = 1.7 \text{ July–September}$$
$$S_4 = 0.5 \text{ October–December}$$

The resulting forecasts including trend and seasonal (FITS) for the four quarters of 1980 are:

$$\text{FITS}_9 = 1,675 \times .3 = 502.5$$
$$\text{FITS}_{10} = 1,750 \times 1.5 = 2,625.0$$
$$\text{FITS}_{11} = 1,825 \times 1.7 = 3,102.5$$
$$\text{FITS}_{12} = 1,900 \times .5 = 950$$

Example. As another illustration of the decomposition procedure, we can use a simple graphical example.

Assume the history of data as follows:

Quarter	Amount	Quarter	Amount
I–1978	300	I–1979	520
II–1978	200	II–1979	420
III–1978	220	III–1979	400
IV–1978	530	IV–1979	700

This data is plotted in Exhibit 4.6. Note that we can fit a straight line through the data with a value of about 225 for the first quarter of 1978 and 610 for the fourth quarter of 1979.[8] We could read off all the intermediate points, but it is simpler to write the equation which is

$$\text{Trend}_t = 170 + 55t$$

This was derived from the intercept 170 plus a rise of $(610 - 170) \div 8$ periods. Next we can derive a seasonal index by comparing the actual data with the trend line as in Exhibit 4.7. The same quarters in each year average together to develop an index.

---

[8] Or use regression analysis covered later in this chapter.

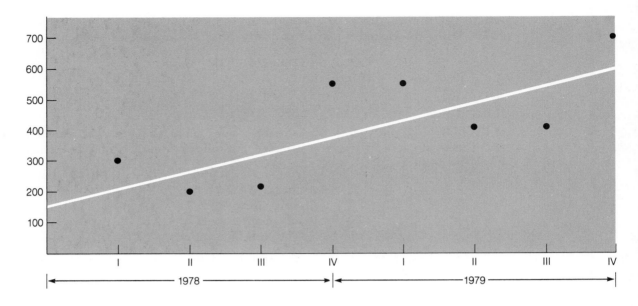

EXHIBIT 4.6
A plot of quarterly demand history

The remaining amount which differs from the actual and forecasted we can attribute to random error, unless we perform further analysis or have additional knowledge as to its cause. We could also determine the range of error which is a standard measurement in regression analysis techniques. Finally, we can compute the forecast for 1980 as follows:

$$FITS_t = Trend \times Seasonal$$

I–1980 $FITS_9 = [170 + 55(9)]1.25 = 831$
II–1980 $FITS_{10} = [170 + 55(10)]0.78 = 562$
III–1980 $FITS_{11} = [170 + 55(11)]0.70 = 543$
IV–1980 $FITS_{12} = [170 + 55(12)]1.25 = 1038$

Linear regression analysis

Linear regression analysis is used in forecasting major occurrences or items, say, for example, a product or product line as opposed to simple exponential smoothing which is primarily used to forecast parts and supplies. The major restriction in using linear regression forecasting is, as

EXHIBIT 4.7
Computing a seasonal factor from the actual data and trend line

Quarter		Actual amount	From trend equation $T_t = 170 + 55t$	Ratio of actual ÷ trend	Seasonal factor (average of same quarters in both years)
I	1978	300	225	1.33	
II		200	280	.71	I–1.25
III		220	335	.66	II–0.78
IV		530	390	1.36	III–0.69
					IV–1.25
I	1979	520	445	1.17	
II		420	500	.84	
III		400	555	.72	
IV		700	610	1.15	

the name implies, that past data and future projections are assumed to fall about a straight line. While this does limit its use, sometimes a shorter period of data will allow linear regression analysis with good results; for example, over a 10- or 20-year period, past history indicates a growth trend. If all the years are used, the next year's project will be low due to the earlier data. By using only the past several years, the forecast will be much closer. Part of the linear regression procedure develops an estimate of how well the line fits the data and thus indicates a range of error.

Linear regression "regresses" one variable on another variable. For example, we know that consumption is a function of income. If we let Y represent consumption (the dependent variable) and x represent income (the independent variable), the linear model becomes

$$Y = a + bx$$

where

y or Y = consumption
a = the y intercept
b = the slope of the line
x = income

The uppercase Y is used to denote consumption as computed by the equation, and the lowercase y is consumption as directly observed in the data.

The accepted method to determine which line is the best fit is the "least squares" method. This technique seeks to minimize the sum of the squares of the distance between each unit of data and its corresponding point on the assumed line. Exhibit 4.8 shows five data points defining consumption levels (y) for specific income levels (x). If we draw a straight line through the general area of the points, we can show the difference between consumption at the data point (y) and the corresponding point

EXHIBIT 4.8
Fitting a least squares regression line to data of consumption as a function of income

Y or y

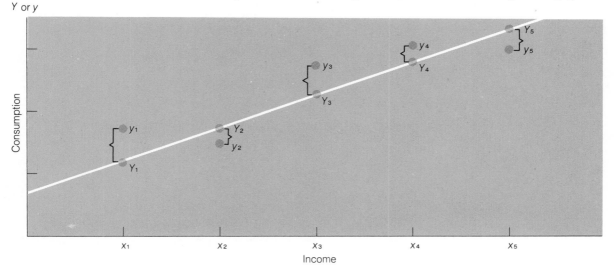

(Y) on the line. The sum of the squares of the differences between the plotted data points and the line points is

$$(y_1 - Y_1)^2 + (y_2 - Y_2)^2 + (y_3 - Y_3)^2 + (y_4 - Y_4)^2 + (y_5 - Y_5)^2$$

The best line to use is the one that minimizes this total.

We will not delve into the derivation of the equations but will simply state them. The equation for a straight line is $Y = a + bx$, and the problem is to determine the values for *a* and *b*. Mathematically, they are

$$a = \bar{y} - b\bar{x}$$

$$b = \frac{\Sigma xy - n\bar{x}\bar{y}}{\Sigma x^2 - n\bar{x}^2}$$

where

$a =$ the *y* intercept
$b =$ the slope of the line
$\bar{y} =$ the average of all *y*'s
$\bar{x} =$ the average of all *x*'s
$x =$ the *x* value at each data point
$y =$ the *y* value at each data point
$n =$ the number of data points
$Y =$ the value of the dependent variable computed with the regression equation

EXHIBIT 4.9
Annual number of housing starts

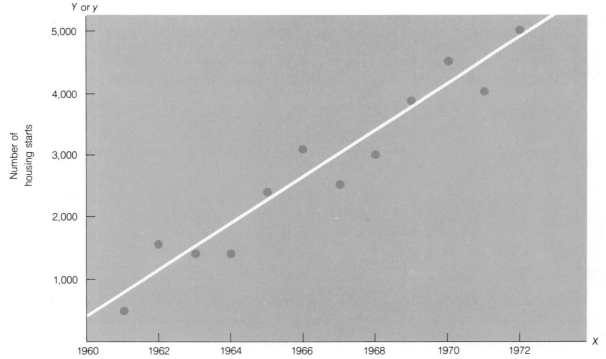

The standard error of estimate, or how well the line fits the data, is

$$S_{yz} = \sqrt{\frac{\sum_{i=1}^{n} (y_i - Y_i)^2}{n}}$$

This is the same expression as that for the standard deviation of an arithmetic mean. To illustrate the procedure for determining a regression line, a sample problem will be presented.

Example. The history of housing starts within a particular community for the years 1960 to 1972 is shown in Exhibit 4.9. The coordinates of each data point are listed in the first two columns of Exhibit 4.10.

To determine the least squares regression line, we must first compute the slope b. Procedurally, the easiest way to do this is in tabular form, and the complete calculations are shown in Exhibit 4.10. (The last column has nothing to do with developing the line equation but is there for convenience in calculating the standard error, S_{yx}.) The final equation for the least squares line is shown as $Y = -21,230 + 361x$. In order to draw this line on Exhibit 4.9, we can pick two values of x, solve for Y at these points, and draw a straight line. Two convenient points are the extremes of the data, where $x = 60$ and $x = 72$. Solving the equation for Y (above)

EXHIBIT 4.10
Least squares analysis for the number of annual housing starts

Housing starts y	Year x	xy	x^2	y^2	For computation of error (from equation $Y = a + bx$) Y
400	'60	24,000	3,600	160,000	430
600	'61	36,600	3,721	360,000	791
1,550	'62	96,100	3,844	2,402,500	1,152
1,500	'63	94,500	3,969	2,250,000	1,513
1,500	'64	96,000	4,096	2,250,000	1,874
2,400	'65	156,000	4,225	5,760,000	2,235
3,100	'66	204,600	4,356	9,610,000	2,596
2,600	'67	174,200	4,489	6,760,000	2,957
2,900	'68	197,200	4,624	8,410,000	3,318
3,800	'69	262,200	4,761	14,440,000	3,679
4,500	'70	315,000	4,900	20,250,000	4,040
4,000	'71	284,000	5,041	16,000,000	4,401
4,900	'72	352,800	5,184	24,010,000	4,762
33,750	858	2,293,200	56,810	112,662,500	

$$\bar{x} = \frac{\Sigma x}{n} = \frac{858}{13} = 66$$

$$\bar{y} = \frac{\Sigma y}{n} = \frac{33,750}{13} = 2,596.15$$

$$b = \frac{\Sigma xy - n\bar{x}\bar{y}}{\Sigma x^2 - n\bar{x}^2} = \frac{2,293,200 - 13(66)(2,596.15)}{56,810 - 13(66)^2} = 361$$

$$a = \bar{y} - b\bar{x} = 2,596.15 - (361)(66) = -21,230$$

Therefore
$$Y = a + bx$$
$$Y = -21,230 + 361x$$

at these two values of x gives $Y = 430$ (at $x = 60$) and $Y = 4,762$ (at $x = 72$).

The standard error of estimate is computed from the first and last columns of Exhibit 4.10. From the equation

$$S_{yx} = \sqrt{\frac{\sum\limits_{i=1}^{n}(y_i - Y_i)^2}{n}}$$

we can compute S_{yx} as

$$S_{yx} = \sqrt{\frac{(400-430)^2 + (600-791)^2 + (1,550-1,152)^2 \ldots (4,900-4,762)^2}{13}}$$

$$S_{yx} = 319.8$$

To forecast the number of housing starts for 1973, then, from the final straight line equation

$$Y = -21,230 + 361(x)$$
$$Y_{73} = 21,230 + 361(73) = 5,123$$

Therefore the expected number of housing starts for 1973 is 5,123, with a standard error estimate of 319.8.[9]

This regression analysis is the least squares method, containing one dependent and one independent variable and fitting a straight line to the data. There is also curvilinear regression analysis—fitting, as implied, a curve rather than a straight line to explain the data.

Seasonal adjustment

The data which were used to construct a linear regression line may contain a monthly or seasonal influence. In projecting the regression line into the future, then, correction must be made to adjust the forecast up or down depending on the particular period of interest. The method is much the same as was done earlier in the chapter under multiplicative seasonal variation. That is, the actual data is divided by the regression-equation derived amount to yield the seasonal factor (also called seasonal index).

Example. To abbreviate the amount of data, we have only listed the first several months for two consecutive years in Exhibit 4.11. The regression equation derived from a least squares analysis of the data points was $Y = 100 + 5X$ where X is the month. The resulting seasonal factor was derived by dividing the actual data point by the computed regression

---

[9] An equation for the standard error which is often easier to compute is:

$$S_{yx} = \sqrt{\frac{\sum y^2 - a\sum y - b\sum xy}{n}}.$$

Using data from Exhibit 4.10,

$$S_{yx} = \sqrt{\frac{112,662,500 - (-21,230)(33,750) - 361(2,293,200)}{13}} = 319.82$$

EXHIBIT 4.11
Computing a seasonal factor from a regression line

Month	Period	Actual data point	From regression equation $Y = 100 + 5X$	Actual $\div Y$	Seasonal factor average of same month in both years
1978					
January 1		120	105	1.14	
February 2		100	110	0.91	
March 3		90	115	0.78	
April 4		85	120	0.71	January 1.16
.					February 0.93
.					March 0.82
.					April 0.74
1979					
January 13		195	165	1.18	
February 14		160	170	0.94	
March 15		150	175	0.86	
April 16		140	180	0.78	
.					
.					
.					

amount for each month. Since undoubtedly some other component is present in the data, such as cyclical or random, the standard procedure averages the results of the same months in each year.

If we wish to forecast sales for January and February of 1980, they would be.

January 1980 (period 25) Forecast $= [Y = 100 + 5(25)] \times 1.16 = 261$
February 1980 (period 26) Forecast $= [Y = 100 + 5(26)] \times .93 = 214$

Multiple regression analysis

Another forecasting method is multiple regression analysis, in which a number of variables are considered, together with the effects of each on the item of interest. For example, in the home-furnishings field, the effects of the number of marriages, disposable income, housing starts, and trend can be expressed in a multiple regression equation,[10] as

$$S = B + B_m (M) + B_h (H) + B_i (I) + B_t (T)$$

where

$S =$ Gross sales for year
$B =$ Base sales, a starting point from which other factors have influence
$M =$ Marriages during the year
$H =$ Housing starts during the year
$I =$ Annual disposable personal income
$T =$ Time trend (first year $= 1$, second $= 2$, third $= 3$, and so forth)

B_m, B_h, B_i, and B_t represent the influence on expected sales due to the number of marriages and housing starts, income, and trend.

---

[10] G. C. Parker and Edelberto L. Segura, "How to Get a Better Forecast," *Harvard Business Review*, vol. 49, no. 2 (March–April 1971), pp. 99–109.

Forecasting by multiple regression is very appropriate when a number of factors influence a variable of interest—in this case, sales. Its difficulty lies with the data gathering, and particularly with the mathematical computation. Fortunately, standard programs for multiple regression analysis are available for most computers, relieving the need for tedious manual calculation.

FORECAST ERRORS

Demand for a product is generated through the interaction of a number of factors. Because this interaction is too complex to describe accurately in a model, all forecasts will certainly contain some error. In discussing the forecast errors, it is convenient to distinguish between *sources of error* and the *measurement of error*.

Sources of error

When we talk about statistical errors, such as in regression analysis, we are referring to the deviations of our observations from our regression line. It is common to attach a confidence band (i.e., statistical control limits which will be described in Chapter 10), to the regression line to reduce the unexplained error. However, when we then use this regression line as a forecasting device by projecting it into the future, the error may not be correctly defined by the projected confidence band. This is so simply because the confidence interval is based on past data; it may or may not hold for projected data points and therefore cannot be used with the same confidence. Experience has shown that the actual errors tend to be greater than those predicted from forecast models.

Errors can be classified as *bias* or *random*. Bias errors occur when a consistent "mistake" is made. Sources of bias are: failure to include the right variables; using the wrong relationships among variables; employing the wrong trendline; shift of seasonal demand from its historic calendar occurrence; and the existence of some undetected secular trend.

Random errors can be defined as those that cannot be explained by the forecast model employed. There is a bit of irony in this statement, though, since, if one desires to minimize the error in explaining past data, he can use a sophisticated model such as a Fourier series with a large number of terms. While this can reduce the forecasting model's error on the data to almost zero, it may do no better in forecasting future demand than a simpler model with a higher error.

Measurement of error

Several of the common terms used to describe the degree of error are: standard error, mean squared error (or variance), and mean absolute deviation. In addition, tracking signals may be used to indicate the existence of any positive or negative bias in the forecast.

Standard error was defined in the linear regression section of this chapter. Since the standard error is the square root of a function, it is often more convenient to use the function itself. This is called the mean squared error, or variance.

The mean absolute deviation (MAD) was in vogue in the past but subsequently was ignored in favor of standard deviation and standard error measures. In recent years, MAD has made a comeback because of its simplicity and usefulness in obtaining tracking signals (discussed below).

The mean absolute deviation (MAD) is computed using the differences between the actual demand and the forecasted demand without regard to sign. It is equal to the sum of the absolute deviations divided by the number of data points, or, stated in equation form,

$$\text{MAD} = \frac{\sum\limits_{t=1}^{n} \left| A_t - F_t \right|}{n}$$

where

$t =$ Period number
$A =$ Actual demand for the period
$F =$ Forecasted demand for the period
$n =$ Total number of periods
$\|$ is a symbol used to indicate the absolute value disregarding positive and negative signs

When the errors that occur in the forecast are normally distributed (the usual case), the mean absolute deviation relates to the standard deviation as,

1 standard deviation

$$= \sqrt{\frac{\pi}{2}} \times \text{MAD} \text{ where } \pi = 3.1416, \text{ or approximately } 1.25 \times \text{MAD}$$

or conversely,

$$1 \text{ MAD} = 0.8 \text{ standard deviation}$$

The standard deviation is the larger unit of measure. If the MAD of a set of points was found to be 75 units, then the standard deviation would be 60 units. And, in the usual statistical manner, if control limits were set at plus or minus 3 standard deviations (or $\pm$ 3.75 MADs), then 99.7 percent of the points would fall within these limits.

As previously mentioned, a *tracking signal* is a measurement that indicates whether the forecast average is keeping pace with any genuine upward or downward changes in demand. A tracking signal can be calculated using the arithmetic sum of forecast deviations divided by the mean absolute deviation. Exhibit 4.12 illustrates the procedure for computing MAD and the tracking signal for a six-month period wherein the forecast had been set at a constant 1,000 and the actual demands that occurred are as shown. In this example, the forecast, on the average, was off by 66.7 units and the tracking signal was equal to 3.3 mean absolute deviations.

EXHIBIT 4.12
EXHIBIT 4.12
Computing the mean absolute deviation (MAD), the running sum of forecast errors (RSFE), and the tracking signal from forecasted and actual data

Month	Forecast	Actual	Actual deviation	Running sum of forecast errors (RSFE)	Absolute deviation
1	1,000	950	−50	−50	50
2	1,000	1,070	+70	+20	70
3	1,000	1,100	+100	+120	100
4	1,000	960	−40	+80	40
5	1,000	1,090	+90	+170	90
6	1,000	1,050	+50	+220	50
	Total absolute deviation				= 400

Mean absolute deviation (MAD) = 400 ÷ 6 = 66.7

$$\text{Tracking signal} = \frac{\text{RSFE}}{\text{MAD}} = \frac{220}{66.7} = 3.3 \text{ MADs}$$

Acceptable limits for the tracking signal depend on the size of the demand being forecasted (high volume or high revenue items should be monitored frequently) and the amount of personnel time available (lower acceptable limits cause more forecasts to be out of limits and therefore require more time to investigate). Exhibit 4.13 shows the area within the control limits for a range of zero to four MADs.

The sum of the actual forecast errors in a perfect forecasting model would be expected to be zero; that is, the random errors that result in overestimates should be offset by errors that are underestimates. The tracking signal would then also be zero, indicating an unbiased model, neither leading nor lagging the actual demands.

Often, MAD is used to forecast errors. It might then be desirable to make the MAD more sensitive to recent data. A useful technique to do this is to compute an exponentially smoothed MAD as a forecast for the next period's error range. The procedure is similar to single exponential smoothing previously covered in this chapter. The value of the MAD forecast is to provide a range of error; in the case of inventory control, this is useful in setting safety stock levels.

$$\text{MAD}_t = \alpha \, |A_{t-1} - F_{t-1}| + (1 - \alpha) \, \text{MAD}_{t-1}$$

where

MAD_t = Forecasted MAD for the tth period
α = Smoothing constant (normally in the range of 0.05 to 0.15)
A_{t-1} = Actual demand in the period $t-1$
F_{t-1} = Forecasted demand for period $t-1$

EXHIBIT 4.13
The percentages of points included within the control limits for a range of 0 to 4 MADs

Control limits

Number of MADs	Related number of standard deviations	Percentage of points lying within control limits
±1	0.798	57.048
±2	1.596	88.946
±3	2.394	98.334
±4	3.192	99.856

FOCUS FORECASTING

Focus forecasting is the creation of Bernie Smith,[11] who claims that this method of forecasting is a revolutionary new concept. He uses it primarily in finished-goods inventory management, and he has laid such significant claims to its success that we feel obligated to include a coverage of the topic here. Smith makes a strong and substantiated argument that statistical approaches used in forecasting do not give the best results. He states that simple techniques that work well on past data will also prove the best in forecasting the future. We will explain all this in greater detail.

Methodology of focus forecasting

There are two components of the focus forecasting system: (1) several simple forecasting strategies and (2) computer simulation of these strategies on past data.

Examples of simple forecasting strategies could include the following:

A. Whatever we sold in the past three months is what we will probably sell in the next three months.

B. What we sold in the same three-month period last year, we will probably sell in that three-month period this year. (This would account for seasonal effects.)

C. We will probably sell 10 percent more in the next three months than we sold in the last three months.

D. We will probably sell 50 percent more over the next three months than we did for the same three months last year.

E. Whatever percentage change we had last year in the past three months will probably be the same percentage change we will have over last year in the next three months.

These are continually applied rules but may be changed as desired and new ones added at will.

The second part of the process is computer simulation. In order to use the system, a data history should be available; for example, 18 to 24 months of data. The simulation process then uses each of the forecasting strategies to predict some recent *past* data. The strategy which did best in predicting the past is the strategy that will be used to predict the future. Following is an exercise used by Smith.[12]

Example. Exhibit 4.14 shows demands for an 18-month period. (Try to guess what the demand might be for July, August, and September, and compare what you have found to the actual data which will be presented later.)

---

[11] Bernard T. Smith and Oliver W. Wight, *Focus Forecasting: Computer Techniques for Inventory Control* (Boston: CBI Publishing Co., 1978).

[12] We chose to use this exercise since it is real data from the records of American Hardware Supply Company where Smith is inventory manager. This forecasting exercise has been played by many people: buyers for American Hardware, inventory consultants, and over 500 participants at the national meeting of the American Production and Inventory Control Society. Further, data for the remainder of the year exist which allow for checking the results.

EXHIBIT 4.14
**Demand in units
for a broiler pan**

	Last year	This year
January	6	72
February	212	90
March	378	108
April	129	134
May	163	92
June	96	137
July	167	
August	159	
September	201	
October	153	
November	76	
December	30	

Using focus forecasting, we will first apply forecasting strategy A—whatever we sold in the last three months is what we will probably sell in the next three months. (We are using the terms demand and sales interchangeably assuming demands culminated in actual sales.) We first test this strategy on the past three months; that is,

$$\text{Forecast (April, May, June)} = \text{Demand (January + February + March)}$$
$$= 72 + 90 + 108 = 270$$

Since what actually occurred was 363 (134 + 92 + 137), the forecast was 270/363 = 74 percent, or in other words, it was 26 percent low.

Try another strategy, say strategy E—whatever percentage change we had over last year in the past three months will probably be the same percentage change we will have over last year in the next three months.

Forecast (April + May + June)

$$= \frac{\text{Demand (January + February + March) this year}}{\text{Demand (January + February + March) last year}} \times$$

$$\text{Demand (April + May + June) last year.}$$

$$= \frac{72 + 90 + 108}{6 + 212 + 378} \times (129 + 163 + 96)$$

$$= \frac{270}{596} (388) = 175.77$$

What actually occurred during April, May, and June this year was 363 so the forecast was 175/363, or only 48 percent of the actual demand.

Since strategy A was better in predicting the past three months, we will use that strategy in predicting July, August, and September of this year. Using strategy A, whatever we sold in the last three months is what we will probably sell in the next three months.

$$\text{Forecast (July + August + September)} = \text{Demand (April + May + June)}$$
$$= 134 + 92 + 137$$
$$= 363$$

The actual demand for the period was 357. Exhibit 4.15 shows the completed demand history for this year and serves as a basic for comparison.

These forecasts are then reviewed and modified (if necessary) by buyers or inventory control personnel who have responsibility over these items.

Exhibit 4.16 shows the forecasts for a moving three month period made with strategy A along with the actual values.

Smith states that in all the forecast simulations he has run using variations of exponential smoothing including adaptive smoothing, focus forecasting gave significantly better results.

EXHIBIT 4.15
Demand in units for a broiler pan

	Last year	This year
January	6	72
February	212	90
March	378	108
April	129	134
May	163	92
June	96	137
July	167	120
August	159	151
September	201	86
October	153	113
November	76	97
December	30	40

EXHIBIT 4.16
Focus forecasts for the broiler pan

Three-month period	Focus strategy	Forecast	Actual
July, August, September	A	363	357
August, September, October	A	349	350
September, October, November	A	408	296

Developing a focus forecasting system

Some suggestions in developing a focus forecasting system are:

1. Don't try to add a seasonality index. Let the forecasting system find that out by itself because, especially with new items, seasonality may not apply until the pipeline is filled and the system is stable. The forecasting strategies can handle it.
2. When a forecast is unusually high or low (such as two or three times the previous period, or the previous year if there is seasonality) print out an indicator such as the letter R telling the person affected by this demand to review it. Don't just disregard unusual demands since they may, in fact, be valid changes in the demand pattern.[13]
3. Let the people who will be using the forecasts participate in creating the strategies (such as buyers or inventory planners). Smith plays his

[13] Statistical forecasting routines, such as IBM's IMPACT, filter out unusual demands by calculating a mean and standard deviation for all the data. Data falling outside the 95 percent confidence interval are considered highly questionable and are disregarded.

"can you outguess focus forecasting" game with all the company's buyers. Using two years data and 2,000 items, focus forecasting makes forecasts for the past six months. Buyers are asked to forecast the past six months using any strategy they prefer. If they are consistently better than the existing forecasting strategies, the buyer's strategy is added to the list.

4. Keep the strategies simple. In that way they will be easily understood and trusted by users of the forecast.

In summary, it appears that focus forecasting has significant merit when demand is generated outside the system, such as in forecasting end-item demand, spare parts, and materials and supplies used in a variety of products.

Computer time apparently is not very large since Smith forecasts 100,000 items every month using his focus forecasting strategies.

COMPUTER PROGRAMS

There are many forecasting programs available commercially. Some of these exist as library routines within a computer, some may be purchased separately from a vendor, and some forecasting routines are part of larger programs. Following are brief descriptions of several of them.

General Electric's *Time Series Forecasting* programs FCST1 and FCST2 are basically straightforward models. The FCST1 is intended where monthly data show a linear growth trend. A trend line is derived by least squares regression analyses. A seasonal factor is then determined by comparing the actual data points to the corresponding points on the regression line. The final forecast is the result of multiplying the trend line by the seasonal factor.

The FCST2 uses yearly data and creates several forecasts with four different methods of exponential smoothing. The program then points out which method produced the best forecast on past data. The FCST2 does not account for seasonal variation.

The Consumer Goods System (COGS) of IBM is a forecasting and inventory-control program which is specifically oriented to the manufacturing, process and distribution industries. The forecasting portion computes expected demands, and the inventory portion computes order quantities and when to order and ship items.

The COGS program is quite sophisticated. It starts by fitting a least squares regression line to past data; then, adaptive smoothing places more emphasis on recent data. The user supplies two smoothing constants, a normal one and a higher value which will be used when significant forecast errors are detected. The regression line supplies the starting value and trend. The cyclical elements (including seasonal) are fitted to a curve using Fourier analysis. Fourier analysis is a series which contains sines and cosines and can therefore closely fit a waveform to data points.

The forecasting technique used in IBM's Inventory Management Program and Control Technique (IMPACT) is described in Chapter 15. IMPACT is a program designed for users in the distribution system, such as wholesalers.

CONCLUSION

Forecasting is fundamental to any planning effort. In the short run, one needs to predict the requirements for materials, products, services, or other resources in order to respond to changes in demand. These forecasts permit adjusting schedules and varying labor and materials. In the long run, forecasting is required as a basis for strategic changes, such as developing new markets, developing new products or services, and expanding or creating new facilities.

For long-term forecasts which lead to heavy financial commitments, great care should be taken to derive the forecast. Several approaches should be used. Exhibit 4.17 summarizes the common forecasting techniques. Causal methods such as regression analysis or multiple regression analysis are beneficial. These provide a basis for discussion. Economic factors, product trends, growth factors, competition, as well as a myriad of other possible variables will need to be considered and the forecast adjusted to reflect the influence of each.

Short- and intermediate-term forecasting, such as required for inventory control and manpower and material scheduling, may be satisfied with simpler models, such as exponential smoothing with perhaps an adaptive feature or a seasonal index. In these applications, there are usually thousands of items being forecasted. The forecasting routine should therefore be simple and run quickly on a computer. The routines should also detect and respond rapidly to definite short-term changes in demand while at the same time ignoring the occasional spurious demands. Exponential smoothing, when monitored by management to control the constant alpha, is an effective technique.

Focus forecasting appears to offer a reasonable approach to short-term, forecasting, say, monthly or quarterly but certainly less than a year. If there is one thing focus forecasting does offer, it is close monitoring and rapid response. Quick detection and response certainly would be assured if one of the strategies used was something such as: "Demand for the next period is equal to the demand for the last period."

In summary, forecasting is tough. A perfect forecast is like a hole-in-one in golf: they are great to get but we should be satisfied just to get close to the cup—or to push the metaphor—just to land on the green. The ideal philosophy is create the best forecast that you reasonably can and then hedge by maintaining flexibility in the system to account for the inevitable forecast error.

EXHIBIT 4.17
Forecasting techniques and common models

I.	Qualitative	Subjective; judgmental. Based on estimates and opinions.
	Delphi method	Group of experts responds to questionnaire. A moderator compiles results and formulates new questionnaire again submitted to the group. Thus, there is a learning process for the group as they receive new information and there is no influence of group pressure or dominating individual.
	Market research	Sets out to collect data in a variety of ways (surveys, interviews, etc.) to test hypotheses about the market. This is typically used to forecast long-range and new-product sales.
	Panel consensus	Free open exchange at meetings. The idea is that discussion by the group will produce better forecasts than any one individual. Participants may be executives, sales people, or customers.
	Historical analogy	Ties what is being forecast to a similar item. Important in planning new products wherein a forecast may be derived by using the history of a similar product.
	Grass roots	Derives a forecast by compiling input from those at the end of the hierarchy who deal with what is being forecast. For example, an overall sales forecast may be derived by combining inputs from each sales person who is closest to his or her own territory.
II.	Time series analysis	Based on the idea that the history of occurrences over time can be used to predict the future.
	Simple moving average	A time period containing a number of data points is averaged by dividing the sum of the point values by the number of points. Each, therefore, has equal influence.
	Weighted moving average	Specific points may be weighted more or less than the others, as seen fit by experience.
	Exponential smoothing	Recent data points are weighted more with weighting declining exponentially as data becomes older.
	Regression analysis	Fits a straight line to past data generally relating the data value to time. Most common fitting technique is "least squares."
	Box Jenkins technique	Very complicated but apparently the most accurate statistical technique available. Relates a class of statistical models to data and fits the model to the time series by using Bayesian posterior distributions. Time consuming and expensive.
	Shiskin time series	(Also called X-11). Developed by Julius Shiskin of the Census Bureau. An effective method to decompose a time series into seasonals, trends, and irregular. It needs at least three years of history. Very good in identifying turning points, for example, in company sales.
	Trend projections	Fits a mathematical trend line to the data points and projects it into the future. Best known as least squares regression technique.

EXHIBIT 4.17 *(continued)*	III. Causal		Tries to understand the system underlying and surrounding the item being forecast. For example, sales may be affected by advertising, quality, and competitors.
		Regression analysis	Similar to least squares method in time series but may contain multiple variables. Basis is that forecast is *caused* by the occurrence of other events.
		Econometric models	Attempts to describe some sector of the economy by a series of interdependent equations.
		Input/output models	Focuses on sales of each industry to other firms and governments. Indicates the changes in sales which a producer industry might expect because of purchasing changes by another industry.
		Leading indicators	Statistics which move in the same direction as the series being forecast but move before the series, such as an increase in the price of gasoline indicating a future drop in the sale of large cars.
	IV. Simulation models		Dynamic models, usually computer based, which allow the forecaster to make assumptions about the internal variables and external environment in the model. Depending on the variables in the model, the forecaster may ask such questions as: What would happen to my forecast if price increased by 10 percent? What effect would a mild national recession have on my forecast?

REVIEW AND DISCUSSION QUESTIONS

1. Give some very simple rules you might use to "manage demand" for a firm's product. (An example is "one to a family.")

2. What strategies are used by the following businesses to influence demand? Supermarkets, airlines, hospitals, banks, and cereal manufacturers.

3. Forecasting using exponential smoothing, adaptive smoothing, and exponential smoothing including trend each require starting values to get the equations going. How would you select the starting value for, say, F_{t-1}.

4. From the choice of simple moving average, weighted moving average, exponential smoothing, and regression analysis, which forecasting technique would you consider the most accurate? Why?

5. Give some examples that you can think of which have a multiplicative seasonal trend relationship.

6. What is the main disadvantage of daily forecasting using regression analysis?

7. What are the main problems with using adaptive exponential smoothing in forecasting?

8. How is a seasonal index computed from a regression line analysis?

9. Discuss the basic differences between the mean absolute deviation (MAD) and the standard deviation.

10. What implications do the existence of forecast errors have for the search for ultrasophisticated statistical forecasting models?

11. What are "focused forecasting's" strongest selling points?

PROBLEMS

1. Carter Bathing Suit Company feels that it has been consistently way off in its forecasts for bathing-suit sales. Bathing suits are highly seasonal and with a short sales cycle. The production-distribution time is too long to detect excesses or shortages and respond. Accurate forecasting is therefore critical. Sales by quarters for the years 1977–79 are as follows.

1977		*1978*		*1979*	
Quarter	*Sales in units*	*Quarter*	*Sales in units*	*Quarter*	*Sales in units*
I	3,000	I	4,000	I	3,000
II	35,000	II	42,000	II	50,000
III	10,000	III	12,000	III	15,000
IV	2,000	IV	3,000	IV	3,000

a. Develop an equation for the trend line by hand fitting a line through the points.
b. Develop an equation for a best-fit line through the points using regression analysis.
c. Forecast sales for each quarter of 1980 and 1981.

2. Sunrise Baking Company markets doughnuts through a chain of food stores and has been experiencing over- and underproduction because of forecasting errors. The following data are their demands in dozens of doughnuts for the past four weeks. The bakery is closed Saturday, so Friday's production must satisfy both Saturday and Sunday demand.

	4 weeks ago	*3 weeks ago*	*2 weeks ago*	*Last week*
Monday	2,200	2,400	2,300	2,400
Tuesday	2,000	2,100	2,200	2,200
Wednesday	2,300	2,400	2,300	2,500
Thursday	1,800	1,900	1,800	2,000
Friday	1,900	1,800	2,100	2,000
Saturday Sunday	2,800	2,700	3,000	2,900

Make a forecast for this week on the following basis:
a. Daily, using simple four-week moving average.
b. Daily, using a weighted average of 0.40, 0.30, 0.20, and 0.10 for the past four weeks.
c. By least squares regression for Wednesday, Thursday, and Friday.

3. In planning its purchases of ingredients, Sunrise Baking Company makes a weekly forecast for each product. Its bread production had been forecast

for last week at 22,000 loaves; however, only 21,000 loaves were actually demanded.

a. Using exponential smoothing with $\alpha = 0.10$, what would Sunrise's forecast be for this week?

b. Supposing this week's demand actually turns out to be 22,500, what would the new forecast be for the following week?

4. With the present popularity of ecology, the Ponce de Leon Purified Water Company has found that demand for its spring water dispensers has been growing. It appears that its present water sources will not be sufficient, and it would like to have some idea of its future needs in order to advise Tiny Peachfork, its divining-rod specialist, how many new springs he must find. De Leon's demands for spring water for last year were as follows.

Month	Demand	Month	Demand
January	4,200 gal.	July	5,300 gal.
February	4,300 gal.	August	4,900 gal.
March	4,000 gal.	September	5,400 gal.
April	4,400 gal.	October	5,700 gal.
May	5,000 gal.	November	6,300 gal.
June	4,700 gal.	December	6,000 gal.

a. Using least squares regression analysis, what would you estimate demand to be for December of next year? Construct a graph showing the two-year period.

b. To be reasonably confident of having adequate water, de Leon decides to use three standard errors of estimate for safety. What water supply should it plan on having on hand?

5. The historical demand for a product is: January, 80; February, 100; March, 60; April, 80; and May, 90.

a. Using a simple four-month moving average, what is the forecast for June? If June experienced a demand of 100, what would your forecast be for July?

b. Using single exponential smoothing with $\alpha = 0.20$, if the forecast for January had been 70, compute what the exponentially smoothed forecast would have been for the remaining months through June.

c. Using least squares regression analysis, compute a forecast for June, July, and August.

1. Using a weighted moving average with weights of 0.30, 0.25, 0.20, 0.15, and 0.10, what is June's forecast?

6. Using the demand for broiler pans shown in Exhibit 4.14 and simple exponential smoothing with a smoothing constant alpha of 0.3, forecast sales for the second, third, and fourth quarters of last year and the first, second, and third quarters of this year. Start with the first quarter forecast of last year equal to 596 (what actually occurred).

How well did your exponential forecasts predict the actual demands which occurred?

7. Below are given the actual demands for a product for the past six quarters. Using the forecasting strategies A to E listed in the text, find the best strategy to use in predicting the seventh quarter.

	Quarter			
	I	*II*	*III*	*IV*
Last year	1,200	700	900	1,100
This year	1,400	1,000		

SELECTED BIBLIOGRAPHY

Berry, William L.; Mabert, Vincent A.; and Marcus, Myles "Forecasting Teller Window Demand With Exponential Smoothing," *Journal of the Academy of Management,* vol. 22, no. 1 (March 1979), pp. 129–37.

Box, George E. P., and Jenkins, Gwilym M. *Time Series Analysis: Forecasting and Control.* San Francisco: Holden-Day, 1970.

Bowerman, Bruce L., and O'Connall, Richard T. *Forecasting and Time Series.* North Scituate, Mass.: Duxbury Press, 1979.

Brown, Robert G. *Decision Rules for Inventory Management.* New York: Holt, Rinehart and Winston, 1967.

_____ *Smoothing, Forecasting, and Prediction of Discrete Time Series.* Englewood Cliffs, N.J.: Prentice-Hall, 1963.

_____ *Statistical Forecasting for Inventory Control.* New York: McGraw-Hill Book Company, 1959.

Chambers, John C.; Mullick, Satinder K.; and Smith, Donald D. "How to Choose the Right Forecasting Technique." *Harvard Business Review,* vol. 49, no. 4 (July–August 1971), pp. 45–74.

Chan, Hung, and Hayya, Jack "Spectral Analysis in Business Forecasting," *Decision Sciences,* vol. 7, no. 1 (January 1976), pp. 137–51.

Dancer, Robert, and Gray, Clifford "An Evaluation of Constant and Adaptive Computer Forecasting Models for Inventory Control," *Decision Sciences,* vol. 8, no. 1 (January 1977), pp. 228–38.

General Electric Company. *Time Series Forecasting FCST1, FCST2.* Publication 5104.09.

Gross, Charles W., and Peterson, Robin T. *Business Forecasting,* Boston: Houghton Mifflin Company, 1976.

International Business Machines Corporation. *Forecasting and Modeling Systems.* Publication GH19-4000-0.

_____ *Consumer Goods System—Forecasting.* Publication GH20–0722–4.

_____ *Consumer Goods System—Forecasting.* Publication SH20–0804–4.

_____ *Management Operating System. Forecasting, Materials Planning and Inventory Management.* Publication GE20-0031-0.

Mabert, Vincent A. "Forecast Modification Based Upon Residual Analysis: A Case Study of Check Volume Estimation." *Decision Sciences,* vol. 9, no. 2 (April 1978), pp. 285–96.

Parker, G. C., and Segura, Edelberto L. "How to Get a Better Forecast." *Harvard Business Review,* vol. 49, no. 2 (March–April 1971), pp. 99–109.

Roberts, S. D., and Reed, R. "The Development of a Self-Adaptive Forecasting Technique," *AIIE Transactions,* vol. 1, no. 4 (1969), pp. 314–22.

Smith, Bernard T. *Focus Forecasting: Computer Techniques for Inventory Control.* Boston: CBI Publishing Co. Inc., 1978.

Thomopoulis, Nick T. *Applied Forecasting Methods.* Englewood Cliffs, N.J.: Prentice-Hall, 1980.

Trigg, D. W., and Leach, D. H. "Exponential Smoothing With an Adaptive Response Rate," *Operational Research Quarterly,* vol. 18 (1967), pp. 53–59.

Wheelwright, Stephen, and Makridakis, Spyros *Forecasting Methods for Management,* New York: John Wiley & Sons, 2d ed., 1977.

Wybark, D. Clay "A Comparison of Adaptive Forecasting Techniques," *The Logistics Transportation Review,* vol. 9, no. 1 (1973), pp. 13–26.

Chapter 5

FINANCIAL ANALYSIS

The basic tools of cost and investment analysis find usefulness in all aspects of the design and operation of a productive system. While we recognize the existence of a firm's multiple goals, such as growth, competitive position, safety of income, corporate perpetuity, and so on, in this chapter we concentrate on the economic objective of selecting among the least-cost or highest-profit alternatives. Some basic investment concepts, such as sunk costs, opportunity costs, and depreciation, are presented, as well as an introduction to cash flow budgeting. In addition, the more commonly used methods of ranking investment alternatives are treated in example form.

CONCEPTS AND DEFINITIONS

A few basic concepts drawn from the fields of economics, accounting, and finance are utilized in making investment decisions. Those included in the following discussions, while not difficult, are nonetheless essential for understanding the material in later sections.

Fixed costs. A fixed cost is any expense that remains constant regardless of the level of output. Although no cost is truly fixed, many types of expense are virtually fixed over a wide range of output. Examples of commonly incurred fixed costs are rent, property taxes, most types of depreciation, insurance payments, and salaries of top management.

Variable costs. Variable costs are expenses that fluctuate directly with changes in the level of output. Often, variable costs can be traced to

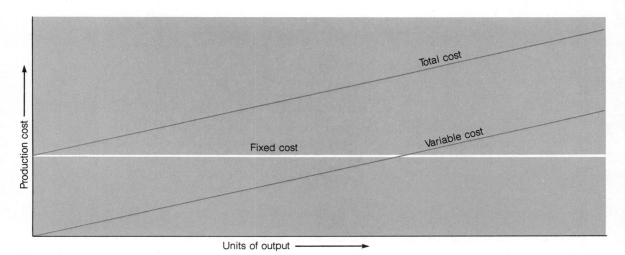

EXHIBIT 5.1
**Fixed and
variable cost
components of
total cost**

each unit produced. For example, each additional unit of sheet steel produced by United States Steel requires a specific amount of material and
labor. The incremental cost of this additional material and labor can be
isolated and assigned to each unit of sheet steel produced. Many overhead
expenses are also variable, inasmuch as utility bills, maintenance expense,
and so forth will vary with production level.

Exhibit 5.1 illustrates the fixed and variable cost components of total
cost. Note that total cost increases at the same rate as variable costs since
fixed costs are constant.

Sunk costs. Sunk costs are expenses which have *no effect* on a decision
and therefore should not be taken into account in considering investment
alternatives. There are two types of sunk costs—past expenditures, which
cannot be recovered or are unaffected by the decision, and costs that apply
equally to all alternatives under consideration.

As an example of the first type, suppose an ice cream manufacturing
firm occupies a rented building and is considering making sherbet in the
same building. If the company enters sherbet production, its cost accountant will assign some of the rental expense to the sherbet operation. However, the building rent remains unchanged and therefore is not a relevant
expense to be considered in making the decision. The rent is *sunk;* that
is, it will continue to exist and will not change in amount regardless of
the decision.

The second type of sunk cost is an expense that is common to all alternatives being considered, and therefore provides no basis for choice among
them. All Seven-Eleven stores, a national chain of convenience grocery
stores, are of uniform size and design. If the cost of building these stores
is the same throughout a geographic area, construction costs are not an

element to be considered by Seven-Eleven's management in choosing where to locate its stores in the area.

Opportunity cost. Opportunity cost is the benefit *foregone,* or advantage *lost,* which results from choosing one course of action over the *best known alternative* course of action. It is the *difference* between the best choice and any alternative. The opportunity cost of attending college is the highest salary the student could command if he or she chose to work instead. Alternatively, the opportunity cost of not attending college is the increased earning power one gives up in the long run by not holding a college degree. A person interested solely in maximizing his lifetime earnings would base his decision on attending college on which of the two opportunity costs was highest.

Let's examine a more specific example. Suppose a firm has $100,000 to invest and two alternatives of comparable risk present themselves, each requiring a $100,000 investment. Investment A will net $25,000; investment B will net $23,000. Investment A is clearly the better choice, with a $25,000 net return. If the decision is made to invest in B instead of A, the opportunity cost of B then is $2,000, which is the benefit foregone.

Investment possibilities cannot be put into proper perspective unless the opportunity costs are considered.

Risk and expected value. Risk is inherent in any investment, since the future can never be predicted with absolute certainty. It is a rare occurrence indeed when expected outcome and actual outcome coincide perfectly. To deal with this uncertainty, mathematical techniques for incorporating probability provide some assistance. Expected value, for example, is the expected outcome multiplied by the probability of its occurrence. Recall that in the example above, the expected outcome of alternative A was $25,000 and B, $23,000. Suppose the probability of A's actual outcome is 80 percent while B's probability is 90 percent. The expected values of the alternatives are determined as follows:

$$\text{Expected outcome} \times \begin{array}{c}\text{Probability that actual}\\\text{outcome will be the}\\\text{expected outcome}\end{array} = \text{Expected value}$$

Investment A: $25,000 × 0.80 = $20,000
Investment B: $23,000 × 0.90 = $20,700

Investment B is now seen to be the better choice, with a net advantage over A of $700. Risk is always present when dealing with the future and should be explicitly incorporated into the decision-making process where possible.

Economic life and obsolescence. When a firm invests in an income-producing asset, the productive life of the asset is estimated. For accounting purposes, the asset is depreciated over this period. It is assumed that the asset will perform its function during this time and then be considered obsolete or "worn out" and replacement will be required. This view of asset life rarely coincides with reality. Production techniques and technological improvements frequently render a machine obsolete long before its productive live has been exhausted.

Assume that a machine expected to have a productive life of ten years is purchased. If at any time during the ensuing ten years a new machine is developed that can perform the same task more efficiently or economically, the old machine has become obsolete. Whether it is "worn out" or not is irrelevant.

The economic life of a machine is the period over which it provides the best method for performing its task. When a superior method is developed, the machine has become obsolete. Thus, the stated book value of a machine can be a meaningless figure.

Suppose a machine with an estimated ten-year life is purchased for $10,000 and will be depreciated by $1,000 per year to a zero salvage value. At the end of the fifth year, the machine will be carried at $5,000. If a superior machine has become available, the $5,000 book value does not reflect the true value of the present machine. Technological obsolescence has reduced its value for prospective buyers and also makes the use of such equipment costly by creating high opportunity costs.

Generally, economic lives are very short, and for machinery, may not exceed more than five or six years on the average.

Depreciation. Depreciation is an accounting procedure used to periodically reduce the value of an asset on the company books. The value of any capital asset—buildings, machinery, and so forth—decreases as its useful life is expended. *Amortization* is a term often used interchangeably with the term *depreciation.* Through convention, however, depreciation refers to the allocation of cost due to the physical or functional deterioration of *tangible* (physical) assets, such as buildings or equipment, while amortization refers to the allocation of cost over the useful life period of *intangible* assets, such as patents, leases, franchises, or goodwill.

Depreciation procedures may not reflect an asset's true value at any point in its life since obsolescence may at any time cause a large difference between true value and book value. Also, since depreciation rates significantly affect taxes, a firm may choose a particular method from the several alternatives with more consideration for its effect on taxes than its ability to make the book value of an asset reflect the true resale value.

Five commonly used methods of depreciation are described below. All methods, however, are computed by using three basic criteria:

1. Cost of the asset
2. Estimated life of the asset
3. Estimated salvage value

Straight-line method. Under this method, an asset's value is reduced in uniform annual amounts over its estimated useful life. The general formula is:

$$\text{Annual amount to be depreciated} = \frac{\text{Cost} - \text{Salvage value}}{\text{Estimated useful life}}$$

A machine costing $10,000, with an estimated salvage value of zero and an estimated life of ten years, would be depreciated at the rate of $1,000 per year for each of the ten years. If its estimated salvage value at the end of the ten years is $1,000, the annual depreciation charge is:

$$\frac{\$10,000 - \$1,000}{10} = \$900$$

Sum-of-years'-digits (SYD) method. The purpose of the SYD method is to reduce the book value of an asset rapidly in early years and at a lower rate in the later years of its life. The procedure is best shown by the following example:

Cost of new asset $17,000
Estimated useful life . . . . 5 years
Estimated salvage value . . . . . . $ 2,000

First, determine the amount to be depreciated:

$$\text{Cost} - \text{Salvage value} = \$17,000 - \$2,000 = \$15,000$$

Second, total the number of years represented by *each year* in the asset's estimated useful life:

$$1 + 2 + 3 + 4 + 5 = 15$$

Third, depreciate the asset by $\frac{5}{15}$ after the first year, $\frac{4}{15}$ after the second year, and so on, down to $\frac{1}{15}$ in the last year. As a check on computation, the total of the fractions should equal one, and the annual depreciation charges should equal the total amount to be depreciated. The example is illustrated in the accompanying table.

Year	Yearly depreci- ation rate		Amount to be depreciated		Yearly depreci- ation charge	Stated value at end of year
1	5/15	×	$15,000	=	$ 5,000	$10,000
2	4/15	×	15,000	=	4,000	6,000
3	3/15	×	15,000	=	3,000	3,000
4	2/15	×	15,000	=	2,000	1,000
5	1/15	×	15,000	=	1,000	0
Total	1				$15,000	

The accelerated depreciation during early years can be advantageous for two reasons. First, the effect of rapid technological obsolescence is reflected in the quickly falling book value; second, the rapid rate of depreciation provides early tax deductions, which may increase profits. In certain instances, however, the Internal Revenue Service does not allow the use of the SYD method.

Declining-balance method. This method also achieves an accelerated depreciation. The asset's value is decreased by reducing its book value by a constant percentage each year. The percentage rate used is often selected as the one that will just reduce book value to salvage value at the end of the asset's estimated life. In any case, the asset should never be reduced below estimated salvage value. Use of the declining balance method and allowable rates is controlled by Internal Revenue Service regulations. As a simplified illustration, the preceding example is used in the next table with an arbitrarily selected rate of 40 percent. Note that depreciation is based on full cost *not* cost minus salvage value.

Year	Depreciation rate	Beginning book value	Depreciation charge	Accumulated depreciation	Ending book value
1	0.40	$17,000	$6,800	$ 6,800	$10,200
2	0.40	10,200	4,080	10,880	6,120
3	0.40	6,120	2,448	13,328	3,672
4	0.40	3,672	1,469	14,797	2,203
5		2,203	203	15,000	2,000

In the fifth year, reducing book value by 40 percent would have caused it to drop below salvage value. Consequently, the asset was depreciated by only $203, which decreased book value to salvage value.

Double-declining-balance method. Again, for tax advantages, the double-declining-balance method offers higher depreciation early in the life span. Double-declining-balance method uses a percentage twice the straight-line for the life span of the item but applies this rate to the undepreciated original cost. The method is the same as the declining-balance method above, but the term *double-declining-balance* means double the straight-line rate. Thus, equipment with a ten-year life span would have a straight-line depreciation rate of 10 percent per year and a double-declining-balance rate (applied to the undepreciated amount) of 20 percent per year.

Depreciation-by-use method. The purpose of this method is to depreciate capital investment in proportion to its use. It is applicable, for example, to a machine that performs the same operation many times. The life of the machine is not estimated in years but rather in terms of the total number of operations it may reasonably be expected to perform before wearing out. Suppose that a metal-stamping press has an estimated life of 1 million stamps and costs $100,000. The charge for depreciation per stamp is then $100,000/1,000,000, or $0.10. Assuming a zero salvage value, the depreciation charges are as shown on the next table.

Year	Total yearly stamps	Cost per stamp	Yearly depreciation charge	Accumulated depreciation	Ending book value
1	150,000	$0.10	$15,000	$ 15,000	$85,000
2	300,000	0.10	30,000	45,000	55,000
3	200,000	0.10	20,000	65,000	35,000
4	200,000	0.10	20,000	85,000	15,000
5	100,000	0.10	10,000	95,000	5,000
6	50,000	0.10	5,000	100,000	0

This depreciation-by-use method is an attempt to gear depreciation charges to actual use and thereby coordinate expense charges with productive output more accurately. Also, since a machine's resale value is related to its remaining productive life, it is hoped that book value will approximate resale value. The danger, of course, is that technological improvements will render the machine obsolete, in which case book value will not reflect true value.

THE EFFECTS OF TAXES

The tax rates and the method of applying them occasionally change. The most recent tax rates for corporations, which became effective on January 1, 1979, changed the method slightly to resemble the personal income tax graduated rates. In addition, the rates were lowered to stimulate the economy. (It is interesting to note that in the year and a half since then—July 1980—the economy was so stimulated that inflation and interest rates reached all time highs. Severe restraining measures were therefore taken to cool the economy down.)

The corporate tax rates are as follows:

Net income	Tax rate
0–$ 25,000	17%
$25,001–$ 50,000	$ 4,250 + 20% of the amount over $25,000
$50,001–$ 75,000	9,250 + 30% of the amount over $50,000
$75,001–$100,000	16,750 + 40% of the amount over $75,000
Greater than $100,000	26,750 + 46% of the amount over $100,000

This favors small businesses when compared to the pre-1979 taxes. Tax rates had been 48 percent of all income over $50,000. In 1978, a firm with a $100,000 net income would have paid $34,500 taxes. In 1979, this dropped to $26,750.

For large corporations, the average tax rate approaches the maximum of 46 percent. For this reason, all large firms employ specialists to deal with tax-associated problems. Avoidance of a tax yields a direct increase in profit. Tax avoidance, however, is not tax evasion. It is accomplished by choosing a form of organization and structuring investments in such a way as to minimize the firm's tax liability.

When choosing among investment proposals, tax considerations often prove to be the deciding factor since depreciation expenses directly affect taxable income and therefore profit. Consider the following example. Firms A and B both earn net incomes of $100,000 before depreciation expenses are considered. The depreciation expense for firm A is $50,000 while that for B is only $20,000. Because of the graduated tax rate, profit for A will exceed the profit for B by $9,500. The calculations are shown in the following table.

		Firm A	Firm B
1.	Income before depreciation expenses and taxes	$100,000	$100,000
2.	Depreciation expense	50,000	20,000
3.	Income before taxes	$ 50,000	$ 80,000
4.	Taxes from schedule above	9,250	18,750
5.	Net income	$ 40,750	$ 61,250
6.	Funds available for reinvestment [(5) + (2)]	$ 90,750	$ 81,250

The advantage of using accelerated depreciation methods is apparent. Large tax deductions for depreciation in early years provide an added source of funds for reinvestment. One qualification must be mentioned, however. Large deductions in early years necessitate small ones in later years. This could be disadvantageous if tax rates are expected to increase significantly in the future. Even in this case, though, the time value of money may offset the effects of any future tax-rate increases.

In recent years, firms have been able to employ what is termed an *investment tax credit*. A tax credit allows a direct reduction in tax liability. Note that this is a deduction from taxes payable and not simply a reduction in taxable income.

Currently, the tax credit authorizes that for new machinery and equipment with a life of seven years or more, 10 percent of the cost may be deducted from the firm's tax liability. Thus, if a firm purchases new equipment for $100,000, it is permitted to reduce its tax payment by $10,000 in the year the purchase is made. (For machinery and equipment with a five- to seven-year life, $6\frac{2}{3}$ percent may be deducted; for three to five years, $3\frac{1}{3}$ percent may be deducted.) The tax credit offers a high incentive for firms to invest, and it is a proven spur to the national economy. Though originally intended to be put into effect during periods of economic recession, it has been so effective that the Senate Finance Committee has voted to make the 10-percent tax credit permanent.[1]

There are other incentives also. For example, a business energy credit may allow an additional 10 percent allowance. Tax factors such as these verify the need to stay on top of current tax laws and try to predict future changes which may affect current investments and accounting procedures.

CASH MANAGEMENT AND BUDGETING

Companies, though otherwise financially sound, are frequently forced into bankruptcy because they lack the cash needed to carry on their normal business operations. In a stable company, this may occur due to a drop in sales revenue at a time when other sources of ready cash, such as loans or convertible assets, are lacking. In a company experiencing rapid

---

[1] "Panel Supports Tax Break of 10% Being Continued," *The Wall Street Journal* (May 24, 1976), p. 4.

growth, this situation typically arises for two reasons. The first is the delay between investment in new productive facilities and the receipt of revenue derived from sales—a transitional period when a firm's cash needs often are most acute. The second is the tieup of funds in inventories—transit stocks, safety stocks, in-process inventory, and so on. As demand for the product increases, the demand for inventory rises at an even more rapid rate to supply wholesale and retail warehouses and fill the marketing pipelines. This, coupled with the delays inherent in the production-distribution process, puts an overwhelming strain on the firm's cash resources. Clearly, cash budgeting to meet these and similar contingencies is a must. The ensuing discussion, using as an example a firm producing a seasonal product, considers how this is done.

A cash budgeting example

Outdoor Recreation Products, Inc. (ORP) manufactures fishing rods and reels and experiences peak sales during the spring and summer months. To prepare for the period of high sales, the firm must purchase the raw materials needed for production about five months prior to the selling season. Cash expenditures will be large during this period, while at the same time sales revenue will be very low. To project cash needs, a cash budget is formulated. This budget will project future cash needs on a month-by-month basis. With knowledge of its future cash needs, the firm may, if necessary, avoid liquidity problems by negotiating a bank loan well ahead of time.

The following data for ORP are given as a basis for formulating a cash budget. Highest production levels will be maintained from December through April, and highest sales levels will occur between March and July. The firms expects to pay its bills one month after incurring them and to receive payments on sales as follows: 50 percent one month after sales are made and 50 percent two months after sales are made. Procedurally, a worksheet is first drawn up that accounts only for cash outflow due to the purchase of raw materials and for cash inflow resulting from sales. Then, with the work sheet as a 'basis, a cash budget that accounts for all causes of cash flow is developed. A cash budget for Outdoor Recreation Products is shown in Exhibit 5.2.

The cash budget for ORP shows why a business with a highly fluctuating cash level requires periodic external financing to carry on normal operations. The cash deficit is at a maximum in April, and the company will need to borrow at least $133,000 to maintain a safe cash level and ensure liquidity. Management is thus provided a tool with which to determine how much additional funds are necessary during any given month. Beginning in July, cash will exceed the level desired, and ORP can begin to repay the loan.

In general, sales require financing. The more cyclical a firm's sales, the greater the amount of financing that will be required. Outdoor Recreation could avoid financing only by holding very large cash reserves during the year in anticipation of the heavy need for cash during the months

EXHIBIT 5.2

Outdoor Recreation Products, Inc.

WORK SHEET

	November	December	January	February	March	April	May	June	July	August	September
Sales	$10,000	$10,000	$16,000	$50,000	$80,000	$100,000	$100,000	$80,000	$80,000	$30,000	$20,000
Collections											
1st month after sales		5,000	5,000	8,000	25,000	40,000	50,000	50,000	40,000	40,000	15,000
2nd month after sales			5,000	5,000	8,000	25,000	40,000	50,000	50,000	40,000	40,000
Total Collections		$ 5,000	$10,000	$ 13,000	$ 33,000	$ 65,000	$ 90,000	$100,000	$90,000	$ 80,000	$ 55,000
Purchases of raw materials	$25,000	$30,000	$35,000	$40,000	35,000	25,000	10,000	6,000	4,000	4,000	4,000
Payments (1 month after purchases)		25,000	30,000	35,000	40,000	35,000	25,000	10,000	6,000	4,000	4,000

CASH BUDGET

	November	December	January	February	March	April	May	June	July	August	September
Revenues (collections)		$ 5,000	$10,000	$ 13,000	$ 33,000	$ 65,000	$ 90,000	$100,000	$90,000	$ 80,000	$ 55,000
Payments											
Purchases		$25,000	$30,000	$ 35,000	$ 40,000	$ 35,000	$ 25,000	$ 10,000	$ 6,000	$ 4,000	$ 4,000
Salaries		10,000	12,000	15,000	15,000	12,000	10,000	5,000	5,000	5,000	5,000
Rent and leases		2,000	2,000	2,000	2,000	2,000	2,000	2,000	2,000	2,000	2,000
Long-term debt retirement								30,000			
Income taxes						20,000					
Total Payments		$37,000	$44,000	$ 52,000	$ 57,000	$ 69,000	$ 37,000	$ 47,000	$13,000	$ 11,000	$ 11,000
Net cash increase (decrease) during month		($32,000)	($34,000)	($39,000)	($24,000)	($4,000)	$53,000	$53,000	$77,000	$69,000	$44,000
Beginning cash		10,000	(22,000)	(56,000)	(95,000)	(119,000)	(123,000)	(70,000)	(17,000)	60,000	129,000
Cumulative cash		(22,000)	(56,000)	(95,000)	(119,000)	(123,000)	(70,000)	(17,000)	60,000	129,000	173,000
Desired level of cash (safety level to ensure liquidity)		10,000	10,000	10,000	10,000	10,000	10,000	10,000	10,000	10,000	10,000
Excess cash (or additional financing required)*		($32,000)	($66,000)	($105,000)	($129,000)	($133,000)	($80,000)	($27,000)	$50,000	$119,000	$163,000

* Cumulative less desired.

of high production. However, the opportunity cost of holding cash in such quantity is high. Therefore, it may be in the firm's best interests to invest its excess cash in capital assets that yield higher rates of return and to borrow funds to finance production.

BREAK-EVEN ANALYSIS

Break-even analysis is used to determine the volume of sales (either in dollars or units of output) that must be achieved for the firm to break even; that is, to neither earn profits nor incur losses. The sales volume—in units or dollar amount—that gives this result is termed the *break-even point,* and calculation of the break-even point is quite simple. The accompanying formula is used to determine the break-even point in units of output.

$$\text{Break-even point in units} = \frac{\text{Total fixed costs}}{\text{Unit price} - \text{Variable cost per unit}}$$

Since variable costs are assumed to be the same for each unit of output, subtracting variable costs from price yields the amount of revenue or *contribution* each unit makes toward the coverage of fixed costs. Fixed costs, of course, remain constant regardless of the level of output. The break-even point will be achieved when sales produce just enough revenue above variable costs to cover fixed costs.

Suppose a product is priced at $10 and the variable cost is $6 per unit. If total fixed costs are $1,000, the break-even point in units of output sold is

$$\text{Break-even point in units} = \frac{TFC}{P - VC} = \frac{\$1,000}{\$10 - \$6} = 250$$

The result is easily verified. Total costs = $1,000 fixed costs + $6 variable cost × 250 units = $1,000 + $1,500 = $2,500. Total revenue is $10 selling price × 250 units, or $2,500.

We can also look at the break-even point as the point where revenue equals variable costs plus fixed costs. If N is the number of units sold,

$$\text{Revenue} = \text{Variable costs} + \text{Fixed costs}$$
$$10N = 6N + 1,000$$
$$N = 250 \text{ units}$$

The analysis can be extended to allow for a profit goal. To the numerator in the formula, a desired level of profit is added to the fixed costs. The result gives the sales in units required to attain a given level of profit. Using the figures above and assuming a profit goal of $3,000, the required sales in units is

Units required to yield a desired level of profit

$$= \frac{\text{Total fixed costs} + \text{Desired profit level}}{\text{Price} - \text{Variable costs}} \quad (1)$$

Units required to yield a $3,000 profit

$$= \frac{\$1,000 + \$3,000}{\$10 - \$6} = 1,000 \qquad (2)$$

The sale of 1,000 units will yield a before-tax profit of $3,000.

The relationships among costs, level of output, and revenue are shown graphically in Exhibit 5.3. Reference to such a graph provides a quick picture of profits (or losses) as they may be expected to change with output.

It will now be shown how break-even analysis assists in pricing decisions. Suppose a firm produces a product with variable costs of $6 per unit and incurs fixed costs totaling $1,000. Because management is debating the price and can't decide whether to set a price of $9 or $10 for the product, the accounting department constructs a graph to assist management in making the decision. The same formulas developed earlier have been used to construct Exhibit 5.4. Break-even occurs at 250 units when the selling price is $10 and at 333 units when the price is $9. Which price is chosen will depend on the firm's estimated demand curve for the product. Beyond 250 units, any level of sales yields greater profits if a $10 price is used. But suppose the firm feels it can sell 250 units when

EXHIBIT 5.3
Relationships among costs, output, and profit (fixed costs = $1,000; variable costs = $6 per unit; selling price = $10 per unit)

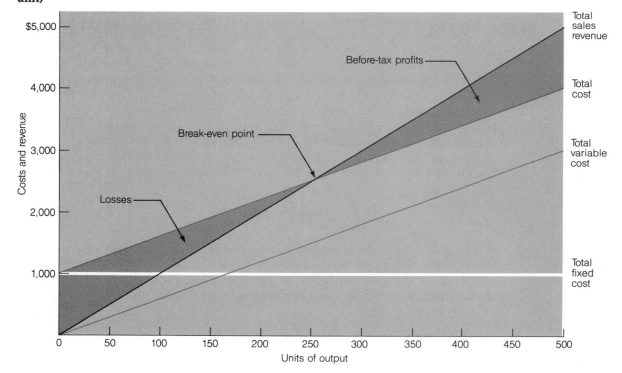

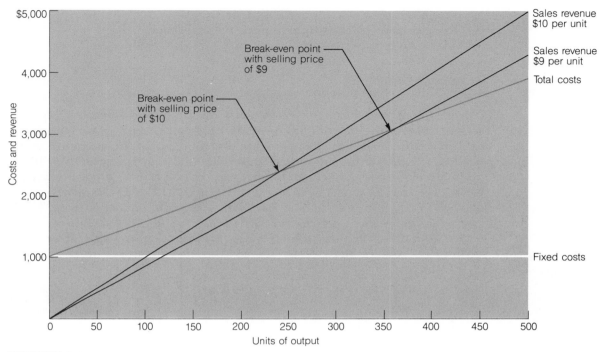

EXHIBIT 5.4
Comparative relationship among costs, output, sales revenues, and profits when varying selling prices are used (fixed costs = $1,000; variable cost = $6 per unit; selling price A = $9 per unit; selling price B = $10 per unit)

the price is $10 and 450 units if the product is priced at $9. The firm will break even using a $10 price and earn a profit using the $9 price. Alternatively, suppose 450 units can be sold at $10 and that sales will be 500 units if the price is $9. In this case, notice that a larger profit can be earned if a $10 price is set, even though 50 additional units could be sold if the price were $9.

Once again, the price to be selected will depend on management's estimate of how much the market will absorb at each price. Break-even analysis does not indicate which price should be selected; rather, it aids management in making the decision by providing a picture of profits at various prices and levels of sales.

CHOOSING AMONG SPECIFIC INVESTMENT PROPOSALS

The capital investment decision has become highly rationalized, as evidenced by the variety of techniques available for its solution. In contradistinction to pricing or marketing decisions, the capital investment decision can usually be made with a higher degree of confidence because the variables affecting the decision are relatively well known and can be quantified with fair accuracy.

Investment decisions may be grouped into six general categories:

1. Purchase of new equipment and/or facilities.
2. Replacement of existing equipment or facilities.
3. Make-or-buy decisions.
4. Lease-or-buy decisions.
5. Temporary shutdown or plant-abandonment decisions.
6. Addition or elimination of a product or product line.

Investment decisions are made with regard to the lowest acceptable rate of return on investment. As a starting point, the lowest acceptable rate of return may be considered to be the cost of investment capital needed to underwrite the expenditure. Certainly an investment will not be made if it does not return at least the cost of capital. Investments are generally ranked according to the return they yield in excess of their cost of capital. In this way a business with only limited investment funds can select investment alternatives that yield the highest *net* returns. (Net return is defined here as the earnings an investment yields after gross earnings have been reduced by the cost of the funds used to finance the

EXHIBIT 5.5
Priority among investment alternatives

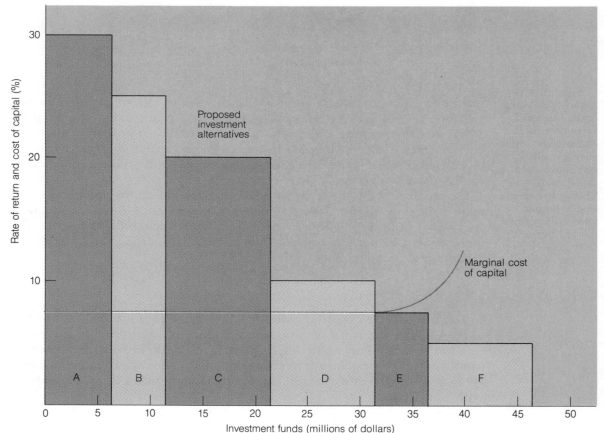

investment.) In general, investments should not be made unless the return in funds exceeds the *marginal* cost of investment capital (marginal cost is defined as the incremental cost of each new acquisition of funds from outside sources).

A general view of the investment problem is presented graphically in Exhibit 5.5. In constructing this graph, the assumption is made that the marginal cost of capital is a constant 8 percent up to $30 million and increases rapidly thereafter. Given these alternatives, which should be selected? Clearly, since the alternative with the highest rate of return should be selected first, a firm which has $20 million to invest should select *A, B,* and *C,* in that order. If it has $30 million, it should select alternatives *A* through *D.* Since the remaining alternatives' cost of capital is in excess of net return, they should not be chosen. In this situation, $30 million is the maximum cutoff point for investments.

A major problem in choosing among alternatives is encountered when the expected lives of the investments differ. Comparison is easier and more accurate if the economic lives of the alternatives under consideration are the same. We will deal with this problem later, when we consider some specific proposals.

Several types of costs are used in capital investment decisions: (1) fixed costs, (2) variable costs, (3) opportunity costs, (4) sunk costs, and (5) avoidable costs. (The first four have been defined previously.)

Avoidable costs include any expense that will *not* be incurred if an investment is made but that *must* be incurred if the investment is not made. Suppose a company owns a metal lathe that is not in working condition but is needed for the firm's operations. Since the lathe must be repaired or replaced, the repair costs are avoidable if a new lathe is purchased. Avoidable costs reduce the cost of a new investment because they will not be incurred if the investment is made. Avoidable costs are an example of how it is possible to "save" money by spending money.

INTEREST RATE EFFECTS

There are two basic ways to account for the effects of interest accumulation: one way is to compute the total amount created over the time period as the *compound value,* and the other way is to remove the interest rate effect over time by reducing all future sums to present-day dollars, or the *present value.*

Compound value

The compound value of a sum, say $10, is the value of the sum after it earns an annual rate of interest over a specified period. The sum earns interest during each period on the initial value *and* on the interest earned in the preceding periods. For example, the compound value of $10 earning 5 percent interest after three years is $11.58 and is derived as follows. The value of $10 after one year is $10 + ($10) (0.05) = $10.50, or $10

$(1 + 0.05) = \$10.50$. Thus, the value of a sum after any year is the beginning value times one plus the interest rate (i).

Year	Adding in interest rate $(1 + i)$	Value at beginning of year	Value at end of year
1	$(1 + 0.05) \times \$10.000 = \$10.500$		
2	$(1 + 0.05) \times \$10.500 = \$11.025$		
3	$(1 + 0.05) \times \$11.025 = \$11.576$ or $\$11.58$		

The process used to arrive at the $11.58 figure is generalized below, where V = value at the end of a specific year, P = principal, or value at the beginning of a specific year, i = the interest rate, and the subscript represents the length of the compounding period:

$$V_3 = P_3 (1 + i) = P_1 (1 + i)^3$$
$$= \$10.00 (1 + 0.05)^3$$
$$= \$10.00 (1.158)$$
$$= \$11.58$$

Thus the general formula for compound value is:

$$V_n = P_1(1 + i)^n$$

In practice, it is not necessary to compute compound values. Compound value tables are available that list the compound value for a number of years and various interest rates. Using Exhibit 5.6, we see that the value of $1 at 5 percent interest after three years is $1.158. Multiplying this figure by $10 gives $11.58, as computed previously. (Note: Exhibits 5.6 through 5.9 will be found as an appendix of this chapter.)

The compound value of an *annuity* is found in a similar manner. An *annuity* is the receipt of a constant sum each year for a specified number of years. Usually an annuity is received at the end of a period and does not earn interest during that period. Therefore, an annuity of $10 for three years would bring in $10 at the end of the first year (allowing the $10 to earn interest if invested for the remaining two years), $10 at the end of the second year (allowing the $10 to earn interest for the remaining one year), and $10 at the end of the third year (with no time to earn interest). If the annuity receipts were placed in a bank savings account at 5 percent interest, the total or compound value of the $10 at 5 percent for the three years would be:

Year	Receipt at end of year		Compound interest factor $(1 + i)^n$		Value at end of third year
1	$10.00	$\times$	$(1 + 0.05)^2$	=	$11.02
2	10.00	$\times$	$(1 + 0.05)^1$	=	10.50
3	10.00	$\times$	$(1 + 0.05)^0$	=	10.00
					$31.52

The general formula for finding the compound value of an annuity is

$$S_n = R(1+i)^{n-1} + R(1+i)^{n-2} + \ldots + R(1+i)^1 + R$$
$$= R[(1+i)^{n-1} + (1+i)^{n-2} + \ldots + (1+i)^1 + 1]$$

where

S_n = compound value of an annuity
R = periodic receipts in dollars
n = length of the annuity in years

Applying this formula to the above example, we get:

$$S_n = R[(1+i)^2 + (1+i) + 1]$$
$$= \$10[(1+0.05)^2 + (1+0.05) + 1]$$
$$= \$10 \,(3.152)$$
$$= \$31.52$$

Compound value tables for annuities are available to simplify computation. Exhibit 5.7 lists the compound value factor of $1 for 5 percent after three years as 3.152. Multiplying this factor by $10 yields $31.52.

Present value   Compound values are used to determine the value of a sum after a specified period has elapsed. Present-value procedures accomplish just the reverse. They are used to determine the current value of a sum or stream of receipts expected to be received in the future. Most investment decision techniques utilize present-value concepts rather than compound values. Since decisions affecting the future are made in the present, it is better to convert future returns into their present value at the time the decision is being made. In this way, investment alternatives are placed in better perspective in terms of current dollars.

An example will make this more apparent. If a rich uncle offers to make you a gift of $100 today or $250 after ten years, which should you choose? You must determine whether the $250 in ten years will be worth more than the $100 now. Suppose that you base your decision on the rate of inflation in the economy and believe that inflation averages 10 percent per year. By deflating the $250, you can compare its relative purchasing power with $100 received today. Procedurally, this is accomplished by solving the compound formula for the present sum, P, where V is the future amount of $250 in 10 years at 10 percent. The compound value formula is

$$V = P(1+i)^n$$

Dividing both sides by $(1+i)^n$ gives:

$$P = \frac{V}{(1+i)^n}$$
$$= \frac{250}{(1+0.10)^{10}}$$
$$= \$96.39$$

This shows that, at a 10 percent inflationary rate, $250 in ten years will be worth 96.39 today. The rational choice, then, is to take the $100 now.

The use of tables is also standard practice in solving present-value problems. With reference to Exhibit 5.8, the present-value factor for $1 received 10 years hence is 0.386. Multiplication of this factor by $250 yields $96.50.

The present value of a future sum includes compounding at a specific interest rate, just as do compound value procedures. The difference lies in the fact that compounding takes place in reverse. The practice of reducing future sums or income streams to present values by using specified interest rates is often referred to as *discounting*. The discounted value of $250 after ten years at 10 percent is $96.39. This is the same as *present value,* and the terms are generally interchangeable.

The present value of an annuity is the value of an annuity to be received over a future period expressed in terms of the present. The process of finding it is simply the reverse of finding the compound value of an annuity. Again, the purpose is to deal with values in the present rather than in the future. To find the value of an annuity of $100 for three years at 10 percent, find the factor in the present-value table which applies to 10 percent in *each* of the three years in which the amount is received and multiply each receipt by this factor. Then sum the resulting figures. Remember that annuities are usually received at the end of each period.

Year	Amount received at end of year		Present-value factor at 10%		Present value
1	$100	×	0.909	=	$ 90.90
2	100	×	0.826	=	82.60
3	100	×	0.751	=	75.10
Total receipts	$300		Total P.V. =		$248.60

The general formula used to derive the present value of an annuity is

$$A_n = R\left[\frac{1}{(1+i)} + \frac{1}{(1+i)^2} + \cdots + \frac{1}{(1+i)^n}\right]$$

where

A_n = present value of an annuity of n years
R = periodic receipts
n = length of the annuity in years

Applying the formula to the above example gives

$$A_n = \$100\left[\frac{1}{(1+0.10)} + \frac{1}{(1+0.10)^2} + \frac{1}{(1+0.10)^3}\right]$$
$$= \$100\,(2.488)$$
$$= \$248.80$$

The $248.80 result differs from the answer obtained above because of rounding in the table of present-value factors. Tables for the present value of an annuity are also available. The present-value factor for an annuity of $1 for three years at 10 percent (from Exhibit 5.9) is 2.487. Since our sum is $100 rather than $1, we multiply this factor by $100 to arrive at $248.70. Again, the slight variance from the previous answers results from rounded figures in the table.

When the stream of future receipts is uneven, the present value of each annual receipt must be calculated. The present values of the receipts for all years are then summed to arrive at total present value. This process can sometimes be tedious, but it is unavoidable. Discounted at 10 percent, the total present value of $100 received in one year, $400 in two years, and $200 in five years would be as shown on the accompanying table.

Year	Receipt		Present-value factor at 10%		Present value
1	$100	×	0.909	=	$ 90.90
2	400	×	0.826	=	330.40
3	. . .		. . . .		. . . . .
4	. . .		. . . .		. . . . .
5	200	×	0.621	=	124.20
	$700				$545.50 = Total P.V.

METHODS OF RANKING INVESTMENTS

Payback period

The payback method ranks investments according to the time required for each investment to return earnings equal to the cost of the investment. The rationale underlying the use of payback is that the sooner that investment capital can be recovered, the sooner it can be reinvested in new revenue-producing projects. Thus, supposedly, a firm will be able to get the most benefit from its available investment funds.

Consider two alternatives requiring a $1,000 investment each. The first will earn $200 per year for six years; the second will earn $300 per year for the first three years, and $100 per year for the next three years. The two alternatives are outlined in the accompanying table.

Year	Alternative A Investment = $1,000 Cash inflow	Alternative B Investment = $1,000 Cash inflow
1...................	$ 200	$ 300
2...................	200	300
3...................	200	300
4...................	200	100
5...................	200	100
6...................	200	100
	$1,200	$1,200

If alternative A is selected, the initial investment of $1,000 will be recovered at the end of the fifth year. The income produced by B will total $1,000 after only four years. The selection of *B* will permit reinvestment of the full $1,000 in new revenue-producing projects one year sooner than *A* and under this method, should be selected.

The payback method is declining in popularity as the sole measure in investment decisions. It is still frequently used, however, in conjunction with other methods to give an indication of the time commitment of funds. The major problems with payback are that it does not consider income beyond the payback period and it ignores the time value of money. Consider the investment alternatives shown in the next table.

Year	Investment A Cost: $20,000 Cash inflow	Investment B Cost: $20,000 Cash inflow	Investment C Cost: $20,000 Cash inflow
1	$6,000	$4,000	$5,000
2	6,000	4,000	5,000
3	6,000	4,000	5,000
4	6,000	4,000	5,000
5	6,000	4,000	4,000
6	—	4,000	4,000
7	—	4,000	4,000
8	—	4,000	4,000
9	—	4,000	—
10	—	4,000	—
Payback period	3.33 years	5 years	4 years
Total receipts	$30,000	$40,000	$36,000
Present value at 12%	$21,630	$22,600	$22,909

On the basis of payback, investment *A* represents the best alternative since it will return the original investment of $20,000 in only 3⅓ years. If, however, the firm discounts the cash flow of each investment by the cost of capital, in this case 12 percent, investment *C* is the most attractive of the three.[2] While investment *B* will return more in actual dollars than either *A* or *C,* its present value is less than that for *C.* Total earnings do not afford the best basis for decision because, as with payback, the time value of money is ignored. The present value of the three income streams offers the best method of comparison because the alternatives can be compared in terms of their value at the same point in time.

Net present value

The net present-value method is commonly used in business. Under this method, decisions are based on the amount by which the present value of a projected income stream exceeds the cost of an investment. (Refer to the previous example.) The present values of the income streams, discounted at the cost of capital, exceed the cost of the investments by the amounts shown in the accompanying table.

---

[2] This example ignores the availability of cash for reinvestment, which is obviously higher for alternative *A.* This problem is discussed again in this chapter under "Ranking investments with uneven lives," (page 124).

	Investment A	Investment B	Investment C
Present value of total cash flows	$21,630	$22,600	$22,909
Cost of investment	20,000	20,000	20,000
Net present value	$ 1,630	$ 2,600	$ 2,909

Investment *C*, at $2,909, yields the highest net present value and should be selected.

Now consider a case where the costs of investments differ. A firm is considering two alternative investments, the first costing $30,000 and the second, $50,000. The expected yearly cash income streams are shown in the next table.

Year	Alternative A Cost: $30,000 Cash inflow	Alternative B Cost: $50,000 Cash inflow
1	$10,000	$15,000
2	10,000	15,000
3	10,000	15,000
4	10,000	15,000
5	10,000	15,000

To choose between alternatives *A* and *B*, find which alternative has the highest net present value. Assume an 8 percent cost of capital.

> Alternative A:
> 3.993 (P.V. factor) × $10,000 = $39,930
> Less cost of investment   =   30,000
> Net present value   = $ 9,930
>
> Alternative B:
> 3.993 (P.V. factor) × $15,000 = $59,895
> Less cost of investment   =   50,000
> Net present value   = $ 9,895

Investment *A* is the better alternative. Its net present value exceeds that of investment *B* by $35 ($9,930 − $9,895 = $35).

Internal rate of return   The internal rate of return may be defined as the interest rate that equates the present value of an income stream with the cost of an investment. There is no procedure or formula that may be used directly to compute the internal rate of return—it must be found by interpolation or iterative calculation.

Suppose we wish to find the internal rate of return for an investment costing $12,000 that will yield a cash inflow of $4,000 per year for four years. We see that the present value factor sought is

$$\frac{\$12,000}{\$4,000} = 3.000$$

and we seek the interest rate that will provide this factor over a four-year period. The interest rate must lie between 12 percent and 14 percent because 3.000 lies between 3.037 and 2.914 (in the fourth row of Exhibit 5.9). Linear interpolation between these values, according to the following equation

$$i = 12 + (14 - 12) \frac{(3.037 - 3.000)}{(3.037 - 2.914)}$$
$$= 12 + 0.602 = 12.602\%$$

gives a good approximation to the actual internal rate of return.

When the income stream is discounted at 12.6 percent, the resulting present value closely approximates the cost of investment. Thus the internal rate of return for this investment is 12.6 percent. The cost of capital can be compared with the internal rate of return to determine the net rate of return on the investment. If, in this example, the cost of capital were 8 percent, the net rate of return on the investment would be 4.6 percent.

The net present-value and internal rate-of-return methods involve procedures that are essentially the same. They differ in that the net present-value method enables investment alternatives to be compared in terms of the dollar value in excess of cost whereas the internal rate-or-return method permits comparison of rates of return on alternative investments.

In most instances, each method will rank a series of alternatives in an identical manner. Sometimes, however, when investments are unequal amounts, the two methods will give different results. Such an instance is given below, where we assume a 7 percent cost of capital.

Year	Alternative A Cost: $55,000 Cash flows	Alternative B Cost: $75,000 Cash flows
1	$15,000	$20,000
2	15,000	20,000
3	15,000	20,000
4	15,000	20,000
5	15,000	20,000

Internal rates of return:
   Investment A:
      P.V. factor = $55,000/$15,000 = 3.667
      Internal rate of return = approximately 11.3% (interpolated in Exhibit 5.9)

   Investment B:
      P.V. factor = $75,000/$20,000 = 3.750
      Internal rate of return = approximately 10.4% (interpolated in Exhibit 5.9)

Net present values (cost of capital = 7%):

   Investment A: Investment B:
      4.100 × $15,000   = $61,500   4.100 × $20,000   = $82,000
      Cost of investment = 55,000   Cost of investment = 75,000
      Net present value = $ 6,500   Net present value = $ 7,000

The internal rate-of-return method would indicate that *A* should be chosen, while the net present-value method points to *B* as the best alternative. Because no clear answer can be given as to which investment should be made, the decision will depend heavily upon other factors, such as the relative risk of the two investments or the presence of other investment alternatives. As an example of the latter, suppose the firm had another alternative that would require a $20,000 investment. If the total net present value of alternative *A* and the $20,000 investment were greater than the net present value of *B*, *A* should be chosen.

Many times there are investment analyses which include nonconstant benefit streams. This problem may be even further confounded by uncertain projections as brought about, for example, by changing technology which tends to make future replacement costs and income streams uncertain. An excellent discussion of this type problem is contained in the Bowman and Fetter reference at the end of this chapter. Their approach avoids the unequal investment lives issue by looking at infinite life, or continual replacement. Since this evaluation is done each year, the latest knowledge about costs and changing technology can be incorporated into the analysis.

Depreciation and cash flow

The examples have thus far referred to investment earnings as cash flows. The reason for this is that only the actual cash flow produced by an investment is relevant to the investment decision process. Earnings before depreciation and tax adjustments do not represent the actual benefits realized by a firm. Consequently, the expected income from an investment must be adjusted to represent only the realizable cash inflow before ranking can take place.

Assume that a machine costing $10,000 has an expected life of five years and is expected to produce gross earnings of $4,000 each year. With straight-line depreciation, no salvage value for the machine, and a 50 percent tax rate, the annual cash inflow in *each* of the five years will be

Gross earnings	$4,000
Less: Depreciation expense	2,000
Income before taxes	$2,000
Less: Taxes at 50%	1,000
Net income	$1,000
Plus: Depreciation expense	2,000
Cash inflow	$3,000

In this example, with the straight-line method, the net present value of the investment, using a 10 percent cost of capital, is:

$$(3.791 \times \$3,000) - \$10,000 = \$1,373$$

Contrast this with the sum-of-years'-digits method of depreciation, which provides large cash flows in the early years of an investment's life. This will result in higher present values of income streams because the larger cash flows in the early years will not be affected by discounting as greatly as the smaller flows in later years. Under the SYD method, the cash flow for each year must be calculated separately since the flows will differ and therefore cannot be treated as an annuity. The results of applying the SYD method are summarized in the accompanying table.

Year	Present-value factor		Cash flow		Present value
1	0.909	×	$3,667	=	$ 3333.30
2	0.826	×	3,333	=	2753.06
3	0.751	×	3,000	=	2253.00
4	0.683	×	2,667	=	1821.56
5	0.621	×	2,333	=	1448.79
					$11,609.71 or $11,610

Also,

$$\text{Net present value} = \$11,610 - \$10,000 = \$1,610$$

Use of the SYD method in preference to the straight-line method increases net present value by $237 ($1,610 − $1,373 = $237).

Ranking investments with uneven lives

When proposed investments have the same life expectancy, comparison among them, using the preceding methods, will give a reasonable picture of their relative value. When lives are unequal, however, the net present-value and internal rate-of-return methods share a crucial shortcoming. In the example that used the payback method, notice that investment A has a life expectancy half that of B. When A is exhausted at the end of the fifth year, management would presumably reinvest the $20,000 cost. If this is done, the earnings on the new investment over the next five years must be compared with the earnings on B for years six through ten if a true comparison between A and B is to be made. Suppose $20,000 is reinvested (after investment A expires) in investment A', which has a life expectancy of five years. Since the reinvested $20,000 is the *same* $20,000 that was originally invested over the ten-year period, the investment funds used to finance A and A' are equal to the investment in B, that is, $20,000.

The problem, then, concerns the rate of return on A' over years six through ten. The earnings on A' must be estimated before A can be compared with B. But how can this be done when A' does not even exist at the time of decision? The answer is that it cannot be done with specificity; yet some standard for comparison is needed for ranking to occur.

One approach is to assume that the second investment (A' in this case) will return just the cost of capital. Another approach would be to use the internal rate-of-return method. If a firm operates with a 20 percent cutoff rate of return, it would be assumed that the new investment, A', would earn the minimum acceptable rate of return, 20 percent. Which percentage to use depends on the historical rate of return on the firm's investments and its policy regarding cutoff rates of return. A third approach would be to assume new investments to be exact duplicates of the original in cost and cash inflow. In that case, unequal lives can be resolved by taking multiples of investments over an identical period (e.g., two investments in A at five years each compared to one in B for ten years).

These approaches still do not provide a completely satisfactory method for dealing with investments having unequal lives. One immediately striking shortcoming is the assumption that machine A', purchased five years hence, will be equivalent to machine A, purchased today. On the contrary, technological improvements can generally be expected to make A' the better and more productive machine and may provide a higher cash inflow. On the other hand, inflationary pressures may substantially increase the purchase price of A'.

No estimate dealing with investments unforeseen at the time of decision can be expected to reflect a high degree of accuracy. Still, the problem must be dealt with, and these approaches afford a reasonable basis for proceeding with ranking.

EXAMPLES OF INVESTMENT DECISIONS

An expansion decision

Problem. William J. Wilson Ceramic Products, Inc., leases plant facilities in which firebrick is manufactured. Because of rising demand, Wilson could increase sales by investing in new equipment to expand output. The selling price of $10 per brick will remain unchanged if output and sales increase. Based on engineering and cost estimates, the accounting department provides management with the following cost estimates based on an annual increased output of 100,000 bricks.

Cost of new equipment having an expected life of five years	$500,000
Equipment installation cost	20,000
Expected salvage value	0
New operation's share of annual lease expense	10,000
Annual increase in utility expenses	40,000
Annual increase in labor costs	160,000
Annual additional cost for raw materials	40,000

The sum-of-years'-digits method of depreciation will be used and taxes are paid at a rate of 40 percent. Mr. Wilson's policy is not to invest capital in projects earning less than a 20 percent rate of return. Should the proposed expansion be undertaken?

Solution. Compute cost of investment:

Acquisition cost of equipment	$500,000
Equipment installation costs	20,000
Total cost of investment	$520,000

Determine yearly cash flows throughout the life of the investment:

The lease expense is a sunk cost. It will be incurred whether or not the investment is made and is therefore irrelevant to the decision and should be disregarded. Annual production expenses to be considered are utility, labor, and raw materials. These total $600,000 per year.

Annual sales revenue is $10 × 10,000 units of output, or $1,000,000. Yearly income before depreciation and taxes is thus $1,000,000 gross revenue less $600,000 expenses, or $400,000.

Determine the depreciation charges to be deducted from the $400,000 income each year using the SYD method (sum-of-years' digits = 1 + 2 + 3 + 4 + 5 = 15):

Year	Proportion of $500,000 to be depreciated				Depreciation charge
1	5/15	×	$500,000	=	$166,667
2	4/15	×	500,000	=	133,333
3	3/15	×	500,000	=	100,000
4	2/15	×	500,000	=	66,667
5	1/15	×	500,000	=	33,333
Accumulated depreciation				=	$500,000

Find each year's cash flow when taxes are 40 percent. Cash flow for only the first year is illustrated:

Earnings before depreciation and taxes		$400,000
Deduct: Taxes at 40%	$160,000	
Add: Tax benefit of depreciation expense (0.4 × 166,667)	66,667	93,333
Cash flow (1st year)		$306,667

Determine present value of the cash flows:

Since Wilson demands at least a 20 percent rate of return on investments, multiply the cash flows by the 20 percent present-value factor for each year. The factor for each respective year must be used because the cash flows are not an annuity.

Year	Present-value factor		Cash flow		Present value
1	0.833	×	$306,667	=	$255,454
2	0.694	×	293,333	=	203,573
3	0.579	×	280,000	=	162,120
4	0.482	×	266,667	=	128,533
5	0.402	×	253,334	=	101,840
Total present value of cash flows (discounted at 20%)				=	$851,520

Find whether net present value is positive or negative:

Total present value of cash flows $851,520
Total cost of investment   520,000
Net present value $331,520

Decision. Net present value is positive when returns are discounted at 20%. Wilson will earn an amount in excess of 20% on the investment. The proposed expansion should be undertaken.

A replacement decision

Problem. For five years Bennie's Brewery has been using a machine that attaches labels to bottles. The machine was purchased for $4,000 and is being depreciated over ten years to a zero salvage value using straight-line depreciation. The machine can be sold now for $2,000. Bennie can buy a new labeling machine for $6,000 that will have a useful life of five years and cut labor costs by $1,200 annually. The old machine will require a major overhaul in the next few months. The cost of the overhaul is expected to be $300. If purchased, the new machine will be depreciated over five years to a $500 salvage value using the straight-line method. The company will invest in any project earning more than the 12% cost of capital. The tax rate is 40%. Should Bennie's Brewery invest in the new machine?

Solution. Determine the cost of investment:

Price of the new machine $6,000
  Less: Sale of old machine $2,000
            Avoidable overhaul costs   300   2,300
Effective cost of investment $3,700

Determine the increase in cash flow resulting from investment in the new machine:

Yearly cost savings = $1,200.
Differential depreciation:
  Annual depreciation on old machine:

$$\frac{\text{Cost} - \text{Salvage}}{\text{Expected life}} = \frac{\$4,000 - \$0}{10} = \$400$$

Annual depreciation on new machine:

$$\frac{\text{Cost} - \text{Salvage}}{\text{Expected life}} = \frac{\$6,000 - \$500}{5} = \$1,100$$

Differential depreciation = $1,100 − $400 = $700
Yearly net increase in cash flow into the firm:

Cost savings $1,200
   Deduct: Taxes at 40% $480
   Add: Advantage of increase in depreciation
      (0.4 × $700)   280   200
Yearly increase in cash flow $1,000

Determine total present value of the investment:

The five-year cash flow of $1,000 per year is an annuity.
Discounted at 12 percent, the cost of capital, the present value is

$$3.605 \times \$1,000 = \$3,605$$

The present value of the new machine, if sold at its salvage value of $500 at the end of the fifth year, is

$$0.567 \times \$500 = \$284$$

Total present value of the expected cash flows:

$$\$3,605 + \$284 = \$3,889$$

Determine whether net present value is positive:

Total present value $3,889
Cost of investment   3,700
Net present value .... $ 189

Decision. Bennie's Brewery should make the purchase because the investment will return slightly more than the cost of capital.

Note: The importance of depreciation has been shown in this example. The present value of the yearly cash flow resulting from operations is *only*

(Cost savings − Taxes)   (Present value factor)
   ($1,200 − $480)   ×   (3.605)   = $2,596

This figure is $1,104 less than the $3,700 cost of the investment. Only a very large depreciation advantage makes this investment worthwhile. The total present value of the advantage is $1,009:

(Tax rate × Differential depreciation)   (P.V. factor)
      (0.4 × $700)   ×   (3.605)   = $1,009

A make-or-buy decision

Problem. The Triple X Company manufactures and sells refrigerators. It makes some of the parts for the refrigerators and purchases others. The engineering department believes it might be possible to cut costs by manufacturing one of the parts currently being purchased for $8.25 each. The firm uses 100,000 of these parts each year, and the accounting department compiles the following list of costs based on engineering estimates.

Fixed costs will increase by $50,000.

Labor costs will increase by $125,000.

Factory overhead, currently running $500,000 per year, may be expected to increase 12 percent.

Raw materials used to make the part will cost $600,000.

Given the above estimates, should Triple X make the part or continue to buy it?

Solution. Find total cost incurred if the part were manufactured:

Additional fixed costs	$ 50,000
Additional labor costs	125,000
Raw materials cost	600,000
Additional overhead costs = 0.12 × $500,000	60,000
Total cost to manufacturer	$835,000

Find cost per unit to manufacture:

$$\frac{\$835,000}{100,000} = \$8.35 \text{ per unit}$$

Decision. Triple X should continue to buy the part. Manufacturing costs exceed the present cost to purchase by $0.10 per unit.

A lease-or-buy decision

Problem. George Sprott is a small businessman who has need for a pickup truck in his everyday work. He is considering buying a truck for $3,000. If he buys the truck, he believes he will be able to sell it for $1,000 at the end of four years, so he will depreciate $2,000 of the truck's value on a straight-line basis. Sprott can borrow $3,000 from the bank and repay it in four equal annual installments at 6 percent interest. However, a friend advises him that he may be better off to lease a truck if he can get the same terms from the leasing company that he receives at the bank. Assuming that this is so, should Sprott buy or lease the truck? Taxes are 40 percent.

Solution. Find the cost to buy:

The bank loan is an installment loan at 6 percent interest, so the payments constitute a four-year annuity. Divide the amount of the loan by the present value factor for a four-year annuity at 6 percent interest to find the annual payment. Multiply the annual payments by four to find the total payment.

$$\frac{\$3,000}{3.465} = \$866 \text{ annual payment}$$
$$4 \times \$866 = \$3,464 \text{ total payment}$$

Next, find the present value of the cost of the loans:

(1) Year	(2) Yearly payment	(3) Interest at 6%	(4) Payment on principal	(5) Remaining balance	(6) Depreciation
1	$866	$180	$686	$2,314	$500
2	866	139	727	1,587	500
3	866	95	771	816	500
4	866	50	816	. . .	500

(7) Tax deductible expense (3) + (6)	(8) Tax saving 0.4 × (7)	(9) Cost of owning (2) − (8)	(10) Present-value factor	(11) Present value (9) × (10)
$680	272	$594	0.943	$ 560
639	256	610	0.890	543
595	238	628	0.840	527
550	220	646	0.792	497
Total present value of payments				$2,127

$$\text{Present value of salvage} = 0.792 \times \$1,000 = \$792$$
$$\text{Present value of cost of loan} = \$2,127 - \$792 = \$1,335$$

Find the cost to lease:

(1) Year	(2) Lease payment	(3) Tax saving 0.4 × 866	(4) Least cost after taxes (2) − (3)	(5) Present-value factor at 6%	(6) Present value (4) × (5)
1	$866	$346	$520	0.943	$ 490
2	866	346	520	0.890	463
3	866	346	520	0.840	437
4	866	346	520	0.792	411
Total present value of lease payments (present value of cost to lease)					$1,801

Compare present values of cost to buy and cost to lease:

Present value of cost to lease $1,801
Present value of cost to buy   1,335
Advantage of buying . . . . $ 466

Decision. Mr. Sprott should buy the truck.

Note: Again, the importance of depreciation may be noted. When Sprott purchases the truck, he gains the tax advantages to be had from depreciation. If the truck were leased, the lessor would depreciate the truck and gain advantage thereby. Sprott was also aided by being able to reduce the cost of buying by the present value of the salvage (or disposal) value of the truck.

In general, depreciation and salvage value reduce the cost of buying. However, if an asset is subject to rapid obsolescence, it may be less expensive to lease. This example should not be taken as a general demonstration of the virtues of buying rather than leasing. In many cases, leasing is less expensive than buying.

REVIEW AND DISCUSSION QUESTIONS

1. Break-even analysis is typically simplified by using constant-unit variable cost, revenue, and fixed cost. What would you expect realistic cost and revenues to be, and what would a break-even chart look like?

2. A supply of cash is necessary to operate any firm. Why is the need for cash especially high and critical in a rapidly growing firm?

3. If a firm is short of capital, what action might it take to conserve the capital it has and to obtain more?

4. Explain why the marginal cost for borrowing money increases. Why might the cost also be high for borrowing small amounts?

5. Are there any reasons for using present-value analysis rather than "future-value" analysis?

6. Why might a decision maker like to see the payback analysis as well as the rate of return and the net present value?

7. Discuss why the comparison of alternative investment decisions is especially difficult when the investment choices have different life lengths.

8. Compare the advantages and disadvantages of each depreciation method.

PROBLEMS

1. Analysis of the market indicates with relative certainty that a minimum 10,000 units of a product could be sold at $4.20 per unit. However, if the price was reduced to $4 per unit, a minimum of 12,000 units could be sold.

   Fixed costs   = $10,000
   Fixed OH and G&A = $3,000
   Direct labor   = $1.50/unit
   Direct material   = $1.00/unit

   a. Using break-even analysis, determine the break-even point.
   b. Which of the two prices would you establish to maximize profits at the expected minimum sales levels?

2. The cost of producing between 1,500 units and 2,500 units of a product consists of $25,000 fixed cost and $10-per-unit variable cost. With the selling price at $20 per unit, what is the break-even point? Suppose the price per unit was increased to $25. How does this affect the break-even point?

3. A new machine has a cost of $24,000, an estimated economic life of eight years, and a salvage value of $4,000 at the end of the eight-year period. Assume that the annual operating costs will be $3,000 per year and that the going rate of interest is 10 percent.
   What is the present value of new expenditures for the machine?

4. Joseph Collins, a part-time inventor, apparently has come up with a very practical new and efficient design for an electric generator powered by wind. It is a surprisingly simple unit based on turbine design principles. He formed JoCo Wind Power Company and would now like to start producing and marketing his generators.

   Joe made several experimental models and so has a good handle on costs and supply sources. He has had several offers of working capital from interested investors but he would have had to give up almost half of his ownership. Thus, to retain complete stock ownership, he wants to start small and then increase capacity as his working capital allows.

   Joe has already contacted a bank for a loan, and they seemed quite interested in giving him one. The bank asked for a cash flow budget so they could judge the feasibility of his plans as well as determine how much cash he would need to borrow. Although he has a little savings, Joe would like to borrow the full amount and keep his savings "just in case."

   Joe intends to begin production on January 11 with the following production rates?

January 11, 18, 25; February 1, 8	10 per week
February 15, 22, 29; March 2, 9, 16, 23, 30	20 per week
April 6, 13, 20, 27; May 4, 11, 18, 25	40 per week

   The unit is made with a housing, blades, and a kit of parts.
   Blades cost $57 per unit.
   Housings cost $160 per unit.
   Parts cost $132 per unit.
   Labor costs

   For the first five weeks, one person can make all ten for $150 (or $15 per unit).
   When the rate reaches 20 per week, labor cost is $250 (or $12.50 per unit).
   At 40 units per week, labor cost becomes $500 per week (still $12.50 per unit).
   Blades are ordered from Germany and have a six-week lead time. The first order will be placed on December 1, so blades would arrive on time for January 11 production. Blades are paid for on arrival (therefore, the first payment would be made January 11).
   Housing units and parts are paid for weekly.
   Joe and his wife attend trade shows displaying their generator and estimate a $100-per-week advertising and show expense.
   Joe's salary is to be a low $150 per week through March 30 in order to conserve capital. On April 6, his salary is to be raised to $300.
   Revenue. Generators sell for $550 each. There is a $100 deposit at the signing of the order. The balance of $450 is paid on delivery. Joe's wife says she can sign up sales at least as fast as the production rate. (In this cash budget we will assume sales are the same rate as production.)
   Delivery of completed units is one week after the order from January 11 to April 6. No deliveries are to be made on April 13 as the delivery schedule intentionally skips a week to build up inventory. (Lead time for this one time is then two weeks.)

Joe needs a flatbed truck to make deliveries. The truck costs $6,000 used, and he will need equipment to handle the generators which costs another $1,000.

Rent, utilities, and gas cost $1,000 per month for January, February, and March. In April, more space will be needed, and the cost will increase to $1,500 per month (payable in the first week of the month).

Create a cash budget for January 11 through May 25. What amount of cash will Joe need to borrow? Does it look as though he may have a successful product? If you can, create a balance sheet as of March 31 and June 30. (Extend the same 40-unit rate through June.)

5. A full page ad appears in the paper showing why you should buy a Jugular XVI automobile. The Jugular XVI is compared to several significantly cheaper models of other manufacturers, and in all cases, the percent of original price that the used Jugulars are selling for is higher than the other models. The car manufacturer obviously is trying to project the impression that the car loses little value since its resale value stays so high. We will compare two models: the Jugular XVI and the Monument MK II.

	Jugular XVI		Monument MK II	
	Original price	Present retail value based on the "Greybook"	Original price	Present retail value based on the "Greybook"
1975	$15,000	90%	$ 9,000	80%
1980	$27,000 (new price)		$14,000 (new price)	

The retail value is expressed as a percent of original price by the advertiser to stress a point. The 1975 car, for example, sold new for $15,000 in 1975 and now (1980) has a resale value of $13,500, or 90 percent of the original price.

Make a financial judgment as to which car is the best buy. Assume that one of each car was bought in 1975 and that insurance, maintenance, and tax rates are the same for both (likely not true). The two buyers each had $15,000; one bought the Jugular and spent all his money; the other buyer bought the Monument and invested his remaining $6,000 in an investment which yielded an annual rate of 10 percent. Use a five-year period (1975–80).

6. Suppose a product is priced at $50 and the variable cost is $30 per unit. If the total fixed costs are $20,000, what is the break-even point in units of output sold?

7. What is the depreciation expense for the third year, using the sum-of-the-years'-digit method for the following cost (below) of a new machine?

Cost of machine $35,000
Estimated life .... 6 years
Estimated salvage value .... $ 5,000

8. Disregarding tax considerations, is it cheaper to buy or to lease a piece of equipment with the following costs for a five-year term?

	To buy	To lease
Purchase (or lease) cost	$50,000	$10,000/yr.
Annual operating cost	4,000/yr.	4,000/yr.
Maintenance cost	2,000/yr.	0
Salvage value at end of 5 years	$20,000	0

Interest value of money is 10 percent

9. A new piece of office equipment must be purchased, and the choice has been narrowed down to two styles, each capable of meeting the intended needs. With a ten-year horizon and an interest rate of 8 percent, which equipment should be purchased?

	Equipment A	Equipment B
Initial cost	$10,000	$7,000
Salvage value (10 years hence)	4,000	2,000
Estimated annual operation and maintenance cost ...	1,000	1,500

10. The university is accepting bids for the hot dog and cold drink concession at the new stadium. The contract is for a five-year period, and it is your feeling that a bid of $40,000 will win the contract. A preliminary analysis indicates that annual operating costs will be $35,000 and average annual sales will be $50,000. The contract can be written off during the five years. Taxes are at the 40 percent rate, and your goal is to make a 20 percent return on your investment.

    a. Will you meet your goal if you use straight-line depreciation?

    b. Would you meet your goal using sum-of-the-years'-digits depreciation?

11. Because of the high demand for single-residence housing, Ackerman, Ballard, and Chessen decided to enter the construction business. As in any new business, they are faced with a variety of investment decisions. For example: should they buy raw land and develop it themselves, or should they purchase building lots in developed areas? Should they buy tools and equipment, or should they lease them? Should they employ crews of their own, or should they subcontract most of the work? In terms of price range, should they produce a large number of low-price homes or a small number of high-price homes?

    To analyze the first question, "Should ABC buy and develop raw land, or should it buy lots with existing services?" Ackerman, after careful analysis of the city's growth direction, found a 40-acre parcel in a prime area that could be purchased for $115,000. However, roads would have to be put in and ditches dug for sewers, water, gas, and underground electric services. Also, the entire area would have to be graded and surveyed. This work would start immediately, at a cost of $100,000, to be paid at the rate of $25,000 at the end of each of the first four months (for a total of $100,000). The 40 acres would be divided into ⅓-acre lots to provide a total of 120 lots. The first lots would be available for use or for sale in four months, and the expectations are that the entire area could be sold at a constant rate of ten lots per month until all lots are sold (120/10 = 12 months).

    Disregarding tax considerations and assuming that funds may be borrowed at a savings and loan institution at an 8 percent interest rate, what average price would ABC have to charge in order to obtain a present-value profit of $40,000? (Note: The present value of an annuity of $1 for 12 monthly increments at a simple 8 percent annual interest rate is $11.50.) The present value (on a monthly scale) of $1 based on a simple annual interest rate of 8 percent is

End of month	Present value at 8 percent
1	$0.9933
2	0.9868
3	0.9803
4	0.9740
5	0.9677
6	0.9615
7	0.9554
8	0.9493
9	0.9433
10	0.9375
11	0.9316
12	0.9259

12. ABC would like to build some homes on its lots and is now looking at ways to obtain needed equipment, such as mixers, a pickup truck, a flatbed truck, a compressor, a Payloader with a backhoe, mortar boxes, forms, scaffolding, and a variety of miscellaneous items. There are three ways to obtain this equipment: buy it new, buy it used, or lease it. Looking at only the Payloader under the alternatives of buy new or lease, which alternative should ABC select? (The Payloader has a life span of 10 years; however, intentions are to sell it after five years to avoid the high cost of upkeep.) A bank loan has been set up for five years with equal annual loan payments. The cost of capital is 8 percent, and the tax rate is expected to be 40 percent.

Buy new

Purchase cost	$11,000
Maintenance and insurance	$ 500/year
Economic life	10 years
Salvage value after 5 years	$ 4,000
Depreciation method: double-declining-balance	

Lease

Lease cost on 5-year contract: $3,000/year
Operating costs are identical in either option.

Note: In double-declining-balance, the rate is double the straight-line schedule. To illustrate: for a ten-year life, straight-line depreciation is 10 percent and DDB is as follows:

Year	Rate of depreciation (double the 10%)		Beginning book value		Depreciation	Ending book value
1	0.20	×	$1,000	=	$200	$800
2	0.20	×	800	=	160	640
3	0.20	×	640	=	128	512
4	0.20	×	512	=	102	410

13. A parcel of land has been set aside by ABC to be the site of future construction. At the present time, ABC is interested in determining whether it should build $35,000 or $60,000 houses on the parcels as "speculative homes" (homes completed by a builder and available for sale to any buyer, as opposed to homes which are constructed at the request of a particular buyer). The $60,000 homes take longer to build and sell at a lower rate than the lower-price homes; however, each one yields a higher profit margin. For either type of house, the cost of capital is 8 percent.

Expenses incurred in building the $35,000 homes are as follows:

Cost of land .... $5,000 (immediate payment)
Time to complete home .... 3 months
Building cost of $20,000 incurred as
    1st month 40%
    2nd month 40%
    3rd month 20%

A contingency allocation to cover the expected loss of 5 percent for material theft is included in the building cost. The average time required to sell a home is one month after completion. The entire amount of $35,000 is paid in cash either by the buyer or the new mortgage holder.

Expenses incurred for the $60,000 homes are as follows:

Cost of land .... $9,000 (immediate payment)
Time to complete home .... 5 months
Building cost of $30,000 incurred as
    1st month 20%
    2nd month 30%
    3rd month 20%
    4th month 20%
    5th month 10%

The average time needed to sell the home is three months after completion, when the entire $60,000 is received in cash.

Assignment: Employ present-value analysis to help ABC make the decision as to which type of house it should build. (Use the monthly present-value figures provided in problem 11.)

14. ABC is planning to start one of each house discussed in the previous problem. At the completion of each house, they will start another one of the same style, and so on. The land must be paid for at the start of the project, and when the home is sold, the full selling price is to be paid to ABC by the buyer or the new mortgage holder.

Using the data from problem 13, construct a cash budget for ABC for the next 12 months. (In preparing the budget, disregard taxes and interest costs.) If all funds are borrowed, what amount of outside financing should ABC arrange for?

15. ABC's business has been going so well that the firm decides to diversify with a sideline business. Ballard, an experienced cabinet maker, has a great deal of know-how in making cabinets for kitchens and vanities for bathrooms. (Counter tops would be subcontracted because of the specialized equipment needed for molding and pressing.) The company is anticipating

putting out a standard line of cabinets available in birch, walnut, mahogany, or oak veneer at no extra charge.

Three manufacturing methods are feasible for producing the cabinets. The first is largely manual, the second uses some semiautomated equipment, and the third is largely automatic. The equipment can be leased, so the fixed cost includes leasing or depreciation, overhead, and all other fixed burdens.

	Manual	Semiautomatic	Mostly automated
Annual fixed cost	$15,000	$35,000	$80,000
Variable costs per complete kitchen			
Materials	350	350	350
Direct labor	350	270	130
Crating and shipping	120	110	100
Variable cost per unit	$ 820	$ 730	$ 580

The wholesale price of these units will be $1,100 each. (The installed cost for the homeowner will be between $2,200 and $2,800.)

a. Construct a break-even chart for each of the three methods. If sales are expected to be 200 units per year, which manufacturing method should ABC choose?

b. ABC feels that if it sets a price of $1,000 per unit, it should be able to sell 350 units. Which production method should then be selected? How much profit will it realize?

16. In adding a new product line, a firm needs a new piece of machinery. An investigation of suitable equipment for the production process has narrowed the choice to the two machines listed below.

	Machine A	Machine B
Type of equipment	General purpose	Special purpose
Installed cost	$8,000	$13,000
Salvage value	800	3,000
Annual labor cost	6,000	3,600
Estimated life (years)	10	5

Assume that at the end of five years, a comparable replacement for machine B will be available. Using present-value analysis with a 10 percent interest rate, which machine would you choose?

SELECTED BIBLIOGRAPHY

Anthony, Robert N., and Welsch, Glenn A. *Fundamentals of Management Accounting.* Homewood, Ill.: Richard D. Irwin, Inc., 1977.

Archer, Stephen H.; Choate, G. Marc; and Racette, George. *Financial Management.* New York: John Wiley & Sons, 1979.

Bowman, Edward H., and Fetter, Robert B. *Analysis for Production and Operations Management.* Homewood, Ill.: Richard D. Irwin, Inc., 1967 (pp. 386–95).

Gitman, Lawrence J. *Principles of Managerial Finance.* New York: Harper & Row, 1979.

Martin, John D.; Keown, Arthur J.; Petty, J. William; and Scott, David E. Jr. *Basic Financial Management.* Englewood Cliffs, N.J.: Prentice-Hall, 1979.

Solomon, Eyra, and Pringle, John J. *An Introduction to Financial Management.* Santa Monica, Calif.: Goodyear Publishing Co., 1980.

Van Horne, James C. *Financial Management and Policy.* 3d ed. Englewood Cliffs, N.J.: Prentice-Hall, 1974.

Welsch, Glenn A., and Anthony, Robert N. *Fundamentals of Financial Accounting.* Homewood, Ill.: Richard D. Irwin, Inc., 1977.

Wert, James E., and Henderson Jr., Glenn V. *Financing Business Firms.* Homewood, Ill.: Richard D. Irwin, Inc., 1979.

Weston, J. Fred, and Brigham, Eugene F. *Essentials of Managerial Finance.* Hinsdale, Ill.: The Dryden Press, 1979.

APPENDIX: INTEREST TABLES

EXHIBIT 5.6
Compound sum of $1

Year	1%	2%	3%	4%	5%	6%	7%
1	1.010	1.020	1.030	1.040	1.050	1.060	1.070
2	1.020	1.040	1.061	1.082	1.102	1.124	1.145
3	1.030	1.061	1.093	1.125	1.158	1.191	1.225
4	1.041	1.082	1.126	1.170	1.216	1.262	1.311
5	1.051	1.104	1.159	1.217	1.276	1.338	1.403
6	1.062	1.126	1.194	1.265	1.340	1.419	1.501
7	1.072	1.149	1.230	1.316	1.407	1.504	1.606
8	1.083	1.172	1.267	1.369	1.477	1.594	1.718
9	1.094	1.195	1.305	1.423	1.551	1.689	1.838
10	1.105	1.219	1.344	1.480	1.629	1.791	1.967
11	1.116	1.243	1.384	1.539	1.710	1.898	2.105
12	1.127	1.268	1.426	1.601	1.796	2.012	2.252
13	1.138	1.294	1.469	1.665	1.886	2.133	2.410
14	1.149	1.319	1.513	1.732	1.980	2.261	2.579
15	1.161	1.346	1.558	1.801	2.079	2.397	2.759
16	1.173	1.373	1.605	1.873	2.183	2.540	2.952
17	1.184	1.400	1.653	1.948	2.292	2.693	3.159
18	1.196	1.428	1.702	2.026	2.407	2.854	3.380
19	1.208	1.457	1.754	2.107	2.527	3.026	3.617
20	1.220	1.486	1.806	2.191	2.653	3.207	3.870
25	1.282	1.641	2.094	2.666	3.386	4.292	5.427
30	1.348	1.811	2.427	3.243	4.322	5.743	7.612

Year	8%	9%	10%	12%	14%	15%	16%
1	1.080	1.090	1.100	1.120	1.140	1.150	1.160
2	1.166	1.188	1.210	1.254	1.300	1.322	1.346
3	1.260	1.295	1.331	1.405	1.482	1.521	1.561
4	1.360	1.412	1.464	1.574	1.689	1.749	1.811
5	1.469	1.539	1.611	1.762	1.925	2.011	2.100
6	1.587	1.677	1.772	1.974	2.195	2.313	2.436
7	1.714	1.828	1.949	2.211	2.502	2.660	2.826
8	1.851	1.993	2.144	2.476	2.853	3.059	3.278
9	1.999	2.172	2.358	2.773	3.252	3.518	3.803
10	2.159	2.367	2.594	3.106	3.707	4.046	4.411
11	2.332	2.580	2.853	3.479	4.226	4.652	5.117
12	2.518	2.813	3.138	3.896	4.818	5.350	5.936
13	2.720	3.066	3.452	4.363	5.492	6.153	6.886
14	2.937	3.342	3.797	4.887	6.261	7.076	7.988
15	3.172	3.642	4.177	5.474	7.138	8.137	9.266
16	3.426	3.970	4.595	6.130	8.137	9.358	10.748
17	3.700	4.328	5.054	6.866	9.276	10.761	12.468
18	3.996	4.717	5.560	7.690	10.575	12.375	14.463
19	4.316	5.142	6.116	8.613	12.056	14.232	16.777
20	4.661	5.604	6.728	9.646	13.743	16.367	19.461
25	6.848	8.623	10.835	17.000	26.462	32.919	40.874
30	10.063	13.268	17.449	29.960	50.950	66.212	85.850

EXHIBIT 5.6
(continued)

Year	18%	20%	24%	28%	32%	36%
1	1.180	1.200	1.240	1.280	1.320	1.360
2	1.392	1.440	1.538	1.638	1.742	1.850
3	1.643	1.728	1.907	2.067	2.300	2.515
4	1.939	2.074	2.364	2.684	3.036	3.421
5	2.288	2.488	2.932	3.436	4.007	4.653
6	2.700	2.986	3.635	4.398	5.290	6.328
7	3.185	3,583	4.508	5.629	6.983	8.605
8	3.759	4.300	5.590	7.206	9.217	11.703
9	4.435	5.160	6.931	9.223	12.166	15.917
10	5.234	6.192	8.594	11.806	16.060	21.647
11	6.176	7.430	10.657	15.112	21.199	29.439
12	7.288	8.916	13.215	19.343	27.983	40.037
13	8.599	10.699	16.386	24.759	36.937	54.451
14	10.147	12.839	20.319	31.691	48.757	74.053
15	11.974	15.407	25.196	40.565	64.359	100.712
16	14.129	18.488	31.243	51.923	84.954	136.97
17	16.672	22.186	38.741	66.461	112.14	186.28
18	19.673	26.623	48.039	85.071	148.02	253.34
19	23.214	31.948	59.568	108.89	195.39	344.54
20	27.393	38.338	73.864	139.38	257.92	468.57
25	62.669	95.396	216.542	478.90	1033.6	2180.1
30	143.371	237.376	634.820	1645.5	4142.1	10143.

Year	40%	50%	60%	70%	80%	90%
1	1.400	1.500	1.600	1.700	1.800	1.900
2	1.960	2.250	2.560	2.890	3.240	3.610
3	2.744	3.375	4.096	4.913	5.832	6.859
4	3.842	5.062	6.544	8.352	10.498	13.032
5	5.378	7.594	10.486	14.199	18.896	24.761
6	7.530	11.391	16.777	24.138	34.012	47.046
7	10.541	17.086	26.844	41.034	61.222	89.387
8	14.758	25.629	42.950	69.758	110.200	169.836
9	20.661	38.443	68.720	118.588	198.359	322.688
10	28.925	57.665	109.951	201.599	357.047	613.107
11	40.496	86.498	175.922	342.719	642.684	1164.902
12	56.694	129.746	281.475	582.622	1156.831	2213.314
13	79.372	194.619	450.360	990.457	2082.295	4205.297
14	111.120	291.929	720.576	1683.777	3748.131	7990.065
15	155.568	437.894	1152.921	2862.421	6746.636	15181.122
16	217.795	656.84	1844.7	4866.1	12144.	28844.0
17	304.914	985.26	2951.5	8272.4	21859.	54804.0
18	426.879	1477.9	4722.4	14063.0	39346.	104130.0
19	597.630	2216.8	7555.8	23907.0	70824.	197840.0
20	836.683	3325.3	12089.0	40642.0	127480.	375900.0
25	4499.880	25251.	126760.0	577060.0	2408900.	9307600.0
30	24201.432	191750.	1329200.	8193500.0	45517000.	230470000.0

EXHIBIT 5.7
Sum of an annuity of $1 for N years

Year	1%	2%	3%	4%	5%	6%
1	1.000	1.000	1.000	1.000	1.000	1.000
2	2.010	2.020	2.030	2.040	2.050	2.060
3	2.030	3.060	3.091	3.122	3.152	3.184
4	4.060	4.122	4.184	4.246	4.310	4.375
5	5.101	5.204	5.309	5.416	5.526	5.637
6	6.152	6.308	6.468	6.633	6.802	6.975
7	7.214	7.434	7.662	7.898	8.142	8.394
8	8.286	8.583	8.892	9.214	9.549	9.897
9	9.369	9.755	10.159	10.583	11.027	11.491
10	10.462	10.950	11.464	12.006	12.578	13.181
11	11.567	12.169	12.808	13.486	14.207	14.972
12	12.683	13.412	14.192	15.026	15.917	16.870
13	13.809	14.680	15.618	16.627	17.713	18.882
14	14.947	15.974	17.086	18.292	19.599	21.051
15	16.097	17.293	18.599	20.024	21.579	23.276
16	17.258	18.639	20.157	21.825	23.657	25.673
17	18.430	20.012	21.762	23.698	25.840	28.213
18	19.615	21.412	23.414	25.645	28.132	30.906
19	20.811	22.841	25.117	27.671	30.539	33.760
20	22.019	24.297	26.870	29.778	33.066	36.786
25	28.243	32.030	36.459	41.646	47.727	54.865
30	34.785	40.568	47.575	56.085	66.439	79.058

Year	7%	8%	9%	10%	12%	14%
1	1.000	1.000	1.000	1.000	1.000	1.000
2	2.070	2.080	2.090	2.100	2.120	2.140
3	3.215	3.246	3.278	3.310	3.374	3.440
4	4.440	4.506	4.573	4.641	4.770	4.921
5	5.751	5.867	5.985	6.105	6.353	6.610
6	7.153	7.336	7.523	7.716	8.115	8.536
7	8.654	8.923	9.200	9.487	10.089	10.730
8	10.260	10.637	11.028	11.436	12.300	13.233
9	11.978	12.488	13.021	13.579	14.776	16.085
10	13.816	14.487	15.193	15.937	17.549	19.337
11	15.784	16.645	17.560	18.531	20.655	23.044
12	17.888	18.977	20.141	21.384	24.133	27.271
13	20.141	21.495	22.953	24.523	28.029	32.089
14	22.550	24.215	26.019	27.975	32.393	37.581
15	25.129	27.152	29.361	31.772	37.280	43.842
16	27.888	30.324	33.003	35.950	42.753	50.980
17	30.840	33.750	36.974	40.545	48.884	59.118
18	33.999	37.450	41.301	45.599	55.750	68.394
19	37.379	41.446	46.018	51.159	63.440	78.969
20	40.995	45.762	51.160	57.275	72.052	91.025
25	63.249	73.106	84.701	98.347	133.334	181.871
30	94.461	113.283	136.308	164.494	241.333	356.787

EXHIBIT 5.7
(continued)

Year	16%	18%	20%	24%	28%	32%
1	1.000	1.000	1.000	1.000	1.000	1.000
2	2.160	2.180	2.200	2.240	2.280	2.320
3	3.506	3.572	3.640	3.778	3.918	4.062
4	5.066	5.215	5.368	5.684	6.016	6.362
5	6.877	7.154	7.442	8.048	8.700	9.398
6	8.977	9.442	9.930	10.980	12.136	13.406
7	11.414	12.142	12.916	14.615	16.534	18.696
8	14.240	15.327	16.499	19.123	22.163	25.678
9	17.518	19.086	20.799	24.712	29.369	34.895
10	21.321	23.521	25.959	31.643	38.592	47.062
11	25.733	28.755	32.150	40.238	50.399	63.122
12	30.850	34.931	39.580	50.985	65.510	84.320
13	36.786	42.219	48.497	64.110	84.853	112.303
14	43.672	50.818	59.196	80.496	109.612	149.240
15	51.660	60.965	72.035	100.815	141.303	197.997
16	60.925	72.939	87.442	126.011	181.87	262.36
17	71.673	87.068	105.931	157.253	233.79	347.31
18	84.141	103.740	128.117	195.994	300.25	459.45
19	98.603	123.414	154.740	244.033	385.32	607.47
20	115.380	146.628	186.688	303.601	494.21	802.86
25	249.214	342.603	471.981	898.092	1706.8	3226.8
30	530.312	790.948	1181.882	2640.916	5873.2	12941.0

Year	36%	40%	50%	60%	70%	80%
1	1.000	1.000	1.000	1.000	1.000	1.000
2	2.360	2.400	2.500	2.600	2.700	2.800
3	4.210	4.360	4.750	5.160	5.590	6.040
4	6.725	7.104	8.125	9.256	10.503	11.872
5	10.146	10.846	13.188	15.810	18.855	22.370
6	14.799	16.324	20.781	26.295	33.054	41.265
7	21.126	23.853	32.172	43.073	57.191	75.278
8	29.732	34.395	49.258	69.916	98.225	136.500
9	41.435	49.153	74.887	112.866	167.983	246.699
10	57.352	69.814	113.330	181.585	286.570	445.058
11	78.998	98.739	170.995	291.536	488.170	802.105
12	108.437	139.235	257.493	467.458	830.888	1444.788
13	148.475	195.929	387.239	748.933	1413.510	2601.619
14	202.926	275.300	581.859	1199.293	2403.968	4683.914
15	276.979	386.420	873.788	1919.869	4087.745	8432.045
16	377.69	541.99	1311.7	3072.8	6950.2	15179.0
17	514.66	759.78	1968.5	4917.5	11816.0	27323.0
18	700.94	1064.7	2953.8	7868.9	20089.0	49182.0
19	954.28	1491.6	4431.7	12591.0	34152.0	88528.0
20	1298.8	2089.2	6648.5	20147.0	58059.0	159350.0
25	6053.0	11247.0	50500.0	211270.0	824370.0	3011100.0
30	28172.0	60501.0	383500.0	2215400.0	11705000.0	56896000.0

EXHIBIT 5.8
Present value of $1

Year	1%	2%	3%	4%	5%	6%	7%	8%	9%	10%	12%	14%	15%
1	.990	.980	.971	.962	.952	.943	.935	.926	.917	.909	.893	.877	.870
2	.980	.961	.943	.925	.907	.890	.873	.857	.842	.826	.797	.769	.756
3	.971	.942	.915	.889	.864	.840	.816	.794	.772	.751	.712	.675	.658
4	.961	.924	.889	.855	.823	.792	.763	.735	.708	.683	.636	.592	.572
5	.951	.906	.863	.822	.784	.747	.713	.681	.650	.621	.567	.519	.497
6	.942	.888	.838	.790	.746	.705	.666	.630	.596	.564	.507	.456	.432
7	.933	.871	.813	.760	.711	.665	.623	.583	.547	.513	.452	.400	.376
8	.923	.853	.789	.731	.677	.627	.582	.540	.502	.467	.404	.351	.327
9	.914	.837	.766	.703	.645	.592	.544	.500	.460	.424	.361	.308	.284
10	.905	.820	.744	.676	.614	.558	.508	.463	.422	.386	.322	.270	.247
11	.896	.804	.722	.650	.585	.527	.475	.429	.388	.350	.287	.237	.215
12	.887	.788	.701	.625	.557	.497	.444	.397	.356	.319	.257	.208	.187
13	.879	.773	.681	.601	.530	.469	.415	.368	.326	.290	.229	.182	.163
14	.870	.758	.661	.577	.505	.442	.388	.340	.299	.263	.205	.160	.141
15	.861	.743	.642	.555	.481	.417	.362	.315	.275	.239	.183	.140	.123
16	.853	.728	.623	.534	.458	.394	.339	.292	.252	.218	.163	.123	.107
17	.844	.714	.605	.513	.436	.371	.317	.270	.231	.198	.146	.108	.093
18	.836	.700	.587	.494	.416	.350	.296	.250	.212	.180	.130	.095	.081
19	.828	.686	.570	.475	.396	.331	.276	.232	.194	.164	.116	.083	.070
20	.820	.673	.554	.456	.377	.312	.258	.215	.178	.149	.104	.073	.061
25	.780	.610	.478	.375	.295	.233	.184	.146	.116	.092	.059	.038	.030
30	.742	.552	.412	.308	.231	.174	.131	.099	.075	.057	.033	.020	.015

Year	16%	18%	20%	24%	28%	32%	36%	40%	50%	60%	70%	80%	90%
1	.862	.847	.833	.806	.781	.758	.735	.714	.667	.625	.588	.556	.526
2	.743	.718	.694	.650	.610	.574	.541	.510	.444	.391	.346	.309	.277
3	.641	.609	.579	.524	.477	.435	.398	.364	.296	.244	.204	.171	.146
4	.552	.516	.482	.423	.373	.329	.292	.260	.198	.153	.120	.095	.077
5	.476	.437	.402	.341	.291	.250	.215	.186	.132	.095	.070	.053	.040
6	.410	.370	.335	.275	.227	.189	.158	.133	.088	.060	.041	.029	.021
7	.354	.314	.279	.222	.178	.143	.116	.095	.059	.037	.024	.016	.011
8	.305	.266	.233	.179	.139	.108	.085	.068	.039	.023	.014	.009	.006
9	.263	.226	.194	.144	.108	.082	.063	.048	.026	.015	.008	.005	.003
10	.227	.191	.162	.116	.085	.062	.046	.035	.017	.009	.005	.003	.002
11	.195	.162	.135	.094	.066	.047	.034	.025	.012	.006	.003	.002	.001
12	.168	.137	.112	.076	.052	.036	.025	.018	.008	.004	.002	.001	.001
13	.145	.116	.093	.061	.040	.027	.018	.013	.005	.002	.001	.001	.000
14	.125	.099	.078	.049	.032	.021	.014	.009	.003	.001	.001	.000	.000
15	.108	.084	.065	.040	.025	.016	.010	.006	.002	.001	.000	.000	.000
16	.093	.071	.054	.032	.019	.012	.007	.005	.002	.001	.000	.000	
17	.080	.030	.045	.026	.015	.009	.005	.003	.001	.000	.000		
18	.089	.051	.038	.021	.012	.007	.004	.002	.001	.000	.000		
19	.030	.043	.031	.017	.009	.005	.003	.002	.000	.000			
20	.051	.037	.026	.014	.007	.004	.002	.001	.000	.000			
25	.024	.016	.010	.005	.002	.001	.000	.000					
30	.012	.007	.004	.002	.001	.000	.000						

EXHIBIT 5.9
**Present value
of an annuity
of $1**

Year	1%	2%	3%	4%	5%	6%	7%	8%	9%	10%
1	0.990	0.980	0.971	0.962	0.952	0.943	0.935	0.926	0.917	0.909
2	1.970	1.942	1.913	1.886	1.859	1.833	1.808	1.783	1.759	1.736
3	2.941	2.884	2.829	2.775	2.723	2.673	2.624	2.577	2.531	2.487
4	3.902	3.808	3.717	3.630	3.546	3.465	3.387	3.312	3.240	3.170
5	4.853	4.713	4.580	4.452	4.329	4.212	4.100	3.993	3.890	3.791
6	5.795	5.601	5.417	5.242	5.076	4.917	4.766	4.623	4.486	4.355
7	6.728	6.472	6.230	6.002	5.786	5.582	5.389	5.206	5.033	4.868
8	7.652	7.325	7.020	6.733	6.463	6.210	6.971	5.747	5.535	5.335
9	8.566	8.162	7.786	7.435	7.108	6.802	6.515	6.247	5.985	5.759
10	9.471	8.983	8.530	8.111	7.722	7.360	7.024	6.710	6.418	6.145
11	10.368	9.787	9.253	8.760	8.306	7.887	7.499	7.139	6.805	6.495
12	11.255	10.575	9.954	9.385	8.863	8.384	7.943	7.536	7.161	6.814
13	12.134	11.348	10.635	9.986	9.394	8.853	8.358	7.904	7.487	7.103
14	13.004	12.106	11.296	10.563	9.899	9.295	8.745	8.244	7.786	7.367
15	13.865	12.849	11.938	11.118	10.380	9.712	9.108	8.559	8.060	7.606
16	14.718	13.578	12.561	11.652	10.838	10.106	9.447	8.851	8.312	7.824
17	15.562	14.292	13.166	12.166	11.274	10.477	9.763	9.122	8.544	8.022
18	16.398	14.992	13.754	12.659	11.690	10.828	10.059	9.372	8.756	8.201
19	17.226	15.678	14.324	13.134	12.085	11.158	10.336	9.604	8.950	8.365
20	18.046	16.351	14.877	13.590	12.462	11.470	10.594	9.818	9.128	8.514
25	22.023	19.523	17.413	15.622	14.094	12.783	11.654	10.675	9.823	9.077
30	25.808	22.397	19.600	17.292	15.373	13.765	12.409	11.258	10.274	9.427

Year	12%	14%	16%	18%	20%	24%	28%	32%	36%
1	0.893	0.877	0.862	0.847	0.833	0.806	0.781	0.758	0.735
2	1.690	1.647	1.605	1.566	1.528	1.457	1.392	1.332	1.276
3	2.402	2.322	2.246	2.174	2.106	1.981	1.868	1.766	1.674
4	3.037	2.914	2.798	2.690	2.589	2.404	2.241	2.096	1.966
5	3.605	3.433	3.274	3.127	2.991	2.745	2.532	2.345	2.181
6	4.111	3.889	3.685	3.498	3.326	3.020	2.759	2.534	2.339
7	4.564	4.288	4.039	3.812	3.605	3.242	2.937	2.678	2.455
8	4.968	4.639	4.344	4.078	3.837	3.421	3.076	2.786	2.540
9	5.328	4.946	4.607	4.303	4.031	3.566	3.184	2.868	2.603
10	5.650	5.216	4.833	4.494	4.193	3.682	3.269	2.930	2.650
11	5.988	5.453	5.029	4.656	4.327	3.776	3.335	2.978	2.683
12	6.194	5.660	5.197	4.793	4.439	3.851	3.387	3.013	2.708
13	6.424	5.842	5.342	4.910	4.533	3.912	3.427	3.040	2.727
14	6.628	6.002	5.468	5.008	4.611	3.962	3.459	3.061	2.740
15	6.811	6.142	5.575	5.092	4.675	4.001	3.483	3.076	2.750
16	6.974	6.265	5.669	5.162	4.730	4.033	3.503	3.088	2.758
17	7.120	5.373	5.749	4.222	4.775	4.059	3.518	3.097	2.763
18	7.250	6.467	5.818	5.273	4.812	4.080	3.529	3.104	2.767
19	7.366	6.550	5.877	5.316	4.844	4.097	3.539	3.109	2.770
20	7.469	6.623	5.929	5.353	4.870	4.110	3.546	3.113	2.772
25	7.843	6.873	6.097	5.467	4.948	4.147	3.564	3.122	2.776
30	8.055	7.003	6.177	5.517	4.979	4.160	3.569	3.124	2.778

Chapter

6

CAPACITY PLANNING AND FACILITY LOCATION

*"Factories in the United States operated at 84.2 percent
of capacity last month, the Federal Reserve Board
reported, the same as in the previous two months."*

The Wall Street Journal
March 18, 1980, p. 1

Does this mean that the surveyed companies have 15.8 percent capacity left and would therefore have to refuse orders once they operate at 100 percent? Are they talking about capacity for a 40-hour week or with a second shift? If they became automated, could they increase to 200 percent? Pretty clearly, the answer to these questions is, "it all depends." What it all depends on is what definition one uses for capacity, of course; but it also depends on the means by which those factories manage their capacity. In this chapter, we will provide an operations management definition of capacity, present some important capacity concepts and calculation methods, and then discuss how capacity fits into overall production planning for the firm. We will also discuss some approaches to determining how the facilities which provide that capacity are located.

AN OM DEFINITION OF CAPACITY

A dictionary definition of capacity is "the ability to hold, receive, store, or accommodate." In a general business sense, it is most frequently viewed as the amount of output which a system is capable of achieving at a particular time. An operations management view tends to modify these definitions to account for the factors which determine output achieved. That is, when looking at capacity, operations managers need to look at both resource inputs *and* product outputs. The reason is that, for planning purposes, real (or effective) capacity is dependent upon what is to be

147

produced. For example, a firm which makes multiple products inevitably can produce more of one kind than of another with a given level of resource inputs. Thus, while factory management may state that their facility has 10,000 labor hours available per year, they are also thinking that these labor hours can be used to make either 50,000 X's or 20,000 Y's (or what is more likely, some mix of X's and Y's). This reflects their knowledge of what their current technology and labor force inputs can produce and the product mix which is to be demanded from these resources. An operations management view also emphasizes the time dimension of capacity. This is evidenced in the common distinction drawn between long-range, intermediate-range, and short-range capacity planning (see Exhibit 6.1). Finally, capacity planning itself has different meanings to individuals at different levels within the operations management hierarchy. The vice president of manufacturing is concerned with aggregate capacity of all factories within the firm, the plant manager is concerned with the capacity of the individual plant, and the first-level supervisor is concerned with capacity of the equipment and manpower mix at the department level. Thus, while there is no one with the job title of "capacity manager," there are several managerial positions charged with the effective use of capacity.

EXHIBIT 6.1
Time horizons for capacity planning

Capacity planning is generally viewed in three time durations:
Long range—greater than one year. Where productive resources take a long time to acquire or dispose of, such as buildings, equipment, or facilities. Long-range capacity planning requires top management participation and approval.
Intermediate range—monthly or quarterly plans for the next 6 to 18 months. Here, capacity may be varied by such alternatives as hiring, layoffs, new tools, minor equipment purchases, and subcontracting.
Short range—less than one month. This is tied into the daily or weekly scheduling process and involves making adjustments to eliminate the variance between planned output and actual output. This includes alternatives such as overtime, personnel transfers, alternate production routings.

In summary, capacity is a relative term which, in an operations management context, may be defined as *the amount of resource inputs available relative to output requirements at a particular time.* Note that this definition makes no distinction between efficient and inefficient use of capacity. In this respect, it is consistent with the way in which the government, through the Bureau of Economic Analysis, defines "maximum practical capacity" used in its surveys: "That output attained within the normal operating schedule of shifts per day and days per week *bringing in* [sic.] high cost inefficient facilities."[1] (This definition is the one used by the Federal Reserve Board in *The Wall Street Journal* news brief.)

---

[1] In gathering capacity statistics, the Bureau of Economic Analysis asks the following questions of surveyed firms: (1) At what percentage of manufacturing capacity did your company operate in (month and year)? and (2) At what percentage of (month and year) manufacturing capacity would your company have preferred to operate in order to achieve maximum profits or other objectives? See "Survey of Current Business," *U.S. Department of Commerce Journal.*

IMPORTANT CAPACITY CONCEPTS

Best operating level

The term *capacity* implies an attainable rate of output but says nothing about how long that rate can be sustained. Thus, if we say that a given plant has a capacity of X units, we don't know if this is its one-day peak or its six-month average. To avoid this problem, the concept of "best operating level" is used. This is the level of capacity for which the process was designed and thus is the volume of output at which the average unit cost is at a minimum. This is depicted in Exhibit 6.2.

EXHIBIT 6.2
Best operating level

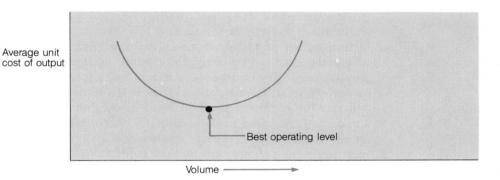

Economies of scale

The basic notion is well known: as a plant gets larger and volume increases, the average cost per unit of output drops because each succeeding unit absorbs part of the fixed costs. This reduction in average unit cost continues until the plant gets so big that coordination of material flows and manpower becomes so expensive that new sources of capacity must be found. This concept can be related to best operating levels by comparing the average unit cost of different sized plants. Exhibit 6.3 shows the best operating levels for 100, 200, and 300 unit (per year) plants. The average unit cost is shown as dropping from best operating level to best operating level as we move from 100 to 300 units. *Dis-economies* of scale would be

EXHIBIT 6.3
Economies of scale

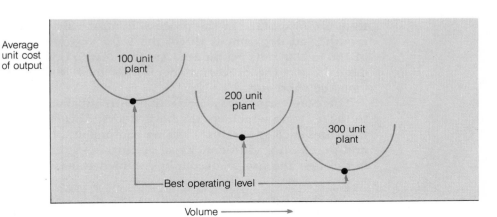

evidenced if we had, say, a 400-unit plant where cost was higher than for the 300-unit plant. However, moving to the right along any of the three average cost curves would not be evidence of dis-economy of scale because the plant size has not increased, rather it would indicate that management has tried to get more from the plant than it can most efficiently provide.

Capacity focus

Skinner[2] has suggested that a production facility works best when it focuses on a fairly limited set of production objectives. This means, for example, that a firm should not expect to excel in every aspect of manufacturing performance—cost, quality, flexibility, new-product introductions, reliability, short lead times, and low investment. Rather, it should select a limited set of tasks which contribute the most to corporate objectives. Capacity comes into play here in at least two respects. One is in the type of capacity chosen—for example, is it sufficiently flexible to handle a variety of different products, or is it inflexible but geared to rapid production of a limited product line? The other is the philosophy by which capacity is handled organizationally. A focused plant may very well have separate suborganizations, equipment and process policies, work-force management policies, production control methods, and so forth for different products—even if they are made under the same roof. This, in effect, permits finding the best operating level for each component of the organization and thereby carries the focus concept down to the operating level.

Capacity balance

It is essential in capacity planning to make sure that each stage in the production system is designed so that one does not slow production in stages which precede it or follow it—that is, to assure that the capacity across the entire system is in balance. In a perfectly balanced process, the output of stage one provides the exact input requirement for stage two, stage two's output provides the exact input requirement for stage three, and so on. In practice, however, achieving such a perfect design is difficult if not impossible. One reason is that the basic operating levels for each stage generally differ. For instance, department one may operate most efficiently over a range of 90 to 110 units per month while department two, the next stage in the process, is most efficient at 75 to 85 units per month, and department three, the third stage, works best over a range of 150 to 200 units per month. Another reason is that variability in product demand and the processes themselves may lead to imbalance, at least over the short run.

There are various ways of dealing with imbalance. One is to add capacity to those stages which are the bottlenecks. This can be done by temporary measures such as overtime, leasing equipment, or going outside the system and purchasing additional capacity through subcontracting. Another way is through the use of decoupling, which can take several forms. One is

---

[2] Wickham Skinner, "The Focused Factory," *Harvard Business Review* (May–June 1974) pp. 113–21.

to set up buffer inventories so that interdependence between two groups can be loosened (e.g., department X furnishes work-in-process, and department Y uses this to make the final product). A buffer inventory may be set up so that department X places its components in a big bin ahead of Y's needs. If X falls behind, Y will have the inventory to draw upon. A second approach is to decouple by duplicating the facilities of one department upon which another is dependent. For example, many departments may maintain a backup Xerox machine in case central duplicating bogs down; a hospital operating room maintains a backup generator in case of power failure; or the sales division may maintain a reserve pool of gasoline in case the central motor pool runs dry.

Throughput effects

While the amount of available resources relative to the type of product to be produced sets certain limits on production system output, the sheer quantity of orders also greatly affects system productivity. That is, when the amount of work in process gets above a certain level, the finished goods output rate begins to drop off. This throughput effect is due to the inability of management to coordinate the increased materials flows, physical impedance from having too much inventory on the floor, and extended backlogs in front of bottleneck operations.

In coping with this problem, management must accept the counter intuitive proposition that *to increase system output one must reduce system input.* Obviously, this solution doesn't set well when, for example, a company is striving to get all the business it can and *appears* to have adequate capacity when measured by available machine or labor hours. Alas, "you can't fool mother nature," and therefore, the only ways to get around throughput log jams is to cut down on incoming orders going into production or to buy more capacity.

Calculating capacity requirements

In essence, the determination of how many units (e.g., labor hours or machines) of capacity is required over a given time period is made by taking the ratio of demand to the capacity of *one* resource unit. Thus, if 500 labor hours are required to meet demand for, say, one month and an individual worker puts in 160 hours per month, then 3.125 workers are required. In practice, however, a number of additional factors must be considered in deriving this requirement.

In a mathematical format, the following equations state the hours and resource units needed to meet some demand. Included in the equations are such factors as productivity and efficiency. The first equation computes standard resource hours, the second computes actual resource hours, and the third, the number of resource units.

The total number of standard resource hours needed to meet the demand for x different products with N_i of each is equal to the time needed to set up and produce each unit plus the time to set up each batch as

$$H_{std} = \sum_{i=1}^{x} [O_i(T_i + S_i) + B_i N_i]$$

where,

H_{std} = total number of standard hours needed to meet demand
O_i = the number of output units of x required
T_i = standard operating time per unit of x
S_i = standard set-up time per unit of output x
B_i = standard time to set up a batch of x
N_i = number of batches of x required
x = product number; for example, product 1, product 2 . . .

The actual resource hours needed are the standard resource hours adjusted for efficiencies and productivity or

$$H_{act} = \frac{H_{std}}{E_o P_w E_m}$$

where,

H_{act} = actual resource hours needed
E_o = organizational efficiency
P_w = operator productivity
E_m = machine efficiency, maintenance factor, or breakdown factor

The number of units of resource needed (machines, equipment, or workers) is equal to the actual resource hours needed divided by the number of hours available per unit of resource.

$$N_r = \frac{H_{act}}{H_{avail}}$$

where

N_r = number of units of resource required (equipment, machines, or workers)
H_{avail} = number of hours available per unit of resource during the time period.

Example. A company has a demand for 200 units of a product. There are 22 working days per month. Standard operating time per unit is eight hours, and it takes one half hour to set up each unit. The 200 units will be processed in ten batches. At the end of each batch, the machine must be recalibrated before the next batch is run; this set-up time takes four hours. Organizational efficiency is estimated at 95 percent, and machines operate at 90 percent efficiency—that is, while machines are operated at recommended speed they encounter maintenance delays of 48 minutes per day. The machines are to be run eight hours per day and the machine operators are working at standard rate (1.00).

How many machines are needed to meet monthly demand?

$$H_{std} = \sum_{i=1}^{x} [O_i(T_i + S_i) + B_i N_i]$$

There is only one product, so $x = 1$, and

$$H_{std} = 200(8 + 0.5) + 4(10) = 1{,}740 \text{ standard hours}$$

$$H_{act} = \frac{H_{std}}{E_o P_w E_m} = \frac{1740}{.95(1.0).90} = 2{,}035.1 \text{ actual hours}$$

$$N_r = \frac{H_{std}}{H_{avail}} = \frac{2035.1}{22(8)} = 11.56 \text{ machines}$$

Whether this should be rounded to 12 machines with some idle time or 11 machines with the operator working some overtime is a judgment based on the costs of each. If costs entailed in the 12th machine (depreciation cost, maintenance, overhead, and so forth) are less than the overtime costs (or incentive costs to have operators and machines work faster), then the 12th machine should be utilized.

Calculating capacity utilization

Capacity utilization for a component U_c (i.e., resource input) of the U_s by the formula

$$U_s = \frac{\text{Actual output}}{\text{System capacity}}$$

Capacity utilization for a component U_s (i.e., resource input) of the system can be calculated by the formula

$$U_c = \frac{\text{System actual output}}{\text{Component capacity}}$$

Thus, if a system produces 150 units per month with a capacity of 200 units per month,

$$U_s = \frac{150}{200} = 75\%$$

and if workers X and Y are *capable* of producing their share of 210 and 220 units, respectively,

$$U_c \text{ for worker X} = \frac{150}{210} = 71\%$$

and

$$U_c \text{ for worker Y} = \frac{150}{220} = 68\%$$

Note that even if the system were working at full capacity, both workers would still be underutilized.

DEVELOPING A CAPACITY PLAN—AN EXAMPLE FROM BANKING

The major short-run capacity planning issue in banks as well as other labor-intensive services is in setting staff levels. This example illustrates how central clearing houses and back-office operations of larger branches treat this problem. Basically, management wants to derive a staffing plan which (1) requires the least number of workers to accomplish the daily work load and (2) minimizes the variance between actual output and planned output.

In structuring the problem, bank management defines inputs (checks, statements, investment documents, and so forth) as "products," which are routed through different processes or "functions" (sorting, encoding, microfilming, and so forth).

In solving the problem, a monthly demand forecast is made by product for each function. This is converted to labor hours required per function, which in turn is converted to workers required per function. These figures are then tabled, summed, and adjusted by an absence and vacation factor to give planned hours. Then they are divided by the number of hours in the work day to yield the number of workers required. This is what the banks term a capacity plan. (See Exhibit 6.4.) This plan becomes the basis for a departmental staffing plan which gives the workers required, workers available, variance, and managerial action (in light of variance). (See Exhibit 6.5.)

EXHIBIT 6.4
Daily capacity requirements

Product	Daily Volume	Receive P/H	Receive H_{std}	Pre-process P/H	Pre-process H_{std}	Microfilm P/H	Microfilm H_{std}	Verify P/H	Verify H_{std}	Totals H_{std}
Checks	2,000	1,000	2.0	600	3.3	240	8.3	640	3.2	16.8
Statements	1,000	—	—	600	1.7	250	4.0	150	6.6	12.3
Notes	200	30	6.7	15	13.3	—				20.0
Investments	400	100	4.0	50	8.0	200	2.0	150	2.7	16.7
Collections	500	300	1.7			300	1.9	60	8.4	11.8
Total hours required			14.4		26.3		16.0		20.9	67.6
Times 1.25 (absences and vacations)			18.0		32.9		20.0		26.2	
Divided by 8 hours equals: staff required			2.3		4.1		2.5		3.3	

Note: P/H indicates production rate per hour; H_{std} indicates required hours.

EXHIBIT 6.5
Staffing plan

Function	Staff required	Staff available	Variance ($\pm$)	Management actions
Receive	2.0	2.0	0	None
Pre-process	4.1	4.0	−0.1	Use overtime
Microfilm	2.5	3.0	+0.5	Use excess to verify
Verify	3.3	3.0	−0.7	Get 0.5 from microfilm, Use overtime for 0.2

In addition to their use in day-to-day planning, the capacity and staffing documents provide information for controlling operations, scheduling individual workers, comparing capacity utilization with other branches, and for starting up new branches.

CAPACITY AND PRODUCTION PLANNING IN MANUFACTURING

Exhibit 6.6 shows an overview of a production and capacity planning system for manufacturing. Its elements will now be briefly described.

Corporate production planning provides the overall direction for the firm's production for a year or more into the future. Such planning takes into account significant changes in the market and major financial requirements of the production system. Its primary outputs are operating budgets for departments involved in production, finance and marketing, and commitments for major expansion of capacity.

Manufacturing aggregate production planning specifies output requirements by major product groups either in labor hours required or in units of production for monthly periods for up to 18 months out. Its focus is on production rates, work force levels, and inventories (see Chapter 13).

Master production scheduling generates the amounts and need dates for the manufacture of specific end products. The master production schedule is

EXHIBIT 6.6
Overall view of the production and capacity planning system

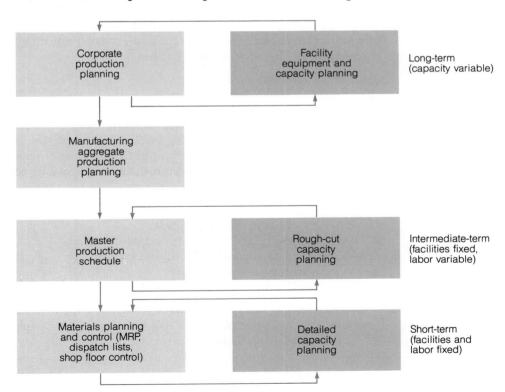

usually fixed over the short run (six to eight weeks); that is, it is a firm schedule of what is to be produced and generally cannot be changed. Beyond six to eight weeks, various changes may be made with essentially complete revisions possible after six months (see Chapter 14).

Materials planning and control includes materials requirements planning, (Chapter 16) which breaks down, or "explodes," end-product requirements into their constituent materials and components and specifies when each is needed relative to the master schedule. Dispatch lists represent one of the tangible documents which initiate actual production; shop flow control refers to the techniques by which materials and orders are kept on schedule (see Chapter 14).

Facilities planning examines the requirements for new plant and equipment for the next five to ten years. Because these decisions are long-term, capacity is treated as a variable for corporate planning purposes. Facilities planning is what top management usually views as capacity planning.

Rough-cut capacity planning is intermediate term and reviews the master production schedule to make sure that production facilities are available and that there are no obvious bottlenecks which would require the master production schedule to be changed. As the name suggests, this is a "rough-cut" view of available production.

Detailed capacity planning deals with evaluating and adjusting capacity availability at each work center for purposes of short-term scheduling. This is the area of capacity planning which has attracted the greatest interest of production control people. We will discuss scheduling in light of capacity constraints in the scheduling chapter.

FACILITIES PLANNING

Facilities planning involves determining how big a facility is to be (its capacity) and where the facility is to be located. Because it deals with the commitment of a sizable amount of financial resources over an extended period of time, its outcome has significant implications for every organization.

Wheelwright sees five key decisions in facility planning:

1. How much capacity to provide.
2. When capacity should be added or dropped.
3. What kind of capacity (facilities) to provide.
4. Where to locate the capacity.
5. How to accomplish the desired facilities plan.[3]

In determining how much capacity to provide, the previously mentioned concepts of economies of scale, capacity balance, and capacity focus pertain as do the ways of calculating capacity requirements.

---

[3] Steven C. Wheelwright, *Capacity Planning and Facilities Choice* (Boston: Division of Research, Harvard Business School, 1979), pp. 1–7.

The determination of when capacity should be added or dropped depends upon market conditions and corporate strategy. Deciding what kind of capacity to add is (in Wheelwright's opinion), the least well-handled of the five in practice. He cautions against merely duplicating existing facilities and argues for a careful review of all decisions made with respect to existing operations. This would include, for example, an examination of production processes, production control system, and the organization of the manufacturing function. Where to locate the capacity entails examining transportation costs and regional costs of alternative locations (we will discuss these shortly). Finally, how to accomplish the facilities plan entails both deciding on how capacity requirements will be met with respect to major facilities and managing the transition from existing facilities to the new facility.

Evaluating alternative facilities using decision trees

A useful tool for evaluating facility alternatives (as well as many other types of decisions) is the decision tree. We will demonstrate its use via the classic example developed by Magee.[4]

Stygrain Chemical Industries has developed a new product which has an estimated life of ten years. Stygrain must build either a large plant or a small plant to produce the product; the choice depends on the size of the market demand.

If Stygrain builds a large plant, it is committed to this decision for the life of the product. If it builds a small plant and the product turns out to be successful, Stygrain still has the option of expanding the plant in two years.

The list of assumptions and conditions are as follows:

1. A large plant involves a $3 million investment.
2. A small plant involves a $1.3 million investment.
3. If demand is high, a large plant would yield $1 million annual return.
4. If demand is low, a large plant would only yield $100,000 annually because of high fixed costs and inefficiencies.
5. If demand is low, a small plant would be economical and would yield $450,000 annually.
6. If demand is high, a small plant could expand in two years at an additional cost of $2.2 million.
7. If demand is high, a small plant which did not expand would yield $450,000 for two years, but this would drop to $300,000 per year because compeition would be attracted to produce the product.
8. If after two years the small plant expanded and the demand remained high, cash flow would be $700,000 per year.
9. If after two years the small plant expanded but the demand dropped low, the estimated cash flow would be $50,000 per year.

4 John F. Magee, "Decision Trees for Decision Making," *Harvard Business Review* (July–August 1964), pp. 126–38.

10. Marketing estimates for the product demand are:
    High demand for all ten years—60 percent
    High demand for two years, low demand
       for eight years—10 percent
    Low demand for all ten years—30 percent
       Therefore chances of an initial high demand is 60 + 10 = 70 percent
       Chances of an initial high demand then low demand is 10 ÷ 70 =
          14 percent
       Then chances of an initial high demand staying high is 60 ÷ 70 =
          86 percent.

Exhibit 6.7 shows the decision tree for this problem where the square node denotes a decision point and a circle node denotes a chance occurrence.

EXHIBIT 6.7
Decision tree for plant expansion example

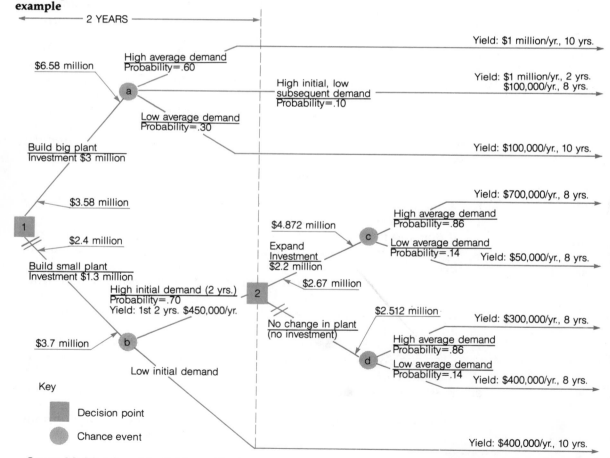

Source: Modified from John F. Magee, "Decision Trees for Decision Making," *Harvard Business Review* (July–August 1964), pp. 126–38.

In Exhibit 6.7 the following values occur at various points:

Node a. 0.60 ($1 million × 10 years) . . . . . = 6.00 million
        +0.10 ($1 million × 2 years
            + $100,000 × 8 years) . . . . = 0.28
        +0.30 ($100,000 × 10 years) . . . . = 0.30
                                            = $6.58 million

Decision point 1, build big plant

    $6.58 million less $3 million
        = 3.58 million

Node c. 0.86 ($700,000 × 8 years) . . . . = 4.816 million
        +0.14 ($50,000 × 8 years) . . . . . . = 0.056
                                            $4.872 million

Node d. 0.86 ($300,000 × 8 years) . . . . = 2.064 million
        +0.14 ($400,000 × 8 years) . . . . . = 0.448
                                            $2.512 million

Decision point 2, "expand plant" branch of decision tree would have a value of $4.872 million, less $2.2 million investment, or a value of $2.672 million. Since this is larger than the "no change in plant" decision of Node d, that branch would be severed, and the value at decision point 2 is $2.672 million.

Node b. 0.70 ($450,000 × 2 years
            + $2.672 million) . . . . = 2.5
        +0.30 (400,000 × 10 years) . . . . . = 1.2 million
                                            $3.7 million

Decision point 1, "build small plant" has a value of $3.7 million minus the $1.3 million investment for a net $2.4 million. The alternatives at decision point 1 are to either build a big plant which would net $3.58 million or build a small plant which would net $2.4 million. The choice is obviously to build the large plant.

In this example of a capacity decision analysis, the cost of capital or interest rates were not included to simplify the presentation. Because of the high fluctuating interest rates of recent years, they clearly should be included in an actual application. The appropriate tables to use are in Chapter 5, Financial Analysis.

FACILITY LOCATION

Facility location is one of the most important decisions a firm has to make. A misplaced machine can usually be moved to where it belongs at a relatively small cost. A misplaced factory, on the other hand, involves significant long-term costs. Hicks and Kumtha offer the following hypothesis: "The more aggregate a facilities planning mistake (e.g., a factory, a department, a machine), the more costly it will be, the less likely it will be changed, and the longer it will affect the operation."[5]

For manufacturers, the facility location problem is broadly categorized into factory location and warehouse location. Within this categorization, we may be interested in locating the firm's first factory or warehouse or locating a new factory or warehouse relative to the locations of existing facilities. The general objective in choosing a location is to select that site or combination of sites that minimizes three classes of costs—regional costs, distribution costs, and raw-material and supplies cost. Regional costs are those associated with a given locale and include land, construction, labor, and state and local expenses. Distribution costs are those directly related to the shipping of supplies and products to customers and other branches of the distribution network. Raw-material and supply costs refer to the availability and costs of production inputs including energy and water as well as the lead time to acquire these inputs. Since the location of the initial factory is usually determined by the historical context of the firm, economic analysis of facility location has focused on the problem of adding warehouses or factories to the existing production-distribution system.

Plant location methods

When new plant locations are to be considered, the sequence of analysis follows the major decisions listed in Exhibit 6.8. That is, the company moves step-by-step from market region to ultimate site using selected decision criteria to narrow the search.

The evaluation of alternative regions, subregions, and communities is commonly termed *macro analysis,* and the evaluation of specific sites in the selected community is termed *micro analysis.*

Commonly used tools in selecting a subregion (such as a small state or county) are linear programming, grid methods, simulation, and simple point-rating systems. Traditional financial techniques are employed at all levels of analysis.

Linear programming. Using the transportation method discussed in Chapter 7, linear programming finds an optimum location for a new plant by substituting, one at a time, each candidate location into a transportation matrix. The location that minimizes the sum of the transportation costs between that facility and all other existing plants and warehouses is then selected. This method is really quite easy to use but requires that alternative locations be identified before a solution can be found.

Grid methods. These methods also focus on finding a location which minimizes transportation costs between the new facility and existing facilities, supply sources, and markets.

They set up a grid with horizontal (M_H) and vertical (M_V) coordinates

---

[5] Philip E. Hicks and Areen M. Kumtha, "One Way to Tighten Up Plant Location Decisions," *Industrial Engineering* (April 1971), pp. 19–23.

Decision unit   Major decision   Selected decision criteria

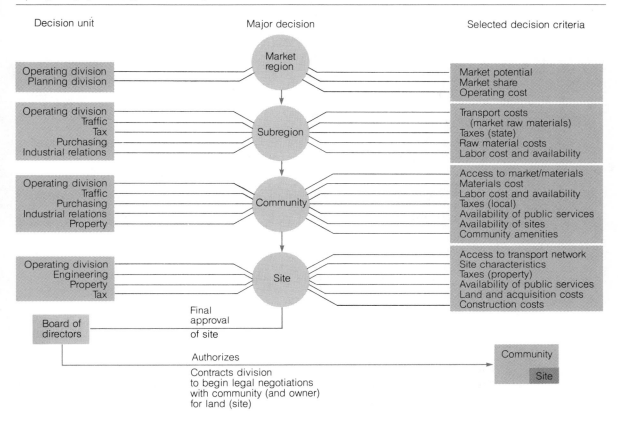

Operating division Planning division	Market potential Market share Operating cost

Market region

Operating division Traffic Tax Purchasing Industrial relations	Transport costs (market raw materials) Taxes (state) Raw material costs Labor cost and availability

Subregion

Operating division Traffic Purchasing Industrial relations Property	Access to market/materials Materials cost Labor cost and availability Taxes (local) Availability of public services Availability of sites Community amenities

Community

Operating division Engineering Property Tax	Access to transport network Site characteristics Taxes (property) Availability of public services Land and acquisition costs Construction costs

Site

Board of directors — Final approval of site

Authorizes

Contracts division to begin legal negotiations with community (and owner) for land (site)

Community
Site

Source: Thomas M. Carroll and Robert D. Dean, "A Bayesian Approach to Plant-Location Decisions", *Decision Sciences,* vol. 11, no. 1 (January 1980), p. 87.

EXHIBIT 6.8
Plant search:
Company XYZ

specified for each existing plant and solve analytically for the best coordinates for the new plant.

One of the more useful of these grid techniques is termed the *center of gravity approach.* This technique can be readily understood by the following solved example taken from Coyle and Bardi.[6]

Exhibit 6.9 depicts a grid which has been superimposed over the exact geographic locations of a firm's raw material sources *(RM)* and finished goods markets *(FG)* and is scaled by miles (0 to 1,000) on each axis. Exhibit 6.9B gives volume and distance data for these sources and markets.

The concept underlying this technique is best visualized as a series of strings to which are attached weights corresponding to the weight of raw materials provided by each source and of finished goods sold at each market. The strings are threaded through holes in a flat surface; the holes correspond to the location of the sources and markets. The other end of

[6] John J. Coyle and Edward J. Bardi, *The Management of Logistics,* 2d ed. (St. Paul: The West Publishing Company, 1980), pp. 294–98.

EXHIBIT 6.9
A. Grid loca-
tions of raw
materials and
markets

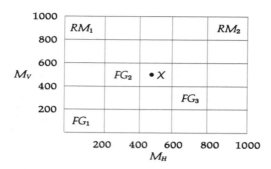

RM = raw material source locations
FG = finished good market location
X = least cost location

B. Example
data for center of
gravity analysis

	Tons	Rate/ton/mile	Grid location
FG_1	50	$1.00	100,100
FG_2..........	50	$1.00	300,500
FG_3	50	$1.00	700,300
RM_1	100	$ .50	100,900
RM_2	100	$ .50	900,900

the strings are tied together and the weights are then permitted to exert
their respective pulls on the knot. The end of the strings will finally reach
an equilibrium: this equilibrium will be the center of mass (gravity) or
the ton-mile center.

   This problem can be solved mathematically by solving in rectilinear
distances for the following equation, first for the horizontal coordinate
and then for the vertical coordinate.

$$M_H \text{ or } M_V = \frac{\sum_1^n R_i D_i FG_i + \sum_1^m r_i d_i RM_i}{\sum_1^n R_i FG_i + \sum_1^m r_i RM_i}$$

where

M_H = horizontal distance coordinate
M_V = vertical distance coordinate
n = identity of each particular finished good
m = identity of each particular raw material
R_i = FG transportation rate per unit of distance for FG_i
D_i = distance from 0 point on grid to the location of finished good (i)
FG_i = weight (volume) of finished goods sold in market (i)
RM_i = weight (volume) of raw material purchased at source (i)
r_i = RM transportation rate per unit of distance for RM_i
d_i = distance from 0 point on grid to the grid location of raw material (i)

That is, we simply find the horizontal and vertical coordinates by the relationship expressed in the equation above which is:

$$M_H \text{ or } M_V = \frac{\Sigma \, [\text{transportation rate} \times \text{distance} \times \text{volume shipped}]}{\Sigma \, [\text{transportation rate} \times \text{volume shipped}]}$$

Substituting the data from Exhibit 6.11 into the original formulas we get

$$M_H = \frac{\begin{array}{l}(1)(100)(50) + (1)(300)(50) + (1)(700)(50) + \\ (.5)(100)(100) + (.5)(900)(100)\end{array}}{(1)(50) + (1)(50) + (1)(50) + (.5)(100) + (.5)(100)} = 420$$

$$M_V = \frac{\begin{array}{l}(1)(100)(50) + (1)(500)(50) + (1)(300)(50) + \\ (.5)(900)(100) + (.5)(900)(100)\end{array}}{(1)(50) + (1)(50) + (1)(50) + (.5)(100) + (.5)(100)} = 540$$

Thus the least-cost location for the plant is at 420 miles in the horizontal direction and 540 miles in the vertical direction (as indicated on the grid as point X).

The major limitations of the center of gravity method just shown are that it assumes linear transportation costs and rectilinear distances. In practice, transportation costs do increase with distance but not proportionately since shipment rates tend to taper out as distance increases. Rectilinear distances are unrealistic over long hauls because transportation routing logically follows a shortest path direct line rather than horizontal and vertical moves. Within cities, which usually have square blocks, rectilinear distances are close to actual mileage covered. However, despite these problems, the method can provide a good first-cut location with a minimum of effort.

Simulation. This method entails running a mathematical model of a system on a computer in order to predict the behavior of that system under different operating conditions. Shycon[7] suggests that the best way to solve the location problem for a plant or warehouse is to simulate a number of locations and vary the number of facilities. The simulation model he has developed examines the impact on different locations of such factors as raw-material availability, production rates, total transportation costs, warehousing costs, inventory levels, and customer requirements. One advantage of the simulation approach is that it can deal realistically with nonlinear cost functions. Exhibit 6.10, for example, shows that in the typical case, transportation cost from the plant to each warehouse increases only very gradually as the number of warehouses increases. On the other hand, transportation cost from the warehouses to customers decreases dramatically as the number of warehouses increases since more warehouses means more local shipments rather than over-the-road ship-

[7] Harvey N. Shycon, "Site Location Analysis, Cost, and Consumer Considerations" (Proceedings of the Seventeenth Annual International Conference, American Production and Inventory Control Society, 1974), pp. 337–38.

A. Transportation : Primary (plants to warehouse)

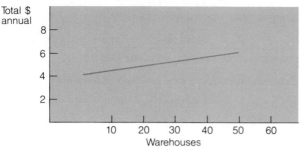

B. Transportation : Secondary (warehouse to customer)

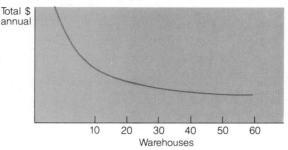

Source: Harvey N. Shycon, "Site Location Analysis, Cost, and Consumer Considerations" (Proceedings of the Seventeenth Annual International Conference, American Production and Inventory Control Society, 1974), pp. 337–38.

EXHIBIT 6.10
Transportation cost (A) from the factory or plant to a varying number of warehouses, (B) from a varying number of warehouses to the customer

ping. It is doubtful that direct mathematical procedures would account for these types of costs in a practical way. In relating the value of his simulation, Shycon states that in over three dozen applications "the benefits have been almost universally great,"[8] He goes on further to say:

> The simulation approach enables comparative evaluations of a wide number of locations, of a large number of combinations of locations, of questions concerning what to manufacture, of what to stock at each location, and of questions of what markets to serve. In addition, it enables evaluations of varying cost levels and varying customer service levels.[9]

Factor-rating systems. These are perhaps the most widely used of the general location techniques because they provide a mechanism to combine diverse factors in an easy-to-understand format. Three common types of factor-rating schemes are:[10]

1. Assigning equal weights to all factors and evaluating each location along the factor scale.
2. Assigning variable weights to each of the factors and evaluating each location along the factor scale.
3. Assigning variable weights to each factor. The locations are then rated by a common scale for each factor. The location point assignment for the factor is then obtained by multiplying the location rating for each factor by the factor weight.

Examples of the above are:

1. A manufacturer of fabricated metal products selected 50 factors by which to rate 12 sites. Each site was assigned a rating of zero to ten points for each factor. The sum of the assigned factor points constituted the site rating by which it could be compared to other sites.

---

[8] Ibid., p. 347.

[9] Ibid.

[10] Modified from Ruddel Reed, Jr., *Plant Location, Layout, and Maintenance,* Irwin Series in Operations Management (Homewood, Ill.: Richard D. Irwin, Inc., 1967), pp. 21–22.

2. A refinery assigned the following comparative ratings to major factors:

Fuels 330
Power availability and reliability 200
Labor climate 100
Living conditions 100
Transportation 50
Water supply 10
Climate 50
Supplies 60
Tax policies and laws 20
Site 10

Each site was then rated against each factor and a point assignment of zero to the maximum factor value assigned. The sums of assigned points for each site were then compared and that site with the maximum number of points selected.

3. Rating weights of from one to five were assigned to ten factors as follows:

Labor climate 5
Community facilities 3
Site 1
Power availability and reliability 2
Tax plans 2
Residential housing 3
Distance from (city) 1
Available work force 2
Available commercial transportation 1
Available tooling and plating vendors 1

For each of the factors, the site could receive zero to ten points. The factor points assigned were then multiplied by the factor weight above to find the site factor value. The sum of the resulting site factor values were used to compare sites.

In some instances, an attempt is made to combine cost and noncost factors. This results in a modification of one of the three methods as, for example, is shown in Exhibit 6.11 (which is a modification of the second technique). Here, a conversion of cost to points is made where in this case, the lower the cost, the higher the points assigned.

EXHIBIT 6.11
Reduced point-rating table

	Location		
	Tucson, Arizona	Tempe, Arizona	Maximum possible points
Tangibles			
Distribution cost	200	210	250
Labor cost	90	80	100
Intangibles			
Site availability	100	100	100
University assistance	20	10	20
Total	410	400	

One of the major problems with simple point-rating schemes is that they do not account for the wide range of costs which may occur within each factor. For example, there may be only a few hundred dollars difference between the best and worst locations on one factor and several thousands of dollars difference between the best and the worst on another. The first factor may have the most points available to it but provide little help in making the location decision; the latter may have few points available but potentially show a real difference in the value of locations. To

EXHIBIT 6.12
**Cost analysis
example**

Operating expenses	Present location versus recommended communities			
	Present location	Community A	Community B	Community C
Transportation				
Inbound	$ 202,942	$ 212,209	$ 207,467	$ 220,009
Outbound	480,605	361,268	393,402	365,198
Labor				
Hourly direct and indirect	$1,520,943	$1,339,790	$1,146,087	$1,223,416
Fringe benefits	304,189	187,571	126,070	159,044
Plant overhead				
Rent or carrying costs	$ 271,436	$ 290,000	$ 280,000	$ 295,000
Real estate taxes	43,345	39,000	34,000	39,000
Personal property and other				
locally assessed taxes	16,899	—	—	8,500
Fuel for heating	19,260	11,000	9,500	13,000
Utilities				
Power	$ 56,580	$ 61,304	$ 41,712	$ 49,007
Gas............................	18,460	19,812	13,767	16,633
Water..........................	12,474	8,200	4,500	4,500
Treatment of				
effluent	6,376	—	2,300	—
State factors				
State taxes........................	$ 67,811	$ 73,400	$ 44,920	$ 71,000
Workmen's compen-				
sation insurance	30,499	24,000	14,000	17,000
Total........................	$2,051,819	$2,627,554	$2,317,725	$2,481,307
Savings through construction of				
new plant				
New plant layout		($ 210,000)	($ 210,000)	($ 210,000)
Reduced materials handling		(38,000)	(38,000)	(38,000)
Elimination of present local interplant				
movements		(60,000)	(60,000)	(60,000)
Reduced public warehousing		((30,000))	(30,000)	(30,000)
Reduced super visory personnel		(27,000)	(27,000)	(27,000)
Savings through new				
construction		($ 365,000)	($ 365,000)	($ 365,000)
Annual operating costs	$3,051,819	$2,262,554	$1,952,752	$2,116,307
Potential annual savings over				
present location		$789,265	$1,099,094	$935,512
Percentage of savings		25.9 %	36.0 %	30.7 %

Source: "New Plants and Expansions, End of Tunnel May be in Sight," *Factory* (September 1975), p. 57.

deal with this problem, Hicks and Kumtha[11] suggest that points possible for each factor be derived using a weighting scale based upon standard deviations of costs rather than "raw" cost amounts. The advantage of this is that it centers on the variation of costs as opposed to ranges and thereby focuses attention on factors where alternative locations have significant differences. For instance, if labor costs at all locations are close together, then the use of standard deviations would "automatically" reduce the importance of labor cost as a criterion (i.e., fewer points would be allocated to it). This method seems logical and the interested reader should consult the original publication.

Financial analysis. Cost analyses have to be performed before any location decision is finalized. Exhibit 6.12, taken from *Factory* magazine, presents an actual cost analysis used by a company contemplating the relocation of its plant. Break-even analysis and present-value calculations are also widely used for locational decisions.

LOCATING SERVICE FACILITIES

In service organizations, the facility location decision is also a major one, but as a rule, the choice of a locale is based upon nearness to the customer rather than on resource considerations. With the shift in the U.S. economy away from manufacturing and toward service, there is little question that the opening of new service facilities has become far more common than the opening of new factories and warehouses. Indeed, there are few communities in which rapid population growth has not been paralleled by a concurrent rapid growth in municipal services, franchises, and entertainment facilities.

Locating service outlets— an heuristic method

A common problem encountered by service-providing organizations is deciding how many service outlets to establish within a geographical area and where within that geographical area the service outlets are to be located. The problem is complicated by the fact that there are usually a large number of possible locations and several options in the absolute number of service centers that can be selected. Thus, attempting to find a good solution, much less an optimum one, can be extremely time-consuming, even for a relatively small problem. For example, there would be 243 possible solutions for a problem involving choosing among one, two, or three retail outlets to serve four geographically dispersed customer populations, even where there are only three possible locations for the outlets. To illustrate one approach to searching for feasible solutions to such problems, an heuristic method based on one described by Khumawala[12] will be applied to a sample problem.

[11] Philip E. Hicks and Areen M. Kumtha, "One Way to Tighten Up Plant Location Decisions" *Industrial Engineering* (April 1971), pp. 19–23.

[12] Basheer M. Khumawala, "An Efficient Algorithm for Central Facilities Location" (Paper No. 357, Krannert School of Industrial Administration, Purdue University, July 1972).

Example. Suppose that a medical consortium wishes to establish two clinics to provide medical care for people living in four communities in central Ohio. Assume that the sites under study are in each community and that the population within each community is evenly distributed within the community's boundaries. Further, assume that the potential use of the clinics by members of the various communities has been determined and weighting factors reflecting the relative importance of serving members of the population of each community have been developed. (This information is given in Exhibit 6.13 below.) The objective of the problem can be stated as follows: find the two clinics that can serve all communities at the lowest weighted-travel distance cost.

EXHIBIT 6.13
Distances, population, and relative weights

From community	To clinic A	B	C	D	Population of community	Relative weighting of population
1	0	11	8	12	10,000	1.1
2	11	0	10	7	8,000	1.4
3	8	10	0	9	20,000	0.7
4	9.5	7	9	0	12,000	1.0

Procedure. Step 1: Construct a weighted population-distance table from initial data table (Exhibit 6.14).

EXHIBIT 6.14
Weighted population distances (distance × population × weighting factor) in thousands

From community	To clinic A	B	C	D
1	0	121	88	132
2	123.2	0	112	78.4
3	112	140	0	126
4	114	84	108	0

Step 2: Circle the smallest non-zero number in each row. Draw an arrow from that number to the zero in its row. This zero identifies the column (clinic) which can be eliminated at the lowest added cost of providing service to that clinic's community. Record the cost of eliminating that clinic. Draw a line through the column associated with the clinic with the lowest cost to indicate its elimination.

Community	Clinic A	B	C	D
1	0	121	(88)	132
2	123.2	0	112	(78.4)
3	(112)	140	0	126
4	114	(84)	108	0

Cost of eliminating clinic:

A	B	C	D
88	78.4	112	84

Step 3: Subtract the smallest circled number from itself and all remaining numbers in its row and construct a matrix reflecting this subtraction and the elimination of the clinic. If the specified number of clinics remaining open is now achieved, stop, otherwise repeat steps 2 and 3.

	Clinic		
Community	A	C	D
1	0	88	132
2	44.8	33.6	0
3	112	0	126
4	114	108	0

(subtractions made in row 2)

One more clinic must be eliminated, so we repeat steps 2 and 3. Step 2 (repeated):

	Clinic		
Community	A	C	D
1	0	88	132
2	44.8	33.6	0
3	112	0	126
4	114	108	0

Cost of eliminating clinic:

A	C	D
88	112	33.6
		108
88	112	141.6	Totals

Step 3 (repeated):

	Clinic	
Community	C	D
1	0	44
2	33.6	0
3	0	126
4	108	0

The problem is now solved: Clinic C serves communities 1 and 3; clinic D serves communities 2 and 4. The total cost of the solution (in population weighted distance) is 88 + 78.4, or 166.4.

LOCATING MOBILE SERVICES USING SIMULATION

Below is a brief review of three simulation studies performed by OM graduate students at the University of Arizona. These studies provide a flavor of the types of issues which must be considered in locating home bases and deploying service vehicles.

Tucson Fire Department

Tucson, for the past decade or so, has been the fastest or nearly the fastest growing city in the United States. As a consequence, it is necessary to continually plan services well in advance of their need. In the case of fire stations, plans are made based on 15-year projections (which seem to become obsolete every five years because of rapid growth).

In fire departments, a major portion of the planning effort is in the investigation and deployment of fire-fighting resources. Three important deployment policies are:

1. Location policies—how many units of each type (engines and ladders) should be located in each area.
2. Dispatching policies—how many units of each type of equipment should be sent to each incident.
3. Relocation policies—when units in one area have been deployed, which available units should be moved in from which other stations to provide continued coverage.

Fire department effectiveness may be directly measured in terms of loss of life, personal and property damage. Correlating these measures with alternate location and deployment policies is next to impossible. Instead, surrogate measures are used which reflect the Fire Department's activity rather than the consequences. Examples of such measures are: the number of units responding, the time to reach the incident, the number of responses made by each unit, the number of times each unit was called upon but not available, and the proportion of time each unit is active.

Policies are evaluated on how they affect the measures given the same consequences. If at a particular incident, one policy produces a smaller response time vector than that for another policy, then it is assumed that the former policy is "best," even though we do not know the precise relationship between response time and losses.

A private ambulance service

A private ambulance service was analyzed and the firm's operation modeled and simulated. This ambulance service had four types of calls.

1. Private (emergency and nonemergency).
2. County (emergency and nonemergency).
3. Death calls (contract nonemergency service for mortuaries).
4. No-ticket calls (emergency response but the call is cancelled after a short period of time).

For emergency calls, speed in the time to arrive at the scene is a major criterion. One questionable activity with ambulance services is that a rotation system is often used with hospitals as to "who gets the next case." Thus, even though the response time for the ambulance to arrive may be fast, the hospital that the patient is taken to is usually not the closest one and often quite distant from the scene.

The data concerning times, number of calls of various types, frequency distributions, sources of calls, point of dispatch, response times, destinations, and so forth were obtained from the firm's records. Financial data were included to obtain profit and loss statements.

The simulation showed, as expected, that to achieve a fast response time, idle time was high (or utilization low). As more ambulances were added to the existing system, the response time was quicker, the number of calls transferred to a competitor decreased, but profit went down. From the standpoint of private industry operating under government controls (county, in this case), the ambulance service was required to operate at a nonoptimal level. That is, in order to provide a response time that met the county requirements, the ambulance service needed more ambulances and crews than it would have chosen if maximizing profit were its primary objective.

An interesting sidelight in this case was that the graduate students who developed the model became so knowledgeable about the costs and operations of the ambulance firm that they were called before the State Corporation Commission to testify concerning a proposed rate increase.

A taxicab company

A taxicab simulation model was built to study the effects on profit of changing such controllable variables as the number of cabs, search distance—how far a cab should go from its present position to pick up a fare, and initial cab positioning in light of such existing uncontrollable variables as demand, destination, driving speeds (some control over this), costs to operate, and rate of fare (set by State Corporation Commission).

The program used a series of matrices to determine demand and distribution of demand by day, zone, and time period. Profits were computed for various combinations of numbers of cabs, search distances, and cab positioning.

Summary note on simulation models

Several highly sophisticated mathematical models exist today for locating mobile services. Unfortunately, understanding them is often difficult and trying to use them usually requires that one be an expert on that model. By contrast, a great deal of information can be gained from relatively simple simulation models which can be created in as short a time as several man-months of labor. Beyond this range, however, each remaining increment of information becomes increasingly more expensive both in manpower, computer time, and in the time to construct the model. Therefore, one often has to decide whether the remaining increments such as 5, 10, or 15 percent increases in the system performance are worth several times or more in costs required to create a more elaborate model.

CONCLUSION

Capacity and facilities planning for manufacturing firms are so interrelated that for many, they constitute one decision. In services, capacity and facilities are by convention less closely aligned because so much of service system capacity is tied up in people and hence is variable in the short run. Clearly, however, even for service systems, capacity is finite at some point. Both Disneyland and our favorite bar reach a point at peak demand periods where there is inadequate capacity to serve all customers (at least at a level where they are willing to remain to get served).

Plant location, though presented as a one-time decision, is for many firms an on-going evaluation process. Shifting tax rates, low-cost labor, and quality of life all combine to raise the question, "Should we move?" The answer for a number of firms is "yes" as evidenced in recent years by major firms moving their main operations to sun-belt states and foreign countries. In this regard, it should be noted that industrial powers such as Japan and West Germany view the United States as a desirable place to locate their operations. For these countries, the motivation is not so much to obtain low-cost labor but rather to strengthen their hold on a particular market through achieving the benefits of proximity. Check to see in which country your 1981 Volkswagon was made.

REVIEW AND DISCUSSION QUESTIONS

1. What is the relationship between capacity planning, facilities planning, and plant location?

2. Does it make sense to say that a particular plant is working at 110 percent of capacity?

3. What are some practical limits to economies of scale—that is, when should a plant stop growing?

4. What are some capacity balance problems faced by the following organizations or facilities:
    a. An airline terminal.
    b. A university computing center.
    c. An automobile assembly line.

5. Why does cutting down on the input to a system often lead to an increase in its output?

6. What are some major capacity considerations in a hospital? How do they differ from those of a factory?

7. Describe in your own words how capacity requirements planning is done in the bank example given in the chapter.

8. Develop a list of five major reasons why a new electronics firm should move into your city or town.

PROBLEMS

1. Ohio Gozimus Restaurants, a Japanese chain home officed in Cleveland, is seeking the optimum balance between their dining room and bar facilities. Like most restaurants, they make a substantial profit on their bar drinks and want to make certain that every dinner party which enters the restaurant will have ample time to drink in the bar before they move to the dining room.

    An industry survey indicates that the average customer has two drinks with the second drink being delivered 24 minutes after the customer has arrived in the bar. The restaurant's own records indicate that a typical dinner party consists of four people and averages one hour in the dining room.

Assuming that all customers will need tables of four (or equivalent seating) in the bar, what is the optimum ratio of tables in the bar relative to tables in the dining room?

2. An electronics firm has just won a contract to manufacture two products (A and B) for the government. The firm has three major departments—design, manufacture, and test. The design department has finished its work, and now it is up to manufacturing to actually start production.

The contract stipulates that 1,000 A's and 2,000 B's must be made over the next 30 *working days*. It is management's objective to produce the product on straight time (i.e., an eight-hour work day). Other data about the case are as follows.

Standard time per unit of A	20 hours
Standard time per unit of B	5 hours
Set-up time per unit A	3 hours
Set-up time per unit of B	2 hours
Number of batches	1 for A and 1 for B
Standard set-up time per batch of A	16 hours
Standard set-up time per batch of B	10 hours
Organizational efficiency including operator productivity	80%

a. How many workers are required to complete the project on time?

b. Halfway through the project, the government asks if you can add another 300 A's to the contract. Assume that you can react instantaneously by pulling workers off other projects. (This will entail a separate batch of A.) For this remaining 15 days, how many additional workers are required?

3. Art Fern, owner of Tea Time Movies, Inc., is trying to decide whether to lease a movie theater at a site near the Ventura Freeway in Hollywood or build a new four-screen theater near a fork in the Slauson Freeway in Inglewood. The theater will be built on state-leased land which will be part of a new expanded intersection in ten years. Thus, there is no salvage value at the termination of the ten-year period.

The initial lease will run for a period of two years. If the owner is satisfied at that time, he will extend the lease for an additional eight years. Art attaches a 50-50 probability to this renewal. If the lease is cancelled, Art knows of another theater nearby which will be available for leasing, but the lease will be 30 percent more than the present site. Given this information and the information below, develop a decision tree to help Art choose between these sites (Use a ten-year planning horizon.) Disregard the cost of capital.

Decision variables	Hollywood site	Probability	Inglewood site	Probability
Cost to lease per year	$250			
Cost to build			$1,000,000	
Gross revenue per year				
High ticket sales	700,000	0.5	400,000	0.5
Medium ticket sales	500,000	0.3	300,000	0.3
Low ticket sales	300,000	0.2	200,000	0.2
Operating costs per year	200,000		200,000	

✓ 4.   Ev and Ron are looking for a short-cut method to determine where to place
       their new book warehouse. With reference to the grid in Exhibit 6.15, their
       present print shops are shown as P_1 and P_2 and their current book distributors
       are shown as B_1 and B_2. The annual number of loads, the transportation
       rates, and the exact grid locations are given below. Use the center of gravity
       method to help these fellows out.

	Loads	Rate/ton/mile	Grid location
P_1	700	$1	10, 40
P_2	900	$1	20, 30
B_1	400	$1	30, 50
B_2	500	$1	40, 60

EXHIBIT 6.15

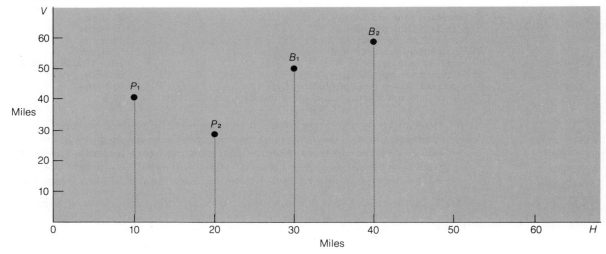

X 5.   A drug store chain plans to open four stores in a medium-size city. However,
       funds are limited, so only two can be opened this year. (a) Given the following
       tableau showing the weighted population distance costs for each of the four
       areas and four store sites, select the two to be opened up first. (b) If additional
       funds become available, which store should be the third to open?

		Store 1	Store 2	Store 3	Store 4
Geographic area	1	0	20	160	60
	2	80	0	40	80
	3	120	80	0	100
	4	80	100	60	0

CASE: COMMUNITY HOSPITAL* ———————————————————————————

In 1979, Community Hospital, which had served the downtown area of a large West Coast city for over a quarter century, closed and then built a new, modern short-term general hospital in a thinly populated area about 30 miles west of the city. The new hospital, also named Community Hospital, was located on a parcel of land owned by the original hospital for many years.

This new hospital, which opened Oct. 1, 1979, is a four-story structure that includes all of the latest innovations in health care technology. The first floor houses the emergency department; intensive care unit; operating room; radiology, laboratory, and therapy departments; pharmacy; and housekeeping and maintenance facilities and supplies, as well as other supportive operations. All administrative offices, such as the business office, medical-record department, special services, and so forth, are located on the second floor, as are the cafeteria and food service facilities. The two upper floors contain patient rooms divided into surgical, medical, pediatric, and obstetric units.

Community Hospital has a total capacity of 177 beds assigned as follows:

Unit	Number of beds
Surgical	45
Medical	65
Pediatrics	35
Obstetrics	20
Intensive care	12

For the first six months of the hospital's operation, things were rather chaotic for the administrator, Jim Jones. All of his time was occupied with the multitude of activities that go along with starting a new facility, seeing that malfunctioning equipment is repaired, arranging for new staff to be hired and trained, establishing procedures and schedules, making necessary purchasing decisions, and attending endless conferences and meetings.

All during this period, Mr. Jones had been getting some rather disturbing reports from his controller, Bob Cash, regarding Community Hospital's financial situation. But he decided that these financial matters would simply have to wait until things had settled down.

Finally, in April, Mr. Jones asked Mr. Cash to prepare a comprehensive report on the hospital's financial position and to make a presentation to himself and his new assistant administrator, Tim Newman, who had recently received a degree in hospital administration.

In his report, Mr. Cash stated: "As you both know, we have been running at an operating cash deficit since we opened last October. We expected, of course, to be losing money at the start until we were able to establish ourselves in the community and draw in patients. We certainly were right. During our first month, we lost almost $221,000. Last month, in March, we lost $58,000.

"The reason, of course, is pretty straightforward. Our income is directly related to our patient load. On the other hand, our expenses are fixed and are running at about $235,000 a month for salaries and wages, $75,000 a month for supplies

---

* Reprinted with permission from *Hospital Cost Containment Through Operations Management*, published by the American Hospital Association. Copyright 1980.

and equipment, and another $10,000 a month in interest charges. Our accumulated operating deficit for the six months we've been here totals $715,000, which we've covered with our bank line of credit. I suppose we can continue to borrow for another couple of months, but after that I don't know what we're going to do."

Mr. Jones replied, "As you said, Bob, we did expect to be losing money in the beginning, but I never expected the loss to go on for six months or to accumulate to almost three-quarters of a million dollars. Well, at least last month was a lot better than the first month. Do you have any figures showing the month-to-month trend?"

Bob Cash laid the following worksheet on the table:

Community Hospital's six-month operating statement, October 1979–March 1980 ($000)

	1979			1980			
	October	November	December	January	February	March	Total
Income	$ 101	$ 163	$ 199	$ 235	$ 245	$ 262	$ 1,205
Expenses (excluding interest)							
Salaries, wages	232	233	239	235	236	236	1,410
Supplies, others	80	73	74	75	73	75	450
Total	312	306	313	310	309	310	1,860
Interest	10	10	10	10	10	10	60
Operating loss	$(221)	$(153)	$(124)	$(85)	$(74)	$(58)	$(715)
Average daily census	42	68	83	98	102	109	
Occupancy	24%	38%	47%	55%	58%	62%	

QUESTIONS

1. Evaluate the situation at Community Hospital with respect to trends in daily census, occupancy rate, and income.
2. Has there been any change in revenue per patient-day over the six-month period (assuming a 30-day month)?
3. At what capacity level will the hospital achieve breakeven?
4. What questions might one raise about the constant level of salaries and supplies relative to past and future operations?

SELECTED BIBLIOGRAPHY

Belt, Bill "Integrating Capacity Planning and Control." *Production and Inventory Management,* vol. 17, no. 1 (First quarter 1976), pp. 9–25.

Berry, William L.; Vollmann, Thomas E.; and Whybark, D. Clay *Master Production Scheduling.* American Production and Inventory Control Society, Inc., 1979.

Carroll, Thomas M., and Dean, Robert D. "A Bayesian Approach to Plant Location Decisions." *Decision Sciences,* vol. 11, no. 1 (January 1980), p. 87.

Coyle, John J., and Bardi, Edward J. *The Management of Logistics,* 2d ed. St. Paul: The West Publishing Company, 1980, pp. 294–98.

Graziano, Vincent J. "Production Capacity Planning—Long Term." *Production and Inventory Management,* vol. 15, no. 2 (Second Quarter 1974), pp. 66–80.

Plossl, George W., and Wight, Oliver W. "Capacity Planning and Control." *Production and Inventory Management* (Third Quarter 1973), pp. 31–67.

Shycon, Harvey N. "Site Location Analysis, Cost and Customer Service Consideration." Proceedings of the Seventeenth Annual International Conference, American Production and Inventory Control Society, 1974, pp. 335–47.

Skinner, Wickham. "The Focused Factory." *Harvard Business Reveiw* (May–June 1974), pp. 113–21.

Wheelwright, Stephen C., ed. *Capacity Planning and Facilities Choice: Course Module.* Boston: Harvard Business School, 1979.

Chapter

7

LINEAR PROGRAMMING

Linear Programming refers to several related mathematical techniques that are used to allocate limited resources among competing demands in an optimal way. LP is the most popular of the approaches falling under the general heading of mathematical optimization techniques,[1] and, as will become apparent in subsequent chapters, it has been applied to a myriad of production management problems.[2] In this chapter, we shall discuss the simplex method (which can solve any type of linear programming problem) and the graphical, transportation, and assignment methods (which are useful in dealing with certain special cases). In addition to illustrating how linear programming methods lead to an optimum solution for a given problem, we will discuss shadow prices and some of the other valuable "free information" provided by the simplex method.

THE LINEAR PROGRAMMING MODEL

The linear programming problem entails an optimizing process in which nonnegative values for a set of decision variables $X_1, X_2 \ldots X_n$ are selected so as to maximize (or minimize) an objective function in the form

$$\text{Maximize (minimize) } Z = C_1 X_1 + C_2 X_2 + \ldots + C_n X_n$$

subject to resource constraints in the form

---

[1] Dynamic programming and nonlinear programming are two other well known (but generally more complicated) forms of optimization techniques.

[2] See Exhibit 7.21 for a summary of uses.

$$A_{11} X_1 + A_{12} X_2 + \ldots + A_{1n} X_n \leq B_1$$
$$A_{21} X_1 + A_{22} X_2 + \ldots + A_{2n} X_n \leq B_2$$
$$\cdot$$
$$\cdot$$
$$\cdot$$
$$A_{m1} X_1 + A_{m2} X_2 + \ldots + A_{mn} X_n \leq B_m$$

where C_j, A_{ij}, and B_i are given constants.

Depending upon the problem, the constraints may also be stated with equal-to signs ($=$) or greater-than-or-equal-to signs ($\geq$).

For linear programming to be applicable, the following conditions must exist.

1. The objective function and each constraint equation must be linear. This excludes exponents and cross products in the problem statement and implies proportionality; for example, if it takes three people to produce one unit, it takes six people to produce two in the same time.
2. The constants must be known and assumed to be deterministic. In other words, the probability associated with the occurrence of any C_j, A_{ij}, and B_i value is presumed to be 1.0.
3. The decision variables must be divisible; that is, a feasible solution would permit half a unit of X_1, a quarter unit of X_2, and so forth to be produced. (This obviously would eliminate such situations as scheduling air flights, since sending up half an airplane is not possible.)[3]

GRAPHICAL LINEAR PROGRAMMING

Though limited in application to problems involving two decision variables (or three variables for three-dimensional graphing), graphical linear programming provides a quick insight into the nature of linear programming and illustrates what takes place in the general simplex method described later.

We will describe the steps involved in the graphical method in the context of a sample problem, that of the Puck and Pawn Company, which manufactures hockey sticks and chess sets. Each hockey stick yields an incremental profit of $2 and each chess set an incremental profit of $4. A hockey stick requires four hours of processing at machine center A and two hours at machine center B. A chess set requires six hours at machine center A, six hours at machine center B, and one hour at machine center C. Machine center A has a maximum of 120 hours of available capacity per day, machine center B has 72 hours, and machine center C has 10 hours.

If the company wishes to maximize profit, how many hockey sticks and chess sets should be produced per day?

[3] In such situations, the technique of integer programming, yielding only whole numbers in its solution, is often applied.

1. *Formulate the problem in mathematical terms.* If H is the number of hockey sticks and C is the number of chess sets, the objective function may be stated as follows:

$$\text{Maximize } Z = \$2H + \$4C \text{ (profit)}$$

The maximization will be subject to the following constraints:

$$4H + 6C \leq 120 \text{ (machine center A)}$$
$$2H + 6C \leq 72 \text{ (machine center B)}$$
$$1C \leq 10 \text{ (machine center C)}$$
$$H, C \geq 0 \text{ (nonnegativity requirement)}$$

2. *Plot constraint equations.* The constraint equations are easily plotted by letting one variable equal zero and solving for the axis intercept of the other. (The inequality portions of the restrictions are disregarded for this step.) For the machine center A constraint equation, then, when $H = 0$, $C = 20$, and when $C = 0$, $H = 30$. For the machine center B constraint equation, when $H = 0$, $C = 12$, and when $C = 0$, $H = 36$. For the machine center C constraint equation, $C = 10$ for all values of H. These lines are graphed in Exhibit 7.1.

EXHIBIT 7.1
Graph of hockey stick and chess set problem

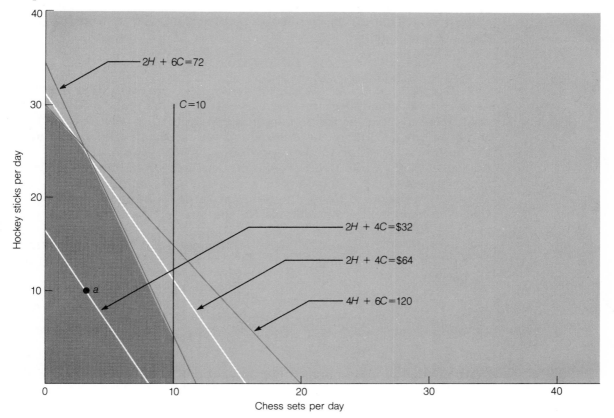

3. Determine the area of feasibility. The direction of inequality signs in each constraint determines the area wherein a feasible solution will be found. In this case, all inequalities are of the less-than-or-equal-to variety, which means that it would be impossible to produce any combination of products that would lie to the right of any constraint line on the graph. The region of feasible solutions is shaded on the graph and forms a convex polygon. A convex polygon exists when a line drawn between any two points in the polygon stays within the boundaries of that polygon. If this condition of convexity does not exist, the problem is either incorrectly set up or not amenable to linear programming.

4. Plot the objective function. The objective function may be plotted by assuming some arbitrary total profit figure and then solving for the axis coordinates, as was done for the constraint equations. Another term for the objective function, when used in this context, is the *iso-profit* or *equal contribution line,* because it shows all possible production combinations for any given profit figure. For example, from the light line closest to the origin on the graph, we can determine all possible combinations of hockey sticks and chess sets that will yield \$32 by picking a point on the line and reading the number of each product that can be made at that point The combination yielding \$32 at point *a* would be 10 hockey sticks and 3 chess sets. This can be verified by substituting $H = 10$ and $C = 3$ in the objective function:

$$\$2(10) + \$4(3) = \$20 + \$12 = \$32$$

5. Find the optimum point. It can be shown mathematically that the optimum combination of decision variables will always be found at an extreme point (corner point) of the convex polygon. In Exhibit 7.1 there are four corner points (excluding the origin), and we can determine which one is the optimum by either of two approaches. The first approach is to find the values of the various corner solutions algebraically. This entails simultaneously solving the equations of various pairs of intersecting lines and substituting the quantities of the resultant variables in the objective function. For example, the calculations for the intersection of $2H + 6C = 72$ and $C = 10$ would be as follows.

Substituting $C = 10$ in $2H + 6C = 72$ gives $2H + 6(10) = 72$, $2H = 12$, or $H = 6$. Substituting $H = 6$ and $C = 10$ in the objective function, we get:

$$\begin{aligned}
\text{Profit} &= \$2H + \$4C \\
&= \$2(6) + \$4(10) \\
&= \$12 + \$40 \\
&= \$52
\end{aligned}$$

A variation of this approach is to read the *H* and *C* quantities directly from the graph and substitute these quantities into the objective function, as shown in the previous calculation. The drawback in this approach is that in problems with a large number of constraint equations, there will be many possible points to evaluate, and the procedure of testing each one mathematically is somewhat inefficient.

The second and generally preferred approach entails using the objective function or iso-profit line directly to find the optimum point. The procedure involves simply drawing a straight line *parallel* to any arbitrarily selected initial iso-profit line so that the iso-profit line is farthest from the origin of the graph. (In cost minimization problems, the objective would be to draw the line through the point closest to the origin.) In Exhibit 7.1, the light line labeled $2H + $4C = $64 intersects the most extreme point. Note that the initial arbitrarily selected iso-profit line is necessary in order to display the slope[4] of the objective function for the particular problem. This is important since a different objective function (try profit $= 3H + 3C$) might indicate that some other point is farthest from the origin. Given that $2H + $4C = $64 is optimum, the amount of each variable to produce can be read from the graph: 24 hockey sticks and 4 chess sets. No other combination of the products will yield a greater profit.

THE SIMPLEX METHOD

The simplex method[5] is an algebraic procedure that, through a series of repetitive operations, progressively approaches an optimum solution. Theoretically, the simplex method can solve a problem consisting of any number of variables and constraints, although for problems containing more than, say, four variables or four constraint equations, the actual calculations are best left to the computer. In this regard, however, it is well worth the effort to go through the simplex method manually a few times in order to fully understand and utilize the data provided by a computer.

Six-step solution procedure

There are a number of technical steps in the simplex method, and each one will be described in detail and summarized at the end of the section. We will use the hockey stick and chess set problem to demonstrate the procedure involved.

Step 1: Problem formulation. Recall that we had

$$\text{Maximize } Z = \$2H + \$4C \text{ (profit)}$$

subject to

$$4H + 6C \le 120 \text{ (machine center A constraint)}$$
$$2H + 6C \le 72 \text{ (machine center B constraint)}$$

---

[4] The slope of the objective function is -2. If

$p = \text{profit},$
$p = \$2H + \$4C; \$2H = p - \$4C; H = p/2 - 2C.$ Thus the slope is -2.

[5] *Simplex* does not mean "simple"; it is a term used in n-space geometry.

$$1C \leq 10 \text{ (machine center C constraint)}$$
$$H, C \geq 0 \text{ (nonnegativity requirement)}$$

Step 2: Set up initial tableau with slack variables in solution. To use the simplex method requires two major adjustments to the problem as stated: *(a)* the introduction of slack variables and *(b)* the establishment of a solution table or tableau.

Introduce slack variables. Each constraint equation is expanded to include a slack variable. A slack variable, which may be thought of as an idle resource in a practical sense, computationally represents the amount required to make one side of a constraint equation equal to the other—in other words, to convert the inequalities to equalities. For our problem, we need three slack variables: S_1 for the first constraint equation, S_2 for the second, and S_3 for the third.

The constraint equations appear as follows.

$$4H + 6C + 1S_1 = 120$$
$$2H + 6C + 1S_2 = 72$$
$$1C + 1S_3 = 10$$

So that all variables are represented in each equation, each slack variable not originally associated with a constraint equation is given a zero coefficient and added to that equation. Adjusting the system of equations in this way gives

$$4H + 6C + 1S_1 + 0S_2 + 0S_3 = 120$$
$$2H + 6C + 0S_1 + 1S_2 + 0S_3 = 72$$
$$0H + 1C + 0S_1 + 0S_2 + 1S_3 = 10$$

Note that the variable H, with a zero coefficient, is entered in the third equation to ensure that it also will be represented in all equations. Likewise, the objective function reflects the addition of slack variables, but since they yield no profit, their coefficient is $0:

$$Z = \$2H + \$4C + \$0S_1 + \$0S_2 + \$0S_3$$

Construct initial tableau (see Exhibit 7.2). A tableau is a convenient way of setting up the problem for simplex computation. A tableau provides the following information.

1. The variables which are in the solution at that point.
2. The profit associated with the solution.
3. The variable (if any) that will add most to profit if brought into the solution.
4. The amount of reduction in the variables in the solution which results from introducing one unit of each variable. This amount is termed the *substitution rate.*
5. The worth of an additional unit (e.g., hour) of resource capacity. This is referred to as a *shadow price.*

The first four features will be discussed in reference to the first tableau; the last one will be considered later.

The top row of Exhibit 7.2 contains the C_j's, or the contribution to total profit associated with the production of one unit of each alternative product. This row is a direct restatement of the coefficients of the variables in the objective function, and therefore remains the same for all subsequent tableaus. The first column, headed by C_j, merely lists, for convenience, the profit per unit of the variables included in the solution at any stage of the problem.

EXHIBIT 7.2
Initial tableau of the hockey stick and chess set problem

C_j	C_j row	$2	$4	$0	$0	$0	
Column	Solution mix	H	C	S_1	S_2	S_3	Quantity
$0	S_1	4	6	1	0	0	120
$0	S_2	2	6	0	1	0	72
$0	S_3	0	1	0	0	1	10 ←
	Z_j	$0	$0	$0	$0	$0	$0
	$C_j - Z_j$	$2	$4	$0	$0	$0	
			↑				

The variables chosen for the first tableau are listed under "solution mix." As can be seen, only slack variables are considered in the initial solution, and their profit coefficients are zero, which is indicated by the aforementioned C_j column.

The constraint variables are listed to the right of "solution mix," and under each one is the particular variable's coefficient in each constraint equation. That is, 4, 6, 1, 0, and 0 are the coefficients of the machine center A constraint; 2, 6, 0, 1, and 0 for machine center B; and 0, 1, 0, 0, and 1 for machine center C.

Substitution rates can be ascertained from the numbers as well. For example, consider 4, 2, and 0, listed under H in the third column. For every unit of product H introduced into the solution, four units of S_1, two units of S_2, and zero units of S_3 must be withdrawn from the solution in order to stay within the problem constraints.

The entries in the "quantity" column refer to how many units of each resource are available in each machine center. In the initial tableau, this is a restatement of the right-hand side of each constraint equation. With the exception of the value in the quantity column, the Z_j values in the second row from the bottom refer to the amount of *gross* profit that is given up by introducing one unit of that variable into the solution. The subscript j refers to the specific variable being considered. The Z_j value under the quantity column is the total profit for the solution. In the initial solution of a simplex problem, all values of Z_j will be zero because no real product is being produced (all machines are idle), and hence, there is no gross profit to be lost if they are replaced.

The bottom row of the tableau contains the *net* profit per unit, obtained by introducing one unit of a given variable into the solution. This row is designated the $C_j - Z_j$ row. The procedure for calculating Z_j and each $C_j - Z_j$ is demonstrated in Exhibit 7.3.

The initial solution to the problem is read directly from Exhibit 7.2: the company will "produce" 120 units of S_1 72 units of S_2 and 10 units of S_3. The total profit from this solution is $0. Thus, no capacity has yet been allocated and no real product produced.

EXHIBIT 7.3
Calculations of Z_j and $C_j - Z_j$

C_j H	C_j C	C_j S_1	C_j S_2	C_j S_3	C_j Quantity
$\$0 \times 4 = 0$	$\$0 \times 6 = 0$	$\$0 \times 1 = 0$	$\$0 \times 0 = 0$	$\$0 \times 0 = 0$	$\$0 \times 120$
$+$	$+$	$+$	$+$	$+$	$+$
$\$0 \times 2 = 0$	$\$0 \times 6 = 0$	$\$0 \times 0 = 0$	$\$0 \times 1 = 0$	$\$0 \times 0 = 0$	$\$0 \times 72$
$+$	$+$	$+$	$+$	$+$	$+$
$\$0 \times 0 = \underline{0}$	$\$0 \times 1 = \underline{0}$	$\$0 \times 0 = \underline{0}$	$\$0 \times 0 = \underline{0}$	$\$0 \times 1 = \underline{0}$	$\$0 \times \underline{10}$
$Z_H = \$0$	$Z_C = \$0$	$Z_{S_1} = \$0$	$Z_{S_2} = \$0$	$Z_{S_3} = \$0$	$Z_Q = \$0$

$C_j - Z_j$ calculations:
$C_H - Z_H = \$2 - 0 = \$2$
$C_C - Z_C = \$4 - 0 = \$4$
$C_{S_1} - Z_{S_1} = \$0 - 0 = \$0$
$C_{S_2} - Z_{S_2} = \$0 - 0 = \$0$
$C_{S_3} - Z_{S_3} = \$0 - 0 = \$0$

Step 3: Determine which variable to bring into solution. An improved solution is possible if there is a positive value in the $C_j - Z_j$ row. Recall that this row provides the net profit obtained by adding one unit of its associated column variable in the solution. In this example, there are two positive values to choose from: $2, associated with H, and $4, associated with C. Since our objective is to maximize profit, the logical choice is to pick the value of the largest payoff to enter the solution, so variable C will be introduced. The column associated with this variable is termed the *optimum column* and is designated by the small arrow beneath column C in Exhibit 7.2. (It should be emphasized that only one variable at a time can be added in developing each improved solution.)

Step 4: Determine which variable to replace. Given that it is desirable to introduce C into the solution, the next question is to determine which variable it will replace. To make this determination, we divide each amount in the Quantity column by the amount in the comparable row of the C column and choose the variable associated with the smallest quotient as the one to be replaced:

For the S_1 row: $120/6 = 20$
For the S_2 row: $72/6 = 12$
For the S_3 row: $10/1 = 10$

Since the smallest quotient is 10, S_3 will be replaced, and its row is identified by the small arrow to the right of the tableau in Exhibit 7.2.

This is the maximum amount of C that can be brought into the solution; that is, production of more than 10 units of C would exceed the available capacity of machine C. This can be verified mathematically by considering the constraint $C \leq 10$ and visually by examining the graphical representation of the problem in Exhibit 7.1. The graph also shows that the 20 and 12 are the C intercepts of the other two constraints, and if $C \leq 10$ were removed, the amount of C introduced could be increased by 2 units.

EXHIBIT 7.4
Calculation of new row values for entering variable

		C					
		6					
		6					
S_3	0	①	0	0	0	10	$0/1 = 0$, $1/1 = 1$, $0/1 = 0$, $0/1 = 0$, $1/1 = 1$, $10/1 = 10$
	$4						

Step 5: Calculate new row values for entering variable. The introduction of C into the solution requires that the entire S_3 row be replaced. The values for C, the replacing row, are obtained by dividing each value presently in the S_3 row by the value in column C in the same row. This value is termed the *intersectional element* since it occurs at the intersection of a row and column. This intersectional relationship is abstracted from the rest of the tableau and the necessary divisions are shown in Exhibit 7.4.

Step 6: Revise remaining rows. The new third-row values (now associated with C) are 0, 1, 0, 0, 1, and 10, which in this case are identical to those of the old third row.

The introduction of a new variable into the problem will affect the values of the remaining variables, and a second set of calculations must be performed to update the tableau. Specifically, we want to determine the effect of introducing C on the S_1 and S_2 rows. These calculations can be carried out by using what is termed the *pivot method* or by algebraic substitution. The pivot method is a more mechanical procedure and is generally used in practice, while algebraic substitution is more useful in explaining the logic of the updating process. The procedure using the pivot method to arrive at new values for S_1 and S_2 is shown in Exhibit 7.5. (In essence, the method subtracts six times row 3 from both the S_1 and S_2 rows.)

Updating by algebraic substitution entails substituting the entire equation for the entering row into each of the remaining rows and solving for the revised values for each row's variable. The procedure, summarized in Exhibit 7.6, illustrates the fact that linear programming via the simplex method is essentially the solving of a number of simultaneous equations.

Isolating the variable coefficients yields the same values for the new S_1 row as did the pivot method: 4, 0, 1, 0, −6, 60.

The results of the computations carried out in steps 3 through 6, along with the calculations of Z_j and $C_j - Z_j$ are shown in the revised tableau,

EXHIBIT 7.5
Pivot method

Old S_1 row	−	(Intersectional element of old S_2 row ×	Corresponding element of new C row)	Updated = S_1 row	Old S_2 row	−	(Intersectional element of old S_2 row ×	Corresponding element of new C row)	Updated = S_2 row
4	−	(6	× 0)	= 4	2	−	(6	× 0)	= 2
6	−	(6	× 1)	= 0	6	−	(6	× 1)	= 0
1	−	(6	× 0)	= 1	0	−	(6	× 0)	= 0
0	−	(6	× 0)	= 0	1	−	(6	× 0)	= 1
0	−	(6	× 1)	= −6	0	−	(6	× 1)	= −6
120	−	(6	× 10)	= 60	72	−	(6	× 10)	= 12

Exhibit 7.7. In mathematical programming terminology, we have completed one "iteration" of the problem.

In evaluating this solution, we note two things: the profit is \$40, but, more important, further improvement is possible since there is a positive value in the $C_j - Z_j$ row.

Second iteration. The entering variable is H since it has largest $C_j - Z_j$ amount (2). The replaced variable is S_2 since it has the smallest quotient when the Quantity column values are divided by their comparable amounts in the H column:

$$S_1 = 60/4 = 15, \; S_2 = 12/2 = 6, \; S_3 = 10/0 = \infty$$

Values of entering *(H)* row are

$$2/2 = 1, \; 0/2 = 0, \; 0/2 = 0, \; 1/2 = 1/2, \; -6/2 = -3, \; 12/2 = 6$$

Updated S_1 row from Exhibit 7.8: 0, 0, 1, −2, 6, 36.
Updated C row from Exhibit 7.8: 0, 1, 0, 0, 1, 10. Using the result from Exhibit 7.8, we obtain the third tableau: Exhibit 7.9.

EXHIBIT 7.6
Algebraic substitution

To find new values for S_1,
1. Reconstruct old S_1 row as a constraint with slack variables added (from first tableau):
$$4H + 6C + 1S_1 + 0S_2 + 0S_3 = 120$$
2. Write entering row as a constraint with slack variables added (these are the values computed in Exhibit 7.4):
$$0H + C + 0S_1 + 0S_2 + 1S_3 = 10$$
3. Rearrange entering row in terms of C, the entering variable:
$$C = 10 - S_3$$
4. Substitute $10 - S_3$ for C in the first equation (the old S_1 row) and solve for each variable coefficient:
$$4H + 6(10 - S_3) + 1S_1 = 120$$
$$4H + 60 - 6S_3 + 1S_1 = 120$$
$$4H + 1S_1 - 6S_3 = 120 - 60$$
$$4H + 1S_1 - 6S_3 = 60$$

or

$$4H + 0C + 1S_1 + 0S_2 - 6S_3 = 60$$

EXHIBIT 7.7
Second tableau of the hockey stick and chess set problem

C_j		$2	$4	$0	$0	$0	
	Solution mix	H	C	S_1	S_2	S_3	Quantity
$0	S_1	4	0	1	0	-6	60
$0	S_2	2	0	0	1	-6	12 ←
$4	C	0	1	0	0	1	10
	Z_j	$0	$4	$0	$0	$ 4	$40
	$C_j - Z_j$	$2	$0	$0	$0	$-4	
		↑					

Examination of the third tableau indicates that further improvement is possible by introducing the maximum amount of S_3 that is technically feasible. As can be seen below the tableau, the maximum amount of S_3 that can be brought into the solution is 6 units because of the limited supply of S_1.

EXHIBIT 7.8
Updating S_1 and C rows

Old S_1 row	$-$	(Intersectional element of old S_1 row $\times$ Corresponding element in new H row)	New S_1 = row	Old C row	$-$	(Intersectional element of old C row $\times$ Corresponding element of new H row)	New C = row
4	$-$	(4 $\times$ 1)	= 0	0	$-$	(0 $\times$ 1)	= 0
0	$-$	(4 $\times$ 0)	= 0	1	$-$	(0 $\times$ 0)	= 1
1	$-$	(4 $\times$ 0)	= 1	0	$-$	(0 $\times$ 0)	= 0
0	$-$	(4 $\times$ ½)	= -2	0	$-$	(0 $\times$ ½)	= 0
-6	$-$	(4 $\times -3$)	= 6	1	$-$	(0 $\times -3$)	= 1
60	$-$	(4 $\times$ 6)	= 36	10	$-$	(0 $\times$ 6)	= 10

EXHIBIT 7.9
Third tableau of hockey stick and chess set problem

C_j		$2	$4	$0	$0	$0	
	Solution mix	H	C	S_1	S_2	S_3	Quantity
$0	S_1	0	0	1	-2	6	36 ←
$2	H	1	0	0	½	-3	6
$4	C	0	1	0	0	1	10
	Z_j	$2	$4	$0	$ 1	$-2	$52
	$C_j - Z_j$	$0	$0	$0	$-1	$ 2	
						↑	

$$36/6 = 6$$
$$6/-3 = -2 \text{ (negative)}[6]$$
$$10/1 = 10$$

---

[6] Since there are three constraint equations, there must be three variables with nonnegative values in the solution. Therefore a negative amount cannot be considered for introduction into the solution.

Replacing S_1 by S_3 and performing the updating operations yields the tableau shown in Exhibit 7.10. As can be seen from $C_j - Z_j$ row of this tableau, no further improvement is possible, and an optimum solution ($H = 24$, $C = 4$) has been achieved in three iterations.

EXHIBIT 7.10
Fourth tableau of the hockey stick and chess set problem (optimum solution)

C_j		$2	$4	$0	$0	$0	
	Solution mix	H	C	S_1	S_2	S_3	Quantity
$0	S_3	0	0	⅙	$-\frac{1}{3}$	1	6
$2	H	1	0	½	$-\frac{1}{2}$	0	24
$4	C	0	1	$-\frac{1}{6}$	⅓	0	4
	Z_j	$2	$4	$ ⅓	$ ⅓	$0	$64
	$C_j - Z_j$	$0	$0	$$-\frac{1}{3}$$	$$-\frac{1}{3}$$	$0	

Summary of steps in the simplex method

1. Formulate problem in terms of an objective function and a set of constraints.
2. Set up initial tableau with slack variables in the solution mix and calculate the Z_j and $C_j - Z_j$ rows.
3. Determine which variable to bring into solution (largest $C_j - Z_j$ value).
4. Determine which variable to replace (smallest ratio of quantity column to its comparable value in the optimum column).
5. Calculate new row values for entering variable and insert into new tableau (row to be replaced plus intersectional element).
6. Update remaining rows and enter into new tableau; compute new Z_j and $C_j - Z_j$ rows (old row minus intersectional element of old row times corresponding element in new row). If no positive $C_j - Z_j$ value is found, solution is optimum. If there is a positive value of $C_j - Z_j$, repeat steps 3 to 6.

Minimization problems. An identical procedure is followed for solving minimization problems. Since the objective is to minimize rather than maximize, a negative $C_j - Z_j$ value indicates potential improvement; therefore the variable associated with the largest negative $C_j - Z_j$ value would be brought into solution first. Additional variables must be brought in to set up such problems, however, since minimization problems include greater-than-or-equal-to constraints, which must be treated differently from less-than-or-equal-to constraints, which typify maximization problems. (See section dealing with greater-than-or-equal-to and equal-to constraints in the simplex, later in this chapter.)

Search path followed by the simplex method

As mentioned in the description of the graphical solution to the sample problem, the optimum solution to linear programming problems is obtained by finding the extreme corner point. The simplex procedure always starts at a feasible solution, searches for the most profitable direction to follow, and hops from point to point of intersecting lines (or planes in multidimensional space). The evaluation of a corner point takes one iteration, and

EXHIBIT 7.11
**Graph of hockey
stick and chess
set problem
showing succes-
sive corner eval-
uations**

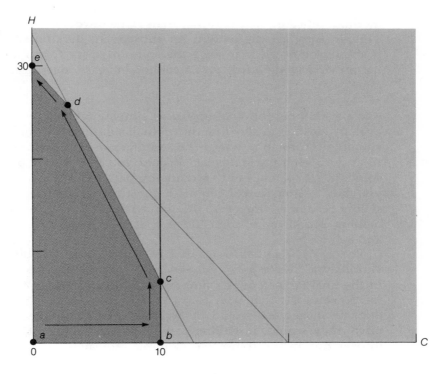

when the furthermost point is reached (in the case of profit maximization
problems as shown by the next point's decreasing profit), the solution is
complete.

Consider the graph of the example problem shown in Exhibit 7.11,
where the simplex method began at point a (profit = $0). In the first
iteration, 10 units of C were introduced at point b (profit = $40). In the
second iteration, 6 units of H were introduced at point c (profit = $52).
The third iteration left the problem at point d (profit = $64), which is
optimum. Note that the solution procedure did not calculate profit for
all corners of this problem. It did, however, *look ahead*—by virtue of the
$C_j - Z_j$ calculations—to see if further improvement was possible by moving
to another point (point e), but no improvement was indicated by such a
change. These two characteristics—evaluating corner points and looking
ahead for improvements—are the essential features of the simplex method.

Another feature that is also characteristic of the basic simplex method
is that it does not necessarily converge on the optimum point by the
shortest route around the feasible area. Reference to the graph will show
that if the solution procedure had proceeded along the path $a \longrightarrow e \longrightarrow$
d, an optimum would have been reached in two iterations rather than
three.

The reason why this route was not followed was that the profit per
chess set was higher than for a hockey stick, and therefore, the simplex

method indicated that C, rather than H, be introduced in the first iteration. This, in turn, set the pattern for subsequent iterations to points c and d. It should be noted that since the solution space forms a convex polygon (as previously defined), profit cannot increase, decrease, and then again increase.

Shadow prices and breaking constraints (ranging)

By examining the final (optimal) simplex tableau, we can learn a great deal. In addition to showing the optimal solution, the final tableau provides valuable information about the resources used. Specifically, it enables us to answer such questions as "Would you like to buy any more of a resource?" "If so, what price would you pay?" and "How many units would you buy at that price?" Similar questions can be answered relative to selling resources, for even though a resource may be currently used in making products, at some price it is worthwhile to forego production and sell it.

The $C_j - Z_j$ values associated with the slack variables are referred to variously as *shadow prices, marginal values, incremental values,* or *break-even prices.* In the final tableau of the simplex example in Exhibit 7.10, shadow prices for S_1 were \$1/3 or 33¢, $S_2 - $\$1/3 or 33¢, and $S_3 - $\$0. Above each price, management would be willing to sell resources, and below each price, they would be willing to buy. Let us take another look at all the information in the completed example tableau.

Referring to Exhibit 7.10, note that the solution is $H = 24$, $C = 4$, $S_1 = 0$, $S_2 = 0$, $S_3 = 6$. An identity column (having entries of zero and the number 1), has that variable at the top of the column in solution in the row where the 1 is. Since S_1 and S_2 do not have identity columns below, they are not in solution and therefore equal to zero.

To answer the question: Would you buy any S_1? S_1 is a resource which the shadow price shows as having a value of one third of a dollar. Therefore, you would buy S_1 if the price is less than \$1/3.

How many units would you buy?

Note that equations can be written vertically in this matrix as well as horizontally. That is,

$$S_1 = \frac{1}{6}S_3 + \frac{1}{2}H - \frac{1}{6}C$$

Therefore, if we add one unit of S_1, we gain $\frac{1}{6}S_3$, we gain $\frac{1}{2}H$, but we *lose* $\frac{1}{6}C$. This relationship is termed the substitution rate, as previously mentioned. The number of S_1 we can bring in is limited by the number of C's we have to give up. Since there are 4 C, giving them up at the rate of $\frac{1}{6}$ at a time means we can buy $4/\frac{1}{6} = 24$ units of S_1. At that point we have no more C (but we have gained $12H$ and $4S_3$).

Would you buy S_2? Yes, if the price is less than \$1/3 or 33¢.

How many would you buy? Since

$$S_2 = -\frac{1}{3}S_3 - \frac{1}{2}H + \frac{1}{3}C$$

we give up $\frac{1}{3}S_3$ and $\frac{1}{2}H$ for each S_2 we buy. Our limit, then, is whichever one we run out of first. We have $6S_3$, so $6/\frac{1}{3} = 18$. We have $24H$, so $24/\frac{1}{2} = 48$. We would therefore buy 18 units of S_2 at a price less than 33¢.

Would you buy S_3? Yes, if the price is less than 0. (We would be paid to haul it away.)

How many would you buy? Since there are no limiting negative numbers, the answer is infinity. (Which explains why we create so much garbage and the collection agency has an unlimited desire to collect it when being paid.)

The counter question to those just covered: Would you sell resource S_1? Yes, if the price is greater than $\$\frac{1}{3}$.

How many would you sell? The same reasoning applies as in buying, except the signs change. For example.

$$S_1 = \frac{1}{6}S_3 + \frac{1}{2}H - \frac{1}{6}C$$

If we subtract S_1, then we subtract $\frac{1}{6}S_3$, we subtract $\frac{1}{2}H$, and we *add* a $\frac{1}{6}C$ (since we subtract a negative $\frac{1}{6}C$). Our limit in selling is whichever we run out of first—giving up $\frac{1}{6}S_3$ for each S_1 is $6/\frac{1}{6} = 36$; giving up $\frac{1}{2}H$ for each S_1 is $24/\frac{1}{2} = 48$. Our limit, therefore, is selling a maximum of 36 S_1.

In selling S_2, the signs change so we would gain $\frac{1}{3}S_3$ and $\frac{1}{2}H$ but lose $\frac{1}{3}C$. We have 4 C so giving them up $\frac{1}{3}$ at a time is $4/\frac{1}{3} = 12$. Therefore, we would sell 12 S_2 if the price was greater than $\$\frac{1}{3}$.

S_3 has a shadow price of 0, and we have 6 units on hand. We would therefore be willing to sell the 6 units at any positive price.

Exhibit 7.12 shows another completed tableau without some unneeded numbers.

EXHIBIT 7.12
Final tableau for buy and sell questions

x	y	S_1	S_2	S_3	
0	1	$\frac{1}{2}$	0	$-\frac{1}{2}$	50
0	0	-5	1	2	100
1	0	0	0	1	300
		$-\$1.50$	0	$-\$2.50$	

The questions and answers concerning buying and selling are as follows:

Would you buy S_1? Yes, if price $< \$1.50$.
  How many would you buy? $100/5 = 20$ units
Would you buy S_2? Yes, if price < 0.
  How many would you buy? ∞
Would you buy S_3? Yes if price $< \$2.50$.
  How many would you buy? $50/\frac{1}{2} = 100$

Would you sell S_1? Yes, if price > \$1.50.
How many would you sell? 50/½ = 100
Would you sell S_2? Yes, if price > 0.
How many would you sell? All we have, which is 100.
Would you sell S_3? Yes, if price > \$2.50.

How many would you sell? 100/2 = 50 or $\dfrac{300}{1}$ = 300. Sell 50.

Dealing with greater-than-or-equal-to and equal-to constraints in the simplex.

Greater-than-or-equal-to constraints (≥) and equal-to constraints (=) must be handled somewhat differently from the less-than-or-equal-to constraints (≤) in setting up and solving simplex problems.

Recall that with ≤ constraints, we added a slack variable to convert the inequality to an equality. For example, in converting the inequality $4H + 6C \leq 120$ to an equality, we added S_1, giving us $4H + 6C + S_1 = 120$. Now suppose that the sign was changed to a greater-than-or-equal-to sign yielding $4H + 6C \geq 120$. Initially, one would surmise that subtracting a slack variable would convert this to an equality and it would be written as $4H + 6C - 1S_1 = 120$. Unfortunately, this adjustment would lead to difficulties in the simplex method for the reason that the initial simplex solution starts with fictitious variables and hence a negative value ($-1S_1$) would be in the solution—a condition not permitted in linear programming. To overcome this problem, the simplex procedure requires that a different type of variable—an artificial variable—be added to each equal-to- or greater-than-equation. An artificial variable may be thought of as representing a fictitious product having a very high cost, which, though permitted in the initial solution to a simplex problem, would never appear in the final solution. Defining A as the artificial variable, the constraint given above would now appear as

$$4H + 6C - 1S_1 + 1A_1 = 120$$

And assuming that we were minimizing cost in the objective function rather than maximizing profit, it would appear as

$$\$2H + \$4C + \$0S_1 + \$MA_1$$

where \$$M$ is assumed to be a very large cost, for example, \$1 million.[7] (Note also that S_1 is added to the objective function even though it is negative in the constraint equation.)

An artificial variable must also be included in constraints with equality signs. For example, if $4H + 6C = 120$, this must be changed to $4H + 6C + 1A_1 = 120$ to satisfy the simplex requirement that each constraint equation have a nonnegative variable in the initial solution. It would be reflected

---

[7] When a ≥ or = constraint is encountered in a maximization problem, an artificial variable is assumed to have a large negative profit coefficient in the *objective function* to assure that it would not appear in the final solution.

in the objective function, again as MA_1, but would have no slack variable accompanying it in the constraint equation.

Procedurally, where such constraints exist, the simplex method starts with artificial variables in the initial solution but otherwise treats them the same as it would real or slack variables.

TRANSPORTATION METHOD

The transportation method is a simplified special case of the simplex method. It gets its name from its application to problems involving transporting products from several sources to several destinations.[8] The two common objectives of such problems are (1) minimize the cost of shipping n units to m destinations or (2) maximize the profit of shipping n units to m destinations. There are three general steps in solving transportation problems, and we will discuss each one in the context of a simple example.

Suppose the Puck and Pawn Company has four factories supplying four warehouses and its management wants to determine the minimum-cost shipping schedule for its monthly output of chess sets. Factory supply, warehouse demands, and shipping costs per case of chess sets are as shown in Exhibit 7.13.

EXHIBIT 7.13
Data for chess set transportation problem

					Shipping costs per case (in $)			
Factory	Supply	Warehouse	Demand	From	To E	To F	To G	To H
A	15	E	10	A	25	35	36	60
B	6	F	12	B	55	30	45	38
C	14	G	15	C	40	50	26	65
D	11	H	9	D	60	40	66	27

Step 1: Set up transportation matrix

The transportation matrix for this example appears in Exhibit 7.14, where supply availability at each factory is shown in the far right-hand column and the warehouse demands are shown in the bottom row. The unit shipping costs are shown in the small boxes within the cells. It is important at this step to make sure that the total supply availabilities and total demand requirements are equal. In this case they are both the same, 46 units, but quite often there is an excess supply or demand. In such situations, in order for the transportation method to work, a "dummy" warehouse or factory must be added. Procedurally, this entails the insertion of an extra row (for an additional factory) or an extra column (for an additional warehouse). The amount of supply or demand required by the dummy will be equal to the difference between the row and column totals. For example, the problem below might be restated to indicate a total

---

[8] For other applications, see Exhibit 7.21.

EXHIBIT 7.14
Transportation matrix for chess set problem

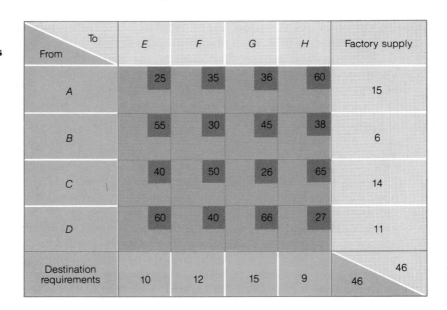

From \ To	E	F	G	H	Factory supply
A	25	35	36	60	15
B	55	30	45	38	6
C	40	50	26	65	14
D	60	40	66	27	11
Destination requirements	10	12	15	9	46 / 46

demand of 36 cases, and therefore, a new column would be inserted with a demand of 10 cases to bring the total up to 46 cases. The cost figures in each cell of the dummy row would be set at zero, and therefore, any units "sent" there would not incur a transportation cost. Theoretically, this adjustment is equivalent to the simplex procedure of inserting a slack variable in a constraint inequality to convert it to an equation, and, as in the simplex, the cost of the dummy would be zero in the objective function.

Step 2: Make initial allocations

Initial allocation entails assigning numbers to cells in order to satisfy supply and demand constraints. There are several methods for carrying this out, and we shall describe two: the northwest-corner method and Vogel's approximation method (VAM).

Northwest-corner method of allocation. The northwest-corner method, as the name implies, begins allocation by starting at the northwest corner of the matrix and assigning as much as possible to cells in the first row.[9] The procedure is then repeated for the second row, third row, and so on, until all row and column requirements are met. Exhibit 7.15 shows a northwest-corner solution. (Cell *A-E* was assigned first, *A-F* second, *B-F* third, and so forth.)

Inspection of Exhibit 7.15 indicates some high-cost cells were assigned and some low-cost cells bypassed by using the northwest-corner method.

[9] It is important that as many units as possible be assigned to each cell in order to meet the requirements of having no more than $m + n - 1$ filled cells, where m = number of rows and n = number of columns. If more than this number is used, the problem will have excess routes and be difficult to optimize.

EXHIBIT 7.15
Northwest corner assignment

From / To	E	F	G	H	Factory supply
A	25 10	35 5	36	60	15
B	55	30 6	45	38	6
C	40	50 1	26 13	65	14
D	60	40	66 2	27 9	11
Destination requirements	10	12	15	9	46 / 46

Total cost = 10($25) + 5($35) + 6($30) + 1($50) + 13($26) + 2($66)
+ 9($27) = $1,368

Indeed, this is to be expected since this method ignores costs in favor of following an easily programmable allocation algorithm.[10]

VAM method of allocation. The VAM method, in contrast to the northwest corner method, uses the cost figures as additional information in making an initial allocation and generally provides an optimum or near optimum initial solution.[11] The procedure in using VAM is as follows.

1. For each row and column, find and list the differences between the two lowest-cost cells. (Include the costs associated with any dummy row or column in finding these differences.)
2. Choose the largest difference of a row or column.
3. Assign the maximum possible amount to the lowest cost cell in the selected row or column. By definition, this allocation will satisfy a row or column requirement.[12] If a tie exists in these different figures (or VAM numbers), allocate to the lowest cost cell in any of the tied rows or columns. If the lowest costs are also tied, allocate to one of them arbitrarily.
4. Repeat 1 through 3, eliminating from consideration those rows or columns that have been satisfied, until all supply and demand requirements are met.

[10] For this reason, the northwest-corner method is easy to computerize but is generally inefficient for manual calculation.

[11] It has been reported that VAM will yield an optimum solution about 80 percent of the time. (Those instances where it doesn't are typically encountered on examinations.)

[12] When a row *and* a column are satisfied by a single allocation, the problem is degenerate, and adjustments must be made to the matrix to evaluate the solutions. These adjustments will be discussed later under "degeneracy."

VAM will now be applied to the sample problem above, and Exhibit 7.16 shows the data. Note that rows and columns have been extended to show VAM numbers—that is, the difference between the two lowest-cost cells in each row and column. The first allocation, to cell *A-E*, was made on the basis of the VAM number 15, shown in the first added row under column *E*. The VAM numbers were then recalculated, and the second allocation, to cell *C-G*, was made on the basis of VAM number 24 in the second added column. The third allocation, to cell *D-H*, was made on the basis of VAM number 13 in the third added column. The fourth allocation, to cell *D-F*, was made on the basis of VAM number 26 in the fourth added column. The fifth allocation, to cell *B-F*, was made on the basis of VAM number 15 in the fifth added column. The sixth allocation, to *A-F*, was made on the basis of VAM number 1 in the sixth added column. The final allocation, to cell *A-G*, was made on the basis of inspection; there were no other cells available, and one unit was required to satisfy the remaining supply and demand requirements.

EXHIBIT 7.16
VAM assignment of chess set problem

To \ From	E	F	G	H	Factory supply	VAM numbers trial					
						1	2	3	4	5	6
A	25 / 10	35 / 4	36 / 1	60	15	10	1	1	1	1	1
B	55	30 / 6	45	38	6	8	8	8	15	15	--
C	40	50	26 / 14	65	14	14	24	--	--	--	--
D	60	40 / 2	66	27 / 9	11	13	13	13	26	--	--
Destination requirements	10	12	15	9	46 / 46						

VAM numbers trial

E	F	G	H
15	5	10	11
--	5	10	11
--	5	9	11
--	5	9	--
--	--	--	--

Total cost = 10($25) + 4($35) + 1($36) + 6($30) + 14($26) + 2($40) + 9($27) = $1,293

In comparing the two approaches—the northwest-corner method and VAM—we find that VAM yields a lower cost initial solution to the problem. The total cost for the VAM solution is $1,293, which is $75 less than the northwest-corner solution.

Logic of the VAM method. Each VAM number may be thought of as a penalty cost incurred from selecting some cell other than the lowest cost cell for allocation. For example, the VAM number 10 in the first added column may be interpreted as the penalty cost of selecting *A-F* rather than *A-E*. Likewise, VAM number 15 in the first added row represents the penalty cost of selecting *C-E* over *A-E.* The same logic may be applied to selecting the greatest difference (largest VAM number) from the entire matrix as the basis for allocation. That is, if the largest penalty cost is 15 for a column and 13 for a row, $2 is saved by allocating to the lowest cost cell in the column rather than the row.

VAM also may be used in maximization problems. In such cases, the VAM numbers would represent the difference between the two highest profit cells in each row or column. The allocation would then be made to the highest profit cell within the row or column with the largest VAM number. Each VAM number may be thought of as profit forgone by not allocating to the highest profit cell.

**Step 3:
Develop
optimum
solution**

To develop an optimum solution in a transportation problem entails evaluating each unused cell to determine whether a shift into it is advantageous from a total-cost standpoint. If it is, the shift is made, and the process is repeated. When all cells have been evaluated and appropriate shifts made, the problem is solved.

Stepping stone method of evaluation. One approach to making this evaluation is the stepping stone method. The term *stepping stone* appeared in early descriptions of the method in which unused cells were referred to as "water" and used cells as "stones"—from the analogy of walking on a path of stones half submerged in water. The method will now be applied to the northwest-corner solution to the sample problem, as shown in Exhibit 7.15.

Step a: Pick any empty cell.

Step b: Identify the closed path leading to the cell. A "closed path" consists of horizontal and vertical lines leading from an empty cell back to itself.[13] In the closed path there can only be one empty cell which we are examining. The 90 degree turns must therefore occur at those places which meet this requirement. Two closed paths are identified in Exhibit 7.17. Closed path *a* is required to evaluate empty cell *B-E;* closed path *b* is required to evaluate empty cell *A-H.*

Step c: Move one unit[14] *into the empty cell from a filled cell at a corner of the*

---

[13] If assignments have been made correctly, the matrix will have only one closed path for each empty cell.

[14] More than one unit could be used to test the desirability of a shift. However, since the problem is linear, if it is desirable to shift one unit, it is desirable to shift more than one, and vice versa.

EXHIBIT 7.17
Stepping stone method—identification of closed paths

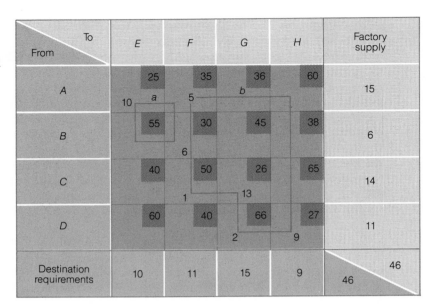

closed path and modify the remaining filled cells at the other corners of the closed path to reflect this move. "Modifying" entails adding to and subtracting from filled cells in such a way that supply and demand constraints are not violated. This requires that one unit always be subtracted in a given row or column for each unit added to that row or column. Thus, the following additions and subtractions would be required for path *a.*

Add one unit to *B-E* (the empty cell).
Subtract one unit from *B-F.*
Add one unit to *A-F.*
Subtract one unit from *A-E.*

And, for the longer path *b,*

Add one unit to *A-H* (the empty cell).
Subtract one unit from *D-H.*
Add one unit to *D-G.*
Subtract one unit from *C-G.*
Add one unit to *C-F.*
Subtract one unit from *A-F.*

Step d: Determine desirability of the move. This is easily done by *(a)* summing the cost values of the cells to which a unit has been added, *(b)* summing the cost values of the cells from which a unit has been subtracted, and *(c)* taking the difference between the two sums to determine if there is a cost reduction. If the cost is reduced by making the move, as many units as possible should be shifted out of the evaluated filled cells into the empty cell. If the cost is increased, no move should be made and the empty cell should be crossed out or otherwise marked to show that it has been evaluated. (A large plus sign is typically used to denote a cell that has been evaluated and found undesirable in cost-minimizing problems. A large minus sign is used for this purpose in profit-maximizing problems.) For cell B-E, the pluses and minuses are as follows.

+		−	
$55	(B-E)	$30	(B-F)
35	(A-F)	25	(A-E)
$90		$55	

For cell A-H:

+		−	
$ 60	(A-H)	$27	(D-H)
66	(D-G)	26	(C-G)
50	(C-F)	35	(A-F)
$176		$88	

Thus in both cases it is apparent that no move into either of the empty cells should be made.

Step e: Repeat steps a–d until all empty cells have been evaluated. To illustrate the mechanics of carrying out a move, consider cell D-F and the closed path leading to it, which is a short one: C-F, C-G, and D-G. The pluses and minuses are

+		−	
$40	(D-F)	$ 50	(C-F)
26	(C-G)	66	(D-G)
$66		$116	

Since there is a savings of $50 per unit from shipping via D-F, as many units as possible should be moved into this cell. In this case, however, the maximum amount that can be shifted is one unit—because the maximum amount added to any cell may not exceed the quantity found in the lowest-amount cell from which a subtraction is to be made. To do otherwise would violate the supply and demand constraints of the problem. Here we see that the limiting cell is C-F, since it contains only one unit. The revised matrix, showing the effects of this move and the previous evaluations, is presented in Exhibit 7.18. Applying the stepping stone method to the remaining unfilled cells and making shifts where indicated[15] yields an optimum solution, which is the same solution as the initial VAM solution.

Degeneracy. Degeneracy exists in a transportation problem when the number of filled cells is less than the number of rows plus the number of columns minus one (i.e., $m + n - 1$). Degeneracy may be observed

[15] Actually, only one more shift is required—to cell A-G.

EXHIBIT 7.18
Revised transportation matrix

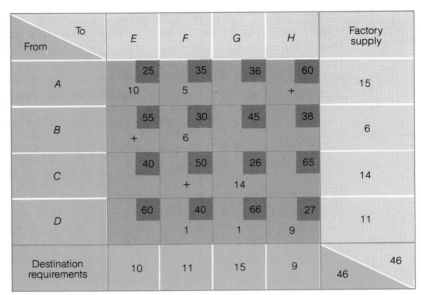

Total cost = 10($25) + 5($35) + 6($30) + 14($26) + 1($40)
+ 1($66) + 9($27) = $1,318

during the initial allocation when the first entry in a row or column satisfies *both* the row and column requirements. Degeneracy has no effect on real-world implications of the problems (i.e., a shipping schedule without degeneracy is no better than one with it), but it requires some adjustment in the matrix in order to evaluate the solution achieved. The form of this adjustment involves inserting some value in an empty cell in order that a closed path be developed to evaluate other empty cells. This value may be thought of as an infinitely small amount, having no direct bearing on the cost of the solution.

Procedurally, the value (often denoted by the Greek letter theta, θ) is used in exactly the same manner as a real number except that it may initially be placed in any empty cell, even though row and column requirements have been met by real numbers. A degenerate transportation problem showing an optimum minimum cost allocation is presented in Exhibit 7.19, where we can see that if θ were not assigned to the matrix, it would be impossible to evaluate several cells (including the one where it is added). Once a θ has been inserted into the solution, it will remain there until it is removed by subtraction or until a final solution is reached.

While the choice of where to put a θ is arbitrary, it saves time if it is placed in such a location that it may be used to evaluate as many cells as possible without being shifted. In this regard, the reader should verify that θ is optimally allocated in Exhibit 7.19.

Alternate optimum solutions. When the evaluation of an empty cell

EXHIBIT 7.19
Degenerate transportation problem with theta added

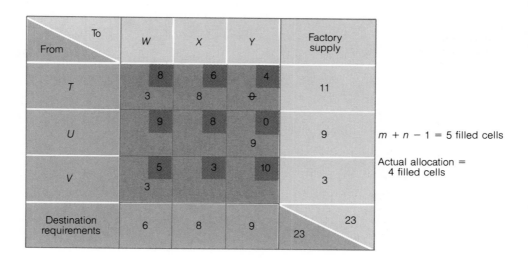

$m + n - 1 = 5$ filled cells

Actual allocation = 4 filled cells

yields the same cost as the existing allocation, an alternate optimum solution exists.[16] In such cases, management is given additional flexibility and is thereby able to invoke nontransportation cost factors in deciding on a final shipping schedule. (A large zero is commonly placed in an empty cell that has been identified as an alternate optimum route.)

ASSIGNMENT METHOD

The assignment method is described in detail in Chapter 14, so we will treat it only briefly here. This special form of linear programming is applied to situations where there are n supply sources and n demand uses (e.g., five jobs on five machines) and the objective is to minimize or maximize some measure of effectiveness. Assignment problems are quite similar to transportation problems, but the fact that each allocation in an assignment problem simultaneously satisfies a row and column requirement makes all such problems multidegenerate. The transportation problem specified in Exhibit 7.14 can be translated into an assignment-problem if we specify that each factory must ship *all* of its supply to one and only one warehouse. This adjustment, of course, eliminates a major part of the problem, but on rare occasions where row and column requirements are identical, the assignment method can be employed to save computation time.

Exhibit 7.20 illustrates how the transportation problem would appear if it were cast as an assignment problem. Here the cell entries are the transportation costs, with those circled indicating the optimum assignments as determined by the simple algorithm described in Chapter 14. The fact that minimum cost values fall on a diagonal is coincidental. Note also

---

[16] Assuming that all other cells are optimally assigned.

EXHIBIT 7.20
**Assignment ma-
trix for modified
transportation
problem**

From \ To	E	F	G	H
A	$25	$35	$36	$60
B	$55	$30	$45	$38
C	$40	$50	$26	$65
D	$60	$40	$66	$27

that the structure of the assignment problem precludes having more than one assignment in a row or column.

Typical operations management applications of linear programming

Exhibit 7.21 summarizes some typical operations management applications of linear programming according to the particular technique by which the application is usually carried out.

Again, the simplex method can be applied to any of the situations presented in the table; however, it is generally more expedient to employ the transportation or the assignment method if the problem lends itself to these forms.

CONCLUSION

This chapter has dealt mainly with the mechanics of solution procedures for linear programming problems. In practice, however, formulating the objective function and constraints is the usual stumbling block in using linear programming methods, and certainly, a chapter of equal length could be written on how to abstract data from a real-world situation and translate it into a form suitable for linear programming. In addition, there has been a great deal of development in variants of linear programming that overcome some of the inherent limitations of the simplex model. A particularly noteworthy innovation is *goal programming,* which is capable of solving linear programming type problems having multiple goals (e.g., profit, quality, and satisfaction). See the Lee and Moore bibliographical reference for an introduction to the methodology. Also of note is the development in linear programming computer programs that, in addition to solving large problems, provide a variety of collateral information for sensitivity analysis. IBM's Mathematical Programming System and Honeywell's Linear Pro-

EXHIBIT 7.21

Typical operations management applications of linear programming*

*Simplex**

Aggregate production planning: Finding the minimum cost production schedule, including rate change costs, given constraints on size of work force and inventory levels

Product planning: Finding the optimum product mix where several products have different costs and resource requirements (e.g., finding the optimum blend of constituents for gasolines, paints, human diets, animal feeds)

Product routing: Finding the optimum routing for a product that must be processed sequentially through several machine centers, with each machine in a center having its own cost and output characteristics

Process control: Minimizing the amount of scrap material generated by cutting steel, leather, or fabric from a roll or sheet of stock material

Inventory control: Finding the optimum combination of products to stock in a warehouse or store

Transportation

Aggregate production planning: Finding the minimum cost production schedule, taking into account inventory carrying costs, overtime costs, and subcontracting costs

Distribution scheduling: Finding the optimum shipping schedule for distributing products between factories and warehouses or warehouses and retailers

Plant location studies: Finding the optimum location of a new plant by evaluating shipping costs between alternative locations and supply and demand sources

Materials handling: Finding the minimum cost routings of material handling devices (e.g., forklift trucks) between departments in a plant and of hauling materials from a supply yard to work sites by trucks, with each truck having different capacity and performance capabilities

Assignment

Scheduling: Minimum cost assignment of trucks to pickup points and ships to berths

Worker assignments: Minimum cost assignment of men to machines and to jobs

* The graphical method is not included since it may be applied in the same situations as simplex if the problem has fewer than three variables.

gramming System are two such programs. Finally, there is ongoing development of mathematical techniques which can be applied to linear programming problems, such as the widely publicized "Ellipsoid Algorithm."[17]

REVIEW AND DISCUSSION QUESTIONS

1. What structural requirements of a problem are needed in order to solve it by linear programming?

2. What type of information is provided in a solved simplex tableau?

3. What type of information is provided by shadow prices?

4. What are slack variables? Why are they necessary in the simplex method? When are they used in the transportation method?

5. It has been stated in this chapter that an optimum solution for a simplex problem always lies at a corner point. Under what conditions might an equally desirable solution be found anywhere along a constraint line?

6. What is a convex polygon? How is it identified?

7. How do you know if a transportation problem is degenerate? What must be done if a degenerate problem is to be tested for optimality?

8. What is the basic rationale of the VAM method? How does the relative magnitude of cost or profit values in a transportation problem affect the effectiveness of the VAM method?

9. Why is an assignment problem multidegenerate?

PROBLEMS

1. Two products, X and Y, both require processing time on machines I and II. Machine I has 200 hours available, and machine II has 400 hours available. Product X requires 1 hour on machine I and 4 hours on machine II. Product Y requires 1 hour on machine I and 1 hour on machine II. Each unit of product X yields $10 profit and each unit of Y yields of $5 profit. These statements reduce to the following set of equations:

$$X + Y \leq 200$$
$$4\,X + Y \leq 400$$

Maximize
$$10\,X + 5\,Y.$$

Solve the problem graphically showing the optimal utilization of machine time.

2. Solve problem 1 using the simplex method.

3. Following is a set of linear equations. Solve *graphically* for the optimum point.

---

[17] See, for example, "Fascinatin' Algorithm," *Scientific American* (January 1980), pp. 80, 84.

$$4A + 6B \geq 120$$
$$2A + 6B \geq 72$$
$$B \geq 10$$

Minimize $2A + 4B$.

4. Solve the following problem using the graphical method of linear programming.

$$5X + 4Y \leq 40$$
$$3X + 2Y \geq 12$$
$$5X + 12Y \geq 60$$

Minimize $3x + Y$.

5. The cook at Kiddie Land Lakeside Resort has a problem and needs your help. First, he knows how to cook only three dishes. Secondly, he has been told to use the ingredients on hand to make up meals having the highest nutritional value possible. (This is so that Kiddie Land can advertise that the resort is not only a place where the kids can have fun but also that it is a healthy place for them.)

The cook currently has 40 pounds of ingredient A available, 30 pounds of ingredient B, and 60 pounds of ingredient C. Each unit of recipe 1 calls for 1 pound of A, ½ pound of B, and 1 pound of C. Each unit of recipe 2 calls for 2 pounds of B and 1 pound of C. Each unit of recipe 3 requires 1 pound of A, 1 pound of B, and 2 pounds of C. If one unit of recipe 1 contains 15 nutritional units, one unit of recipe 2 contains 30 nutritional units, and one unit of recipe 3 contains 25 nutritional units, how many units of each recipe should the cook make in order to maximize the nutritional value of the meals made.

Write out the objective function and the set of constraint equations. Do not solve.

6. Solve problem 5 using the simplex method.

7. Logan Manufacturing wants to mix two fuels (A and B) for its trucks in order to minimize cost. It needs no less than 3,000 gallons in order to run its trucks during the next month. It has a maximum fuel storage capacity of 4,000 gallons. There are 2,000 gallons of fuel A and 4,000 gallons of fuel B available. The mixed fuel must have an octane rating of no less than 80.

When mixing fuels, the amount of fuel obtained is just equal to the sum of the amounts put in. The octane rating is the weighted average of the individual octanes, weighted in proportion to the respective volumes.

The following is known: fuel A has an octane of 90 and costs 20¢ per gallon; fuel B has an octane of 75 and costs 13⅓¢ per gallon.

a. Write out the equations expressing the above information.
b. Solve the problem graphically, giving the amount of each fuel to be used. State any assumptions necessary to solve the problem.

8. A diet is being prepared for the University of Arizona dorms. The objective is to feed the students at the least possible cost, but the diet must have between 1,800 and 3,600 calories. No more than 1,400 calories can be starch, and no less than 400 can be protein. The varied diet is to be made of two foods, A and B. Food A costs $0.75 per pound and contains 600 calories, 400 of which are protein and 200 starch. No more than 2 pounds of food

A can be used per resident. Food B costs $0.15 per pound and contains 900 calories, of which 700 are starch, 100 are protein, and 100 are fat.

a. Write out the equations representing the above information.

b. Solve the problem graphically for the amounts of each food which should be used.

9. The following tableau shows a completed simplex maximization problem.

X	Y	Z	S_1	S_2	S_3	
4	0	0	7	2	1	400
−7	0	1	−2	−4	0	100
3	1	0	5	1	0	200
			−10	−7	0	

a. Which variables are in solution and what are their values?

b. From the tableau, answer the following questions about buying and selling resources:

    (1) Would you buy any S_1? If so, at what price? How many would you buy?

    (2) Answer (1) for S_2 and S_3.

    (3) Would you sell any S_1? If so, at what price? How many would you sell?

    (4) Answer (3) for S_2 and S_3.

10. Following is a solved simplex tableau.

A	B	C	S_1	S_2	S_3	
0	0	−2	−4	2	1	300
1	0	3	−2	2	0	500
0	1	−1	1	−2	0	100
0	0	0	−7	−2	−4	

a. What are the values of each variable (A, B, C, S_1, S_2, S_3)?

b. From the tableau, answer the following questions about buying and selling resources:

    (1) Would you buy any S_1? If so, at what price? How many would you buy?

    (2) Answer (1) for S_2 and S_3.

    (3) Would you sell any S_1? If so, at what price? How many would you sell?

    (4) Answer (4) for S_2 and S_3.

11. Find the optimal solution for the following transportation-type linear programming problem.

Sources	Availability	Destinations	Required
A	200	D	300
B	300	E	125
C	150	F	140

Transportation costs

$AD = \$10$	$BD = \$4$	$CD = \$9$
$AE = \$12$	$BE = \$13$	$CE = \$14$
$AF = \$4$	$BF = \$15$	$CF = \$2$

12. You are trying to create a budget to optimize the use of a portion of your disposable income. You have a maximum of $700 per month which is to be allocated to food, shelter, and entertainment. The amount spent on food and shelter combined must be less than $500. The amount spent on shelter alone must be less than $100. Entertainment cannot exceed $300 per month. Each dollar spent on food has a satisfaction value of 2, each dollar spent on shelter has a satisfaction value of 3, and each dollar spent on entertainment has a satisfaction value of 5.

Assuming a linear relationship, use the simplex method of linear programming to determine the optimum allocation of your funds.

13. Minimize the following three transportation problems.

A.

From \ To	W	X	Y	Supply
A	8	15	3	15
B	5	10	9	7
C	6	12	10	6
Demand	12	8	8	28 / 28

B.

From \ To	D	E	F	G	Supply
A	17	12	32	4	300
B	9	18	7	11	700
C	3	21	14	9	400
Demand	200	500	350	350	1400 / 1400

C.

From \ To	E	F	G	H	Dummy	Supply
A	44	50	48	49	0	70
B	45	50	48	51	0	30
C	45	51	50	51	0	180
D	48	54	50	52	0	110
Demand	90	40	75	100	85	390 / 390

14. Following is a *solved* simplex tableau:

A	B	C	S_1	S_2	S_3	
1	4	0	3	0	−4	60
0	−3	0	−2	1	2	100
0	7	1	1	0	−5	120
	−8	0		0	−3	

   a.   From the tableau, $A = ?$, $B = ?$, $C = ?$, $S_1 = ?$, $S_2 = ?$, $S_3 = ?$.
   b.   Answer the following questions about S_1, S_2, and S_3:

	S_1	S_2	S_3
Would you buy any?			
At what price?			
How many would you buy?			
Would you sell any?			
At what price?			
How many would you sell?			

15. Maximize the following two transportation problems.

A.

From \ To	D	E	F	Supply
A	4	6	4	11
B	9	8	5	9
C	5	3	10	3
Demand	6	8	9	23 / 23

B.

From \ To	D	E	F	G	H	Supply
A	1	4	10	4	10	52
B	8	2	8	2	1	20
C	10	1	8	8	2	20
Demand	16	22	4	19	31	92 / 92

SELECTED BIBLIOGRAPHY

Avriel, Mordecai *Nonlinear Programming: Analysis and Methods.* Englewood Cliffs, N. J.: Prentice-Hall, Inc., 1976.

"Fascinatin' Algorithm." *Scientific American,* "Science and Citizen" section (January 1980), pp. 80, 84.

Gass, Saul I. *Linear Programming: Methods and Applications.* New York: McGraw-Hill Book Company, 1975.

Lee, Sang M., and Moore, Laurence J. *Introduction to Decision Science.* New York: Petrocelli/Charter, 1975.

"Linear Programming Discovery." *Science* 206 (November 30, 1979), p. 1022.

Metzger, Robert W. *Elementary Mathematical Programming.* New York: John Wiley & Sons, 1965.

Naylor, Thomas H.; Byrne, Eugene T.; and Vernon, John R. *Introduction to Linear Programming: Methods and Cases.* San Francisco: Wadsworth Publishing Co., 1971.

Plane, Donald R., and Kochenberger, Gary A. *Operations Research for Managerial Decisions.* Homewood, Ill.: Richard D. Irwin, Inc., 1972.

Rothenberg, Ronald I. *Linear Programming.* New York: Elsevier North Holland, Inc., 1979.

Thompson, Gerald L. *Linear Programming.* New York: Macmillan Co., 1971.

Chapter 8

LAYOUT OF THE
PHYSICAL SYSTEM

The layout decision entails determining the placement of departments, work stations, machines, and stock-holding points within a productive facility. Its general objective is to arrange these elements in such a way as to assure a smooth work flow (in a factory) or a particular traffic pattern (in a service organization). The inputs to the layout decision are:

1. Specification of objectives of the system in terms of output and flexibility.
2. Estimation of product or service demand on the system.
3. Processing requirements in terms of number of operations and amount of flow between departments and work centers.
4. Space availability within the facility itself.

Each of these inputs are, in fact, outputs of process selection and capacity planning as discussed in previous chapters. In our treatment of layout in this chapter, we will examine how layouts are developed under various formats (or work flow structures). Our emphasis will be on quantitative techniques used in locating departments within a facility and on work station arrangements and balance in the important area of assembly lines. Before embarking on this discussion, however, it is useful to note the marks of a good layout listed in Exhibit 8.1.

BASIC LAYOUT FORMATS

The format by which departments and components within departments are arranged may be viewed either in terms of work flow or the function of the productive system. Looking first at work flow formats, we can

EXHIBIT 8.1
**Marks of A good
plant layout***

1. Planned materials flow pattern.
2. Straight-line layout (or an adaptation thereof).
3. Building constructed (or altered) around a preplanned layout design.
4. Straight, clear, marked aisles.
5. Backtracking kept to a minimum.
6. Related operations close together.
7. Production time predictable.
8. Minimum of scheduling difficulties.
9. Minimum of goods-in-process.
10. Easy adjustment to changing conditions.
11. Plans for expansion.
12. Maximum ratio of actual processing time to overall production time.
13. Good quality with minimum inspection.
14. Minimum materials handling distances.
15. Minimum of manual handling.
16. No unnecessary rehandling of materials.
17. Materials handled in unit loads.
18. Minimum handling between operations.
19. Materials delivered to production employees.
20. Materials efficiently removed from the work area.
21. Materials handling being done by indirect labor.
22. Orderly material handling and storage.
23. Good housekeeping.
24. Busy employees, working at maximum efficiency.

* Source: James M. Apple, *Plant Layout and Materials Handling*, 2d ed. (New York: Ronald Press, 1963), p. 11.

specify three basic types: product layout, process layout, and fixed-position layout.

A *product layout* is one in which the components are arranged according to the progressive steps by which the product is made. Conceptually, the flow is an unbroken line from raw material input to finished goods. This type of layout is exemplified in automobile assembly, food processing, and furniture manufacture.

A *process (or functional) layout* is one in which the components are grouped according to the general function they perform, without regard to any particular product. Custom job shops, department stores, and hospitals are generally arranged in this manner.

A *fixed-position layout* is one in which the product, by virtue of its bulk or weight, remains at one location. The equipment required for product manufacture is moved to the product rather than vice versa. Sound stages on a movie lot, aircraft assembly shops, and shipyards typify this mode of layout.

With respect to the classification of layouts by productive system function, we can mention three common types: storage layout, marketing layout, and project layout.

Storage layout refers to the relative placement of the layout components in a warehouse or storeroom. It differs from other types of layout in that it is designed to fulfill an inventory function rather than to operate directly on the product or service being created.

Marketing layout refers to layouts whose components are arranged in such a fashion as to facilitate the sale of a product rather than its production. Retail stores, supermarkets, convention exhibits, and customer display rooms utilize this type of layout.

Project layout refers to the arrangement of components in "one shot" situations, such as those developed around building, dam, and highway construction sites. Although project layouts are identical in most respects to fixed-position layouts, the latter are characterized by a fixed facility that is designed to turn out more than one of a given product. A project layout, on the other hand, must be planned around the particular terrain where the work is being carried out and, in many cases, is subject to shifts in location as the project progresses.

It should be noted at this point that many layouts are designed with more than one function in mind, and therefore, functional combinations are common. For example, a supermarket, though primarily arranged on the basis of marketing criteria, displays more than one line of brand items on its shelves and therefore, is partly a storage layout. In addition, combinations of work flow and functional arrangements are quite common. A cafeteria represents not only layout by function (marketing) but layout by work flow (a food assembly line). Finally, many production facilities have more than one type of layout format. A factory, for instance may carry out machining in a process-oriented layout and perform assembly operations on a product-oriented basis.

QUANTITATIVE LAYOUT ANALYSIS

Of the several formats discussed, process formats, along with assembly line balancing (a special case of product layout), have been most heavily subjected to analysis, with the result that a number of quantitative techniques have been developed to aid in their solution. These formats have received wide attention not only because of their extensive employment in productive systems but also because they present challenging theoretical problems in combinatorial mathematics. We shall consider several of these techniques in depth.

Process layout   The most common approach in developing a process layout is to arrange departments consisting of like components so as to optimize their relative placement. In many installations, optimal placement often means that the *material handling* costs for the total layout are minimized by placing departments that have large amounts of interdepartment traffic adjacent to one another. For example, in a steel mill producing custom items, this rationale might dictate the placement of finishing machines (such as high-tolerance turret lathes) next to rough machining facilities since many items follow this sequence of manufacture. In many situations, however, the concept of material handling cost must be broadened to include the cost of the individuals who carry the material. In the steel mill, for instance, it might be desirable to have the tool crib area near the skilled machinists in order to minimize the time they are away from their machines. In a large insurance office, it might be desirable to have files (or computer terminals) on the insured persons close to the underwriter's desk.

The general approach to process layout and some of the unique problems it poses can be illustrated by the following example. Suppose that we want to arrange the eight departments of a toy factory in order to minimize the interdepartmental material handling cost. Initially, let us make the simplifying assumption that all departments have the same amount of space, say, 40 feet by 40 feet and that the building is 80 feet wide and 160 feet long (and thus compatible with the former dimensions). The first thing we would want to know is the nature of the flow between departments and the way the material is transported. If the company has another factory that makes similar products, information about flow patterns might be abstracted from the records. On the other hand, if this is a new-product line, such information would have to come from routing sheets (see Chapter 2) or from estimates by knowledgeable personnel such as process or industrial engineers. Of course these data, regardless of their source, will have to be modified to reflect the nature of future orders over the projected life at the proposed layout.

Let us assume, further, that the information is available and we find that all material is transported in a standard-size crate by forklift truck, one crate to a truck (which constitutes one "load"). Now suppose that transportation costs are $1 to move a load between adjacent departments and $1 extra for each department in between. The expected loads between

EXHIBIT 8.2
Interdepartmental flow

	1	2	3	4	5	6	7	8	Department	Activity
1		175	50	0	30	200	20	25	1	Shipping and receiving
2			0	100	75	90	80	90	2	Plastic molding and stamping
3				17	88	125	99	180	3	Metal forming
4					20	5	0	25	4	Sewing department
5						0	180	187	5	Small toy assembly
6							374	103	6	Large toy assembly
7								7	7	Painting
8									8	Mechanism assembly

Flow between departments (number of moves)

EXHIBIT 8.3
Building dimensions and departments

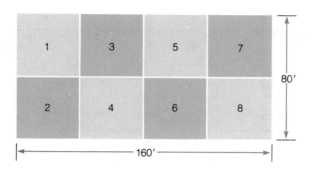

departments for the first year of operation are tabulated in Exhibit 8.2; the available plant space is depicted in Exhibit 8.3.

Given this information, our first step is to illustrate the nature of the interdepartmental flow by a schematic model, such as that in Exhibit 8.4. This provides the basic layout pattern, which we will try to improve.

The second step is to determine the cost of this layout by multiplying the material handling cost by the number of loads moved between each department. Exhibit 8.5 presents this information, which is derived as follows. The annual material handling cost between departments 1 and 2 is $175 ($1 × 175 moves), $60 between departments 1 and 5 ($2 × 30 moves), $60 between departments 1 and 7 ($3 × 20 moves), and so forth.

Step three entails a search for departmental changes that will reduce costs. Looking at the graph and the cost matrix, it would appear desirable to place departments 1 and 6 closer together since their high move-distance costs can be substantially reduced by making them adjacent to each other. However, creation of this adjacency requires the shifting of several other

EXHIBIT 8.4
Interdepartmental flow graph with number of annual movements

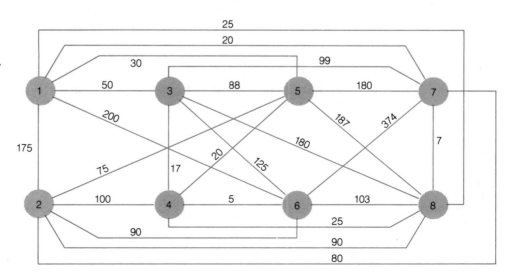

EXHIBIT 8.5
**Cost matrix—
first solution**

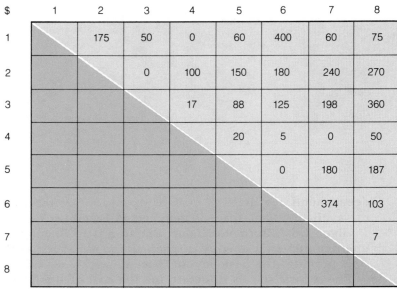

$	1	2	3	4	5	6	7	8
1		175	50	0	60	400	60	75
2			0	100	150	180	240	270
3				17	88	125	198	360
4					20	5	0	50
5						0	180	187
6							374	103
7								7
8								

Total cost: $3,474

departments, thereby affecting their move-distance costs and the total cost of the second solution. Exhibit 8.6 shows the revised layout resulting from the relocation of department 6 and an adjacent department (department 4 is arbitrarily selected for this purpose). The revised cost matrix for the exchange, with the cost changes circled, is given in Exhibit 8.7— where the total cost is $262 *greater* than in the initial solution. Clearly, the fact that the distance between departments 6 and 7 was doubled accounts for the major part of the cost increase. This points out the fact that, even in a small problem, it is rarely easy to make the correct "obvious move" on the basis of casual inspection.

Thus far, we have shown only one exchange among a large number of potential exchanges; in fact, for an eight-department problem there are 8! (or 40,320) possible arrangements. Therefore, the procedure we have employed would have only a remote possibility of achieving an optimum

EXHIBIT 8.6
**Revised interde-
partmental flow
graph (only in-
terdepartmental
flow having ef-
fect on cost is de-
picted)**

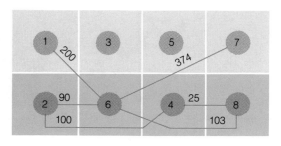

EXHIBIT 8.7
**Cost matrix—
second solution**

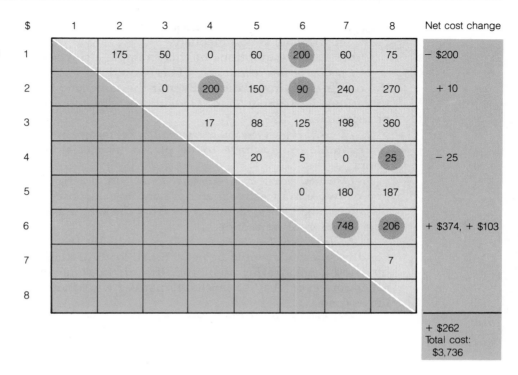

$	1	2	3	4	5	6	7	8	Net cost change
1		175	50	0	60	200	60	75	− $200
2			0	200	150	90	240	270	+ 10
3				17	88	125	198	360	
4					20	5	0	25	− 25
5						0	180	187	
6							748	206	+ $374, + $103
7								7	
8									

+ $262
Total cost:
$3,736

combination in a "reasonable" number of tries. Nor does our problem stop here.

Suppose that we *do* arrive at a good cut-and-try solution solely on the basis of material handling cost, such as that shown in Exhibit 8.8 (whose total cost is $3,244). We would note, first of all, that our shipping and receiving department is near the center of the factory—an arrangement that probably would not be acceptable. Note also that the sewing department is next to the paint department, introducing the hazard that lint, thread, and cloth particles might drift onto painted items. Further, small-toy assembly and large-toy assembly are located at opposite ends of the plant, which would increase travel time for assemblers, who very likely would be needed in both departments at various times of the day, as

EXHIBIT 8.8
A feasible layout

Small toy assembly	Mechanism assembly	Shipping and receiving	Large toy assembly
5	8	1	6
Metal forming	Plastic molding and stamping	Sewing	Painting
3	2	4	7

well as the travel time of supervisors, who might otherwise supervise both departments simultaneously.

Other basic assumptions of this example also could be challenged:

1. Equality of department size.   This would be an exception rather than the rule in most installations. Even if the same amount of area is allocated to various departments, L or U shapes may be more suitable than squares or rectangles.

2. No restriction on location of equipment.   Forming and stamping equipment, for example, might have to be placed in special rooms on high-stress floors.

3. Unlimited access to departmental areas.   In practice, there may be only one or two entrances for material handling purposes, so that actual travel distances might differ significantly from the simple assumption of distances as a function of adjacency.

4. Material handling method.   It is quite likely that a variety of material handling methods would be used. Small loads of material might be moved by hand trucks rather than forklifts or, in some instances, by belt or roller conveyor. Any of these alternatives would affect interdepartmental move costs.

Systematic Layout Planning.   In certain types of layout problems, numerical flow of items between departments is either impractical to obtain or really does not reveal the qualitative factors that may be crucial to the placement decision. In these situations, the technique known as Systematic Layout Planning (SLP)[1] is commonly used. The technique requires the creation of a relationship chart showing the degree of importance of having each department located adjacent to every other department. From this chart is developed an activity relationship diagram similar to an interdepartmental flow graph used for illustrating material handling between departments. The activity relationship diagram is then adjusted by trial and error until a satisficing adjacency pattern is obtained. This pattern, in turn, is modified department-by-department to meet building space limitations. Exhibit 8.9 illustrates the technique as applied to a simple five-department problem involving the laying out of a floor of a department store.

Computerized layout techniques.   It should be apparent at this point that making a *good* process layout entails the simultaneous solution of mathematical, economic, and technological problems—any one of which may be highly complex in its own right. To come to grips with this problem, researchers work with computer-based models that, in a general sense, follow the approach in our simple example. In addition, however, they provide for more sophisticated measurements of flow and permit adjustments for a variety of constraints, such as building construction features (for example, stairwells and elevators) and fixed departmental locations. These models also have the capability of dealing with the *re*layout problem,

---

[1] See the Muther and Wheeler bibliographical reference.

EXHIBIT 8.9
Systematic Layout Planning for a floor of a department store

A. Relationship chart (based upon Tables B and C)

From	To				Area (sq. ft.)
	2	3	4	5	
1. Credit dept.	I / 6	U / —	A / 1,6	U / —	100
2. Toy dept.		U / —	I / 1	A / 1,6	400
3. Wine dept.			A / 2,3	E / 1	300
4. Camera dept.				X / 1	100
5. Candy dept.					100

Letter	← Closeness rating
Number	← Reason for rating

B.

Code	Reason*
1	Type of customer
2	Ease of supervision
3	Common personnel
4	Contact necessary
5	Share same space
6	Psychology

*Others may be used.

C.

Value	Closeness	Line code*	Color code†
A	Absolutely necessary	══════	Red
E	Especially important	═════	Orange
I	Important	════	Green
O	Ordinary closeness OK	────	Blue
U	Unimportant		None
X	Undesirable	/\/\/\	Brown

* Used for example purposes only.
† Used in practice.

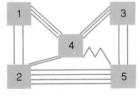

Initial relationship diagram (based upon Tables A and C)

5 2 4
  3 1

Initial layout based upon relationship diagram (ignoring space and building constraints)

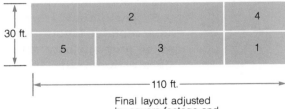

Final layout adjusted by square footage and building size

which is often far more demanding than the initial layout case we have discussed. The characteristics of these computerized approaches are summarized in Exhibit 8.10.

The best choice among the methods described in Exhibit 8.10 depends on the particular objectives and characteristics of the layout problem under study; therefore, to provide guidelines for specific situations would be a massive undertaking. However, certain features of these techniques should be understood prior to application:

1. ALDEP and CORELAP, as defined by their developers, employ preference ratings that have the advantage of being inclusive in terms of the features that are important in department location. On the other hand, the scoring techniques used in these methods require the quantification of subjective preferences, which is inherently risky. Both approaches employ the "Muther scale" as used in SLP, which assumes, for instance, that the weights of 4 ("absolutely essential to be located near department") and 3 ("essential to be located near department") maintain their relative numeric position in any situation. Clearly, this is a tenuous assumption.

CRAFT avoids this problem by using cost per unit distance between department centroids as its criterion. However, this approach depends upon the assumption that cost per unit distance is the appropriate measure and that department centroids are the approximate material pickup and delivery points. Both of these assumptions are open to question.

2. CRAFT requires that the user provide a feasible initial layout. The program then modifies this layout by exchanging departments two or three at a time until no further reduction in total material handling cost is possible. A second initial layout might then be developed and the program run again. This interactive process is repeated until a satisfactory layout is obtained.

ALDEP either generates a series of random layouts within the program and selects the one with the best preference score or generates one random layout and makes pairwise departmental exchanges until no further improvement can be made in the preference score.

CORELAP simply generates a predetermined number of random layouts and selects the one with the best "total closeness rating" (preference score).

3. The outputs from each program must be "hand smoothed" to make an acceptable layout. For instance, the best layout developed by the computer program may show departments that have very long and narrow sides or more than four sides—characteristics that might be undesirable in practice.

4. ALDEP, CORELAP, and CRAFT are heuristic programs; that is, they do not investigate every possible departmental arrangement, nor do they necessarily yield optimal solutions. Therefore, regardless of which technique is selected, the chances of a good layout are greatly enhanced by generating a large number of possible layouts.

Extent of application of computerized layout programs. A 1975 survey by the Facilities Planning and Design Division of AIIE, American

Institute of Industrial Engineers, indicated that out of 75 division members, about one out of three respondents have had some experience with computerized layout programs. Eighty-three percent of the users stated that they used one of the methods either to generate alternative layouts or to evaluate alternative layouts. The main problem encountered with them was getting accurate input data in the precise form for computer manipulation. However, in commenting on this finding, Tompkins and Moore note that, "If [the data] has been too indefinite for the computer, perhaps it should be questioned in developing layouts manually."[2]

Intradepartmental layout

In factories and low-contact services, the placement of machines, desks, storage areas, and so forth within a department is determined by a combination of engineering requirements (e.g., 20 square feet for each lathe) and material flow patterns (e.g., accounts-receivable desks next to billing desks).

In high contact systems, the location of equipment is predicated on more subjective factors which often lie within the realm of the marketeer rather than the operations manager. For instance, it is doubtful that questions of material flow are dominant in Nunn-Bush's Brass Boot stores which are designed to recreate the atmosphere of a Victorian English club:

> Customers relax in leather-covered seats beneath tinkling chandeliers. Goblets of red wine and piped-in sitar music stimulate the buying hormones . . . Orgiastic collection (of shoes) . . . designed to blow your mind.[3]

In a similar vein, many new branch banks are designed not around flow patterns, but rather to convey an atmosphere of "cheerful rectitude" through the use of "open offices." Unfortunately for some banks, flow patterns have been ignored to such an extent that customers negotiating for a loan are compelled to detail their financial histories in the midst of other customers going to and from teller's windows or other open desks. Similar problems have been observed in a study of a claims and adjustment department of a large insurance firm.[4]

Product layout— assembly lines

The distinguishing characteristic between product layout and process layout is the pattern of work flow. In process layout, the pattern can be highly variable. Product layout, on the other hand, is highly predictable because it is a function of the manufacturing stages of the product itself. For this reason, the relative location of departments within a product-oriented system and the positioning of components within a product-ori-

[2] James A. Tompkins and James M. Moore, *Computer Aided Layout: A User's Guide*, publication no. 1, Facilities Planning and Design Division, American Institute of Industrial Engineers, 1977, p. 2.

[3] "Sex, Wine, and Sitars: Shoe Fashion for the Groovy Male," *Journal of Footwear Management* (Spring 1970), p. 22.

[4] A. Szilagyi, W. Holland, and C. Oliver, "Keys to Success With Open Plan Offices," *Management Review* (August 1979), p. 38.

EXHIBIT 8.10
Summary of three computerized layout techniques*

Required inputs	Problem size handled	Outputs	Measure of effectiveness	Distinguishing features
ALDEP: (Automated Layout Design Program)†				
1. Size and number of each department to be located in the building	1. 63 departments	1. Layout matrix with departments and aisles drawn by plotter (58 layouts were plotted for sample 11-department problem, each entailing 1.03 minutes on IBM 7090 computer)	1. Maximum preference score (for all layouts generated)	1. Program can layout a multistory building up to 3 floors
2. Description of building dimensions, which must include areas assigned to specific building features (aisles, stairwells, etc.). These data are fed into program in form of a matrix		2. Preference score for each layout		2. Departmental exchanges may be made randomly or according to criteria
3. Preference table giving relative department location preferences, denoted by letters A, B, C, V, E, X, which range from "absolutely essential" (A) to "undesirable" (F). Letters are then converted to a numerical scale; i.e., A = 4, B = 2, etc.				3. Departments are exchanged 2 at a time
				4. Authors favor using the program in concert with a layout planner who, at various stages, inserts departments into intermediate layouts
4. Control cards to activate subroutines, such as "number of layouts to be tried"				5. Best suited for relayout problems

CORELAP (Computerized Relationship Layout Planning)‡

Inputs	Capacity	Output	Objective	Comments
1. Relationship chart similar to preference chart used in ALDEP	1. 70 departments with over 1,000 interdepartmental relationships	1. Numerical layout matrix printout	1. Maximum total closeness rating (for all layouts tested)	1. Not confined to any particular building shape
2. Building width-length ratio		2. Can use digital plotter, such as CALCOMP plotter (27-department problem solved in 2.46 minutes on IBM 7090 computer)		2. Yields near optimum solutions according to authors
3. Departmental area restrictions				3. Requires little computer time
4. Size of area modules to be manipulated to form each department				
5. Number of modules per department				

CRAFT (Computerized Relative Allocation of Facilities Technique)§

Inputs	Capacity	Output	Objective	Comments
1. Initial block layout	1. 40 departments	1. Block layout, shaped to conform to building dimensions	1. Minimum total material handling cost	1. Final solution is function of initial layout
2. Load matrix (tabulation of loads, e.g., materials, which flow between all combinations of departments)		2. Cost of each solution leading up to final solution (22-department problem solved in 0.62 minutes on IBM 7090 computer)		2. Later versions exchange departments 3 at a time rather than 2 at a time, as in ALDEP and CORELAP
3. Material handling cost matrix (handling costs between departments)				3. Distances computed between department centroids
				4. Limited to single-story building
				5. Departments can be fixed in location

* An expanded comparison of these techniques is presented in Richard L. Francis and John A. White, *Facility Layout and Location* (Englewood Cliffs, N.J.: Prentice-Hall, 1974), pp. 95–141.

† Jarrold M. Seehof and Wayne O. Evans, "Automated Layout Design Programs," *Journal of Industrial Engineering*, vol. 18, no. 12 (December 1967), pp. 690–95.

‡ Robert S. Lee and James M. Moore, "CORELAP—Computerized Relationship Layout Planning," *Journal of Industrial Engineering*, vol. 18, no. 3 (March 1967), pp. 195–200.

§ Elwood S. Buffa, Gordon C. Armour, and Thomas E. Vollmann, "Allocating Facilities with CRAFT," *Harvard Business Review* (March–April 1964), pp. 136–50.

ented department present less of a challenge than in process layouts. Nevertheless, the layout planner is confronted with a challenging problem in a special case of product layout—the assembly line. The objective of such a layout is to achieve a smooth flow of product assembly with minimum idle time on the part of workers who man the line. Essentially, this is a question of workload equalization, and thus, the term *assembly line balancing* is used to denote the problem area.

Assembly line balancing

In most instances, the initial layout of the assembly line is based on the output required from the line. Once the line has been established, however, the assembly line balancing problem is to a large degree a scheduling problem. These two opposing starting points—a given desired output versus a given established line—may be expressed as the following formulation of the assembly line balancing problem:

Find (a) the minimum number of work stations for a given cycle time.
or
Find (b) the minimum cycle time for a given number of work stations. (A "work station" is a specified location for performance of a given amount of work usually, but not always, manned by one operator, and "cycle time" is the elapsed time between units coming off the line.)

If we are dealing with (a), our problem is a layout problem since we must determine the number of work stations required to achieve the specified cycle time. If we are dealing with (b), we have a scheduling problem since we know the number of work stations and therefore the essential nature of the layout. In practice, however, those who design assembly line systems rarely make this layout-scheduling distinction because the solution procedures—that is, line balancing methods—treat (a) and (b) together once the type and length of the assembly line are specified.

To illustrate the nature of the assembly line balancing problem and methods for its solution, we will again employ the example of the toy factory. This time, however, our focus will be on the large-toy assembly department, in which we consider how a toy wagon might be assembled on a belt conveyor line.[5] To perform the analysis, we would require a list of the assembly tasks that go into making each unit, their operation time, and their sequence restrictions. In addition, we would need an estimate of the desired cycle time. This information, which is generally based on assembly chart data (see Chapter 2) and a demand forecast, is presented in Exhibit 8.11. To visualize the sequence relationships more easily, refer to the precedence graph in Exhibit 8.12.

Before we proceed to balance the line, we can make the following obser-

---

[5] As any parent of small children will attest, bicycles, tricycles, and wagons are rarely assembled at the factory. This example is selected as much from wishful thinking as for simplicity in conveying line balancing concepts.

EXHIBIT 8.11
**Assembly steps
and times for
model J wagon**

Task	Performance time (in seconds)	Description	Tasks that must precede
A.......	45	Position near axle support and hand fasten 4 screws to nuts	—
B.......	11	Insert rear axle	A
C.......	9	Tighten rear axle support screws to nuts	A, B
D	50	Position front axle assembly and hand fasten with 4 screws to nuts	—
E.......	15	Tighten front axle assembly screws	D
F	12	Position rear wheel #1 and fasten hub cap	A, B, C
G.......	12	Position rear wheel #2 and fasten hub cap	A, B, C
H	12	Position front wheel #1 and fasten hub cap	D, E
I	12	Position front wheel #2 and fasten hub cap	D, E
J	8	Position wagon handle shaft on front axle assembly and hand fasten bolt and nut	A, B, C, D, E, F, G, H, I
K.......	9	Tighten bolt and nut	J

Cycle time determination:
Demand per day *(D):* 500 wagons
Productive time per day *(P):* 420 minutes
Total time for all tasks *(T):* 195 seconds

Cycle time *(C)* in seconds $= \dfrac{60P}{D} = \dfrac{60 \times 420}{500} = \dfrac{25{,}200}{500} = 50.4$ seconds

Theoretical minimum number of work stations *(N)* $= \dfrac{DT}{60P} = \dfrac{500 \times 195}{25{,}200} = \dfrac{97{,}500}{25{,}200} = 3.87$

vations about the range of cycle times we might use. At one extreme, the 50 seconds associated with task D is the shortest cycle time we could employ if we do not split this task among two or more workers. At the other extreme, the longest cycle time (assuming no penalty for extra tool handling and operator movements) would be the sum of all of the assembly task times: 195 seconds. This would be the figure when one operator does the entire assembly. Finally, if this problem had no sequential restrictions, there would be 11! (or 39,916,800) possible task-performance arrangements. However, the sequence requirements in this situation would substantially reduce the number of possible arrangements.

Referring to Exhibit 8.11, we note that the cycle time required to meet the hypothesized demand of 500 units per day is 50.4 seconds. Thus, our objective is to find the minimum *actual* number of work stations re-

EXHIBIT 8.12
**Precedence graph
for model J
wagon**

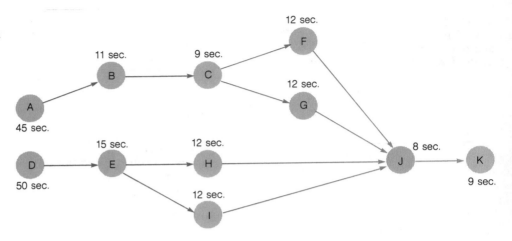

quired to meet this cycle time. ("Actual" is emphasized because—although we have calculated the *theoretical* minimum number of stations in Exhibit 8.11—we will not be able to balance exactly to this number since we are designing for an integral number of stations.) Further, the precedence constraints and the problem of trying to combine whole elements within each work station may necessitate more work stations than the theoretical minimum. Given a cycle time, the first step in balancing the line is to decide upon a rule by which tasks may be allocated to the different work stations. In this example we have selected two simple rules:

1. First allocate those tasks that have the largest number of following tasks.
2. First allocate those tasks that have the longest operation time.

To make the first balance, we will use rule 1 and break ties with rule 2. The reverse procedure will be followed for the second balance.

Utilizing rule 1, we initially array the tasks in the following order:

Task	Number of following tasks
A	6
B or D	5
C or E...............	4
F, G, H, or I	2
J	1
K	0

Tasks are then assigned in sequence to stations, subject to precedence restrictions (that is, a task cannot be selected until all prior tasks in the sequence have been assigned) and to cycle time constraints (task time must be less than the remaining unassigned station time). The balance achieved and station idle time are shown in Exhibit 8.13.

EXHIBIT 8.13
Balance made according to largest number of following tasks rule

	Task	Task time (in seconds)	Remaining unassigned time (in seconds)	Feasible remaining tasks	Task with most followers	Task with longest operation time
Station 1	A	45	5.4 idle	none		
Station 2	D	50	0.4 idle	none		
Station 3	B	11	39.4	C, E	C, E	E
	E	15	24.4	C, H, I	C	
	C	9	15.4	F, G, H, I	F, G, H, I	F, G, H, I
	F*	12	3.4 idle	none		
Station 4	G	12	38.4	H, I	H, I	H, I
	H*	12	26.4	I		
	I	12	14.4	J		
	J	8	6.4 idle	none		
Station 5	K	9	41.4 idle	none		

* Denotes task arbitrarily selected where there is a tie between longest operation times.

Utilizing rule 2, our initial array of tasks would be: D, A, E, (F, G, H, or I), B, (C or K), J. Station assignments and idle time are shown in Exhibit 8.14.

Analyzing the two balances achieved, we see that rule 1, supplemented with rule 2, resulted in a given station balance with a total of 57 seconds of idle time. Rule 2, supplemented with rule 1, yielded a four-station balance with a total idle time of 6.6 seconds and clearly is preferable in this case. The obvious question at this point is: Would we expect similar results in other line balancing problems? About all we can say is "It depends."

It depends mainly on the number of tasks being considered and their order strength (that is, the extent of precedence constraints), which, unfortunately, interact to such an extent that it is impossible to provide general guidelines. Moreover, other useful heuristic rules apply task-weighting

EXHIBIT 8.14
Balance made according to longest-operation time rule

	Task	Task time (in seconds)	Remaining unassigned time (in seconds)	Feasible remaining tasks	Task with longest time	Task with most followers
Station 1	D	50	0.4 idle	none		
Station 2	A	45	5.4 idle	none		
Station 3	E	15	35.4	B, H, I	H, I	H, I
	H*	12	23.4	B, I	I	
	I	12	11.4	B		
	B	11	0.4 idle	none		
Station 4	C	9	41.4	F, G	F, G	F, G
	F*	12	29.4	G		
	G*	12	17.4	J		
	J	8	9.4	K		
	K	9	0.4 idle	none		

* Denotes task arbitrarily selected where there is a tie between the number of following tasks.

techniques and may perform as well or better than our rule 2.[6] In practice, probably the best strategy is to try several different rules if the problem is relatively small, say, fewer than 30 tasks. For larger problems, computerized techniques employing more elaborate weighting procedures[7] or mathematical programming approaches[8] would be warranted.[9]

Our previous example developed the best balance for a specific cycle time. Management, however, is also extremely interested in the sensitivity of the line to changes in production rate and number of work stations. By varying the cycle time length and the size of the work force, we can derive an "efficiency" relationship between the line idle time and line productive time. This entails generating a number of balances over a range of cycle times and quantitatively solving for measures of efficiency. Once these calculations are made, a graph is constructed from which the efficiency of any cycle time–work force combination may be determined.

Using the wagon line, we might investigate combinations from 50 seconds (1.2 units per minute) to, say, 70 seconds (0.86 units per minute). Our measure of efficiency may be obtained as follows.

$$\text{Efficiency } (E) = \frac{\sum_{i=1}^{11} t_i}{nc}$$

where

$t_i =$ Time per task, $i = 1, 2, 3, \ldots 11$
$n =$ Actual number of work stations
$c =$ Selected cycle time

Thus, for the balance achieved by rule 1,

$$E = \frac{195}{(5)(50.4)} = 0.77, \text{ or } 77\%$$

And for rule 2:

$$E = \frac{195}{(4)(50.4)} = 0.97, \text{ or } 97\%$$

These efficiencies,[10] along with others obtained from different balances, are plotted in Exhibit 8.15.

---

[6] Commonly employed heuristic rules are given in Ignall and Buxey et al. bibliographical references.

[7] See Helgeson-Birnie and Mastor bibliographical references.

[8] See Buffa-Miller, Moore, and Wu bibliographical references.

[9] A discussion of the extent of use of formal, published assembly line balancing techniques is presented in R. B. Chase, "Survey of Paced Assembly Lines," *Industrial Engineering,* vol. 6, no. 2 (February, 1974), pp. 14–18.

[10] An alternative way of denoting the effectiveness of a given balance is to specify the "balance delay," or idle time which results from that balance. This is calculated as: $(1 - \text{efficiency})$.

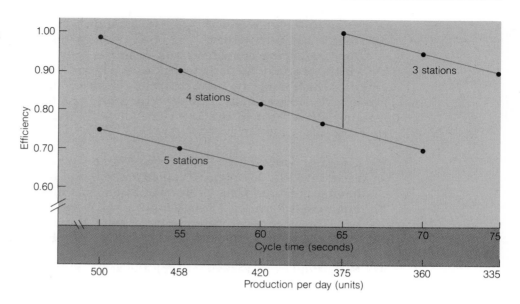

EXHIBIT 8.15
**Efficiency graph
of selected *n-c*
combinations**

It is apparent in evaluating this graph that it would be inefficient to use five work stations unless the bottleneck operation, *D,* is reduced below 50 seconds. Likewise, it would be inefficient to use four stations when 65 seconds (or more) is an acceptable cycle time. In addition, although 100 percent efficiency is possible in this example—when $c = 65$ and $n = 3$—with only a slight loss in efficiency, a substantial increase in output may be made by adding one man and balancing the line at 50 seconds.

Factors other than those represented on the graph also affect the ultimate line balance choice. Labor considerations, such as keeping the work force intact, may dictate that the line be run at an output level that will result in substantial idle time. If only enough parts and subassemblies are available for 420 wagons per day, this volume is too large for a three-station balance, but an alternate choice of running the line at higher speeds for less than a full day may cause inventory and coordination problems. Considerations such as these abound in practice. Indeed, an argument can be made that these problems are of such significance that top management should acquire more than a casual understanding of line balancing concepts *before* a line technology is selected.[11]

Deliberate imbalance of assembly lines. Under certain situations, it has been found desirable to deliberately unbalance assembly lines by having shorter operations at work stations in the middle of the line than at the front and back. The logic is that operator variability leads to work buildup toward the center of the line, and hence, to clear this out, shorter

---

[11] See Richard B. Chase, "Strategic Considerations in Assembly Line Selection," *California Management Review,* vol. 18, no. 1 (Fall 1975), pp. 17–23.

operation times are required by middle stations. This high-low-high time differential has been termed "the bowl phenomenon."[12]

Other balancing considerations. Time is only one of several criteria by which jobs may be assigned to work stations. A partial list of other criteria, which might be used separately or in conjunction with time, are given below. Procedurally, these criteria would be admitted to the "feasible remaining task" list in the same fashion as if they were precedence or time criteria.

1. Operator wage rates: Since it is common practice to pay operators according to their highest skilled tasks, costs may be kept down by having premium tasks performed at one station.
2. Equipment location: Tasks requiring the same tools or machines may be assigned to a special equipment work station.
3. Parts space: Tasks would be allocated so that bulky parts would not be used excessively at any one work station.
4. Parts similarity: Tasks requiring the same parts might be grouped together so as to minimize the number of storage locations along the line.
5. Social-psychological factors: To achieve a sense of completion by the operator, tasks may be combined into meaningful wholes. Tasks may also be grouped so as to facilitate two people working together.
6. Task characteristics: Dirty tasks, such as painting, oiling, or greasing, may be located in the same area, while imcompatible tasks, such as painting and sanding, should be separated.

Finally, we have assumed that the task times used in balancing are deterministic; however, since assembly lines are operated by people rather than by machines, this assumption is far from warranted in practice. Indeed, we would expect to find variations in the time required by a worker to perform the same task, rather than a constant time repeatedly achieved. Further, the magnitude of this variance differs from operator to operator and even for the same operator on different days.[13]

Computerized line balancing. Companies engaged in assembly methods commonly employ a computer for line balancing. While it appears that most of these firms develop their own computer programs, commercial package programs are also widely applied. One of these is General Electric's *Assembly-Line Configuration (ASYBL$)*, which uses the "ranked positional weight" rule in selecting tasks for work stations. Specifically, this rule states that tasks are assigned according to their positional weights, where

---

[12] See Torig E. El-Rayah, "The Efficiency of Balanced and Unbalanced Production Lines," *International Journal of Production Research*, vol. 17, no. 1 (1979), pp. 61–75.

[13] See Brennecke and the Kottas–Lau bibliographical references for methods of dealing with this problem.

EXHIBIT 8.16
Sample computer output

```
ENTER ØPTIØN NUMBER?3

ENTER TARGET EFFICIENCY?.85


TØTAL EFFICIENCY   =   82 %
STANDARD DEVIATIØN=      0.0153
TARGET CYCLE TIME  =    0.347
MINIM. CYCLE TIME  =    0.343
NØ. ØF STATIØNS =   19

TØTAL EFFICIENCY   =   80 %
STANDARD DEVIATIØN=      0.0175
TARGET CYCLE TIME  =    0.368
MINIM. CYCLE TIME  =    0.368
NØ. ØF STATIØNS =   18

TØTAL EFFICIENCY   =   75 %
STANDARD DEVIATIØN=      0.0214
TARGET CYCLE TIME  =    0.417
MINIM. CYCLE TIME  =    0.415
NØ. ØF STATIØNS =   17
```

Source: General Electric Company, *Assembly-Line Configuration, ASYBL$ User's Guide* (1975), p. 28.

a positional weight is the time for a given task plus the task times of all those which follow it. Thus, the task with the highest positional weight would be assigned to the first work station (subject to time, precedence, and zoning constraints). As is typical with such software, the user has several options in terms of how the problem is to be solved. Exhibit 8.16 illustrates a portion of program output when a target level of efficiency is used as a basis for deriving and comparing different balances for a 35-task assembly line. (The program can handle up to 450 tasks.) Note the trade-offs that take place as the number of work stations changes. In this case, the larger number of work stations allows for a better balance and, therefore, a higher efficiency.

A recent development in computerized line balancing is the MUST algorithm which can generate about 100 different balance solutions of equal quality for single product lines. The big advantage of this is that it eliminates the time-consuming process of making manual adjustments to work station assignments which are often necessary when there is only one solution to work from. The Dar-El and Rubinovitch reference explains how the program works.

When should a company switch to straight-line production? Volume is the primary determinant of when a company should shift from process to product layout (or vice versa). That is, the volume must be there before sufficient equipment and labor utilization will exist to justify the necessary duplication of machines and worker specialization. The general cost-volume trade-off cast as a make-or-buy decision is illustrated in Exhibit 8.17.

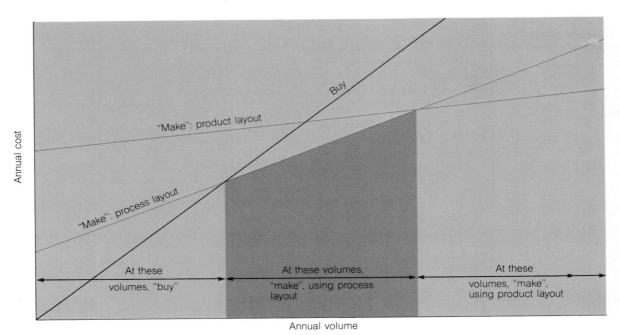

Source: Robert A. Olsen, *Manufacturing Management: A Quantitative Approach* (Scranton, Pa.: International Textbook Co. 1968), p. 314.

EXHIBIT 8.17
**Cost-volume re-
lationships for
alternative lay-
outs**

CONCLUSION

Although we have tended to deal with the plant layout problem in isolation, the reader should be aware that the selected physical layout has great impact not only on the things that one can see, such as product flow and worker placement, but on the less obvious elements of organization structure and communication flow. The operational effect of these unseen factors is to broaden the criteria by which the layout is derived.

Much has been written about the relative advantages of product and process layouts. As noted above, the evaluation centers on a trade-off between expected volume and desired machine utilization. Where demand is high for a homogeneous product line, the decision tends toward product layout since redundant equipment can be justified. On the other hand, where a wide variety of items is produced, fewer machines of a given type are required and process layout is generally preferred. Other factors, however, must also be considered in the decision: variation in demand, need for flexibility, supervision requirements, labor-force composition, and available plant space.[14] For these and other reasons, most factory installations are blends of the two types of flow formats, and management often makes it a point to continually evaluate the desirability of changing the flow formats. (In the case of functional layout formats, comparison is not particularly relevant; by definition, each is intended for a different purpose.)

In conclusion, we listed marks of a good layout at the beginning of this chapter. Below are some indications of a bad plant layout (or poor scheduling, or both):

1. Crowded conditions.
2. Production bottlenecks.
3. Backtracking.
4. Much work-in-process inventory.
5. Unexplainable delays and idle time.
6. Large number of people moving material.
7. Lost materials.
8. "Lost" workers.
9. Frequent accidents.

Some indicators of a bad layout in a high-contact service system are

1. Low sales volume per square foot of facility.
2. Excessive noise, poor lighting.
3. Imbalance between waiting areas and service areas.
4. Poor housekeeping.
5. Excessive waits for service.
6. Inaccessible or crowded support services (restrooms, waiting areas).
7. Excessive walking and material movement.
8. Customer dissatisfaction with the service experience.

REVIEW AND DISCUSSION QUESTIONS

1. How does the presence or absence of the customer in the production process affect the criteria used in making the layout decision?

2. What are the major inputs to the layout decision?

3. Contrast the measures of effectiveness used in assembly line balancing problems and process layout problems.

4. What is the importance of product homogeneity in choosing between product and process layout?

5. How do you determine the idle-time percentage from a given assembly line balance?

---

[14] For more complete discussions of these factors, see the Buffa-Miller and Moore bibliographical references.

6. Why is it often impossible to claim optimality for a particular process layout configuration?

7. What information of particular importance do route sheets and process charts (discussed in Chapters 2 and 3) provide to the layout planner?

8. What do you see as the key differences between ALDEP, CORELAP, and CRAFT?

9. Why is it that efficiency graphs (such as that shown in Exhibit 8.15) appear as sawtooth graphs? What is the nature of the trade-off they depict?

10. Under what conditions is the scheduling problem equivalent to the layout problem?

11. Give some examples of marketing layout problems you have encountered as a customer.

12. If you get a chance, ask a construction foreman how he or she decides on the placement of components at a construction site.

13. What advice would you give a supermarket manager about where he or she should locate a slow-moving item?

14. What are the major differences between the minimum material flow approach and the SLP approach to process layout?

PROBLEMS

1. Task Masters, Inc. manufactures a line of disciplinary devices including cattle prods, hobbles, and cages. The owner, Lash Whipley, is contemplating the opening of a new building to meet what appears to be an ever increasing demand for handcuffs in certain large cities. (Demand is correlated with leather sales.) The decision he is confronted with is whether he should buy these cuffs from subcontractors and use the building for quality control tests, painting on the company logo (which we won't describe), final packaging, and so forth; or to go into production using either a process or product layout.

   Given the following information, what course of action or policy would you recommend based upon a break-even analysis?

Alternatives	Fixed cost	Unit cost*
Buy.........................	$ 50,000/year	$10
Make: process layout	75,000/year	$ 7
Make: product layout	110,000/year	$ 4

   * Linear up to 50,000 units per year, which is maximum expected demand.

2. A University advising office has four rooms, each one dedicated to dealing with specific problems: petitions (room A), schedule advising (room B), grade complaints (room C), and student council (room D). The office is 80 feet long and 20 feet wide. Each room is 20 feet by 20 feet. The present location of rooms is A, B, C, D; that is, a straight line. The load summary shows the number of contacts that each advisor in a room has with other advisors in the other rooms. Assume that all advisors are equal in this value.

Load summary: AB = 10, AC = 20, AD = 30, BC = 15, BD = 10, CD = 20.

a. Evaluate this layout according to one of the methods in the chapter.

b. Improve the layout by exchanging functions within rooms. Show your amount of improvement using the same method as in a.

3. The following tasks must be performed on an assembly line in the sequence and times specified below.

Task	Task time (seconds)	Tasks which must precede
A	50	—
B	40	—
C	20	A
D	45	A,C
E	20	A,C
F	25	A,C,D
G	10	A,C,E
H	35	A,B,C,D,E,F

a. Draw the schematic diagram.

b. What is the theoretical minimum number of stations required to meet a forecasted demand of 400 units per eight-hour day?

c. Select a balancing rule and balance the line in the minimum number of stations to produce 400 units per day.

4. See if you can develop a departmental arrangement for the toy factory example in this chapter whose material handling cost would be less than $3,244.

5. Develop a set of efficiency graphs for 2, 3, and 4 stations for the assembly line depleted by the following precedence diagram. Assume a seven-hour day. Task times are in seconds.

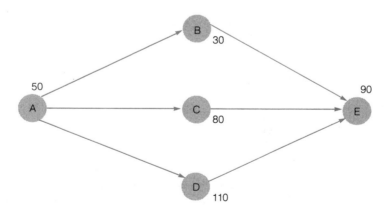

6. The Royal University of Dorton was created for the purpose of providing higher education for the aristocracy of the kingdom, the sons and daughters of resident foreign dignitaries, and other loyal and influential subjects. The regent of the country and university (Queen Harriet) has allocated a rectangular (40 by 80 feet) portion of the first floor of the south wing of the Imperial

Palace for the purpose of constructing lecture halls, laboratories and so forth. The interior layout was designed by Mr. S. L. P. Craft, and is one of the first examples of flexible layout by means of modular partitions in Dorton. The basic module is 10 feet square, and the tentative design is shown in Exhibit 8.18.

EXHIBIT 8.18
Current layout of the Royal University of Dorton

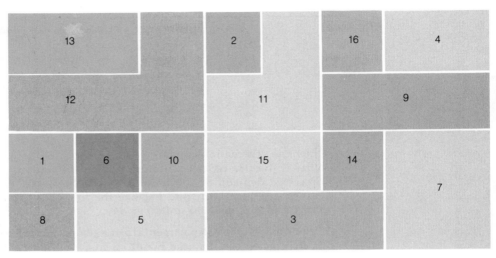

Number	Activity	Number	Activity
1	Entrance	9	Accounting
2	Meditation	10	Electrical engineering
3	Basketweaving*	11	Psychology
4	Calculus	12	Assertiveness training
5	Arithmetic	13	Humanities
6	Finance	14	Art
7	Production management	15	Philosophy
8	Economics	16	Exit

* Location must remain fixed due to its proximity to the fountain for soaking the weaving material.

Unlike most American universities, Dorton has only six categories of students. The members of each category are assigned the same classes and schedules during their years at the university. Each class meets for 50 minutes each day, and the students are required to proceed directly to their next class. The schedule for the current semester is indicated in Exhibit 8.19.

The architect is interested in gaining the favor of the queen and has contracted for you to verify his layout and suggest improvements. He has asked you to:

a. Prepare a flow matrix for the class sequence similar to the load summary shown in Exhibit 8.2.

b. Determine the cost of the existing layout in terms of walking. (Since the architect wishes to gain favor with the queen, he values each foot walked by the recent children of the queen as equivalent to two feet walked by the children from a previous marriage and to four feet walked by all others.)

   c. Create a better layout, keeping room areas the same and fitting into a 40 by 80-foot rectangular space. *Note:* the entrance and exit must remain in the same position.

EXHIBIT 8.19
Dorton University's semester schedule

Category	Number of students	8	9	10	11	12	1	2	3	4	5	6
		Classroom										
1. Queen's children	8	15	4	7	11	6	10	12	13	2	9	8
2. Queen's children (by a previous marriage)	4	3	14	5								
3. Merchants' children	32	5	9	6	8	11	7					
4. Nobles' children	25	12	3	13	7	4						
5. Children of idle rich	42	7	12	14	13	3						
6. Children of foreign officials	17	2	7	4	10	15	6	14				

Class meeting time

7. Given the following data on the task precedence relationships for an assembled product and assuming the tasks cannot be split, what is the theoretical minimum cycle time? Assume a cycle time of seven minutes.

Task	Performance time in minutes	Tasks that must precede
A	3	—
B	6	A
C	7	A
D	5	A
E	2	A
F	4	A,C,B
G	5	A,C
H	5	A,B,C,D,E,F,G

   a. Determine the minimum number of work stations needed to achieve this cycle time using the "ranked positional weight" rule.

   b. Determine the minimum number of stations needed to meet a cycle time of ten minutes according to the "largest number of following tasks" rule.

   c. Compute the efficiency of the balances achieved.

8. Sketch the floor plan and identify the location of major items of furniture and appliances at your residence.

   a. Specify the bases for placing the components in their present positions.

   b. Develop a hypothetical layout that would optimize your utilization of facilities. Be sure to specify the measure of effectiveness you will use in your analysis.

9. S. L. P. Craft, would like your help in developing a layout for a new outpatient clinic to be built in Dorton. Based upon analysis of another recently built

Interdepartmental flow and closeness ratings

Departments	2	3	4	5	6	Area requirement (sq. ft.)
1 Reception	A / 2	O / 5	E / 200	U / 0	O / 10	100
2 X-ray		E / 10	I / 300	U / 0	O / 8	100
3 Surgery			I / 100	I / 0	A / 4	200
4 Examining rooms (5)				U / 0	I / 15	500
5 Lab					O / 3	100
6 Nurses' station						100

clinic, he obtains the following data for (1) number of trips made by patients between departments on a typical day (shown above diagonal line), and (2), the closeness ratings (defined in Exhibit 8.9c) between departments as specified by the new clinic's physicians (below diagonal). The new building will be 60 feet by 20 feet.

a. Develop an interdepartmental flow graph which minimizes patient travel.
b. Develop a "good" relationship diagram using Systematic Layout Planning.
c. Choose either of the layouts obtained in a or b and sketch the departments to scale within the building.
d. Will this layout be satisfactory to the nursing staff? Explain.

SELECTED BIBLIOGRAPHY

Axler, Bruce H. *Food Service: A Managerial Approach.* New York: D. C. Heath and Co., 1979.

Brennecke, Donald "Two Parameter Assembly Line Balancing Models," in *Models and Analysis for Production Management,* ed. Michael P. Hottenstein. Scranton, Pa.: International Textbook Co., 1968, pp. 215–35.

Buffa, E. S.; Armour, G. C.; and Vollmann, T. E. "Allocating Facilities with CRAFT," *Harvard Business Review* (March–April 1964), pp. 136–58.

——— and Miller, Jeffery *Production Inventory Systems: Planning and Control.* rev. ed. Homewood, Ill.: Richard D. Irwin, Inc., 1979.

Buxey, G. M.; Slack, N. P.; and Wild, R. "Production Flow System Design— A Review," *AIIE Transactions,* vol. 5, no. 1 (March 1973), pp. 37–48.

Chase, R. B. "Survey of Paced Assembly Lines," *Industrial Engineering,* vol. 6, no. 2 (February 1974), pp. 14–18.

———. "Strategic Considerations in Assembly-Line Selection," *California Management Review,* vol. 18, no. 1 (Fall 1975), pp. 17–23.

Dar-El, E. M., and Rubinovitch, Y. "MUST— A Multiple Solutions Technique for

Balancing Single Model Assembly Lines." *Management Science,* vol. 25, no. 11 (November 1979), pp. 1105–14.

Francis, R. L., and White, J. A.   *Facility Layout and Location: An Analytical Approach.* Englewood Cliffs, N.J.: Prentice-Hall , 1974.

Helgeson, W. B., and Birnie, D. P.   "Assembly Line Balancing Using the Ranked Positional Weight Technique," *Journal of Industrial Engineering,* vol. 12, no. 6 (November–December 1961), pp. 394–98.

Ignall, Edward J.   "A Review of Assembly Line Balancing," *Journal of Industrial Engineering,* vol. 16, no. 4 (July–August 1965), pp. 244–54.

Kottas, J. F., and Lau, H.   "A Cost-Oriented Approach to Stochastic Line Balancing," *AIIE Transactions,* vol. 5, no. 2 (June 1973), pp. 164–71.

Lee, Robert S., and Moore, James M.   "CORELAP—Computerized Relationship Layout Planning," *Journal of Industrial Engineering,* vol. 18, no. 3 (March 1967), pp. 195–200.

Mastor, Anthony A.   "An Experimental Investigation and Comparative Evaluation of Production Line Balancing Techniques," *Management Science,* vol. 16, no. 11 (July 1970), pp. 728–46.

Moore, James M.   *Plant Layout and Design.* New York: Macmillan Co., 1962.

Muther, Richard   *Practical Plant Layout.* New York: McGraw-Hill Book Company, 1955.

Muther, Richard, and Wheeler, John D.   "Simplified Systematic Layout Planning," *Factory,* vol. 120, nos. 8, 9, 10 (August, September, October 1962), pp. 68–77, 111–19, 101–13.

Seehof, Jarrold M., and Evans, Wayne O.   "Automated Layout Design Program," *Journal of Industrial Engineering,* vol. 18, no. 12 (December 1967), pp. 690–95.

Thompkins, James, A., and Moore, James M.   *Computer Aided Layout: A User's Guide.* Publication no. 1, Facilities Planning and Design Division, American Institute of Industrial Engineers, Inc., Atlanta: AIIE, Inc., 1978.

Wu, Nesa L. J.   "Multiple Decision Role Line Balancing Technique (MDR)." Proceedings of the 11th Annual Meeting, American Institute for Decision Sciences, New Orleans, 1979, pp. 386–88.

Chapter 9

WAITING LINE THEORY

The other line moves faster[1]
Barbara Ettorre, *Harpers,* August 1974.

Waiting line or queuing theory was originated in the early 1900s by the Danish mathematician, A. K. Erlang, who employed it to study problems of telephone traffic. Since that time, and especially since the end of World War II, waiting line theory has had extensive application in industry and has become a standard tool of operations management.

In this technical note we will present the basic elements of a waiting line situation and provide the standard "steady-state" formulas for solving waiting line problems. While we will discuss some of the statistical aspects of the subject, the mathematics used to derive the formulas are somewhat involved and will not be considered here. Readers interested in such derivations are encouraged to consult the references at the end of the chapter.

THE WAITING LINE PROBLEM

A waiting line situation arises whenever arrivals at a service facility desire similar services. Such situations, of course, exist in virtually every productive system and are a fact of life in even the most prosaic human activities.

Central to the waiting line problem is a trade-off decision—that is,

---

[1] This is known as Ettorre's observation. The full version is: "The Other Line Moves Faster—this applies to all lines—bank, supermarket, toll booth, customs, and so on. And don't try to change lines. The other line—the one you were in originally—will then move faster."

comparing the extra cost of providing more rapid service (more traffic lanes, additional checkout stands, and so forth) with the inherent costs of waiting (lost customers, larger waiting rooms, longer waiting lines, and so forth). In some instances, this cost trade-off decision is straightforward. For example, if we find that the total time our employees spend in line waiting to use a copying machine would otherwise be spent in productive activity, we could compare the cost of adding an additional machine to the value of employee time saved. The decision could then be reduced to dollar terms and the choice easily made.

On the other hand, suppose that our waiting line problem centers upon the demands of the patients for beds in a hospital. We can compute the cost of additional beds by summing the costs for building construction, additional equipment required, and increased maintenance. But what is on the other side of the scale? Here we are confronted with the problem of trying to place a dollar figure on a patient's need of a hospital bed and finding none available. While we can arrive at an estimate of lost hospital income, what about the human cost arising from this lack of adequate hospital care?

Consider another waiting line that forms every fall—the registration line in college. If we desire to speed the registration process by adding more service lines, the college will incur additional costs in paying more clerks and student assistants. To be weighed against this additional cost to the college is the time saved by the students—a commodity that defies economic quantification. Some may state that the cost of a student's standing in line is a negligible factor in the university budget, although the student will be reluctant to agree that his or her time has no value.

In summary, these two examples show that the mere existence of a trade-off does not guarantee that it can be adequately quantified or that it will be explicitly considered in decision making. Of course, such considerations extend far beyond waiting line problems.

WAITING LINE CHARACTERISTICS

Exhibit 9.1 depicts a conceptual framework for viewing the various characteristics of waiting line problems. A detailed examination of these characteristics, under the major framework headings, is given in Exhibit 9.2. The ensuing discussion is devoted to elaboration upon each of these items.

I. Population source

The source of arrivals at a service system may be a *finite* or an *infinite* population. A factory has a finite number of machines that may require repair—that is, become *arrivals* to the repair facility or repair crew. A physician has a finite number of regular patients. In practical terms, an infinite population, in contrast, is one that is large in *comparison* to the service system. Thus, for a barbershop, 200 customers may be treated as an infinite

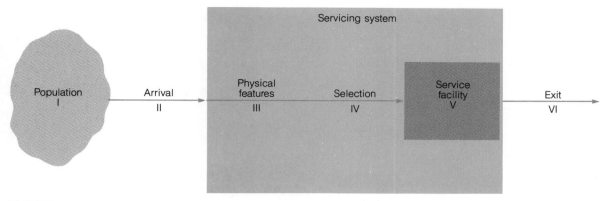

Servicing system

EXHIBIT 9.1
Framework for viewing waiting line situations

population, but at least several hundred thousand vehicles would be required to constitute an infinite population for the California freeway system.

II. Arrival characteristics

Pattern. The arrivals at a system are far more *controllable* than is generally recognized. Barbers may decrease their Saturday arrival rate (and supposedly shift it to other days of the week) by charging an extra 50 cents for adult haircuts and/or charging adult prices for children's haircuts. Department stores run sales during the off-season or "one-day-only" sales in part for purposes of control. Airlines offer "excursion" and off-season

EXHIBIT 9.2
Characteristics of waiting line problems

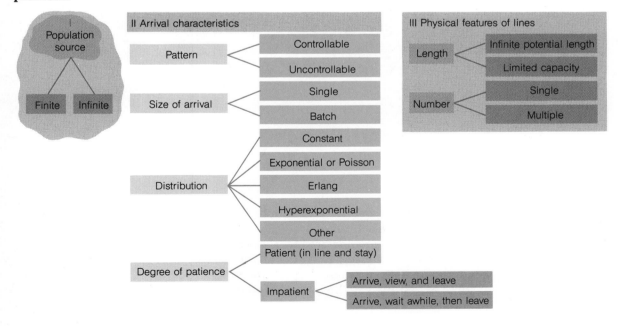

EXHIBIT 9.2
(continued)

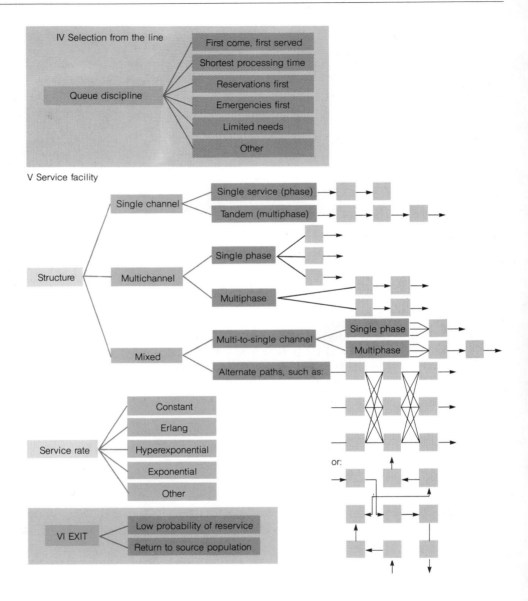

rates for similar reasons. The simplest of all arrival-control devices is the posting of business hours.

Some service demands are clearly *uncontrollable,* such as emergency medical demands on a city's hospital facilities. However, even in these situations, the arrivals at emergency rooms in specific hospitals are controllable to some extent by, say, keeping ambulance drivers informed of each hospital's status.

EXHIBIT 9.3
**Constant
arrival pattern
with time
interval = *t* and
variance = 0**

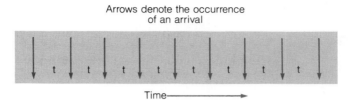

Arrows denote the occurrence
of an arrival

Time——————→

Size of arrival units. A *single arrival* may be thought of as one unit when a unit is defined as the smallest number handled. A single arrival on the floor of the New York Stock Exchange (NYSE) is 100 shares of stock; a single arrival at an egg-processing plant might be a dozen eggs or a flat of two and a half dozen.

A *batch arrival* is some multiple of the unit, as a block of 1,000 shares on the NYSE, a case of eggs at the processing plant, or a party of five at a restaurant.

Distribution of arrivals. A *constant* arrival distribution is periodic, with exactly the same time period between successive arrivals (see Exhibit 9.3). In productive systems, about the only arrivals that truly approach a constant interarrival period are those that are subject to machine control.

Two views can be taken of any arrival process. Either we can look at the time between successive arrivals to gain some insight into the probabilities of particular times between arrivals, or we may set some specific length of time *(T)* and seek to determine how many arrivals might occur within that length of time (Exhibit 9.4).

In the first case, when arrivals at a service facility occur on a purely random fashion, a plot of the interarrival times yields an *exponential* distribution such as that shown in Exhibit 9.5. The mathematical formula for this class of distributions is

$$f(t) = \lambda e^{-\lambda t} \tag{1}$$

In equation (1), the probability *f(t)* is often written as P_t. This equation, graphed in Exhibit 9.5 for single arrivals, shows that short intervals between arrivals are more probable than long intervals. The curve can be used in two ways: first, it directly shows the probability that there will be at least *t* units of time until the next arrival, or second, the probability that the next arrival will occur in a time of *t* or less can be computed as

EXHIBIT 9.4
**Variable arrival
pattern**

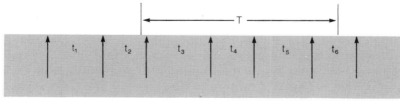

Time ——————→

EXHIBIT 9.5
**Exponential
distribution of
$\lambda e^{-\lambda t}$ where
$\lambda = 1$**

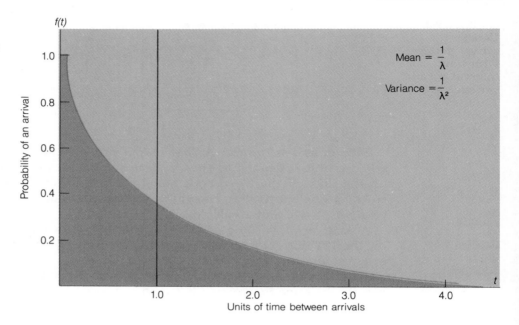

one minus the value read off the curve. The following table shows the
probability of the next arrival for several values of t in Exhibit 9.5.

t	Probability that the next arrival will occur in t minutes or more. (Read directly from Exhibit 9.5) $f(t)$	Probability that the next arrival will occur in t minutes or less $[1 - f(t)]$
0 minutes	1.0	$1 - 1.0 = 0$
1 minute	0.35	$1 - 0.35 = 0.65$
2 minutes	0.15	$1 - 0.15 = 0.85$
4 minutes	0	$1 - 0 = 1.0$

In the second case, where one is interested in the number of arrivals during
some time period T, the distribution appears as in Exhibit 9.6 and is obtained by finding the probability of n arrivals during T. If the arrival
process is random, the distribution is the *Poisson*, and formula 2 applies.

$$P_T(n) = \frac{(\lambda T)^n e^{-\lambda T}}{n!} \tag{2}$$

Equation (2) shows the probability of exactly n arrivals in time T. For
example, if the mean arrival rate of units into a system is 3 per minute
($\lambda = 3$) and we want to find the probability that exactly 5 units will
arrive within a 1 minute period ($n = 5$, $T = 1$), we have,

$$P_{1,5} = \frac{(3 \times 1)^5 e^{-3 \times 1}}{5!} = \frac{3^5 e^{-3}}{120} = 2.025 e^{-3} = 0.101$$

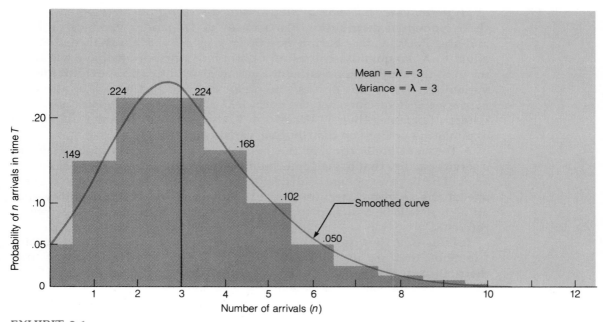

EXHIBIT 9.6
**Poisson
distribution
for $\lambda T = 3$**

That is, there is a 10.1 percent chance that there will be 5 arrivals in any one minute interval.

Although often shown as a smoothed curve, as in Exhibit 9.6, the Poisson distribution is a discrete distribution (the curve becomes smoother as n becomes larger). The distribution is discrete because n refers, in our example, to the number of arrivals in a system, and this must be an integer (for example, there cannot be 1.5 arrivals).

Parameters of the exponential and Poisson distributions. The exponential and Poisson distributions can be derived from one another. The mean and variance of the Poisson are equal and denoted by λ. The mean of the exponential is $1/\lambda$ and its variance is $1/\lambda^2$. (Remember: the time between arrivals is exponentially distributed and the number of arrivals per unit of time is Poisson distributed.)

Negative exponential and Poisson tables. Appendixes E and F provide tables for the negative exponential distribution (or natural logarithms) and the Poisson distribution. You might wish to see if you can obtain the same values from these tables that we obtained from solving the formulas for $f(t)$ and $P_T(n)$.[2] Note that the tables can be used in exactly the same way for analyzing service times and service rates as they are for arrivals. However, by convention, the term μ is used instead of λ when referring to service.

---

[2] The Poisson distribution in Appendix F is cumulative; that is, the probability for c = 5, for example, includes the probability of 0, 1, 2, 3, 4, and 5 arrivals. Therefore, to find the probability that c is equal to exactly 5, subtract the probability of $c = 4$ from the probability of $c = 5$.

Hyperexponential and hyperpoisson distributions. As noted above, the exponential distribution has a mean of $1/\lambda$ and a variance of $1/\lambda^2$, and the Poisson distribution has both a mean and a variance that are equal to λ. Frequently, empirically observed distributions have the same mean as the simple exponential or Poisson distributions but exhibit greater variability. When this occurs, the prefix *hyper* is used to denote them. A *hyperexponential* variance has the form j/λ^2 and a *hyperpoisson* variance is $j\lambda$, where j is greater than 1. When $j = 1$, the variances become the simple exponential or Poisson distribution variances.

A frequent application of the hyperexponential distribution occurs in a service facility that has several channels with differing exponential service rates. The hyperexponential distribution that results is the weighted average of the service distribution of each channel and the probability that an arrival will be assigned to that channel (see the Saaty bibliographical reference).

Erlang distributions. The term *Erlang* applies to a class of density functions that are useful in representing a variety of interarrival time distributions. The generic function for any Erlang distribution is

$$f(t) = \frac{K\lambda (K\lambda t)^{K-1} e^{-K\lambda t}}{(K-1)!} \qquad (3)$$

All such distributions have a mean of $1/\lambda$ and a variance of $1/K\lambda^2$. In this formula, K is any positive integer and is used to distinguish one Erlang distribution from another; that is, if $K = 1$, we would be referring to a first-order Erlang distribution, if $K = 2$, to a second-order Erlang distribution, and so forth.

Depending on which value of K is selected, a distribution may be shaped to approximate the actual observed data. Examining the extremes of this equation, we note that when $K = 1$, the time to observe one arrival reduces to $\lambda e^{-\lambda t}$, which is in fact the exponential distribution. When K becomes very large, the variance becomes zero, which means that the time between arrivals becomes constant. Exhibit 9.7 shows several Erlang distributions with $\lambda = 1$.

Goodness of fit. Several methods can be used to determine whether or not the observed pattern of arrivals (or services) matches one of the above distributions. In many instances, a graph of the data may be sufficient. However, if more certainty is deemed necessary, then statistical tests for goodness of fit (e.g., chi-square) should be applied.[3] If the distributions clearly do not fit the Poisson-exponential model, then simulation techniques (Chapter 12) are probably necessary to solve the queuing problem at hand.

---

[3] For a good discussion of curve fitting methods applied to queuing see Walter C. Giffin, *Queueing: Basic Theory and Applications* (Columbus, Ohio: Grid Publishing Company, Inc., 1978), chapter 13.

EXHIBIT 9.7
Erlang distributions with λ = 1

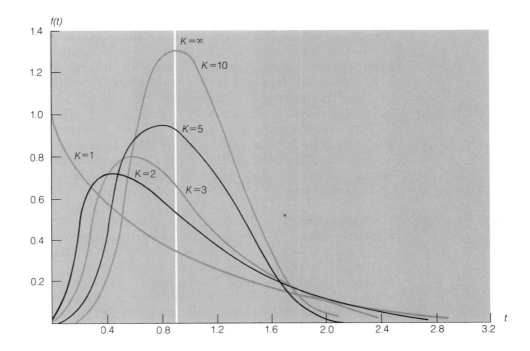

Degree of patience. A *patient* arrival is one who waits as long as necessary until the service facility is ready to serve him. (Even if arrivals grumble and behave *im*patiently, the fact that they wait is sufficient to label them as patient arrivals for purposes of waiting line theory.)

There are two classes of *impatient* arrivals. The first class arrives, surveys both the service facility and the length of the line, and then decides to leave. The second class arrives, views the situation and joins the waiting line, and then, after some period of time, departs. The behavior of the first type is termed *balking* and the second is termed *reneging.*

III. Physical features of lines

Length. In a practical sense, an infinite line is very long in terms of the capacity of the service system. Examples of *infinite potential length* are a line of vehicles backed up for miles at a bridge crossing, or customers waiting to purchase tickets at a theater who must form a line around the block.

Such systems as gas stations, loading docks, and parking lots have *limited line capacity* due to legal restrictions or physical space characteristics. This complicates the waiting line problem not only in terms of service system utilization and waiting line computations but in terms of the shape of the actual arrival distribution as well. The arrival who is denied entry into the line because of lack of space may rejoin the population for a later try, or he may seek service elsewhere. Either action makes an obvious difference in the finite population case.

Number of lines. A *single line* or single file is, of course, one line only. The term *multiple lines* refers either to the single lines that form in front of two or more servers or to single lines that converge at some central redistribution point. The disadvantage of multiple lines in a busy facility is that arrivals often will shift lines if several previous services have been of short duration or if those customers currently in other lines appear to require a short service time. Although the overall characteristics of the facility and the expected waiting time of a customer remain the same, the variability within customers' waiting time will increase if customers are not equally skilled in the art of switching lines. When this inequality exists, the effect is the same as if special priorities are given to a particular class of customer.

IV. Selection from the waiting line

Queue discipline. A queue discipline is a priority rule, or set of rules, for determining the order of service to customers in a waiting line. As will be discussed with respect to scheduling in Chapter 14, the rules selected can have a dramatic effect on the system's overall performance. In waiting line situations, the number of customers in line, the average waiting time, the range of variability in waiting time, and the efficiency of the service facility are just a few examples of factors that are affected by the choice of priority rules.

Probably the most common priority rule is *first-come first-served* (FCFS). This rule states that the customers in line are served on the basis of their chronological arrival; no other characteristics have any bearing on the selection process. This is popularly accepted as the "fairest" rule, but in practice, it discriminates against the arrival requiring a short service time. A common example occurs in the supermarket, where the shopper with a single item must either wait a long time or rely on the largesse of those ahead of him who may have shopping baskets full of groceries (express lines are mentioned below under "line structuring rules").

Reservations first, emergencies first, highest-profit customer first, largest orders first, best customers first, longest waiting time in line, and *soonest promised date* are other examples of priority rules. As will be seen in Chapter 14, each rule has attractive features as well as shortcomings.

Line structuring rules. "Single transactions only" (as in a bank) or "limited needs" (such as a quick checkout in a market) are directives that are similar to priority rules, though in reality they are methodologies for structuring the line itself. Such lines are formed of a specific class of customers with similar characteristics. Within each line, however, priority rules still apply (as before) to the method of selecting the next customer to be served. A classic case of line structuring is the fast checkout line for customers with six items or less in a busy supermarket. Interestingly enough, the advantage of such a separate line is mainly psychological, since the same service could be achieved by permitting people who buy six items or less to go to the head of the line.

V. Service facility

Structure. The physical flow of items to be serviced may go through a single line, multiple lines, or some mixtures of the two. The choice of format depends partly on the volume of customers served and partly on the restrictions imposed by sequential requirements as to the order in which service must be performed.

Single channel, single phase. This is the simplest type of waiting line structure, and straightforward formulas are available to solve the problem for standard distribution patterns of arrival and service. When the distributions are nonstandard, the problem is easily solved by computer simulation. A typical example of a single-channel, single-phase situation is the one-person barbershop.

Single channel, multiphase. A carwash is an illustration of this multiphase case, for a series of services—vacuuming, wetting, washing, rinsing, drying, window cleaning, and parking—is performed in a fairly uniform sequence. A critical factor in the single-channel case with service in series is the amount of buildup of items allowed in front of each service, which in turn constitutes separate waiting lines.

Because of the inherent variability in service times, the optimal situation in terms of maximizing the utilization of the service station is to allow the building of an infinite waiting line in front of each station. The worst situation is that in which no line is permitted and only one customer at a time is allowed. When no sublines are allowed to build up in front of each station, as in a car wash, the utilization of the overall service facility is governed by the probability that a long service time will be required by any one of the servers in the system. This problem is common in most product-oriented systems, such as assembly lines. In process-oriented systems, such as job shops, the processing of orders in lots—rather than singly—permits maximum utilization of the server by allowing the inventory of available items to absorb the variation in performance time.

Multichannel, single phase. Tellers' windows in a bank and checkout counters in high-volume department stores exemplify this type of structure. The difficulty with this format is that the uneven service time given each customer will result in unequal speed or flow among the lines. This, in turn, results in some customers' being served before others who arrived earlier as well as in some degree of line shifting. Varying this structure to assure the servicing of arrivals in chronological order would entail the forming of a single line, from which, as a server becomes available, the next customer in the queue is assigned to that server.

The major problem of this structure is that it requires rigid control of the line to maintain order and to direct customers to available servers. In some instances, assigning numbers to customers in order of their arrival helps alleviate this problem. (We will discuss some other options in Chapter 18.)

Multichannel, multiphase. This case is similar to the one above except that two or more services are performed in sequence. The admission of patients in a hospital follows this pattern because a specific sequence of steps is usually followed: initial contact at the admissions desk, filling out forms, making identification tags, obtaining a room assignment, escorting the patient to the room, and so forth. Since several servers are usually available for this procedure, more than one patient at a time may be processed.

Mixed. Under this general heading, we may consider two subcategories: *(a) multi-to-single-channel structures* and *(b) alternate path structures.* Under *(a),* we find either lines that merge into one for single-phase service, as at a bridge crossing where two lanes merge into one, or lines that merge into one for multiple-phase service, such as subassembly lines feeding into a main line. Under *(b),* we encounter two structures that differ in directional flow requirements. The first is similar to the multiple-channel-multiple-phase case, except that (1) there may be switching from one channel to the next after the first service has been rendered and (2) the number of channels and phases may vary—again—after performance of the first service.

The second structure has no flow restrictions, and customers arriving at this facility may obtain whatever services are required and in any sequence. This is the job shop format, and here we encounter a very complex scheduling problem. To date, there are no known methods for obtaining an optimal solution for such problems. Most progress has been through computer simulation that uses a variety of configurations and priority rules (see Chapter 12).

Service rate. The rationale underlying these distributions is similar to the descriptions under the heading "distribution of arrivals." A *constant* service time rule states that each service takes exactly the same time. As in constant arrivals, this characteristic is generally limited to machine-controlled operations. Analogous to their use in arrival rates, the *Erlang* and *hyperexponential* distributions are used to represent service times when they appear to be better approximations of the observed rate than is a simpler distribution.

A frequently used illustration of the *Erlang* distribution employs a single-channel, multi service situation. However, the conditions that must be met for the Erlang approximation are so severe as to make practical application rare. The distribution applies only when each service in the series is exponentially distributed with the same mean and no time delay is allowed between them. An example will illustrate the restrictions in one application. Suppose that, in rebuilding machines, one repairman has a sequence of five operations to perform. If his service time for *each* operation is exponentially distributed, with *each* having the same average completion time, the Erlang equations may be used to solve the problem (with K equal to the number of services, or five in this example). Such conditions, however, are seldom found in practice.

The *exponential* distribution is frequently used to approximate the actual service distribution. This practice, however, may lead to incorrect results in that relatively few service situations are closely represented by the exponential function since the service facility must be capable of performing services of very short duration relative to the average time of service. Telephone usage (the original subject of queuing theory) is one of the few systems that embodies this feature, and therefore, it is well approximated by the exponential. This is so because telephone usage may range from a few seconds—where the user picks up the receiver and replaces it, having changed his mind about making the call, or where the user dialed the first number wrong and starts over again—to a conversation of an hour or more.

Even in telephony, however, this distribution has its peculiarities. For example, it has been shown that there is a noticeable variation between the actual service time and the exponential approximation between 20 and 30 seconds. This happens in the case of a caller who, having dialed a number, waits for an answer to determine whether the call is to the correct destination and whether the party he or she is calling is available. Another deviation from the exponential approximation occurs with toll calls when a minimum charge is made for a specific number of minutes. If the caller is charged for three minutes' usage, there is an observed tendency on the part of the caller to approach that minimum rather than complete the call in one or two minutes.

Most other types of services also have some "practical" minimum time. A clerk in a checkout line may have a three-minute average service time but a one-minute minimum time. This is particularly true where another checkout aisle provides quick service. Likewise in a barbershop, while the average service time of a barber may be 20 minutes, he rarely cuts hair or gives a shave in less than 10 or more than 45 minutes.

Hence, these and similar types of services that have strong time dependency are poorly characterized by the exponential curve. Unfortunately, data collectors on a given problem frequently group their data in increments so that, when they are plotted as a histogram, the exponential approximation seems valid. If smaller time increments were taken, however, the inapplicability of the distribution would be obvious at the lower time values.

VI. Exit

Once a customer is served, two exit fates are possible: (1) he can *return to the source population* and immediately become a competing candidate for service again or (2) he may enter a category with a *low probability of reservice*. The first case can be illustrated by a machine which has been routinely repaired and returned to duty but may break down again; the second can be illustrated by a machine that has been overhauled or modified and has a low probability of reservice over the near future. In a lighter vein, we might refer to (1) as the "recurring-common-cold case" and to (2) as the "appendectomy-only-once case."

It should be apparent that when the population source is finite, any change in the service performed on customers who return to the population will modify the arrival rate at the service facility. This, of course, will alter the characteristics of the waiting line under study and necessitate reanalysis of the problem.

SAMPLE PROBLEMS

This section contains solved problems using the standard models and queuing formulas found in the literature. However, in using these formulas, it should be kept in mind that they are steady-state formulas derived on the assumption that the process under study is ongoing. Thus, they may provide inaccurate results when applied to initial operations such as the manufacture of a new product or the start of a business day by a service firm. (Exhibits 9.8 and 9.9 give models and notation.)

Model 1

Western National Bank is considering opening a drive-in window for customer service. Management estimates that customers will arrive for service at the rate of 15 per hour. The teller whom it is considering to staff the window can service customers at the rate of one every three minutes.

Assuming Poisson arrivals and exponential service, find

1. Utilization of the teller.
2. Average number in the waiting line.
3. Average number in the system.
4. Average waiting time in line.
5. Average waiting time in the system including service.

Solution (using model 1 equations from Exhibit 9.10).
1. The average utilization of the teller is

$$\rho = \frac{\lambda}{\mu} = \frac{15}{20} = 75 \text{ percent}$$

2. The average number in the waiting line is

$$\bar{n}_l = \frac{\lambda^2}{\mu(\mu - \lambda)} = \frac{(15)^2}{20(20 - 15)} = 2.25 \text{ customers}$$

3. The average number in the system is

$$\bar{n}_s = \frac{\lambda}{\mu - \lambda} = \frac{15}{20 - 15} = 3 \text{ customers}$$

4. Average waiting time in line is

$$\bar{t}_l = \frac{\lambda}{\mu(\mu - \lambda)} = \frac{15}{20(20 - 15)} = 0.15 \text{ hour or 9 minutes}$$

5. Average waiting time in the system is

$$\bar{t}_s = \frac{1}{\mu - \lambda} = \frac{1}{20 - 15} = 0.2 \text{ hour or 12 minutes}$$

EXHIBIT 9.8
Properties of some specific waiting line models

Model	Layout	Service phase	Source population	Arrival pattern	Queue discipline	Service pattern	Permissible queue length	Typical example
(1)	Single channel	Single	Infinite	Poisson	FCFS	Exponential	Unlimited	Drive-in teller at bank, one-lane toll bridge
(2)	Single channel	Single	Infinite	Poisson	FCFS	Constant	Unlimited	Automatic car wash, roller coaster rides in amusement park
(3)	Single channel	Single	Infinite	Poisson	FCFS	Exponential	Limited	Ice cream stand, cashier in a restaurant
(4)	Single channel	Single	Infinite	Poisson	FCFS	Any distribution	Unlimited	Empirically derived distribution of flight time for a transcontinental flight
(5)	Single channel	Single	Infinite	Poisson	FCFS	Erlang	Unlimited	One-man barbershop
(6)	Multiple channel	Single	Infinite	Poisson	FCFS	Exponential	Unlimited	Parts counter in auto agency, two-lane toll bridge
(7)	Single channel	Single	Finite	Poisson	FCFS	Exponential	Unlimited	Machine breakdown and repair in a factory

EXHIBIT 9.9
Infinite queuing notation (infinite)

σ = Standard deviation

λ = Arrival rate

μ = Service rate

$\dfrac{1}{\mu}$ = Average service time

$\dfrac{1}{\lambda}$ = Average time between arrivals

ρ = Potential utilization of the service facility (defined as λ/μ)

$\bar{n}_l$ = Average number waiting in line

$\bar{n}_s$ = Average number in system (including any being served)

$\bar{t}_l$ = Average time waiting in line

$\bar{t}_s$ = Average total time in system (including time to be served)

K = Kth distribution in the Erlang family of curves

n = Number of units in the system

M = Number of identical service channels

Q = Maximum queue length (sum of waiting space and service space)

P_n = Probability of exactly n units in system

P_w = Probability of waiting in line

Finite queuing notation (based on Peck and Hazelwood tables)

D = Probability that an arrival must wait in line

F = Efficiency factor, a measure of the effect of having to wait in line

H = Average number of units being serviced

J = Population source less those in queuing system $(N - n)$

L = Average number of units in line

M = Number of service channels

n = Average number of units in queuing system (including the one being served)

N = Number of units in population source

P_n = Probability of exactly n units in queuing system

T = Average time to perform the service

U = Average time between customer service requirements

W = Average waiting time in line

X = Service factor, or proportion of service time required

EXHIBIT 9.10
Equations for models in Exhibit 9.8 (see Exhibit 9.9 for explanation of notation)

Model 1

$$\bar{n}_l = \frac{\lambda^2}{\mu(\mu-\lambda)} \qquad \bar{t}_l = \frac{\lambda}{\mu(\mu-\lambda)} \qquad P_n = \left(1-\frac{\lambda}{\mu}\right)\left(\frac{\lambda}{\mu}\right)^n$$

$$\bar{n}_s = \frac{\lambda}{\mu-\lambda} \qquad \bar{t}_s = \frac{1}{\mu-\lambda} \qquad \rho = \frac{\lambda}{\mu}$$

Model 2

$$\bar{n}_l = \frac{\lambda^2}{2\mu(\mu-\lambda)} \qquad \bar{t}_l = \frac{\lambda}{2\mu(\mu-\lambda)}$$

$$\bar{n}_s = \bar{n}_l + \frac{\lambda}{\mu} \qquad \bar{t}_s = \bar{t}_l + \frac{1}{\mu}$$

Model 3

$$\bar{n}_l = \left(\frac{\lambda}{\mu}\right)^2 \left[\frac{1-Q\left(\frac{\lambda}{\mu}\right)^{Q-1}+(Q-1)\left(\frac{\lambda}{\mu}\right)^{Q}}{\left(1-\frac{\lambda}{\mu}\right)\left(1-\left(\frac{\lambda}{\mu}\right)^{Q}\right)}\right]$$

$$\bar{n}_s = \frac{\lambda}{\mu} \left[\frac{1-(Q+1)\left(\frac{\lambda}{\mu}\right)^{Q}+Q\left(\frac{\lambda}{\mu}\right)^{Q+1}}{\left(1-\frac{\lambda}{\mu}\right)\left(1-\left(\frac{\lambda}{\mu}\right)^{Q+1}\right)}\right] \qquad P_n = \left[\frac{1-\frac{\lambda}{\mu}}{1-\left(\frac{\lambda}{\mu}\right)^{Q+1}}\right]\left(\frac{\lambda}{\mu}\right)^{n}$$

Model 4

$$\bar{n}_l = \frac{\left(\frac{\lambda}{\mu}\right)^2+\lambda^2\sigma^2}{2\left(1-\frac{\lambda}{\mu}\right)} \qquad \bar{t}_l = \frac{\frac{\lambda}{\mu^2}+\lambda\sigma^2}{2\left(1-\frac{\lambda}{\mu}\right)}$$

$$\bar{n}_s = \bar{n}_l + \frac{\lambda}{\mu} \qquad \bar{t}_s = \bar{t}_l + \frac{1}{\mu}$$

Model 5

$$\bar{n}_l = \frac{K+1}{2K}\cdot\frac{\lambda^2}{\mu(\mu-\lambda)} \qquad \bar{t}_l = \frac{K+1}{2K}\cdot\frac{\lambda}{\mu(\mu-\lambda)}$$

$$\bar{n}_s = \bar{n}_l + \frac{\lambda}{\mu} \qquad \bar{t}_s = \bar{t}_l + \frac{1}{\mu}$$

Model 6

$$\bar{n}_l = \frac{\lambda\mu\left(\frac{\lambda}{\mu}\right)^{M}}{(M-1)!(M\mu-\lambda)^2}P_0 \qquad \bar{t}_l = \frac{P_0}{\mu M M!\left(1-\frac{\lambda}{\mu M}\right)^2}\left(\frac{\lambda}{\mu}\right)^{M}$$

$$\bar{n}_s = \bar{n}_l + \frac{\lambda}{\mu} \qquad \bar{t}_s = \bar{t}_l + \frac{1}{\mu}$$

$$P_0 = \frac{1}{\displaystyle\sum_{n=0}^{M-1}\frac{\left(\frac{\lambda}{\mu}\right)^{n}}{n!}+\frac{\left(\frac{\lambda}{\mu}\right)^{M}}{M!\left(1-\frac{\lambda}{\mu M}\right)}} \qquad P_w = \left(\frac{\lambda}{\mu}\right)^{M}\frac{P_0}{M!\left(1-\frac{\lambda}{\mu M}\right)}$$

Model 7

This is a finite queuing situation that is most easily solved by using finite tables. These tables, in turn, require the manipulation of specific terms (see Exhibit 9.9 for notation).

$$X = \frac{T}{T+U} \qquad H = FNX \qquad L = N(1-F)$$

$$P_n = \frac{N!}{(N-n)!}X^n P_0 \qquad J = NF(1-X)$$

$$W = \frac{L(T+U)}{N-L} = \frac{LT}{H} \qquad F = \frac{T+U}{T+U+W}$$

$$n = L + H$$

Because of limited space availability and a desire to provide an acceptable level of service, the bank manager would like to assure, with 95 percent confidence, that not more than three cars will be in the system at any one time. What is the present level of service for the three-car limit? What level of utilization of the teller must be attained and what must be the service rate of the teller to assure the 95 percent level of service?

Solution. The present level of service for three cars or less is the probability that there are 0, 1, 2, or 3 cars in the system.

From Model I, Exhibit 9.10:

$$P_n = \left(1 - \frac{\lambda}{\mu}\right)\left(\frac{\lambda}{\mu}\right)^n$$

at $n = 0$ $P_0 = (1 - {}^{15}\!/_{20})({}^{15}\!/_{20})^0 = 0.250$
at $n = 1$ $P_1 = (\frac{1}{4})$ $({}^{15}\!/_{20})^1 = 0.188$
at $n = 2$ $P_2 = (\frac{1}{4})$ $({}^{15}\!/_{20})^2 = 0.141$
at $n = 3$ $P_3 = (\frac{1}{4})$ $({}^{15}\!/_{20})^3 = \underline{0.106}$

                                         0.685 or 68.5 percent

The probability of having more than three cars in the system is 1.0 minus the probability of three cars or less ($1.0 - 0.685 = 31.5$ percent).

For a 95 percent service level to three cars or less, this states that $P_0 + P_1 + P_2 + P_3 = 95$ percent.

$$0.95 = \left(1 - \frac{\lambda}{\mu}\right)\left(\frac{\lambda}{\mu}\right)^0 + \left(1 - \frac{\lambda}{\mu}\right)\left(\frac{\lambda}{\mu}\right)^1 + \left(1 - \frac{\lambda}{\mu}\right)\left(\frac{\lambda}{\mu}\right)^2 + \left(1 - \left(\frac{\lambda}{\mu}\right)\right)\left(\frac{\lambda}{\mu}\right)^3$$

$$0.95 = \left(1 - \frac{\lambda}{\mu}\right)\left[1 + \frac{\lambda}{\mu} + \left(\frac{\lambda}{\mu}\right)^2 + \left(\frac{\lambda}{\mu}\right)^3\right]$$

We can solve this by trial and error for values of $\frac{\lambda}{\mu}$. If $\frac{\lambda}{\mu} = 0.50$:

$$0.95 \stackrel{?}{=} 0.5(1 + 0.5 + 0.25 + 0.125)$$
$$0.95 \neq 0.9375$$

With $\frac{\lambda}{\mu} = 0.45$,

$$0.95 \stackrel{?}{=} (1 - 0.45)(1 + 0.45 + 0.203 + 0.091)$$
$$0.95 \neq 0.96$$

With $\frac{\lambda}{\mu} = 0.47$,

$$0.95 \stackrel{?}{=} (1 - 0.47)(1 + 0.47 + 0.221 + 0.104) = 0.95135$$
$$0.95 \approx 0.95135$$

Therefore, with the utilization $\left(\rho = \frac{\lambda}{\mu}\right)$ of 47 percent, the probability of three cars or less in the system is 95 percent.

To find the rate of service required to attain this 95 percent service level, we simply solve the equation $\lambda/\mu = 0.47$, where λ = number of arrivals per hour. This gives $\mu = 32$ per hour.

That is, the teller must serve approximately 32 people per hour—a 60 percent increase over the original 20-per-hour capability—for 95 percent confidence that not more than three cars will be in the system. Perhaps service may be speeded up by modifying the method of service, adding another teller, or limiting the number of types of transactions available at the drive-in window. It should also be noted that, with the condition of 95 percent confidence that three or fewer cars will be in the system, the teller will be idle 53 percent of the time.

Model 2

The Robot Company franchises combination gas and carwash stations throughtout the United States. Robot follows a policy of giving a free carwash for a fill-up of gasoline or, for a wash alone, charging $0.50. Past experience shows that the number of customers that have carwashes following fill-ups is about the same as for a wash alone. The average profit on a gasoline fill-up is about $0.70, and the cost of the carwash to Robot is $0.10. Robot stays open 14 hours per day.

Robot has three power units and drive assemblies, and a franchisee must determine which unit he prefers. Unit I can wash cars at the rate of one every five minutes and is leased for $12 per day. Unit II, a larger unit, can wash cars at the rate of one every four minutes but costs $16 per day. Unit III is the largest unit available, costing $22 per day, and can wash a car in three minutes.

The franchisee estimates that customers will not wait for more than an average five minutes in line for a carwash. A longer time will cause Robot to lose the gasoline sales as well as the carwash sale.

If the estimate of customer arrivals resulting in washes at the franchisee's proposed location is 10 per hour, which wash unit should be selected?

Solution. Using Unit I, calculate the average waiting time of customers in the wash line (μ for Unit I $= 12$ per hour). From the Model 2 equations (Exhibit 9.10),

$$\bar{t} = \frac{\lambda}{2\mu(\mu - \lambda)} = \frac{10}{2(12)(12 - 10)} = 0.208 \text{ hour or } 12.5 \text{ minutes}$$

For Unit II at 15 per hour,

$$\bar{t} = \frac{10}{2(15)(15 - 10)} = 0.067 \text{ hour or } 4 \text{ minutes}$$

If waiting time is the only criterion, Unit II should be purchased. However, before we make the final decision, we must look at the profit differential between both units.

The installation of Unit I would result in some customers balking and reneging because of the 12.5-minute wait. And although this greatly complicates the mathematical analysis, we can gain some estimate of lost sales with Unit I by inserting $t = 5$ minutes or $\frac{1}{12}$ hour (the average length of time customers will wait) and solving for λ. This would be the effective arrival rate of customers:

$$\bar{t}_i = \frac{\lambda}{2\mu(\mu - \lambda)}$$

$$\lambda = \frac{2\bar{t}_i\mu^2}{1 + 2\bar{t}_i\mu}$$

$$\lambda = \frac{2(\frac{1}{12})(12)^2}{1 + 2(\frac{1}{12})(12)} = 8 \text{ per hour}$$

Therefore, since the original estimate of λ was 10 per hour, an estimated two customers per hour will be lost. Lost profit of 2 customers per hour $\times$ 14 hours $\times$ $\frac{1}{2}$ ($0.70 fill-up profit + $0.40 wash profit) = $15.40 per day.

Since the additional cost of Unit II over Unit I is only $4 per day, the loss of $15.40 profit obviously warrants the installation of Unit II.

The original constraint of a five-minute maximum wait is satisfied by Unit II. Therefore Unit III is not considered unless the arrival rate is expected to increase in the future.

Model 3

A drive-through ice cream stand has space for a four-car line, including the car being served (the stand is on a main thoroughfare and the line cannot extend onto the street). The average arrival rate of potential customers is 40 cars per hour, and the service rate in filling the ice cream orders is 50 cars per hour. Average profit on ice cream purchased per car is $0.50. Additional driveway space is available from the owner of the lot next door at a leased rate of $5 per day. The stand is open 14 hours per day.

Assuming Poisson arrivals and exponential service, should space be rented in the adjacent lot? If so, how many spaces?

Solution. This is a limited queue-length problem and the Model 3 formulas are applicable. The easiest approach to solving this problem is to assume an increasing number of auto spaces and compare the additional profit generated by each space. Additional spaces will be rented until the profit becomes less than the $5 cost of rental.

Ice cream will be served to customers at the rate of 50 cars per hour any time there are cars in the system. To find the amount of time there are customers, we can solve for the probability of zero in the system and subtract this from 1. This will give us the percent of time ice cream is served.

From Model 3, (Exhibit 9.10):

$$P_n = \left[\frac{1 - \frac{\lambda}{\mu}}{1 - \left(\frac{\lambda}{\mu}\right)^{Q+1}} \right] \left(\frac{\lambda}{\mu}\right)^n$$

For the probability of zero cars in the system, with four spaces on the premises ($Q = 4$):

$$P_0 = \left[\frac{1 - \dfrac{\lambda}{\mu}}{1 - \left(\dfrac{\lambda}{\mu}\right)^{Q+1}} \right] \left(\frac{\lambda}{\mu}\right)^0 = \left[\frac{1 - \dfrac{40}{50}}{1 - \left(\dfrac{40}{50}\right)^5} \right] 1 = \frac{0.2}{1 - 0.328} = 0.298$$

And ice cream is being served $1 - 0.298 = 0.702$, or 70.2 percent of the time.

When one space is rented ($Q = 4 + 1 = 5$),

$$P_0 = \left[\frac{0.2}{1 - \left(\dfrac{40}{50}\right)^6} \right] = 0.271$$

Service is then being carried out $(1 - 0.271) = 0.729$, or 72.9 percent of the time, or an increase of 2.8 percent $(72.9 - 70.2)$. In profit, this is worth

$$0.028 \, (50 \text{ cars per hour} \times 14 \text{ hours per day} \times \$0.50 \text{ per car}) = \$9.80$$

When a second space is rented ($Q = 4 + 2 = 6$),

$$P_0 = \left[\frac{0.2}{1 - \left(\dfrac{40}{50}\right)^7} \right] = 0.253$$

and the facility is busy $1 - 0.253 = 0.747$, or 74.7 percent of the time.

Thus, the additional space increases the utilization of the stand by 1.8 percent $(74.7\% - 72.9\%)$ and increases profit by $6.30 (0.018) (50 \times 14 \times \$0.50)$. Since this amount is greater than the $5 rental charge, the space should be rented.

A third rented space, with $Q = 4 + 3 = 7$, gives

$$P_0 = \left[\frac{0.2}{1 - \left(\dfrac{40}{50}\right)^8} \right] = 0.241$$

and $1 - 0.241 = 0.759$.

Increased service is 1.2 percent $(75.9\% - 74.7\%)$ and added profit is $(50 \times 0.012 \times 14 \times \$0.50)$ or $4.20. The third space should not be rented since it would incur an $.80 loss ($5 - $4.20).

The optimal solution, then, is to rent just two spaces. The profit will be $261.45 per day $(0.747) (50 \times 14 \times \$0.50)$—quite reasonable for a good location.

We can also obtain some other useful information about the ice cream stand. The average number of cars in the system, both in line and being served, when two rented spaces are added, is

$$\bar{n}_s = \frac{\lambda}{\mu}\left[\frac{1-(Q+1)\left(\dfrac{\lambda}{\mu}\right)^Q + Q\left(\dfrac{\lambda}{\mu}\right)^{Q+1}}{\left(1-\dfrac{\lambda}{\mu}\right)\left(1-\left(\dfrac{\lambda}{\mu}\right)^{Q+1}\right)}\right]$$

$$\bar{n}_s = \frac{40}{50}\left[\frac{1-(6+1)\left(\dfrac{40}{50}\right)^6 + 6\left(\dfrac{40}{50}\right)^7}{\left(1-\dfrac{40}{50}\right)\left[1-\left(\dfrac{40}{50}\right)^7\right]}\right]$$

$$\bar{n}_s = 2.15 \text{ cars}$$

It is interesting to note that if an unlimited waiting line were possible, the increase in the efficiency (working time) of the ice cream stand would be increased by only 5.3 percent (the efficiency for an infinite line is $\rho = \lambda/\mu = \frac{4}{5} = 0.80$, or 80%). The average number of cars in the system, on the other hand, would almost double since $\dfrac{\lambda}{\mu-\lambda} = 4$ for the infinite case, as opposed to 2.15, as found above for a maximum of six cars.

Model 4   The C. J. Ballard Company is entering its second year in building residential homes. In transferring to this city, you, as an individual, are considering contracting with Ballard to build a home, but first you would like some idea of the completion time in order to plan the sale of your old home and time the cross-country move to this new home.

From your discussions, you found that Ballard completed 10 homes last year. To speed the building time span, Ballard uses one basic floor plan so that it can prepour the concrete floor slabs on selected lots. This saves not only the time of excavating, form building, laying the service lines (plumbing, electrical conduit, and air-conditioning return ducts), and pouring concrete but also the time necessary for concrete curing. Ballard has only a small crew of workmen and, therefore, builds only one house at a time, carrying it to completion before starting the next one.

Once a customer has picked the lot and signed the contract, Ballard is able to build a house from its various style plans in about a month. Actual figures for completion time per home last year were 30, 32, 29, 34, 27, 29, 29, 33, 30, and 31 calendar days.

Although Ballard built just 10 homes last year, it has the capability of building 12 homes per year ($\mu = 12$). Further investigation shows that of the various people who discuss home building with Ballard, nine actually contract with the firm. These contracts appear to be randomly distributed (Poisson) through the year ($\lambda = 9$).

Estimate the completion time of your home if you should sign a contract.

Solution. Without any justification for assuming a common frequency distribution curve for the building time (such as exponential, normal, or Erlang), we can use the equation from basic statistics to estimate the mean and variance of service times.

$$\bar{X} = \frac{\sum\limits_{i=1}^{N} X_i}{N} \tag{1}$$

where

$\bar{X}$ = the average time
X = the actual time data point
i = the identification of each time element
N = the number of time elements

$$\sigma^2 = \frac{\sum\limits_{i=1}^{N} (X_i - \bar{X})^2}{N} \tag{2}$$

σ_2 = variance of the distribution

Using the data given in the problem and equation 1 (above), we get:

$$\bar{X} = \frac{30 + 32 + 29 + 34 + 27 + 29 + 29 + 33 + 30 + 31}{10} = 30.4 \text{ days}$$

From Equation 2, we get:

$$\sigma^2 = \frac{\begin{array}{l}(30 - 30.4)^2 + (32 - 30.4)^2 + (29 - 30.4)^2 + (34 - 30.4)^2 \\ + (27 - 30.4)^2 + (29 - 30.4)^2 + (29 - 30.4)^2 + (33 - 30.4)^2 \\ + (30 - 30.4)^2 + (31 - 30.4)^2\end{array}}{10}$$

$$\sigma^2 = \frac{0.16 + 2.56 + 1.96 + 12.96 + 11.6 + 1.96 + 1.96 + 6.76 + 0.16 + 0.36}{10}$$

$$\sigma^2 = \frac{40.44}{10} = 4.044 \text{ days, or } 0.01105 \text{ year}$$

From Exhibit 9.10, Model 4, we see that

$$\bar{t}_s = \frac{\dfrac{\lambda}{\mu^2} + \lambda\sigma^2}{2\left(1 - \dfrac{\lambda}{\mu}\right)} + \frac{1}{\mu}$$

$$\bar{t}_s = \frac{\dfrac{9}{(12)^2} + 9(0.01105)}{2\left(1 - \dfrac{9}{12}\right)} + \frac{1}{12}$$

$$\bar{t}_s = 0.3239 + 0.0833 = 0.4072 \text{ year, or } 148 \text{ days}$$

Under the assumption of the problem—that is, that homes are built in the order of their contract signing (first come, first served)—you will have to wait 148 days, or almost five months, for your home to be built. (This example shows that "logical guesses" in queuing problems are often wide of the mark. Intuitively, one might have estimated the time from contract signing to completion to be about two months.)

Ballard's average number of active contracts (homes waiting to be started plus any being built) is

$$\bar{n}_s = \frac{\left(\dfrac{\lambda}{\mu}\right)^2 + \lambda^2 \sigma^2}{2\left(1 - \dfrac{\lambda}{\mu}\right)} + \frac{\lambda}{\mu}$$

$$\bar{n}_s = \frac{2\left(\dfrac{9}{12}\right)^2 + (9)^2(0.01105)}{2\left(1 - \dfrac{9}{12}\right)} + \frac{9}{12}$$

$$\bar{n}_s = 2.914 + 0.75$$

$$\bar{n}_s = 3.664 \text{ contracts}$$

Model 5

The barber at the one-man Speedway Barbershop averages 15 minutes per haircut. Customers arrive at the shop in Poisson fashion with a mean arrival rate of two per hour. Suppose you want a haircut and you have an appointment with your tax accountant 30 minutes after you arrive at the shop.

Assuming that it is a three-minute walk to your appointment location from the shop and that haircutting time is Erlang distributed with $K = 3$, would you expect to be on time to meet your accountant?

Solution. Given that $\lambda = 2$ arrivals per hour and $\mu = 4$ haircuts per hour, the problem is simply to determine the expected time in the system, $\bar{t}_s$. Using the $\bar{t}_s$ formula from Exhibit 9.10, Model 5, we have

$$\bar{t}_s = \frac{K+1}{2K} \cdot \frac{\lambda}{\mu(\mu - \lambda)} + \frac{1}{\mu}$$

Substituting

$$\bar{t}_s = \frac{3+1}{2(3)} \cdot \frac{2}{4(4-2)} + \frac{1}{4}$$

we get

$$\bar{t}_s = \frac{1}{6} + \frac{1}{4} = \frac{5}{12} \text{ of an hour, or 25 minutes}$$

Thus you should make your appointment (if you don't dawdle along the way).

Model 6

In the service department of the Glenn-Mark Auto Agency, mechanics requiring parts for auto repair or service present their request forms at the parts department counter. The parts clerk fills a mechanic's request

Continuing Education and Extension
UNIVERSITY OF MINNESOTA

Department of Extension Classes
REGISTRATION FORM

DEPARTMENT	COURSE NO.	SECTION	CREDIT	GRADE BASE			Graduate Credit Requested
				A/N	S/N	AUD	If you have been adm Minnesota and are no check this box
IEOR	5000	2		☑	☐	☐	PAG

DAY	HOUR	LOCATION	ROOM	COURSE TITLE AS APPEARS IN BULLETIN			COURSE TOTAL
TTh	6-9	ME	302	Evaluation Aux 1301			1062

TUITION	SPECIAL FEES	COURSE FEES	LATE FEE	
106.00				TUITION DEFERRED

U OF M STUDENT I.D. #

266817

NAME LAST	FIRST	MIDDLE	BIRTH DATE (USE NUMERIC
Peterson	Lee	Paul	MONTH / DAY

LOCAL STREET ADDRESS (INCLUDE APT. NO. IF APPROPRIATE)

845 Weeks Ave

SOCIAL SECURITY NO

CITY	STATE ABBREV	ZIP CODE	HOME PHONE
Mpls	Mn	55414	379-707

OCCUPATION	BUSINESS PHONE
Student	

while he waits. Mechanics arrive in a random (Poisson) fashion at the rate of 40 per hour, and a clerk can fill requests at the rate of 20 per hour (exponential). If the cost for a parts clerk is $2 per hour and the cost for a mechanic is $4.50 per hour, determine the optimum number of clerks to staff the counter. (Because of the high arrival rate, an infinite source may be assumed.)

Solution. First, assume that three clerks will be utilized because only one or two clerks would create long lines (since $\lambda = 40$ and $\mu = 20$). From Exhibit 9.10, Model 6

$$P_0 = \frac{1}{\sum\limits_{n=0}^{M-1} \frac{\left(\frac{\lambda}{\mu}\right)^n}{n!} + \frac{\left(\frac{\lambda}{\mu}\right)^M}{M!\left(1 - \frac{\lambda}{\mu M}\right)}}$$

with $M = 3$.

$$P_0 = \frac{1}{\sum\limits_{n=0}^{2} \frac{\left(\frac{40}{20}\right)^n}{n!} + \frac{\left(\frac{40}{20}\right)^3}{3!\left(1 - \frac{40}{20(3)}\right)}}$$

$$P_0 = \frac{1}{\frac{(2)^0}{0!} + \frac{(2)^1}{1!} + \frac{(2)^2}{2!} + \frac{(2)^3}{3!\left(1 - \frac{2}{3}\right)}} = \frac{1}{1 + 2 + 2 + 4} = 0.111$$

The average number in line is

$$\bar{n}_l = \frac{\lambda \mu \left(\frac{\lambda}{\mu}\right)^M}{(M-1)!(M\mu - \lambda)^2} P_0$$

$$\bar{n}_l = \frac{40(20)\left(\frac{40}{20}\right)^3}{(3-1)![3(20) - 40]^2}(0.111) = \frac{800(8)}{2(60 - 40)^2}(0.111)$$

$$\bar{n}_l = \frac{6400}{800}(0.111) = 0.888 \text{ mechanic}$$

At this point, we see that we have an average of 0.888 mechanic waiting all day. For an eight-hour day at $4.50 per hour, there is a loss of mechanic's time worth 0.888 mechanic × $4.50 per hour × 8 hours = $31.97.

Our next step is to recalculate the waiting time if we add another parts clerk. We will then compare the added cost of the additional employee with the time saved by the mechanics. Using our P_0 equation, when $M = 4$:

$$P_0 = \cfrac{1}{\displaystyle\sum_{n=0}^{3} \frac{(2)n}{n!} + \cfrac{(2)^4}{4!\left(1 - \cfrac{4}{2(4)}\right)}}$$

$$P_0 = \cfrac{1}{\cfrac{(2)^0}{0!} + \cfrac{(2)^1}{1!} + \cfrac{(2)^2}{2!} + \cfrac{(2)^3}{3!} + \cfrac{16}{24\left(1 - \cfrac{1}{2}\right)}}$$

$$P_0 = \cfrac{1}{1 + 2 + 2 + \cfrac{8}{6} + \cfrac{8}{6}} = 0.130$$

$$\bar{n}_l = \frac{40(20)(2)^4}{(4-1)![4(20) - 40]^2}(0.130)$$

$$\bar{n}_l = \frac{800(16)}{6(80 - 40)^2}(0.130)$$

$\bar{n}_l = 1.333 \times 0.130 = 0.173$ mechanic in line

$0.173 \times \$4.50 \times 8$ hours $= \$6.23$ cost of mechanic's waiting in line

Value of mechanics' time saved is $\$31.97 - \$6.23 = \$25.74$

Cost of additional parts clerk is 8 hr. $\times$ \$2/hr.   =   16.00

Cost reduction by adding 4th clerk $ 9.74

This problem could be expanded to consider the addition of runners to deliver parts to mechanics, so that the problem would be to determine the optimal number of runners. This, however, would have to include the added cost of lost time due to errors in parts receipts. For example, a mechanic would recognize a wrong part at the counter and obtain immediate correction whereas the parts runner may not.

Model 7   Studies of a bank of four weaving machines at the Loose Knit textile mill have shown that, on average, each machine needs adjusting every hour and that the current serviceman averages 7½ minutes per adjustment.

Problem. Assuming Poisson arrivals, exponential service, and a machine idle time cost of $40 per hour, determine if a second serviceman (who also averages 7½ minutes per adjustment) should be hired at a rate of $7 per hour.

Solution. This is a finite queueing problem that can be solved by using finite queuing tables. The approach in this problem is to compare the costs due to machine downtime (either waiting in line or being serviced) and the cost of one repairman, to the cost of machine downtime and two repairmen. We do this by finding the average number of machines that are in the service system and multiply this number by the downtime cost per hour. To this we add the repairmen's cost.

Before we proceed we will first define some terms:

N = the number of machines in the population
M = the number of repairmen
T = the time required to service a machine
U = the average time a machine runs before requiring service
X = the service factor, or proportion of service time required for each machine ($X = T/(T + U)$)
L = the average number of machines waiting in line to be serviced
H = the average number of machines being serviced

The values that will be determined from the finite tables are:

D, the probability that a machine needing service will have to wait
F, the efficiency factor, which is a measure of the effect of having to wait in line to be serviced

The tables are arranged according to three variables: N, population size; X, service factor; and M, the number of service channels (repairmen in this problem). To look up a value, first find the table for the correct N size, then search the first column for the appropriate X, and finally find the line for M. D and F are then read off. (In addition to these values, other characteristics about a finite queuing system can be found by using the finite formulas.)

To solve the problem above, consider Case I with one repairman, and Case II with two repairmen.

Case I: One repairman. From the problem statement,

$$N = 4$$
$$M = 1$$
$$T = 7\frac{1}{2} \text{ minutes}$$
$$U = 60 \text{ minutes}$$

$$X = \frac{T}{T + U} = \frac{7.5}{7.5 + 60} = 0.111$$

From Exhibit 9.12, the correct table for $N = 4$, F is interpolated as being approximately 0.957 at $X = 0.111$ and $M = 1$.

The number of machines waiting in line to be serviced is L, where

$$L = N(1 - F) = 4(1 - 0.957) = 0.172 \text{ machines}$$

The number of machines being serviced is H, where

$$H = FNX = 0.957(4)(0.111) = 0.425 \text{ machines}$$

Exhibit 9.11 shows the cost resulting from the machine unproductive time and the cost of the repairman.

EXHIBIT 9.11
A comparison of downtime costs for service and repair of a population of four machines

Number of repairmen	Number of machines down (H + L)	Cost per hour for machines down (H + L) × \$40/hour	Cost of repairmen \$7/hour each	Total cost per hour
1	0.597	\$23.88	\$ 7.00	\$30.88
2	0.451	18.04	14.00	32.04

Case II: Two repairmen.

From Exhibit 9.11, at $X = 0.111$ and $M = 2$, $F = 0.998$

The number of machines waiting in line, L, is

$$L = N(1 - F) = 4(1 - 0.998) = 0.008 \text{ machines}$$

The number of machines being serviced, H, is

$$H = FNX = 0.998(4)(0.111) = 0.443 \text{ machines}$$

EXHIBIT 9.12
Finite queuing tables

POPULATION 4

X	M	D	F	X	M	D	F	X	M	D	F
.015	1	.045	.999		1	.479	.899	.400	3	.064	.992
.022	1	.066	.998	.180	2	.088	.991		2	.372	.915
.030	1	.090	.997		1	.503	.887		1	.866	.595
.034	1	.102	.996	.190	2	.098	.990	.420	3	.074	.990
.038	1	.114	.995		1	.526	.874		2	.403	.903
.042	1	.126	.994	.200	3	.008	.999		1	.884	.572
.046	1	.137	.993		2	.108	.988	.440	3	.085	.986
.048	1	.143	.992	.200	1	.549	.862		2	.435	.891
.052	1	.155	.991	.210	3	.009	.999		1	.900	.551
.054	1	.161	.990		2	.118	.986	.460	3	.097	.985
.058	1	.173	.989		1	.572	.849		2	.466	.878
.060	1	.179	.988	.220	3	.011	.999		1	.914	.530
.062	1	.184	.987		2	.129	.984	.480	3	.111	.983
.064	1	.190	.986		1	.593	.835		2	.498	.864
.066	1	.196	.985	.230	3	.012	.999	.480	1	.926	.511
.070	2	.014	.999		2	.140	.982	.500	3	.125	.980
	1	.208	.984		1	.614	.822		2	.529	.850
.075	2	.016	.999	.240	3	.014	.999		1	.937	.492
	1	.222	.981		2	.151	.980	.520	3	.141	.976
.080	2	.018	.999		1	.634	.808		2	.561	.835
	1	.237	.978	.250	3	.016	.999		1	.947	.475
.085	2	.021	.999		2	.163	.977	.540	3	.157	.972
	1	.251	.975		1	.654	.794		2	.592	.820
.090	2	.023	.999	.260	3	.018	.998		1	.956	.459
	1	.265	.972		2	.175	.975	.560	3	.176	.968
.095	2	.026	.999		1	.673	.780		2	.623	.805
	1	.280	.969	.270	3	.020	.998		1	.963	.443
.100	2	.028	.999		2	.187	.972	.580	3	.195	.964
	1	.294	.965		1	.691	.766		2	.653	.789
.105	2	.031	.998	.280	3	.022	.998		1	.969	.429
	1	.308	.962		2	.200	.968	.600	3	.216	.959
.110	2	.034	.998		1	.708	.752		2	.682	.774
	1	.321	.958	.290	3	.024	.998		1	.975	.415
.115	2	.037	.998		2	.213	.965	.650	3	.275	.944
	1	.335	.954		1	.725	.738		2	.752	.734
.120	2	.041	.997	.300	3	.027	.997		1	.985	.384
	1	.349	.950		2	.226	.962	.700	3	.343	.926
.125	2	.044	.997		1	.741	.724		2	.816	.695
	1	.362	.945	.310	3	.030	.997		1	.991	.357
.130	2	.047	.997		2	.240	.958	.750	3	.422	.905
	1	.376	.941		1	.756	.710		2	.871	.657
.135	2	.051	.996	.320	3	.033	.997		1	.996	.333
	1	.389	.936		2	.254	.954	.800	3	.512	.880
.140	2	.055	.996		1	.771	.696		2	.917	.621
	1	.402	.931	.330	3	.036	.996		1	.998	.312
.145	2	.058	.995		2	.268	.950	.850	3	.614	.852
	1	.415	.926		1	.785	.683		2	.954	.587
.150	2	.062	.995	.340	3	.039	.996		1	.999	.294
	1	.428	.921		2	.282	.945	.900	3	.729	.821
.155	2	.066	.994		1	.798	.670		2	.979	.555
	1	.441	.916	.360	3	.047	.994	.950	3	.857	.786
.160	2	.071	.994		2	.312	.936		2	.995	.526
	1	.454	.910		1	.823	.644				
.165	2	.075	.993	.380	3	.055	.993				
	1	.466	.904		2	.342	.926				
.170	2	.079	.993		1	.846	.619				

EXHIBIT 9.12
(continued)

POPULATION 5

X	M	D	F
.012	1	.048	.999
.019	1	.076	.998
.025	1	.100	.997
.030	1	.120	.996
.034	1	.135	.995
.036	1	.143	.994
.040	1	.159	.993
.042	1	.167	.992
.044	1	.175	.991
.046	1	.183	.990
.050	1	.198	.989
.052	1	.206	.988
.054	1	.214	.987
.056	2	.018	.999
	1	.222	.985
.058	2	.019	.999
	1	.229	.984
.060	2	.020	.999
	1	.237	.983
.062	2	.022	.999
	1	.245	.982
.064	2	.023	.999
	1	.253	.981
.066	2	.024	.999
	1	.260	.979
.068	2	.026	.999
	1	.268	.978
.070	2	.027	.999
	1	.275	.977
.075	2	.031	.999
	1	.294	.973
.080	2	.035	.998
	1	.313	.969
.085	2	.040	.998
	1	.332	.965
.090	2	.044	.998
	1	.350	.960
.095	2	.049	.997
	1	.368	.955
.100	2	.054	.997
	1	.386	.950
.105	2	.059	.997
	1	.404	.945
.110	2	.065	.996
	1	.421	.939
.115	2	.071	.995
	1	.439	.933
.120	2	.076	.995
	1	.456	.927
.125	2	.082	.994
	1	.473	.920
.130	2	.089	.993
	1	.489	.914
.135	2	.095	.993

X	M	D	F
	1	.505	.907
.140	2	.102	.992
	1	.521	.900
.145	3	.011	.999
	2	.109	.991
	1	.537	.892
.150	3	.012	.999
	2	.115	.990
	1	.553	.885
.155	3	.013	.999
	2	.123	.989
	1	.568	.877
.160	3	.015	.999
	2	.130	.988
	1	.582	.869
.165	3	.016	.999
	2	.137	.987
	1	.597	.861
.170	3	.017	.999
	2	.145	.985
	1	.611	.853
.180	3	.021	.999
	2	.161	.983
	1	.638	.836
.190	3	.024	.998
	2	.177	.980
	1	.665	.819
.200	3	.028	.998
.200	2	.194	.976
	1	.689	.801
.210	3	.032	.998
	2	.211	.973
	1	.713	.783
.220	3	.036	.997
	2	.229	.969
	1	.735	.765
.230	3	.041	.997
	2	.247	.965
	1	.756	.747
.240	3	.046	.996
	2	.265	.960
	1	.775	.730
.250	3	.052	.995
	2	.284	.955
	1	.794	.712
.260	3	.058	.994
	2	.303	.950
	1	.811	.695
.270	3	.064	.994
	2	.323	.944
	1	.827	.677
.280	3	.071	.993
	2	.342	.938
	1	.842	.661
.290	4	.007	.999
	3	.079	.992

X	M	D	F
	2	.362	.932
.300	1	.856	.644
	4	.008	.999
	3	.086	.990
	2	.382	.926
	1	.869	.628
.310	4	.009	.999
	3	.094	.989
	2	.402	.919
	1	.881	.613
.320	4	.010	.999
	3	.103	.988
	2	.422	.912
	1	.892	.597
.330	4	.012	.999
	3	.112	.986
	2	.442	.904
	1	.902	.583
.340	4	.013	.999
	3	.121	.985
	2	.462	.896
	1	.911	.569
.360	4	.017	.998
	3	.141	.981
	2	.501	.880
	1	.927	.542
.380	4	.021	.998
	3	.163	.976
	2	.540	.863
	1	.941	.516
.400	4	.026	.997
	3	.186	.972
	2	.579	.845
	1	.952	.493
.420	4	.031	.997
	3	.211	.966
	2	.616	.826
	1	.961	.471
.440	4	.037	.996
	3	.238	.960
	2	.652	.807
	1	.969	.451
.460	4	.045	.995
	3	.266	.953
	2	.686	.787
	1	.975	.432
.480	4	.053	.994
	3	.296	.945
	2	.719	.767
	1	.980	.415
.500	4	.063	.992
	3	.327	.936
	2	.750	.748
	1	.985	.399
.520	4	.073	.991
	3	.359	.927

X	M	D	F
	2	.779	.728
	1	.988	.384
.540	4	.085	.989
	3	.392	.917
	2	.806	.708
	1	.991	.370
.560	4	.098	.986
	3	.426	.906
	2	.831	.689
	1	.993	.357
.580	4	.113	.984
	3	.461	.895
	2	.854	.670
	1	.994	.345
.600	4	.130	.981
	3	.497	.883
	2	.875	.652
	1	.996	.333
.650	4	.179	.972
	3	.588	.850
	2	.918	.608
	1	.998	.308
.700	4	.240	.960
	3	.678	.815
	2	.950	.568
	1	.999	.286
.750	4	.316	.944
	3	.763	.777
.800	2	.972	.532
	4	.410	.924
	3	.841	.739
	2	.987	.500
.850	4	.522	.900
	3	.907	.702
	2	.995	.470
.900	4	.656	.871
	3	.957	.666
	2	.998	.444
.950	4	.815	.838
	3	.989	.631

From L. G. Peck and R. N. Hazelwood, *Finite Queueing Tables* (New York: John Wiley & Sons, 1958), pp. 3–4.

The costs for the machines being idle and for the two repairmen are shown in Exhibit 9.11. The final column of Exhibit 9.11 indicates that retaining just one repairman is the best choice. The hourly costs with one repairman are $30.88 versus hourly costs of $32.04 with two repairmen.

REVIEW AND DISCUSSION QUESTIONS

1. How might waiting line theory apply to plant layout?

2. Distinguish between a *channel* and a *phase*.

3. What is the major cost trade-off which must be made in managing waiting line situations?

4. What assumptions are necessary to employ the formulas given in Model 1?

5. In what way might the first-come first-served rule be "unfair" to the customers waiting for service in a bank or hospital?

6. Define, in a practical sense, what is meant by an exponential service time.

7. Would you expect the exponential distribution to be a good approximation of service times for
   a. Buying an airline ticket at the airport?
   b. Riding a merry-go-round at a carnival?
   c. Checking out of a hotel?
   d. Completing a mid-term exam in your OM class?

8. Would you expect the Poisson distribution to be a good approximation of
   a. Runners crossing the finish line in the Boston Marathon?
   b. Arrival times of the students in your OM class?
   c. Arrival times of the bus to your stop at school?

PROBLEMS

1. Greased Lightening Lube Pits operates a fast lube and oil change garage. On a typical day, customers arrive at the rate of three per hour, and lube jobs are performed at an average rate of one every 15 minutes. The mechanics operate as a team on one car at a time.
   Assuming Poisson arrivals and exponential service, find
   a. Utilization of the lube team.
   b. The average number of cars in line.
   c. The average time a car waits before it is lubed.
   d. The total time it takes to go through the system (i.e., waiting in line plus lube time.)

2. The Better Food for Everyone (BFFE) Automat Company supplies vended food to a large university. Since, out of anger and frustration, students kick the machines at every opportunity, management has a constant repair problem. The machines break down at an average of three per hour, and the breakdowns are distributed in a Poisson manner. Downtime costs the company $25/hour/machine, and each maintenance worker gets $4 per hour. One worker can service machines at an average rate of five per hour, distributed exponentially; two workers, working together, can service seven per hour, distributed exponentially; and a team of three workers can do eight per hour, distributed exponentially.
   What is the optimum maintenance crew size for servicing the machines?

3. Irving Impresario, the manager of the Frenetic Flick movie theater, has some questions about the efficiency of his operation. Since he knows of your quantitative abilities, he asks you for your assistance. Further, since he knows you are independently wealthy and therefore indifferent to money, he promises

to reward you with a date with your favorite movie star, Carla Curvy or Marvin Macho, if you can help him.

Irving gives you the following data. The theater has a single-ticket booth and a cashier who is capable of maintaining a mean service rate of 200 customers per hour—distributed according to an exponential distribution. Arrivals are assumed to be Poisson distributed with a mean arrival rate of 150 per hour.

To help Irving (and to get the date), determine the following.

a. The average number of people waiting in line to purchase tickets.
b. The average number of people in the system (either waiting in line or being waited on).
c. The probability of having a waiting line.
d. The average time the arrival waits in line to get to the ticket window.
e. The average time an arrival spends in the system.

4. Big Jack's drive-through hamburger service is planning to build another stand at a new location and must decide how much land to lease to optimize returns. Leased space for cars will cost $1,000 per year per space. Big Jack is aware of the highly competitive nature of the quick-food service industry and knows that if his drive-in is full, customers will go elsewhere. The location under consideration has a potential customer arrival rate of 30 per hour (Poisson). Customer's orders are filled at the rate of 40 per hour (exponential) since Big Jack prepares food ahead of time. The average profit on each arrival is $0.60, and the stand is open from noon to midnight every day. How many spaces for cars should be leased?

5. A cafeteria serving line has a coffee urn from which customers serve themselves. Arrivals at the urn follow a Poisson distribution at the rate of three per minute. In serving themselves, customers take about 15 seconds, exponentially distributed.

a. How many customers would you expect to see on the average at the coffee urn?
b. How long would you expect it to take to get a cup of coffee?
c. What percentage of time is the urn being utilized?
d. What is the probability that there would be three or more people in the cafeteria?

If the cafeteria installs an automatic vendor that dispenses a cup of coffee at a constant time of 15 seconds, how does this change your answers to a and b?

6. An engineering firm retains a technical specialist to assist five design engineers working on a project. The help that the specialist gives the engineers ranges widely in terms of time consumption. Some answers he has available in memory, others require computation, and still others require significant search time. On the average, each request for assistance takes the specialist one hour.

The engineers require help from the specialist on the average of once each day. Since each assistance takes about an hour, each engineer can work for seven hours, on the average, without assistance. One further point: engineers needing help do not interrupt the specialist when he is already involved with another problem, but rather wait until he is finished.

Treat this as a finite queueing problem and answer the following questions:

a. How many engineers, on the average, are waiting for the technical specialist for help?

b. What is the average time that an engineer has to wait for the specialist to get to him?

c. What is the probability that an engineer will have to wait in line for the technical specialist?

7. A graphics reproduction firm has four units of equipment that are automatic, but occasionally become inoperative because of the need for supplies, maintenance, or repair. Each unit requires service roughly twice each hour, or more precisely, each unit of equipment will run an average of 30 minutes before needing service. Service times vary widely, ranging from a simple service (such as hitting a restart switch or repositioning paper) to more involved equipment disassembly. The average service time, however, is 5 minutes.

Equipment downtime results in a loss of $20 per hour. The one attendant that is employed is paid $3 per hour.

Using finite queueing analysis, answer the following questions:

a. What is the average number of units in line?

b. What is the average number of units still in operation?

c. What is the average number of units being serviced?

d. The firm is considering adding another attendant at the same $3 rate. Should they do it?

SELECTED BIBLIOGRAPHY

Giffin, Walter C. *Queueing: Basic Theory and Applications.* Columbus, Ohio: Grid Publishing, Inc., 1979.

Gross, Donald, and Harris, Carl M. *Fundamentals of Queuing Theory.* New York: John Wiley & Sons, 1974.

Kleinrock, L. *Queueing Systems, Volume 2: Computer Applications.* New York: John Wiley & Sons, 1976.

Morse, Phillip M. *Queues, Inventories, and Maintenance.* New York: John Wiley & Sons, 1958.

Panico, J. A. *Queueing Theory.* Englewood Cliffs, N.J.: Prentice-Hall, 1969.

Saaty, T. L. *Elements of Queueing Theory.* New York: McGraw-Hill Book Company, 1961.

Thierauf, R. J., and Klekamp, R. C. *An Introduction to Quantitative Methods for Decision Making.* New York: Holt, Rinehart, and Winston, 1974.

Wagner, Harvey. *Principles of Operations Research,* 2d ed. Englewood Cliffs, N.J.: Prentice-Hall, 1975.

Chapter

10

DESIGN OF THE QUALITY CONTROL SYSTEM

Extensive sales and jobs have already been lost [mainly to Japan] for quality reasons. However, the West has long believed these losses to be due to price competition. Originally, this belief was entirely valid. Lately, the quality competition has been growing while price competition has been declining. This trend has yet to be understood by the majority of the economic analyses in the West and especially by the press.[1]

This statement from a leading expert in quality control serves to underline the importance of quality control (QC) to the U.S. economy and why it has become a major source of concern to operations management. Quality control was one of the first fields to be approached scientifically by business organizations. The procedures used by quality control specialists have evolved apace with the evolution of production processes and statistics so that now "Q.C." is perhaps the most highly refined support area of general manufacturing. Indeed, a glance at a recent quality control journal should readily indicate the depth and breadth of the procedures by which contemporary quality control is performed. From a management perspective, quality control can be viewed as consisting of two classes of decisions: strategic decisions and tactical decisions. Strategic decisions are those that must be made at the highest (or corporate) level of the organization and, in effect, determine the influence of quality control in the long-run operation of the firm. These decisions are:

---

[1] J. M. Juran, "Japanese and Western Quality—A Contrast (Part 1)," *Quality*, February 1979, p. 14.

1. Organizational role of the quality control function.
2. Quality of product design.

The tactical decisions relate to the means by which quality control is conducted on a day-by-day basis and include:

1. Degree of conformance to product design specifications.
2. Acceptance sampling procedures.
3. Process control procedures.
4. Location and frequency of inspection activities.
5. Personnel considerations.

In this chapter, we will initially discuss quality control by developing the seven strategic and tactical decisions listed above. Then we will consider the role of quality in several service industries, and present some examples of commercial quality control computer programs for acceptance sampling and process control. We will conclude with a discussion of the Japanese approach to quality control with particular reference to "quality circles."

ROLE OF THE QUALITY CONTROL FUNCTION

Prior to the early 1900s, quality control was loosely organized in business enterprises. Generally, the inspection function was performed by a worker who reported to the line foreman, who, in addition, was responsible for detecting errors and correcting the manufacturing process. As organizations grew in size and inspection became more technical, there was a tendency to group inspectors together and make them responsible to an inspection foreman or chief inspector, who reported to the manufacturing manager. Not until the 1920s, was the importance of quality in all areas of organization performance firmly realized and quality responsibility consolidated as a separate function, often on the same level as the manufacturing manager. The most recent trend, strongly evidenced in large manufacturing companies, is to place quality responsibility on a par with other major corporate functions. Such an organization structure placement is shown in Exhibit 10.1, along with some duties of the quality function.

The pervasiveness of quality control inputs throughout one company's product development cycle can be seen in Exhibit 10.2. The QA in the center stands for "quality assurance," a program for "prevention, detection and correction of product defects that would cause customer dissatisfaction."[2]

At the left of Exhibit 10.2, outside the main figure, the generation of a product idea is symbolized, perhaps originating in the market research department. Design engineers, management, and other personnel discuss this idea in relation to its manufacturability and marketability as a finished product. If the anticipated selling price and manufacturing costs are reason-

---

[2] P. J. Ernster, "Quality Assurance Assures Customer Satisfaction," *Quality Progress*, no. 1 (January 1970), pp. 21–24.

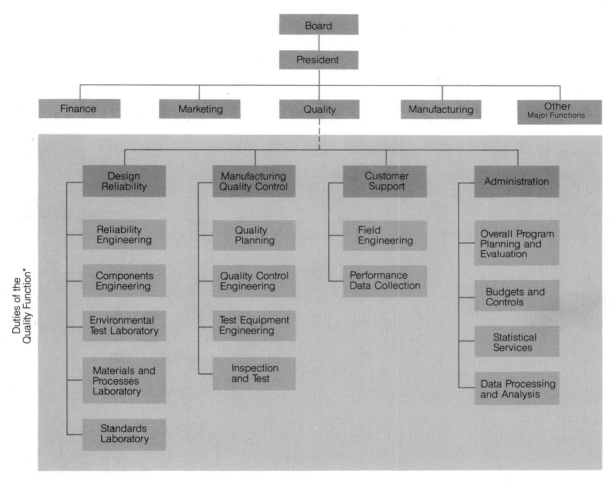

*From J. M. Duran and Frank M. Gryna, Jr., *Quality Planning and Analysis* (New York: McGraw-Hill Book Company, 1970), p. 96.

EXHIBIT 10.1
Organizational structures that emphasize the quality responsibility

able, the proposal is presented to the appropriate level of management for approval. A functional design is made without any regard for the appearance of the product (called a "breadboard"). Interest is solely in designing a product to operate as intended. Once this breadboard design is accepted, a prototype is made of the complete product, incorporating the breadboard design and styling for appearance. Designs are released and necessary materials ordered. Several products are made, and the process is viewed closely for improvements in design or in production methods and equipment. This small product run is frequently performed by the design and development staff. When results of the pilot run are satisfactory, the product is released to the production staff. Production commences, and in due course, the product is delivered to the customer.

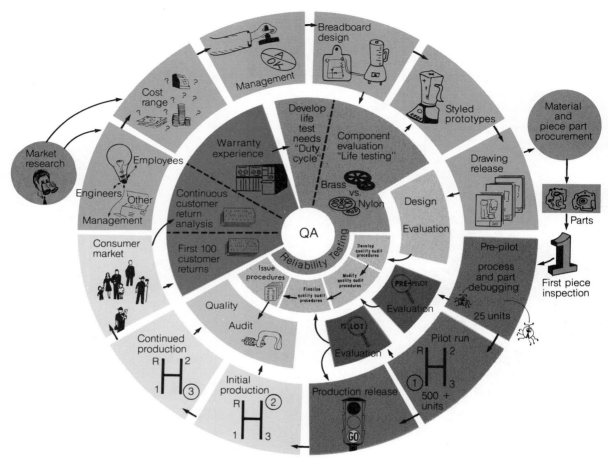

EXHIBIT 10.2
Quality inputs from product inception through use analysis

Quality decisions occurred throughout the above sequence—in parts evaluation, reliability testing, design evaluation, inspections, and analysis of customers' use of the product. The cycle may be partially repeated if feedback from the customers indicates a need for changes in the product.

Objectives of the quality control function

Quality control objectives typically include reducing the scrap rate, reducing the number of returns from customers, maintaining the desired degree of comformance to product design, increasing the average level of outgoing product quality, and decreasing the amount of defective raw materials from vendors. They also include keeping the cost of controlling quality within reason.

Quality control objectives should be set down in specific terms and for a prescribed period. The following might be the quality control goals of a firm for the coming year.

1. Reduce the number of customer complaints to 3 percent.
2. Reduce the number of customer returns to 2 percent.
3. Reduce the maximum rework level to 5 percent.
4. Lower the per unit quality control and inspection costs by 10 percent.
5. Conduct a monthly program for training and updating inspection personnel.

At the end of the year, success or failure in meeting these objectives must be seriously analyzed. The objectives may be either extended or revised for the following year.

QUALITY OF PRODUCT DESIGN

Quality of product design refers to the product's inherent worth as defined by its component cost, its manufacturing cost, and its value in the eyes of the consumer. In some sense, a product's design quality can be measured by comparing it to competing products in terms of three quality concepts—grade, fitness for use, and consistency.

Grade. To most persons, quality implies such attributes as smoothness; purity of color or texture, taste, or odor; closeness of fit; small number of flaws; reliability; range of operation; and so forth. In this sense, quality is used to imply grade. One might say that the quality of a Rolls-Royce is higher than that of a Chevrolet or that the quality of a New York-cut steak graded USDA Prime is higher than one graded USDA Choice. Grade classifies characteristics into groupings: grades 1, 2, 3, 4 and so forth, or A, B, C, D, or USDA Prime, Choice, Good, Fancy, or Commercial.

The confusing part of grading is that universal standards do not always exist and the grading system may be made by someone other than the ultimate user—perhaps the producer, wholesaler, retailer, or an association. Therefore grade A might seem to imply that it is the producer's top grade, whereas he also has AA, AAA, and perhaps AAAA. In liquors, for example, one might be happy buying the "3 Star" grade—until he discovers the "5 Star," or finds that the top quality (with limited distribution) is actually "7 Star" grade.

Fitness for use. This quality concept refers to the degree to which a product satisfies the user. The user's satisfaction generally depends on three factors: the grade itself, the consistency of quality within that grade, and, for a functioning item, its reliability and maintainability. To elaborate on the last factor, a product should function for some specified time under specified conditions, and repair service and replacement parts should be available (unless, of course, the product is not expected to undergo repair, as in the case of "throwaway" items like nonrefillable lighters or inexpensive radios).

Consistency. Products or services are designed, and the output of this design stage is a set of specifications for each component of the product. How well the finished product meets the design specifications is called the "quality of conformance" and will be discussed in more detail later. What often is more important to the customer, however, is the consistency of succeeding units of the product relative to certain key criteria.

Consider two automobile service agencies, one that usually does high-quality service but occasionally botches a job and a second agency that consistently does mediocre work. The customer may care little about either agency's quality design or conformance level; the decision he is faced with is trading off the probability of excellent versus bad service by one agency and the high likelihood of an average job by the other.

Or consider the plight of students attempting to ascertain what material is covered in a particular college course. Should they refer to the catalog for a course description, hoping that the "quality of conformance" is high; that is, that the course actually conforms to the description? Should they try to find out if a new course description has been developed? Or should they try to find out from other sources if the course has been consistently taught in the same fashion, regardless of the description? In many cases, consistency may be more important than quality of conformance.

QUALITY OF CONFORMANCE

Quality of conformance quite simply refers to the degree to which a product meets its design specifications. As mentioned in Chapter 2, the output of the design stage is a set of specifications for each component of the product. Specifications generally contain a specific measurement and also an acceptable range or tolerance: the diameter of a steel shaft may be specified as 1.000 inch $\pm$ 0.005. To produce this shaft, the decision must be made as to how well the machinery process should meet the specifications as designed—that is, what the quality of conformance should be. If a very expensive machining process is chosen, perhaps it may be able to produce virtually all shafts to 1 inch $\pm$ 0.003. It would then be producing to a high degree of conformance but also to a higher quality than originally designed. The amount of reject work would decrease—but at the added cost of a more expensive production process. Conversely, if the process output is in the other direction—that is, an inexpensive process that produces output ranging far outside the 1 inch $\pm$ 0.005—then the production process would cost less but the costs due to rejects, customer complaints, product failures and so forth, would increase. Exhibit 10.3 shows this relationship of process cost and costs due to the product's not meeting the specifications related to the degree of conformance. Optimal conformance is found where total cost is at the minimum.

Quality of conformance greatly affects product assembly. If all parts of a certain type conform to specifications, the operator may select any at random. If conformance is poor and parts vary outside specifications, "fitting" is required; that is, individual parts must be selected to fit together. For example, if steel shafts with poor conformance are to be used with bearings, the operator will have to search for larger bearings to fit the

EXHIBIT 10.3
**Degree of
conformance
to design
specifications**

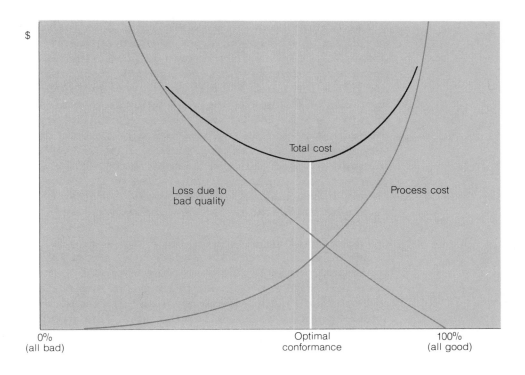

larger shafts and smaller bearings for the undersize shafts. While this practice often is used for better fit, problems may be experienced by the user at some future time if he must replace the shaft. Overconformance, on the other hand, while perhaps contributing to a "better" product, is usually more costly to produce.

ACCEPTANCE SAMPLING PROCEDURES

Acceptance sampling is performed to determine what percentage of products conform to specifications. These products may be items received from another company and evaluated by the receiving department or they may be components that have passed through a processing step and are evaluated by company personnel either in production or later in the warehousing function. Acceptance sampling is based upon the statistical concept that a random sample of appropriate size will have within it a proportional representation of all items in the parent population. One estimates product quality through sampling in order to determine whether or not complete (100%) inspection should be part of the manufacturing process. (The economics of this decision are discussed in the section entitled "costs to justify inspection.") There are two general ways of describing the degree of conformance to design quality in acceptance sampling (and process control). One measures attributes, and the other measures variables.

The differentiation between attributes and variables may be described as follows. Two clear-cut types of observations are possible: an item of production or service may be recognized as *either good or bad,* or it may be measured to determine *how much it varies* from other units or from the design specifications. The first type is usually termed *sampling by attributes.* Examples of this are testing lamp bulbs to determine whether they light or not; checking the buttons on a shirt in a laundry (if all are present, the shirt is passed on for pressing; if not, it goes to sewing); testing a stereo tape player (if the frequency response falls within a specified range, the unit is passed, if not, it is set aside for repair). The use of attributes in acceptance sampling is usually based on the binomial statistical distribution. In process control, attributes of a product or service are used to determine a proportion which, in turn, may be used to construct a control chart.

The second type, measuring the *amount* of deviation of an observation, is called *sampling by variables.* Rather than accept the shirt if all buttons are present or reject it if one or more are missing, the interest may be in the actual number of buttons missing. The stereo examination might include the plotting of a frequency-amplitude response curve to obtain the actual output characteristics, rather than just an accept-reject decision. Actual measurement of the particular variable has considerable usefulness if analysis and control of the productive process is of interest. Variables sampling is based on the normal statistical distribution.

Design of a single sampling plan for attributes

Acceptance sampling is executed through the development and operation of a sampling plan. In this section, we will illustrate the planning procedures for a single sampling plan—that is, a plan in which the quality of conformance is determined from the evaluation of one sample. (Other plans may be developed using two or more samples on which to base the accept–reject decision.)

A single sampling plan is defined by n and c, where n is the number of units in the sample, and c is the acceptance number. The size of n may vary from one up to all of the items in the lot (usually denoted as N) from which it is drawn. The acceptance number c denotes the maximum number of defective items that can be found in the sample before the lot is rejected. Values for n and c are determined by the interaction of four factors that quantify the objectives of the producer of the product and the consumer of the product. The objective of the producer is to assure that the sampling plan has a *low probability of rejecting good lots.* Lots are defined as "good" if they contain no more than a specified level of defectives, termed the *acceptable quality level* (AQL). The objective of the consumer is to assure that the sampling plan has a *low probability of accepting bad lots.* Lots are defined as "bad" if the percentage of defectives is greater than a specified amount, termed *lot tolerance percent defective* (LTPD). The probability associated with rejecting a good lot is denoted by the Greek letter alpha (α) and is termed the *producer's risk.* The probability associated

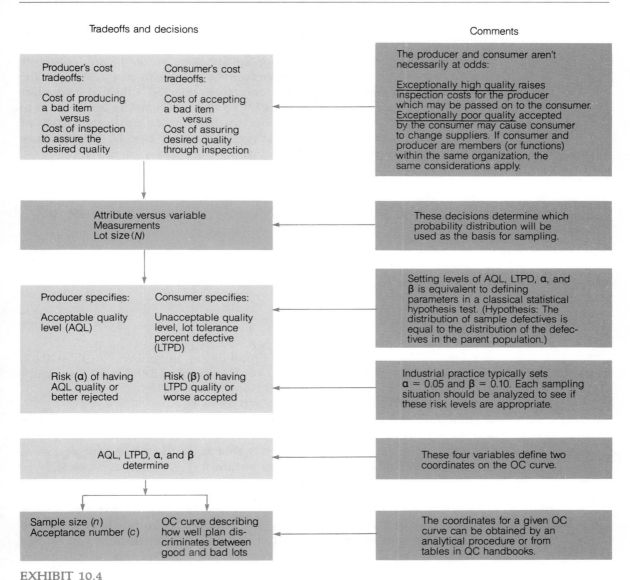

Tradeoffs and decisions

Comments

Producer's cost tradeoffs:

Cost of producing a bad item
versus
Cost of inspection to assure the desired quality

Consumer's cost tradeoffs:

Cost of accepting a bad item
versus
Cost of assuring desired quality through inspection

The producer and consumer aren't necessarily at odds:

Exceptionally high quality raises inspection costs for the producer which may be passed on to the consumer. Exceptionally poor quality accepted by the consumer may cause consumer to change suppliers. If consumer and producer are members (or functions) within the same organization, the same considerations apply.

Attribute versus variable
Measurements
Lot size (N)

These decisions determine which probability distribution will be used as the basis for sampling.

Producer specifies:

Acceptable quality level (AQL)

Consumer specifies:

Unacceptable quality level, lot tolerance percent defective (LTPD)

Setting levels of AQL, LTPD, α, and β is equivalent to defining parameters in a classical statistical hypothesis test. (Hypothesis: The distribution of sample defectives is equal to the distribution of the defectives in the parent population.)

Risk (α) of having AQL quality or better rejected

Risk (β) of having LTPD quality or worse accepted

Industrial practice typically sets $\alpha = 0.05$ and $\beta = 0.10$. Each sampling situation should be analyzed to see if these risk levels are appropriate.

AQL, LTPD, α, and β determine

These four variables define two coordinates on the OC curve.

Sample size (n)
Acceptance number (c)

OC curve describing how well plan discriminates between good and bad lots

The coordinates for a given OC curve can be obtained by an analytical procedure or from tables in QC handbooks.

EXHIBIT 10.4
Trade-offs and decisions in sampling plan development

with accepting a bad lot is denoted by the letter beta (β) and is termed the *consumer's risk*. The selection of particular values for AQL, α, LTPD, and β is an economic decision based upon a cost trade-off. The nature of this trade-off and subsequent decisions in sampling plan development are summarized in Exhibit 10.4.

The following example using an excerpt from a standard acceptance sampling table illustrates how these four parameters—AQL, α, LTPD, and β—are used in developing a sampling plan.

Example. The Old C.B. Company of Shaky-town manufactures citizens'-band radios. These units use the speakers made by a subsidiary in Chi-town. The subsidiary producing the speakers works to an acceptable quality level (AQL) of 2% defectives and is willing to run a 5% risk (α) of having lots of this level or fewer defectives rejected. Old C.B. considers lots of 8% or more defectives (LTPD) to be unacceptable and wants to assure that they will accept such poor quality lots no more than 10% of the time (β). A convoy has just delivered a lot of size N. What values of n and c should be selected to determine the quality of this lot?

EXHIBIT 10.5
Excerpt from a sampling plan table for $\alpha = 0.05$, $\beta = 0.10$

(1) c	(2) $LTPD \div AQL$	(3) $(n) \cdot (AQL)$
0	44.890	0.052
1	10.946	0.355
2	6.509	0.818
3	4.890	1.366
4	4.057	1.970
5	3.549	2.613
6	3.206	3.286
7	2.957	3.981
8	2.768	4.695
9	2.618	5.426

Solution. The parameters of the problem are as follows: AQL = 0.02, $\alpha = 0.05$, LTPD = 0.08, and $\beta = 0.10$. We can use Exhibit 10.5 to find c and then n.

First divide LTPD by AQL ($0.08 \div 0.02 = 4$).

Then find the ratio in column 2 that is equal to or just greater than that amount (i.e., 4). This value is 4.057, which is associated with $c = 4$.

Finally, find the value in column 3 that is in the same row as $c = 4$, and divide that quantity by AQL to obtain n ($1.970 \div 0.02 = 98.5$).

The appropriate sampling plan is: $c = 4$, $n = 99$.

OC curves

While the sampling plan meets our requirements for the extreme values of good and bad quality, we can not readily determine how well the plan discriminates between good and bad lots at intermediate values. For this reason, sampling plans are generally displayed graphically through the use of operating characteristic (OC) curves. These curves, which are unique for each combination of n and c simply illustrate the probability of accepting lots with varying percent defectives. The procedure we have followed in developing the plan, in fact, specifies two points on an OC curve—one point defined by AQL and $1 - \alpha$, and the other point defined by LTPD and β. Curves for common values of n and c can be computed or obtained from available tables.[3]

[3] See, for example H. F. Dodge and H. G. Romig, *Sampling Inspection Tables—Single and Double Sampling* (New York: John Wiley & Sons, 1959), and Superintendent of Documents, *Military Standard Sampling Procedures and Tables for Inspection by Attributes* (MIL-STD-105D) (Washington, D.C.: U.S. Government Printing Office).

EXHIBIT 10.6
Computing the probability of acceptance of a lot using a sample of $n = 99$, various values of p, $c = 4$, and the Poisson table in Appendix F

P	$\times$	n	$=$	Pn	P_a(from Poisson table at $c = 4$)
.01	$\times$	99	$=$	.99	.996
.02	$\times$	99	$=$	1.98	.947
.03	$\times$	99	$=$	2.97	.815
.04	$\times$	99	$=$	3.96	.629
.05	$\times$	99	$=$	4.95	.440
.06	$\times$	99	$=$	5.94	.285
.07	$\times$	99	$=$	6.93	.173
.08	$\times$	99	$=$	7.92	.105
.09	$\times$	99	$=$	8.91	.055
.10	$\times$	99	$=$	9.90	.029
.11	$\times$	99	$=$	10.89	.015
.12	$\times$	99	$=$	11.98	.008

An OC curve can be computed from a binomial distribution. However, if n is large and p is small, a Poisson distribution can be used as an approximation to the binomial since a binomial computation is cumbersome and Poisson tables are readily available.

A binomial process applies to either/or choices, such as in attributes sampling where a unit is determined to be either good or bad. The equation for a binomial distribution is

$$P(r) = \frac{n!}{r!(n-r)!} \, p^r (1-p)^{n-r}$$

where p is the probability that an r will occur on any single trial. $P(r)$, then, is the probability of exactly r events (frequently called "successes") occurring in n trials.

The Poisson distribution is described in Chapter 9 and further discussed in Chapter 12. Poisson tables, such as Appendix F at the end of the book, are cumulative and save a good deal of computational time when substituted for the binomial.

To illustrate the construction of an OC curve using the Poisson tables, we will use the example just presented, where $n = 99$ and $c = 4$. The columns in Appendix F are in terms of the acceptance number c (so we will be using the numbers in the column $c = 4$). The rows are pn, which are the number of defects we would expect to find in each sample. We will vary the percent defective from 1 percent to 8 percent (or .01 to .08) holding $n = 99$. Exhibit 10.6 shows the computations with the probability of acceptance values in the last column. These values of P_a can be plotted against the proportion defective (first column), and the result is the OC curve shown in Exhibit 10.7.

Shaping the OC curve. Ideally we would like to have an OC curve that discriminates perfectly between good and bad lots—such as in Exhibit 10.8. In practice, however, such a plan is possible only with complete inspection of all items and, therefore, really not a sampling plan. As an alternative, a sampling plan may be selected which is steep in the region

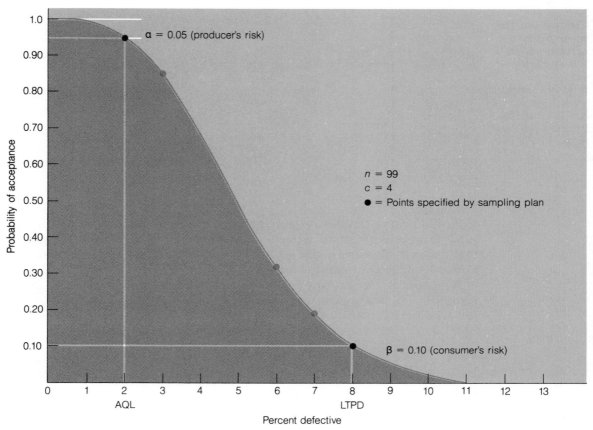

EXHIBIT 10.7
Operating characteristic curve for AQL = 0.02, α = 0.05, LTPD = 0.08, β = 0.10

of most interest and is derived by varying n and c. Increasing the sample size n will steepen the curve for any given c, as in Exhibit 10.9. By keeping n the same and decreasing c, the OC curve also becomes steeper, moving closer to the origin, as in Exhibit 10.10.

In selecting any sampling plan, the cost of sampling must be weighed against the losses that would be incurred if no sampling were performed. A sampling plan is then computed or selected from a source of plans, by choosing the sample size n and the allowable rejects c that most closely fit the specific needs.[4]

Average outgoing quality

When the same sampling plan is used repeatedly, the average outgoing quality (AOQ) of the product or service can be calculated if any lot that fails to pass the sampling plan is completely inspected. AOQ generally

---

[4] See, for example, H. F. Dodge and H. G. Romig, *Sampling Inspection Tables—Single and Double Sampling,* 2d ed. (New York; John Wiley & Sons, 1959).

EXHIBIT 10.8
Ideal discriminating sampling plan

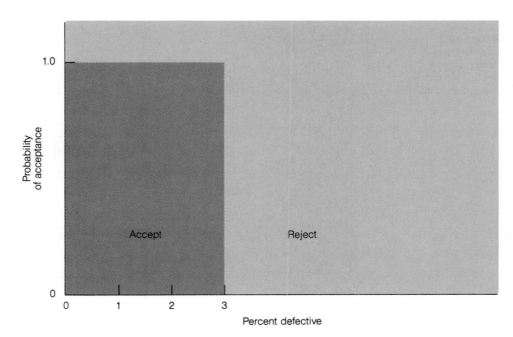

applies to the producer, however, since the consumer may simply reject the lot and send it back rather than perform a complete inspection of all items in bad lots.

If defective items are removed but not replaced (thereby reducing the lot size), the average quality is

EXHIBIT 10.9
Effect of increasing the sample size from n_1 to n_2 with the same c

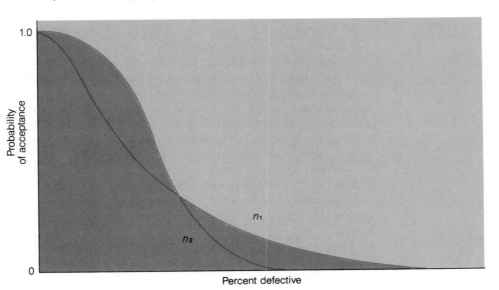

EXHIBIT 10.10
**Effect of
increasing c
from c_1 to c_4
with the same
sample size n**

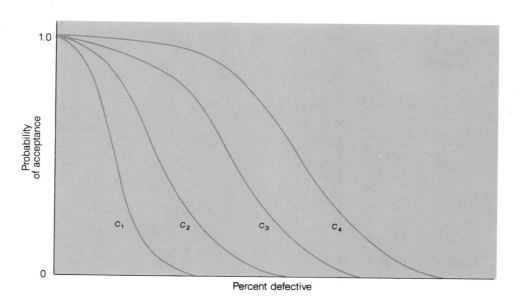

$$AOQ = \frac{P_a p(N-n)}{N - pn - p(1-P_a)(N-n)}$$

where P_a is the probability of acceptance, p is the fraction defective, N is the lot size, and n is the sample size.

If defective items are replaced with good ones (thereby returning the lot to its original size, N),

$$AOQ = \frac{P_a p(N-n)}{N}$$

What does the average outgoing quality look like for a sampling plan? To derive one we can start with the OC curve in Exhibit 10.7 and suppose that the lot size N is 1,000 units and that any defective units found during inspection are replaced with good units (so that the lot size remains the same). Then, using the probability of acceptance derived in Exhibit 10.6 and the equation for AOQ, we compute the values in Exhibit 10.11. These values are then plotted in Exhibit 10.12 as the average outgoing quality as a function of incoming quality. Note that both the axes are in terms of percent *defective*. An average outgoing quality of 1 percent means that the product is 99 percent good. The maximum AOQ (called the *average outgoing quality limit* or AOQL) is about 2.5 percent (97.5 percent good units) when the incoming quality is about 4 percent defective. The reason the curve is shaped the way it is, is as follows: If incoming quality is good so that the lot is accepted based on the sample tested, then outgoing quality is about the same as incoming quality. As the incoming quality gets worse, more and more samples will fail, and these bad lots will have

EXHIBIT 10.11
Average outgoing quality using the data in Exhibit 10.6 and assuming $N = 1,000$ and $n = 99$

$$\frac{P_a p (N-n)}{N} = AOQ$$

P	$\times$	P_a	$\times$	$(N-n)$	$\div$	N	$=$	AOQ
.01	$\times$	.996	$\times$	901	$\div$	1,000	$=$	.0090
.02	$\times$	.950	$\times$	.	$\div$	.	$=$	.0171
.03	$\times$	.815	$\times$	.	$\div$	.	$=$	.0220
.04	$\times$	.629	$\times$	.	$\div$	.	$=$	.0227
.05	$\times$	.440	$\times$	.	$\div$	.	$=$	.0198
.06	$\times$	.285	$\times$	.	$\div$	.	$=$	.0154
.07	$\times$	.173	$\times$	.	$\div$	.	$=$	.0109
.08	$\times$	.105	$\times$	.	$\div$	.	$=$	.0076
.09	$\times$	.055	$\times$	.	$\div$	.	$=$	.0045
.10	$\times$	.029	$\times$	.	$\div$	.	$=$	.0026
.11	$\times$	.015	$\times$	.	$\div$	.	$=$	.0015
.12	$\times$	.008	$\times$	.	$\div$	.	$=$	.0009

to be completely inspected. The worse the incoming quality gets, the better the outgoing quality would be since lots will have to be 100 percent tested. If a producer's output is so bad that all samples fail, all lots will be completely tested, and the quality sent out will be perfect (assuming all defective units are detected and removed during the testing).

The effects of lot size

The percent that the sample size is of the total size of the lot has relatively little effect on the quality of protection. In Exhibit 10.13, note that the five curves drawn were each based on a sample size of $n = 20$ and $c = 0$. However, the lot size ranged from 50 to 1,000. Thus, the ratio of sample size to lot size ranged from 40 percent to 2 percent. In fact, if the lot size N were infinity (and therefore the sample size zero percent of the lot), the quality of protection would be about the same. From Exhibit 10.13, the probability of acceptance of a 5 percent defective lot when $N = 1,000$ is 0.355. At $N = \infty$, the probability is 0.358. For a 10 percent defective lot the probabilities for acceptance when $N = 1,000$ and $N = \infty$ are 0.119 and 0.122, respectively.

EXHIBIT 10.12
Average outgoing quality (AOQ) versus incoming quality

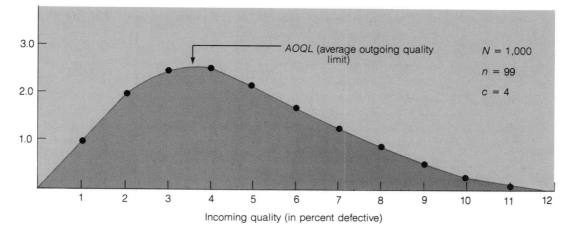

AOQL (average outgoing quality limit)

$N = 1,000$
$n = 99$
$c = 4$

Incoming quality (in percent defective)

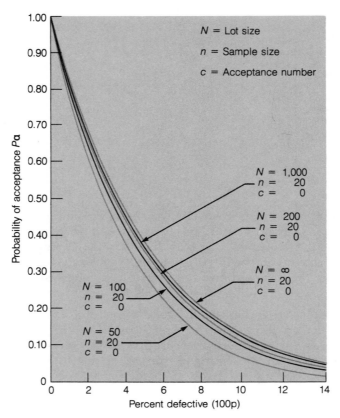

Source: Adapted from Eugene L. Grant, *Statistical Quality Control*
(New York: McGraw-Hill Book Company, 1964), pp. 335–36.

What this means, quite simply, is that so long as the lot size is several times the sample size, it makes very little difference how large the lot is. We could take a sample of 50 from a lot of 500, 5,000 or 100,000 and get essentially the same results.

Suppose the lot size is less than several times the sample size. What happens? If an OC curve or sampling plan based on an infinite lot size is used (a common practice) the consumer achieves a higher quality than asked for. The penalty, though, is against the producer in that more good lots are rejected. Again referring to Exhibit 10.13, note that at a β (probability of acceptance) of 10 percent, the consumer sampling 20 out of 50 is protecting himself with a defective rate (LTPD) of 8.5 percent, whereas at a lot size of ∞, he is using a LTPD of 10.9 percent.

**Costs to
justify
inspection**

Total (100 percent) inspection is justified when the cost of a loss incurred by not inspecting is greater than the cost of inspection. For example, suppose a faulty item results in a $10 loss. If the average percentage of defective items in a lot is 3 percent, the expected cost due to faulty items is 0.03 × \$10, or \$0.30 each. Therefore, if the cost of inspecting each item is less than \$0.30, the economic decision is to perform 100 percent inspection. Not all defective items will be removed, however, since inspectors will pass some bad items and reject some good ones.[5]

The purposes of a sampling plan are to test the lot to either (1) find its quality, or (2) assure that the quality is what it is supposed to be. Thus, if you already know the quality (such as the 0.03 given in the example above), you do not sample for defects. Either you inspect all of them to remove the defects or don't inspect any of them and let the rejects pass into the process. The choice simply depends on the cost to inspect, and the cost incurred by passing a reject.

Sequential sampling plans

Rather than selecting a sample from a lot and inspecting all items in the sample to make the accept-reject decision, a sequence of smaller samples may be used. The advantage of such a sequence is that fewer items need be inspected for the same degree of accuracy. Such series of samples are termed *sequential sampling plans*. The limit in sequential sampling plans is the plan that inspects items one at a time. In a sequential sampling plan, the results are accumulated and a decision is made to (1) reject the lot, (2) accept the lot, or (3) inspect another item.

Wald, who instituted one of the well-known sequential plans, estimated that this sequential plan could reduce the average sample size by about one-half, as compared to a single sampling plan.[6] His plan entailed a decision each time an item was inspected and required three inputs—the producer's risk (α), the consumer's risk (β), and a "sequential probability ratio." This ratio is a method of keeping score and is also the probability of getting a particular sample result if the material is of p_2' quality compared to the probability of getting the result if the material were p_1' quality. In practice, it is not necessary to compute this ratio. Instead, a chart or form may be constructed from sampling limits. Then each inspection result is plotted until the lot is accepted or rejected.

The limit lines of a sequential plan are defined by

$$X_1 = sn + h_2$$

and

$$X_2 = sn - h_1$$

where

---

[5] Sometimes inspectors are tested by being subjected to inspection of test lots with a known number of defectives. At Federal Reserve banks, for example, unfit and counterfeit bills are inserted into incoming bundles of bills from commercial banks as a means of appraising the performance of bill counters.

[6] A. Wald, *Sequential Analysis* (New York: John Wiley & Sons, 1947).

$$h_1 = \frac{\log\left(\frac{1-\alpha}{\beta}\right)}{\log\left[\frac{p_2'(1-p_1')}{p_1'(1-p_2')}\right]}$$

$$h_2 = \frac{\log\left(\frac{1-\beta}{\alpha}\right)}{\log\left[\frac{p_2'(1-p_1')}{p_1'(1-p_2')}\right]}$$

$$s = \frac{\log\left(\frac{1-p_1'}{1-p_2'}\right)}{\log\left[\frac{p_2'(1-p_1')}{p_1'(1-p_2')}\right]}$$

Tables are available so that it is not necessary to compute the values of h_1, h_2, and s through the formulas (see Chapter Appendix, page 324). The following example illustrates the method of constructing a sequential sampling plan.

Assume that the producer's risk α is 5 percent at the point where p_1' is 0.01; that is, the producer wants a 95 percent probability of accepting as good any lots of items that are 1 percent or less defective. Further, assume that β is 10 percent and p_2' is 0.06; that is, the consumer wants only a 10 percent chance of accepting any lots that are 6 percent or more defective.

Using the Appendix to this chapter, the appropriate values can be read off at $p_1' = 0.01$ and $p_2' = 0.06$. Corresponding values are $h_2 = 1.5678$, $h_1 = 1.2211$, and $s = 0.02811$.

Since the control chart is linear, to draw the chart requires the definition of two points for each line. One convenient point is the vertical axis where $n = 0$; that is, where no items have yet been sampled.

At $n = 0$,

$$X_1 = sn + h_2$$
$$= 0 + 1.5678$$
$$= 1.5678$$
$$X_2 = sn - h_1$$
$$= 0 - 1.2211$$
$$= -1.2211$$

A second point is chosen at another convenient location, say where $n = 100$. Then, at $n = 100$,

$$X_1 = sn + h_2$$
$$= (0.02811)(100) + 1.5678$$
$$= 2.811 + 1.5678$$
$$= 4.3788$$

$$X_2 = sn - h_1$$
$$= (0.02811)(100) - 1.2211$$
$$= 2.811 - 1.2211$$
$$= 1.5899$$

These are plotted on Exhibit 10.15, and the points are connected to form the boundaries for the plan. Both the accept and reject regions lie above the horizontal axis, so that for this example, no acceptance of a lot is possible until at least 44 units have been inspected.

If one prefers, a table can be made showing the decisions rather than referring to the graph. Exhibit 10.14 was derived from Exhibit 10.15.

EXHIBIT 10.14
Accept or reject decisions over a range of defects and numbers sampled

Range of n	Reject when number of defectives found is:	Range of n	Accept when number of defectives found is:
2–15	2	0–43	No decision possible. Continue sampling.
16–51	3		
52–86	4	44–80	0
87–121	5	81–114	1
		115–150	2

EXHIBIT 10.15
Sequential sampling plan with $\alpha = 0.05$ at $p_1' = 0.01$ and $\beta = 0.10$ at $p_2' = 0.06$

The following example is based on Exhibit 10.15 and/or Exhibit 10.14. Two lots, 1 and 2, are inspected on an item-by-item basis, resulting in the following action (these examples are plotted in Exhibit 10.15).

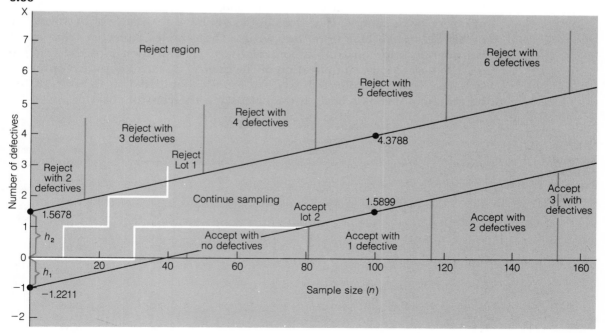

```
Lot 1:  Items   1–10    OK          Lot 2:  Items   1–30    OK
                  11    Defective                      31    Defective
                12–23   OK                           32–81   OK
                  24    Defective           Action: Accept lot 2
                25–40   OK
                  41    Defective
         Action: Reject lot 1
```

PROCESS CONTROL PROCEDURES

Process control is concerned with monitoring quality *while the product or service is being produced.* Typical objectives of process control plans are: (1) to provide timely information on whether currently produced items are meeting design specifications; and (2) to detect shifts in the process which signal that future products may not meet specifications. The actual control phase of process control occurs when corrective action is taken, such as a worn part replaced, a machine overhauled, or a new supplier found. Process control concepts, especially statistically based control charts, have seen wide use outside the factory. The following example, in fact, illustrates how a control chart for attributes (called a "*p*-chart") is developed and used in the context of employee performance monitoring.

Process control using attribute measurements

Suppose one wants to establish some control device for keypunch operators with which he could monitor their performance over time. After the key punching has been verified, suppose further that he randomly selects 200 cards out of each punched box and notes the number of errors made. By dividing the number of errors by 200, he may then derive the fraction of errors in the sample. If he does not as yet have a measure of performance of his keypunch operators, he can use the samples collected from all of his operators to construct a control chart. He can then plot the fraction on his chart to gain an indication of the quality of each keypunch operator. If he has initially collected, say, 30 samples (as listed in Exhibit 10.16), he may use this as a basis for constructing the control chart.

EXHIBIT 10.16
Number of keypunch errors for samples of size $n = 200$

Sample number	Number of errors	Fraction defective (number errors/200)	Sample number	Number of errors	Fraction defective (number errors/200)
1	4	0.02	16	17	0.085
2	8	0.04	17	9	0.045
3	12	0.06	18	13	0.065
4	10	0.05	19	12	0.06
5	14	0.07	20	14	0.07
6	9	0.045	21	14	0.07
7	11	0.055	22	12	0.06
8	13	0.065	23	21	0.105
9	14	0.07	24	13	0.065
10	8	0.04	25	12	0.06
11	10	0.05	26	13	0.065
12	11	0.055	27	12	0.06
13	7	0.035	28	7	0.035
14	11	0.055	29	14	0.07
15	12	0.06	30	11	0.055

The overall fraction defective $(\bar{p})$, standard deviation (s_p), and upper and lower control limits are calculated as follows:

$$\bar{p} = \frac{\text{Total number of defects from all samples}}{\text{Number of samples} \times \text{Sample size}}$$

$$\bar{p} = \frac{348}{30 \times 200} = 0.058$$

$$s_p = \sqrt{\frac{\bar{p}(1 - \bar{p})}{n}}$$

$$s_p = \sqrt{\frac{0.054636}{200}} = 0.0165$$

The most common confidence limits are 99.0 and 99.7 percent or where the chance of an occurrence is one in 100 and 3 in 1,000, respectively. From a two-tailed normal distribution table, 99 percent of the area under the curve is included in the mean plus-or-minus 2.58 standard deviations, and 99.7 percent includes the mean plus-or-minus 3.0 standard deviations. For a confidence of 99 percent, limits are placed at $\bar{p} \pm 2.58 s_p$. Thus

$$\text{UCL} = \bar{p} + 2.58 s_p = 0.10057$$
$$\text{LCL} = \bar{p} - 2.58 s_p = 0.01543$$

The control limits and individual sample results are plotted in Exhibit 10.17. Performance of the keypunch operators can now be observed over time, and by identifying the source of the sample, the output of individual operators vis-à-vis the group average can be compared. Note, for instance, that sample 23 is outside the control limits. We can expect one out of 100 to be out since that's where we set the control limits. With one out of 30 samples out of the limits (sample 23), we can't be sure yet that there is a problem. However, we should carefully watch the process. If, say, sample 55 was also out, then 2 out of 55 would signal an investigation as to the cause.

Suppose, as additional information, that the industry average for key-punch operators classified as "good" is 5 percent errors ± 2 percent (with 99 percent confidence). These limits can also be placed on the graph to give an additional measure of control. (The limits are plotted as 3 and 7 percent.) Such a control chart, if occasionally updated for $\bar{p}$ and s_p, will give a running measure of performance and progress over time.

Process control using variable measurements

The development of process control techniques (and acceptance sampling plans) using variables parallels the development procedures using attributes. The statistical manipulations in using variables are somewhat more involved, however, and are beyond the scope of this discussion. Worthy of mention, though, is a valuable type of control chart that is particularly useful in variable measurement situations. Termed a *dynamic control chart*, it is highly appropriate when there is a predictable trend in process output over time. Frequently, when equipment has been set up

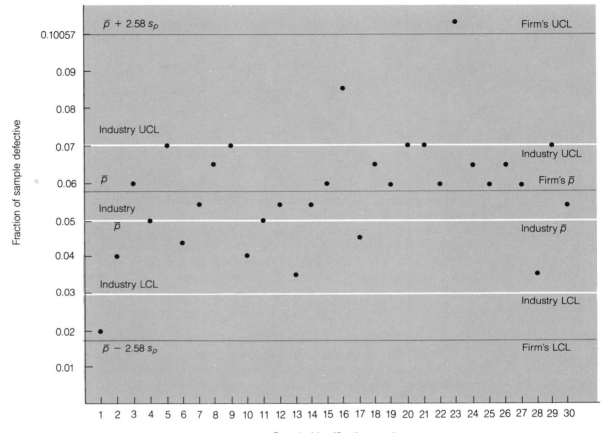

EXHIBIT 10.17
Control chart of keypunch operators (sample size n = 200; firm's own $\bar{p}$, LCL, and UCL calculated from 30 samples; industry $\bar{p}$, LCL, and UCL plotted from known industrywide operator performance)

and operation begun, tool wear or other changes in the system cause measurements of the product output to shift. A dynamic control chart may be constructed to determine the initial setup position to assure that the process is performing as expected. In addition, the chart will indicate when the process should be temporarily halted for machine readjustment.

Either of two charts can be used for dynamic control: *(a)* an $\bar{X}$ chart, on which the means of small samples (perhaps four or five items) are plotted, or *(b)* a chart for sequential sampling, such as for measuring every 10th or 20th item. The sequential plan is easiest because only one unit at a time is plotted and no computations are involved. Exhibit 10.18 shows a sequential dynamic control chart for the following example: Suppose a particular part to be manufactured has the specified diameter of 1.000 ± 0.010 inch, and the output from the particular machine to be used can be represented by a normal distribution with σ = 0.001 inch. Suppose further that 3σ is established as the control limits; that is, 99.73 percent

EXHIBIT 10.18
Dynamic control chart for process control

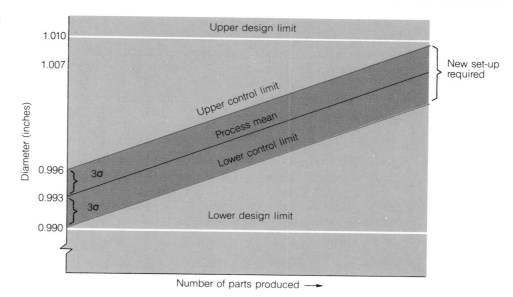

of the parts produced will fall within design specifications. The problem, then, is to develop a control chart for sequential unit sampling (parts get larger as production continues).

The procedure is as follows. Since the lower design limit allows a diameter as small as 0.990 inch (1.000 − 0.010), 0.003 (3σ) is simply added to 0.990 to arrive at the initial machine setup of 0.993 inch. The first parts produced should then vary from 0.990 to 0.996 inch. Subsequent parts would be expected to fall within the band, as illustrated in Exhibit 10.18. If they do not fall in this band, the equipment may be examined for possible slippage or wear of bearings or other parts, depending on how the output shifts.

Dynamic control charts of this type find their greatest use for long production runs which require periodic resetting of tools.

LOCATION AND FREQUENCY OF INSPECTION ACTIVITIES

Location of inspection activites
Inspection is required for both acceptance sampling and process control. The decision of where in the production process such inspections must be performed depends on the cost of inspecting at any given location versus the cost of allowing a defective product to continue throughout the production cycle. Performing a cost analysis on each potential inspection location is a significant undertaking for many firms, and mathematical techniques and computer programs to solve the problem are still being developed. Baker[7] suggests that the problem of locating inspection stations

---

[7] Eugene M. Baker, "Why Plan Your Inspection?" *Quality Progress* (July 1975), pp. 22–27.

can be alleviated by starting with the end product and charting (using an engineering process flow chart) each characteristic in the product that requires inspection. "Then decide at what point in the manufacturing cycle that particular characteristic could first be inspected."[8] (Rules of thumb are: "Do each inspection as early in the manufacturing cycle as possible," and "Perform each inspection only once.") This information is noted on the flow chart for each characteristic. "Then work backwards through the manufacturing cycle doing the same thing at each point along the way. At completion, a clear pattern of inspection points will be defined. Finally, each potential inspection point is evaluated to decide whether it is economical to move it to a later point in the process."[9] (Specific sampling plans and process control procedures are then determined for the selected inspection points.) An example of a process chart showing the final location of inspection points in the manufacture of recording cassettes is illustrated in Exhibit 10.19.

Frequency of inspection activities

Once the decision has been made as to which inspection is to be done, the next problem is to determine how often it is to be done. Again, a tradeoff is involved between the cost of inspection and the cost of defective products and added work caused by not detecting defective components. This problem has been discussed by Meske.[10] A systematic way of determining the frequency of inspection requires four factors of the particular manufacturing situation:

1. The delay interval—the time in hours between initiation of an inspection and the termination of the loss it discovered. (Contributing to this interval are the time to get authorization to stop the process, to prepare a reject tag, to adjust a machine, and so forth).
2. The reliability interval—the average time in hours between process failures for a given job.
3. Manufacturing loss—the cost per hour of defects to the company as reflected in rework, sorting, scrap, wasted labor and machine time, and so forth.
4. Inspection cost—the cost per units of the inspection act.

Economic inspection interval model. In constructing any model, the first step is to develop a functional relationship between the variables of interest and the measure of effectiveness. In this case, since we are concerned with cost, the following equation would pertain.

$$TC = \frac{R}{I}C + M\left(\frac{I}{2} + D\right)$$
$$= \frac{R}{I}C + M\frac{I}{2} + MD$$

---

[8] Ibid., p. 23.

[9] Ibid., p. 24.

[10] See "A Management Standard for Economic Inspection," *Quality* (January 1976), pp. 28–30.

EXHIBIT 10.19
Location and type of inspection points for recording cassette manufacture

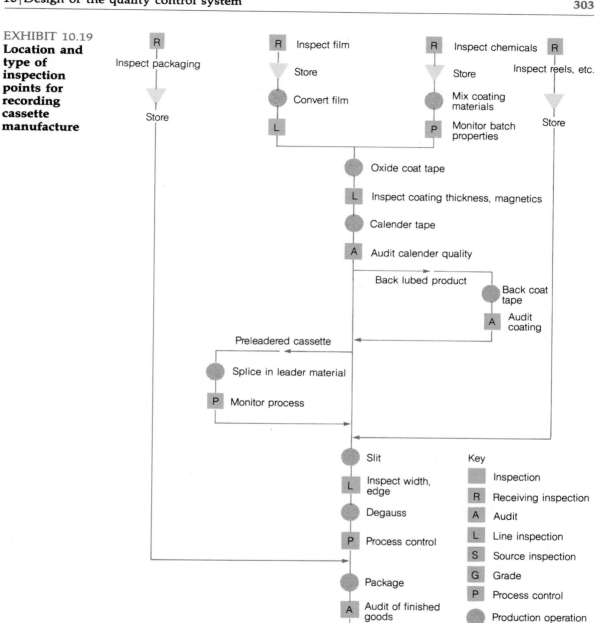

Source: Eugene M. Baker, "Why Plan Your Inspection?" *Quality Progress*, (July, 1975), p. 23.

where

TC = Total cost per reliability interval
R = Reliability interval in hours
D = Delay interval in hours
C = Inspection cost per unit
I = Inspection interval in hours (the optimum value is termed the
        Economic Inspection Interval—EII or I_{opt})
M = Manufacturing loss per hour

A defective unit may be produced at the beginning of the inspection interval (just after the last inspection) or at the end (just prior to inspection). On the average, therefore, the defect will occur $I/2$ hours after an inspection. Adding to this the delay interval D (the time required to respond to the defect) gives a cost per defect of $M(I/2 + D)$ on the right-hand side of the equation. Also in this equation is $(R/I)C$, the cost of inspection per reliability interval (the actual number of inspections during the reliability interval R/I times the cost of each inspection, C). These cost relationships are shown graphically in Exhibit 10.20.

The second step in the model development is to find that inspection interval I for which total cost is a minimum. In the basic model, this

EXHIBIT 10.20
Total cost based on the size of inspection interval

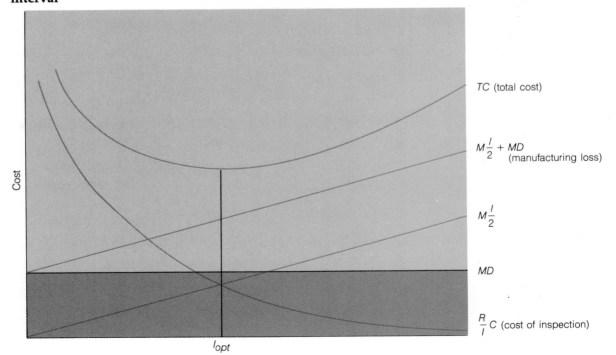

TC (total cost)

$M\dfrac{I}{2} + MD$ (manufacturing loss)

$M\dfrac{I}{2}$

MD

$\dfrac{R}{I}C$ (cost of inspection)

I_{opt}
Inspection interval (*I*)

Cost

may be done by simple algebra since MD is not a decision variable and, hence, not a factor in the inspection interval decision. Then with reference to Exhibit 10.20, total cost is minimum at the point where $\frac{R}{I}C = M\frac{I}{2}$ which in turn is solved as follows:

$$RC = M\frac{I^2}{2}$$

$$2\,RC = MI^2$$

$$I^2 = \frac{2\,RC}{M}$$

$$I_{opt} = \sqrt{\frac{2\,RC}{M}}$$

Example. A three-shift operation evaluated over a five-week period encompassed a total running time of 555 hours. During this period, 10 rejections occurred, and the average reliability interval was therefore 55.5 hours. The delay interval was 15 minutes, and the manufacturing loss was $44 per hour. The inspection cost was $14 per hour, and the inspection time was 2 minutes. The inspection cost per unit is $14 ÷ 30 inspections per hour, or $0.47.

Reliability interval $(R) =$ 55.5 hours
Delay interval $(D) =$ 15/60 or 0.25 hour
Inspection cost $(C) =$ $0.47 per unit
Manufacturing loss $(M) =$ $44 per hour

The economic inspection interval is

$$I_{opt} = \sqrt{\frac{2RC}{M}} = \sqrt{\frac{2(55.5)(0.47)}{44}}$$

$$= 1.089 \text{ hour}$$

The total cost over a reliability interval of 55.5 hours will be

$$TC = \frac{R}{I}C + M\frac{I}{2} + MD$$

$$= \frac{55.5(0.47)}{1.089} + \frac{44(1.089)}{2} + 44(0.25)$$

$$= 23.95 + 23.95 + 11.0$$

$$= \$58.90$$

The total cost for a shift or for any other given period can be easily calculated from the total cost per reliability interval determined above. For example, the total cost for the 555-hour period will be

$$\frac{58.90(555)}{(55.5)} = \$589.0$$

In this analysis, however, one must bear in mind that the per unit inspection cost may not be accurate since it assumes a per unit cost derived by dividing the cost per hour by the inspection rate. The inspector may be a fixed cost, or there may be travel time involved such that to inspect just one unit every 1.089 hour may be much higher than $0.47. If this is the case, the per-unit inspection cost more than likely could be obtained or estimated and this figure used for computation instead.

PERSONNEL CONSIDERATIONS

Management, job design, and wage payment present special problems in quality control. First, quality control is often a staff department in large organizations, and therefore, the quality control manager's authority is limited to advising the production area in matters of quality. Even if the quality control manager is in a line position, as is shown in Exhibit 10.1, his or her role should be one of accommodation with the production area to assure that the QC function does not impede the production process. This need for accommodation, however, may conflict with quality requirements, and the inherent adversary relationship between quality control and various production departments may evolve into hostility. Thus, the quality control manager must have human relations skills as well as technical competence of his or her department is to maximize its contribution to organizational goals.

Second, inspection work, which comprises the major portion of quality control activities, is often both demanding and monotonous. Therefore, finding ways of making inspection jobs more attractive is a continuing job-design problem. Third, finding the appropriate basis for wage payment for inspection tasks is a difficult problem. Incentive plans basing inspectors' pay on the number of defects discovered may result in wide variations in their income and/or rejecting items which are marginally good. To include the "good" items rejected as an added factor makes for a complicated pay scheme. Hourly pay plans, on the other hand, tend to reduce vigilance by removing the direct monetary reward for finding poor quality items. In practice, plans combining incentives with hourly pay are employed to cope with these problems. (See Chapter 11 for a more extensive discussion of the general topics of job design and wage payment.)

As a final comment, there is a tendency in most firms to hold the worker responsible for poor quality work. However, W. L. Deming (a leading figure in QC) takes a strong counter position. He separates the production process into two parts—the system, over which management has control, and the workers, who are under their own control. From his experience, he attributes 85 percent of the variation in quality to the system, and only 15 percent of the variation to workers. He points out that the system may be at fault in many ways: using low-quality materials, failing to keep equipment maintained, failing to provide an adequate working environment, using poor routing sequences, having standards too tight, and putting too much pressure to get work out, to name but a few possibilities. Clearly, since the system is designed by management, it is management's responsibility to correct these problems. Moreover, of the 15 percent of the problems which are assignable to workers, most are due to such things as lack of training, inability to perform the task, and lack of understanding of the job—factors which are in part management's responsibility.

QUALITY CONTROL FACTORS IN SERVICE INDUSTRIES

As stated previously, to develop a quality control program, five points must be specifically stated: (1) What is to be inspected? (2) Where it is to be inspected? (3) How is the inspection to be performed? (4) What are the units of measurement? and (5) What are the criteria for acceptance or rejection?

When an area has not previously been subjected to statistical quality control, cost factors are frequently difficult to compute and inadequate to use as a sole basis for justifying the inspection procedure. Poor quality may have such a variety of impacts on the organization that it is useful,

EXHIBIT 10.21 Some essential features of a hospital quality control system	Points of inspection	Examples of what to look for	Consequences of deviations	Possible method of inspection
	Lab tests	Accuracy in reading	Inaccurate diagnosis, possibly serious consequences	Chief lab technician samples completed tests. Automatic equipment checked for reasonable readings and tests on known samples
	Pharmacy	Expiration dates of medications; accuracy in requests	Ranging from minor to fatal	Complete recheck. Pharmacist fills prescriptions, checks, and packages; questions MD on large dosages
	House-keeping	Cleanliness	Dirty areas increase likelihood of infection	Supervisor checks against standards
	Operating rooms	Sterile conditions; correct equipment, surgical procedures, scrubbing, attire	Lawsuits, malpractice, possible death or injury, loss of image	Armband verifies correct patient for surgery; verify chart and surgical procedure; sponge and instrument count
	Admissions	Verify information with patient; forms all filled in	Usually minor inconveniences or later questions	If computerized, verified by techniques such as format of insurance numbers, age of children versus age and marital status of patient

EXHIBIT 10.21
(continued)

Points of inspection	Examples of what to look for	Consequences of deviations	Possible method of inspection
Billing	Insurance claims filed, late billings, accuracy in amount	Lost money or late receipts	Compare patients' stay with billing date and insurance filing
Nursing service	Up-to-date charts, medication on time, correct medication, temperature and pulse readings on time, progress reports	Discomfort, delayed patient recovery, degrading to image	Supervisor checks work; incident reports reviewed daily
Laundry	Cleanliness, on-time schedule	Degrades image, possible contamination	Supervisor inspects linen
Food service	Quality of precooked food, method of preparation, meals on time and satisfactory	Patient satisfaction, hospital's image	Dietician inspects all food; prepackaged frozen food sampled for diet constraints and quality; patient complaints observed
Outpatient	Available facilities, degree of usage	Crowding or underutilization	Perhaps emergency room department may review
Central supply	Stocking of linens, surgical instruments, syringes; sterility of supplies	Delays, infection from unsterilized items	Tapestrip indicating sterilization performed. Indicator to determine if packages opened or leaking; packages dated
Medical staff	Competence, accuracy in diagnosis, acceptable surgery or service	Lawsuits, malpractice suits, hospital image, patient death or injury	Adequate observation by specialists before hospital privileges granted. Analysis of procedures reviewed on all difficult cases. Tissue committee reviews all charts for pathology reports

as a first step, to create a list stating the consequences of poor quality in various operational areas. For a typical hospital, for example, the major effect of poor quality in the laundry may be the degradation of the hospital's image—a minor offense. Poor quality of the medical staff, however, may result in the death of patients and lawsuits, as well as injury to the hospital's image. In either case, a table of this type, which broadly states the consequences of bad quality, is useful in establishing a priority hierarchy and indicates which areas should be dealt with first when planning an overall quality control program.

Health care   Nearly all quality control procedures may be used in the health care industry, where one often hears such comments as "Traditional scientific methods do not apply when a human life is at stake" or "No price can be placed on human life." Statements like these have no rhyme or reason. Indeed, the fact that this industry *does* deal with human life makes it all the more important to use the best available techniques to determine and assure acceptable quality levels. Exhibit 10.21 lists some essential features of a hospital quality control system.

Banking

Banks, at the present time, do not use a significant amount of statistical quality control. Generally, various ratios or account compositions are compared to some established norm. This norm may be determined by legal regulation or by an individual bank's policy.

Although formal statistical sampling plans are not generally used in banks, sampling is periodically performed on savings and checking accounts. The quality of a loan portfolio, however, is observed primarily

EXHIBIT 10.22
Some essential features of a bank quality control system

Points of inspection	Examples of what to look for	Consequences of deviations	Possible method of inspection
Loan ratio	Too low or too high	Loss of profit, inadequate funds	Complete tabulation, compared to standard
Equity base	Small or large	Committed to lower-yield, less risky use of funds; high equity permits greater risk	Routine reports
Liquidity ratio	Ratio of short term to total	High-ratio loss of potential profit; Low-ratio inability to meet withdrawals or make new loans	Tabulation compared to norm
Loan portfolio	Collateral backing, degree of risk, term length	Possible defaults	Internal audits, also audits by Federal Reserve and state for some banks
Margin	Adequate reserves	Violation of regulation	Routine observation
Savings accounts	Accuracy	Not serious to bank but creates unhappy customers, loss of prestige and business	Sampling of accounts
Checking accounts	Accuracy, overdrawn accounts	As above, plus possible losses on overdrafts if honored	Routine sampling plus flagged accounts
Savings to total deposits	Ratio	High ratio results in higher interest costs	Occasional observation
Teller operations	Shortages, overages, neatness, manners	Loss of prestige	Daily tally sheets, general subjective observation

by examining the larger loans, usually those over 1 percent or 0.1 percent of the total loan portfolio. A bank's status and operation in some areas is periodically spotchecked by an internal audit team, but these examinations are not statistically based. Certain bank functions, such as investment portfolios and maintenance of liquidity ratios, are not handled at branch offices. The home office retains the responsibility for unit banks in branch banking. Correct liquidity ratios are maintained by the home office by periodically issuing general guidelines to the branches, such as "No personal notes over 90 days," "No commercial loans," or "Improvement loans only to customers' owner-occupied residences." Exhibit 10.22 lists some essential features of a bank quality control system.

Insurance companies

A large part of an insurance company's operations involve record processing and accounting, and statistical quality control can be readily applied to the many similar accounts. Standardized forms can be examined; repeated errors may indicate the probability of improper or vague wording. Billing, premium payments, and claims are easily sampled to determine accuracy. However, systematic sampling, rather than random sampling, is easier to use. For example, if the degree of confidence from a sampling plan stipulates that 10 percent of the accounts should be sampled, a "system" can be used—one that inspects each account ending in zero, for example. Some of the essential features of a quality control system are shown in Exhibit 10.23.

EXHIBIT 10.23

Some essential features of an insurance company quality control system

Points of inspection	Examples of what to look for	Consequences of deviations	Possible method of inspection
Mailroom	Correct routing	Loss of time and/or item	Inspection and tabulation of errors
Processing of subscriber applications	Legibility, correct spelling, reasonableness of data	Expensive reprocessing. Policies awarded to unqualified or at wrong premium rates	Examination by supervisor; use of sampling and control charts for error trends
Premium-due billing	Accuracy in amount, assurance that customer is actually billed	Loss of customer goodwill. Unintentional policy lapsing	Sampling by supervisor
Receipt of premium payments	Unreasonable amounts, invalid codes, improper data	Financial losses, lapsed policies, loss of customers	Inspection by supervisor
Claims	Policy number and code validity. Accuracy in claim	Customer complaints, loss of company image, poor service, increased correspondence with customer, financial loss to company	Random sampling by supervisor; 100 percent inspection of large claims

COMPUTER PROGRAMS FOR QUALITY CONTROL

The advent of computers has added a new dimension in relieving most of the tedious calculations formerly required to install and maintain a quality control system. A wide variety of computer programs is available in both batch processing and by time sharing via a remote terminal. All computer manufacturers and many computer service companies make computer programs available to customers. The following examples illustrate just a few of the many programs available from one of these companies:[11]

Program	Description
ML105$	Determines sampling plan to fit combinations of AOQL, lot size, etc., and randomly determines which parts to sample according to military standard
TABF1$ 414F1$	Performs analysis of samples with variability unknown, standard deviation method according to Mil-Std-414.
HISTO$	Produces sample statistics and plots a histogram with variable scaling.
MLBIN$	Evaluates multiple level sampling plans where user inspects a number of parts from a large lot and accepts, rejects, or resamples bases on the number of defectives found (binomial distribution).
RANDM$	Randomly selects parts for inspection for a specified lot and sample size. Eliminates inspector bias in determining which items to inspect.
OCBIN$	Plots the operating characteristic curve or probability of acceptance as a function of the number of defectives (binomial distribution). User supplies the sample size and number of defectives required to reject the lot.
PCHRT$	Provides a control chart on the reject rate. The program determines the upper and lower control limits and plots a control chart for the data provided.
CONLM$	Determines confidence limits and sample statistics on a process average.

To illustrate the ease in using these programs, two examples will be given, one producing an operating characteristic curve (OC) and the second plotting a control chart.

1. Sampling by attributes with a double sampling plan. A shipment has just be received and a decision must be made to accept or reject the lot. The inspected items are declared either good or bad. A double sampling plan is considered as follows.

Take a sample size of 15. If none or one is bad, accept the lot. If three or more are bad, reject the lot. If two are bad, take a second sample.

Then, with a second sample size of 10, accept the lot only if all 10 units are good; otherwise reject it.

The problem is to plot the operating characteristic curve and determine the average quality level. Exhibit 10.24 shows the terminal/human interac-

---

[11] TIME/WARE Corp., 688 Main Street, Redwood City, CA 94063. Appreciation is extended for permission to reproduce portions of its *Quality Control Package-User's Manual.*

EXHIBIT 10.24
Computer terminal output of the program MLBIN$

MULBIN   06:59   03/26/70

INPUT THE NUMBER OF LEVELS IN YOUR SAMPLING PLAN. EG 2
? 2

INPUT THE SIZE OF THE FIRST SAMPLE, THE NUMBER OF REJECTS
WHICH WILL CAUSE RESAMPLING, AND THE NUMBER OF REJECTS
WHICH WILL CAUSE REJECTION OF THE LOT
? 15,2,3

INPUT THE SIZE OF THE LAST LOT AND THE TOTAL NUMBER OF
REJECTS WHICH WILL CAUSE REJECTION OF THE LOT   EG 20,5
? 10,3

```
LOT                PERCENT CHANCE OF ACCEPTING THE LOT
 %               10   20   30   40   50   60   70   80   90  100
DEF.     %      !....!....!....!....!....!....!....!....!....!....!
0        100  -                                                   *
2.5      98.4-                                                  *
5        91  -                                               *
7.5      78.7-                                          *
10       64.2-                                     *
12.5     50  -                               *
15       37.5-                         *
17.5     27.2-                     *
20       19.2-                 *
22.5     13.2-             *
25        6.9-         *
27.5      5.9-        *
30        3.6-      *
32.5      2.4-  *
35        1.5- *
37.5      0.9-*
40        0.5-*
42.5      0.3-*
45        0.2-*
47.5      0.1-*
```

THE A.O.Q.L. OVER THE SPECIFIED RANGE IS 6.42

DO YOU WANT TO SEE THE A.O.Q. AND THE AVE. # SAMPLED?   YES

% DEF.	A.O.Q.	AVE. # SAMPLED
0	0	10
2.5	2.38	13.51
5	4.07	15.88
7.5	4.79	16.98
10	4.75	17.14
12.5	4.28	16.72
15	3.65	16.01
17.5	3	15.2
20	2.41	14.38
22.5	1.91	13.62
25	1.49	12.94
27.5	1.14	12.35
30	0.87	11.85
32.5	0.65	11.44
35	0.48	11.1
37.5	0.34	10.82
40	0.24	10.61
42.5	0.17	10.44
45	0.11	10.31
47.5	0.08	10.22
50	0.05	10.15
52.5	0.03	10.1
55	0	10.06

tion. The underlined portions are those input by the person. All other parts are computer printout.

2. Control chart for the number of defects.[12]   A number of characteristics are to be inspected in each unit of output, with each defect carrying equal

---

[12] A *u* chart is a control chart where $u = \frac{c}{k}$, *c* is the total number of defects in any sample, and *k* is the number of inspection units in the sample.

weight. A control chart is to be instituted that will display the results from examining a daily random sample of 10 parts to determine if the process is in control (i.e., within acceptable limits).

Data on the number of defects for the past 20 days are:

Day	Number of defects	Number in sample	Day	Number of defects	Number in sample
1	20	10	11	7	10
2	18	10	12	26	10
3	16	10	13	22	10
4	30	10	14	20	10
5	35	10	15	35	10
6	18	10	16	18	10
7	26	10	17	16	10
8	14	10	18	8	10
9	40	10	19	15	10
10	8	10	20	16	10

EXHIBIT 10.25
Computer terminal output of the program UCHRT$

```
RUN

UCHRT$          19:48      06/04/70

ENTER THE NUMBER OF SAMPLES?   20
INPUT, ONE SAMPLE AT A TIME, THE NUMBER OF DEFECTS
AND THE NUMBER OF UNITS INSPECTED
SAMPLE # 1 ?   20,10
SAMPLE # 2 ?   18,10
SAMPLE # 3 ?   16,10
SAMPLE # 4 ?   30,10
SAMPLE # 5 ?   35,10
SAMPLE # 6 ?   18,10
SAMPLE # 7 ?   26,10
SAMPLE # 8 ?   14,10
SAMPLE # 9 ?   40,10
SAMPLE #10 ?    8,10
SAMPLE #11 ?    7,10
SAMPLE #12 ?   26,10
SAMPLE #13 ?   22,10
SAMPLE #14 ?   20,10
SAMPLE #15 ?   35,10
SAMPLE #16 ?   18,10
SAMPLE #17 ?   16,10
SAMPLE #18 ?    8,10
SAMPLE #19 ?   15,10
SAMPLE #20 ?   16,10


                        U CHART

        0.685009              2.3425              4
VAL.    :....:....:....:....:....:....:....:....:....:
  2     :                   *:                   :
  1.8   :              *     :                   :
  1.6   :           *        :                   :
  3     :                    :          *        :
  3.5   :                    :                   :*
  1.8   :              *     :                   :
  2.6   :                    :       *           :
  1.4   :         *          :                   :
  4     :                    :                   :      *
  0.8   : *                  :                   :
  0.7   :*                   :                   :
  2.6   :                    :          *        :
  2.2   :                    :  *                :
  2     :                   *:                   :
  3.5   :                    :                   :*
  1.8   :              *     :                   :
  1.6   :           *        :                   :
  0.8   : *                  :                   :
  1.5   :          *         :                   :
  1.6   :              *     :                   :
```

Exhibit 10.25 shows the computer output. As in the previous example, the underlined portions are those input by the terminal operator.

Control limits for the chart are set at 3 sigma, implying that 99.7 percent of the data should fall within these limits. Since three units out of 20 are outside limits, the process would be suspected to be out of control (since the average number outside should be three out of 1,000). Three other units of data fall just inside the lower limit. With this wide scatter at both the lower and upper limit, the process would be examined for some cause of the wide variance. A machine, for example, would be suspected of worn gears, bearings, or loosening of parts.

CONCLUSION: QC IN JAPAN

The opening quote in this chapter is but one acknowledgement of Japan's QC success. Others are found in the technical literature (recent QC handbooks and journals), magazines (*Business Week,* June 30, 1980), and television documentaries ("If the Japanese Can Why Can't We?," an NBC white paper broadcast in June, 1980).

The basic thrust of Japan's QC philosophy is combining extensive statistical analysis techniques (such as those discussed in this chapter) with a strong top-to-bottom instructional program. The statistical techniques were brought to Japan in the 1950s by William Edwards Deming, a consultant and New York University professor from the United States. Through his lecturing and consulting, the importance of detailed study of machine tolerances, simplification of quality tests, avoidance of operator-caused defects, and plantwide participation in quality control efforts was recognized by Japanese industry. Thus, in contrast to its post-World War II record of shoddy craftsmanship, Japan combined its national traits of diligence and teamwork with statistical methodology to become the world's leader in consumer-product quality in the 1970s.[13]

The Japanese QC Circle

The QC Circle is the backbone of the motivational side of Japanese quality control. It is a group of workers and work leaders within a single company department which meet once or more a month to study ways of improving quality. Juran describes the development and activities of QC Circles as follows:

> The first step in the formation of QC Circles is an offer by a company to provide to the work force, training in analysis of quality problems and in participaton in QC Circles. Employee participation is voluntary, and about half of the work force does volunteer. Once formed, the Circle embarks on study of projects. These projects may be nominated by the management or by the circle itself.

---

[13] The United States continues to dominate in the quality of its high-technology products such as lasers, chemical synthesizing equipment, and advanced electronics.

Training of the Circle and study of the first project proceed simultaneously. The training takes several forms:

1. Training "by the book." Using manuals, the *QC Textbook For Foremen,* etc., the Circle is instructed in a number of all purpose techniques: pareto analysis to identify the "vital few," cause-and-effect diagram (the Ishikawa diagram) to map out the variables, and statistical tools (histograms, graphs, control charts, process capability study, scatter diagram, binomial probability paper).

2. Training through study of projects worked out by other QC Circles. The journal *Gemba to QC (Quality Control for the Foreman)* is a source of many such projects and is studied at circle meetings.

3. Training during the working out of the project itself through assistance from supervisors, engineers, and others; case report presentation meetings; submission of case reports for action and for publication.[14]

Juran also notes that a Circle averages about three project completions per year, with savings per project averaging $5,000 (according to reports at Japanese QC conventions).[15]

Management's relationship to QC Circles (and Japanese QC in general) is an important one. Upper-level management prepares annual quality plans and monitors achievement of QC Circle projects throughout the year. They also provide a strong leadership role through tangible support of QC improvement efforts. Unlike the United States where QC is generally a staff responsibility, most Japanese middle managers and foremen have QC skills, and thus, QC staffs are small, and formal QC departments rare.

The Japanese success in quality control raises some interesting questions for U.S. organizations, the main one being: "Can we do it here?" The Japanese culture is based upon cooperation rather than confrontation. They view their competition as being other countries rather than other Japanese firms. In fact, strong government backing of Japanese industry as a totality has led observers to refer to the country as "Japan, Inc." Western countries, even those with a socialist orientation, do not come close to presenting the united front that the Japanese do. Thus, it would appear unlikely that the United States, with its heterogeneous culture and laissez-faire history, would ever adopt the Japanese approach as a national program interlocking all organizations.

On the other hand, some U.S. firms such as Motorola are now applying Japanese concepts with good success. Moreover, there is nothing saying that a government-sanctioned award for productivity and quality improvement such as the Deming Prize (given annually to outstanding Japanese

---

[14] J. M. Juran, *Quality Control Handbook* (New York: McGraw-Hill Book Company, 1974), pp. 18–36.

[15] Ibid., p. 46–49.

firms) can not be instituted here. In any event, whether or not the United States goes the "whole nine yards" in replicating the Japanese approach, it does seem to us that two aspects of their philosophy must be considered if we are to remain competitive in quality in the medium- to low-technology products where the Japanese excel:

1. A raised quality consciousness and participation in quality control by all members of the organization.
2. A concerted effort on the part of management to train themselves and their work force in the technical side of quality control. For whatever reasons, U.S. upper and middle management too often have been satisfied to limit their role in QC to "policy development" and delegate quality responsibility to a department or staff. An attitude of "we'll leave it to QC" seems to prevail. It is our belief that it is high time for management to get serious about quality, which, among other things, means that we will have to master the statistical quality control techniques that we developed and the Japanese have internalized.

Perhaps the objectives of the successful International Telephone and Telegraph (ITT) program might be considered as a model for other U.S. firms:

1. Establish a competent quality management program in every operation, both manufacturing and service.
2. Eliminate suprise nonconformance problems.
3. Reduce the cost of quality.
4. Make [our firm] the standard for quality—worldwide.[16]

REVIEW AND DISCUSSION QUESTIONS

1. Discuss some of the difficulties encountered in trying to define quality. State some ways in which a definition may be possible.

2. Ideally, what is the optimal quality level that should be sought by a firm?

3. What is your response to the often-heard comment that one should strive to achieve the highest quality possible?

4. Why should the general level of product quality be set by corporate-level management rather than by a lower level?

5. What responsibilities does a firm have to its customers to guarantee the quality of its products?

6. Should a company be legally responsible for its output of defective products (for example, a pacemaker implant, a steering mechanism in an automobile, children's toys)?

---

[16] Philip B. Crosby, *Quality is Free: The Art of Making Quality Certain* (New York: McGraw-Hill Book Company, 1979), p. 7.

7. Discuss the flow of events described in the overall quality assurance program depicted in Exhibit 10.2.

8. How might you determine at what organizational level the manager of quality control should be placed?

9. In order to have a quality control system, what basic quantities must be specified?

10. Suppose, as assistant administrator of a hospital, you were asked to propose a quality control plan for next year and one for five years hence. What might these plans look like?

11. Briefly summarize how sampling by attributes differs from sampling by variables.

12. What is the meaning of producer's risk and consumer's risk?

13. When is the cost for inspection justified, or when is it not worthwhile to institute an inspection procedure?

14. How might quality control procedures be used in the following types of services: airline, auto dealership, physician's office, drug store, and department store?

15. If QC Circles are so good in Japan, why have they not been widely instituted here in the United States?

16. Why is the average outgoing quality AOQ for producer always better (on the average) than the quality actually produced?

PROBLEMS

1. Completed forms from a particular department of an insurance company were sampled on a daily basis as a check against the quality of performance of that department. In order to establish a tentative norm for the department, one sample of 100 units was collected each day for 15 days as follows:

Sample	Sample size	Number of forms with errors
1	100	4
2	100	3
3	100	5
4	100	0
5	100	2
6	100	8
7	100	1
8	100	3
9	100	4
10	100	2
11	100	7
12	100	2
13	100	1
14	100	3
15	100	1

  a. Develop a *p*-chart using a 95 percent confidence interval (1.96 sigma).
  b. Plot the 15 samples collected.
  c. What comments can you make about the process?

2. A survey was conducted to determine the quality of TV programs on Channel 7, as perceived by random samples of shoppers at a local shopping center. Ten samples were taken over a ten-week period with the single question of: "Are you generally satisfied with the quality of TV programs on Channel 7?" The answer was simply tallied as yes, or other (which included no, undecided, and so forth).

Week number	Number of yes answers	Sample size
1	40	100
2	50	100
3	35	100
4	50	100
5	45	100
6	40	100
7	50	100
8	45	100
9	30	100
10	45	100

  a. Construct a *p*-chart of the survey data at a 95 percent confidence.
  b. The director of programming at Channel 7 changed the program composition and, in three samples which were later taken, found the yes answers to be 60, 50, and 65 for the same sample sizes of 100. What comments can you make?

3. Output from a process contains 0.02 defective units. Defective units which go undetected into final assemblies cost $25 each to replace. An inspection process, which would detect and remove all defectives, can be established to test these units. However, the inspector, who can test 20 units per hour, will entail a wage rate of $8 per hour, including fringe benefits. Should an inspection station be established to test all units?
  a. What is the cost to inspect each unit?
  b. What is the benefit (or loss) from the inspection process?

4. A company is producing component parts which it is using later in its production process. The department producing the products has defined its acceptable quality level as 3 percent defective. For later installation, the using department has a lot-tolerance percent defective of 8 percent.
  a. Specify the sampling plan; that is, what is the *c* and *n*?
  b. What does this mean in English; that is, tell what an inspector does?

5. As the newly appointed assistant administrator at a local hospital, your first project is to investigate the quality of the patient meals put out by the food-service department. You then conduct a ten-day survey by submit-

ting a simple questionnaire to the 400 patients with each meal requiring that they simply check off that the meal was either satisfactory or unsatisfactory. For simplicity in this problem, assume that the response was 1,000 returned questionnaires from the 1,200 meals each day. The results ran as follows:

	Number of unsatisfactory meals	Sample size
December 1	74	1,000
December 2	42	1,000
December 3	64	1,000
December 4	80	1,000
December 5	40	1,000
December 6	50	1,000
December 7	65	1,000
December 8	70	1,000
December 9	40	1,000
December 10	75	1,000
	600	10,000

a. Construct a p-chart based on the questionnaire results, using a confidence interval of 95.5 percent, which is two standard deviations.

b. What comments can you make about the results of the survey?

6. Management is trying to decide whether part A, which is produced with a consistent 3 percent defective, should be inspected. If part A is not inspected, the 3 percent defectives will go through a product assembly phase and have to be replaced later. If all part A's are inspected, *one third* of the defectives will be found, thus raising the quality to 2 percent defectives.

a. Should the inspection be done if the cost of inspecting is $0.01 per unit and the cost of replacing a defective in the final assembly is $4.00?

b. Suppose the cost of inspecting is $0.05 per unit rather than $0.01. Would this change your answer in a? (Show calculations for a and b. A simple yes or no is inadequate.)

7. Large scale integrated (LSI) circuit chips are made in one department of an electronics firm. These chips are then incorporated into analog devices which are then encased in epoxy. The yield is not particularly good for LSI manufacture, so the AQL specified by that department is .15 while the LTPD acceptable by the assembly department is .40.

a. Develop a sampling plan.

b. Explain what the sampling plan means; that is, how would you tell someone to do the test?

8. Parts are produced in one part of a production process to be used later in the assembly of the final product. If items are inspected, the cost of the inspector's wages, fringe benefits, and materials total $10 per hour. The inspector can inspect ten units per hour and units are produced at a 95 percent yield (i.e., .05 defectives). Defective units which pass on through the system must be replaced later at a cost of $12 each.

Question: Assuming that the inspector could detect all the existing defects should an inspector be retained at point A?

9. In order to correctly fit parts which are to be engaged in a product, design limits are set which define the upper and lower acceptable measurements. If the upper limit of one part was defined as 0.5050 inches and the lower design limit as 0.4950, the problem is to determine the initial setting of the machine. In this process, as the tool wears, parts get larger and larger as more parts are made.

   Since the time to reset the process is quite long, it is desirable to make the original setting in such a way so as to run the process as long as possible without resetting.

   The machine itself produces parts which vary from the setting with a standard deviation of 0.0002 inches. Further, you would like to set the machine such that 99 percent of the first parts are acceptable and shut down the machine when 99 percent of the last parts are acceptable (sigma = 2.58).

   Draw a control chart showing the initial setting and point of shutdown.

10. A test is to be made to accept or reject a shipment of items. Since items are destroyed during the test, a sequential sampling plan is to be used.

    Design a sequential sampling plan where the producer's risk is 5 percent and the consumer's risk is 10 percent. The percent defectives for the producer (p_1) is 1 percent and the percent defective for the consumer (p_2) is eight percent.

    What is the minimum number of units which must be tested to accept the lot?

    What is the minimum number of units which must be tested to reject the lot?

11. A sequential sampling plan is to be designed to minimize the number of units which must be tested in an acceptance sampling plan.

    Design a plan in which there is a producer's risk of 95 percent for accepting any lots with 2 percent defective and a consumer's risk of 90 percent that it will not accept any lots of more than 5 percent defective ($p_1 = .02$; $p_2 = .05$)

    What is the minimum number of units which must be tested to accept the lot?

    What is the minimum number of units which must be tested to reject the lot?

12. An inspector on an assembly line is currently inspecting parts as they pass his/her station at the line rate of 130 per hour. From the past experience of this inspector, 4 percent of the units coming to this point have been defective and have been removed from the line. It was noted that if the defective part was not removed at this point, it would cost $2.00 for time and materials to replace it later. The cost of the inspector is $9.00 per hour (wages plus fringe benefits).

    a. Should the inspection point be continued?
    b. What would the yield (or number of defects) have to be to be impartial to whether the parts are inspected or not at this point?

13. The state and local police departments are trying to analyze crime rate areas so that they can shift their patrols from areas with decreasing crime rates to areas that are increasing. The city and county have been geographically segmented into areas containing 5,000 residences. The police recognize that all crimes and offenses are not reported; people either "do not want to become involved," consider the offenses too small to report, are too embarrassed to make a police report, or do not take the time—among other reasons. Every month, because of this, the police are contacting by phone a random sample of 1,000 of the 5,000 residences for data on crime (the respondents are guaranteed anonymity). The data collected for the past 12 months for one area are as follows.

Month	Crime incidence	Sample size	Crime rate
January	7	1,000	0.007
February	9	1,000	0.009
March	7	1,000	0.007
April	7	1,000	0.007
May	7	1,000	0.007
June	9	1,000	0.009
July	7	1,000	0.007
August	10	1,000	0.010
September	8	1,000	0.008
October	11	1,000	0.011
November	10	1,000	0.010
December	8	1,000	0.008

Construct a p-chart for 95 percent confidence (1.96σ), and plot each of the months. If the next three months show crime incidences in this area as

$$January \quad = 10 \text{ (out of 1,000 sampled)}$$
$$February = 12 \text{ (out of 1,000 sampled)}$$
$$March \quad = 11, \text{ (out of 1,000 sampled)}$$

what comments can you make regarding the crime rate?

14. Some of the citizens complained to city councilmen that there should be equal protection under the law against the occurrence of crimes. The citizens' arguments stated that this "equal protection" should be interpreted as indicating that high-crime areas should have more police protection than low-crime areas. Therefore, police patrols and other methods for preventing crime (such as street lighting or "cleaning up" abandoned areas and buildings) should be used proportionately to crime occurrence.

In a fashion similar to problem 1, the city has been broken down into 20 geographical areas, each containing 5,000 residences. The 1,000 sampled from each area showed the following incidence of crime during the past month.

Area	Number of crimes	Sample size	Crime rate
1	14	1,000	0.014
2	3	1,000	0.003
3	19	1,000	0.019
4	18	1,000	0.018
5	14	1,000	0.014
6	28	1,000	0.028
7	10	1,000	0.010
8	18	1,000	0.018
9	12	1,000	0.012
10	3	1,000	0.003
11	20	1,000	0.020
12	15	1,000	0.015
13	12	1,000	0.012
14	14	1,000	0.014
15	10	1,000	0.010
16	30	1,000	0.030
17	4	1,000	0.004
18	20	1,000	0.020
19	6	1,000	0.006
20	30	1,000	0.030
	$\overline{300}$		

Suggest a reallocation of crime protection effort, if indicated, based upon a p-chart analysis. In order that you may be reasonably certain in your recommendation, select a 95 percent confidence level (i.e., 1.96σ).

15. A process has been set up to make bearings for a line of washing-machine motors. In order to fit correctly, the inside diameter of the bearings must be 0.7000 inch plus-or-minus 0.0050 inch. The machinery has a natural variation in output of $\sigma = 0.0005$ inch (normally distributed), and the diameter of the bearings get smaller as the tool wears.

   a. Construct a dynamic control chart for accepting 99 percent of the output (2.58σ) for the longest period of time before the tool must be replaced.

   b. If the process mean shifts 0.001 inch for every 100 bearings made, how many may be made before the process must be stopped for a tool change?

16. Defective units which are not detected in an inspection station cost $20 to repair later. If the quality of the units coming in to the station is 0.95, the inspector can inspect 100 units per hour, and the inspector is paid $5 per hour, should the inspection station be abolished (i.e., should inspection at this point be performed at all)?

17. Testing one of the new line-of-sight ground-to-ground missiles entails the actual firing and destruction of the missile. Thus, it is desirable to test as few units as possible in order to accept or reject a lot. A sequential sampling plan offers the advantages of a small test number.

   a. Design a sequential sampling plan such that the missile manufacturer has a 95 percent probability of accepting any lots with 0.5 percent defectives and the consumer (the Army) has a 90 percent assurance that it will not accept any lots that have more than 3 percent defective (i.e., $\alpha = .05$, $\beta = 0.10$, $p_1 = 0.005$, $p_2 = 0.03$).

   b. What minimum number of units must be tested in order to accept the lot? Suppose one defective missile was found; how large a sample must be tested?

18. A company currently using an inspection process in their material receiving department is trying to install an overall cost reduction program. One of the reductions considered is the elimination of one of the inspection positions. This position tests material which has a defective content on the average of 0.04. By inspecting all items, the inspector is able to remove all defects. The inspector can inspect 50 units per hour. Hourly rate including fringe benefits for this position is $9 per hour. If the inspection position is eliminated, defects will go into product assembly and will have to be replaced later at a cost of $10 each when they are detected in final product testing.

  a. Should this inspection position be eliminated?

  b. What is the cost to inspect each unit?

  c. Is there benefit (or loss) from the current inspection process? How much?

SELECTED BIBLIOGRAPHY

Baker, E. M. "Why Plan Your Inspection?" *Quality Progress* (July 1975), pp. 22–27.

Benich, J. J., and Enrick, N. L. "Inspectors Get Worse Before They Get Better," *Quality Progress* (January 1975), pp. 23–24.

Charbonneau, Harvey C., and Webster, Gordon L. *Industrial Quality Control.* Englewood Cliffs, N.J.: Prentice-Hall, Inc., 1978.

Duncan, Acheson J. *Quality Control and Industrial Statistics.* 4th ed. Homewood, Ill. Richard D. Irwin, Inc., 1974.

Juran, J. M., and Gryna, F. M. *Quality Planning and Analysis.* New York: McGraw-Hill Book Company, 1970.

Smith, Martin R. *Quality Sense.* New York: AMACOM Division of American Management Association, 1979.

APPENDIX: CHARACTERISTICS OF SEQUENTIAL TESTS OF BINOMIAL DISTRIBUTION

Characteristic quantities of sequential tests of the binomial distribution computed for various combinations of p_1', p_2', $\alpha = 0.05$, and $\beta = 0.10$*	p_1'	p_2'	h_2	h_1	s	$\bar{n}_0$	$\bar{n}_1$	$\bar{n}_{p_1'}$	$\bar{n}_s$	$\bar{n}_{p_2'}$
	0.005	0.01	4.1398	3.2245	0.007216	447	5	1,289	1,863	1,222
		0.02	2.0624	1.6064	0.01084	149	3	244	309	185
		0.03	1.5906	1.2389	0.01400	89	2	122	143	82
		0.04	1.3664	1.0643	0.01693	63	2	79	87	49
		0.05	1.2305	0.9585	0.01970	49	2	58	61	33
		0.06	1.1371	0.8857	0.02237	40	2	45	46	25
		0.07	1.0679	0.8318	0.02496	34	2	37	36	19
	0.010	0.03	2.5829	2.0118	0.01824	111	3	216	290	181
		0.04	2.0397	1.5887	0.02172	74	3	120	153	92
		0.05	1.7510	1.3639	0.02499	55	2	81	98	58
		0.06	1.5678	1.2211	0.02811	44	2	60	70	40
		0.07	1.4391	1.1209	0.03113	37	2	47	53	30
		0.08	1.3426	1.0458	0.03406	31	2	38	43	24
	0.015	0.03	4.0796	3.1776	0.02166	147	5	423	612	402
		0.04	2.8716	2.2367	0.02554	88	3	188	258	163
		0.05	2.3307	1.8153	0.02917	63	3	113	149	92
		0.06	2.0169	1.5710	0.03263	49	3	79	100	61
		0.07	1.8089	1.4089	0.03596	40	2	60	74	44
	0.02	0.03	6.9527	5.4154	0.02467	220	8	1,027	1,565	1,073
		0.04	4.0495	3.1541	0.02889	110	5	314	455	300
		0.05	3.0509	2.3763	0.03282	73	4	164	228	146
		0.06	2.5348	1.9743	0.03655	55	3	106	142	89
		0.07	2.2146	1.7250	0.04012	43	3	76	99	61
		0.08	1.9941	1.5532	0.04359	36	3	58	74	45
		0.09	1.8315	1.4265	0.04696	31	2	47	58	35
		0.10	1.7056	1.3285	0.05025	27	2	39	47	28

Abridged with permission from Table 2.23 of Statistical Research Group, Columbia University, *Sequential Analysis of Statistical Data: Applications* (New York: Columbia University Press, 1945), pp. 2.39–2.42.

Chapter
11

JOB DESIGN AND
WORK MEASUREMENT

The direct labor force accounts for a sizable percentage of the cost of production and, as such, represents a major concern in the design and operation of a production system. In this chapter, we will discuss a variety of approaches used in designing, measuring, and compensating the work of this group.

JOB DESIGN

Perhaps the most challenging (and perplexing) design activity encountered by the productive system is the development of the jobs that each worker and work group are to perform. This is so for at least three reasons:

1. There is often an inherent conflict between the needs and goals of the worker and work group and the requirements of the transformation process.

2. The unique nature of each individual results in a wide range of attitudinal, physiological, and productivity responses in performing any given task.

3. The changing character of the work force and the work itself which lays open to question the traditional models of worker behavior and the efficacy of standard approaches to work development. (But we have come a long way—see Exhibit 11.1.)

In this section, we will explore these and other issues in job design and present some guidelines for carrying out the job-design function.

<table>
<tr><td>

EXHIBIT 11.1
Contrasting approaches to job design

</td><td>

Frederick W. Taylor recounts his "motivation" of his trusty worker, Schmidt (in *Principles of Scientific Management*, 1910):

</td></tr>
</table>

> "Schmidt, are you a high-priced man?"
>
> "Vell, I don't know vat you mean."
>
> "Oh yes you do. What I want to know is whether you are a high-priced man or not. . . . What I want to find out is whether you want to earn $1.85 a day or whether you are satisfied with $1.15, just the same as all those cheap fellows are getting?"
>
> "Vell, yes I vas a high-priced man."
>
> "Now come over here. You see that pile of pig iron?"
>
> "Yes."
>
> "You see that car?"
>
> "Yes."
>
> "Well, if you are a high-priced man, you will load that pig iron on that car tomorrow for $1.85."
>
> "You see that man over there?" . . . Well, if you are a high-priced man, you will do exactly as this man tells you tomorrow, from morning till night. When he tells you to pick up a pig and walk, you pick it up and you walk, and when he tells you to sit down and rest, you sit down. You do that straight through the day. And what's more, no back talk."

* * * * * * * *

William F. Dowling describes job redesign at Phillips N.V. in the Netherlands (in Job Redesign on the Assembly in "Farewell to the Blue-Collar Blues?" *Organizational Dynamics*, Autumn 1973).

The truck chassis assembly groups have real decision-making power. Production groups of 5 to 12 workers with related job duties decide among themselves how they will do their jobs, within the quality and production standards defined by higher management; they can rotate job assignments— do a smaller or larger part of the overall task. At the same time, the jobs of all members of the production groups were enlarged making them jointly responsible for simple service and maintenance activities, housekeeping, and quality control in their work area, duties formally performed by staff personnel.

<table>
<tr><td>

Job design defined

</td><td>

Job design may be defined as the function of specifying the work activities of an individual or group in an organizational setting. Its objective is to develop work assignments that meet the requirements of the organization and the technology and that satisfy the personal and individual requirements of the job holder. The term *job* (in the context of nonsupervisory work) and the activities subsumed under it are defined below.

</td></tr>
</table>

1. *Micromotion:* the smallest work activities, involving such elementary movements as reaching, grasping, positioning, or releasing an object.
2. *Element:* an aggregation of two or more micromotions, usually thought of as a more or less complete entity, such as picking up, transporting, and positioning an item.

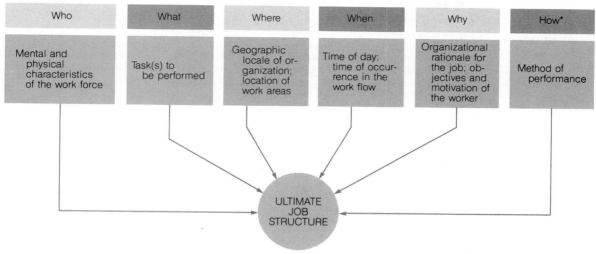

Who	What	Where	When	Why	How*
Mental and physical characteristics of the work force	Task(s) to be performed	Geographic locale of organization; location of work areas	Time of day; time of occurrence in the work flow	Organizational rationale for the job; objectives and motivation of the worker	Method of performance

ULTIMATE JOB STRUCTURE

*See work measurement in this chapter.

EXHIBIT 11.2
Factors in job design

3. *Task:* an aggregation of two or more elements into a complete activity, such as wiring a circuit board, sweeping a floor, cutting a tree.
4. *Job:* the set of all tasks that must be performed by a given worker. A job may consist of several tasks, such as typing, filing, and taking dictation, as in secretarial work, or it may consist of a single task, such as attaching a wheel to a car, as in automobile assembly.

Job design is a complex function because of the variety of factors that enter into arriving at the ultimate job structure. Decisions must be made as to who is to perform the job, where it is to be performed, and how it is to be performed. And, as can be seen in Exhibit 11.2, each of these factors may have additional considerations.

PSYCHOSOCIAL CONSIDERATIONS IN JOB DESIGN

Degree of labor specialization

Specialization of labor is the two-edged sword of job design. On the one hand, specialization has made possible high-speed, low-cost production, and, from a materialistic standpoint, has greatly enhanced our standard of living. On the other hand, it is well known that extreme specialization, such as that encountered in mass production industries, often has serious adverse effects on the worker, which in turn are passed on to the production system. In essence, the problem is the determination of how much specialization is enough; that is, at what point do the disadvantages outweigh the advantages? (See Exhibit 11.3.)

Recent research suggests that the disadvantages dominate the advantages much more commonly than was thought in the past. However, simply stating that for purely humanitarian reasons specialization should be

EXHIBIT 11.3
Advantages and disadvantages of specialization of labor

Advantages of specialization

To management:
1. Rapid training of the work force
2. Ease in recruiting new workers
3. High output due to simple and repetitive work
4. Low wages due to ease of substitutability of labor
5. Close control over work flow and work loads

To labor:
1. Little responsibility for output
2. Little mental effort required
3. Little or no education required to obtain work

Disadvantages of specialization

To management:
1. Difficulty in controlling quality since no one person has responsibility for entire product
2. "Hidden" costs of worker dissatisfaction, arising from
   a. turnover
   b. absenteeism
   c. tardiness
   d. grievances
   e. intentional disruption of production process

To labor:
1. Boredom stemming from repetitive nature of work
2. Little gratification from the work itself because of small contribution to each item.
3. Little or no control over the work pace, leading to frustration and fatigue (in assembly-line-type situations)
4. Little opportunity to progress to a better job since significant learning is rarely possible on fractionated work
5. Little opportunity to show intiative through developing better methods or tools
6. Local muscular fatigue due to use of the same muscles in performing the task
7. Little opportunity for communication with fellow workers due to layout of the work area

avoided is a risky assertion. The reason, of course, is that people differ in what they want from their work and what they are willing to put into it. Some workers prefer not to make decisions about their work, some like to daydream on the job, and others are simply not capable of performing more complex work. Still, as was pointed out earlier, there is a good deal of frustration on the part of the work force with the way many jobs are structured, leading researchers and thoughtful businessmen to try different approaches to job design. Two popular contemporary approaches are job enlargement and socio-technical systems.

Job enlargement

Job enlargement generally entails making adjustments to a specialized job so as to make it more interesting to the job holder. A job is said to be enlarged *horizontally* if the worker performs a greater number or variety of tasks, and it is said to be enlarged *vertically* if the worker is involved in planning, organizing, and inspecting his or her own work. Horizontal job enlargement is intended to counteract oversimplification and to permit the worker to perform a "whole unit of work." Vertical enlargement (often termed *job enrichment*) attempts to broaden the workers' influence in the transformation process by giving them certain "managerial powers" over their own activities.

A brief example of horizontal job enlargement, undertaken by IBM's French affiliate in the subassembly of counters used on tabulators, follows:

> The jobs originally had been divided among 13 workers, each doing a fragmentary operation. These were semi-skilled men who were bored with their jobs and were anxious to advance. The jobs were enlarged by successively consolidating the 13 stages into 7, and then into 4 jobs. As an ancillary part of the program, the workers were given theoretical and practical training on Saturdays for a period of six weeks. Because of the enlarged jobs and the weekend training, the workers were initiated into the lowest order of the skilled class. Also, the workers were reported to like having fuller jobs and feeling responsible to the customer for the quality of their work.[1]

Sociotechnical systems   Consistent with the job-enlargement philosophy but focusing more on the interaction between technology and the work group is the sociotechnical systems approach. This approach attempts to develop jobs which adjust the needs of the production process technology to the needs of the worker and work group. The term *sociotechnical system* was developed from studies of weaving mills in India and coal mines in England in the early 1950s. In these studies, it was discovered that work groups could effectively handle many production problems better than management by being permitted to make their own decisions on scheduling, work allocation among members, bonus sharing, and so forth. This was found to be particularly true when there were variations in the production process requiring quick reactions by the group or when the work of one shift overlapped with the work of other shifts.

Since these pioneering studies, the sociotechnical approach has been applied in many countries, though often under the heading of "autonomous work groups" or "industrial democracy" projects.

One of the major philosophical points which underlies these studies is that the individual or the work group requires a logically integrated pattern of work activities that incorporates the following job design principles:

> *Task variety.* An attempt must be made to provide an optimum variety of tasks within each job. Too much variety can be inefficient for training and frustrating for the employee. Too little can lead to boredom and fatigue. The optimum level is one which allows the employee to take a rest from a high level of attention or effort while working on another task or, conversely, to allow him to stretch himself after periods of routine activity.
>
> *Skill variety.* Research suggests that employees derive satisfaction from using a number of different kinds and levels of skill.
>
> *Feedback.* There should be some means for informing employees quickly

---

[1] Georges Friedmann, *The Anatomy of Work* (New York: Free Press of Glencoe, 1960), p. 48.

when they have achieved their targets. Fast feedback aids the learning process. Ideally, employees should have some responsibility for setting their own standards of quantity and quality.

Task identity. Sets of tasks should be separated from other sets of tasks by some clear boundary. Whenever possible, a group or individual employee should have responsibility for a set of tasks which is clearly defined, visible, and meaningful. In this way, work is seen as important by the group or individual undertaking it, and others understand and respect its significance.

Task autonomy. Employees should be able to exercise some control over their work. Areas of discretion and decision taking should be available to them.[2]

Following a sociotechnical approach to job design by implementing some of the more controversial guidelines may create a certain amount of malaise in the typical organization. For example, if one accepts the notion that groups may be able to self-organize and function autonomously more successfully if their activities are not completely prescribed, production management personnel and industrial engineers who are charged with the job-design function must be able to adjust to such a loose-rein situation. And whether they will be able to do so depends jointly on management's philosophy toward such an approach and their own security in their changed organizational role. Indeed, this is more than a small challenge to industrial engineers because, historically, they have been weaned on a "one-best-way" philosophy—that is, for every job there is a "preferred" structure, and it is the *industrial engineer's* function to find it and implement it. Similarly, management may perceive that it is relinquishing some of its power to direct and control its work force and therefore may do so with great reluctance—a response which is not lost on the average worker.

Experiments in job design

Exhibit 11.4, reproduced from *Work in America*, provides a concise summary of a few experiments in job restructuring and management in a variety of firms in several countries; in most of the cases cited, the changes took hold and are no longer viewed by the companies as "trial runs." Examination of "Techniques used" (item 5 on the table) indicates a diversity in design approaches used, yet underlying all of the innovations is a provision for increased independence on the part of the worker in doing his or her job.

PHYSICAL CONSIDERATIONS IN JOB DESIGN

Beyond the psychosocial aspects of job design, another aspect of the topic warrants consideration, namely, the physical side. Indeed, while motivation and work-group structure strongly influence worker performance, they may be of secondary importance if the job is too demanding or is

---

[2] This summary is taken from Enid Mumford and Mary Weir, *Computer Systems in Work Design—the ETHICS Method* (New York: Halsted Press, 1979), p. 42.

otherwise ill-designed from a physical standpoint. In this section, we will examine the physical side of work in terms of its demands on the individual and then consider one approach to job design utilizing physiological criteria.

Work task continuum

One way of viewing the general nature of the physical requirements inherent in work is through the rough continuum in Exhibit 11.5. In this typology, *manual tasks* are defined as tasks that entail stress on large muscle groups in the body and lead to overall fatigue, as measured by increases in the vital functions. In this context, the body is viewed as a heat engine that is supplied by fuel—food and liquids—and uses oxygen for its transformation into energy. *Motor tasks* are controlled by the central nervous system, and their measure of effectiveness is the speed and precision of movements. While these tasks lead to fatigue, the effect is localized in the smaller muscle groups, such as the fingers, hands, and arms and, hence, cannot be adequately measured by indices of *general* fatigue. (In measuring the physiological stress of motor tasks, researchers are investigating the use of electromyography, which records the changes in electrical potential in the involved muscular extremity; that is, the hands, arms, and fingers.) *Mental tasks* involve rapid decision making based upon certain types of stimuli, such as "blips" on a radar screen or defects in a product. Here the measure of effectiveness is generally some combination of time to respond and number and kind of error. Research into this type of work is usually predicated on concepts from the discipline of information theory, and as might be expected by the nature of the tasks, much of the source work has been provided by military agencies.

As noted in Exhibit 11.5, motor tasks and mental tasks fall under the heading *human engineering,* while the study of the physical aspects of work in general is called *ergonomics* (from the Greek noun for "work" and the Greek verb for "to manage"). Of the three categories, the analysis of strenuous manual work (approached through the discipline of work physiology) will now be discussed.

There are some compelling reasons why, even in the age of mechanization, we should study strenuous manual work:

First, it is unlikely for economic reasons that we will ever succeed in eliminating all strenuous (or heavy) work. In many instances, manpower is far less costly and far more versatile than machine power. Indeed, the rising cost of energy may force some organizations to revert to manual work.

Second, even though we now engage in fewer heavy tasks, the ones that remain may be critical to the functioning of certain production systems. For example, a worker may be in charge of loading and unloading a bank of machines that may represent a sizable investment, and if he does not adequately perform his function, the resulting loss in output could be just as great as if the work were inefficiently performed by hand by a large number of workers.

EXHIBIT 11.4
Experiments in job design

	Organization			
	Netherlands PTT	*Kaiser Aluminum Corporation Ravenswood, W.Va.*	*Bankers Trust Company New York*	*Operations Division, Bureau of Traffic— Ohio Department of Highways*
1. *Establishment(s) or employee groups*	Clerical workers— data collection.	Maintenance workers in reduction plant.	Production typists in stock transfer operations.	Six field construction crews.
2. *Year initiated*	Not specified.	1971	1969	Not specified.
3. *Number employees affected*	100	60	200	Not specified.
4. *Problem*	Jobs were routine. Workers and supervisors were both "notably uninterested" in their work.	Productivity was low. There were walkouts and slowdowns.	Production was low and quality poor. Absenteeism and turnover were high and employee attitudes were poor . . . Jobs were routine, repetitive and devoid of intrinsic interest . . . Too much overseeing.	Low productivity and poor quality of performance.
5. *Technique used*	Jobs were enlarged to comprise a whole collaborative process (e.g., listing, punching, control punching, corrections, etc.) instead of a single stage of this process.	Time clocks were removed and supervision virtually eliminated. Workers now decide what maintenance jobs are to be done and in what priority and keep their own time cards.	Typists were given the opportunity (1) to change their own computer output tapes, (2) to handle typing for a specific group of customers, (3) to check their own work, and (4) to schedule their own work. Training was given in these areas.	Three experimental groups were established, each with a different degree of self-determination of work schedules. Crews were unaware that they were participating in an experiment.

6. *Human results*	88% of the workers in the experimental group said the work had become more interesting.	"Morale has improved along with pride in workmanship," says the maintenance chief.	A quantitative survey disclosed improved attitudes and greater satisfaction.	Data showed that as participation increased, so did morale.
7. *Economic results*	There was a 15% increase in output per man-hour.	Tardiness is now "nonexistent." Maintenance costs are down 5.5%. Maintenance work is done with more "quality."	Absenteeism and tardiness were reduced while production and quality increased. Job enrichment programs were extended.	There was no significant changes in productivity.
8. *Reference(s)*	Wilson, N. A. B., *On The Quality of Working Life,* A Personal Report to the NATO Committee on Challenges of Modern Society, p. 36	Thompson, Donald B., "Enrichment in Action Convinces Skeptics," *Industry Week,* Feb. 14. 1971	Detteback, William W., Assistant Vice Pres. Bankers Trust, and Kraft, Philip, Partner; Roy W. Walters Associates, "Organization Change Through Job Enrichment," *Training and Development Journal,* August 1971	Powell, Reed M., and Schlacter, John L., "Participative Management: A Panacea?" *Academy of Management Journal,* June 1971, pp. 165–73

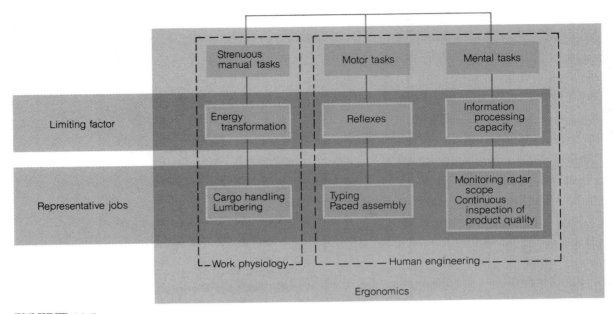

EXHIBIT 11.5
**Work task
continuum**

Third, space and weight limitations often make mechanization impossible, as in mining operations, cargo handling aboard aircraft, and in certain types of construction work.

Finally, it is a fact that large numbers of people in parts of the United States, as well as the rest of the world, are employed in predominantly heavy manual work. Inefficiency in their use can be a grave waste of human resources.

**Work
physiology**

Work physiology is essentially the application of physiological techniques to manual work. The techniques are predicated on the assumption that certain physiological changes take place during work and that, by observing these changes, the level of physical stress can be determined. Unlike traditional industrial engineering practice, where performance time is the criterion of work intensity (e.g., the faster the work, the more fatiguing it is to the worker), work physiology attempts to determine directly, and express by physiological indices, the true fatigue engendered by the work.

The physiological indices most widely used by work physiologists are heart rate and oxygen consumption rate converted to calories per unit of time. Other indices, such as sweat rate, lactic acid concentration in the blood, and body temperature, have also been used but for various reasons are impractical for industrial application. The remainder of this discussion focuses on how heart rate and oxygen consumption can be employed in work-stress evaluation.

Heart rate (in beats per minute) is a familiar way of gauging physiological

EXHIBIT 11.6
**Calorie
requirements for
various activities**

Type of activity	Typical energy cost in calories per minute
Sitting at rest	1.7
Writing	2.0
Typing	2.3
Medium assembly work	2.9
Shoe repair	3.0
Machining	3.3
Ironing	4.4
Heavy assembly work	5.1
Chopping wood	7.5
Digging	8.9
Tending furnace	12.0
Walking upstairs	12.0

Source: *Bioastronautics Data Book,* Paul Webb, ed. (Washington, D.C.: Scientific and Technical Information Division, National Aeronautics and Space Administration, 1964).

stress, and we have some reliable guidelines for its use. One is that the maximum sustainable heart rate for an eight-hour work day is about 115 beats per minute for the "average" worker. He could exceed this level for a short period of time but then would have to cease working to permit his body to recover. Of prime importance in this recovery process is the need for the working muscles to get a fresh supply of oxygen through the blood and rid themselves of the body's main waste product, carbon dioxide.

Oxygen consumption, converted to calories per unit of time, is the basic measure for determining the energy expended by the body at work.[3] Expressing oxygen consumption as calories has become common practice even in underdeveloped countries because of the need to establish the minimum amount of food required to enable a worker to function effectively. Thus calories provide the basis for an input-output equation for broad-scale nutritional planning. With respect to the maximum sustainable calorie consumption level, most authorities agree that five calories per minute represents a conservative upper limit. The approximate number of calories required per minute for various activities is shown in Exhibit 11.6. Clerical or assembly tasks, which may entail a high level of localized fatigue, are not well suited for heart rate or oxygen consumption analyses.

**The work
environment**

Several factors in the work environment may affect job performance—such as illumination, noise, temperature and humidity, and composition of the air. Though each is worthy of discussion, space does not permit

[3] It is not necessary to use both heart and energy expenditure rate in every situation. However, while heart rate determinations are generally easier to make, this index is highly sensitive to environmental factors such as temperature and humidity. Therefore, unless these factors are relatively constant over the work day, it may prove difficult to obtain a true picture of job stress by heart rate alone.

thorough treatment of these topics, and the interested reader is therefore referred to the A.S.H.R.A.E., Chapanis, and McCormick works listed at the end of the chapter. It should be pointed out also that these factors have a strong bearing on the safety and general health of the worker and, therefore, have been subjected to legal regulation through the Occupational Safety and Health Act of 1970.

METHODS, MEASUREMENT, AND PAYMENT

". . . brook no idleness. Stand over them (the fieldworkers) during their work, and brook no interruptions. Do not distract your fieldworkers."[4]

In this section, our focus shifts from delineating the boundaries and general character of the job to the specifics of job performance. In particular, we wish to consider:

1. How the work should be accomplished (work methods).
2. How performance may be evaluated (work measurement).
3. How workers should be compensated (wage payment plans).

WORK METHODS

In our development of the productive system, we have defined the tasks that must be done by workers. But *how* should they be done? Years ago, production workers were craftsmen who had their own (sometimes secret) methods for doing work. However, as products became more complicated, as mechanization of a higher order was introduced, and as output rates increased, the responsibilities for work methods were necessarily transferred to management. It was no longer logical or economically feasible to allow individual workers to produce the same product by different methods. Further, work specialization brought much of the concept of craftwork to an end as less-skilled workers were employed on the simpler tasks.

In contemporary industry, the responsibility for developing work methods in large firms is typically assigned either to a staff department that is designated "methods analysis" or to an industrial engineering department. In small firms, this activity is often performed by individual specialists who report to the production manager.

The principal approach to the study of work methods is the construction of charts (such as operations charts, man/machine charts, activity charts) in conjunction with time study or standard time data. The choice of which charting method to use depends on the activity level of the task; that is, whether the focus is on (1) the overall productive system, (2) the stationary

---

[4] Samuel N. Kramer, *Sumerians: Their History, Culture and Character* (Chicago: University of Chicago Press, 1963).

EXHIBIT 11.7
Work methods design aids

Activity	Objective of study	Study techniques
Overall productive system	Eliminate or combine steps; shorten transport distance; identify delays	Flow diagram, process chart
Stationary worker at fixed work place	Simplify method; minimize motions	Operations charts, simo charts; apply principles of motion economy
Worker interacts with equipment	Minimize idle time; find number or combination of machines to balance cost of man and machine idle time	Activity chart, man-machine charts
Worker interacts with other workers	Maximize productivity; minimize interference	Activity charts, gang process charts

worker at a fixed work place, (3) a worker interacting with equipment, or (4) a worker interacting with other workers (see Exhibit 11.7). (Several of these charting techniques were introduced in Chapter 2, where they were used to aid process selection.)

Overall productive system

The objective in studying the overall productive system is to identify delays, transport distances, processes, and processing time requirements in order to simplify the entire operation. Once the process has been charted, the following questions may be asked.

What is done? Must it be done? What would happen if it were not done?

Where is the task done? Must it be done at that location or could it be done somewhere else?

When is the task performed? Is it critical that it be done then or is there flexibility in time and sequence? Could it be done in combination with some other step in the process?

How is the task done? Why is it done this way? Is there another way?

Who does the task? Can someone else do it? Should the worker be of a higher or lower skill level?

These thought-provoking questions usually lead to elimination of much of the unnecessary work, as well as to simplifying the remaining work, by combining a number of processing steps and changing the order of performance.

Use of the *process chart* is valuable in studying an overall system, though care must be taken to follow the same item throughout the process. The subject may be a product being manufactured, a service being created, or a person performing a sequence of activities. An example of a process chart (and flow diagram) for a clerical operation is shown in Exhibit 11.8. Common notation in process charting is given in Exhibit 11.9.

EXHIBIT 11.8
Flow diagram and process chart of an office procedure— present method*

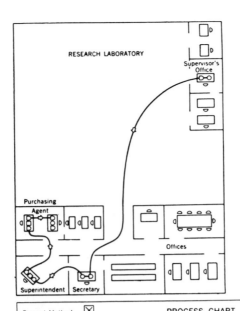

RESEARCH LABORATORY

Supervisor's Office

Purchasing Agent

Offices

Superintendent   Secretary

PROCESS CHART

Present Method ☒
Proposed Method ☐

SUBJECT CHARTED ___ Requisition for small tools ___
Chart begins at supervisor's desk and ends at typist's desk in
purchasing department

DEPARTMENT ___ Research laboratory ___

DATE _____
CHART BY J. C. H.
CHART NO. R 136
SHEET NO. 1 OF 1

DIST. IN FEET	TIME IN MINS.	CHART SYMBOLS	PROCESS DESCRIPTION
		●⇨☐D▽	Requisition written by supervisor (one copy)
		○⇨☐D▽	On supervisor's desk (awaiting messenger)
65		○⇨☐D▽	By messenger to superintendent's secretary
		○⇨☐D▽	On secretary's desk (awaiting typing)
		●⇨☐D▽	Requisition typed (original requisition copied)
15		○⇨☐D▽	By secretary to superintendent
		○⇨☐D▽	On superintendent's desk (awaiting approval)
		○⇨■D▽	Examined and approved by superintendent
		○⇨☐D▽	On superintendent's desk (awaiting messenger)
20		○⇨☐D▽	To purchasing department
		○⇨☐D▽	On purchasing agent's desk (awaiting approval)
		○⇨■D▽	Examined and approved
		○⇨☐D▽	On purchasing agent's desk (awaiting messenger)
5		○⇨☐D▽	To typist's desk
		○⇨☐D▽	On typist's desk (awaiting typing of purchase order)
		●⇨☐D▽	Purchase order typed
		○⇨☐D▽	On typist's desk (awaiting transfer to main office)
		○⇨☐D▽	
		○⇨☐D▽	
105		3 4 2 8	Total

* Requisition is written by supervisor, typed by secretary, approved by superintendent, and approved by purchasing agent; then a purchase order is prepared by a stenographer.

Source: Ralph M. Barnes, *Motion and Time Study* (New York: John Wiley & Sons, 1968) pp. 76–79.

EXHIBIT 11.9
**Common
notation in
process charting**

●	Operation. Something actually is being done. This may be work on a product, some support activity or anything that is directly productive in nature.
➡	Transportation. The subject of the study (product, service, or person) moves from one location to another.
▪	Inspection. The subject is observed for quality and correctness.
◗	Delay. The subject of the study must wait before starting the next step in the process.
▼	Storage. The subject is stored, such as finished products in inventory or completed papers in a file. Frequently, a distinction is made between temporary storage and permanent storage by inserting a T or P in the triangle.

**Stationary
worker at a
fixed work
place**

Many work tasks require the work to remain at the same place. When the nature of the work is primarily manual (e.g., sorting, inspecting, making entries, or assembly operations), the focus of work design is on simplifying the work method and making the required operator motions as few and as easy as possible.

There are two basic ways to determine the best method when studying a single worker who is performing an essentially manual task. The first is to search among the workers and find the one who performs the job best. That person's method is then accepted as the standard, and others who would work on that job are trained to perform it in the same way. This was basically F. W. Taylor's approach, though after determining the best method, he searched for "first-class men" to perform according to the method. (A "first-class man" possessed the natural ability to do much more productive work in a particular task than the average. Men who were not "first class" were transferred to other jobs.) The second way to determine the best method is to observe the performance of a number of workers, analyze in detail each step of their work, and pick out the superior features of each worker's performance. This results in a composite method that combines the best elements of the group studied. This was the procedure used by Frank Gilbreth, the "father of motion study," to determine the "one best way" to perform a work task.

Whereas Taylor observed actual performance to find the best method, Frank Gilbreth and his wife Lillian relied on movie film. Through "micro-motion analysis"—observation of the filmed work performance frame by frame—the Gilbreths studied work very closely and defined its basic elements, which were termed *therbligs* (Gilbreth spelled backward, with the *t* and *h* transposed). Their study led to the rules or principles of motion economy listed in Exhibit 11.10.

Once the motions for performing the task have been identified, an *operations chart* may be made, listing the operations and their sequence of performance. For greater detail, a *simo* (*simultaneous motion*) *chart* may be constructed, which lists not only the operations but also the times for both left and right hands. This chart may be assembled from data collected

EXHIBIT 11.10
Principles of motion economy (checksheet for motion economy and fatigue reduction)

Use of the human body

1. The two hands should begin as well as complete their motions at the same time.
2. The two hands should not be idle at the same time except during rest periods.
3. Motions of the arms should be made in opposite and symmetrical directions, and should be made simultaneously.
4. Hand and body motions should be confined to the lowest classification with which it is possible to perform the work satisfactorily.
5. Momentum should be employed to assist the worker wherever possible, and it should be reduced to a minimum if it must be overcome by muscular effort.
6. Smooth continuous curved motions of the hands are preferable to straight-line motions involving sudden and sharp changes in direction.
7. Ballistic movements are faster, easier, and more accurate than restricted or "controlled" movements.
8. Work should be arranged to permit easy and natural rhythm wherever possible.
9. Eye fixations should be as few and as close together as possible.

Arrangement of the work place

10. There should be a definite and fixed place for all tools and materials.
11. Tools, materials, and controls should be located close to the point of use.
12. Gravity feed bins and containers should be used to deliver material close to the point of use.
13. Drop deliveries should be used wherever possible.
14. Materials and tools should be located to permit the best sequence of motions.
15. Provisions should be made for adequate conditions for seeing. Good illumination is the first requirement for satisfactory visual perception.
16. The height of the work place and the chair should preferably be arranged so that alternate sitting and standing at work are easily possible.
17. A chair of the type and height to permit good posture should be provided for every worker.

Design of tools and equipment

18. The hands should be relieved of all work that can be done more advantageously by a jig, a fixture, or a foot-operated device.
19. Two or more tools should be combined wherever possible.
20. Tools and materials should be pre-positioned whenever possible.
21. Where each finger performs some specific movement, such as in typewriting, the load should be distributed in accordance with the inherent capacities of the fingers.
22. Levers, crossbars, and hand wheels should be located in such positions that the operator can manipulate them with the least change in body position and with the greatest mechanical advantage.

Source: Ralph M. Barnes, *Motion and Time Study* (New York: John Wiley & Sons, 1968), p. 220.

with a stopwatch, from analysis of a movie film of the operation, or from predetermined motion time data (discussed later in the chapter). Many aspects of poor design will be immediately obvious: a hand being used as a holding device (rather than a jig or fixture), an idle hand, or an exceptionally long time for positioning.

EXHIBIT 11.11
Man-machine activity chart*

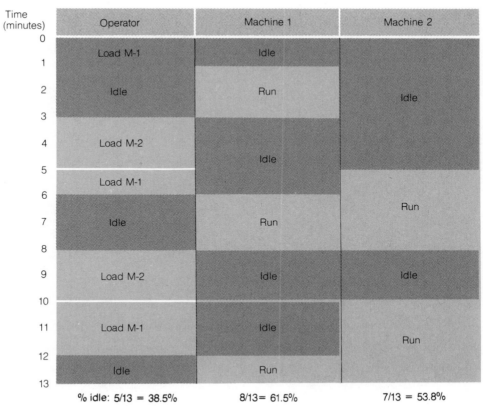

Time (minutes)	Operator	Machine 1	Machine 2
0			
	Load M-1	Idle	
1			
2	Idle	Run	Idle
3			
4	Load M-2		
		Idle	
5			
	Load M-1		
6			Run
7	Idle	Run	
8			
9	Load M-2	Idle	Idle
10			
11	Load M-1	Idle	Run
12			
	Idle	Run	
13			
% idle:	5/13 = 38.5%	8/13 = 61.5%	7/13 = 53.8%

* Machines unload automatically and perform the same function. M–2 has twice the capacity of M–1.

Load and run times: Load: M–1 = 1 minute, M–2 = 2 minutes.
Run: M–1 = 2 minutes, M–2 = 3 minutes.

Worker interacting with equipment

When a person and equipment operate to perform the productive process, interest focuses on the efficient utilization of the person's time and equipment time. When the working time of the operator is less than the equipment run time, a *man-machine chart* is a useful device in analysis. If the operator can operate several pieces of equipment, the problem is to find the most economical combination of operator and equipment. This optimum point occurs when the combined cost of the idle time of a particular combination of equipment and the idle time for the worker is at a minimum.

Man-machine charts are always drawn to scale, the scale being time as measured by length. Exhibit 11.11 gives an example of a man-machine chart for one operator running two machines. Note that a better utilization of machine capacity is possible through changing the loading sequence.

EXHIBIT 11.12
Activity chart of emergency tracheotomy

	Nurse	First doctor	Orderly	Second doctor	Nurse supervisor	Scrub nurse
0						
1	Detects problem / Notifies doctor					
2	Gets mobile cart					
3		Makes diagnosis				
4						
5	Notifies nurse supervisor					
6		Assists patient to breathe			Opens OR / Calls scrub nurse	
7	Notifies second doctor / Notifies orderly			Assures availability of laryngoscope and endotracheal tube		
8	Moves patient to OR	Moves to OR	Moves patient to OR			Moves to OR / Sets up equipment
9		Scrubs				
10		Dons gown and gloves		Operates laryngoscope and inserts endotracheal tube		
11						
12		Performs tracheotomy		Calls for IPPB machine		
13						
14						
15						
16						

Data taken from Harold E. Smalley and John Freeman, *Hospital Industrial Engineering* (New York: Reinhold Publishing Co., 1966), p. 409.

Workers interacting with other workers

A great amount of our productive output in manufacturing and service industries is performed by teams. The degree of interaction may be as simple as one operator handing a part to another—or as complex as a cardiovascular surgical team of doctors, nurses, anesthesiologist, operator of an artificial heart machine, X-ray technician, standby blood donors, and pathologist (and perhaps a minister to pray a little).

An *activity* or a *gang process chart* is useful in plotting the activities of each individual on a time scale similar to that of the man-machine chart. A gang process chart is usually employed to trace the interaction of a number of men with machines of a specified operating cycle with the objective of finding the best combination of men and machines. An activity chart is less restrictive and may be used to follow the interaction of any group of operators, with or without equipment being involved. In addition, they are often used for the study and definition of each operator in an ongoing repetitive process, and they are extremely valuable in developing a standardized procedure for the accomplishment of a specific task. Exhibit 11.12, for example, shows an activity chart for a hospital's emergency routine in performing a tracheotomy (opening a patient's throat surgically to allow him to breathe), where detailed activity analysis is of major importance and any delay could be fatal.

WORK MEASUREMENT

"When you can measure it, you know something about it."—Lord Kelvin.

The efficient operation of any firm is predicated on some knowledge of how long it takes to make a product or perform a service. Without some indication of the time requirements,

1. Costs could not be estimated, and therefore, prices could not be quoted.
2. Budgets could not be made.
3. Evaluation of performance would not be possible since there would be no basis for comparison.
4. Incentive plans and merit increases become unpredictable.

There are four accepted ways to derive the time required in the performance of a human task:

1. Time study (stopwatch and micromotion analysis).
2. Elemental standard time data.
3. Predetermined motion-time data.
4. Work sampling.

Each of these methods has some advantages over the others and has particular areas of application. Exhibit 11.13 lists these methods and relates them to a general class of jobs. Note that the use of historical records to estimate future performance rather than a formal method is generally bad practice. Experience has shown that tasks which are performed without any formal analysis range very widely in "fairness." Some tasks are very

EXHIBIT 11.13
Types of work measurement applied to differing tasks

Type of Work	*Major methods of determining task time*
Very short interval, highly repetitive	Film analysis
Short interval, repetitive	Stopwatch time study; predetermined motion-time data
Task in conjunction with machinery or other fixed-processing-time equipment ...	Elemental data
Infrequent work or work of a long cycle time	Work sampling

easy (allowed times are too long) and some are too difficult (inadequate time is allowed). Therefore good practice requires that production tasks be measured formally, using one of the four methods stated.

Time study

Time study was formalized by Frederick W. Taylor in 1881. Since Taylor's time, volumes have been written on time study, and the technique is undoubtedly the most widely used of the quantitatively based methods of work measurement.

A time study is generally made with a stopwatch, although in some instances film analysis or a timed recording device may be used. Procedurally, the job or task to be studied is separated into measurable parts or elements, and each element is timed individually. After a number of repetitions, the collected times are averaged. (The standard deviation may be computed to give a measure of variance in the performance times.) The averaged times for each element are added, and the result is the performance time for that operator. However, to make this operator's time usable for all workers, a measure of speed or "performance rating" must be included to "normalize" the job. The application of a rating factor gives what is called "normal" time. For example, if an operator performs a task in 2 minutes and the time study analyst estimates him or her to be performing about 20 percent faster than normal, the normal time would be computed as 2 minutes + 0.20(2 minutes), or 2.4 minutes. In equation form,

Normal time = Observed performance time per unit × Performance rating

In the above example, denoting normal time by NT,

$$NT = 2(1.2) = 2.4 \text{ minutes}$$

When an operator is observed for a period of time, the number of units produced during this time, along with the performance rating, gives the normal time as

$$NT = \frac{\text{Time worked}}{\text{Number of units produced}} \times \text{Performance rating}$$

"Standard time" is derived by adding allowances to "normal time" for personal needs (washroom and coffee breaks, and so forth), unavoidable work delays (equipment breakdown, lack of materials, and so forth), and worker fatigue (physical or mental). Two such equations are

$$\text{Standard time} = \text{Normal time} + (\text{Allowances} \times \text{Normal time})$$

or

$$ST = NT(1 + \text{Allowances}) \qquad (1)$$

and

$$ST = \frac{NT}{1 - \text{Allowances}} \qquad (2)$$

Equation (1) is most often used in practice. If one presumes that allowances should be applied to the total work period, then equation (2) is the correct one. To illustrate, suppose that the normal time to perform a task is one minute and that allowances for personal needs, delays, and fatigue total 15 percent; then, by equation (1),

$$ST = 1(1 + 0.15) = 1.15 \text{ minutes}$$

In an eight-hour day, a worker would produce 8 × 60/1.15, or 417 units. This implies 417 minutes working and 480 − 417 (or 63) minutes for allowances.

With equation (2),

$$ST = \frac{1}{1 - 0.15} = 1.18 \text{ minutes}$$

In the same eight-hour day, 8 × 60/1.18 (or 408) units are produced with 408 working minutes and 72 minutes for allowances. Depending on which equation is used, there is a difference of 9 minutes in the daily allowance time.

As mentioned previously, preparatory to making a time study, the task is broken down into elements or parts. Some general rules for this breakdown are:

1. Define each work element short in duration but long enough so each can be timed with a stopwatch and the time can be written down.
2. If the operator works with equipment that runs separately—that is, the operator performs a task and the equipment runs independently—separate the actions of the operator and of the equipment into different elements.
3. Define any delays by the operator or equipment into separate elements.

Exhibit 11.14 shows a time study of ten cycles of a four-element job. For each element, there is a space for the watch reading in 100ths of a minute (R) and each element subtracted time (T). The value for T is obtained after the time study observations are completed, since in this case, the watch is read continuously.[5] T denotes the average time for each element.

---

[5] Not suprisingly, this is called the "continuous method" of timing. When the watch is reset after each element is recorded, it is called the "snapback method."

EXHIBIT 11.14

Time Study Observation Sheet		

Identification of operation	Assemble 24" × 36" chart blanks	Date 10/9

Began timing: 9:26 Ended timing: 9:32	Operator 109	Approval *BgR*	Observer *fDT*

Element description and breakpoint			Cycles											Summary			
			1 0.00	2	3	4	5	6	7	8	9	10	ΣT	$\bar{T}$	RF	NT
1	Fold over end (grasp stapler)	T	.07	.07	.05	.07	.09	.06	.05	.08	.08	.06	.68	.07	.90	.06
		R	.07	.61	.14	.67	.24	.78	.33	.88	.47	.09				
2	Staple five times (drop stapler)	T	.16	.14	.14	.15	.16	.16	.14	.17	.14	.15	1.51	.15	1.05	.16
		R	.23	.75	.28	.82	.40	.94	.47	.05	.61	.24				
3	Bend and insert wire (drop pliers)	T	.22	.25	.22	.25	.23	.23	.21	.26	.25	.24	2.36	.24	1.00	.24
		R	.45	.00	.50	.07	.63	.17	.68	.31	.86	.48				
4	Dispose of finished chart (touch next sheet)	T	.09	.09	.10	.08	.09	.11	.12	.08	.17	.08	1.01	.10	.90	.09
		R	.54	.09	.60	.15	.72	.28	.80	.39	.03	.56				
5		T												0.55 normal– minute for cycle		
		R														
6		T														
		R														
7		T														
		R														
8		T														
		R														
9		T														
		R														
10		T														
		R														

Normal cycle time ___0.55___ + Allowance ___(0.55 × 0.143) or 0.08___ = Std. time ___0.63 min./pc.___

Completed time study observation sheet for study of "assembly chart blanks." From E. V. Krick, *Methods Engineering* (New York: John Wiley & Sons, 1962), p. 246.

EXHIBIT 11.15
Guide to number of cycles to be observed in a time study

When time (hours) per cycle is more than	Minimum number of cycles of study (activity)		
	Over 10,000 per Year	1,000 to 10,000	Under 1,000
8.000	2	1	1
3.000	3	2	1
2.000	4	2	1
1.000	5	3	2
0.800	6	3	2
0.500	8	4	3
0.300	10	5	4
0.200	12	6	5
0.120	15	8	6
0.080	20	10	8
0.050	25	12	10
0.035	30	15	12
0.020	40	20	15
0.012	50	25	20
0.008	60	30	25
0.005	80	40	30
0.003	100	50	40
0.002	120	60	50
under 0.002	140	80	60

Source: Benjamin W. Niebel, *Motion and Time Study*, 6th ed. (Homewood, Ill.: Richard D. Irwin, Inc., 1976), p. 325.

The standard time (calculated according to equation 1) is given at the bottom of the time study sheet.

How many observations is enough? Time study is really a sampling process in that we take relatively few observations as being representative of many subsequent cycles to be performed by the worker. Based upon a great deal of analysis and experience, Niebel's table shown in Exhibit 11.15 indicates that "enough" is a function of cycle length and number of repetitions of the job over a one-year planning period.

Elemental standard-time data

Elemental standard-time data tables contain performance times for operations that are common to many applications. The time data within each table are generally single-time entries that summarize more detailed analysis obtained through time study, as in the following example.

Suppose a company produces nozzles and we are concerned with establishing time standards for drilling the orifice in each nozzle. There are many sizes of nozzles, a variety of materials, varied openings with both single and multiple holes and different-size holes, and a range in the precision of hole sizes. The number of possible combinations is overwhelming. It should be obvious that each possible nozzle configuration need not be studied. There are many similarities among the various nozzles, so that common time-data tables may be compiled.

The basic procedure for drilling all nozzles may be:

1. Place nozzle in jig, tighten, and position.
2. Insert drill into chuck and prepare to drill hole.
3. Drill hole.
4. Raise drill.
5. Reposition jig.
6. Drill second hole.
7. Repeat 4, 5, and 6 until required holes are drilled.
8. Raise drill and remove from chuck.
9. Remove nozzle from jig.

Also, a detailed time study of item 1, "Place nozzle in jig, tighten, and position," may contain the studied elements of

a. Clean jig.   d. Tighten front set screw.
b. Pick up nozzle and place in jig.   e. Position jig under drill.
c. Tighten right set screw.   f. Tighten clamp.

Practice may show that the resulting standard time for placing all nozzles in the jig can be adequately described by three or four size categories. Therefore a standard data table for item 1, "Place nozzle in jig, tighten, and position," may be reduced to a single line with the standard time for each of the three or four sizes.

The time requiried for element 3, "Drill hole," will depend on three factors: material composition (e.g., brass, steel), drill size and type, and hole depth. Each material composition would constitute a separate part of the table, the vertical column would list drill descriptions and sizes, and the horizontal lines would list hole depths. Thus to find the standard time to drill a hole, one would identify the material, find the appropriate drill size and hole depth, and read off the standard time.

The same procedure is followed for the remainder of the required operations. The standard time for each operation is obtained from a table that has been compiled from earlier time studies. Given the existence of these standard data tables, the time for drilling any nozzle (whether or not previously produced) may be derived by describing the nozzle configuration and extracting the time from the tables. Such elemental-data tables may be compiled for any series of operations that have commonality among various tasks. This avoids the need for separate time studies.

Predetermined motion-time data systems

To set a standard time for performing a task by using predetermined motion-time systems (PMTS), one divides the total task into elements, rates the difficulty of each element, looks in the tables for the time allowed for each element, and then adds all the element times together. PMTS systems are based on three assumptions:

1. That the time required by many individuals performing the same work element will fall into the bell-shaped normal distribution.
2. That the times required for performance of the separate elements are additive; that is, the expected time required for completion of the

total task is equal to the sum of the times required to complete the separate elements.

3. That the time study analyst has the ability to describe accurately the procedure to do the work task, to break down the task into appropriate elements, and to apply the degree of difficulty that correctly determines the allowable fatigue rest time.

The three most often used predetermined motion-time data systems are *methods time measurement* (MTM), *basic motion time study* (BMT), and *work factor*.

To illustrate PMTS data, Exhibit 11.16 presents a sample of MTM data. This table describes the element "reach," stipulating the different times allowed for varying conditions. Companies that are in the consulting business and use PMTS to set time standards for their customers state that their systems are more accurate than stopwatch time study. Their reasoning stems from the fact that PMTS data have been accumulated through observing many individuals, and therefore, each element of data (the time it takes to extend the arm a specified distance, for example) is the average of a large number of observations and highly accurate.

However, there are several challenges to PMTS accuracy. First, the work force in a specific location may not be the same as the work force population from which the PMTS data were derived. Second, to set a time standard, the analyst must break down the task into elements and identify them correctly. Different analysts, using the same PMTS system, perceive the

EXHIBIT 11.16
MTM predetermined motion-time data for the hand and arm movement "reach" (1 TMU = .0006 minutes)

REACH—R

Distance Moved Inches	Time TMU				Hand In Motion		CASE AND DESCRIPTION
	A	B	C or D	E	A	B	
¾ or less	2.0	2.0	2.0	2.0	1.6	1.6	**A** Reach to object in fixed location, or to object in other hand or on which other hand rests.
1	2.5	2.5	3.6	2.4	2.3	2.3	
2	4.0	4.0	5.9	3.8	3.5	2.7	
3	5.3	5.3	7.3	5.3	4.5	3.6	**B** Reach to single object in location which may vary slightly from cycle to cycle.
4	6.1	6.4	8.4	6.8	4.9	4.3	
5	6.5	7.8	9.4	7.4	5.3	5.0	
6	7.0	8.6	10.1	8.0	5.7	5.7	
7	7.4	9.3	10.8	8.7	6.1	6.5	**C** Reach to object jumbled with other objects in a group so that search and select occur.
8	7.9	10.1	11.5	9.3	6.5	7.2	
9	8.3	10.8	12.2	9.9	6.9	7.9	
10	8.7	11.5	12.9	10.5	7.3	8.6	
12	9.6	12.9	14.2	11.8	8.1	10.1	**D** Reach to a very small object or where accurate grasp is required.
14	10.5	14.4	15.6	13.0	8.9	11.5	
16	11.4	15.8	17.0	14.2	9.7	12.9	
18	12.3	17.2	18.4	15.5	10.5	14.4	
20	13.1	18.6	19.8	16.7	11.3	15.8	
22	14.0	20.1	21.2	18.0	12.1	17.3	**E** Reach to indefinite location to get hand in position for body balance or next motion or out of way.
24	14.9	21.5	22.5	19.2	12.9	18.8	
26	15.8	22.9	23.9	20.4	13.7	20.2	
28	16.7	24.4	25.3	21.7	14.5	21.7	
30	17.5	25.8	26.7	22.9	15.3	23.2	

job differently and will therefore come up with different element descriptions and, consequently, different times. Third, along with the element breakdown, the analyst must stipulate the degree of difficulty involved in performing that work element. (In the work factor system, this is called a *work factor,* and it indicates the amount of control or weight needed for performance of the task; in the MTM system, this is stated as "cases," which give the particular times allowed, depending on the precision needed to perform the task or the degree of performance difficulty.) Studies have shown that analysts vary in their ratings of job difficulty. In summary, the combined effects of these factors often result in a significant variation in the standard times derived—differences in the description of what is involved in the job and differences in the difficulty perceived by the analysts.

In practice, many companies use both predetermined motion-time analysis and stopwatch time study and compare the results. A practical sequence that is used in industry is to plan operations by using predetermined motion-time data and to follow up with stopwatch time study after the operations have been in existence for a while and operators have become experienced.[6]

Work sampling

As the name suggests, work sampling involves observing a portion or sample of the work activity. Then, based on the findings in this sample, some statements can be made about the activity. For example, if we were to observe a fire department rescue squad at 100 random times during the day and found it to be involved in a rescue mission for 30 of the 100 times (en route, on site, or returning from a call), we would estimate that the rescue squad spends 30 percent of its time directly on rescue mission calls. (The time it takes to make an observation depends on what is being observed. Many times only a glance is needed to determine the activity, and the majority of studies require only several seconds' observation.)

Observing an activity even 100 times may not, however, provide the accuracy desired in the estimate. In order to refine this estimate, three main issues must be decided (these points will be discussed later in this section, along with an example):

1. What level of statistical confidence is desired in the results?
2. How many observations are necessary?
3. Precisely when should the observations be made?

The three primary applications for work sampling are

1. *Ratio delay:* to determine the activity-time percentage for personnel or equipment. For example, interest may be in the amount of time a machine is running or idle.

---

[6] For a complete treatment of the latest in MTM (computer use, and so forth), see the Karger and Bayha bibliographical reference.

2. *Performance measurement:* to develop a performance index for workers. When the amount of work time is related to the quantity of output, a measure of performance is developed. This is useful for periodic performance evaluation.
3. *Time standards:* to obtain the standard time for a task. When work sampling is used for this purpose, however, the observer must be experienced since he must attach a performance rating to his observations.

The number of observations required in a work sampling study can be fairly large, ranging from several hundred to several thousand, depending on the activity and the desired degree of accuracy. Although the number of observations required in a work sample can be computed from formulas, the easiest way is to refer to a table such as Exhibit 11.17, which gives the number of observations needed for a 95 percent confidence level in terms of absolute error. *Absolute error* is the actual range of the observations. For example, if the percentage of time a clerk is idle is 10 percent and the designer of the study is satisfied with a 2.5 percent range (or the true percentage lies within 7.5 to 12.5 percent), the number of observations required for the work sampling study is 576. A 2 percent error (or an interval of 8 to 12 percent) would require 900 observations.

The steps involved in making a work sampling study are:

1. Identify the specific activity or activities that are the main purpose for the study. For example, a study may be made to determine the percentage of time equipment is working, idle, or under repair.
2. Estimate the proportion of time of the activity of interest to the total time (e.g., that the equipment is working 80 percent of the time). These estimates can be made from the analyst's knowledge, past data, reliable guesses from others, or a pilot work-sampling study.
3. State the desired accuracy in the study results.
4. Determine the specific times when each observation is to be made.
5. At two or three intervals during the study period, recompute the required sample size by using the data collected thus far. Adjust the number of observations as deemed appropriate.

From a procedural standpoint, the number of observations to be taken in a work sampling study is usually divided equally over the study period. Thus, if 500 observations are to be made over a ten-day period, the observations are usually scheduled at 500/10, or 50 per day. Each day's observations are then assigned a specific time by using a random number table.

Work sampling applied to nursing.   There has been a long-standing argument that a large amount of nurses' hospital time is spent on nonnursing activities. This, the argument goes, creates an apparent shortage of well-trained nursing personnel, a significant waste of talent, a corresponding loss of efficiency, and increased hospital costs, since nurses' wages are the highest single cost in the operation of a hospital. Further, pressure is growing for hospitals and hospital administrators to contain costs. With

EXHIBIT 11.17

Determining the number of observations required for a given absolute error at various values of p, with a 95% confidence level*

Percentage of total time occupied by activity or delay, p	Absolute error					
	±1.0%	±1.5%	±2.0%	±2.5%	±3.0%	±3.5%
1 or 99	396	176	99	63	44	32
2 or 98	784	348	196	125	87	64
3 or 97	1,164	517	291	186	129	95
4 or 96	1,536	683	384	246	171	125
5 or 95	1,900	844	475	304	211	155
6 or 94	2,256	1003	564	361	251	184
7 or 93	2,604	1157	651	417	289	213
8 or 92	2,944	1308	736	471	327	240
9 or 91	3,276	1456	819	524	364	267
10 or 90	3,600	1600	900	576	400	294
11 or 89	3,916	1740	979	627	435	320
12 or 88	4,224	1877	1056	676	469	344
13 or 87	4,524	2011	1131	724	503	369
14 or 86	4,816	2140	1204	771	535	393
15 or 85	5,100	2267	1275	816	567	416
16 or 84	5,376	2389	1344	860	597	439
17 or 83	5,644	2508	1411	903	627	461
18 or 82	5,904	2624	1476	945	656	482
19 or 81	6,156	2736	1539	985	684	502
20 or 80	6,400	2844	1600	1024	711	522
21 or 79	6,636	2949	1659	1062	737	542
22 or 78	6,864	3050	1716	1098	763	560
23 or 77	7,084	3148	1771	1133	787	578
24 or 76	7,296	3243	1824	1167	811	596
25 or 75	7,500	3333	1875	1200	833	612
26 or 74	7,696	3420	1924	1231	855	628
27 or 73	7,884	3504	1971	1261	876	644
28 or 72	8,064	3584	2016	1290	896	658
29 or 71	8,236	3660	2059	1318	915	672
30 or 70	8,400	3733	2100	1344	933	686
31 or 69	8,556	3803	2139	1369	951	698
32 or 68	8,704	3868	2176	1393	967	710
33 or 67	8,844	3931	2211	1415	983	722
34 or 66	8,976	3989	2244	1436	997	733
35 or 65	9,100	4044	2275	1456	1011	743
36 or 64	9,216	4096	2304	1475	1024	753
37 or 63	9,324	4144	2331	1492	1036	761
38 or 62	9,424	4188	2356	1508	1047	769
39 or 61	9,516	4229	2379	1523	1057	777
40 or 60	9,600	4266	2400	1536	1067	784
41 or 59	9,676	4300	2419	1548	1075	790
42 or 58	9,744	4330	2436	1559	1083	795
43 or 57	9,804	4357	2451	1569	1089	800
44 or 56	9,856	4380	2464	1577	1095	804
45 or 55	9,900	4400	2475	1584	1099	808
46 or 54	9,936	4416	2484	1590	1104	811
47 or 53	9,964	4428	2491	1594	1107	813
48 or 52	9,984	4437	2496	1597	1109	815
49 or 51	9,996	4442	2499	1599	1110	816
50	10,000	4444	2500	1600	1111	816

* Number of observations is obtained from the formula for the distribution of a proportion:

$$Sp = 2 \sqrt{\frac{p(1-p)}{N}} \text{ or, in terms of } N, \ N = \frac{4p(1-p)}{Sp^2}$$

where

Sp = Desired absolute accuracy
p = Percentage occurrence of activity or delay being measured
N = Number of random observations (sample size)
2 = Number of standard deviations to give desired confidence level (95% $\cong$ 2 standard deviations)

the above in mind, let us use work sampling to test the hypothesis that a large portion of nurses' time is spent on nonnursing duties.

Assume at the outset that we have made a list of all the activities that are part of nursing and will make our observations in only two categories: nursing and nonnursing activities. (An expanded study could list *all* nursing activities to determine the portion of time spent in each.)[7] Therefore, when we observe a nurse during the study and find her performing one of the duties on the nursing list, we simply place a tally mark in the nursing column. If we observe her doing anything besides nursing, we place a tally mark in the nonnursing column.

We can now proceed to plan the study. Assume that our estimate (or the estimate of the nursing supervisor) is that nurses spend 60 percent of their time in nursing activities. Assume, further, that we would like to be 95 percent confident that the findings of our study will be within the absolute error range of plus or minus 3 percent; that is, that if our study shows nurses spend 60 percent of their time on nursing duties, we are 95 percent confident that the true percentage lies between 57 and 63 percent. From Exhibit 11.17, we find that 1,067 observations are required for 60 percent activity time and ±3 percent error. If our study is to take place over ten days, we will start with 107 observations per day.

In order to determine when each day's observations are to be made, we use a random number table in a manner similar to the example in the Technical Note on simulation. If the study extends over an eight-hour shift, we can assign numbers to correspond to each consecutive minute.[8] The list in Exhibit 11.18 shows the assignment of numbers to corresponding minutes. For simplicity, since each number corresponds to one minute, a three-number scheme is used wherein the second and third number correspond to the minute of the hour. A number of other schemes would also be appropriate.[9]

EXHIBIT 11.18

Time	Assigned numbers
7:00– 7:59 A.M.	100–159
8:00– 8:59 A.M.	200–259
9:00– 9:59 A.M.	300–359
10:00–10:59 A.M.	400–459
11:00–11:59 A.M.	500–559
12:00–12:59 A.M.	600–659
1:00– 1:59 P.M.	700–759
2:00– 2:59 P.M.	800–859

[7] Actually, there is much debate on what constitutes nursing activity. For instance, is talking to a patient a nursing duty?

[8] For this study, it is likely that the night shift (11 P.M. to 7 A.M.) would be run separately since the nature of nighttime nursing duties is considerably different from daytime duties.

[9] If a number of studies are planned, a computer program may be used to generate a randomized schedule for the observation times.

If we refer to a random number table and list three-digit numbers, we can assign each number to a time. The random numbers shown in Exhibit 11.19 demonstrate the procedure.

EXHIBIT 11.19

Random number	Corresponding time from the preceding list
669	nonexistent
831	2:31 P.M.
555	11:55 A.M.
470	nonexistent
113	7:13 A.M.
080	nonexistent
520	11:20 A.M.
204	8:04 A.M.
732	1:32 P.M.
420	10:20 A.M.

This procedure is followed to generate 107 observation times, and the times are rearranged chronologically for ease in planning. Rearranging the times determined in Exhibit 11.19 gives the total observations per day shown in Exhibit 11.20.

EXHIBIT 11.20

Observation	Scheduled time	Nursing activity ($\checkmark$)	Nonnursing activity ($\checkmark$)
1	7:13 A.M.		
2	8:04 A.M.		
3	10:20 A.M.		
4	11:20 A.M.		
5	11:55 A.M.		
6	1:32 P.M.		
7	2:31 P.M.		

To be perfectly random in this study, we should also "randomize" the nurse we observe each time (the use of various nurses minimizes the effect of bias). In the study, our first observation is made at 7:13 A.M. for nurse X. We walk into her area and, on seeing her, check either a nursing or a nonnursing activity. Each observation need be only long enough to determine the class of activity—in most cases only a glance. At 8:04 A.M. we observe nurse Y. We continue in this way to the end of the day and the 107 observations. At the end of the second day (and 214 observations), we decide to check for the adequacy of our sample size.

Let's say we made 150 observations of nurses working and 64 of them not working, which gives 70.1 percent working. From Exhibit 11.17, this corresponds to 933 observations. Since we have already taken 214 observations, we need take only 719 over the next eight days, or 90 per day.

When the study is half over, another check should be made. For instance, if days 3, 4, and 5 showed 55, 59, and 64 working observations, the cumulative data would give 328 working observations of a total 484, or a 67.8 percent working activity. Exhibit 11.17 shows the sample size to be about 967, leaving 483 to be made—at 97 per day—for the following five days. Another computation should be made before the last day to see if another adjustment is required. If after the tenth day several more observations are indicated, these can be made on day 11.

If at the end of the study we find that 66 percent of nurses' time is involved with what has been defined as nursing activity, there should be an analysis to identify the remaining 34 percent. Approximately 12 to 15 percent is justifiable for coffee breaks and personal needs, which leaves 20 to 22 percent of the time that must be justified and compared to what the industry considers ideal levels of nursing activity. To identify the nonnursing activities, a more detailed breakdown could have been originally built into the sampling plan. Otherwise, a follow-up study may be in order.

Setting time standards using work sampling. As mentioned earlier, work sampling can be used to set time standards. To do this, the analyst must record the subject's performance rate (or index) along with working observations. The additional data required and the formula for calculating standard time are given in Exhibit 11.21.

EXHIBIT 11.21
Deriving a time standard using work sampling

Information	Source of data	Data for one day
Total time expended by operator (working time and idle time)	Time cards	480 min.
Number of parts produced	Inspection Department	420 pieces
Working time in percent	Work sampling	85%
Idle time in percent	Work sampling	15%
Average performance index	Work sampling	110%
Total allowances	Company time-study manual	15%

$$\text{Standard time per piece} = \frac{\binom{\text{Total time in minutes}}{} \times (\text{Working time}) \times (\text{Performance index})}{\text{Total number of pieces produced}} \times \frac{1}{1 - \text{Allowances}}$$

$$= \left(\frac{480 \times 0.85 \times 1.10}{420}\right) \times \left(\frac{1}{1 - 0.15}\right) = 1.26 \text{ minutes}$$

Source: R. M. Barnes, *Work Sampling*, 2d ed. (New York: John Wiley & Sons, 1966), p. 81.

Advantages of work sampling over time study.

1. Several work sampling studies may be conducted simultaneously by one observer.
2. The observer need not be a trained analyst unless the purpose of the study is to determine a time standard.
3. No timing devices are required.
4. Work of a long cycle time may be studied with fewer observer hours.
5. The duration of the study is longer, so that the effects of short-period variations are minimized.

6. The study may be temporarily delayed at any time with little effect.
7. Since work sampling needs only instantaneous observations (made over a longer period), the operator has less chance to influence the findings by changing his or her work method.

When the cycle time is short, time study rather than work sampling is more appropriate. One drawback of work sampling is that it does not provide as complete a breakdown of elements as time study. Another difficulty with work sampling is that observers, rather than follow a random sequence of observations, tend to develop a repetitive route of travel. This may allow the time of the observations to be predictable and thus invalidate the findings. A third factor—a potential drawback—is that the basic assumption in work sampling is that all observations pertain to the same static system. If the system is in the process of change, work sampling may give misleading results.

WAGE INCENTIVE PLANS

For the majority of people in our work force, money remains a strong—if not the strongest—motivator. In this section, we will consider some of the common wage incentive plans that attempt to relate the individual's desire for additional income to the organization's need for productive efficiency.

There is no clear-cut way to categorize wage incentive plans. One possibility is to classify plans into those that are established by management and those which are participative plans, in which workers play a large part. The first includes the traditional plans, which have time or unit production as the basis. The participative plans may use the same measurements, but they differ in that worker committees perform a great deal of the design and analysis. Plans in each category will now be examined more closely.

Plans established by management

Four subcategories of plans under this heading are:

1. Plans based on time worked.
2. Plans based on work output.
3. Plans based on either 1 or 2 that have some provision for gain sharing or bonuses.
4. Plans based on general performance of the worker or the firm over an extended time period; that is, indirect payment plans and "fringe benefits."

Exhibit 11.22 lists each of these subcategories with several of the best-known plans.

Type of plan	Method of payment

EXHIBIT 11.22
Wage payment plans for direct labor

Type of plan	Method of payment
Time based	Straight hourly or day rate, straight salary
Piece rate	Straight piece rate, standard hour
Gain sharing or bonus	Halsey plan, Rowan plan, Gantt task and bonus plan, measured day rate, 100 percent bonus (most used)
Indirect payments (fringe benefits) ...	Yearly bonus, profit sharing, pension plans, stock distribution, paid insurance, holidays, vacations

Minimum wage plans. These are in common use today. Such plans are desirable where, for example, a new employee is learning the job or where conditions beyond the workers' control often prevent production (through a lack of materials, power, and so forth). To illustrate, assume a worker's base hourly rate is $3 per hour and during the week he or she works on a variety of jobs, each with a different piece rate. On each of these jobs, he or she is guaranteed at least the base rate. If the rate is achieved, payment is at the piece rate. Now suppose the worker completes a job consisting of 25 pieces, at a rate of $0.60 per piece, in four hours. The worker's wages would be the larger of base rate ($4 \times \$3 = \$12$) or piece rate ($25 \times \$0.60 = \$15$). Thus in this case, he or she would be paid $15 for the four hours' work.

Gain sharing or bonus plans. Plans in this category guarantee a base rate and divide any amount in excess of this base between management and the worker. Among such plans are the Halsey plan, which guarantees the standard rate and shares higher output on a 50–50 or ⅓–⅔ basis between the worker and management; the Rowan plan, which is similar to the Halsey plan except that it pays at a decreasing rate and has an upper limit of twice the standard rate; and the Gantt task and bonus plan, which pays a person a guaranteed day rate as a minimum, with a 20–50 percent premium for higher performance. Although quite popular around the turn of the century, these plans are no longer widely used.

Measured day work is used today and is gaining in popularity. It is similar to other plans in rewarding increased production, but the major difference is a longer period for measurement—one to three months. If the policy is to measure work over a two-month period, for example, a worker's performance is tabulated and this establishes the pay rate for the next two-month period. The worker's performance during the next two-month period determines his or her pay rate for the third two-month period and so forth. The advantage of this plan, from a worker's standpoint, is that his or her paycheck remains relatively constant, and a few bad days during the period may be made up.

Indirect payments. Most of the entries in this category are familiar fringe benefits: extra holidays, vacations, company-paid insurance premiums, relocation allowances, company contributions to pension plans, and so forth. When nonproductive time is included (rest breaks, coffee breaks, washup, and so forth), fringe benefits throughout industry average about 25 percent of each employee's wages.

There are a variety of other incentive plans, such as stock options, stock warrants, bonuses, interest-free loans, and so forth, but in general, they are not worker oriented; rather, they are intended to attract and hold top management.

Time-based plans. In this class, the straight pay rates (hourly, daily, or weekly) are payments to the worker in direct relationship to time spent on the job. Thus if the hourly rate is $4.50 per hour and a worker puts in a 40-hour week, he or she receives a week's pay of $40 \times \$4.50$, or $180. Variations of this plan, now rarely used, had rates hinged to productivity and incorporating different hourly rates for different levels of output.

Piece-rate plans. Here a worker is paid strictly on the basis of performance. A straight piece rate pays for the number of units completed. If a worker completes 100 units a day and the rate is $0.30 per unit, his or her earnings are $\$0.30 \times 100$, or $30.

Standard-hour plans. Standard-hour plans are the most widely used of all incentive plans. To use this plan, each job must have a standard amount of time assigned to do the job. If the worker does it in less time, he/she earns more pay. For example, rather than specify a sum of money per unit as in the piece-rate plan, a job of 100 units may be assigned ten standard hours for completion. If the worker completes this job in eight hours and his base rate is $6 per hour, earnings would be $60 for that day.

Automobile mechanics work on standard hour plans; however, in the auto repair business it is called *flat-rate hours.* If you need a tune-up, your ticket writer at the service shop might look it up in his book of standard hours and tell you that the charge is 2½ hours of labor. A good tune-up man should be able to do the job easily in 1½ hours and thus earn an hour extra pay. You might also find that your automatic transmission overhaul cost you eight hours labor at $24 per hour but you brought it in at 8 A.M. and picked it up after lunch at 1 P.M. with all work performed by one mechanic.

Workers may do a variety of jobs each day. The standard hours for all these jobs are added up daily. At the end of the pay period, the total hours are multiplied by the workers' base rate to determine the paycheck. One major advantage of the standard-hour plan is that it allows different individual base rates to account for experience, seniority in the firm, or any merit-type recognition.

Participative plans

There has been a long-standing attitude on the part of some companies that employees should participate in matters that affect their pay, such as work methods design, job evaluation, wage rates, and evaluation of output. A number of approaches have been made so as to involve workers. The Scanlon and Kaiser plans are the best known; the Eastman Kodak plan is the most recent.

Scanlon plan. In the late 1930s, the Lapointe Machine and Tool Company was on the verge of bankruptcy, but through the efforts of union president Joseph Scanlon and company management, a plan was devised to save the company by reducing labor cost. In essence, this plan starts with the normal labor cost within the firm. Workers are rewarded as a group for any reductions in labor cost below this "normal" base cost. The plan's success depends on the formation of committees of workers throughout the firm whose purpose is to search out areas for cost saving and to devise or suggest ways for improvement. Highly successful results have led to the adoption of this plan by a wide variety of firms.[10]

Kaiser plan. The Kaiser plan was introduced in 1963[11] and was revised in 1967. The basic approach of the plan is a sharing not only of labor cost savings, as in the Scanlon plan, but also of savings from any reductions of material and supply costs. Material and supply cost savings are divided 32.5 percent to the workers and 67.5 percent to the firm. A large number of committees are formed throughout the plant to search out and investigate cost-saving methods. Rewards are distributed on a companywide basis, even though adopted suggestions come from individual workers. The observed results for workers range from a 10.6 to a 35 percent premium over their base wage. Additionally, there was a reduction in absenteeism and wildcat strikes.

Eastman Kodak plan. Barnes describes the premium payment plan used at Eastman Kodak Company.[12] In this plan, a stable wage is paid to workers, replacing the traditional wage incentive plans. Its objective is to bring workers into the discussion of what the goals should be for the individual and the department, how the goals might be attained, and what constitutes a reasonable measure of performance. Wage rates are set at the premium level. Workers, having helped determine the methods, standards, and measures of performance, are expected to produce at that premium rate with less direction. As a result, supervision and paper work have been reduced, incentive rates have been sustained, and there is more satisfaction for each worker through greater participation and self-direction.

CONCLUSION

Despite the fact that job design work methods and measurement in many schools have been eclipsed in popularity by other topics in operations

---

[10] See A. J. Geare, "Productivity from Scanlon-type Plans," *Academy of Management Review,* vol. 1, no. 3 (July 1976), pp. 99–108.

[11] See "The Kaiser Sharing Plan's First Year," *Conference Board Record,* vol. 1, no. 7 (July 1964).

[12] Barnes, *Motion and Time Study,* pp. 688–701.

EXHIBIT 11.23
Use of work measurement and incentive plans*

Percent using time standards	89	Percent using wage incentive plans ..	44
Time study	90	Piece work	40
Elemental data	61	Standard hour	61
PMTS	32	Sharing plan	19
Work sampling	21	Plant-wide bonus	5
Historical estimates	44	Profit sharing	8
Others	3	Others	9

* Rounded; some companies using more than one method.
Source: Robert S. Rice, "Survey of Work Measurement and Wage Incentives," *Industrial Engineering* (July 1977), pp. 18–31.

management, they still have critical importance to the functioning of any productive system. Certainly, all production planning is based directly or indirectly on "standards," which in turn are predicated on at least a minimally satisfying job design for the worker.

In concluding this chapter, it is interesting to note the pervasiveness of work measurement and, to a lesser extent, incentive plans in many organizations both in and out of manufacturing. In a survey by Robert S. Rice (Exhibit 11.23), it was found that out of 1,500 firms (including government and nonmanufacturing), 89 percent used time standards and 44 percent used wage incentive plans. Clearly, the subjects in this chapter are of great practical importance to many organizations.

REVIEW AND DISCUSSION QUESTIONS

1. A management consultant, Roy Walters, occasionally publishes a list of the "Ten Worst Jobs." On one such list, he included the following (in no special order): highway toll collector, car watcher in a tunnel, pool typist, copy-machine operator, bogus-type setter (i.e., type that is not to be used), computer-tape librarian, housewife (not to be confused with mother), and automatic-elevator operator.
   a. With reference to the sociotechnical systems discussion, what characteristics of good job design are absent from each of these jobs?
   b. Do you have any job you might suggest for inclusion in Walters list? What makes this job undesirable?

2. Frederick W. Taylor has been the brunt of criticism by modern specialists on job design. Can you say anything in his defense relative to his handling of Schmidt?

3. Why might the job enlargement and sociotechnical approaches to job design be looked at with skepticism by practising managers and industrial engineers?

4. "Heavy manual work is really such a small component of modern American industry that further study of it is not really necessary." Comment.

5. Chase and Aquilano commonly complain to their families that book writing is hard work and that they should be excused from helping out with the housework so that they can rest. What exhibit in this chapter should they never let their families see?

6. Is there an inconsistency when a company requires precise time standards and encourages job enlargement?

7. Match the following techniques to their most appropriate application

MTM   Purchase of a second washing machine
SIMO chart   Tracing your steps in getting a parking permit
Man-machine chart   Faculty office hours kept
Process chart   Development of a new keyboard for typewriter
Work sampling   Planning the assembly process for a new electronic device

8. You have timed your friend, Lefty, assembling widgets. Her time averages 12 minutes for the two cycles you have timed. She was working very hard, and you believe that none of the nine other operators doing the same job would beat her time. Are you ready to put this time forth as the standard for making an order of 5,000 widgets? If not, what else should you do?

9. Comment on the following:
   a. "Work measurement is old hat. We have automated our office, and now we run every bill through our computer (after our 25 clerks have typed up the IBM cards)."
   b. "It's best that our workers don't know that they are being time studied. That way, they can't complain about us getting in the way when we set time standards."
   c. "Once we get everybody on an incentive plan, then we will start our work measurement program."
   d. "Rhythm is fine for disco dancing, but it has no place on the shop floor."

PROBLEMS

1. Use the following form to evaluate a job you have held relative to the five principles of job design given in the chapter. Develop a numerical score by summing the numbers in parentheses.

	Poor (0)	Adequate (1)	Good (2)	Outstanding (3)
Task variety				
Skill variety				
Feedback				
Task identity				
Task autonomy				

   a. Compute the score for your job. Does the score match your subjective feelings about the job as a whole? Explain.
   b. Compare your score with the scores generated by your classmates. Is there one kind of job that everybody likes and one kind that everybody dislikes?

2. Examine the process chart in Exhibit 11.8. Can you recommend some improvements to cut down on delays and transportations? (Hint: The research laboratory can suggest changes in the requisition form.)

3. Examine the man-machine chart in Exhibit 11.11. Can you develop an alternative loading sequence that will improve capacity utilization?

4. A worker produced 40 parts in 60 minutes of a time study. The time study analyst rated the person as working at a performance rate of 125 percent. Allowances within the company are 15 percent for fatigue and personal time.
    a. What is the normal time?
    b. What is the standard time?

5. A time study was made of an existing job to develop new time standards. A worker was observed for a period of 45 minutes. During that period, 30 units were produced. The analyst rated the worker as performing at a 90 percent performance rate. Allowances in the firm for rest and personal time are 12 percent.
    a. What is the normal time for the task?
    b. What is the standard time for the task?
    c. If the worker produced 300 units in an eight-hour day, what would his/her day's pay be if the basic rate was $6.00 per hour and the premium payment system paid on a 100 percent basis?

6. The following observation times (in seconds) were noted in a time study: 8, 10, 9, 10, 8, 11, 12, 11, 10, 11.
    The worker was rated by the time study analyst at 125 percent. Allowances for this type of work are 20 percent.
    a. Find the normal time.
    b. Find the standard time.

7. A work sampling study is to be conducted over the next 30 consecutive days of an activity in the city fire department. Washing trucks, which is the subject of the study, is to be observed, and it is estimated that this occurs 10 percent of the time. A 3.5 percent accuracy with 95 percent confidence is acceptable. State specifically when observations should be made on *one* day.

8. Felix Unger is a very organized person and wants to plan his day perfectly. To do this, he has his friend Oscar time him on his daily activities. Below are the results of Oscar timing Felix on polishing two pairs of black shoes using the snapback method of timing. What is the standard time for polishing one pair? (Assume a 5 percent allowance factor for Felix to get Oscar an ashtray for his cigar. Account for noncyclically recurring elements by dividing their observed times by the total number of cycles observed.)

Element	Observed times				ΣT	$\overline{T}$	RF	NT
	1	2	3	4				
Get shoe shine kit ...	0.50						1.25	
Polish shoes	0.94	0.85	0.80	0.81			1.10	
Put away kit				0.75			0.80	

9. A total of 15 observations have been taken on a head baker for a school district. The numerical breakdown of her activities are as follows:

Make ready	Do	Clean Up	Idle
2	6	3	4

Based upon this information, how many work sampling observations will be required to determine how much of his time is spent in "doing"? Assume a 5 percent desired absolute accuracy and 99.7 percent confident level.

10. Suppose you want to set a time standard for the baker making her specialty, square donuts. A work sampling study of her on "donut day" yielded the following results.

Time spent (working and idle) .... 320 minutes
Number of donuts produced 5000
Working time .... 280 minutes
Performance rating 125%
Allowances 10%

What is the standard time per donut?

11. A work sampling study was made of an order clerk in order to estimate the percentage of the total week that she spent on each activity (results listed below). In addition to classifying the order-clerk's activity, the observer rated her performance level whenever a sampling observation found her doing one of the productive activities. Since all order forms carried consecutive preprinted numbers, it was an easy matter to determine how many orders the order clerk wrote. Assume that such a check revealed that the order clerk under study wrote 583 orders during the week of the sampling study. Further assume that on the basis of the sampling study, it is determined that the averages of the performance ratings made of her working pace for the four productive activities are those given below. The company policy is to give a personal allowance of 10 percent of the normal time for all office work. From the results of the sampling study, the assumptions given above, and the fact that the order clerk worked a total of 40 hours during the week covered by the sampling study, determine the standard time (minutes per order) for the order writing operation.

Activity	Actual percentage of week	Average performance rating (normal = 100%)
Order writing	52.5%	80%
Filing	12.5%	90%
Walking	15.0%	75%
Receiving instructions	9.6%	100%
Idle	10.4%	—
	100.0%	

12. It is estimated that a bank teller spends about 10 percent of his time in a particular type of transaction. The bank manager would like a work sampling study performed that will show, within plus-or-minus 3 percent, whether the clerk's time is really 10 percent (i.e., from 7 to 13 percent). The manager is well satisfied with a 95 percent confidence level.

From Exhibit 11.17 you observe that, for the first "cut" at the problem, a sample size of 400 is indicated for the 10 percent activity time and plus-or-minus 3 percent absolute error.

State how you would perform the work sampling study. If the study were to be made over a five-day week from the hours of 9 to 5, specify the exact time (in minutes increments) that you would make Monday's observations.

SELECTED BIBLIOGRAPHY

A.S.H.R.A.E.   *Guide and Data Book, 1960: Fundamentals and Equipment.* New York: American Society of Heating, Refrigeration, and Air Conditioning Engineers, 1961.

Barnes, Ralph M.   *Motion and Time Study: Design and Measurement of Work.* 6th ed. New York: John Wiley & Sons, 1968.

Chapanis, Alphonse   *Man-Machine Engineering.* Belmont, Calif.: Wadsworth Publishing Co., 1965.

Chase, Richard, B.   "A Review of Models for Mapping the Socio-Technical System," *AIIE Transactions,* vol. 7, no. 1 (March 1975), pp. 48–55.

Davis, L. E., and Taylor, J. C.   *Design of Jobs.* 2nd ed. Santa Monica, Calif.: Goodyear Publishing Co., 1979.

Dickson, Paul   *The Future of the Workplace.* New York: Weybright and Talley, 1975.

Dunn, J. D., and Rachel, F. M.   *Wage and Salary Administration.* New York: McGraw-Hill Book Company, 1971.

Geare, A. J.   "Productivity from Scanlon-type Plans," *Academy of Management Review,* vol. 1, no. 3 (July 1976), pp. 99–108.

Herbst, P. G.   *Socio-technical Design, Strategies in Multidisciplinary Research.* London: Tavistock Publications, 1974.

Karger, D. W., and Bayha, F. H.   *Engineered Work Measurement.* 3rd ed. New York: Industrial Press, 1977.

McCormick, E. J.   *Human Engineering.* New York: McGraw-Hill Book Company, 1957.

Mumford, Enid and Weir, Mary   *Computer Systems in Work Design—The Ethics Method.* New York: Halstead Press, 1979.

Mundel, Marvin E.   *Motion and Time Study.* 5th ed. Englewood Cliffs, N.J.: Prentice-Hall, 1978.

Niebel, Benjamin W.   *Motion and Time Study.* 6th ed. Homewood, Ill.: Richard D. Irwin, Inc., 1976.

Rice, Robert S.   "Survey of Work Measurement and Wage Incentives," *Industrial Engineering,* (July 1977), pp. 18–31.

Trist, E. L., et al.   *Organizational Choice.* London: Tavistock Publications, 1963.

Terkel, Studs.   *Working.* New York: Pantheon Books, 1972.

Upjohn Institute for Employment Research.   *Work in America.* Cambridge, Mass.: MIT Press, 1973.

Van Der Zwaan, A. H.   "The Sociotechnical Systems Approach: A Critical Evaluation," *International Journal of Production Research,* vol. 13, no. 2 (1975), pp. 149–63.

Chapter

12

SIMULATION

*Simulation is a way of manipulating a model so that
it yields a motion picture of reality*

R. L. Ackoff and M. W. Sasieni[1]

The term *simulation* has various meanings, depending upon the area where it is being applied.[2] In business situations, however, it generally refers to using a digital computer to perform experiments on a model of a real system. Such experiments may be undertaken before the real system is operational so as to aid in its design, or to see how the system might react to changes in its operating rules, or to evaluate the system's response to changes in its structure. Simulation is particularly appropriate to situations where the size and/or complexity of the problem makes the use of optimizing techniques difficult or impossible. Thus, job shops, which are characterized as complex queuing problems, have been studied extensively via simulation, as have certain types of inventory, layout, and maintenance problems (to name but a few). Simulation can also be used in conjunction with traditional statistical and management science techniques.

In addition, simulation is useful in training managers and workers in how the real system operates, in demonstrating the effects of changes in system variables, in real-time control, and in developing new theories about mathematical or organizational relationships. A list of the areas in which simulation methods are currently used is given in Exhibit 12.1.

---

[1] R. L. Ackoff and M. W. Sasieni, *Fundamentals of Operations Research* (New York: John Wiley & Sons, 1967) p. 97.

[2] Webster's defines "to simulate" as "to assume or have the mere appearance of without reality." The following activities represent other types of simulation: dry-run testing of a chemical plant, wind-tunnel testing of a scale model airplane, and business gaming, wherein participants compete in managing hypothetical firms.

EXHIBIT 12.1
Applications of simulation methods

Air traffic control queuing
Aircraft maintenance scheduling
Airport design
Ambulance location and dispatching
Assembly line scheduling
Bank teller scheduling
Bus (city) scheduling
Circuit design
Clerical processing system design
Communication system design
  Computer time sharing
  Telephone traffic routing
  Message system
  Mobile communications
Computer memory-fabrication test-
    facility design
Consumer behavior prediction
  Brand selection
  Promotion decisions
  Advertising allocation
  Court system resource allocation
Distribution system design
  Warehouse location
  Mail (post office)
  Soft drink bottling
  Bank courier
  Intrahospital material flow

Enterprise models
  Steel production
  Hospital
  Shipping line
  Railroad operations
  School district
Equipment scheduling
  Aircraft
Facility layout
  Pharmaceutical center
Financial forecasting
  Insurance
  Schools
  Computer leasing
Insurance manpower hiring decisions
Grain terminal operation
Harbor design

Industry models
  Textiles
  Petroleum (financial aspects)
Information system design
Intergroup communication (sociological studies)
Inventory reorder rule design
  Aerospace
  Manufacturing
  Military logistics
  Hospitals
Job shop scheduling
  Aircraft parts
  Metals forming
  Work-in-process control
  Shipyard
Library operations design
Maintenance scheduling
  Airlines
  Glass furnaces
  Steel furnaces
  Computer field service
National manpower adjustment system
Natural resource (mine) scheduling
  Iron ore
  Strip mining
Parking facility design
Numerically controlled production facility design
Personnel scheduling
  Inspection department
  Spacecraft trips
Petrochemical process design
  Solvent recovery
Police response system design
Political voting prediction
Rail freight car dispatching
Railroad traffic scheduling
Steel mill scheduling
Taxi dispatching
Traffic light timing
Truck dispatching and loading
University financial and operational forecasting
Urban traffic system design
Water resources development

Source: James R. Emshoff and Roger L. Sisson, *Design and Use of Computer Simulation Models* (New York: Macmillan Co., 1972), p. 264.

It is commonly suggested by simulation teachers that the best way to learn about simulation is to simulate. Therefore we will turn to a simple simulation problem and develop the topic as we go along.

A simulation example: Al's fish market

Al, the owner of a small fish market, wishes to evaluate his daily ordering policy for codfish. His current rule is *order the amount demanded the previous day,* but he thinks another rule should be considered as well. Al purchases codfish at $0.20 a pound and sells it for $0.60 a pound. The fish are ordered at the end of each day and are received the following morning. Any fish not sold during the day are thrown away.

From past experience, Al has determined that his demand for codfish has ranged between 30 and 80 pounds per day. He has also kept a record of the relative frequency with which each amount has been demanded and has tabulated this information as follows.

Average demand per day	Relative frequency
35 pounds	1/10
45	3/10
55	2/10
65	3/10
75	1/10

After some deliberation, Al settles on the following ordering rule, which he would like to compare with his current rule: *Each day order the amount of fish that was demanded in the past* (that is, the expected value based on past daily demands) which in this case is

$$(35 \times 1/10) + (45 \times 3/10) + (55 \times 2/10) + (65 \times 3/10) \times (75 \times 1/10)$$
$$= 55 \text{ pounds}$$

Analysis. We will designate Al's current ordering rule as rule 1 and the alternative rule as rule 2. These rules can be stated mathematically, as follows.

$$\text{Rule 1:} \quad Q_n = D_{n-1}$$
$$\text{Rule 2:} \quad Q_n = 55$$

where

$$Q_n = \text{Amount ordered on day } n$$
$$D_{n-1} = \text{Amount demanded the previous day}$$

These ordering rules can be compared in terms of Al's daily profits, which can be stated as follows.

$$P_n = (S_n \times p) - (Q_n \times c)$$

where

P_n = Profit on day n
S_n = Amount sold on day n
p = Selling price per pound
Q_n = Amount ordered on day n (as defined above)
c = Cost per pound

To prepare the problem for simulation at this point requires that we develop some method of generating demand each day in order to compare the two decision rules. One way this could be done is to treat demand

EXHIBIT 12.2

Demand per day	Relative frequency	Probability	Random number interval
35	1/10	0.10	00–09
45	3/10	0.30	10–39
55	2/10	0.20	40–59
65	3/10	0.30	60–89
75	1/10	0.10	90–99

generation as a game of roulette,[3] wherein the roulette wheel would be partitioned in such a way that the slots into which a roulette ball might fall would be associated with specific levels of demand. For example, if the wheel has 100 slots, we might apportion them so that 10 of them represent a demand for 35 pounds, 30 of them represent a demand for 45 pounds, 20 of them represent a demand for 55 pounds, and so forth. Proceeding this way, and using the relative frequencies listed previously, would permit each turn of the wheel to simulate one day of demand for Al's fish.

While a roulette wheel has a certain appeal, a more efficient way of generating demand is to use a probability distribution and a random number table. This approach entails converting the relative frequency values to probabilities. Then specific numbers are attached to each probability value to reflect the proportion of numbers from 00 to 99 that corresponds to each probability entry.[4] For example, 00 to 09 represent 10 percent of the numbers from 00 to 99, 10 to 39 represent 30 percent of the numbers, 40 to 59 represent 20 percent of the numbers, and so on. The probabilities and their associated random numbers (arranged in intervals) are given in Exhibit 12.2.

With this information and a random number table (Exhibit 12.3), we are ready to carry out a hand simulation to determine the relative desirability of ordering rules 1 and 2. If the initial demand for day zero is arbitrarily set at the average demand level of 55 pounds and a 20-day period is selected as the run length, each rule would be tested as follows.

1. Draw a random number from Exhibit 12.3. (The starting point on the table is immaterial, but a consistent, unvaried pattern should be followed in drawing random numbers. Taking the first two digits in each entry in row 1, then row 2, row 3, and so forth would be satisfactory in this regard.)
2. Find the random number interval associated with the random number.
3. Read the daily demand (D_n) corresponding to the random number interval.

---

[3] The term *Monte Carlo*, taken from the name of the famous European gambling casino, is applied to simulation problems in which a chance process is used to generate occurrences in the system.

[4] A *cumulative* probability distribution is sometimes developed to help assure that each random number is associated with only one level of demand. It is our experience, however, that this step, as well as graphing such a distribution, is not necessary in understanding or performing a simulation.

EXHIBIT 12.3
Uniformly distributed random numbers

06433	80674	24520	18222	10610	05794	37515	48619	02866
39208	47829	72648	37414	75755	01717	29899	78817	03500
89884	59051	67533	08123	17730	95862	08034	19473	03071
61512	32155	51906	61662	64130	16688	37275	51262	11569
99653	47635	12506	88535	36553	23757	34209	55803	96275
95913	11045	13772	76638	48423	25018	99041	77529	81360
55804	44004	13122	44115	01691	50541	00147	77685	58788
35334	82410	91601	40617	72876	33967	73830	15405	96554
59729	88646	76487	11622	96297	24160	09903	14041	22917
57383	89317	63677	70119	94739	25875	38829	68377	43918
30574	06039	07967	32422	76791	39725	53711	93385	13421
81307	13314	83580	79974	45929	85113	72208	09858	52104
02410	96385	79007	54039	21410	86980	91772	93307	34116
18969	87444	52233	62319	08598	09066	95288	04794	01534
87803	80514	66800	62297	80198	19347	73234	86265	49096
68397	10538	15438	62311	72844	60203	46412	05943	79232
28520	54247	58729	10854	99058	18260	38765	90038	94200
44285	09452	15867	70418	57012	72122	36634	97283	95943
80299	22510	33517	23309	57040	29285	07870	21913	72958
84842	05748	90894	61658	15001	94055	36308	41161	37341

4. Calculate the amount sold (S_n). If $D_n \geq Q_n$, then $S_n = Q_n$; if $D_n < Q_n$, $S_n = D_n$.
5. Calculate daily profit $[P_n = (S_n \times p) - (Q_n \times c)]$.
6. Repeat steps 1 to 5 until 20 days have been simulated.

The results of this procedure, along with the random numbers (RN) used, are summarized in Exhibit 12.4. We will compare these results with

EXHIBIT 12.4
Hand simulation of Al's fish market

Day	RN	D_n	Rule 1			Rule 2		
			Q_n	S_n	P_n	Q_n	S_n	P_n
0	..	55	..	..	...	..	..	...
1	06	35	55	35	$ 10	55	35	$ 10
2	39	45	35	35	14	"	45	16
3	89	65	45	45	18	"	55	22
4	61	65	65	65	26	"	55	22
5	99	75	65	65	26	"	55	22
6	95	75	75	75	30	"	55	22
7	55	55	75	55	18	"	55	22
8	35	45	55	45	16	"	45	18
9	57	55	45	45	18	"	55	22
10	59	55	55	55	22	"	55	22
11	30	45	55	45	16	"	45	16
12	81	65	45	45	18	"	55	22
13	02	35	65	35	8	"	35	26
14	18	45	35	35	14	"	45	16
15	87	65	45	45	18	"	55	22
16	68	65	65	65	26	"	55	22
17	28	45	65	45	14	"	45	16
18	44	55	45	45	18	"	55	22
19	80	65	55	55	22	"	55	22
20	84	65	65	65	26	"	55	22
Total.		1,120	1,110	1,000	$378	1,100	1,010	$404
Daily average		56	55.5	50.00	$ 18.90	55	50.5	$ 20.20

those achieved by a computer simulation of the problem later in the chapter. We will now develop simulation methodology in detail.

SIMULATION METHODOLOGY

Exhibit 12.5 is a flow chart of the major phases in carrying out a simulation study. To the right of the chart are listed the key factors or decisions that pertain to each phase. In this section, we will develop each of these phases with particular reference to the key factors.

Problem definition

Problem definition for purposes of simulation differs little from problem definition for any other tool of analysis. Essentially, it entails the specification of objectives and the identification of the relevant controllable and uncontrollable variables of the system to be studied. The variables, of course, affect the performance of the system and determine the extent to which the objectives are achieved. The objective of a fish market owner was given as maximizing the profit on sales of codfish. The relevant controllable variable (i.e., under the control of the decision maker) was taken as the ordering rule; the relevant uncontrollable variables were taken as

EXHIBIT 12.5

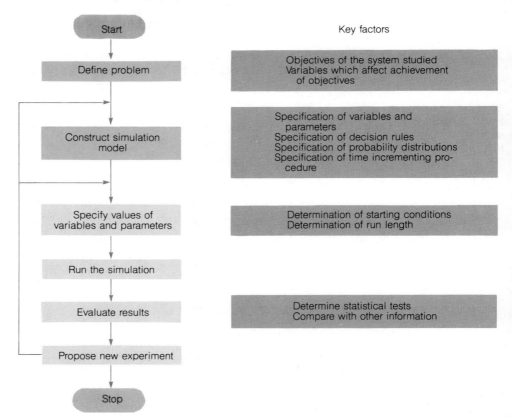

the daily demand levels for codfish and the amount of codfish sold. Other objectives could have been to maximize profit from the sale of all fish or to maximize profit from the sale of herring. Other variables, such as the number of display cases and the use of customer priority rules, could have been identified, and it could be argued that demand could be controlled in part by charging a higher or lower price.

Construct simulation model

A *model* is a representation of a real system. A *simulation model* of a real system is a model in which the system's elements are represented by arithmetic, analogic, or logical processes that can be executed, either manually or by computer, to predict the dynamic properties of the real system.[5] This ability to deal with dynamic systems is one of the features that distinguishes these models from other models used in problem solving. In the fish market problem, an inventory formula, along with appropriate cost data, could have been used to determine the optimum ordering rule, but a simulation run would still be necessary to determine the effects of this rule on a day-to-day basis. Similarly, problems solved through the use of techniques such as queuing theory or linear programming yield only a course of action to follow. It remains for simulation (or the actual operation of the system) to gauge the performance of the solution achieved.

Another feature that distinguishes simulation from these other techniques is the fact that a simulation model must be custom built for each problem situation. (A linear programming model, in contrast, can be used in a variety of situations with only a restatement of the values for the objective function and constraint equations.) The unique nature of simulation models, in turn, means that the procedures discussed below for building and executing a model represent a synthesis of various approaches to simulation and are guidelines rather than rigid rules (such as those developed from rigorous mathematical deduction).

Specification of variables and parameters. The first step in the construction of a simulation model entails determining which properties of the real system are to be allowed to vary and which ones are to remain constant throughout the simulation run. Those allowed to change are termed *variables,* and those held constant are termed *parameters.* In the fish market example, the variables were the amount of fish ordered, the amount demanded, and the amount sold; the parameters were the cost of the fish and the selling price of the fish. In most simulations, the focus is on the status of the variables at different points in time, such as the number of pounds of fish demanded and sold each day.

The determination of which variables from the real system are to be included in the model, as well as how many, depends upon the purpose of the simulation as defined by the problem statement. As a general rule, it is desirable to keep the number of variables as low as possible, at least

---

[5] A simulation can also represent a model of a system as well as the system itself. One might, for example, construct a cost model of an inventory system and, because of intractable analytical problems, estimate the properties of the model by simulation.

during the initial development of the model. This obviously simplifies the writing and debugging of the computer program and facilitates the validation of the model in trial runs. Once the program is tested, additional variables can be added to improve the representation of the system modeled.

Specification of decision rules. Decision or operating rules are sets of conditions under which the behavior of the simulation model is observed. These rules are either directly or indirectly the focus of most simulation studies. In our example, we compared decision rules (in two separate simulations), and thus, they were the focus of the analysis. In other situations, the focus of the study may be to determine what goes on in the system as currently designed, but even here, the way in which the system works is dependent upon the existing decision rules. For example, we may wish to examine the time it takes to process a claim in an insurance office after the introduction of a computerized information system. However, even though the focus of attention is on computer processing time and the manner of routing a claimant's form to and from the computer, the fact that the particular assumptions about the operation must be formalized into decision rules is inescapable.

In many simulations, decision rules are in fact priority rules (for example, which customer to serve first, which job to process first), and in certain situations, they can be quite involved in that they take into account a large number of variables in the system. For example, an inventory ordering rule could be stated in such a way that the amount to order would depend upon the amount in inventory, the amount previously ordered but not received, the amount backordered, and the desired safety stock.

Specification of probability distributions. Two categories of distributions can be used for simulation: empirical frequency distributions and mathematical frequency distributions. In the fish market example, we used an empirical distribution—one derived from observing the relative frequency of various demands for fish. In other words, it is a custom-built demand distribution that is relevant only to our particular problem. It might have happened, however, that the demand for fish closely approximated some known distribution, such as the normal, Poisson, or gamma. If this were the case, data collection and input to the simulation would be greatly simplified.

To illustrate the procedure in using a known distribution, let us suppose that, instead of using the empirical demand distribution for fish (shown in histogram form in Exhibit 12.6A), it was decided that demand could be described by a normal distribution having a mean of 55 and a standard deviation of 10 (Exhibit 12.6B).[6] Under this assumption, the generation

---

[6] In practice, standard "goodness-of-fit" statistical tests, such as chi square, are used to determine how well a particular, known distribution approximates the empirical frequency distribution. It is rather clear in this case, however, that the normal distribution would be a very poor approximation of the empirical distribution and, therefore, should not be used.

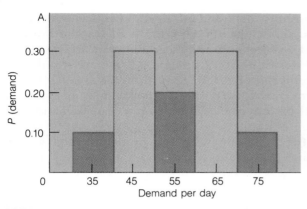

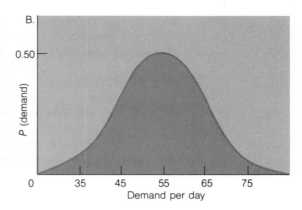

EXHIBIT 12.6

of daily demand would employ a table of randomly distributed *normal* numbers (or deviates) in conjunction with the statistical formula $D_n = \bar{x} + Z_n\sigma$ (terms defined below), derived from the Z transform used to enter a standard normal table.[7] The specific steps are as follows:

1. Draw a five- or six-digit figure from Exhibit 12.7. The entries in this table are randomly developed deviate values that pertain to a normal distribution having a mean of zero and a standard deviation of one. The

EXHIBIT 12.7
Randomly distributed normal numbers

1.23481	.56176	-.23812
1.54221	1.49673	.18124
.19126	1.22318	-1.35882
-.54929	1.00826	-1.45402
1.14463	-2.75470	-.28185
-.63248	1.11241	1.16515
-.29988	-.55806	-.28278
-.32855	-.49094	1.64410
.35331	-.04187	.32468
.72576	-.98726	.34506
.04406	-.26990	.20790
-1.66161	.52304	.70681
.02629	.24826	.16760
1.18250	-1.19941	-.17022
-.87214	1.08497	2.24938
-.23153	.04496	-.95339
-.04776	-.00926	-.96893
-.31052	-.94171	.36915
-.93166	.82752	

[7] The basic formula is $Z = \frac{x - \mu}{\sigma}$, which, when restated in terms of x, appears as $x = \mu + Z\sigma$. We then substituted D_n for x, and $\bar{x}$ for μ in order to relate the method more directly to the sample problem.

term *deviate* refers to the number of standard deviations some value is from the mean and, in this case, represents the number of standard deviations that any day's demand will be from the mean demand. In the above formula for D_n, it would be the value for Z on day n. If we are simulating day 1 and using the first entry in Exhibit 12.7, then $Z_1 = 1.23481$. A negative deviate value means simply that the particular level of demand to be found by using it will be less than the mean not that demand will be a negative value.

2. Substitute the value for Z_1, along with the predetermined values for $\bar{x}$ and σ, into the formula

$$D_n = \bar{x} + Z_n \sigma$$

where

D_n = Demand on day n
$\bar{x}$ = Mean demand (55 in this example)
σ = Estimated standard deviation (10 in this example)
Z_n = Number of standard deviations from the mean

Thus $D_n = 55 + (1.23481)\,(10)$.

3. Solve for D_n:

$$D_n = 55 + 12.3481$$
$$D_n = 67.3481$$

4. Repeat steps 1 to 3, using different normal deviates from the table until the desired number of days have been simulated.

A parallel procedure can be used for other distributions. For example, assume that Al has observed that the demand for lobsters follows a Poisson distribution with a mean (λ) of one every two hours, or .5 per hour. Since the Poisson distribution is generated by solving for different probabilities for a given λ, then the probability of demand for each level of demand must be calculated before random number intervals can be applied. Using the cumulative Poisson distribution in Appendix F, we obtain the following table.

Demand per day for lobsters d_i	Probability of demand $\leq d_i$ from cumulative Poisson table for $\lambda = .5$	Random number intervals
0	0.607	000–606
1	0.910	607–909
2	0.986	910–985
3	0.998	986–997
4	1.000	998–999

If Al wants to simulate the time between lobster sales, he can use an exponential distribution to represent the arrival of customers. The exponential distribution has a mean of $1/\lambda$; therefore, in Al's example with arrivals of .5 per hour, the mean is two lobsters. The time between arrivals *(t)* is defined as

$$t = -\frac{1}{\lambda} \, ln(x)$$

where x is a random number between zero and 1. The natural log is the negative exponential distribution of e^{-x}.

To illustrate using this formula for generating time between arrivals, suppose a random number obtained from a random number table is .75. Then, since $1/\lambda = -2$ and the natural log of .75 $= -.47$ (from the natural log table in Appendix E the distribution of e^{-x}) then

$$t = -2(-.47) = .94 \text{ hours}$$

This says the next lobster purchase will take place .94 hours after the previous one. (Note: if you have a calculator with an *ln* key you can simply enter the random number and hit the *ln* key. This will give you *ln(x)*.)

Specification of time-incrementing procedure. In a simulation model, time can be advanced by one of two methods: (1) fixed-time increments or (2) variable time increments. Under both methods, the concept of a simulated clock is important. In the fixed-time increment method, uniform clock time increments (e.g., minutes, hours, days) are specified and the simulation proceeds by fixed intervals from one time period to the next. At each point in "clock time," the system is scanned to determine if any events are to occur. If they are, the events are simulated, and time is advanced; if they are not, time is still advanced by one unit. This was the method employed in the fish-market example, where one day was the time increment and time would have been advanced even if an event (an order) had not taken place.

In the variable time increment method, çlock time is advanced by the amount required to initiate the next event. This approach would be appropriate in the fish-market example if orders were placed when the inventory of fish reached a certain level rather than being placed at the end of each day.

As for which method is most appropriate, experience suggests that the fixed-time increment is desirable when events of interest occur with regularity or when the number of events is large, with several commonly occurring in the same time period. The variable time increment method is generally desirable in opposite situations, and since it is usually more efficient computationally, it is frequently employed where computer running time is a major concern.[8]

---

[8] It "ignores" time intervals where nothing happens and, therefore, is desirable for simulations covering an extended time period.

Specify
values of
variables and
parameters

Determination of starting conditions. A variable, by definition, will take on different values as the simulation progresses; but some decision must be made at the outset as to the initial values of each one. In our example, since the amount ordered was dependent upon previous orders, we assumed an average value of 55 for demand on day zero. After day zero, the generation of random numbers determined the values for demand in each successive day. An alternative approach would be to start on day 1 and assume no previous demand. For rule 1, however, this would mean that no orders would be placed, since the amount ordered under this rule would be equal to the previous day's demand.

The values for parameters in the example were \$0.60/pound for the price of the fish and \$0.20/pound for the cost of the fish. As mentioned earlier, the value of a parameter does not change during the course of a simulation, but it may be changed as different alternatives are studied in other simulations.

The determination of starting conditions for variables is a major tactical decision in simulation. As McMillan and Gonzales note, "the problem is that the output of the model will be biased by the set of initial values until the model has warmed up or, more precisely, has obtained a steady state where that term is taken to mean an arbitrarily close approximation to the system's equilibrium state."[9]

To cope with this problem, researchers have followed various approaches, such as (1) discarding data generated during the early parts of the run, (2) selecting starting conditions that reduce the duration of the warmup period, or (3) selecting starting conditions that eliminate bias.[10] To employ any of these alternatives, however, implies that the analyst has some idea of the range of output data he is looking for; so in one sense, he is biasing the results by invoking them. On the other hand, one of the unique features of simulation is that it allows judgment to enter into the design and analysis of the simulation; so if the analyst has some information that bears on the problem, it is not necessarily wrong to include it.

Determination of run length. The length of the simulation run depends upon the purpose of the simulation. Perhaps the most common approach is to continue the simulation until it has achieved an equilibrium condition. In the context of the fish-market example, this would mean that simulated demands correspond to their historical relative frequencies. Another approach is to run the simulation for a set period, such as a month, a year, or a decade, and see if the conditions at the end of the period appear reasonable. A third approach is to set run length so that a sufficiently large sample is gathered for purposes of statistical hypothesis testing. This alternative is considered further in the next section.

────────
[9] Claude McMillan and Richard Gonzalez, *Systems Analysis: A Computer Approach to Decision Models* (Homewood, Ill.: Richard D. Irwin, Inc., 1973), p. 496.
[10] Ibid., p. 497.

Determine statistical tests. The types of conclusions that can be drawn from a simulation depend, of course, on the degree to which the model reflects the real system, but they also depend upon the design of the simulation in a statistical sense. Indeed, many researchers view simulation as a form of hypothesis testing with each simulation run providing one or more pieces of sample data that are amenable to formal analysis through inferential statistical methods. For example, we might wish to test the hypothesis that the average amount of fish sold per day is 55 pounds, assuming a normal distribution of demand and a standard deviation of 10 pounds. In order to accept this hypothesis (or, more correctly, fail to reject it) at a particular level of statistical confidence, we would have to run the simulation for a sufficient number of days to satisfy the sample size requirements for the particular statistical test we might employ.[11] Following this approach might well alter both the length of the simulation study and the implications of the results.

In a similar vein, statistical methods could be employed to find the best alternative in a group of several competing alternatives, although in this situation, some rather sophisticated mathematical search routines are required.[12]

Compare with other information. In most situations, the analyst has other information at his disposal with which he can compare his simulation results. Typical sources of such information are past operating data from the real system, operating data from the performance of similar systems, and his own intuitive understanding of the real system's operation. Admittedly, however, the information obtained from these sources is unlikely to be sufficient for validation of the conclusions derived from the simulation, and thus, the only true test of a simulation is how well the real system performs after the results of the study have been implemented: The proof of the pudding is in the eating.

Under this heading fall changes in most of the previously mentioned factors of a simulation model including parameters, variables, decision rules, starting conditions, and run length.

As for parameters, we might be interested in replicating the simulation under, say, several different costs or prices of a product to see if the original simulation result would be applicable if these factors take on new values in the real system.

Trying different decison rules would obviously be in order if the initial rules led to poor results or if these runs yielded new insights into the problem. (The procedure of using the same stream of random numbers, as was done in comparing rules 1 and 2 in the fish-market example, is a

---

[11] Some of the statistical procedures commonly used in evaluating simulation results are analysis of variance, regression analysis, and *t* tests.

[12] See S. W. Schmidt and R. E. Taylor, *Simulation and Analysis of Industrial Systems* (Homewood, Ill.: Richard D. Irwin, Inc., 1970), pp. 517–76.

good general approach in that it sharpens the differences among alternatives and permits shorter runs.) Changing the starting conditions is certainly desirable if the model is sensitive to them or if the first simulation runs were relatively short. In some instances, using the average values obtained from previous runs may be more representative of the real system's starting conditions, and therefore, they would be a desirable input to an experiment in which decision rules or parameter values are being manipulated.

Finally, whether trying different run lengths constitutes a new experiment rather than a replication of a previous experiment depends upon the types of events that occur in the system operation over time. It might happen, for example, that the system has more than one stable level of operation and that reaching the second level is time dependent. Thus, while the first series of runs of, say, 100 periods show stable conditions, doubling the length of the series may provide new and distinctly different, but equally stable, conditions. In this case, then, running the simulation over 200 time periods could be thought of as a new experiment.

Computerization

While the use of a computer is often the only feasible way of performing a simulation study, it brings with it a whole new set of factors about which decisions must be made. Although it is beyond the scope of this book to go into detail about the technical aspects of computer programming, some of these factors bear directly on simulation and therefore should be described. These factors are

1. Computer language selection.
2. Flowcharting.
3. Computer coding and translation.
4. Data generation.
5. Output reports.
6. Validation.

Computer language selection. Computer languages can be divided into general-purpose and special-purpose types. General-purpose languages are FORTRAN, COBOL. PL/1, and BASIC. They have the advantage of being applicable to a wide variety of needs. SIMSCRIPT, GPSS, and GASP are commonly used special-purpose simulation languages that are especially suitable for queuing and scheduling problems since they require less programming time for these types of problems than the general-purpose languages. In addition, they have special output formats and error-checking mechanisms that add to their desirability.

Flowcharting. Flowcharting a simulation program is usually more difficult than flowcharting other kinds of programs since it requires the analyst to visualize how the system responds under dynamic conditions. Indeed, few analysts are brave enough to attempt to code a problem without a flow chart, even if they can develop highly complex static programs without this step.

Coding. Coding refers to translating the flow chart into a computer language. If the programmer is using FORTRAN or some other general-purpose language, the mechanics of writing a computer code are the same as for any mathematical or engineering problem.

Data generation. A considerable amount of theoretical study has been applied to the generation of random numbers in digital computers. The problem is that random number tables use too much space when entered in a computer's memory and that storing them on tape requires too much time. While at first glance random number generation may not appear to be a major endeavor, the fact is that no one method can simultaneously meet the needs for any and all simulations. In particular, such criteria as reproducibility of a previous stream of random numbers, a large quantity of random numbers, true randomness, and computational efficiency cannot be met by any one of the existing methods. For most purposes, though, the built-in random number generators at most computer facilities are adequate. However, if an individual is planning to execute a fairly long simulation program, he or she must have some knowledge of random number generation in order to decide which approach is most desirable for his or her particular purpose.

Output reports. General-purpose languages permit the analyst to specify any type of output report (or data) desired, providing one is willing to pay the price in programming effort. Special-purpose languages, notably GPSS and SIMSCRIPT, have standard routines that can be activated by one or two program statements to print out such data as means, variances, and standard deviations. Regardless of language, however, our experience has been that too much data from a simulation can be as dysfunctional to problem solving as too little, since both situations tend to obscure important, truly meaningful information about the system under study.

Validation. In this context, validation refers to testing the computer program to ensure that the simulation is correct. Specifically, it is a check to see whether the computer code is a valid translation of the flow chart model and whether the simulation model adequately represents the real system. Errors may arise in the program from mistakes in the coding or from mistakes in logic. Mistakes in coding are usually rapidly spotted since the program will most likely not be executed by the computer. Mistakes in logic, however, present more of a challenge. In these cases, the program runs, but it fails to yield correct results.

To deal with this problem, the analyst has three alternatives: (1) have the program print out each calculation and verify these calculations by hand, (2) simulate present conditions and compare the results with the existing system, or (3) pick some point in the simulation run and compare its output to the answer obtained from solving a relevant mathematical model of the situation at that point. While the first two approaches have obvious drawbacks, they are more likely to be employed than the third, since if we had a "relevant" mathematical model in mind, we would probably be able to solve the problem without the aid of simulation.

COMPUTERIZATION OF THE FISH-MARKET EXAMPLE

This problem's flow chart, computer program, and comparative output reports for rules 1 and 2 (based upon 2,000 days) are reproduced in Exhibit 12.8 through Exhibit 12.11.

Comparing the results of this program (written in FORTRAN IV) with the results of the hand simulation, we observe that rule 2 outperformed rule 1 in both cases. For the hand simulation covering 20 days, daily profit for rule 1 ($Q_n = D_{n-1}$) was $18.90 and the average daily profit for rule 2 ($Q_n = 55$) was $20.20. For the computer simulation, average daily profit for rule 1 was $18.05, compared to $19.02 for rule 2. As we can see from the results of the 2,000-day run, the expected profits were overstated in the hand simulation, suggesting that 20 days is too short a time for reliable results.

Looking at the totals for the computer simulation, it is interesting to note that rule 2 yielded $1,944 greater profit than rule 1, yet the amount of fish ordered was 330 pounds *less* under rule 2. This finding would tend to make rule 2 even more attractive if the problem were enriched to include such factors as inventory holding costs and the opportunity cost of funds. Similarly, we note that rule 2 resulted in 3,130 more orders being filled (compared to rule 1), which would enhance the desirability of rule 2 if a stock-out penalty were to be included in the problem.

Research-oriented simulation models

A number of simulation models have been developed as research vehicles and are of historical interest. Under this heading are such classic large-scale models as the Mark I model, developed by the Systems Development Corporation, which shows the effect of various decision rules on an imaginary firm making four products; the Bonini model, developed by Professor Charles P. Bonini of Stanford, which also deals with a hypothetical firm but predicates decision rules on behavioral concepts; and Industrial Dynamics, developed by Professor Jay Forrester of MIT, which employs a special computer language in simulating the information feedback properties of any system. Of these approaches, we will describe only the last one since the other two focus on organization-wide operations rather than operations management.

Industrial dynamics. The term *industrial dynamics* was coined by Forrester to designate "a way of studying the behavior of industrial systems to show how policies, decisions, structure, and delays are interrelated to influence growth and stability."[13]

In its most famous applications, industrial dynamics was applied to production-distribution systems to illustrate the effects of inventory ordering policies and information delays on production rates and inventory levels.

Industrial dynamics simulations showed, for example, that a change

---

[13] Jay W. Forrester, *Industrial Dynamics* (Cambridge, Mass.: MIT Press, 1958), p. 7.

EXHIBIT 12.8
**Simulation flow-
chart for fish
market problem**

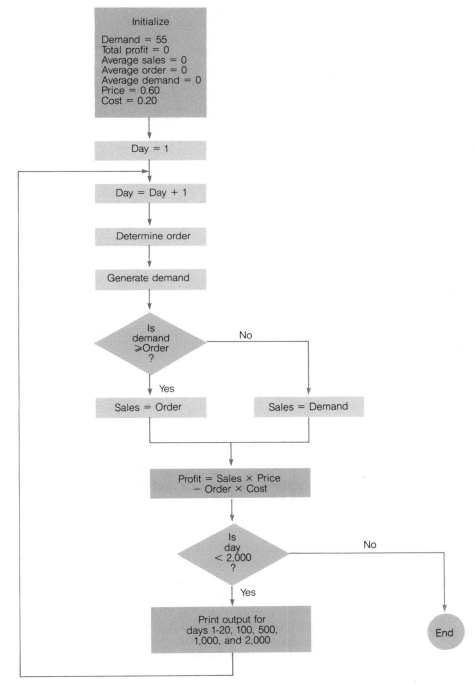

EXHIBIT 12.9
FORTRAN program for simulation of Al's fish market

```
100  PROGRAM FISHMKT (INPUT,OUTPUT)
250  DEMAND=55
260  TPROFIT=0.
265  ADD=0.
270  AOO=0.
275  ASS=0.
300  DO 100 I=1,2000
400  IDAY=I
450  ORDER=55
500  X=RANF(0)*100.
600  IF (X.GE.0.AND.X.LT.10) DEMAND=35
700  IF (X.GE.10.AND.X.LT.40) DEMAND=45
800  IF (X.GE.40.AND.X.LT.60) DEMAND=55
900  IF (X.GE.60.AND.X.LT.90) DEMAND =65
1000 IF (X.GE.90.AND.X.LT.100) DEMAND=75
1050 SALES=DEMAND
1100 IF (DEMAND.GT.ORDER) SALES = ORDER
1200 COST=.20
1300 PRICE =.60
1400 PROFIT=SALES*PRICE-ORDER*COST
1500 TPROFIT=TPROFIT+PROFIT
1550 DAY=IDAY
1560 ADD=ADD+DEMAND
1565 AD=ADD/DAY
1570 AOO=AOO+ORDER
1575 AO=AOO/DAY
1580 ASS=ASS+SALES
1585 AS=ASS/DAY
1600 AVPROF=TPROFIT/DAY
1700 IF(IDAY.GE.1.AND.IDAY.LE.20.OR.IDAY.EQ.100.OR.IDAY.EQ.500)GO TO 99
1800 IF(IDAY.EQ.1000.OR.IDAY.EQ.2000) GO TO 99
1850 GO TO 100
1900 99   PRINT 999,IDAY,DEMAND,AD,ORDER,AO,SALES,AS,PROFIT,AVPROF
2000 999  FORMAT (I5,8F8.2)
2100 100. CONTINUE
2150 PRINT 37,ADD,AOO,ASS,TPROFIT
2175 37 FORMAT(F15.2)
2200 STOP
2300 END
```

in demand at the retail level would become amplified if information about the change went step-by-step through the entire system rather than directly to the factory. The reasons are first, that each decision point in the system (retailer, distributor, warehouse, and factory) tends to react by increasing or decreasing the size of the order placed with the previous stage of the system. If orders go up by 10 percent at the retail level, then the retailer places a reorder of 110 percent of the item in question. This gets passed on to the distributor, who, anticipating an increase in demand, places an order for 110 percent of the order placed by the retailer. If each adds 10 percent all the way to the factory level, this results in a 146 percent increase in production from the 10 percent increase at the retail level. The second reason for the amplification is that there is a time delay involved in conveying and reacting to demand shifts. Thus, if it takes 30 days before the factory personnel begin producing at a higher level, inventories would be depleted at each distribution stage prior to the retailer level. (Imagine then what happens if demand at the retail level drops off by 10 percent after the factory has begun to fill the previous order!)

EXHIBIT 12.10
**Simulation of
fish market—rule
1 output**

```
READY.
450 ORDER=DEMAND
RUN.
PROGRAM TRANSFERRED TO COMPILER
```

Day	Demand	Cumulative Average Demand	Order for Day	Cumulative Average Order	Sales for Day	Cumulative Average Sales	Profit for Day	Cumulative Average Profit
1	35.00	35.00	55.00	55.00	35.00	35.00	10.00	10.00
2	45.00	40.00	35.00	45.00	35.00	35.00	14.00	12.00
3	75.00	51.67	45.00	45.00	45.00	38.33	18.00	14.00
4	45.00	50.00	75.00	52.50	45.00	40.00	12.00	13.50
5	65.00	53.00	45.00	51.00	45.00	41.00	18.00	14.40
6	65.00	55.00	65.00	53.33	65.00	45.00	26.00	16.33
7	65.00	56.43	65.00	55.00	65.00	47.86	26.00	17.71
8	55.00	56.25	65.00	56.25	55.00	48.75	20.00	18.00
9	75.00	58.33	55.00	56.11	55.00	49.44	22.00	18.44
10	55.00	58.00	75.00	58.00	55.00	50.00	18.00	18.40
11	55.00	57.73	55.00	57.73	55.00	50.45	22.00	18.73
12	65.00	58.33	55.00	57.50	55.00	50.83	22.00	19.00
13	45.00	57.31	65.00	58.08	45.00	50.38	14.00	18.62
14	65.00	57.86	45.00	57.14	45.00	50.00	18.00	18.57
15	45.00	57.00	65.00	57.67	45.00	49.67	14.00	18.27
16	45.00	56.25	45.00	56.88	45.00	49.38	18.00	18.25
17	45.00	55.59	45.00	56.18	45.00	49.12	18.00	18.24
18	65.00	56.11	45.00	55.56	45.00	48.89	18.00	18.22
19	65.00	56.58	65.00	56.05	65.00	49.74	26.00	18.63
20	35.00	55.50	65.00	56.50	35.00	49.00	8.00	18.10
100	65.00	55.30	35.00	55.20	35.00	48.20	14.00	17.88
500	75.00	55.24	75.00	55.20	75.00	48.40	30.00	18.00
1000	45.00	55.22	45.00	55.23	45.00	48.52	18.00	18.07
2000	65.00	55.17	35.00	55.16	35.00	48.46	14.00	18.05

```
Total demand    110340.00
Total order     110330.00
Total sales      96930.00
Total profit     36092.00
```

EXHIBIT 12.11
**Simulation of
fish market—rule
2 output**

```
450 ORDER=55
RUN.
PROGRAM TRANSFERRED TO COMPILER
```

Day	Demand	Cumulative Average Demand	Order for day	Cumulative Average Order	Sales for Day	Cumulative Average Sales	Profit for Day	Cumulative Average Profit
1	35.00	35.00	55.00	55.00	35.00	35.00	10.00	10.00
2	45.00	40.00	55.00	55.00	45.00	40.00	16.00	13.00
3	75.00	51.67	55.00	55.00	55.00	45.00	22.00	16.00
4	45.00	50.00	55.00	55.00	45.00	45.00	16.00	16.00
5	65.00	53.00	55.00	55.00	55.00	47.00	22.00	17.20
6	65.00	55.00	55.00	55.00	55.00	48.33	22.00	18.00
7	65.00	56.43	55.00	55.00	55.00	49.29	22.00	18.57
8	55.00	56.25	55.00	55.00	55.00	50.00	22.00	19.00
9	75.00	58.33	55.00	55.00	55.00	50.56	22.00	19.33
10	55.00	58.00	55.00	55.00	55.00	51.00	22.00	19.60
11	55.00	57.73	55.00	55.00	55.00	51.36	22.00	19.82
12	65.00	58.33	55.00	55.00	55.00	51.67	22.00	20.00
13	45.00	57.31	55.00	55.00	45.00	51.15	16.00	19.69
14	65.00	57.86	55.00	55.00	55.00	51.43	22.00	19.86
15	45.00	57.00	55.00	55.00	45.00	51.00	16.00	19.60
16	45.00	56.25	55.00	55.00	45.00	50.63	16.00	19.38
17	45.00	55.59	55.00	55.00	45.00	50.29	16.00	19.18
18	65.00	56.11	55.00	55.00	55.00	50.56	22.00	19.33
19	65.00	56.58	55.00	55.00	55.00	50.79	22.00	19.47
20	35.00	55.50	55.00	55.00	35.00	50.00	10.00	19.00
100	65.00	55.30	55.00	55.00	55.00	50.00	22.00	19.00
500	75.00	55.24	55.00	55.00	55.00	50.02	22.00	19.01
1000	45.00	55.22	55.00	55.00	45.00	50.05	16.00	19.03
2000	65.00	55.17	55.00	55.00	55.00	50.03	22.00	19.02

```
Total demand    110340.00
Total ordered   110000.00
Total sales     100060.00
Total profit     38036.00
```

Industrial Dynamics has been applied to the study of other multistage system problems including food production and population growth. However, its use for other than research has been slight due at first to its unique computer code ("Dynamo") and more recently to the development of simulation models which go beyond simply studying information flow to include forecasting, scheduling, inventory optimization models, and costs.

CONCLUSION

Exhibit 12.12 summarizes the advantages of simulation relative to using the real system for experimentation and relative to using mathematical models for problem solving.

EXHIBIT 12.12

Simulation is desirable when experimentation on the real system	*Simulation is desirable when a mathematical model*
1. would disrupt ongoing activities	1. is not available to handle the problem
2. would be too costly to undertake	2. is too complex or arduous to solve
3. requires many observations over an extended period of time	3. is beyond the capability of available personnel
4. does not permit exact replication of events	4. is not robust enough to provide information on all factors of interest
5. does not permit control over key variables	

The drawbacks of simulation do not lend themselves to tabulation, but they can be summarized as follows. First, simulation models are time consuming to build and require a certain amount of computer experience and expertise on the part of the user. Thus they are not always a practical means for solving many of the problems faced by the production manager. Second, simulation is subject to the same limitations as mathematical models—the impossibility of quantifying certain key variables, the difficulty of casting complex problems in equation form, and so forth. And yet, by virtue of the fact that simulations can be made to run under any type of assumption, such flaws can easily be overlooked. Finally, despite its widespread application, there are very few principles of simulation to guide the user in making decisions on what to include in the model, the length and number of simulation runs, or the general effects that changes in inputs will have on simulation outputs. Thus, at present, simulation must be classified as an art rather than a science.

REVIEW AND DISCUSSION QUESTIONS

1. Why is it that simulation is often referred to as "a technique of last resort?"

2. Give an example of a third rule that Al (of Al's Fish Market) could use in his inventory ordering.

3. What role does statistical hypothesis testing play in simulation?

4. What determines whether a simulation model is valid?

5. Do you have to use a computer to get good information from a simulation? Explain.

6. What methods are used to increment time in a simulation model? Explain how they work.

7. What are the pros and cons of starting a simulation with the system empty? With the system in equilibrium?

8. Distinguish between "known mathematical distributions" and "empirical distributions." What information is needed to simulate using a known mathematical distribution?

9. What is the importance of run length in simulation? Is a run of 100 observations twice as valid as a run of 50? Explain.

10. This chapter is really just a review for you, since you have been simulating for a long time. Consider, for example, the parlor game of Monopoly. What are the variables and parameters of the game? How are random numbers generated? What are some sample decision rules? When is the warm-up period over? If you were to simulate the game on a computer, what are the relevant factors in determining how valid your results would be in subsequent play? Would the results change if each partner (real or simulated) started play with twice as much in his bank account as the rules specify?

PROBLEMS

1. Classroom simulation: Fish Forwarders.

The purpose of this classroom simulation exercise is twofold: (1) to provide further exposure to the concepts of simulation mentioned in the supplement and (2) to focus attention on the problems of decision rule formulation in a dynamic business environment.

Situation. Fish Forwarders supplies fresh shrimp to a variety of customers in the New Orleans area. It places orders for cases of shrimp from fleet representatives at the beginning of each week to meet a demand from its customers at the middle of the week. The shrimp are subsequently delivered to Fish Forwarders and then, at the end of the week, to its customers.

Both the supply of shrimp and the demand for shrimp are uncertain. The supply may vary as much as ±10 percent from the amount ordered, and by contract, Fish Forwarders must purchase this supply. The probability associated with this variation is: −10 percent, 30 percent of the time; 0 percent, 50 percent of the time; and +10 percent, 20 percent of the time. The weekly demand for shrimp is normally distributed with a mean of 800 cases and a standard deviation of 100 cases.

A case of shrimp costs Fish Forwarders $30, and it sells it for $50. Any shrimp not sold at the end of the week are sold to a cat-food company at $4 per case. Fish Forwarders may, if it chooses, order the shrimp "flash-

(1)	(2)	(3)		(4)		(5)	(6)	(7)	(8)		(9)
Week	Flash frozen inventory	Orders placed		Orders received		Available (regular and flash frozen)	Demand (800 + 100Z)	Sales (minimum of demand or available)	Excess		Shortages
		Regular	Flash frozen	Regular	Flash frozen				Regular	Flash	
1											
2											
3											
4											
5											
6											
7		MARDI GRAS					*				
8											
9											
10											
Total											

*Flash frozen only

EXHIBIT 12.13
Simulation worksheet

frozen" by the supplier at dockside, but this raises the cost of a case by $4 and, hence, costs Fish Forwarders $34 per case. Flash-freezing enables Fish Forwarders to maintain an inventory of shrimp, but it costs $2 per case per week to store the shrimp at a local icehouse. The customers are indifferent to whether they get regular or flash-frozen shrimp. Fish Forwarders figures that its shortage cost is equal to its markup; that is, each case demanded but not available costs the company $50 − $30 or $20.

Procedure for play. The game requires that each week a decision be made as to how many cases to order of regular shrimp and flash-frozen shrimp. The number ordered may be any amount.

The steps in playing the game are as follows.

a. Decide on the order amount of regular shrimp and/or flash-frozen shrimp and enter the figures in column 3 of the worksheet (see Exhibit 12.13). Assume that there is no opening inventory of flash-frozen shrimp.

b. Determine the amount that arrives and enter it at *Orders received*. This will be accomplished by the referee's drawing a random number from a uniform random number table (such as that in Exhibit 12.3) and finding its associated level of variation from following random number intervals: 00 to 29 = −10 percent, 30 to 79 = zero percent, and 80 to 99 = +10 percent. If the random number is, say, 13, the amount of variation will be −10 percent. Thus, if you decide to order 1,000 regular cases of shrimp and 100 flash-frozen cases, the amount you would actually receive would be 1,000 − 0.10(1,000), or 900 regular cases, and 100 − 0.10(100), or 90 flash-frozen cases. (Note that the amount of variation is the same for both regular and flash-frozen shrimp.) These amounts are then entered in column 4.

c. Add the amount of flash-frozen shrimp in inventory (if any) to the quantity of regular and flash-frozen shrimp just received and enter this amount in column 5. This would be 990, using the figures provided above.

d. Determine the demand for shrimp. This will be accomplished by the referee's drawing a random normal deviate value from Exhibit 12.3, which he or she enters into the equation at the top of column 6. Thus, if the deviate value is −1.76, demand for the week will be 800 + 100(−1.76) or 624.

e. Determine the amount sold. This will be the lesser of the amount demanded (column 6) and the amount available (column 5). Thus, if a player has received 990 and demand is 624, the quantity entered will be 624 (with 990 − 624, or 366 left over).

f. Determine the excess. The amount of excess is simply that quantity remaining after demand for a given week is filled. Always assume that regular shrimp are sold before the flash-frozen. Thus, if we use the 366 figure obtained above, the excess would include all the original 90 cases of flash-frozen shrimp.

g. Determine shortages. This is simply the amount of unsatisfied demand each period, and it occurs only when demand is greater than sales. (Since all customers use the shrimp within the week in which they are delivered, backorders are not relevant.) The amount of shortages (in cases of shrimp) is entered in column 9.

EXHIBIT 12.14
Profit from Fish Forwarders' operations

Revenue from sales ($50 × Col. 7)	$_____	
Revenue from salvage ($4 × Col. 8 reg.)	$_____	
Total revenue		$_____
Cost of regular purchases ($30 × Col. 4 reg.)	$_____	
Cost of flash-frozen purchases ($34 × Col. 4 flash)	$_____	
Cost of holding flash-frozen shrimp ($2 × Col. 8 flash)	$_____	
Cost of shortages ($20 × Col. 9)	$_____	
Total cost	$_____	
Profit	$_____	

Profit determination. Exhibit 12.14 is provided for determining the profit achieved at the end of play. The values to be entered in the table are obtained by summing the relevant columns of Exhibit 12.13 and making the calculations.

Assignment. Simulate operations for a total of 10 weeks. It is suggested that a 10-minute break be taken at the end of week 5 and the players attempt to evaluate how they may improve their performance. They might also wish to plan an ordering strategy for the week of Mardi Gras, when no shrimp will be supplied.

2. To use an old statistical-type example for simulation, if an urn contains 100 balls of which 10 percent are green balls, 40 percent are red balls, and 50 percent are spotted balls, develop a simulation model of the process of drawing balls at random from the urn. Each time a ball is drawn and its color noted, it is replaced. For your random numbers, use those shown below as you desire.

Simulate drawing 10 balls from the urn. Show which numbers you have used.

26768	83125
42613	55503
95457	47019
95276	84828
66954	08021
17457	36458
03704	05752
56970	05752

3. Marion the librarian provides you with the following traffic pattern of students using the business school library. Students spend an average of ten minutes in each section (except entrance and exit).

Going from	To	Probability
Entrance	Stacks	0.60
	Reference	0.15
	Periodicals	0.20
	Exit	0.05
Stacks	Exit	0.10
	Reference	0.25
	Periodicals	0.25
	Checkout	0.40
Reference	Exit	0.10
	Stacks	0.30
	Periodicals	0.50
	Checkout	0.10
Periodicals	Exit	0.20
	Stacks	0.10
	Reference	0.10
	Checkout	0.60
Checkout	Exit	0.80
	Stacks	0.10
	Reference	0.05
	Periodicals	0.05

a. Simulate the movement of ten students through the library. What is the average time spent by these students in the library?

b. Based upon your simulation, in which section should Marion place a copying machine to maximize student use?

4. A rural clinic receives a delivery of fresh plasma once each week from a central blood bank. Supply varies according to demand from other clinics and hospitals in the region but ranges between 10 to 15 pints of the most widely used blood type, type O. The number of patients per week requiring this blood varies from zero to four, and each patient may need from one to four pints. Given the following delivery quantities, patient distribution, and demand per patient, what will be the number of pints in excess or short for a six-week period? Use Monte Carlo simulation to derive your answer. Consider that plasma is storable.

Delivery quantities		Patient distribution		Demand per patient	
Pints per week	Frequency	Patients per week requiring blood	Frequency	Pints	Frequency
4	0.15	0	0.25	1	0.40
5	0.20	1	0.25	2	0.30
6	0.25	2	0.30	3	0.20
7	0.15	3	0.15	4	0.10
8	0.15	4	0.05		
9	0.10				

5. Larry and Terri are workers on a two-station assembly line. The distribution of activity time at their stations is as follows.

Time (seconds)	Time frequency for Larry (operation 1)	Time frequency for Terri (operation 2)
10	5	4
20	10	5
30	10	6
40	15	7
50	10	10
60	25	8
70	20	6
80	5	4

a. Assign random numbers to the two frequency distributions in such a way that you may simulate operation of the line.

b. Simulate operation of the line for eight items. Use the random numbers given below.

Operation 1		Operation 2	
25	14	36	97
16	01	76	41
82	96	55	13
03	44	25	34

6. Professor Curmudgeon holds office hours from 6 to 8 A.M. once a week for his class of 350 students. The time between students arriving at his office averages three minutes (exponentially distributed), and the time spent with each student follows the pattern shown below:

A students ..... 30 minutes
B students ...... 20 minutes
C students ..... 2 minutes
D students ..... 15 minutes
F students ...... 30 minutes

Assuming that students with any grade average are equally likely to come to his office hours, simulate the arrival and office times for eight students for one 6-to-8-A.M. period. (Hint: Closely follow the method for determining arrival time as covered on pages 378 and 379 of this chapter.)

7. Demand for brake repairs for cars owned by a local driving school ranges from zero to five per week with an average of one per day (Poisson distributed). Use this information to set up a table suitable for simulating daily demand for brake repair.

8. You have been hired as a consultant by a supermarket chain to provide an answer to the basic question: "How many items per customer should be permitted in the fast-checkout line of a supermarket?" This is a nontrivial question for the chain's management because your findings will be the basis for corporate policy for all of its 2,000 stores. (The vice president of operations has given you one month to do the study and two assistants to help you gather the data.)

   In starting this study, you have decided to avoid queuing theory as the tool for analysis (because of your concern about the reliability of its assumptions) and instead have opted for simulation. Given the following data, explain in detail how you would go about your analysis stating (1) the criteria you would use in making your recommendation; (2) what additional data you would need to set up your simulation; (3) how you would gather the preliminary data; (4) how you would set up the problem for simulation; and (5) what factors would affect the applicability of your findings to all of the stores.

   Store locations: The United States and Canada
   Hours of operation: 16 per day
   Average store size: 9 checkout stands including fast checkout
   Available checkers: 7 to 10 (some engage in stocking activities when
                                     not at checkout stand).

SELECTED BIBLIOGRAPHY

Carlson, J. G., and Misshauk, M. J.   *Introduction to Gaming: Management Decision Simulations.* New York: John Wiley & Sons, 1972.

Forrester, Jay W.   *Industrial Dynamics.* New York: John Wiley & Sons, 1961.

House, William C.   *Business Simulation for Decision Making.* New York: PBI Books, 1977.

Harris, Roy D., and Maggard, Michael J.   *Computer Models in Operations Management: A Computer-Augmented System.* New York: Harper & Row, 1972.

McMillan, C., and Gonzalez, R. F.   *Systems Analysis: A Computer Approach to Decision Models.* 3d ed. Homewood, Ill.: Richard D. Irwin, Inc., 1973.

Meier, R. C.; Newell, W. T.; and Pazer, H. L.   *Simulation in Business and Economics.* Englewood Cliffs, N.J.: Prentice-Hall, 1969.

Naylor, T. H., et al.   *Computer Simulation Techniques.* New York: John Wiley & Sons, 1968.

Schrieber, Albert N. ed.   *Corporate Simulation Models.* Seattle: Graduate School of Business Administration, University of Washington, 1970.

Woolsey, G.   "Whatever Happened to Simple Simulation? A Question and Answer," *Interfaces,* vol. 9, no. 4 (August 1979), pp. 9–11.

Chapter 13

DESIGN OF THE PRODUCTION PLANNING SYSTEM

A production planning system contains three major elements: the aggregate production plan, a master production schedule, and a variety of detailed schedules. In this chapter, we will focus on the aggregate plan—what it is and how one derives it. In the next chapter we will consider how this plan is refined (master scheduling) and executed (detailed scheduling).

AGGREGATE PRODUCTION PLANNING

Aggregate production planning is concerned with setting production rates by product group or other broad categories for the intermediate term; that is, for a period of 6 to 18 months (with a year being a suitable figure for most companies). As Wight points out

> The production plan precedes the master schedule. Its prime purpose is to establish a production "rate" that will raise or lower inventories or backlogs as desired and usually keep production relatively stable. It is particularly useful for planning around plant shutdown periods or where sales are seasonal. The master schedule will break this production plan into more specific details so that it can generate specific materials and capacity planning information.[1]

A formal statement of the aggregate planning problem is: given the demand forecast F_t for each period t in the planning horizon which extends

---

[1] Oliver W. Wight, *Production and Inventory Management in the Computer Age* (Boston: Cahners Books, 1974), p. 61.

over T periods, determine the production level P_t, inventory level I_t, and work force level W_t for periods $t = 1, 2, \ldots, T$ which minimize the relevant costs over the planning horizon.[2]

The form of the aggregate plan varies from company to company. In some firms, it is a formalized report containing planning objectives and the planning premises upon which it is based. In other companies, particularly smaller ones, "it may take shape in verbal directives or writings on the back of matchbook covers."[3]

The process by which the plan itself is derived also varies. One common approach is to derive it from the corporate annual plan. A typical corporate plan contains a section on manufacturing which specifies how many units in each major product line need to be produced over the next 12 months to meet the sales forecast. The planner takes this information and attempts to determine how to best meet these requirements in terms of available resources. Alternatively, some organizations combine output requirements into equivalent units and use this as the basis for aggregate planning. That is, a division of say General Motors may be asked to produce so many cars of all types at a particular facility. The production planner would then take the average labor hours required for all models as a basis for the overall aggregate plan. Refinements to this plan, specifically model types to be produced, would be reflected in shorter term production plans.

Another approach is to develop the aggregate plan by simulating various master production schedules and calculating corresponding capacity requirements to see if adequate labor and equipment exist at each work center. If capacity is inadequate, additional requirements for overtime, subcontracting, extra workers, and so forth are specified for each product line and combined into a rough-cut plan. This plan is then modified by cut-and-try or mathematical methods to derive a final and hopefully lower cost plan.

The procedure for doing this has been described by Fisk and Seagle[4] and is shown in the flow chart in Exhibit 13.1. In the exhibit, resource requirement profiles refer to the capacity required in each work center by time period without regard to inventory or existing orders. The production planning profiles provide the required work center production level for each period and use inventory or back orders to meet resource requirements. Planned order releases are the product orders which will be issued in the near future. Aggregate planning models refers to the mathematical techniques we will discuss later in the chapter.

---

[2] J. M. Mellichamp and R. M. Love, "Production Switching Heuristics for the Aggregate Planning Problem," *Management Science*, vol. 24, no. 12 (1978), p. 1242.

[3] M. Nelson, "I Read the Book: The Master Scheduler Did It" (21st Annual American Production and Inventory Control Society Conference Proceedings, 1978), p. 666.

[4] J. C. Fisk and J. P. Seagle, "Integration of Aggregate Planning with Resource Requirements Planning," *Production and Inventory Management* (Third Quarter 1978), pp. 81–91.

EXHIBIT 13.1
The production planning-aggregate planning process

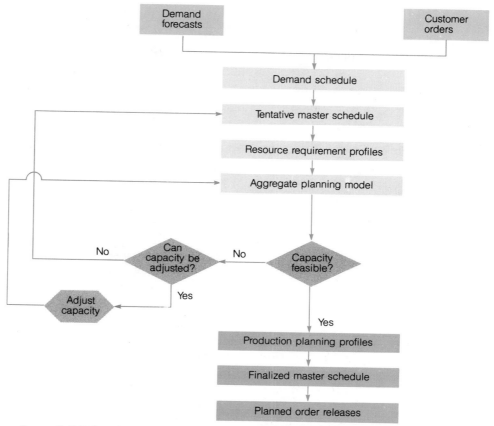

Source: J. C. Fisk and J. P. Seagle, "Integration of Aggregate Planning with Resource Requirements Planning," *Production and Inventory Management* (Third Quarter 1978), p. 87.

Production planning environment

Exhibit 13.2 illustrates the internal and external factors which constitute the production planning environment. In general, the external environment is outside the production planner's direct control. In some firms, demand for the product can be affected (through discounts or advertising), but for the most part, the production planner must live with the sales projections and orders promised by the marketing function. This leaves the internal factors as the variables which can be manipulated in deriving a production plan.

The internal factors themselves differ in terms of their controllability. Current physical capacity (plant and equipment) is usually pretty nearly fixed in the short run; union agreements often constrain what can be done in terms of changing the work force; physical capacity cannot always be increased; and top management may set limits on the amount of money that can be tied up in inventories. Still, there is always some flexibility

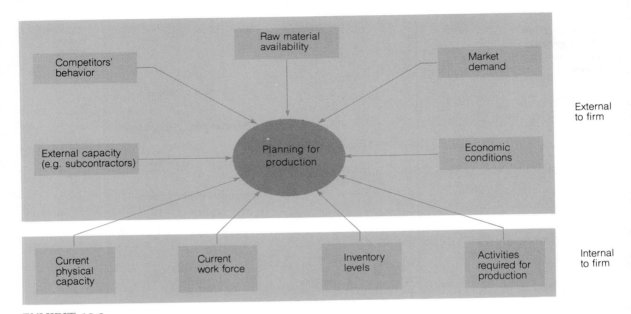

EXHIBIT 13.2
**Required inputs
to the production
planning system**

in managing these factors, and production planners can implement one or a combination of the planning strategies discussed below.

Production planning strategies.   Lee summarizes the following strategies to meet aggregate product demand.

1. Vary the work force size by hiring and laying off employees as demand fluctuates.
2. Maintain a stable work force, but vary the output rate by varying the number of hours worked [through variable work weeks or overtime].
3. Maintain a stable work force and constant output rate, but absorb demand fluctuations by allowing inventory to vary.
4. Allow backlogs (delivery lead times) to increase during periods of increased demand and decrease during periods of decreased demand.[5]

When these are used independently with the effect of utilizing only one variable to absorb demand fluctuations, they are termed "pure strategies;" when they are used in combination, they are termed "mixed strategies." As one might suspect, mixed strategies are more widely applied in industry.

Relevant costs   The costs relevant to aggregate production planning can be categorized as follows:

---

[5] William B. Lee, "Aggregate Production and Inventory Management: Theory, Technique, and Application" (19th Annual American Production and Inventory Control Society Conference Proceedings, 1976), pp. 120–26.

1. Basic production costs. These are the fixed and variable costs incurred in producing a given product type in a given time period. Included are direct and indirect labor costs and regular as well as overtime compensation.
2. Costs associated with changes in the production rate. Typical costs in this category are those involved in hiring, training, and laying off personnel.
3. Inventory holding costs. A major component of the inventory holding cost is the cost of capital tied up in inventory. Other components are storing, insurance, taxes, spoilage, and obsolescence.
4. Backlogging costs. Usually these costs are very hard to measure and include costs of expediting, loss of customer good will, and loss of sales revenues resulting from backlogging.[6]

AGGREGATE PLANNING TECHNIQUES

Most companies use simple "cut-and-try" charting and graphical methods in developing their aggregate plans. Over the last 25 years, researchers have proposed more sophisticated approaches including linear programming, linear decision rules, and various heuristic methods. We will now discuss each of these starting with two examples of a cut-and-try approach.

A cut-and-try example: The C & A Company

Suppose we wish to set up a production plan for the C & A Company for the next six months. In doing this, we want to investigate three different plans with the objective of finding the one with the lowest total cost.

Plan 1: Produce to exact monthly production requirements by varying work force size on regular hours.
Plan 2: Produce to meet expected average demand over the next six months by maintaining a constant work force.
Plan 3: Produce to meet the minimum expected (April) demand using a constant work force on regular time. Subcontract to meet additional output requirements.

Our first step is to set up Exhibit 13.3 which stipulates the production and inventory requirements over the planning horizon. This exhibit is derived using the following information and assumptions:

a. Beginning inventory is 400 units.
b. There is an inventory policy requiring one fourth of a month's forecast in safety stock.
c. Actual demand each month is presumed to be equal to forecasted demand.

---

[6] Arnoldo Hax, "Aggregate Production Planning" in *Handbook of Operations Research,* J. Moder and S. Elmaghraby, eds. (New York: Van Nostrand Reinhold Co., 1978), p. 133.

d. Production requirements (Line 5) are calculated as follows:
    Requirements = Demand + safety stock − beginning inventory
    January requirements = 1,800 + 450 − 400 = 1,850
    February requirements = 1,500 + 375 − 450 = 1,425, and so forth.
e. Company policy prohibits overtime work.

EXHIBIT 13.3
**Aggregate pro-
duction planning
requirements**

	January	February	March	April	May	June
Line 1: Beginning inventory	400	450	375	275	225	275
Line 2: Forecasted demand	1,800	1,500	1,100	900	1,100	1,700
Line 3: Cumulative demand	1,800	3,300	4,400	5,300	6,400	8,100
Line 4: Safety stock	450	375	275	225	275	425
Line 5: Production requirements (Line 2 + Line 4 − Line 1)	1,850	1,425	1,000	850	1,150	1,850
Line 6: Cumulative production required	1,850	3,275	4,275	5,125	6,275	8,125
Line 7: Working days	22	19	21	21	22	20
Line 8: Cumulative working days	22	41	62	83	105	125

Our next step is to set up Exhibit 13.4 which stipulates the relevant costs.

EXHIBIT 13.4
**Costs for C and A
Company**

Manufacturing cost	$100/unit
Inventory holding cost	$1.50/unit/month
Marginal cost of stockout	$5/unit/month
Marginal cost of subcontracting	$2/unit ($102 subcontracting cost less $100 manufacturing cost)
Hiring and training cost	$200/worker
Layoff cost	$250/worker
Labor hours required	5/unit

The third step is to calculate the cost of each plan. This requires a series of simple calculations which are shown in Exhibit 13.5. Note that the headings in each column are different for each plan since each is a different problem requiring its own data and calculations. The strategy for Plan 1 is to produce to exact production requirements by varying the work force size on regular hours. The strategy for Plan 2 is to maintain a constant work force level based on a six-month average demand [(8,125 units × 5 hours each) ÷ (125 days × 8 hours per day) = 41 workers]. Inventory is allowed to accumulate with shortages filled from the next month's production. Plan 3 is based on the strategy of holding the work force constant for a total six-month period at the level to meet the low April demand [(850 units × 6 months × 5 hours per unit) ÷ (125 days × 8 hours per day) = 25 workers] and subcontracting any monthly difference between requirements and production.

The final step is to tabulate and graph each plan and make a comparison of their costs and practicality. From Exhibit 13.6, we can see that making use of subcontracting resulted in the lowest cost (Plan 3). Exhibits 13.7 and 13.8 depict the effects of the three plans. These graphs illustrate the expected results both on a daily rate and on the total production requirement.

Note that we have made one other assumption in this example. That is that the plan can start with any number of workers with no hiring or firing cost. This usually is the case since an aggregate plan draws on existing personnel and we can start the plan that way. However, in an actual application, the availability of existing personnel transferrable from other areas of the firm will change the assumptions in this example.

There are obviously many other feasible plans, some of which would require overtime or a combination of work force change with overtime and some subcontracting. The optimum plan results from a thorough search of a variety of alternatives and takes into account the likely conditions that will exist in the period beyond the 6 month planning horizon.

Aggregate planning applied to services: Tucson Parks and Recreation Department

Charting and graphical techniques are also very useful for aggregate planning in service applications. The following example shows how a city's parks and recreation department could use the alternatives of full-time employees, part-time employees, and subcontracting to meet its commitment to provide a service to the city.

Tucson Parks and Recreations Department has an operation and maintenance budget for fiscal 1980–81 of $9,760,000. The Parks and Recreation Department is responsible for developing and maintaining open space, all public recreational programs, adult sports leagues, golf courses, tennis courts, pools, and so forth. There are 336 full-time-equivalent employees (FTEs) authorized in the department. Of these, 216 are full-time permanent personnel who provide the administration and year-round maintenance to all areas. The remaining 120 positions are all part time—about three quarters of them are used during the summer and the remaining quarter used in the fall, winter, and spring seasons. The three fourths (or 90 positions) show up as approximately 800 part-time summer jobs. These jobs are as life guards, baseball umpires, and instructors in summer programs for children.

Currently, the only parks and recreation work subcontracted amounts to less than $100,000. This is for the golf and tennis pros and for grounds maintenance at the libraries and veterans cemetery.

The option to hire and fire full-time help daily or weekly in order to meet seasonal demand is pretty much out of the question. This is because of the nature of city employment, the probable bad public image, civil service rules, and so forth. However, temporary part-time help is authorized and traditional. Also, it is virtually impossible to have regular employees (non part-time) staff for all the summer jobs. During the summer months, the approximately 800 part-time employees are staffing the many programs which occur simultaneously prohibiting level scheduling over a normal 40-hour week. Also, a wider variety of skills are required than

EXHIBIT 13.5
**Three possible
production plans**

Plan 1*   Exact production; vary work force

Month	(1) Production requirement	(2) Production hours required (1) × 5	(3) Hours per month per worker (days × 8)	(4) Workers required (2) ÷ (3)
January	1,850	9,250	176	53
February	1,425	7,125	152	47
March	1,000	5,000	168	30
April	850	4,250	168	25
May	1,150	5,750	176	33
June	1,850	9,250	160	58

Plan 2†   Constant work force; vary inventory and stockout

Month	(1) Cumulative production requirement	(2) Production hours available (days × 8 × 41 workers)	(3) Units produced (2) ÷ 5	(4) Cumulative production
January	1,850	7,216	1,443	1,443
February	3,275	6,232	1,247	2,690
March	4,275	6,888	1,378	4,068
April	5,125	6,888	1,378	5,446
May	6,275	7,216	1,443	6,889
June	8,125	6,560	1,312	8,201

Plan 3‡   Constant low work force; subcontract

Month	(1) Production requirement	(2) Production hours available (days × 8 × 25 workers)	(3) Units produced (2) ÷ 5	(4) Units subcontracted (1) — (3)
January	1,850	4,400	800	970
February	1,425	3,800	760	665
March	1,000	4,200	840	160
April	850	4,200	840	10
May	1,150	4,400	880	270
June	1,850	4,000	800	1,050
	8,125		5,000	3,125

* Notes for Plan 1:
   Column 4, opening work force is assumed equal to first month's requirement of 53 workers.
† Notes for Plan 2:
   Column 1, taken from Exhibit 13.3, line 6.
   Column 2, the total of 8 hours per day for 41 workers over the number of working days in each month given by Exhibit 13.3, line 7.
   Column 3, the number of production hours available divided by 5 hours' production time for each unit.
   Columns 5–8, as a policy decision in this example to maintain control of the level of stockout protection, shortage costs and inventory costs are based on the planned production requirement, which includes forecast and safety stock. Actually, as far as customer demand is concerned, no shortage occurs until the safety stock is depleted.
‡ Notes for Plan 3:
   Column 2, number of days in each month from Exhibit 13.3, line 7.
   Column 3, each unit requires 5 hours' production time.

EXHIBIT 13.5
(continued)

(5)	(6)	(7)	(8)	(9)
Workers hired	Hiring cost (5) × $200	Workers laid off	Layoff cost (7) × $250	Straight time cost (2) × $4.00
—	—	—	—	$ 37,000
0	0	6	1,500	28,500
0	0	17	4,250	20,000
0	0	5	1,250	17,000
8	1,600	0	0	23,000
25	5,000	0	0	37,000
	$6,600		$7,000	$162,500

(5)	(6)	(7)	(8)	(9)
Units short (1) − (4)	Shortage cost (5) × $5	Units excess (4) − (1)	Inventory cost (7) × $1.50	Straight time cost (2) × $4.00
407	$2,035			$ 28,864
585	2,925			24,928
207	1,035			27,552
		321	$ 482	27,552
		614	921	28,864
		76	114	26,240
	$5,995		$1,517	$161,376

(5)				(9)
Subcontracting cost (4) × $2				Straight time cost (2) × $4.00
$1,940				$ 17,600
1,330				15,200
320				16,800
20				16,800
540				17,600
2,100				16,000
$6,250				$100,000

EXHIBIT 13.6
Comparison of the three plans

Strategy	Plan 1 Exact production; vary work force	Plan 2 Constant work force; vary inventory and stockout	Plan 3 Constant low work force; subcontract
Hiring cost..............	$ 6,600	0	0
Layoff cost..............	7,000	0	0
Excess inventory cost.....	0	1,517	0
Shortage cost............	0	5,995	0
Subcontracting cost	0	0	62,500
Straight time cost	$162,500	$161,376	$100,000
Total costs	$176,100	$168,888	$162,500

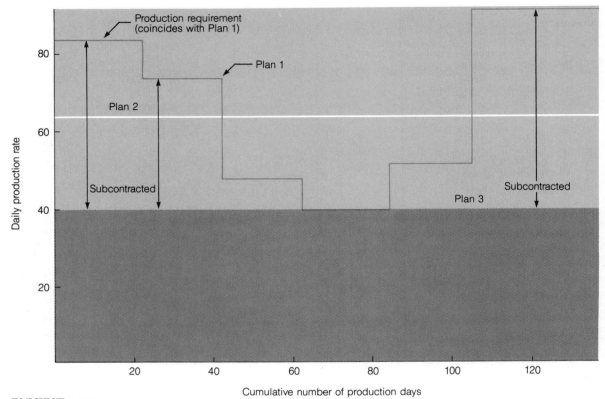

EXHIBIT 13.7
Daily production rates for the three production plans

can be expected from full-time employees (e.g., umpires, coaches, life-guards, teachers of ceramics, guitar, karate, belly dancing, and yoga).

There are three options open to the Parks and Recreation Department in their aggregate planning.

1. The present method, which is to maintain a medium level full-time staff and schedule work during off seasons (such as rebuilding baseball fields during the winter months) and to use part-time help during peak demands.

2. Maintain a lower level of staff over the year and subcontract all additional work presently done by full-time staff (still utilizing part-time help).

3. Maintain an administrative staff only and subcontract all work including part-time help. (This would entail contracts to landscaping firms, pool-maintenance companies, and to newly created private firms to employ and supply part-time help.)

The common unit of measure of work across all areas is Full-Time-Equivalent Jobs or Employees (or FTEs). For example, assume in the same

EXHIBIT 13.8
Three plans for satisfying a production requirement over the number of production days available

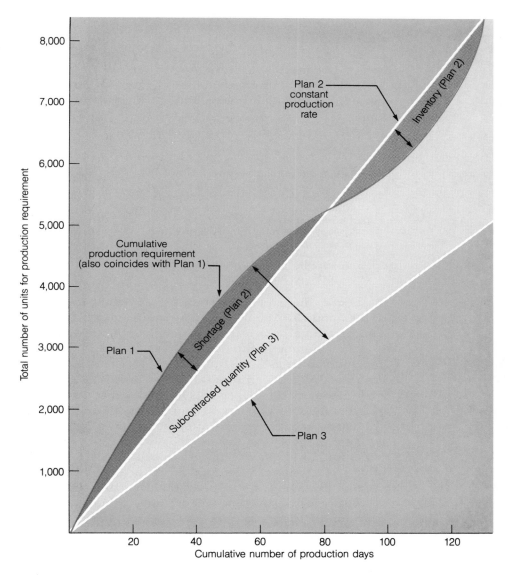

week that, 30 lifeguards worked 20 hours each, 40 instructors worked 15 hours each, and 35 baseball umpires worked 10 hours each. This is equivalent to $(30 \times 20) + (10 \times 15) + (35 \times 10) = 1550 \div 40 = 38.75$ FTEs or full-time-equivalent positions for that week. Although a considerable amount of work load can be shifted to off season, most of the work must be done when required.

Full-time employees consist of three groups: (1) the skeleton group which are key department personnel coordinating with the city, setting policy, determining budgets, measuring performance, and so forth; (2) the administrative group of supervisory and office personnel who are responsible for or whose jobs are directly linked to the direct labor workers; and (3) the direct labor work force of 116 full-time positions. These workers physically maintain the department's areas of responsibility, such as cleaning up, mowing golf greens and ball fields, trimming trees, and watering grass.

Costs required for the determination of the best alternative strategy are:

Full-time direct labor employees
    Average wage rate $4.45 per hour
    Fringe benefits   17% of wage rate
    Administrative costs   20% of wage rate
Part-time employees
    Average wage rate $4.03 per hour
    Fringe benefits   11% of wage rate
    Administrative costs   25% of wage rate
Subcontracting all full-time jobs $1.6 million
Subcontracting all part-time jobs $1.85 million

Demand. June and July are the peak demand seasons in Tucson. Exhibits 13.9 and 13.10 show the high requirements for June and July personnel. The part-time help reaches 575 full-time-equivalent positions (although in actual numbers, this is approximately 800 different employees). The demand shown as "full-time direct" reaches 130 in March when grounds are reseeded and fertilized and then increases to a high of 325 in July. The present method levels this uneven demand over the year to an average of 116 full-time year-round employees by early scheduling of work. As previously mentioned, no attempt is made to hire and layoff full-time workers to meet this uneven demand.

Exhibit 13.11 shows the cost calculations for all three alternatives. Exhibit 13.12 compares the total costs for each alternative.

From this analysis, it appears that the Parks and Recreation Department is already using the lowest-cost alternative (Alternative 1) and should continue to operate as they have been.

Mathematical techniques

Linear programming. Linear programming (LP) is appropriate to aggregate planning if the cost and variable relationships are linear and demand can be treated as deterministic. For the general case, the simplex method can be used. For the special case where hiring and firing are not considerations, the more easily formulated transportation method can be applied.

The applications of an LP transportation matrix to aggregate planning is illustrated by the solved problem in Exhibit 13.13. This formulation is termed a *period model* since it relates production demand to production capacity by periods. In this case, there are four subperiods with demand forecast as 800 units in each. The total capacity available is 3,950 or an excess capacity of 750 (3,950 − 3,200). However, the bottom row of the matrix

EXHIBIT 13.9

Actual demand requirement for full-time direct employees and full-time-equivalent (FTE) part-time employees

	January	February	March	April	May	June	July	August	September	October	November	December	Total
Days..............	22	20	21	22	21	20	21	21	21	23	18	22	252
Full-time employees..........	66	28	130	90	195	290	325	92	45	32	29	60	
Full-time days*..........	1,452	560	2,730	1,980	4,095	5,800	6,825	1,932	945	736	522	1,320	28,897
Full-time-equivalent part-time employees	41	75	72	68	72	302	576	72	0	68	84	27	
FTE days	902	1,500	1,512	1,496	1,512	6,040	12,096	1,512	0	1,564	1,512	594	30,240

Note: Some work weeks are staggered to include weekends, but this does not affect the number of work days per employee.

* Full-time days derived by multiplying the number of days in each month by the number of workers.

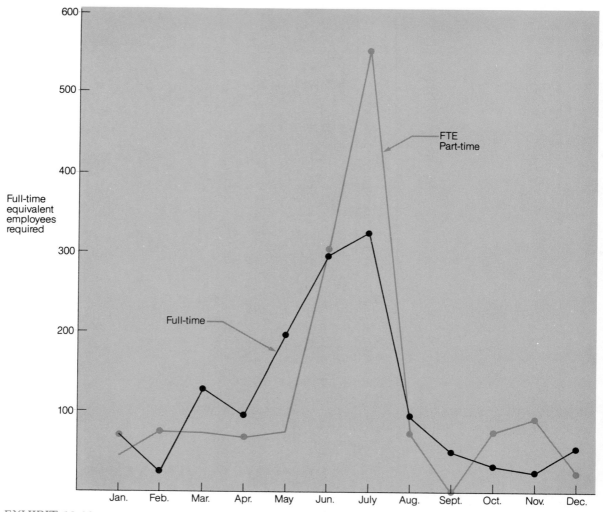

FTE
Part-time

Full-time
equivalent
employees
required

Full-time

Jan.   Feb.   Mar.   Apr.   May   Jun.   July   Aug.   Sept.   Oct.   Nov.   Dec.

EXHIBIT 13.10
Monthly requirement for full-time direct labor employees (other than key personnel) and full-time-equivalent part-time employees

indicates a desire for 500 units in inventory at the end of the planning period, so unused capacity is reduced to 250. The left-hand side of the matrix indicates the means by which production is made available over the planning period: that is, beginning inventory and regular and overtime work during each period. The shaded area indicates that production cannot be backlogged. That is, you can't produce in, say, period 3 to meet demand in period 2 (this is feasible if we allowed backorders). Finally, the costs in each cell are incremented by a holding cost of $5.00 for each period. Thus, if one produces on regular time in period 1 to satisfy demand for period 4, there will be a $15.00 holding cost. Overtime is of course more expensive to start with, but holding costs in this example are not affected

EXHIBIT 13.11
Three possible plans for the Parks and Recreation Department

Alternative 1: Maintain 116 full-time regular direct workers. Schedule work during off seasons to level work load throughout the year. Continue to use 120 full-time-equivalent (FTE) part-time employees to meet high demand periods.

Costs	Days per year (Exhibit 13.9)	Hours (employees × days × 8 hours)	Wages (full-time, $4.45; part-time, $4.03)	Fringe benefits (full-time, 17%; part-time, 11%)	Administrative cost (full-time, 20%; part-time, 25%)
116 full-time regular employees	252	231,176	$1,028,733	$174,885	$205,747
120 part-time employees	252	241,920	974,938	107,243	243,735
Total cost = $2,735,281			$2,003,671	$282,128	$449,482

Alternative 2: Maintain 50 full-time regular direct workers and the present 120 FTE part-time employees. Subcontract jobs releasing 66 full-time regular employees. Subcontract cost, $1,100,000.

Cost	Days per year (Exhibit 13.9)	Hours (employees × days × 8 hours)	Wages (full-time, $4.45; part-time, $4.03)	Fringe benefits (full-time, 17%; part-time, 11%)	Administrative cost (full-time, 20%; part-time, 25%)	Subcontract cost
50 full-time employees	252	100,800	$ 448,560	$ 76,255	$ 89,712	
120 FTE part-time employees subcontracting cost	252	241,920	974,938	107,243	243,735	$1,100,000
Total cost = $3,040,443			$1,423,498	$183,498	$333,447	$1,100,000

Alternative 3: Subcontract all jobs previously performed by 116 full-time regular employees. Subcontract cost $1,600,000. Subcontract all jobs previously performed by 120 full-time-equivalent part-time employees. Subcontract cost $1,850,000.

Cost	Subcontract cost
0 Full-time employees	
0 Part-time employees	
Subcontract—full-time jobs	$1,600,000
Subcontract—part-time jobs	1,850,000
Total	$3,450,000

EXHIBIT 13.12
Comparison of costs for all three alternatives

Description	Alternative 1 — 116 full-time direct labor employees, 120 full-time-equivalent part-time employees	Alternative 2 — 50 full-time direct labor employees, 120 full-time-equivalent part-time employees, subcontracting	Alternative 3 — Subcontracting jobs formerly performed by 116 direct labor full-time employees and 120 FTE part-time employees
Wages	$2,003,671	$1,423,498	—
Fringe benefits	282,128	183,498	—
Administrative costs	449,482	333,447	—
Subcontracting, full-time jobs		1,100,000	$1,600,000
Subcontracting, part-time jobs			1,850,000
Total	$2,735,281	$3,040,443	$3,450,000

EXHIBIT 13.13
Aggregate planning by the transportation method of linear programming

by whether production is on regular time or overtime. The solution shown is an optimum one. The same allocation and evaluation methods (e.g., VAM and stepping stone) applied to the transportation problems shown in Chapter 7 can be applied to the period model.

The transportation matrix is remarkably versatile and can incorporate a variety of aggregate planning factors as described in Exhibit 13.14.

Production periods (sources)		Sales period 1	Sales period 2	Sales period 3	Sales period 4	Ending inventory	Unused capacity	Total capacity
Beginning inventory		0 / 50	5	10	15	20	0	50
1	Regular time	50 / 700	55	60	65	70	0	700
1	Overtime	75 / 50	80 / 300	85	90	95	0	350
2	Regular time	X	50 / 500	55 / 200	60	65	0	700
2	Overtime	X	75	80 / 250	85	90	0	250
3	Regular time	X	X	50 / 350	55 / 350	60	0	700
3	Overtime	X	X	75	80 / 250	85	0	250
4	Regular time	X	X	X	50 / 200	55 / 500	0	700
4	Overtime	X	X	X	75	80	0 / 250	250
Total requirements		800	800	800	800	500	250	3,950

1. *Multiproduct Production.* When more than one product share common facilities, additional columns are included corresponding to each product. For *each month,* the number of columns will be equal to the number of products, and the cost entry in each cell will be equal to the cost for the corresponding product.

2. *Backlogging.* The backlog time and the cost of backlogging can be included by treating the shaded assignments in Exhibit 13.13 as feasible. If a product demanded in period 1 is delivered in period 2, this is equivalent to meeting period 1's demand with production in period 2. For, say, a $10 unit cost associated with such a backlog, the cost entry in the cell corresponding to period 2 regular time row and period 1 column will be $60 ($10 plus the $50 cost of regular-time production in period 2).

3. *Lost sales.* When stockouts are allowed and a part of the demand is not met, the firm incurs opportunity cost equal to the lost revenue. This can be included in the matrix by adding a "lost-sales" row for each period. The cost entry in the cell will be equal to lost revenue per unit.

4. *Perishability.* When perishability does not permit the sale of a product after it has been in stock for a certain period, the corresponding cells in the matrix are treated as infeasible. If the product in Exhibit 13.13 cannot be sold after it has been in stock for two periods, the cells occupying the intersection of period 4 columns and period 1 rows and columns beyond period 3 will be feasible.

5. *Subcontracting.* This can be included by adding a "subcontracting" row for each period. Cost values in each cell would be the unit cost to subcontract plus any inventory holding cost (incremented in the same fashion as regular time and overtime costs).

6. *Learning Effects.* Learning effects result in increased capacity and lower cost per unit. These changes are incorporated by making corresponding adjustments in capacity (total amount available from source) column and cost entry in the cells.

Source: K. Singhal, "A Generalized Model for Production Scheduling by Transportation Method of LP," *Industrial Management,* vol. 19, no. 5 (September–October 1977), pp. 1–6.

Linear decision rule. The linear decision rule (LDR) method was developed in the early 1950s by Holt, Modigliani, Muth, and Simon of the Carnegie Institute of Technology.[7] This method's objective is the derivation of linear equations or "decision rules" that can be used to specify the optimum production rate and work force level over some prescribed production planning horizon. In a well-known study, the developers applied the method to a paint company, for which they devised a month-by-month production plan for a one-year period. The objective of their study was to minimize the expected value of total cost over T months (C_T) where

$$C_T = \text{Regular payroll costs} + \text{Hiring and layoff costs} + \text{Overtime costs} + \text{Inventory costs}$$

From actual company data they derived the following equation:

$$C_T = \sum_{t=1}^{T} \{[340W_t] + [64.3(W_t - W_{t-1})^2]$$
$$+ [0.20(P_t - 5.67W_t)^2 + 51.2P_t - 281W_t]$$
$$+ [0.0825(I_t - 320)^2]\}$$

[7] Charles C. Holt, et al., *Planning Production, Inventories, and Work Force* (Englewood Cliffs, N.J.: Prentice-Hall, 1960).

They argued that each of these cost categories may be approximated by separate quadratic cost curves (as depicted in Exhibit 13.15).[8] Then, based on this presumption, they differentiated each equation and solved for the values at the minimum point. Although the procedure, and especially the proof of the method, is somewhat involved, the result is two equations that, when real data is substituted for the variables, specify work force level and production rate.

It is interesting to look at the form of the two equations (from the paint factory study) developed from their detailed analysis of related costs:

$$P_t = \begin{cases} +0.463\ O_t \\ +0.234\ O_{t+1} \\ +0.111\ O_{t+2} \\ +0.046 O_{t+3} \\ +0.013\ O_{t+4} \\ -0.002\ O_{t+5} \\ -0.008\ O_{t+6} \\ -0.010\ O_{t+7} \\ -0.009\ O_{t+8} \\ -0.008\ O_{t+9} \\ -0.007\ O_{t+10} \\ -0.005\ O_{t+11} \end{cases} + 0.993\ W_{t-1} + 153. - 0.464\ I_{t-1}$$

$$W_t = 0.743\ W_{t-1} + 2.09 - 0.010\ I_{t-1} + \begin{cases} +0.0101\ O_t \\ +0.0088\ O_{t+1} \\ +0.0071\ O_{t+2} \\ +0.0054\ O_{t+3} \\ +0.0042\ O_{t+4} \\ +0.0031\ O_{t+5} \\ +0.0023\ O_{t+6} \\ +0.0016\ O_{t+7} \\ +0.0012\ O_{t+8} \\ +0.0009\ O_{t+9} \\ +0.0006\ O_{t+10} \\ +0.0005\ O_{t+11} \end{cases}$$

where

P_t is the number of units of product that should be produced during the forthcoming month, t;

W_{t-1} is the number of employees in the work force at the beginning of the month (end of the previous month);

I_{t-1} is the number of units or inventory minus the number of units on backorder at the beginning of the month;

W_t is the number of employees that will be required for the current month, t (the number of employees that should be hired is therefore $W_t - W_{t-1}$);

O_t is a forecast of number of units of product that will be ordered for shipment during the current month, t;

O_{t+1} is the same for the next month, $t + 1$, and so forth.

One might be tempted to challenge the equations because the numeric quantities are so specific. In the work force equation, for example, the work force level for next month (W_t) is a function of the work force

---

[8] A quadratic curve is one that is defined by an equation of the second order (i.e., includes one or more squared terms).

A. Regular payroll cost

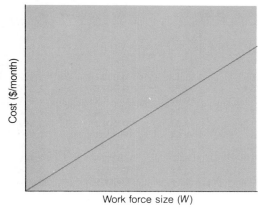

B. Cost for change in work force size

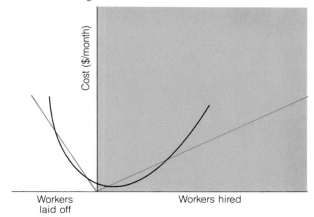

C. Cost of overtime

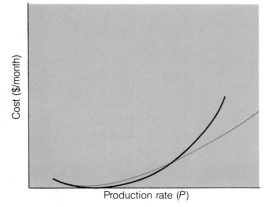

D. Expected inventory, backorder, and set-up costs

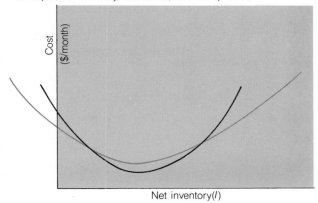

EXHIBIT 13.15
Quadratic cost assumptions (represented by the light lines) in the linear decision rule

last month (W_{t-1}), last month's inventory level (I_{t-1}), the forecast requirements for the next 12 months (O_t to O_{t+11}), *plus* 2.09. To add 2.09 workers to this equation seems too precise, but it must be remembered that this is an optimal solution using the costs the authors developed. There is one bothersome point, however. Notice that in the production equation, the coefficients of the future orders for products are negative beyond O_{t+5}. This states that the need for products during that period has a depressing effect on next month's production schedule. The authors explain this phenomenon by stating that evidently the optimal method to prepare for future orders is first to build up work force slowly then increase production rate gradually.

To illustrate the simplicity in using the equations, suppose that we are given the data in Exhibit 13.16 and must decide on the work force and production rate for next month. In this case, we are at the end of December with a 12-month forecast ahead of us. In using the method, we are planning the production level and work force needs for January.

EXHIBIT 13.16
**Data for linear
decision rule
equations**

Month	(1) Forecast	(2) Coefficient	(3) Forecast effect $(1) \times (2)$	(4) Coefficient	(5) Forecast effect $(1) \times (4)$
		Production equation		Work force equation	
January	240	0.463	111.12	0.0101	2.424
February	250	0.234	58.50	0.0088	2.200
March	270	0.111	29.97	0.0071	1.917
April	290	0.046	13.34	0.0054	1.566
May	310	0.013	4.03	0.0042	1.302
June	320	−0.002	−0.64	0.0031	0.992
July	330	−0.008	−2.64	0.0023	0.759
August	300	−0.010	−3.00	0.0016	0.480
September	280	−0.009	−2.52	0.0012	0.336
October	270	−0.008	−2.16	0.0009	0.243
November	250	−0.007	−1.75	0.0006	0.150
December	240	−0.005	−1.20	0.0005	0.120
			203.05		12.489

Beginning inventory (I_{t-1}) = 160 units
Present work force size (W_{t-1}) = 40 people

Using the same equations as the authors used,

$$P_t = (\text{forecast effect}) + 0.993 W_{t-1} + 153 - 0.464 I_{t-1}$$

From Exhibit 13.16,

$$P_t = 203.05 + 0.993(40) + 153 - 0.464(160) = 321.53$$
$$W_t = 0.743 W_{t-1} + 2.09 - 0.01(I_{t-1}) + (\text{forecast effect})$$
$$= 0.743(40) + 2.09 - 0.01(160) + 12.489$$
$$= 42.70$$

Therefore, our January production schedule is 322 units, and our work force is 43, which means we would have to hire three workers. The total cost for this schedule is $21,220, which is found by substituting the following variables into the equation for C_T: $P_t = 321.53$, $W_{t-1} = 40$, $I_{t-1} = 160$, and $I_t = (P_t + I_{t-1} - 240) = 241.53$. (This gives us the cost for January.)

There are three major drawbacks of the linear decision rule. First, its application is restricted to quadratic cost relationships. Second, the difficulty involved in obtaining the cost information from the firm's operations may be prohibitively tedious. Third, since there are no limitations placed on the variables, it may be possible to generate negative production and work force schedules. (A negative demand would indicate a shipment from the customer to the factory!) The persistence of this technique in the literature is due to its continued use in research as a benchmark against which other planning techniques can be compared.

**Heuristic
techniques**

Management coefficients method. Earlier (Chapter 8) we described a heuristic as a rule of thumb which helps to cope with a particular class of problems (recall our discussion of the CRAFT program for plant layout).

A broader definition of the term would include "methods which help the decision maker learn from his or her own experience and facilitate the development of procedures by which complicated problems can be satisfactorily solved." A classic application of this notion of heuristics is Bowman's management coefficients method in which a manager's past performance is used to devise formal rules for production planning.

In his research, Bowman found that managers made pretty good decisions in their production planning due to their experience and sensitivity to the problem at hand. Where they fell short was not because they were biased (e.g., always produced too much or always kept inventories too low) but rather because they were inconsistent in their decisions. To remedy this inconsistency, Bowman did a multiple regression analysis of past production planning decisions made by managers of the paint company used for the LDR study described in the previous section of this chapter. This analysis yielded coefficients analogous to these derived mathematically for LDR. He then substituted these values into work force and production rate equations (also analogous to those developed for LDR) and compared the costs of the plan with these from actual past performance. The results showed management coefficients to be superior. Subsequent tests using data from a chocolate company and an ice cream company indicated that the approach led to lower costs than those resulting from LDR (although LDR yielded lower costs for the paint company and a candy company). The failure of the optimizing LDR method to "win" in all cases was attributed to the fact that the cost functions used in the LDR model were developed from published, rather than basic, data.

Search decision rules. This method developed by Taubert[9] generates a production plan in stages and seeks to find a minimum cost combination of work force (W) and production (P) levels by evaluating an objective function at each stage. (A stage is a time period such as three months.) Procedurally, an objective function is evaluated at a point, its value compared with previous results, and different combinations of W and P are tried to see if improvement in cost can be made. There is a systematic search for the optimum, but there is no guarantee that it will be found.

The key to search decision rules (SDR) is its use of a pattern search algorithm to seek out the minimum cost point on a complex curve connecting the minimum cost points of all possible schedules. (In mathematical terms, finding the minimum point on a response surface.) The model begins at a base point with trial values selected for P and for W. Given an n-period planning horizon, it would follow a pattern of movement to seek the lowest cost combination for each of these periods. If, for example, it tries one combination and yields an improvement, it would try another combination which moves in the same direction in terms of P and W values. If no improvement is indicated, it goes back to the base point

9 William H. Taubert, "A Search Decision Rule for the Aggregate Scheduling Problem," *Management Science* (February 1968), pp. B343–59.

and starts over in a different direction. If no improvement is indicated in any other direction, the program terminates with the current base point taken as the optimum.

Parametric production planning. The PPP procedure, developed by Jones,[10] also uses a search procedure, but in this case, the objective is to find four parameters which determine how production rate and work force respond to such variables as forecasts and inventories. These parameters are then used in establishing P and W equations similar to those of LDR.

Production switching heuristics. Mellichamp and Love[11] describe an approach to aggregate planning wherein production for the next period, P_t, is determined by a firm's current inventory position. The procedure involves setting three possible production levels: high *(H)*, normal *(N)*, and low *(L)*. If forecast demand indicates that the net production required after taking on-hand and target inventories into account is less than L, produce at L; if it is higher than H, produce at H, and if it is in between H and L, produce at N. The values for H, N, and L are determined by simulating trial values of these three variables using historical demand.

The advantages of this approach are: (1) that it produces P_t, W_t, and I_t decisions with a minimal amount of period-to-period adjustment, (2) it can handle a variety of cost structures, and (3) the search procedure used to find trial values of H, N, and L for simulation is relatively easy and fast (on the computer). The major disadvantage is that it doesn't account for seasonal demand variations very well and to compensate for this shortcoming would increase the model's complexity. Also, in comparative tests, it yields slightly higher cost solutions than LDR and PPP.

Evaluation of mathematical and heuristic techniques

Linear programming is appropriate when the cost and variable relationships are linear or can be cut into approximately linear segments. Linear Decision Rule pertains when these relationships are quadratic. When neither of these conditions is available, then the heuristic approaches should be considered. In evaluating five techniques, a 1974 research study by Lee and Khumawala indicated that SDR provided the best results and in fact outperformed LDR when applied to data from a capital goods firm. (See Exhibit 13.17).

Regarding current application of these techniques in industry, only linear programming has seen wide usage.[12] In commenting upon this issue, Peterson and Silver[13] suggest that the answer lies in the decision-making style of management. The basic issue, in their view, is management's attitude toward models in general. Those companies where modeling is a way of life are likely to try the more sophisticated methods; in those where it

[10] Curtis A. Jones, "Parametric Production Planning," *Management Science* (July 1967), pp. 843–66.

[11] Mellichamp and Love, "Production Switching Heuristics," pp. 1242–1251.

[12] See W. N. Ledbetter and J. F. Cox, "Operations Research in Production Management: An Investigation of Past and Present Utilization," *Production and Inventory Management* (Third Quarter 1977), pp. 84–91.

[13] R. Peterson and E. A. Silver, *Decision Systems for Inventory Management and Production Planning* (New York: John Wiley & Sons, 1979), p. 662.

Source: William B. Lee and Basheer M. Khumawala, "Simulation Testing of Aggregate Production Models in an Implementation Methodology," *Management Science* (February 1974), p. 906.

EXHIBIT 13.17
Comparative profit performance of five aggregate planning approaches

	Imperfect forecast	Perfect forecast
Company decisions	$4,420,000	—
Linear decision rule	$4,821,000	$5,078,000
Management coefficients model	$4,607,000	$5,000,000
Parametric production planning	$4,900,000	$4,989,000
Search decision rule	$5,021,000	$5,140,000

is not, one would suspect that graphical and charting approaches would be used. Somewhere in the middle ground lie companies which have substantial experience in data processing and use the computer primarily for detailed scheduling. In these types of firms, we would expect to see experimentation with alternative cut-and-try plans in developing master schedules as noted in Exhibit 13.18.

EXHIBIT 13.18
Summary data on aggregate planning methods

Methods	Assumptions	
1. Graphical and charting	None	Tests alternative plans through trial and error. Nonoptimal, but simple to develop and easy to understand.
2. Simulation of master schedule	Existence of a computer-based production system	Tests aggregate plans developed by other methods.
3. Linear programming—transportation method	Linearity, constant work force	Useful for the special case where hiring and firing costs are not a consideration. Gives optimal solution.
4. Linear programming—simplex method	Linearity	Can handle any number of variables but often difficult to formulate. Gives optimal solution.
5. Linear decision rules	Quadradic cost functions	Complicated to develop and maintain. Basically a research vehicle used as a benchmark for compari-'son.
6. Management coefficients	Managers are basically good decision makers	Uses statistical analysis of past decisions to make future decisions. Applies, therefore, to just one group of managers, nonoptimal.
7. Search decision rules	Any type of cost structure	Uses pattern search procedure to find minimum points on total cost curves. Complicated to develop, nonoptimal.
8. Parametric production planning	Any type of cost structure	Uses search routine to develop four parameters affecting work force and production rate decisions. Research indicates that it is use effective than SDR, nonoptimal.
9. Production switching heuristic	Any type of cost structure	Uses simulation to establish three alternative production levels. Current inventory position used to choose appropriate level for each period. Nonoptimal.

CONCLUSION

Before leaving the subject of aggregate planning, it is useful to point out some practical considerations.

First, demand variations are a fact of life so the planning system must include sufficient flexibility to cope with such variations. Flexibility can be achieved by developing alternative sources of supply, cross training workers to handle a wide variety of orders, and engaging in more frequent replanning during high demand periods. As Plossl and Wight point out, "It is often practical to maintain a monthly production plan during the inventory building period and then to switch over to a weekly production plan during the peak selling season."[14]

Second, decision rules for production planning should be adhered to once they have been selected. However, they should be carefully analyzed prior to implementation by such checks as simulation of historical data to see what really would have happened if they had been in operation in the past.

Finally, there is a tendency towards inertia in changing production rates since line managers are more attuned to costs of changing than the costs of not changing. "This, of course, is the very reason for having decision rules—delays in changing the production rate can make the amount of change required so large as to be almost impossible to attain."[15]

REVIEW AND DISCUSSION QUESTIONS

1. What are the three basic controllable variables of a production planning problem? What are the four major costs?

2. Distinguish between pure and mixed strategies in production planning.

3. Compare the best plans in the C & A Company and the Tucson Parks and Recreation Department. What do they have in common?

4. Under what conditions would you have to use the general simplex method rather than the period model in aggregate planning?

5. Contrast LDR with management coefficients as techniques for *practical* aggregate planning.

6. How does Search Decision Rule method work?

7. How does management's attitude towards models in general relate to the use of mathematical and heuristic techniques in industry?

8. How does forecast accuracy relate, in general, to the practical application of the aggregate planning models discussed in the chapter?

[14] G. W. Plossl and D. W. Wight, *Production and Inventory Control, Principles and Techniques* (Englewood Cliffs, N.J.: Prentice-Hall, Inc., 1967), p. 235.

[15] Ibid., p. 236.

9. What did Lee and Khumawala's study show to be the *second* best aggregate planning method?

PROBLEMS

1. O. B. Crane is starting production on a secret product called "Perfect 10s." (This product is so hot that he has turned over all responsibility for conehead production to his French affiliate, Beldar Products.) Mr. Crane has asked you to help him with his aggregate planning for this new product and has sent you the following information by registered mail from his hideaway in the Bahamas:

Demand data	January	February	March	April	May	June
Beginning inventory	200					
Forecast demand	500	600	650	800	900	800

Cost data	
Holding cost	$10/Unit/Month
Stockout cost	$20/Unit/Month
Subcontracting cost/unit	$100
Hiring cost/worker	$50
Layoff cost/worker	$100
Labor cost/hour—straight time	$12.50
Labor cost/hour—overtime	$18.75

Production data	
Labor hours/unit	4
Workdays/month	22
Current work force	10

What is the cost of each of the following production strategies?

a. Exact production; vary work force (assuming a starting work force of 10).
b. Constant work force; vary inventory and stockout only (assuming a starting work force of 10).
c. Constant work force by 10; vary overtime only.

2. For problem 1, devise the least costly plan you can. You may choose your starting work force level.

3. Assume that Ichi Ban Enterprises has purchased O. B. Crane's company and has instituted Japanese-style management in which workers are guaranteed a job for life (with no layoffs). Based upon the data in problem 1 (and additional information provided below), develop a production plan for "Perfect 10s" using the transportation period model of linear programming. To keep things simple, plan for the first three months only and convert costs from hours to units in your model. Additional information: overtime is limited to eleven units per month per worker and up to five units per month may be subcontracted at a cost of $100 per unit.

4. Ichi Ban Enterprises is expanding its product line to include "Numero Unos," "Fantastic 4s," and "Figure 8s." These items are to be produced on the same productive equipment (a number cruncher, naturally), and the objective is

to meet the demands for the three products using overtime where necessary. The demand forecast for the next four months, in required hours, is as follows:

Product	April	May	June	July
Unos	800	600	800	1,200
4s	600	700	900	1,100
8s	700	500	700	850

Because the products deteriorate rapidly, there is a high loss in quality and, consequently, a high carryover cost into subsequent periods. Each hour's production carried into future months costs $3 per productive hour of Unos, $4 for 4s, and $5 for 8s.

Production can take place either during regular working hours or during overtime. Regular time is paid at $4 when working on Unos, $5 for 4s, and $6 for 8s. Overtime premium is 50 percent and is limited to half the number of regular-time hours.

The available production capacity for regular time and overtime is

	April	May	June	July
Regular-time	1,500	1,300	1,800	1,700
Overtime	700	650	900	850

a. Set the problem up in matrix form and show appropriate costs.
b. Show a feasible solution.

5. Maple Leaf Ltd., a small, color-TV manufacturer, must come up with a production plan for the next 12 months. Since Maple Leaf is a small concern located in a quiet Canadian city, the owner/president feels that he has an employment obligation to the citizenry. Although he feels free to change the employment level at the start of each year, he feels there should be no further changes. Additionally, all employees should put in full work weeks, even if this is not the lowest-cost alternative. The forecast for the next 12 months is as follows.

Month	Forecast demand	Month	Forecast demand
January	600	July	200
February	800	August	200
March	900	September	300
April	600	October	700
May	400	November	800
June	300	December	900

Manufacturing cost is $200 per set, equally divided between materials and labor. Inventory storage costs are $5 per month. A shortage of sets results in lost sales and is estimated to cost an overall $20 per unit short.

The inventory on hand at the beginning of the planning period is 200 units. Ten labor hours are required per TV set. The work day is eight hours.

Develop an aggregate production schedule for the year using a constant work force. For simplicity, assume 22 working days each month except July, when the plant closes down for three weeks' vacation (leaving seven working days).

6. Develop a production schedule to produce the exact production requirements by varying the work force size for the following problem. Use the example in the chapter shown on Exhibits 13.3 through 13.6 as a guide (Plan 1).

The monthly forecast for product X for January, February, and March is 1,000, 1,500, and 1,200, respectively. Safety stock policy recommends that one half of the forecast for that month be defined as safety stock. There are 22 working days in January, 19 in February, and 21 in March. Beginning inventory is 500 units.

Following are additional data: Manufacturing cost is $200 per unit, storage costs are $3 per unit per month, standard pay rate is $6 per hour, overtime rate is $9 per hour, cost of stockout is $10 per unit per month, marginal cost of subcontracting is $10 per unit, hiring and training cost is $200 per worker, layoff costs are $300 per worker, and production man hours required per unit are 10.

SELECTED BIBLIOGRAPHY

Buffa, Elwood S., and Miller, Jeffrey G. *Production-Inventory Systems: Planning and Control.* 3d. ed. Homewood, Ill.: Richard D. Irwin, Inc., 1979.

Eilon, Samuel. "Five Approaches to Aggregate Production Planning," *AIIE Transactions.* (June 1975).

Fisk, J. C., and Seagle, J. P. "Integration of Aggregate Planning With Resource Requirements Planning," *Production and Inventory Management* (Third Quarter 1978), p. 87.

Greene, James H. *Production and Inventory Control: Systems and Decisions.* Rev. ed. Homewood, Ill.: Richard D. Irwin, Inc., 1974.

Hax, A. C., Majluf, N. S., and Penrock, M. "Diagnostic Analysis of a Production and Distribution System," *Management Science,* vol. 26, no. 9 (1980), pp. 871–89.

Lee, W. B., and Khumawala, B. M. "Simulation Testing of Aggregate Production Planning Models in an Implementation Methodology," *Management Science,* vol. 20, no. 4 (1974), pp. 903–11.

Magee, J. F., and Boodman, D. M. *Production Planning and Inventory Control.* 2d ed. New York: McGraw-Hill Book Company, 1967.

Niland, Powell. *Production Planning, Scheduling, and Inventory Control.* New York: Macmillan Co., 1971.

Peterson, R. and Silver, E. A. *Decision Systems for Inventory Management and Production Planning.* New York: John Wiley & Sons, 1979.

Wight, Oliver W. *Production and Inventory Management in the Computer Age.* Boston, Mass.: Cahners Books, 1974.

Chapter 14

DESIGN OF THE SCHEDULING SYSTEM

Work flow equals cash flow.
William E. Sandman

A schedule is a timetable for performing activities, utilizing resources, or allocating facilities. The process of scheduling can be thought of as the implementation phase of production planning and as a continual activity in the life of a productive system. The purpose of scheduling is to *disaggregate* the general production plan into time-phased weekly, daily, or hourly activities—in other words, to specify in precise terms the planned work load on the productive system in the very short run.

In designing a scheduling system, provision must be made for efficient performance of the following functions:

1. Allocating orders, equipment, and personnel to work centers or other specified locations. Essentially, this is a decision based on a comparison of required capacity with available capacity.
2. Determining the *sequence* of order performance; that is, establishing job priorities.
3. Initiating performance of the scheduled work. This is commonly termed the *dispatching of orders*.
4. Reviewing the status of orders as they progress through the system. This is often referred to as *followup*.
5. *Expediting* late and critical orders.
6. Revising the schedule in light of changes in order status.

Relating these factors on the basis of information flow provides the structure for the generalized scheduling system depicted in Exhibit 14.1. In

EXHIBIT 14.1
Generalized scheduling system

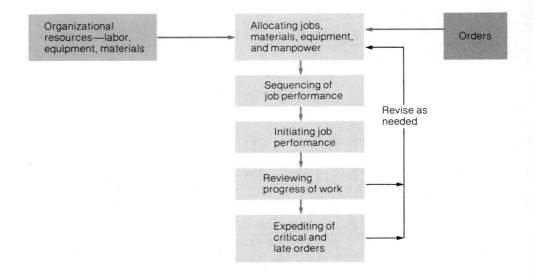

our discussion, we will consider the categories of process flow developed in Chapters 2 and 3. For manufacturing, these are:

Unit—one at a time.

Batch or job shop—each batch or job consists of a finite number of units.

Mass—indefinite or extremely large number of items of homogeneous nature.

Process—continuous processing of primary materials.

and for services:

High contact—primary service product created with the customer in the system.

Low contact—primary service product created in the absence of the customer.

We shall cover scheduling techniques for each of these categories with the exception of low contact services, which in our view are generally amenable to manufacturing scheduling methods.

The heart of a scheduling system is the master schedule. It follows the aggregate plan (Chapter 13) and specifically identifies by period when production or service is to take place. This chapter will open with a discussion of the master schedule and then discuss general scheduling problems in a variety of organizations.

THE MASTER SCHEDULE

The master production schedule is preceded by a demand forecast and a production plan. The production plan created a feasible schedule (usually by product group) while considering such factors as capacity constraints, normal work shifts, holidays, and vacation periods. The master schedule breaks the production plan into greater detail and provides the means to keep a valid schedule by updating it with actual orders as they occur (rather than as they were forecasted) and actual production output (rather than that which had been previously planned). The updated master schedule then becomes an input to detailed scheduling, which specifies when a job should be started, where it is to be performed, and what materials, equipment, and manpower are required. In computerized systems, the master schedule is the input to the Materials Requirements Planning System (MRP), which is discussed in Chapter 16.

Exhibit 14.2 shows a segment of what a master production schedule might look like. All the master schedule does is show how many units of each item must be produced in each period. Note that it is really very simple—except for the fact that there may be several thousand items with production runs distributed throughout a year-long scheduling horizon!

EXHIBIT 14.2
Example of a master production schedule

	Week						Biweekly				
Product	1	2	3	4	. . .	26	27–28	29–30	31–32	. . .	51–52
A	50		100				90		150		
B		70				90		50			
C	100	100		100			150		170		
D	75		90				50	70			
E	50	80		70			100		140		
F	100	50	50				90	90	80		

Each firm varies somewhat in its method of master scheduling. This is partly due to the unit of product they are scheduling (pounds, gallons, units, and so forth) and partly due to the nature of their production (make-for-stock, make-to-order, assemble-to-order, and so forth). The following list of observations was common to eight firms reported by Berry, et al.[1] (These were referred to as "principles" in their book.)

1. The master production schedule (MPS) must agree in total with the aggregate production plan.
2. The MPS drives the entire manufacturing system. (It establishes the production objectives.)

---

[1] Adapted from William L. Berry, Thomas E. Vollmann, and D. Clay Whybark, *Master Scheduling* (Washington, D.C.: American Production and Inventory Control Society, 1979), pp. 11–14.

3. The MPS activity needs to be clearly defined organizationally. (Since the MPS affects the entire manufacturing system and is continually changing, the master scheduler needs clear lines of authority and procedures to resolve conflicts.)

4. All known requirements should be used in preparing the MPS (all needs should be consolidated—backlogs, spare parts, interplant transfers, and so forth).

5. Minimize the number of items that are needed to adequately express the MPS (end items only, major subassemblies, components, or some other level). Too many items increases the difficulty.

6. Stability in the MPS must be managed. (A stable schedule improves performance in plant operations. Too many changes reduces productivity, and too few changes, where necessary, may reduce customer satisfaction.)

7. Closed-loop MRP is important in ensuring a realistic MPS. (Material requirements planning (MRP), presented in Chapter 16, produces a detailed schedule from the master production schedule. When material or resource limitations occur to prevent meeting the schedule, this information must be fed back to change the master schedule.)

8. Safety stock that is incorporated in the MPS should be highly visible to the master scheduler. (When capacity is short, the master scheduler may need to change quantities and shift dates. The scheduler needs to know what is the real demand or forecast and what is safety stock.)

9. The MPS should provide the basis to answer "what-if" questions. (For example, If marketing decided to have a sales promotion on a product line, what effect would this increased demand have on the production system?)

10. The MPS must be easily understood. (All operating and management personnel should know the terminology, the importance, and the procedures to develop and change the master schedule.)

11. The MPS should be evaluated with a formal performance rating system. (The MPS must be feasible, and if it is a good schedule, it should be executed. Performance may be measured in units, percentages, dollar performance, and so forth.)

In summary, the master production schedule is a statement of selected products to be produced and is based on the production plan. Because the entire production function strives to meet this schedule, the MPS should be understood by everyone. Periodic measures should be made to see how well the schedule is being met.

Master scheduling precedes detailed production scheduling. In many respects, the entire sequence from production planning through all phases of scheduling is somewhat hazy. What distinguishes each segment is simply the *time* of performance. In a time sequence, planning (beyond a month) becomes scheduling (daily, weekly, hourly) and scheduling becomes dispatching (actual release of work to be done). There is also expediting, which follows dispatching and is a follow-up either to assure completion on time of high-priority orders or to chase down orders behind schedule.

UNIT SCHEDULING

Unit scheduling consists of scheduling or controlling the production of units which are unique (one of a kind) or which are so large or time consuming they are produced one at a time. This is typically referred to as *project scheduling*.

Project scheduling

A project consists of a set of related jobs usually directed toward some major output and requiring an extensive period of time to perform. Projects may be one of a kind, such as building a custom-designed building or highway interchange, or the production units may be so large or time consuming that they have to be produced one at a time, such as ships or a building of standard design. Typical project scheduling situations are found in the aerospace industry, shipbuilding, large construction operations, and heavy-equipment production. The primary scheduling task in projects is to coordinate the activities and resources (people, material, equipment) so that correct order of activity completion occurs and so that resources are available when needed. Project scheduling, when computerized, permits rescheduling activities and resources when delays (or early completions) are encountered. This is especially important in projects such as highways, dams, building construction, and pipelines which are affected by weather conditions. Exhibit 14.3 shows a simple work flow for a highway construction project.

To maintain adequate control of a project, the schedule should be updated frequently by adding the most recent knowledge about resource availability and activity completion times. Most projects mentioned in this section would have a new schedule run every week or two.

The computerized networking techniques most used in project scheduling are CPM (critical path method) and PERT (program evaluation and review technique). These techniques along with perhaps the newest technique, CPM/MRP, developed by the authors, are the entire subject of Chapter 17 and its supplement. Therefore, we will not discuss them further in this chapter.

Batch or job shop scheduling

When items are produced in "lots" or "batches," a job shop is often the appropriate production system. A job shop scheduling situation exists when a productive facility handles a variety of orders and treats an incoming order as a "mini project." That is, production routing is developed separately for each order, separate records are kept for each job, and the progress of each job through the system is closely monitored. This is not to say that products would not travel through such systems in batches

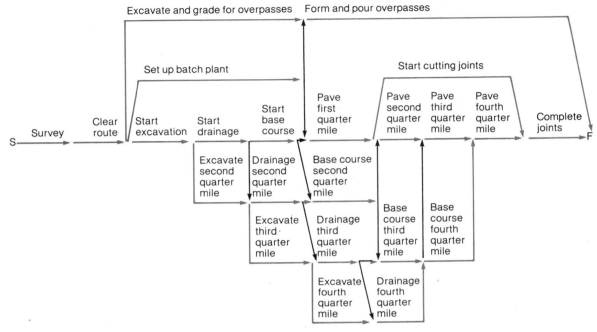

Source: James J. O'Brien, *CPM in the Construction Industry* (New York: McGraw-Hill Book Company, 1969), p. 449.

EXHIBIT 14.3
Basic highway construction flow chart

with other products; indeed, in many instances, individual orders are combined with others as they progress through the various transformation stages. However, because these are special orders with different completion schedules and with different material and service inputs required along the way, it is unlikely that they will take identical routes through the system at identical times.

The job shop scheduling problem has received a great deal of attention in the production literature, although the focus of the vast majority of studies is theoretical rather than applied. Areas of particular interest are as follows:

1. Manner in which jobs arrive.
2. Number and variety of machines in the shop.
3. Number of workers in the shop.
4. Flow pattern of jobs through the shop.
5. Rules by which jobs are allocated to machines.
6. Criteria by which the schedule will be evaluated.

1. Job arrival patterns. Jobs can arrive at the scheduler's desk either in a batch or over a time interval according to some statistical distribution. In the former case, such an arrival pattern is termed *static*, while the latter is termed *dynamic*. Static arrival does not mean that orders are placed by customers at the same moment, only that they are subject to being scheduled at one time. Such a situation is found where a production control clerk makes out a schedule, say, once a week and does not dispatch any jobs until he has all the previous week's incoming orders before him. In the dynamic arrival case, jobs are dispatched as they arrive, and the overall schedule is updated to reflect their effect on the production facility.

2. Number and variety of machines in the shop. The number of machines in the shop obviously affects the scheduling process. If there is but one machine, as in the case of a computer, the scheduling problem is greatly simplified. On the other hand, as the number and variety of machines increase, the more complex the scheduling problem is likely to become if more than one machine operation is to be performed on each job.

3. Number of workers in the shop. A key distinguishing feature in job shops is the number of workers available for work in comparison to the number of machines. If there are more workers than machines or an equal number of workers and machines, the shop is referred to as a *machine-limited system.* If there are more machines than workers, it is referred to as a *labor-limited system.* The machine-limited system has received far and away a greater amount of study, although recent investigations suggest that labor-limited systems are more pervasive in practice. In studying labor-limited systems, the primary areas of concern are the utilization of the worker on several machines and determination of the best way to allocate workers to machines.

4. Flow patterns of jobs through the shop. The pattern of flow through the shop ranges from what is termed a *flow shop,* wherein all the jobs follow the same path from one machine to the next, to a *randomly routed job shop,* where there is no similar pattern of movement from one machine to the next. Most shops fall somewhere in between. The extent to which a shop is a flow shop or a randomly routed job shop can be determined by noting the statistical probability of a job's moving from one machine to the next. For example, Exhibit 14.4A is a "pure" flow shop since the probability of movement from any machine to another machine is 1. On the other hand, Exhibit 14.4B is sometimes referred to as a "pure" random job shop since the transitional flow probabilities are all the same, in this case 0.33.

Obviously, an infinite number of intermediate probabilities are available between the two extreme cases, even for a simple four-machine shop. One interesting and fairly common mixture of the two is the *hybrid job shop,* depicted in Exhibit 14.5. In this case, the movement between departments follows that of a flow shop in that it is unidirectional, but the probability of movement from any machine in department A to any other machine either in department A or in B is equiprobable as in a random job shop. Thus, if a job is on machine 1, it has a 33 percent probability of going to any other machine for further processing, while if a job has progressed to machine 3, it has a 50 percent probability of going to machine 4 and a 50 percent probability of leaving the system.

EXHIBIT 14.4
**Simple job
shop networks**

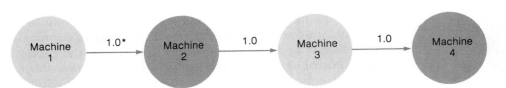

A. Pure flow shop network

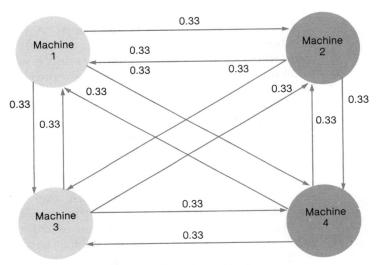

B. Pure random job shop network

* Probability of a job's going from machine *i* to machine *j*.

EXHIBIT 14.5
**Hybrid job
shop network**

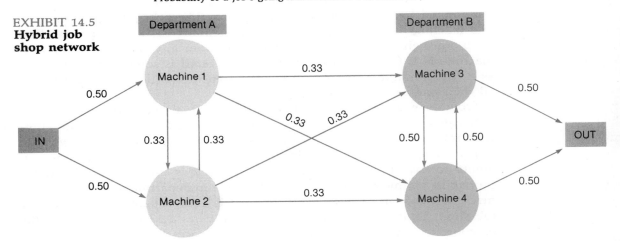

5. Priority rules for allocating jobs to machines. A priority rule is simply a rule for selecting which job is started first on some machine or work center. Examples of simple priority rules are selection of jobs on first-come-first-served, shortest processing time, and earliest due date bases.

Examples of more complex rules are "slack time per remaining operations" (where "slack" is defined as the amount of time remaining before the job must be started if it is to be completed on time), "the shortest operating time to total work time" (i.e., assign the job that has the smallest weighted ratio of processing time to work remaining), and COVERT (delay cost over processing time).

What rules are commonly used in industry? According to Richard Conway,[2] the following rules are widely employed when job lateness is of concern.

1. Assign highest priority to jobs with the earliest due dates.
2. Assign highest priority to the job with the least slack, where "slack" is defined as the time remaining until due date, after deducting the remaining time.
3. Assign highest priority to the job with the earliest due date at that machine. Allowable shop time is divided equally among the operations of the job to obtain the due date for each operation listed in the job route.
4. Assign highest priority to the job that has the least slack per remaining operation. "Slack" is defined as in rule 2 above.[3] That is,

$$\text{Priority} = \frac{\left(\begin{array}{c}\text{Time remaining}\\ \text{before due date}\end{array}\right) - \left(\begin{array}{c}\text{Remaining machine}\\ \text{involvement time}\end{array}\right)}{\text{Number of remaining operations}}$$

Another widely used rule is the critical ratio which is an index number obtained by dividing the time remaining until due date by the work time remaining (including normal delays):

$$\text{Critical ratio} = \frac{\text{Time remaining until due date}}{\text{Work time remaining}}$$

A ratio less than one indicates the job is behind schedule; greater than one indicates completion on time is still feasible.

It has been suggested that many of the assignment rules used in practice come closer to being classified as a longest processing time rule; that is, the longest job first, the second longest second, and so forth. The reason is that many jobs are given a priority based upon their relative importance,

[2] Richard W. Conway, "Priority Dispatching Rules and Job Lateness in a Job Shop," *Journal of Industrial Engineering*, vol. 16, no. 4 (July–August 1965).

[3] New, based upon his experience, states that rule 4 is "by far the most frequently used rule in implemented systems." (See C. Colin New, "Job Shop Scheduling: Who Needs a Computer to Sequence Jobs?" *Production and Inventory Management* (Fourth Quarter 1975), p. 39.

and since importance is often positively correlated with processing time, longer jobs receive higher priorities.

No one rule will be best for every situation. The ultimate choice depends upon how well a particular rule performs according to the criteria by which the schedule is evaluated.

6. Schedule evaluation criteria. A particular schedule can be evaluated in terms of the satisfactory completion of the jobs, utilization of the productive facilities, and meeting of the organization's overall objectives. Research on scheduling has for the most part concentrated on the satisfactory completion of the jobs, utilizing what are termed *local criteria.* In particular, a great deal of study has been given to the relative merits of the various priority rules in meeting such evaluation criteria as minimizing mean job flow time and mean job lateness (both defined below) for some fixed number of jobs that progress through one or more machines.

We will now consider these criteria with respect to a simple scheduling problem involving four jobs that must be processed on one machine (see data below). In scheduling terminology, this class of problems is referred to as an "n job—one-machine problem," or simply $n/1$ ($n = 4$). The theoretical difficulty of this type of problem increases as more machines are considered rather than by the number of jobs that must be processed; therefore, the only restriction on n is that it be a specified, finite number.

Job	Due date	Processing time in days	Job slack (due date— processing time)
A	4 days hence	3	1
B	9 days hence	6	3
C	5 days hence	5	0
D	9 days hence	7	2

Priority rules to be examined are: *(a)* assign jobs according to their minimum slack time, where slack is the amount of time remaining before the job must be started if it is to be completed on time, and *(b)* assign jobs according to shortest processing time. Evaluation criteria are: *(a)* minimum mean flow time, where flow time is the time the job spends in the shop, and *(b)* minimum mean lateness, where lateness is the difference between the time remaining before the job's due date and its flow time.

By the minimum slack priority rule, the jobs would be performed in the following order: C, A, D, B. The effect of these rules, in terms of the evaluation criteria, is shown in Exhibit 14.6. The flow times listed were developed with the aid of the scheduling graphs shown in Exhibit 14.7.

Returning to the schedule results, note that the shortest processing time rule gave better results, not only for flow time criteria but for lateness criteria as well. Is this luck? Not really, for it can be shown mathematically that the shortest processing time rule yields not only a shorter flow time

EXHIBIT 14.6

Job	Flow time	Time until due date	Lateness (flow time— time available)
Minimum slack rule*			
A	8	4	4
B	21	9	12
C	5	5	0
D	15	9	6
Total	49		22
Shortest processing time rule†			
A	3	4	0‡
B	14	9	5
C	8	5	3
D	21	9	12
Total	46		20

* Mean flow time: 49/4 = 12½ days; mean lateness: 22/4 = 5½ days.
† Mean flow time: 46/4 = 11½ days; mean lateness: 20/4 = 5 days.
‡ Job is finished 1 day early.

EXHIBIT 14.7

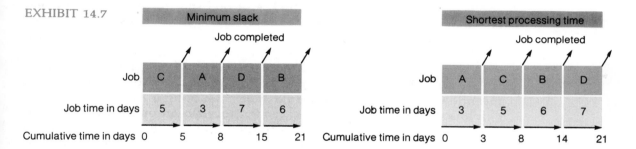

schedule and lateness time schedule than the minimum slack rule but also an optimum solution in terms of both these criteria. Moreover, the shortest processing time rule yields an optimum solution for the *n*/1 case in terms of such other evaluation criteria as mean waiting time and mean completion time. In fact, so powerful is this simple rule that it has been termed "the most important concept in the entire subject of sequencing."[4]

The next step up in the complexity level of job shop types is the *n*/2 flow shop case, where two or more jobs must be processed on two machines in a common sequence. As in the *n*/1 case, there is an approach that leads to an optimum solution according to certain criteria. This approach, termed Johnson's method (after its developer), consists of the following steps.

1. List the operation time for each job on both machines.
2   Select the shortest operation time.

[4] See R. W. Conway, William L. Maxwell, and Louis W. Miller, *Theory of Scheduling* (Reading, Mass.: Addison-Wesley, 1967) for definitions of these terms; quotation on p. 26.

3. If the shortest time is for the first machine, do the job first; if it is for the second machine, do the job last.
4. Repeat steps 2 and 3 for each remaining job until the schedule is complete.

This procedure can be seen in scheduling four jobs through two machines:

Step 1: List operation times.

Job	Operation time on machine 1	Operation time on machine 2
A	3	2
B	6	8
C	5	6
D	7	4

Steps 2 and 3: Select shortest operation time and assign. Job A is shortest on Machine 2 and is assigned first and performed last.

Step 4: Repeat steps 2 and 3. Job D is second shortest on Machine 2 and is assigned second and performed second to last. Job C is third shortest on Machine 1 and is assigned third and performed first. Job B is fourth shortest on Machine 1 and is assigned fourth and performed second.

In summary, the solution sequence is C → B → D → A, and the flow time is 25 days, which is a minimum. Also minimized are total idle time and mean idle time. The final schedule appears in Exhibit 14.8.

Johnson's method has been extended to yield an optimal solution for the $n/3$ case. When flow shop scheduling problems larger than $n/3$ arise (and they generally do), analytical solution procedures leading to optimality are not available. The reason for this is that even though the jobs may arrive in static fashion at the first machine, the scheduling problem becomes dynamic, and series of waiting lines start to form in front of machines downstream.

Queuing theory (Technical note, Chapter 9) discusses approaches to deal with scheduling problems that fall under the "dynamic arrivals" heading. However, in both the static and dynamic cases, Monto Carlo simulation is often the only way of determining the relative merits of different priority rules in real-world situations.

EXHIBIT 14.8

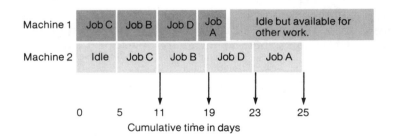

Cumulative time in days

Scheduling with Q-Control*

After just completing several pages of discussions about priority rules, we now will briefly present some of the claims of a successful consultant who says "Don't use priorities to sequence your orders."[5]

Bill Sandman formerly owned and operated his own manufacturing firm where he developed an effective scheduling method. For the past decade, he has been a consultant to industry dealing exclusively with the job shop scheduling problem.

Sandman claims to have studied the job shop problem in over 600 shops. His findings show that the total time a job is in the shop is 10 to 30 times longer than the actual working times required. This means that the balance of the time is spent simply waiting. This wait time lowers productivity primarily because work-in-process is not under ideal management control. While some waiting is obviously necessary, he believes current ratios are far too excessive. What is his solution?

Through controlling the flow of work, Sandman claims to be able to achieve the remarkable results shown in Exhibit 14.9. Both the time to complete an order and the idle work-in-process time decreased by one half while work-in-process doubled. Shop days of actual working time decreased while the labor force increased by 11.9 percent. This was due to a more efficient and smooth working environment wherein more people could work without getting into each other's way.

EXHIBIT 14.9
Improvements shown by users of Q-Control

	Pre-Q-Control	At 5-year point	Change	
Direct labor force	92.00	103.00	11.9%	Increase
Order completion time (in work days)	63.14	33.65	47.0%	Decrease
Shop days of actual working time	9.59	6.25	33.0%	Decrease
Shop days of idle WIP time per order	53.55	26.62	50.75%	Decrease
Work-in-process "turns"	4.15	8.64	107.25%	Increase

These statistics were accumulated by William E. Sandman across a group of clients using Q-Control for five years or more. The statistics present an "average" user profile. In each case, the user was compared to his performance for the year immediately prior to Q-Control use, and then all performance results were averaged.

Traditional approaches to job shop scheduling, says Sandman, are based on "Half-logics," which seek to heavily utilize workers and machines while doing nothing to relieve queue congestion; this queue congestion forces managers to use priorities to try to get jobs completed on time. Priorities make the situation even worse, hence Sandman's statement: ". . . don't use priorities to sequence orders."

---

* Q-Control and Q-Factors are copyrighted © by William E. Sandman Associates, Box 7, Dresher, Pa. 19025.

[5] *Solving the Job Shop Problem* (Dresher, Pa.: Sandman Associates, 1979), p. 7. Also, see William E. Sandman, *How to Win Productivity in Manufacturing* (Dresher, Pa.: Yellow Book of Pennsylvania, Inc., 1980).

Sandman's solution is:

Have a range of acceptable delivery dates for customer orders to allow flexibility in scheduling.

Use a "string of pearls" concept where each shop order is scheduled with all its processing steps threaded on a string, like a pearl necklace.

Simulate on a computer the routing of all the strings of pearls to all work centers to find the best scheduling.

Except for an occasional rebalance to make a better fit, the string is not to be broken. There should be no jobs inserted in the system to disrupt the smooth flow.

Having had several meetings with Bill Sandman, we have distilled some basic principles relating to his success. Exhibit 14.10 shows a list of ten steps or principles (two of which are similar to the list just presented) which should be followed.[6]

EXHIBIT 14.10
Principles of job shop scheduling

1. There is a direct equivalence between work flow and cash flow.
2. The effectiveness of any job shop should be measured by speed of flow through the shop.
3. Schedule jobs as a string, with process steps back to back.
4. A job once started should not be interrupted.
5. Speed of flow is most efficiently achieved by focusing on bottleneck work centers and jobs.
6. Reschedule every day.
7. Obtain feedback each day on jobs that are not completed at each work center.
8. Match work center input information to what the worker can actually do.
9. When seeking improvement in output, look for incompatibility between engineering design and process execution.
10. Certainty of standards, routings, and so forth is not possible in a job shop, but always work towards achieving it.

The assignment method

This technique, a special case of the transportation method of linear programming, can be used in job shop scheduling to allocate people to jobs, jobs to machines, and so forth. Like the Johnson method, the technique is "quick and dirty" and can be applied to problems which have the following characteristics.[7]

1. There are n "things" to be distributed to n "destinations."
2. Each "thing" must be assigned to one and only one "destination."
3. Only one criterion can be utilized—minimum cost, maximum profit, minimum completion time.

---

[6] Developed from a meeting with the authors and Sandman, January 1980.

[7] For more "quick and dirty" techniques, see R. D. Woolsey and H. S. Swanson, *Operations Research for Immediate Application, A Quick & Dirty Manual* (New York: Harper & Row, 1975).

For example, suppose that a scheduler has five jobs that can be performed on any of five machines ($n = 5$) and that the cost of completing each job-machine combination is shown in Exhibit 14.11. The scheduler would like to devise a minimum cost assignment. (There are 5!, or 120, possible assignments.) This problem may be solved by the assignment method, which consists of the following steps.

EXHIBIT 14.11

	Machine				
Job	A	B	C	D	E
I	$5	$6	$4	$8	$3
II	6	4	9	8	5
III	4	3	2	5	4
IV	7	2	4	5	3
V	3	6	4	5	5

EXHIBIT 14.12

Step 1: Row reduction—the smallest number is subtracted from each row.

	Machine				
Job	A	B	C	D	E
I	2	3	1	5	0
II	2	0	5	4	1
III	2	1	0	3	2
IV	5	0	2	3	1
V	0	3	1	2	2

Step 3: Apply line test—the number of lines to cover all zeros is 4; since 5 are required, go to step 4.

	Machine				
Job	A	B	C	D	E
I	2	3	1	3	0
II	2	0	5	2	1
III	2	1	0	1	2
IV	5	0	2	1	1
V	0	3	1	0	2

Optimum solution—by "line test."

	Machine				
Job	A	B	C	D	E
I	1	3	0	2	0
II	1	0	4	1	1
III	2	2	0	1	3
IV	4	0	1	0	1
V	0	4	1	0	3

Step 2: Column reduction—the smallest number is subtracted from each column.

	Machine				
Job	A	B	C	D	E
I	2	3	1	3	0
II	2	0	5	2	1
III	2	1	0	1	2
IV	5	0	2	1	1
V	0	3	1	0	2

Step 4: Subtract smallest uncovered number and add to intersection of lines—using lines drawn in step 3, smallest uncovered number is 1.

	Machine				
Job	A	B	C	D	E
I	1	3	0	2	0
II	1	0	4	1	1
III	2	2	0	1	3
IV	4	0	1	0	1
V	0	4	1	0	3

Optimum assignments and their costs.

Job I to Machine E	$3
Job II to Machine B	$4
Job III to Machine C	$2
Job IV to Machine D	$5
Job V to Machine A	$3
Total cost	$17

1. Subtract the smallest number in each *row* from itself and all other numbers in that row. (There will then be at least one zero in each row).

2. Subtract the smallest number in each *column* from all other numbers in that column.

3. Determine if the *minimum* number of lines required to cover each zero is equal to *n*. If so, an optimum solution has been found, since job-machine assignments must be made at the zero entries and this test proves that this is possible. If the minimum number of lines required is *less* than *n*, go to step 4.

4. Draw the least possible number of lines through all the zeros (these may be the same lines used in step 3). Subtract the smallest number not covered by lines from itself and all other uncovered numbers and add it to the number at each intersection of lines. Repeat step 3.

For the problem above, the steps listed in Exhibit 14.12 would be followed.

Note that even though there are two zeros in three rows and three columns, the solution shown in Exhibit 14.12 is the only one possible for this problem since Job III must be assigned to Machine C to meet the "assign to zero" requirement. Other problems may have more than one optimum solution, depending, of course, on the costs involved.

The nonmathematical rationale of the assignment method is one of minimizing opportunity costs.[8] For example, if we decided to assign Job I to Machine A instead of to Machine E, we would be sacrificing the opportunity to save \$2 (\$5 − \$3). Now this is just a one-to-one comparison, and the assignment algorithm in effect performs such comparisons for the entire set of alternative assignments by means of row and column reduction, as described in steps 1 and 2. It makes similar comparisons in step 4. Obviously, if assignments are made to zero cells, no opportunity cost, with respect to the entire matrix, is incurred.

Monitoring job performance with Gantt charts. The Gantt chart (mentioned earlier) appears in various forms, and several of these are used for monitoring order progress in job shops. An example of a schedule chart, along with conventional Gantt chart symbols, is illustrated in Exhibit 14.13.

---

[8] The underlying rationale of the procedure of adding and subtracting the smallest cell values is as follows: Additional zeros are entered into the matrix by subtracting an amount equal to one of the cells from all cells. Negative numbers, which are not permissible, will occur in the matrix. In order to get rid of the negative numbers, an amount equal to the maximum negative number must be added to each element of the row or column in which it occurs. This results in adding this amount twice to any cell that lies at the intersection of a row and a column that were both changed. The net result is that the lined rows and columns revert to their original amounts, and the intersections increase by the amount subtracted from the uncovered cells. (The reader may wish to prove this to himself by solving the example without using lines.)

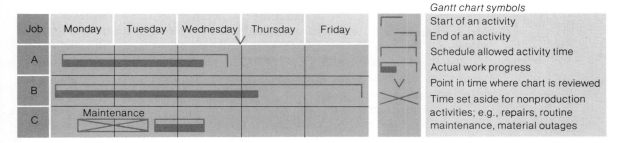

Job	Monday	Tuesday	Wednesday	Thursday	Friday
A					
B					
C	Maintenance				

Start of an activity
End of an activity
Schedule allowed activity time
Actual work progress
Point in time where chart is reviewed
Time set aside for nonproduction activities; e.g., repairs, routine maintenance, material outages

EXHIBIT 14.13
Schedule (or Gantt) chart

In this example, Job A is behind schedule by about four hours, Job B is ahead of schedule, and Job C has been completed, after a delayed start for equipment maintenance.

Computerized job shop scheduling (general shop scheduler program)

A number of computer firms have developed job shop scheduling programs, and many of these programs have been used with a good deal of success in industry. One such program package is the General Shop Scheduler, GJSCH$ developed by the General Electric Company and available on time sharing. The essential features of this program, from the user's point of view, can be described as follows.[9]

The purpose of GJSCH$ is to produce feasible schedules for work activities in situations where a job is moved from work center to work center during its production process. It may be used for direct scheduling of the shop; as a "first cut" picture of shop load, to be later refined by other (perhaps manual) techniques; or as a tool for developing job promise dates. It is generally applicable to shops that are characterized by (1) one-of-a-kind jobs that are processed through several operations in a variety of work centers, (2) little or no production of items for stock, (3) a high incidence of "specials" work, and (4) infrequent repeat orders for items previously produced. Thus, typical applications would be in custom machine shops, maintenance activities, tool and die shops, and foundries.

The program can handle any number of jobs in up to 75 work centers (that is, $n \times 75$ job shop problems). It can schedule "forward" (from today's date forward) or can be "backed off" from the due date. It permits modification of all aspects of work center capacity, and a separate definition of setup time per job. In addition, it permits the inclusion of transit times for a given job between work centers.

The program requires two input files: a machine center file and a job file. The machine center file contains two subfiles. The first describes the on-site machines in terms of their capacity in machine hours; the second describes farm-out centers (i.e., work done outside the shop, usually by

---

[9] Much of this section is drawn from General Electric Company's *User's Guide to General Shop Scheduler GJSCH$* (1970).

subcontractors). Farm-out capacity is expressed in days (and tenths of days), whereas on-site machine capacity is expressed in hours (and tenths of hours). The job file contains a description in hours of the work to be scheduled on each required process. As mentioned above, the program permits inclusion of setup time but will not execute files containing inter-mixed setup/no setup job data.

To operate the program, the user must respond to a series of questions concerning shop capacity, such as the number of days in the week to be scheduled, whether he wishes to change a specific day's capacity for all machines or a specific machine, and so forth. Following these questions (ten in all), the user is interrogated as to the type of scheduling and reporting to be performed. He will be asked the name of the job file to be scheduled, whether it contains setup data and transit times, and what type of schedule he prefers.

The user has the choice of a *finite* schedule or *infinite* load schedules. A *finite* schedule is prepared within the constraints of machine center capacity. "Infinite load" schedules are of two types: one schedules job operations one day apart; the other also schedules jobs one day apart, but the difference between this schedule and machine center capacity is noted. Depending upon the options selected, the user will be asked to respond to as many as eight questions on schedule preparation.

Finally, two reports are generated by GJSCH$. The first is a "job schedule report," detailing the schedule assignments by day, hours, machine center name, and so forth. The second is a "machine center load report," reflecting unassigned time by work center and by day. These reports are shown in Exhibit 14.14, which should be examined with the following points in mind:

Operations numbers are developed by the program and are reflected in the column immediately following *JOB* #.

Operations that will not meet the job due date are flagged with #.

The numbers of remaining hours necessary to complete an operation (on a given day) are reflected in the *REM HRS* column.

Report titles identify the type of schedule (for example, Forward Loading, Due-Date Loading).

Invalid due dates are not handled on the due date schedule; note JOB HI.

In evaluating this fairly representative programming package, we can see that it is easy to use and flexible (the developers indicate that priorities of jobs can be adjusted by physically moving the position of job data within the job file). On the other hand, there are some disconcerting features about this and similar programs. The user does not really know how the schedule is being generated within the computer, and he does not know how good the schedule is. That is, while the program provides a feasible schedule, it may be a far cry from an optimal one. Nevertheless, such packages generally provide better overall scheduling than can be

EXHIBIT 14.14
Job shop scheduler reports

```
                        JOB  SCHEDULE  REPORT
-------------------------------------------------------------------
(NOTE: ITEMS WITH A "#" IN FAR-RIGHT COLUMN WILL NOT MEET DUE DATE)


                  AVAIL CAP. SCH. - FORWARD LOADING
                        STD. TRANSIT TIME

                   MACH   REM    SCH
         JOB#   OP  W.C.   HRS    HRS    SCH.DAY   DUE DATE    #
         ----   --  ----   ----   ----   -------   --------   ---

         ABCD   1   AB01   0.     6.0      324       406
         ABCD   2   AB02   5.2    8.0      325       406
         ABCD   2   AB02   0.     5.2      326       406
         ABCD   3   AB03   0.     7.8      327       406
         ABCD   4   AB01   6.2    10.0     328       406
         ABCD   4   AB01   0.     6.2      329       406

         HI     1   AB01   4.0    4.5      324       301        #
         HI     1   AB01   0.     4.0      325       301        #
         HI     2   AB02   5.2    2.8      326       301        #
         HI     2   AB02   0.     5.2      327       301        #
         HI     3   AB06   0.     7.5      328       301        #
         HI     4   AB02   0.     4.0      329       301        #

         A17    1   AB01   10.0   6.0      325       411
         A17    1   AB01   0.     10.0     326       411

         XX47   2   AB02   8.4    2.8      327       416
         XX47   2   AB02   0.4    8.0      328       416
         XX47   2   AB02   0.     0.4      329       416
         XX47   3   AB03   1.4    8.0      331       416
         XX47   3   AB03   0.     1.4      401       416


-------------------------------------------------------------------


                  MACHINE CENTER LOAD REPORT
-------------------------------------------------------------------

                MACHINE/WORK CENTER LOAD REPORT
                       REGULAR  LOAD
                     WITH  PREV.  CAP.

                  (MACHINES OR WORK CENTERS)
-------------------------------------------------------------------

         DATE   AB01   AB02   AB03   AB04   AB05   AB06
         ----   ----   ----   ----   ----   ----   ----

         324    0.     8.0    8.0    8.0    8.0    8.0
         325    0.     0.     8.0    8.0    8.0    8.0
         326    0.     0.     8.0    8.0    8.0    8.0
         327    10.0   0.     0.2    8.0    8.0    8.0
         328    0.     0.     8.0    8.0    8.0    0.5
         329    3.8    3.6    8.0    8.0    8.0    8.0
         330    0.     0.     0.     0.     0.     0.
         331    10.0   8.0    0.     8.0    8.0    8.0
         401    10.0   8.0    6.6    8.0    8.0    8.0
         402    10.0   8.0    8.0    8.0    8.0    8.0
         403    10.0   8.0    8.0    8.0    8.0    8.0
         404    10.0   8.0    8.0    8.0    8.0    8.0
         405    0.     8.0    0.     0.     0.     0.
         406    0.     0.     0.     0.     0.     0.
         407    10.0   8.0    8.0    8.0    8.0    8.0
         408    10.0   8.0    8.0    8.0    8.0    8.0
         409    10.0   8.0    8.0    8.0    8.0    8.0
         410    10.0   8.0    8.0    8.0    8.0    8.0
```

Source: General Electric Company, *General Shop Schedule, GJSCH$ User's Guide* (1970), pp. 11–12.

done by hand methods and certainly are a boon to firms that cannot afford to develop their own computerized scheduling system.[10]

Scheduling by the runout method

The "runout time" method can be used to determine production runs for a group of items that share the same production facilities or resources. Runout time is that period of time for which previously scheduled production, plus inventory on hand, will satisfy demands for an item. The basic objective of this method is to balance the utilization of production capacity—for example, machine hours—so that the runout time for all items is the same. Production efforts are thereby balanced across the group of items rather than concentrated on a few items (while other items are neglected).

This procedure is illustrated in Exhibit 14.15 for six items, where 96.5 machine hours are available to be scheduled during a week. The aggregate runout time (3.72 weeks) is then used in column 7 to determine the inventories needed at the end of the week if each item is to have a runout time of 3.72 weeks. Column 9 shows units that must be scheduled for production in order to meet these inventory requirements.

Runout time method with lot sizes. In many situations, lot sizes are established to achieve an optimum balance between machine setup costs and inventory holding costs, while in other situations they may be dictated solely by such physical limitations as machine capacity.

The runout time method can be applied in scheduling production in both situations. For instance, consider the example in the previous section but assume that lot sizes have been established.

The objective is to determine the runout time for each item (that time for which previously scheduled production plus inventory on hand will satisfy demands for an item) and then to schedule production in the prescribed lots, starting with the item having the shortest runout time, until the 96.5 machine hours have been scheduled. These runout times are determined in Exhibit 14.16 by dividing the number of items in inventory and in production by forecasted weekly usage.

The 96.5 machine hours would be assigned to items A, F, and C—in that order as shown in Exhibit 14.16 column 5—since these items have the lowest runout times. Notice that the total machine hours required to produce these three items in their respective lot sizes are 102 (column 6). Since only 96.5 machine hours are to be scheduled for the period, the difference of 5.5 hours for item C would be scheduled during the following period.

---

[10] It should be mentioned that when innovations such as computerized scheduling are introduced, a good deal of care should be taken to assure that operating personnel are "sold" on the system. In looking at computer scheduling applications in a variety of facilities, we have observed several cases of a former scheduling system's operating in parallel with its more sophisticated replacement. The reason for this, in general, is that operating personnel were not involved in the development of the new system and hence feel little responsibility for its success.

EXHIBIT 14.15
Runout time calculations

Item	(1) Production time (in machine hours per unit)	(2) Inventory on hand (in units)	(3) Inventory on hand in machine hours (1) × (2)	(4) Forecasted weekly usage (in units)	(5) Forecasted weekly usage in machine hours (1) × (4)
A	0.2	125	25.00	60	12.00
B	0.08	250	20.00	85	6.80
C	0.5	75	37.50	30	15.00
D	0.09	300	27.00	96	8.64
E	0.15	239	35.85	78	11.70
F	0.7	98	68.60	42	29.40
Aggregate totals			213.95		83.54

$$\text{Aggregate runout time} = \frac{\text{Inventory on hand in machine hours (col. 3)} + \text{Available machine hours}}{\text{Forecasted weekly usage (col. 5)}}$$

$$= \frac{213.95 + 96.5}{83.54} = 3.72 \text{ weeks}$$

Item	(6) Runout time (computed above)	(7) Total items required (in units) (4) × (6)	(8) Schedule (total items less beginning inventory) (7) − (2)	(9) Production schedule in machine hours (1) × (8)
A	3.72	223	98	19.6
B	3.72	316	66	5.3
C	3.72	112	37	18.5
D	3.72	357	57	5.0
E	3.72	290	51	7.7
F	3.72	156	58	40.6

EXHIBIT 14.16
Runout time determination for items with established lot sizes

Item	(1) Established production lot size (units)	(2) Inventory on hand (units)	(3) Forecasted weekly usage (units)	(4) Runout time (2) ÷ (3)	(5) Order of scheduling lot size (1) item	(6) Cumulative hours from (1) × Exhibit 14.15 col (1)
A	90	125	60	2.08	A	18
B	150	250	85	2.94	F	67
C	70	75	30	2.5	C	102
D	160	300	96	3.12	B	114
E	100	239	78	3.06	E	129
F	70	98	42	2.33	D	143.4

MASS PRODUCTION SCHEDULING

Though mass production is often thought of as synonymous with automobile production, it appears in other forms as well—in the manufacture of electronic components such as resistors (which are made on automatic equipment), in the forming and assembly of appliances and watches, and in the cutting and sewing of clothing, to name but a few. One way of viewing mass production is to think of it as the extreme case of batch production, where one production order becomes the focus of the production facility for an extended period of time. The physical layout is usually changed to concentrate on flow of the product. Special-purpose equipment, highly specialized tools, and straight-line production are typical in mass production. A *flow shop* is a mass production shop since the arrangement of machines, work centers, transfer equipment, and so forth is intended to facilitate easy flow of the product.

It could be argued, however, that *pure* mass production is a rarity, since even high-volume operations permit variation in the item manufactured. Thus, while a General Motors plant fabricates and assembles Chevrolets, each car may have some special feature making it different from preceding or succeeding cars on the line. Hence, the requirement of product homogeneity in the definition of mass production must be loosely interpreted.

The approach used in scheduling mass production operations depends greatly on the technology by which the product is transformed. If the work is mainly manual and utilizes a production line, as in the assembly stages of telephone manufacture, the scheduling problem becomes one of determining the operator task time required to achieve the desired output rate and then evenly distributing these tasks among the production workers. In such situations, the assembly line balancing techniques discussed in Chapter 8 would be appropriate.

Beyond the balancing problem posed in many mass production operations is the problem of coordinating the flow of materials both to and from the point of transformation, whether that transformation is performed on one large machine, in stages in different departments, or on an assembly line. What management wants to avoid is excessive inventory buildup of raw materials at the initial processing point, in-process inventory at various stages in the process, and finished-goods inventory at the end of the process. At the same time, management also wants to assure that raw materials, subassemblies, and finished goods are always available to assure a smooth flow of production and to meet customer demand. Achieving this balance requires the development of subschedules relating to the ordering of raw materials, the completion time for subassemblies, and the removal of finished products to storage areas. In the case of large products that are expensive to store, the production schedules have to be dovetailed with transportation schedules for outside shipping agencies such as railroads and ships.

Scheduling mass production is similar in respects to process scheduling (discussed next) in that the system is designed with a specified rate of output. For example, if an automobile assembly line was designed with tasks and a cycle time to produce, say, 57 cars per hour, if dealers encounter a sales slump, the manufacturer can not simply decide to slow the line down to, say, 45 or 50 cars per hour to prevent inventory buildup. Such a slow down (or a speed up) entails a complete redesign of all work stations. Manufacturers react to increased demand by working longer (overtime or weekends), not faster. They respond to sales slumps by closing the plant for a week or two; thus news articles such as: "Company X is closing its Detroit plant for two weeks to reduce inventory of unsold cars."

PROCESS SCHEDULING

Separating scheduling from aggregate production planning is extremely difficult in process industries since the desired product output combinations and sequences are generally determined during the planning phase. In an oil refinery, for example, an optimum schedule can be derived for the quantity and mix of various fuels, taking into account the productive capacity, storage costs, and profit by use of the linear programming simplex algorithm. The scheduling problem then becomes one of controlling the refining process from the distillation of crude oil through blending and storage. Typical scheduling problems of priorities, sequencing, and evaluation criteria are essentially answered before the fact.

Some interesting problems in process scheduling are encountered in utilities such as electrical plants. A unique feature of these operations is that the product output cannot be stored, yet it must always be available to meet a continuous though varying demand.

A particular power plant might experience a weekly demand pattern as shown in Exhibit 14.17. The task is to schedule the generators to minimize the operating costs of startup, level, and shutdown operations entailed in meeting these demand variations. The typical basis for such determinations is the incremental cost at various output levels coupled with the incremental costs of changing operating levels. These cost comparisons are ideally suited to computerization. In fact, a substantial number of installations employ computers to monitor the system-loading conditions, to determine the most economical allocation of generation among units, and to send control impulses to each of the units.

Underground mining also presents some interesting scheduling problems since operations have to be carried out in cycles along a changing workface. For example, drilling, blasting, loading, roof bracing, and movement of machines are carried out one after another; however, since the time of each mining operation will vary according to the nature of the deposit, these operations occur not at fixed times but at random intervals. Fortunately, given enough observations of cycle time variations, it is possible to derive statistical distributions that can become inputs to a queuing

EXHIBIT 14.17
Weekly demand pattern for a power plant

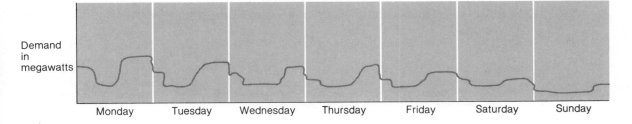

Demand in megawatts

Monday   Tuesday   Wednesday   Thursday   Friday   Saturday   Sunday

theory analysis or a simulation analysis. The findings from such analyses can then be used to derive a schedule for efficient allocation of personnel and machinery at the work area and to determine the timing and sequencing of transportation equipment.

SCHEDULING HIGH-CONTACT SERVICES

In terms of scheduling techniques, most high-contact service systems use very primitive methods that range from appointment lists, to "take a number" systems to determine service priorities. In small service operations, such simple procedures suffice; however, for large, custom service operations, such as hospital and branch banking (which may have several stages), greater effort must go into designing scheduling systems. Banks have made conscious efforts to improve their customer scheduling through the provision of more tellers, drive-in windows, and extended business hours, although their scheduling rules (first-come, first-served) remain unchanged. Hospitals, on the other hand, present a far more difficult area for efficient scheduling. We will now turn to three aspects of hospital operations that have significant scheduling problems—admissions, surgery, and nursing.

Hospital admissions scheduling

Milsum, Turban, and Vertinsky[11] have developed a schematic representation of three admission systems, which they relate to an input-output model consisting of three decision points or "filters." At the top of Exhibit 14.18, we see this input-output model and beneath it, three selected admission (and referral) systems which are found in different parts of the world.

In North America (System A), physicians are granted hospital privileges and make a tentative decision as to which hospital each patient will be sent. This decision is subject to approval by hospital administrators and is monitored by a hospital utilization committee. In Europe, System B is typical of countries in which health care is centralized. Here the referring physician is usually a general practitioner, and full-time specialists at available hospitals screen incoming patients. Also in Europe, System C, first instituted in Rotterdam, utilizes a city-wide Central Admissions Bureau (CAB), which directs patients of referring physicians to any one of several hospitals according to bed availability. (The authors note that this system has several advantages over the other two.)

Four major decision variables come into play in analyzing different scheduling policies. These are cited in Exhibit 14.19 along with the quantitative techniques and measures of system effectiveness that have been applied to the problem.

---

[11] Modified from J. Milsum, E. Turban, and I. Vertinsky, "Hospital Admissions Systems: Their Evaluation and Management," *Management Science*, vol. 19, no. 6 (February 1973), pp. 656–58.

EXHIBIT 14.18
Schematic representation of selected admission systems

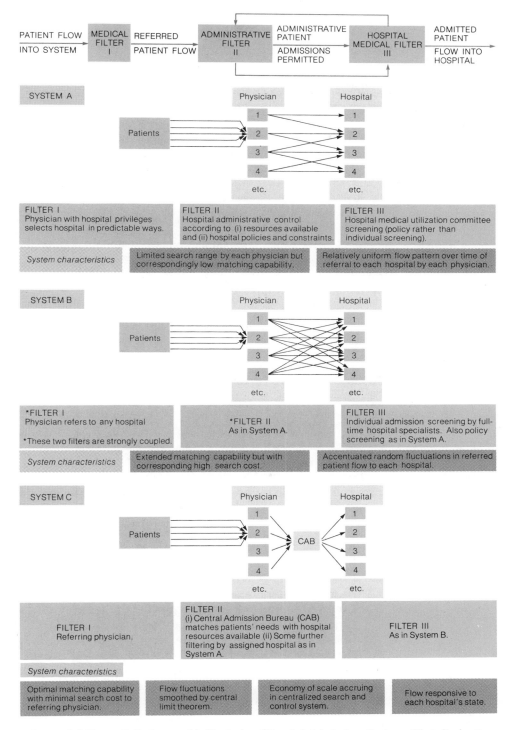

PATIENT FLOW INTO SYSTEM → MEDICAL FILTER I → REFERRED PATIENT FLOW → ADMINISTRATIVE FILTER II → ADMINISTRATIVE PATIENT / ADMISSIONS PERMITTED → HOSPITAL MEDICAL FILTER III → ADMITTED PATIENT FLOW INTO HOSPITAL

SYSTEM A

Physician   Hospital

Patients → 1, 2, 3, 4 etc. → 1, 2, 3, 4 etc.

FILTER I
Physician with hospital privileges selects hospital in predictable ways.

FILTER II
Hospital administrative control according to (i) resources available and (ii) hospital policies and constraints.

FILTER III
Hospital medical utilization committee screening (policy rather than individual screening).

System characteristics
Limited search range by each physician but correspondingly low matching capability.

Relatively uniform flow pattern over time of referral to each hospital by each physician.

SYSTEM B

Physician   Hospital

Patients → 1, 2, 3, 4 etc. → 1, 2, 3, 4 etc.

*FILTER I
Physician refers to any hospital

*These two filters are strongly coupled.

*FILTER II
As in System A.

FILTER III
Individual admission screening by full-time hospital specialists. Also policy screening as in System A.

System characteristics
Extended matching capability but with corresponding high search cost.

Accentuated random fluctuations in referred patient flow to each hospital.

SYSTEM C

Physician   Hospital

Patients → 1, 2, 3, 4 etc. → CAB → 1, 2, 3, 4 etc.

FILTER I
Referring physician.

FILTER II
(i) Central Admission Bureau (CAB) matches patients' needs with hospital resources available (ii) Some further filtering by assigned hospital as in System A.

FILTER III
As in System B.

System characteristics

Optimal matching capability with minimal search cost to referring physician.

Flow fluctuations smoothed by central limit theorem.

Economy of scale accruing in centralized search and control system.

Flow responsive to each hospital's state.

Source: J. Milsum; E. Turban; and I. Vertinsky, "Hospital Admissions Systems: Their Evaluation and Management," *Management Science*, vol. 19, no. 6 (February 1973), p. 649.

EXHIBIT 14.19
Decision variables and techniques used in studies of hospital admissions schedules

Decision variables	Decision making policies	Evaluation technique	Sample measures of effectiveness
Number of patients to be scheduled daily	Schedule a constant number every day	Queuing Simulation	1. Level of occupancy 2. Overflow (overload) 3. Stabilization in bed occupancy 4. Variation in daily admission
	Schedule a variable number each day as a function of bed occupancy		
Feasible admission date for each applicant	Analysis of each applicant Number of patients with same health needs should be assigned to a starting date	Linear programming	Deviation from ideal starting date vs. turning a patient away
Scheduling of operations in operating rooms	1. First came, first served 2. Longest cases first 3. Shortest cases first	Simulation	1. Utilization of facilities 2. Average no. of patients waiting 3. Delayed cases 4. Average overtime per day
Scheduling of a standby emergency hospital	Every nth day, or k_1 consecutive days on with k_2 consecutive days off	Simulation	Stabilization of bed occupancy

Source: Modified from J. Milsum; E. Turban; and I. Vertinsky, "Hospital Admissions Systems: Their Evaluation and Management," *Management Science*, vol. 19, no. 6 (February 1973), pp. 656–58.

Surgery scheduling

Three researchers[12] used simulation to evaluate five strategies for improving the utilization of operating rooms, recovery rooms, and medical personnel. These strategies (justified on the grounds that operating and recovery times are fairly predictable) were as follows:

1. Random input to surgery. This was the strategy currently being followed by the hospital being studied.
2. Preemptive priority according to need for patient's use of recovery room (without regard to length of surgery).
3. Inverted lineup. Patients requiring the longest surgery are served first. (Long surgery typically requires a stay in the recovery room.) Those not requiring the use of the recovery room are operated on last, with their surgery priority determined by longest surgery first.
4. Longest surgery first, but no priority assigned to those not needing recovery rooms.
5. Special categories of patients first according to rule 3. (That is, patients

---

[12] N. Kwak, P. Kuzdrall, and H. Schmitz, "The GPSS Simulation of Scheduling Policies for Surgical Patients," *Management Science*, vol. 22, no. 9 (May 1976), pp. 972–81.

who require major surgery of long duration and recovery room facilities are scheduled first.)

The main findings of the study were that strategies 2 through 5 provided improvements in utilization rates for both surgery and recovery facilities. On average, Strategies 2 through 5 yield schedules requiring 2.4 hours per day less time in staffing recovery than the current strategy. This comes about because patients arrive later in recovery rooms. Following rule 4 would require one less registered nurse and one less operating room technician. The authors point out that the savings in salaries would be greater than the cost of scheduling.

Nurse scheduling

Abernathy, Baloff, and Hershey state, "The key element of effective nurse staffing is a well-conceived procedure for achieving an overall balance between the size of the nursing staff and the expected patient demand."[13] Their procedure, termed "aggregate budgeting," is predicated on a variety of interrelated activities and has a primary output, a short-term schedule. A number of severe practical problems confront hospitals in deriving an effective yet low-cost aggregate budget. These difficulties along with possible remedies are listed in Exhibit 14.20.

EXHIBIT 14.20
General problems in nurse scheduling

Problem	Possible solution
Accuracy of patient load forecast	Forecast frequently and rebudget monthly. Closely monitor seasonal demands, communicable diseases, and current occupancy.
Forecasting nurse availability	Develop work standards for nurses for each level of possible demand (requires systematic data collection and analysis).
Complexity and time to rebudget	Use available computer programs.
Flexibility in scheduling	Use variable staffing: Set regular staff levels slightly above minimum and absorb variation with broad-skilled float nurses, part-time nurses, and overtime.

Though most hospitals still use cut-and-try methods in schedule development, management scientists have applied optimizing techniques to the problem with some success. For example, a linear programming model has been developed[14] that, assuming a known, short-run (that is, three to four days) demand for nursing care, develops a staffing pattern that:

---

[13] W. Abernathy, N. Baloff, and J. Hershey, "The Nurse Staffing Problem: Issues and Prospects," *Sloan Management Review*, vol. 13, no. 1 (Fall 1971).

[14] D. Warner, and J. Prawda, "A Mathematical Programming Model for Scheduling Nursing Personnel in a Hospital," *Management Science*, vol. 19, no. 4 (December 1972), pp. 411–22.

1. Specifies the number of nurses of each skill class to be assigned among the wards and nursing shifts.
2. Satisfies total nursing personnel capacity constraints.
3. Allows for limited substitution of tasks among nurses.
4. Minimizes the cost of nursing care shortage for the scheduling period.

School bus scheduling

The general objectives of bus scheduling are to minimize the number of routes, keep mileage at a minimum, have no overloaded buses, and keep route travel time at or below some acceptable level. Angel et al. have developed a two-stage approach to solve this problem.[15] The first stage consists of collecting data about students (grade, address, and school) and making the assignment of students to pick-up points. Then, utilizing a map, distances between stops and bus travel time between them is obtained. A mathematical programming algorithm is then applied to find the shortest path in time between any pair of bus stops. Also, the number and capacities of the buses, maximum route time in minutes, loading time per student, and allowance for extra time at each stop are obtained. The second stage consists of the actual scheduling, which in essence entails the use of mathematical programming to combine pairs of stops in such a way as to minimize time and distance traveled. The schedule output identifies the number of students, arrival time of the bus, and the time to load the bus for each stop. It also contains summary data about the route on such factors as route time, loading time, driving speed, total students, total stops, and miles driven.

Airline scheduling

One of the most complex standardized service situations is encountered in the airline branch of the transportation industry. Airline scheduling is essentially a list of single-leg flights to which specific aircraft are ultimately routed.[16] Since airplane flight times, refueling times, maintenance times, and so forth are variable, scheduled departure and arrival times will not always be met unless the allowed times are appreciably longer than the average time taken for these activities. Hence the maxim, "The tighter a schedule, the worse its inherent performance."

The scheduling problem encountered by airlines extends beyond the equipment itself. Crew scheduling, for instance, presents a sizable problem: Pilots' salaries are quite high, and thus, it behooves management to make full use of their flying skills each month. Likewise, it is desirable to keep stewardesses working on as many flights as their contracts allow and to avoid "deadheading" and paying for in-transit lodging for airline personnel in general.

---

[15] R. Angel, et al., "Computer Assisted School Bus Scheduling," *Management Science*, vol. 18, no. 6 (February 1973).

[16] Airline scheduling is often confused with airline routing. The distinction is that *scheduling* refers to determining between which places and at what times flights are to be provided while *routing* refers to assigning available plans to those scheduled services in an optimal manner.

In terms of the specific techniques of scheduling, a number of airlines are using computerized Monte Carlo simulation models as a basis for their equipment, manpower, and maintenance schedules. These models have the capability of simultaneously handling such relevant factors as aircraft capacity and availability, maintenance requirements, customer demand, cost per flight, and crew availability, and simulating them in "real time" to arrive at a scheduling decision.[17] By way of example, suppose that a particular plane is in transit and is grounded for minor repairs. The scheduling system would take note of this and determine, via simulation, whether another plane should be dispatched to continue the flight. Entering into this decision (and the simulation) would be the disposition of the original crew (Should it be part of the continuation flight or should it be rerouted?), the effect on other flights of removal of the backup plane, and, of course, the expected time to complete repairs.

Scheduling of airplane landings and takeoffs has also been simulated, and CRT display units are used by flight controllers to evaluate alternative approach paths, runways, and circling patterns in light of existing air traffic and weather conditions. The sophistication of these systems is such that it is possible to obtain a progressive graphic display of simulated alternative airplane locations in the air and on the ground.[18]

CONCLUSION

The objective of this chapter has been to provide some insight into the nature of scheduling and the diversity of systems where it is performed. To date, the most studied area in the scheduling literature is the job shop. This topic has occupied researchers because of the mathematical problems it poses and because the conclusions drawn from its analysis help provide insight into analogous scheduling situations. Now, however, scheduling research, augmented by the computer, has been undertaken in virtually every type of productive system. In manufacturing, its focus has shifted to integrating the short-run scheduling problem with long-term capacity planning in the context of materials requirements planning (see Chapter 16). In services, it has tended to focus on areas of major public concerns—health care, fuel production, and transportation. It seems now that the major constraints in application of scheduling research lie in making the scheduling systems understandable to those who must use them and making them sufficiently flexible to cope with the myriad daily events which can not be planned.

---

[17] An information system is said to operate in "real time" when it has the ability to collect data on events as they occur, to process that data immediately, and to use the new information to influence succeeding events.

[18] Julian Reitman, *Computer Simulation Applications* (New York: John Wiley & Sons, 1971), pp. 367–401.

REVIEW AND DISCUSSION QUESTIONS

1. Distinguish between a job shop, a flow shop, and a hybrid job shop.

2. What is meant by a schedule evaluation criterion?

3. Discuss the role of the master production schedule in the production system.

4. Do you accept the list of 11 principles (or observations) about master scheduling which were used by eight firms.

5. It has been suggested that many of our country's pressing social problems are essentially scheduling problems. Defend this assertion by using some examples.

6. What scheduling rules are commonly used in industry? What is a longest-processing-time rule? Why might it be employed?

7. It is common practice to master schedule by product families rather than specific models. What is the logic behind this?

8. What is Q-control©? What does it try to achieve?

9. In the United States, we make certain assumptions about the customer service priority rules used in banks, restaurants, and retail stores. If you have the opportunity, ask a foreigner what rules are used in his country. To what factors might you attribute the differences, if any?

10. What are some specific advantages of the System C hospital admission structure from the point of view of scheduling? What are some disadvantages of the system from the point of view of the patient? The physician?

11. A patient in a hospital encounters several schedules besides the ones noted in the chapter. What are these other schedules? Suggest how they might conflict with one another for a given patient.

PROBLEMS

1. Mr. Regan has just run across the runout method of scheduling and wonders whether he could apply this technique to allocating expense money among his three children. What he would like to do is to occasionally divide some of the money he might add—say $5, $10, or $20—among his children so that when added to what they currently have, it will cover each of their expenses for the same period of time. Mr. Regan has three children; his son is a freshman in high school and uses $1.95 per day ($.50 each way bus fare plus $.95 for lunch). His daughter is in junior high and uses $1.65 per day (bus fare $.50 each way plus $.65 for lunch). His youngest son is in elementary school and uses $.55 per day (there is a free school bus). Below is the current expense money held by each child along with the scheduled expense just mentioned.

	Expense money in hand	Daily expenses
Eldest son	$3.20	$1.95
Daughter	2.40	1.65
Youngest son	1.80	0.55

Mr. Regan would like to divide $20 among his children so that each would have the same number of days of expense money. Use the runout method to find the appropriate allocation.

2. Joe's Auto Seat Cover and Paint Shop is bidding on a contract to do all the custom work for Smiling Ed's used car dealership. One of the main requirements in obtaining this contract is rapid delivery time, since Ed— for reasons we shall not go into here—wants the cars facelifted and back on his lot in a hurry. Ed has told Joe that if he can refit and repaint five cars which he, Ed, has just received (from an unnamed source) in 24 hours or less, the contract will be his. Below is the time (in hours) required in the refitting shop and the paint shop for each of the five cars. Assuming that cars go through the refitting operations before they are repainted, can Joe meet the time requirements and get the contract?

Car	Refitting time	Repainting time
A	6 hours	3 hours
B	0	4
C	5	2
D	8	6
E	2	1

3. Joe has three cars that must be overhauled by his ace mechanic, Jane. Given the following data about the cars, use Conway's "Rule 4" (least slack per remaining operation) to determine Jane's scheduling priority for each.

Car	Customer pick-up time (hours hence)	Remaining overhaul time (hours)	Remaining operations
A	10	4	Painting
B	17	5	Wheel alignment, painting
C	15	1	Chrome plating, painting, seat repair

4. There are seven jobs which must be processed in two operations: A and B. All seven jobs must go through A and B in that sequence (i.e., A first, then B). Determine the optimal order in which the jobs should be sequenced through the process using the times as follows:

Job	Time required in process A	Time required in process B
1	9	6
2	8	5
3	7	7
4	6	3
5	1	2
6	2	6
7	4	7

5. What is the optimal assignment for the following cost matrix:

Worker \ Task	1	2	3	4
1	9	15	21	27
2	21	18	9	33
3	18	6	12	15
4	30	36	15	27

6. Joe has the opportunity to do a big repair job for a local motorcycle club, "The Cretins." (Their cycles were accidentally run over by a garbage truck.) The compensation for the job is good, but it is very important that the total repair time for the five cycles to be fixed be less than 40 hours. (The leader of the club has stated that he would be very distressed if the cycles were not available for a planned "rumble.") Joe knows from experience that repairs of this type often entail several trips between processes for a given cycle, so estimates of time are difficult to provide. Still, Joe has historical data about the probability that a job will start in each process, processing time in each process, and transitional probabilities between each pair of processes. (The data are tabulated below.)

Process	Probability of job starting in process	Processing time probability (hours)			Probability of going from process to other processes or completion (out)			
		1	2	3	Frame	Engine work	Painting	Out
Frame repair	0.5	0.2	0.4	0.4	—	0.4	0.4	0.2
Engine work	0.3	0.6	0.1	0.3	0.3	—	0.4	0.3
Painting	0.2	0.3	0.3	0.4	0.1	0.1	—	0.8

Given this information, use simulation to determine the repair times for each cycle and display your results on a Gantt chart showing a FCFS schedule. (Assume that only one cycle can be worked on at a time in each process.) Based upon your simulation, what do you recommend Joe do next?

7. A manufacturing facility has five jobs to be scheduled into production. The following table states the processing times plus the necessary wait times and other necessary delays for each of the jobs.

Assume that today is April 3 and the jobs are due on the dates shown:

Job	Days of actual processing time required	Days of necessary delay time	Total time required	Date job due
1	2	12	14	April 30
2	5	8	13	April 21
3	9	15	24	April 28
4	7	9	16	April 29
5	4	22	28	April 27

Question: Determine *two* schedules stating the order in which the jobs are to be done. Use the *critical ratio* priority rule as one of the rules. You may use any other rule for the second schedule so long as you state what the rule is.

8. Jobs A, B, C, D, and E must go through processes I and II in that sequence (i.e., process I first, then process II).

Use Johnson's rule to determine the optimal sequence to schedule the jobs to minimize the total required time.

Job	Required processing time on A	Required processing time on B
A	4	5
B	16	14
C	8	7
D	12	11
E	3	9

• 9. For a variety of reasons, Joe finds himself in charge of what might be referred to as a "captive machine shop" in a government-operated establishment. The machine shop fabricates and paints metal products, including license plates, road signs, window screens, and door frames, and Joe's major responsibility is to balance the utilization of the equipment across all four products in such a way that demand for each product is satisfied. Given the following data, how might Joe schedule the four products in order to achieve this objective for the next week? What would his schedule look like?

Item	Inventory	Production time per unit	Forecasted weekly usage
Window screens	200	0.1 hour	100
Door frames	100	0.06	50
Road signs	70	0.3	60
License plates	150	0.7	125

Available machine hours = 90/week.

10. A textile manufacturer is planning for his next week's production and wants to use the runout method of scheduling. Part of his logic for using the runout method in this case is because he is running the same design on towels, wash cloths, sheets, and pillow cases. He would therefore like to carry the same period amounts in the event the design is changed.

Following are the existing quantities on hand, the production times of each, and the forecasted demands. There are 120 hours of capacity available on the mill in three shifts. (The same machine is used to make all the items, so the problem is to determine which will be made, how many, and how much machine time to allocate to each.)

Item	Number of units on hand	Production time for each in hours	Forecast demand per week
Wash cloths	500	.1	300
Towels	200	.15	400
Sheets	150	.20	200
Pillow cases	300	.15	200

11. The following matrix shows the costs for assigning individuals A, B, C, and D to do jobs 1, 2, 3, and 4. Solve the problem showing your final assignments in order to minimize cost.

	1	2	3	4
A	7	9	3	5
B	3	11	7	6
C	4	5	6	2
D	5	9	10	12

o 12. Joe has achieved a position of some power in the institution in which he currently resides and works. In fact, things have gone so well that he has decided to divide the day-to-day operations of his business activities among four trusted subordinates: Big Louie, Dirty Dave, Baby Face Nick, and Tricky Dick. The question is how he should do this in order to take advantage of his associates' unique skills and to minimize the costs from running all areas for the next year. The following matrix summarizes the costs that arise under each possible combination of men and areas.

	Area			
	1	2	3	4
Big Louie	$1,400	$1,800	$ 700	$1,000
Dirty Dave	600	2,200	1,500	1,300
Baby Face Nick	800	1,100	1,200	500
Tricky Dick	1,000	1,800	2,100	1,500

√13. The following matrix shows the costs of each of four workers performing each of four tasks. Select the optimal assignment of one worker to each task to minimize the total cost of having all tasks completed.

Worker \ Task	1	2	3	4
1	20	36	28	12
2	24	44	12	28
3	8	20	16	24
4	48	36	20	40

14. Having served his time through two editions of this book, Joe was released from his government job. Based on his excellent performance, he was able to land a job as production scheduler in a brand new custom refinishing auto service shop located near the Mexican border. (Oh no! Here we go again!) Techniques have improved in the several years he was out of circulation, so processing times are considerably faster. This system is capable of handling ten cars per day. The flow sequence is: customizing first followed by repainting.

Car	Customizing time (hours)	Painting (hours)
1	3.0	1.2
2	2.0	0.9
3	2.5	1.3
4	0.7	0.5
5	1.6	1.7
6	2.1	0.8
7	3.2	1.4
8	0.6	1.8
9	1.1	1.5
10	1.8	0.7

In what sequence should Joe schedule the cars?

SELECTED BIBLIOGRAPHY

Baker, K. R. *Introduction to Sequencing and Scheduling.* New York: John Wiley & Sons, 1974.

Berry, W. L.; Vollmann, T. E.; and Whybark, D. C. *Master Scheduling.* Washington, D.C.: American Production and Inventory Control Society, 1979, pp. 11–14.

Buffa, E. S. *Operations Management: The Management of Productive Systems.* New York: Wiley/Hamilton, 1976.

Conway, R. W.; Maxwell, William L.; and Miller, Louis W. *Theory of Scheduling.* Reading, Mass.: Addison-Wesley, 1967.

Day, James E., and Hottenstein, Michael P. "Review of Sequencing Research," *Naval Research Logistics Quarterly,* vol. 27, no. 1 (March 1970), pp. 11–39.

Eilon, Samuel *Elements of Production Planning and Control.* New York: Macmillan Co., 1962.

Johnson, S. M. "Optimal Two Stage and Three Stage Production Schedules with Setup Times Included," *Naval Logistics Quarterly,* vol. 1, no. 1 (March 1954), pp. 61–68.

Magee, J. F., and Boodman, D. M. *Production Planning and Inventory Control.* 2d ed. New York: McGraw-Hill Book Company, 1967.

Niland, Powell *Production Planning, Scheduling, and Inventory Control.* New York: Macmillan Co., 1971.

O'Brien, James J. *Scheduling Handbook.* New York: McGraw-Hill Book Company, 1969.

Sandman, W. E., with Hayes, J. P. *How to Win Productivity in Manufacturing.* Dresher, Pa.: Yellow Book of Pennsylvania, Inc., 1980.

Woolsey, R. D., and Swanson, H. S. *Operations Research for Immediate Application, A Quick and Dirty Manual.* New York: Harper & Row, 1975.

Chapter

15

DESIGN OF INVENTORY SYSTEMS FOR INDEPENDENT DEMAND: CLASSICAL MODELS AND PRACTICE

For want of a nail, the shoe was lost . . .

Inventory is the stock of any item or resource used in the creation of an organization. This includes raw materials, work in process finished goods, people, equipment, supplies, and buildings. An *inventory system* is the set of policies and controls which monitors levels of inventory and determines what levels should be maintained, when stock should be replenished, and what order sizes should be placed. A firm cannot exist without inventory, and how well a firm controls its inventory affects how well the firm performs its mission. Inventory represents an investment about which management makes decisions more frequently than other kinds of investment; inventory theory is used to make such investment decisions.

We have divided inventory into two chapters. This chapter introduces some basic concepts and mathematical models essential to designing an inventory system based on independent demand. In Chapter 16, we will present the topic of Materials Requirements Planning, which is based on dependent demand. In both chapters we will discuss commercial computer programs which are commonly used for control of large inventories.

INDEPENDENT VERSUS DEPENDENT DEMAND

From our discussions in Chapter 13, the reader no doubt has recognized the importance in production planning of being able to predict demand. Where demand is known and certain, highly efficient production is possible and practicable; where it is not, compensating mechanisms—varying the work force, subcontracting, and so forth—must be brought into play to cope with uncertainty. An analogous situation exists for inventory control procedures. If the demand for an end item is known, then the demand for component items is also known, and securing the right quantities at the right times of these components is, conceptually at least, a straightforward mechanical process. By way of example, if an auto company knows that it will sell 2,000 cars next month, it knows that it must have in stock or on order 10,000 wheels (including the spares). In this situation, we would say that the number of wheels required is derived from the number of cars to be sold and that demand for wheels is *dependent* on sales of the end item (cars). In contrast, when demand for a product or component is uncertain, then inventory ordering procedures must be modified to account for this by trading off the cost of holding extra inventory with the cost of more frequent ordering. Situations such as these commonly arise in job shops and various service systems (for example, hospital supplies, retailing, book publishing) and are characterized as *independent* demand environments. This chapter is concerned with what may be termed *classical* inventory systems and models that are appropriate for independent demand situations. The reader should note, however, that some of the models are used to solve manufacturing inventory problems, which may also be analyzed using the dependent material requirements planning method covered in Chapter 16.

ROLE OF INVENTORY

As mentioned in the opening sentence of this chapter, the term *inventory* refers to the stock of any item used in the operation of an organization. In its complete scope, inventory would include inputs such as human, financial, energy, equipment, and raw materials; outputs, such as parts, components, and finished goods; and interim stages of the process, such as partially finished goods or work in process. The choice of which items to include in inventory depends on the organization. A manufacturing operation can have an inventory of personnel, machines, and working capital, as well as raw materials and finished goods. An airline can have an inventory of seats, a farm an inventory of uncut wheat, and an engineering firm an inventory of engineering talent.

Two key questions determine whether an item can be classified as inventory:

1. "Can the item be *specifically identified* as different from all other items?" Thus, to be different, the item must be changed in some manner by the process. This may be a change in physical form or shape (casting a steel

housing or milling wheat), a change in the physical or chemical characteristics (hardening the steel housing or enriching the flour), or a change in appearance (painting the housing or bleaching the flour).

2. "Can the item be stored?" *Storability* refers to the ability to be placed into storage for some period of time. "Temporary storage" refers to the brief storage of items in the production area waiting for the next phase. "Permanent storage" generally implies that the item will be physically moved into a storage area and a record kept showing data such as the number of units on hand and date of placement in inventory. Items are withdrawn from permanent inventory either to be used in the productive process or to satisfy an outside demand.

Product inventory versus service inventory

Writers have often wrestled with a definition to distinguish between a "product" and a "service." Most commonly, the differentiation tends to be made along the lines of stating that a product offers a service to the consumer (though the service may be deferred to a later time), while a service is being consumed at the same rate that it is being produced. A major difference between a product and a service is that *a service is not storable.* Thus, for an automobile tune-up service, while specific phases of the service sequence are identifiable (spark plugs changed, points adjusted, carburetor cleaned, and so forth) a tune-up, as such, must be performed on the vehicle and cannot, itself, be stored as inventory. The closest one can come to stocking a service is to prepackage the required components to be used in the service; for example, a package containing a set of spark plugs, a set of points, and a condenser. Therefore, it seems reasonable to define manufacturing inventory in terms of *product output* and service inventory in terms of service *capacity.* If we accept this distinction, we can then expand the definitions as follows:

In manufacturing, inventory generally refers to *inanimate physical entities that contribute to or become part of a firm's product output,* and it is typically classified as:

Raw materials.
Finished products.
Component parts.
Supplies.
Work in process.

In services, inventory refers to the *productive components necessary to administer the service* and may be classified as:

Physical space.
Number of channels or work places.
Service personnel.
Productive equipment.
Parts.
Supplies.

Thus, a beauty salon would list as inventory the number of chairs for operators to work on customers, the number of hair dryers and other appliances used, the stock of supplies, the number of operators, and the number of seats in the waiting room. Wholesalers and retailers would have an inventory of items for sale and the personnel and service capabilities to dispense these items. A repair facility would have an inventory of spare parts and supplies along with the service personnel and available space to perform the repair service. A hospital would have an inventory of rooms, patients' beds, medical supplies, housekeeping supplies, food supplies, medical and nursing staff, and food-service, housekeeping, and maintenance personnel.

The objective of inventory analysis in manufacturing is to specify (1) *when items should be ordered* and (2) *how large the order should be.* In services, the objective of inventory analysis is to specify (1) *which units of productive capacity* should be available to perform the service, and (2) *how many units* are to be available in each time period in order to provide some specified level of service. Determining the particular units, the "When?" and "How many?" decisions in inventory is complicated by the varied purposes of inventory and the variety of costs involved.

PURPOSES OF INVENTORY

A stock of inventory is kept to satisfy the following needs.

1. To maintain independence of operations. If a supply of needed materials is kept at a work center and if the work produced by that center is not immediately needed anywhere else, there is some flexibility in operating that center. Since there are costs for making each new production setup, this independence in operating the center allows management to consider economic production lot sizes.

An assembly line usually does not allow independence since it is fed raw materials to correspond with the line speed and has no work-in-process inventory other than what each worker is working on. The unit in process passes from one person to the next.

2. To meet variation in product demand. If the demand for the product is known precisely, it is feasible (though not necessarily economical) to produce the product to meet the demand exactly. In the usual case, however, demand is not completely known, and a *safety* or *buffer stock* must therefore be maintained to absorb variation.

3. To allow flexibility in production scheduling. The maintenance of higher levels of finished goods inventory relieves the pressure on the production system to get the goods out. This gives longer lead times, which allow not only production planning for smoother flow but permit lower-cost operation through more economical lot size production. High setup costs, for example, favor the production of a larger number of units once the setup has been made.

4. To provide a safeguard for variation in raw material delivery time. When material is ordered from a vendor, delays can occur for a variety of reasons: the normal variation in shipping time, which occasionally will be great; a shortage of materials at the vendor's plant, causing him to backlog orders; an unexpected strike at the vendor's plant or at one of the shipping companies; a lost order; or incorrect or defective material. Depending on the severity of the consequences of material shortage, a safety stock level is determined.

5. To take advantage of economic purchase order size. Obviously, there is a procedural cost for placing an order for goods, and the larger the size of each order, the fewer the number of orders that need be written. The placement of a larger order is also favored by the nonlinearity of shipping costs; that is, the larger the shipment, the lower the per unit cost.

INVENTORY COSTS

In making any decision that will affect inventory size, the following costs must be considered.

Holding (or carrying) costs. This is a broad category that includes the costs for storage facilities, handling, insurance, pilferage, breakage, obsolescence, depreciation, taxes, and the opportunity cost of capital. Obviously, high holding costs tend to favor low inventory levels and frequent replenishment.

Production change (or setup) costs. To make each different product involves obtaining the necessary materials, arranging specific equipment setups, filling out the required papers, appropriately charging time and materials, and moving out the previous stock of material. In addition, other costs may be involved in hiring, training, or layoff of workers, and in idle time or overtime.

If there were no costs or loss of time in changing from the production of one product to another, many small lots of products would be produced. This would reduce inventory levels, with a resulting savings in cost. However, changeover costs usually exist.

Since these costs are frequently difficult to identify within the inventory models that determine the size of lots for production, they are summarized under the catch-all heading of "setup" costs.

Ordering costs. These costs refer to the managerial and clerical costs entailed in preparing the purchase or production order. Common terminology subdivides these into two categories: (1) *header cost,* which is the cost of identifying and issuing an order to a single vendor, and (2) *line cost,* which is the cost for computing each separate item order from the same vendor. Thus, ordering three items from a vendor entails one header cost and three line costs.

Shortage costs. When the stock of an item is depleted, an order for that item must either wait until the stock is replenished or be canceled. There is a trade-off between carrying stock to satisfy demand and the costs resulting from stockout. This balance is sometimes difficult to obtain since it may not be possible to estimate lost profits, or the effects of lost customers, or lateness penalties. Frequently, the amount of the shortage cost is little more than a guess, although it is usually possible to specify the likely range of such costs.

The determination of quantities purchased from vendors or the size of lots submitted to the firm's productive facilities involves a search for the minimum total cost resulting from the combined effects of three individual costs: holding costs, production or ordering costs, and shortage costs. This determination, obtained by using mathematical models, is traditionally conceded to be the essence of inventory theory. This chapter will introduce several specific models to assist in searching for this minimum-cost combination.

INVENTORY SYSTEMS

An inventory system provides the organizational structure and the operating policies for maintaining and controlling goods to be inventoried. The inclusion of one or more inventory models within this system enables the determination of ordering and stocking rules. The system is responsible for ordering and receipt of goods: timing the order placement and keeping track of what has been ordered, how much, and from whom. Further, the system must provide follow-up to enable the answering of such questions as: Has the vendor received the order? Has it been shipped? Are the times correct? Are the procedures established for reordering or returning undesirable merchandise?

Classifying models by fixed-order quantity or fixed-time period

There are two general approaches to inventory systems, which in turn are commonly denoted by the models they employ. These systems, or models, are (1) the *fixed-order quantity* system (also called the economic order quantity, or EOQ) and (2) the *fixed-time period* system (also referred to variously as the *periodic* system, the *periodic review* system, and the *fixed-order interval* system).

The basic distinction between fixed-order quantity models and fixed-time period models is that the former is "event-triggered" while the latter is "time-triggered." That is, a fixed-order quantity model initiates an order when the "event" of reaching a specified reorder level occurs. This event may take place at any time, depending upon the demand for the items considered. In contrast, the fixed-time period model is limited to placing orders at the end of a predetermined time period; hence, the passage of time alone "triggers" the model. This important distinction, along with its resultant effect on the order quantity, Q, is summarized in Exhibit 15.1.

Exhibit 15.2 depicts what occurs when each of the two models is put into use and becomes an operating system. As we can see, the fixed-order quantity system focuses on order quantities and reorder points. Procedurally, each time a unit is taken out of stock, the withdrawal is logged

EXHIBIT 15.1
Fixed-order quantity and fixed-time period differences

Model	Order quantity	When order is placed
Fixed-order quantity (event triggered)	Q-constant (the same amount ordered each time)	R—when quantity on hand reaches the reorder level
Fixed-time period (time triggered)	Q-variable (varies each time order is placed)	T—when the review period arrives

EXHIBIT 15.2
Comparison of fixed-order quantity and fixed-time period reordering inventory systems

and the amount remaining in inventory is immediately compared to the reorder point. If it has dropped to this point, an order for *Q* items is placed. If it has not, the system remains in an idle state until the next withdrawal.

In the fixed-time period system, a decision to place an order is made after the stock has been counted or "reviewed." Whether an order is actually placed depends upon the inventory status at that time.

An interesting feature of this system is that no physical count of items

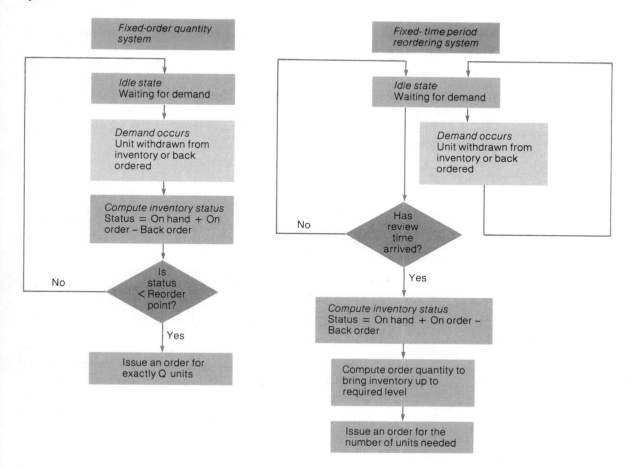

is made after an item is withdrawn—the tallying of inventory occurs only at the time designated for review. As shown in the diagram, this characteristic of fixed-time period systems results in two separate and independent loops: one for placing orders and another for issuing stock. The result of this independence is that inventory protection against stockout must be provided not only for the time between the issuance of a replenishment order and the receipt of the new stock (that is, the lead time) but for the entire period between reviews as well. Thus, in comparing the two systems, the fixed-time period review system will generally require a larger amount of inventory than the fixed-order quantity system. (More will be said about this point later.)

BASIC MODEL TYPES

The inventory models that will be covered in this chapter are broadly organized according to whether the demand is deterministic (known) or probabilistic (uncertain). Within each of these classes, fixed-order quantity and fixed-time period models are then presented.

The first models to be described under conditions of known demand are the simple or fixed-order quantity models, the fixed-order quantity model with usage, and the fixed-order quantity model with backorders allowed. This will be followed by the probabilistic models, which consist of the fixed-order quantity model and the fixed-time period model. A price-break model and a single-period model will then be presented. The last model technique to be presented is the determination of order quantities through marginal analysis.

Deterministic models (conditions of certainty)
The simplest models in this category occur when all aspects of the situation are known with certainty. If the annual demand for a product is 1,000 units, it is precisely 1,000—not 1,000 plus or minus 10 percent. The same is true for setup costs and holding costs. Although the assumption of complete certainty is rarely valid, it provides a good starting point for our coverage of inventory models. In addition, there are times when the errors introduced by assuming certainty are less costly than that incurred in obtaining more precise data or construction of a more complicated probabilistic model. For example, when unit cost or carrying costs are low, a simple model that assumes conditions of certainty is probably adequate.

Fixed-order quantity models. Fixed-order quantity models attempt to determine the specific point, R, at which an order will be placed and the size of that order, Q. The order point, R, is always a specified number of units actually in inventory. The solution to a fixed-order quantity model may stipulate something like this: When the number of units of inventory on hand drops to 36, place an order for 57 more units.

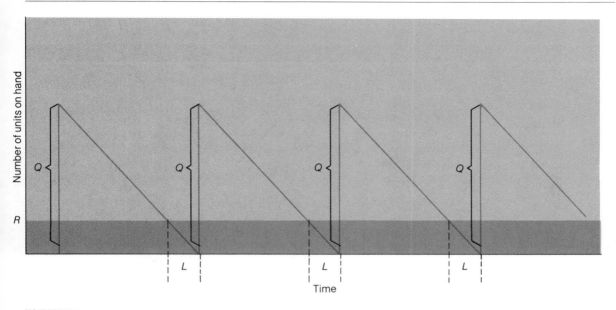

EXHIBIT 15.3
Basic fixed-order quantity model

Exhibit 15.3 and the ensuing derivation of the optimal order quantity are based on the following characteristics of the model:

Demand for the product is constant and uniform through the period.
Lead time (time from ordering to receipt) is constant.
Price per unit of product is constant.
Inventory holding cost is based on average inventory.
Ordering or setup costs are constant, and
All demands for the product will be satisfied (no backorders are allowed).

The "sawtooth effect" relating Q and R in Exhibit 15.3 shows that when inventory drops to point R, a reorder is placed. This order is received at the end of time period L, which does not vary in this model.

In constructing any inventory model, the first step is to develop a functional relationship between the variables of interest and the measure of effectiveness. In this case, since we are concerned with cost, the following equation would pertain.

$$\begin{array}{cccc} \text{Total} & \text{Annual} & \text{Annual} & \text{Annual} \\ \text{annual} = & \text{purchase} + & \text{ordering} + & \text{holding} \\ \text{cost} & \text{cost} & \text{cost} & \text{cost} \end{array}$$

or

$$TC = DC + \frac{D}{Q}S + \frac{Q}{2}H$$

where

$TC =$ Total annual cost
$D =$ Annual demand
$C =$ Purchase cost per unit
$Q =$ Quantity to be ordered (the optimum amount is termed the *economic order quantity*—EOQ—or Q_{opt})
$S =$ Cost of placing an order or making a production setup
$H =$ Annual holding and storage cost per unit of average inventory
$R =$ Reorder point
$L =$ Lead time

On the right-hand side of the equation, DC is the annual purchase cost for the units, $(D/Q)S$ is the annual ordering cost (the actual number of orders placed, D/Q, times the cost of each order, S), and $(Q/2)H$ is the annual holding cost (the average inventory, $Q/2$, times the cost per unit for holding and storage, H). These cost relationships are shown graphically in Exhibit 15.4.

The second step in model development is to find that order quantity, Q, for which total cost is a minimum. With reference to Exhibit 15.4—total cost is minimum at the point where the slope of the curve is zero. Using calculus, the appropriate procedure involves taking the derivative of total cost with respect to Q and setting this equal to zero. For the basic model considered here, the calculations would be as follows.

EXHIBIT 15.4
Annual product costs, based on size of the order

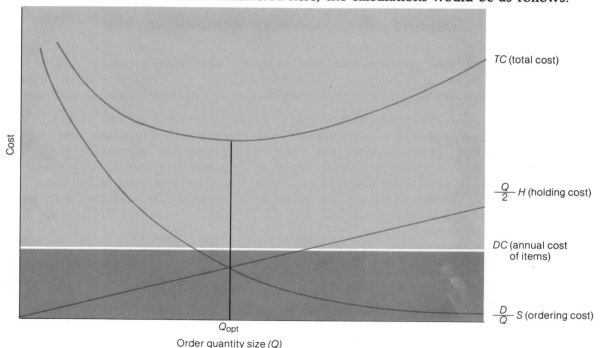

Order quantity size *(Q)*

TC (total cost)

$\frac{Q}{2} H$ (holding cost)

DC (annual cost of items)

$\frac{D}{Q} S$ (ordering cost)

Q_{opt}

Cost

$$TC = DC + \frac{D}{Q}S + \frac{Q}{2}H$$

$$\frac{dTC}{dQ} = 0 + \left(\frac{-DS}{Q^2}\right) + \frac{H}{2} = 0$$

$$Q_{\text{opt}} = \sqrt{\frac{2DS}{H}}$$

Since this simple model assumes constant demand and lead time, no safety stock is necessary, and the reorder point, R, is simply $R = \bar{d}L$ where

$\bar{d}$ = average daily demand [constant] and
L = lead time in days [constant].

Example 15.1. Find the economic order quantity and the reorder point, given the following data:

Annual demand (D) = 1,000 units
Average daily demand $(\bar{d})$ = 1,000/365
Ordering cost (S) = $5 per order
Holding cost (H) = $1.25 per unit per
year
Lead time (L) = 5 days
Cost per unit (C) = $12.50

The optimum order quantity is

$$Q_{\text{opt}} = \sqrt{\frac{2DS}{H}} = \sqrt{\frac{2(1,000)5}{1.25}} = \sqrt{8,000} = 89.4 \text{ units}$$

The reorder point is

$$R = \bar{d}L = \frac{1,000}{365}(5) = 13.7 \text{ units}$$

Rounding to the nearest unit, the inventory policy is as follows: When the number of units in inventory drops to 14, place an order for 89 more. The total annual cost will be

$$TC = DC + \frac{D}{Q}S + \frac{Q}{2}H$$

$$= 1,000(12.50) + \frac{1,000}{89}(5) + \frac{89}{2}(1.25)$$

$$= \$12,611.81$$

Note that in this example, the purchase cost of the units was not required to determine the order quantity and the reorder point.

Simple fixed-order quantity model with usage. Example 15.1 assumed that the quantity ordered would be received in one lot, but frequently this is not the case. In many situations, in fact, production of an inventory item and usage of that item take place simultaneously. This is particularly true where one part of a production system acts as a supplier to another part. For example, while aluminum extrusions are being made to fill an order for aluminum windows, the extrusions are cut and assembled before the entire extrusion order is completed.

The production with usage inventory model is only slightly different from the preceding model. If we let d denote a constant demand rate for some item going into production and p the production rate of that process which uses the item, we may develop the following total cost equation.[1]

$$TC = DC + \frac{D}{Q}S + \frac{(p-d)QH}{2p}$$

Again differentiating with respect to Q and setting the equation equal to zero, we obtain

$$Q_{opt} = \sqrt{\frac{2DS}{H} \cdot \frac{p}{(p-d)}}$$

EXHIBIT 15.5
**Fixed-order
quantity model
with usage
during
production
time**

This model is shown in Exhibit 15.5. We can see that the number of units on hand will always be less than the order quantity, Q.

Example 15.2. Product X is a standard item in a firm's inventory. Final assembly of the product is performed on an assembly line which is in operation every day. One of the components of product X (call it component X_1) is produced in another department. This department, when it

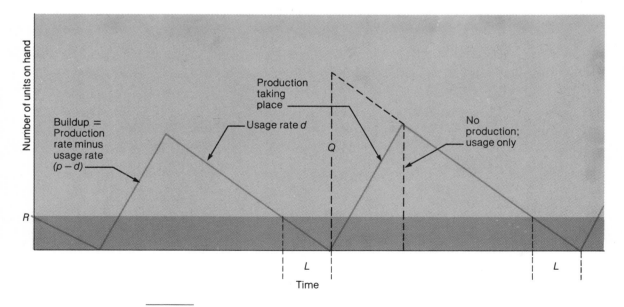

___
[1] Obviously, the production rate must exceed the rate of usage; otherwise Q would be infinite, resulting in continual production.

produces X_1, does so at the rate of 100 units per day. The assembly line uses component X_1 at the rate of 40 units per day.

Given the following data, what is the optimal lot size for production of component X_1?

$$\text{Daily usage rate } (d) = 40 \text{ units}$$
$$\text{Annual demand } (D) = 10{,}000 \text{ (40 units} \times 250 \text{ working days)}$$
$$\text{Daily production } (p) = 100 \text{ units}$$
$$\text{Cost for production setup } (S) = \$50$$
$$\text{Annual holding cost } (H) = \$0.50 \text{ per unit}$$
$$\text{Cost of component } X_1 \ (C) = \$7 \text{ each}$$
$$\text{Lead time } (L) = 7 \text{ days}$$

$$Q_{opt} = \sqrt{\frac{2DS}{H} \cdot \frac{p}{p-d}} = \sqrt{\frac{2(10{,}000)50}{0.50} \cdot \frac{100}{100-40}} = 1{,}826 \text{ units}$$
$$R = dL = 40(7) = 280 \text{ units}$$

This states that an order for 1,826 units of component X_1 should be placed when the stock drops to 280 units.

At 100 units per day, this run will take 18.26 days and will provide a 45.65-day supply for the assembly line (1,826/40). Theoretically, the department will be occupied with other work for the 27.39 days when component X_1 is not being produced.

Simple fixed-order quantity model with backorders. The first model presented in this chapter assumed that all demands would be met (shortages were not allowed). This was done indirectly, by assuming that the cost of running out of stock was infinite. Certainly there are cases where meeting all demands is just not worth the cost of carrying the necessary stock, and the most economical decision is to allow shortages. These shortages are filled as soon as the new order is received. Exhibit 15.6 illustrates this simple model with shortages allowed.

EXHIBIT 15.6
Fixed-order quantity with backorders

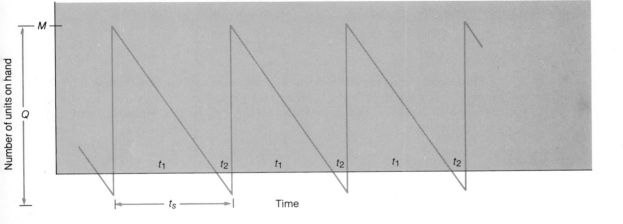

M = Replenishment level (in this case the maximum inventory level at the beginning of each order period)

Q = Quantity to be ordered

t_1 = Time when inventory surplus exists

t_2 = Time when inventory shortage exists

H = Annual holding cost per unit

π = Annual shortage cost per unit

S = Setup or ordering cost

D = Annual demand

The geometry of this model allows us to specify the following relationships. The average inventory cost during time t_1 is

$$\frac{M}{2}Ht_1$$

The average shortage cost during time t_2 is

$$\frac{Q-M}{2}\pi t_2$$

The total cost for the time interval $t_1 + t_2$, wherein one order quantity is ordered and consumed, is

$$\frac{MHt_1}{2} + \frac{Q-M}{2}\pi t_2 + S$$

On an annual basis there are D/Q such periods. Thus, multiplying the above equation by D/Q gives the total annual cost:

$$TC = \frac{D}{Q}\left(\frac{M}{2}Ht_1 + \frac{Q-M}{2}\pi t_2 + S\right)$$

By the geometry of similar triangles and by partial differentiation with respect to Q and M, we obtain

$$Q_{opt} = \sqrt{\frac{2DS}{H}}\sqrt{\frac{H+\pi}{\pi}}$$

$$M = \sqrt{\frac{2DS}{H}}\sqrt{\frac{\pi}{H+\pi}}$$

These equations give the optimal order size and the maximum inventory level (M) for each period. To find the period or cycle time (T), the time between orders, we can substitute D/T for Q in the equation and obtain

$$T = \sqrt{\frac{2S}{DH}}\sqrt{\frac{H+\pi}{\pi}}$$

Example 15.3. A manufacturer is faced with a constant and known demand for his product at the rate of 10,000 per year. The cost to set up for production is $150, and the annual cost to carry the item in inventory is $2 each. If the manufacturer runs out of stock, there is an annual shortage cost of $5 per unit. This shortage will be filled as soon as the new lot is produced. The problem is to determine the optimal order quantity.

$$D = 10,000$$
$$S = 150$$
$$H = 2$$
$$\pi = 3$$

$$Q_{opt} = \sqrt{\frac{2DS}{H}} \sqrt{\frac{H + \pi}{\pi}} = \sqrt{\frac{2(10,000)150}{2}} \sqrt{\frac{2 + 5}{5}}$$
$$= (1,224.8)(1.18) = 1,445.3 \text{ units}$$

The maximum number of units that will be on hand is

$$M = \sqrt{\frac{2DS}{H}} \sqrt{\frac{\pi}{H + \pi}} = 1,224.8(0.845) = 1,035 \text{ units}$$

The number of units by which he will be short at the end of each run is then

$$M - Q = 1,035 - 1,445.3 = -410 \text{ units}$$

The optimum time between placing orders is

$$T = \sqrt{\frac{2S}{DH}} \sqrt{\frac{H + \pi}{\pi}} = \sqrt{\frac{2(150)}{10,000(2)}} \sqrt{\frac{2 + 5}{5}} = 0.145 \text{ year}$$

An order for 1,445 units would be placed every 0.145 year, or about every 7½ weeks.

Probabilistic models (conditions of uncertainty)   The previous models assumed that demand was constant and known. In the majority of cases, though, demand is not constant but varies from day to day. Safety stock must therefore be maintained to provide some level of protection against stockouts. This degree of protection is usually based on one of two criteria; that is, set safety stock (1) at the point that provides some level of customer service (for example, a management policy that 95 percent of the demands will be met directly from stock on hand), or (2) at the point that minimizes the cost of shortages and the cost of carrying added inventory.

In this section, we will first discuss the concept of service level and how to determine safety stocks and reorder points. Then we will discuss two models that contain variation in demand: a probabilistic fixed-order quantity model and a probabilistic fixed-time period model.

Service level. Safety stock is stock which is carried in addition to the expected demand. The amount of safety stock determines the level of meeting demands for the product. A term frequently used in this determination is *service level. Service level,* as we are using it, refers to the number of units of an item demanded which can be supplied from stock currently on hand. Thus, a 95 percent service level means that if the annual demand for an item is 1,000 units distributed over the year, 950 of these units demanded can be supplied immediately; 50 units will be short and the demand will have to wait. (This assumes that orders are small—one or several at a time.)

The general literature on inventory reorder levels and safety stocks contains different and perhaps confusing terms which relate to the service level concept. In a normal distribution of demand, for example, we can talk about:

1.   The *probability* that demand will exceed some specified amount.
2.   The *expected number* of units demanded above some specified amount.

In the first case, a statement might be made something like "There is a 5 percent chance that demand will exceed 30 units." A statement about the second case might be "During the lead time, there will be 2 units short."

The first case, probability of exceeding a value, is the procedure we have used in establishing confidence intervals in quality control (Chapter 10) and in work sampling (Chapter 11). In setting customer service policies, however, it makes more sense to talk about the number of customers who are satisfied, the percentage of orders which are filled directly from stock on hand, or the number of units which we are short. We will now explain these more thoroughly.[2]

Exhibit 15.7 shows the demand distribution for an item. The average demand for the week is 100 units, and the standard deviation is 10 units.

EXHIBIT 15.7
Distribution of weekly demand for an item (mean for the week is 100 units, and standard deviation is 10 units)

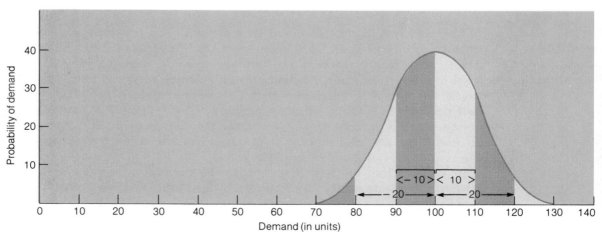

---

[2] For a dozen different ways to define service, see Donald W. Fogarty, and Thomas R. Hoffman, "Customer Service," *Production and Inventory Management*, vol. 21, no. 1 (First Quarter 1980), pp. 70–80.

In the same type of analysis we used in quality control, since this is a normal distribution, we can say that there is a 50 percent chance demand will be greater than 100, an 84 percent chance demand will be greater than 110 (from Appendix D at the end of the book where $z = 1$), a 97.7 percent chance demand will be greater than 120 (Appendix D where $z = 2$), or any other point we may be interested in.

In service level determination, we would like to know how many units there are in some portion of the distribution. For example, at 110 units (one standard deviation above the mean), there is an 84 percent chance that demand will exceed this. But how many units does this mean? How many units would we be short if we stocked 110 units in inventory?

To find the number of units short, we would need to compute the expected demand for all items above 110. We would sum up the probability that 111 is demanded (1 short), plus the probability that 112 is demanded (2 short), and so on. This would give us the expected number in that portion of the distribution, in this case, the number of units we would be short by stocking 110 units.

The expected number within distributions is an integral equation and impractical to solve by hand. Brown has provided tables of expected values which we have included in Exhibit 15.8.[3]

To answer the question: How many units would we be short by stocking 110 units (1 standard deviation above the mean), we look in the table where $z = 1$ and find $E(z) = .0833$. Since this table was constructed for the value of the standard deviation of 1 unit and ours is 10 units, we multiply $E(z)$ by 10 and get $E(z) = .833$ units. This means we would be short less than one unit each week. That would correspond to a service level of $(100 - .833)/100 = 99.2\%$.

Based on the foregoing discussion, we could ask the following question and then procede to answer it: "How do I control my inventory to provide a customer service level of 95 percent?"

First, we need to derive an equation for the expected number of units short.

The number of units short in one year is equal to one minus the desired service level times the annual demand. This is equal to the number of units short per order times the number of orders per year.

Percentage short	$\times$	Annual demand	$=$	Number short per order	$\times$	Number of orders per year
$(1 - P)$	$\times$	D	$=$	$E(z)\sigma_L$	$\times$	$\dfrac{D}{Q}$

which simplifies to

$$E(z) = \frac{(1 - P)Q}{\sigma_L} \tag{1}$$

---

[3] Robert G. Brown, *Decision Rules for Inventory Management* (New York: Holt, Rinehart and Winston, 1967).

EXHIBIT 15.8
Probabilities and partial expectations in the normal probability distribution related to inventory demand and safety stock.

z is the number of standard deviations of safety stock (also called safety factor).

$P(z)$ is the probability that demand will exceed z.

$E(z)$ is the expected number short with a safety stock of z.

$E(-z)$. For negative values of z, use the $E(-z)$ column.

This table is normalized to $z = 1$ and area under the curve $= 1$.

z	$P(z)$	$E(z)$	$E(-z)$
0.00	0.50000	0.39894	0.39894
0.10	0.46017	0.35094	0.45094
0.20	0.42074	0.30690	0.50690
0.30	0.38209	0.26676	0.56676
0.40	0.34458	0.23044	0.63044
0.50	0.30854	0.19780	0.69780
0.60	0.27425	0.16867	0.76867
0.70	0.24196	0.14288	0.84288
0.80	0.21186	0.12021	0.92021
0.90	0.18406	0.10043	1.00043
1.00	0.15866	0.08332	1.08332
1.10	0.13567	0.06862	1.16862
1.20	0.11507	0.05610	1.25610
1.30	0.09680	0.04553	1.34553
1.40	0.08076	0.03667	1.43667
1.50	0.06681	0.02931	1.52931
1.60	0.05480	0.02324	1.62324
1.70	0.04457	0.01829	1.71829
1.80	0.03593	0.01428	1.81428
1.90	0.02872	0.01105	1.91105
2.00	0.02275	0.00849	2.00849
2.10	0.01786	0.00647	2.10647
2.20	0.01390	0.00489	2.20489
2.30	0.01072	0.00366	2.30366
2.40	0.00820	0.00272	2.40272
2.50	0.00621	0.00200	2.50200
2.60	0.00466	0.00146	2.60146
2.70	0.00347	0.00106	2.70106
2.80	0.00256	0.00076	2.80076
2.90	0.00187	0.00054	2.90054
3.00	0.00135	0.00038	3.00038
3.10	0.00097	0.00027	3.10027
3.20	0.00069	0.00019	3.20019
3.30	0.00048	0.00013	3.30013
3.40	0.00034	0.00009	3.40009
3.50	0.00023	0.00006	3.50006
3.60	0.00016	0.00004	3.60004
3.70	0.00011	0.00003	3.70003
3.80	0.00007	0.00002	3.80002
3.90	0.00005	0.00001	3.90001
4.00	0.00003	0.00001	4.00001
4.10	0.00002	0.00001	4.10001
4.20	0.00001	0.00000	4.20000
4.30	0.00001	0.00000	4.30000
4.40	0.00001	0.00000	4.40000
4.50	0.00000	0.00000	4.50000

Source: Robert G. Brown, *Decision Rules for Inventory Management* (New York: Holt, Rinehart, and Winston, 1967), pp. 95–103.

where

P = Service level desired (such as satisfying 95 percent of demand from items in stock)

$(1 - P)$ = Unsatisfied demand

D = Annual demand

σ_L = Standard deviation of demand during lead time

Q = Economic order quantity calculated in the usual way (such as $Q = \sqrt{2DS/H}$)

$E(z)$ = Expected number of units short from a normalized table where the mean $= 0$ and $\sigma = 1$.

Next we need to examine the amount of safety stock required.

Safety stock and reorder point for a specified service level. The time when inventory is vulnerable to a shortage depends on the inventory system used:

1. In a fixed-order quantity system which perpetually monitors the inventory level and places a new order when stock reaches some level R, a shortage can occur during the lead time, which is the time between placing an order and receiving the items. To protect against a shortage, the reorder point is set equal to the average usage during the lead time, plus a safety stock, or,

$$R = \bar{d}L + z\sigma_L \qquad (2)$$

where

R = Reorder point in units

$\bar{d}$ = Average daily demand

L = Lead time in days (time between placing an order and receiving the items)

z = Number of standard deviations for a specified confidence level

σ_L = Standard deviation of usage during lead time.

The term $z\sigma_L$ is the amount of safety stock. Note that the effect of safety stock is to place a reorder sooner. That is, if R without safety stock is 20, then R with 5 units of safety stock is 25. You don't wait until inventory gets down to 20 to place a reorder.

2. In a fixed-time period system, inventory is only counted at particular times, such as every week or every month. It is possible that some large demand will draw the stock down to zero or even negative (with shortages to be supplied as soon as the new stock arrives) right after an order is placed. When the order arrives, it may still not be enough to satisfy the waiting demand. This condition could go unnoticed until the next review period. Then, an order placed for new items still takes time to arrive. Thus, it is possible to be out of stock throughout the entire review period, T, and the order lead time, L.

Reorders are placed at the time of review (T), and the safety stock which must be ordered is

$$\text{Safety stock} = z\sigma_{T+L}$$

Fixed-order quantity model. As mentioned in number 1 above, the danger of stockout in this model occurs only during the lead time; that is, between the time an order is placed and the time it is received. As shown in Exhibit 15.9, an order is placed when the inventory level drops to the reorder point, R. During this lead time (L), a range of demands is possible. This range is determined either from an analysis of past demand data or from an estimate (if past data are not available).

The amount of safety stock depends on the service level desired, as previously discussed. The quantity to be ordered, Q, is calculated in the usual way considering the demand, shortage cost, ordering cost, holding cost, and so forth. Any of the economic fixed-order quantity models previously discussed in this chapter may be used if appropriate for the application. The reorder point is then set to cover the expected demand during the lead time plus a safety stock determined by the desired service level. Thus, the key difference between a fixed-order quantity model under certainty in demand and uncertainty in demand is not in computing the order quantity (both will be the same) but in computing the reorder point.

We will now examine two examples. The difference between them is that in the first, the variation in demand is stated in terms of standard deviation over the lead time, and in the second, it is stated in terms of standard deviation per day.

Example 15.4. Consider an economic order quantity case where annual demand $D = 1,000$ units, economic order quantity $Q = 200$ units, the desired service level $P = .95$, the standard deviation of demand during

EXHIBIT 15.9
Fixed-order quantity model with variation in demand, a constant lead time, and a safety stock

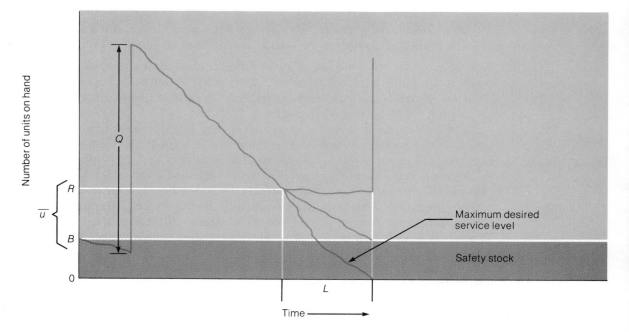

lead time $\sigma_L = 50$ units, and lead time $L = 15$ days. Show the expected number of units out of stock and determine the reorder point.

$$E(z) = \frac{(1 - P)Q}{\sigma_L} = \frac{(1 - .95)200}{50} = .2$$

The expected number short on each order is $E(z)\ \sigma_L = .2(50) = 10$. Since there are five orders per year, this results in 50 units short. (This verifies our achievement of a 95 percent service level since 950 out of 1,000 demand were filled from stock.)

To find the point (R) where orders for new stock should be placed to meet this desired service level, we refer to Exhibit 15.8 and through interpolation at $E(z) = .2$, we find $z = .49$.

In our example, $\bar{d} = 4$ (1,000 over a 250-work-day year), and lead time is 15 days. Therefore, from equation (2)

$$R = \bar{d}L + z\sigma_L$$

$$R = 4(15) + .49(50) = 84.5 \text{ units}$$

This says when the stock on hand gets down to 85 units, order 200 more.

Example 15.5. The daily demand for a product is normally distributed with a mean of 60 and a standard deviation of 7. Further, the source of supply is reliable and maintains a constant lead time of six days. If the cost of placing the order is $10 and annual holding costs are $0.50 per unit, find the order quantity and reorder point to satisfy 95 percent of the customers who place orders during the reorder period. There are no stockout costs, and unfilled orders are filled as soon as the order arrives. Assume sales occur over the entire year.

$$\bar{d} = 60$$
$$\sigma_d = 7$$
$$\bar{D} = 60(365)$$
$$S = \$10$$
$$H = \$0.50$$
$$L = 6$$

The optimal order quantity is

$$Q_{opt} = \sqrt{\frac{2\bar{D}S}{H}} = \sqrt{\frac{2(60)365(10)}{0.50}} = \sqrt{876,000} = 936$$

To compute the reorder point, we need to calculate the amount of product used during the lead time and add this to the safety stock.

The standard deviation of demand during the lead time of six days is calculated from the variance of the individual days. Since each day's demand is independent[4]

---

[4] From basic statistics, the standard deviation of a sum of independent random variables is equal to the square root of the sum of the variances.

$$\sigma_L = \sqrt{\sum_{i=1}^{L} \sigma_{d_i}{}^2} = \sqrt{6(7)^2} = 17.2$$

Next we need to know how many standard deviations are needed for a specified service level. As previously defined

$$E(z) = \frac{Q(1 - P)}{\sigma_L}$$

Therefore

$$E(z) = \frac{936(1 - .95)}{17.2} = 2.721$$

From Exhibit 15.8, interpolating at $E(z) = 2.721$, $z = -2.72$.

The reorder point is

$$\begin{aligned} R &= \bar{d}L + z\sigma_L \\ &= 60(6) + -2.72(17.2) \\ &= 313.2 \text{ units} \end{aligned}$$

To summarize the policy derived in this example, an order for 936 units is placed whenever the number of units remaining in inventory drops to 313.

As shown in these two examples, this technique of determining safety stock levels is relatively simple and straightforward. It allows us to control inventory to meet our desired service levels.

Fixed-time period models. As was mentioned previously, fixed-time period models generate order quantities that vary from period to period, depending on the usage rates. There are many situations where it is more desirable to count inventory and place an order for restocking on a repetitive time basis rather than place orders every time stock drops to the reorder point.

Examples are when vendors make routine visits to customers and take orders for their complete line of products and when buyers want to combine orders to save transportation cost. Still other firms operate on a fixed-time period to facilitate planning, since employees can know—for example—that every two weeks, all the stock on hand from distributor X must be counted.

However, as was also mentioned previously, fixed-time period systems generally require a higher level of safety stock than is required under a fixed-order quantity system. This is so because the order quantity formulas in the latter system assume continual monitoring, with an order immediately placed when the reorder point is reached. In contrast, the standard fixed-time period models assume that inventory is recorded only at the time specified. Therefore, safety stock must be provided to protect against stockouts during the review period itself, as well as during the lead time from order placement to order receipt.

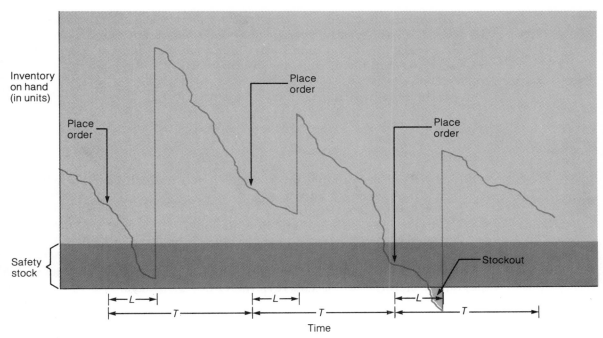

EXHIBIT 15.10
Fixed-time period inventory model with constant review period T and lead time L; inventory is counted and orders are calculated and placed at the beginning of T; order is received at the end of the lead time L

The fixed-time period model under uncertainty provides a safety stock to provide some designated service level. Exhibit 15.10 shows a fixed-time period system with a review cycle of T and a constant lead time L. In this case, demand is randomly distributed about a mean $\bar{d}$. The quantity to order q is

$$q = \bar{d}(T+L) + z\sigma_{T+L} - I \qquad (17)$$

where

average demand over the vulnerable period — $q = \bar{d}(T+L)$

safety stock — $+ z\sigma_{T+L}$

Inventory currently on hand (plus on order, if any) — $-I$

q = Quantity to be ordered
T = The length of time between reviews
L = Lead time—time between placing an order and receiving it
$\bar{d}$ = Forecasted average daily demand over the period $T + L$
z = Number of standard deviations for a specified confidence interval
σ_{T+L} = Standard deviation of demand over the review and lead time
I = Current inventory level (includes items on order)

Note: The demand, lead time, and so forth can be any time period so long as it is consistent throughout the equation.

In this model, demand $(\bar{d})$ can be forecast and revised each review period, if desired, or the yearly average may be used if appropriate. Also the review period T and lead time L can differ from the yearly average because of vacation, shutdown, differing number of work days over the cycle, or weather.

z can be obtained from Exhibit 15.8 since

$$E(z) = \frac{D_T(1 - P)}{\sigma_{T+L}}$$

where

$E(z) =$ Expected number units short from a normalized table where the mean $= 0$ and $\sigma = 1$
$P =$ Service level desired
$D_T =$ Demand during the review period T
$\sigma_{T+L} =$ Standard deviation over the review period and lead time

Example 15.6. Daily demand for a product is ten units with a standard deviation of three units. The review period is 30 days, and lead time is 14 days. Management has set a policy of satisfying 98 percent of demand from items in stock. At the beginning of this review period, there are currently 42 units in inventory.

How many units should be ordered?

$$E(z) = \frac{D_T(1 - P)}{\sigma_{T+L}}$$

The standard deviation during the period $T + L$ is the square root of the sum of the variances for each day, or

$$\sigma_{T+L} = \sqrt{\sum_{i=1}^{T+L} \sigma_{d_i}^2}$$

Since each day is independent,

$$\sigma_{T+L} = \sqrt{(30 + 14)(3)^2} = 19.90$$

In this case demand during the review period (D_T) is $\bar{d}T$. Therefore

$$E(z) = \frac{\bar{d}T(1 - P)}{\sigma_{T+L}} = \frac{10(30)(1 - .98)}{19.90} = 0.30151$$

From Exhibit 15.8 at $E(z) = 0.30151$, by interpolation $z = .21$.
The quantity to order, then is

$$\begin{aligned}
q &= \bar{d}(T + L) + z\sigma_{T+L} - I \\
&= 10(30 + 14) + .21(19.90) - 42 \\
&= 402 \text{ units}
\end{aligned}$$

To satisfy 98 percent of the demand for units, order 402 at this review period.

Special-purpose models

The fixed-order quantity and the fixed-time period models presented thus far differed in their assumptions but had two characteristics in common: (1) the cost of units remained constant for any order size and (2) the reordering process was continuous; that is, the items were ordered and stocked with the expectation that the need would continue. This section presents two new models: the first illustrates the effect on order quantity when unit price changes with order size; the second is a single-period model (sometimes called a *static model*) in which ordering and stocking require a cost trade-off each time. This type of model is amenable to solution by marginal analysis.

Price-break models. Generally, the selling price or cost of an item varies with the order size. This is a discrete or step change rather than a per unit change. For example, wood screws may cost 2¢ each for 1 to 99 screws, $1.60 per 100, and $13.50 per 1,000. In order to determine the optimal quantity of any item to order, the procedure involves simply solving for the economic order quantity for each price and at the point of price change. However, not all of the economic order quantities determined by the formula will be feasible. In the wood-screw example, the EOQ formula might tell us that the optimal decision at the price of 1.6 cents is to order 75 screws. This would be impossible, however, since 75 screws would cost 2¢ each.

The total cost for each feasible economic order quantity and price-break quantity is tabulated, and the Q that leads to the minimum cost is the optimal order size.

If holding cost is based on a percentage of unit price, it may not be necessary to compute economic order quantities at each price. Procedurally, the largest order quantity (lowest unit price) is solved first; if the resulting Q is valid, that is the answer. If not, the next largest order quantity (second lowest price) is derived. If that is feasible, the cost of this Q is compared to the cost of using the order quantity at the price break above, and the lowest cost determines the optimal Q.

Looking at Exhibit 15.11, we see that order quantities are solved from right to left, or from the lowest unit price to the highest, until a valid Q is obtained. Then the order quantity at each price break above this Q is used to find which order quantity has the least cost—the computed Q or the Q at one of the price breaks.

Example 15.7. Consider the following case, where

$D =$ 10,000 units (annual demand)
$S =$ \$20 to place each order
$H =$ 20% of cost (annual carrying cost, storage, interest, obsolescence, etc.)
$C =$ Cost per unit (according to the order size; orders of 0 to 499 units, \$5.00 per unit; 500 to 999, \$4.50 per unit; and 1,000 and up, \$3.90 per unit)

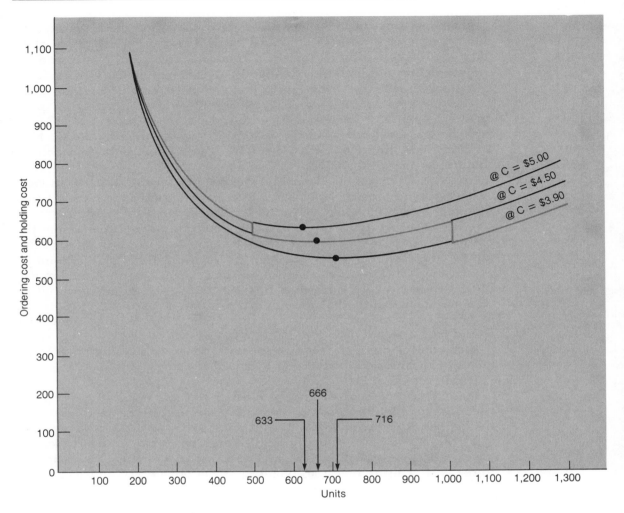

@ C = $5.00
@ C = $4.50
@ C = $3.90

EXHIBIT 15.11
Curves for three separate order quantity models in a three-price break situation (solid line depicts feasible range of purchases)

The appropriate equations from the basic fixed quantity case are

$$TC = DC + \frac{D}{Q}S + \frac{Q}{2}H$$

and

$$Q = \sqrt{\frac{2DS}{H}}$$

Solving for the economic order size at each price, we obtain

@ $C = \$5.00$, $Q = 633$
@ $C = \$4.50$, $Q = 666$
@ $C = \$3.90$, $Q = 716$

In Exhibit 15.11, which displays the cost relationship and order quantity range, note that most of the order quantity-cost relationships lie outside the feasible range and that only a single, continuous range results. This should be readily apparent since, for example, the first order quantity specifies buying 633 units at $5 per unit. However, if 633 units are ordered, the price is $4.50—not $5. The same holds true for the third order quantity, which specifies an order of 716 units at $3.90 each. This $3.90 price is not available on orders of less than 1,000 units.

Exhibit 15.12 itemizes the total costs at the economic order quantities and at the price breaks. The optimal order quantity is shown to be 1,000 units.

EXHIBIT 15.12
Relevant costs in a three-price-break model

	Price break 500	Q = 633 where C = $5	Q = 666 where C = $4.50	C = 716 where C = $3.90	Price break 1,000
Holding cost $\left(\dfrac{Q}{2} H\right)$	$\dfrac{500}{2}(0.20)4.50$ $= \$225$		$\dfrac{666}{2}(0.20)4.50$ $= \$299.70$		$\dfrac{1,000}{2}(0.20)3.90$ $= \$390$
Ordering cost $\left(\dfrac{D}{Q} S\right)$	$\dfrac{10,000(20)}{500}$ $= \$400$	Not feasible	$\dfrac{10,000(20)}{666}$ $= \$300$	Not feasible	$\dfrac{10,000(20)}{1,000}$ $= \$200$
Holding and ordering cost	$625		$600		$590
Item cost (DC)	10,000($4.50)		10,000($4.50)		10,000($3.90)
Total cost	$45,625		$45,599.70		$39,590

One practical consideration in price break problems is that the price reduction from volume purchases frequently makes it seemingly economical to order amounts larger than the EOQ. Thus, one must be particularly careful to obtain a valid estimate of product obsolescence and warehousing costs when applying the model.

Single-period models. Some inventory situations involve placing orders to cover only one demand period or placing orders to cover short lived items at frequent intervals. Sometimes called single period or "newsboy problems" (for example, how many papers should a newsboy order each day), they are amenable to solution through the classic economic approach of marginal analysis. The optimal stocking decision, using marginal analysis, occurs at the point where the benefits derived from carrying the next unit are less than the costs for that unit. Of course, the selection of the specific benefits and costs depends on the problem; for example, we may be looking at costs of holding versus shortage costs, or (as we will develop further) marginal profit versus marginal loss.

In the situation where stocked items are sold, the optimal decision—

using marginal analysis—is to stock that quantity where the profit from the sale or use of the last unit is equal to or greater than the losses if the last unit remains unsold. In symbolic terms, this is the condition where $MP \geq ML$, where

MP = profit resulting from the Nth unit if it is sold
ML = loss resulting from the Nth unit if it is not sold

Marginal analysis is also valid when we are dealing with probabilities of occurrence. In these situations we are looking at expected profits and expected losses. By introducing probabilities, the marginal profit-marginal loss equation becomes

$$P_1(MP) \geq P_2(ML)$$

where P_1 is the probability of the unit's being sold and P_2 is the probability of the unit's not being sold.[5] Since one or the other must occur (the unit is sold or is not sold), $P_1 + P_2$ must equal one, and we can state P_2 (in terms of P_1) as $P_2 = 1 - P_1$.

Our marginal profit-marginal loss equation then becomes

$$P_1(MP) \geq (1 - P_1)ML$$

We can drop the subscript while retaining P as the probability of selling a unit and $1 - P$ as the probability of not selling it. Then, solving for P, we obtain

$$P \geq \frac{ML}{MP + ML}$$

This equation states that we should continue to increase the size of the inventory so long as the probability of selling the last unit added is equal to or greater than the ratio $ML/(MP + ML)$.

Salvage value. Salvage value, or any other benefits derived from unsold goods, can easily be included in the problem. This simply reduces the marginal loss, as demonstrated in the following example.

Example 15.8. A product is priced to sell at $100 per unit, and its cost is constant at $70 per unit. Each unsold unit has a salvage value of $30. Demand is expected to range between 35 and 40 units for the period: 35 units definitely can be sold and no units over 40 will be sold. The demand probabilites and the associated cumulative probability distribution (P) for this situation are shown in Exhibit 15.13.

The marginal profit if a unit is sold is the selling price less the cost, or $MP = \$100 - \$70 = \$30$.

The marginal loss incurred if the unit is not sold is the cost of the unit less the salvage value, or $ML = \$70 - \$30 = \$40$.

---

[5] P is actually a cumulative probability since the sale of the Nth unit depends not only on exactly N being demanded but also on the demand for any number greater than N.

EXHIBIT 15.13

Number of units demanded	(p) Probability of this demand	(P) Probability of selling this unit is	
35	0.10	1 to 35:	1.00
36	0.15	36th:	0.90
37	0.25	37th:	0.75
38	0.25	38th:	0.50
39	0.15	39th:	0.25
40	0.10	40th:	0.10
41	0	41 or more:	0

The optimal number to stock for the period is

$$P \geq \frac{ML}{MP + ML} = \frac{40}{30 + 40} = 0.57$$

According to the cumulative probability table above, the probability of selling the unit must be equal to or greater than 0.57; therefore, 37 units should be stocked. The probability of selling the 37th unit is 0.75. The net benefit from stocking the 37th unit is the expected marginal profit minus the expected marginal loss.

$$\begin{aligned}
\text{Net} &= P(MP) - (1 - P)(ML) \\
&= 0.75(\$100 - \$70) - (1 - 0.75)(\$70 - \$30) \\
&= \$22.50 - \$10.00 = \$12.50
\end{aligned}$$

For the sake of illustration, Exhibit 15.14 shows all possible decisions. From the last column, we can confirm that the optimum decision is 37 units.

EXHIBIT 15.14
Marginal inventory analysis for units having salvage value

(N) Units of demand	(p) Probability of demand	(P) Probability of selling Nth unit	(MP) Expected marginal profit of Nth unit $P(100 - 70)$	(ML) Expected marginal loss of Nth unit $(1 - P)(70 - 30)$	(Net) $(MP) - (ML)$
35	0.10	1.00	$30	0	$30.00
36	0.15	0.90	27	$ 4	23.00
37	0.25	0.75	22.50	10	12.50
38	0.25	0.50	15	20	(5.00)
39	0.15	0.25	7.50	30	(22.50)
40	0.10	0.10	3	36	(33.00)
41	0	0			(40.00)

Note: Expected marginal profit is the selling price of $100 less the unit cost of $70 times the probability the unit will be sold.
Expected marginal loss is the unit cost of $70 less the salvage value of $30 times the probability the unit will not be sold.

PRACTICAL CONSIDERATIONS IN INVENTORY CONTROL

All inventory systems are plagued by two major problems—one, to maintain adequate control over each inventory item, and two, to assure that accurate records are kept of stock on hand. In this section, we will present the ABC inventory system which offers a control technique and inventory cycle counting which can improve record accuracy. We will follow this with a brief description of the IBM IMPACT computer control system.

ABC-type inventory planning

In the 18th century, Villefredo Pareto, in a study of the distribution of wealth in Milan, found that 20 percent of the people controlled 80 percent of the wealth. This logic of the few having the greatest importance and the many having little importance has been broadened to include many situations and is termed the *Pareto Principle*. This is true in our everyday lives (such as, most of the decisions we make are relatively unimportant but a few shape our future), and is certainly true in inventory systems (where a few items account for the bulk of our investment).

Any inventory system must specify when an order is to be placed for an item and how many units to order. In most situations involving inventory control, there are too many items involved for it to be practical to model and give thorough treatment to each item. To get around this problem, the ABC classification scheme divides inventory items into three groupings: high dollar volume (A), moderate dollar volume (B), and low dollar volume (C). This dollar volume is a measure of the importance of an item; that is, an item low in cost but high in volume is usually more important than a high-cost item with low volume.

ABC classification

If the annual usage of items in inventory is listed according to dollar volume, observation of the list will generally show that a small number of items accounts for a large dollar volume and that a large number of items accounts for a small dollar volume. Exhibit 15.15 illustrates the relationship.

EXHIBIT 15.15
Annual usage of inventory by value

Item number	Annual dollar usage	Percent of total value
22	95,000	40.8
68	75,000	32.1
27	25,000	10.7
03	15,000	6.4
82	13,000	5.6
54	7,500	3.2
36	1,500	0.6
19	800	0.3
23	425	0.2
41	225	0.1
	233,450	100.0

The ABC approach divides this list into three groupings by item value, wherein A items consist of roughly the top 15 percent of the items, B items the next 35 percent, and C items the last 50 percent. From observation, it appears that the list in Exhibit 15.16 may be meaningfully regrouped with A including 20 percent (two of the 10), B including 30 percent, and

C including 50 percent. These points show clear delineations between sections. The result of this segmentation is shown in Exhibit 15.16 and is plotted in Exhibit 15.17.

EXHIBIT 15.16
ABC grouping of inventory items

Classification	Item number	Annual dollar usage	Percent of total
A	22, 68	170,000	72.9
B	27, 03, 82	53,000	22.7
C	54, 36, 19, 23, 41	10,450	4.4
		233,450	100.0

The purpose of classifying items into groups is to establish the appropriate degree of control over each item. On a periodic basis, for example, class A items may be more clearly controlled with weekly ordering, B items may be ordered biweekly, and C items may be ordered monthly or bimonthly. Note that the unit cost of items is not related to their classification. An A item may have a high dollar volume through a combination of either low cost and high usage or high cost and low usage. Similarly, C items may have a low dollar volume either because of low demand or low cost. In an automobile service station, gasoline would be an A item with daily tabulation; tires, batteries, oil, grease, and transmission fluid may be B items; and C items would consist of valve stems, windshield wiper blades, radiator caps, hoses, fan belts, oil and gas additives, car wax, and so forth. C items may be ordered every two or three months

EXHIBIT 15.17
ABC inventory classification (inventory value for each group versus the group's portion of the total list)

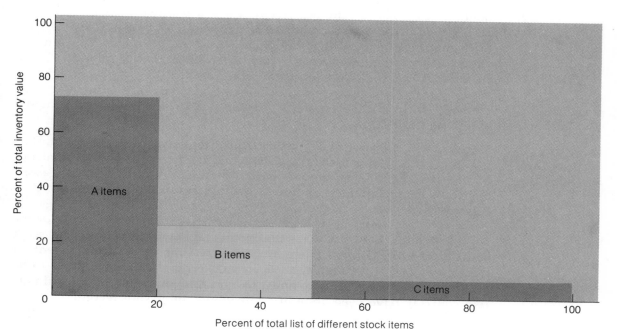

EXHIBIT 15.18
Inventory policies in defining ABC items

Classification	Definition	Safety stock policy (in weeks)		Order quantity policy	
		Manufactured items	Purchased items	Manufactured items	Purchased items
A	More than $1,000/week average usage	2	4	4	6
B	Between $100 and $1,000 per week average usage	4	6	6	10
C	Less than $100 per week average usage	12	16	10	20

or even be allowed to run out before reordering since the penalty for stockout is not serious.

Sometimes, an item may be critical to a system if its absence creates a sizable loss. In this case, regardless of the item's classification, sufficiently large stocks should be kept on hand to prevent runout. One way to assure closer control is to designate this item an A or a B, forcing it into the category even if its dollar volume does not warrant such inclusion.

Exhibits 15.18 and 15.19 show how one firm classifies ABC inventory and computes the cost. Exhibit 15.18 shows the logic they have used. Items are classified according to their weekly dollar volume. Safety stock for each is specified in weeks, as is the quantity to be ordered. This classification was originally derived from their desire to have an ABC breakdown as A—75 percent of dollar usage, B—20 percent, and C—5 percent.

Exhibit 15.19 shows a worksheet which used a 26 percent per year holding cost (0.5 percent per week) and a $50 ordering cost. There are 100 A items, 500 B items, and 2,000 C items. The total weekly cost for managing inventory in this way is shown as $22,650. This firm can test various alternatives (different safety stock levels, order quantities, and so forth) to see the effects on total cost.

In general, ABC analysis will usually reduce inventory costs over other methods which do not spend a greater portion of time on the higher investment items.

Inventory accuracy and cycle counting

Inventory records usually differ from the actual physical count. The question is, how much error is acceptable. If the record shows a balance of 683 part Xs, and an actual count shows 652, is this within reason? Suppose the actual count shows 750, an excess of 67 over the record; is this any better?

Every production or service system must have agreement within some specified range, between what the record says is in inventory and what actually is in inventory. There are many reasons records and inventory may not agree. For example, an open stockroom area allows items to be removed for both legitimate and unauthorized purposes. The legitimate removal may have been done in a hurry and simply not recorded. Sometimes parts are misplaced, turning up months later. Parts are often stored

EXHIBIT 15.19
ABC inventory management work sheet

Total inventory:

Class	S.S.	O.Q./2	Total
A............	$300 M	$300 M	$ 600 M
B............	160 M	120 M	280 M
C............	160 M	60 M	220 M
Total........	$620 M	$480 M	$1100 M

Usage:

Class	% of usage	Usage/week
A............	75	$150 M
B............	20	50 M
C............	5	10 M
Total........	100	$200 M

Safety stock:

Class	Weeks	Usage/week	Inventory	Cost @ .5%
A............	2	$150 M	$300 M	$1500
B............	4	40 M	160 M	800
C............	16	10 M	160 M	800
Total........		$200 M	$620 M	$3100

Order quantity:

Class	Weeks	Usage/week	O.Q.	O.Q./2	Cost @ .5%
A............	4	$150 M	$600 M	$300 M	$1500
B............	6	50 M	240 M	120 M	600
C............	12	10 M	120 M	60 M	300
Total........		$200 M		$480 M	$2400

Per item cost:

Class	Items	$/item	Cost
A............	100	20.00	$2000
B............	500	2.00	1000
C............	2000	.20	400
Total........	2600		$3400

Per order cost:

Class O.Q.	Weeks	O/week	Items	Orders	$/order	Cost
A............	4	.250	100	25	$50	$ 1250
B............	6	.167	500	84	$50	4200
C............	12	.083	2000	166	$50	8300
Total........			2600	275		$13,750

Total cost:

Class	S.S.	O.Q.	Per item	Per order	Total
A............	$1500	$1500	$2000	$ 1250	$ 6250
B............	800	600	1000	4200	6600
C............	800	300	400	8300	9800
Total	$3100	$2400	$3400	$13,750	$22,650

Source: Paul G. Conroy, "Data General ABC Inventory Management," *Production and Inventory Management,* vol. 18, no. 4 (Fourth Quarter 1977), p. 63.

in several locations, but records may be lost or the location recorded incorrectly. Sometimes stock replenishment orders are recorded as received,
though they never were. Occasionally, a group of parts are recorded as
removed from inventory, but a cancelled customer order results in replacing
the parts in inventory without cancelling the record. To keep the production system flowing smoothly without parts shortages and efficiently without excess balances, it is important that records are accurate.

"How can a firm keep accurate up-to-date records?" The first general
rule is to keep the storeroom locked. If only storeroom personnel have
access, and one of their measures of performance when it comes time
for personnel evaluation and merit increases is record accuracy, there is
a strong motivation to comply. Every location of inventory storage—
whether in a locked storeroom or on the production floor—should have
a record-keeping mechanism.

The second helpful way to assure accuracy is to count inventory frequently and match this against records. A widely used method is called
cycle counting.

Cycle counting is a technique where inventory is counted on a frequent
basis rather than once or twice a year. The key to effective cycle counting
and, therefore, in accurate records lies in deciding which items are to be
counted, when, and by whom.

Since most inventory systems these days are computerized, the computer
can be programmed to produce a cycle count notice in the following cases:

1. When the record shows a low or zero balance on hand. (Obviously
    it is easier to count fewer items.)
2. When the record shows a positive balance but a backorder was written
    (indicating a discrepancy).
3. After some specified level of activity.
4. A scheme may be set up which signals a review based on the impor-
    tance of the item such as in the following example.

Annual dollar usage	Review period
$10,000 or more	30 days or less
$3,000–$10,000	45 days or less
$250–3,000	90 days or less
Less than $250	180 days or less

The easiest time for stock to be counted obviously would be when
there is no activity in the stockroom or on the production floor. This
means during the second or third shift when the facility is less busy or
on weekends. If this is not possible, then more careful logging and separation of items is required when doing an inventory count while production
is going on and transactions are occurring.

The counting cycle depends on the available personnel. Some firms
schedule regular stockroom personnel to do the counting during the lull

times of the regular working day. Other firms utilize full-time cycle counters who do nothing but count inventory and resolve differences with the records. While this latter method sounds expensive, many firms believe that this is actually less costly than the usual hectic annual inventory count generally performed during the two- or three-week annual vacation shutdown. (Perhaps the reader has had experience with the latter approach.)

The question of how much error is tolerable between physical inventory and records has been much debated. While some firms strive for 100 percent accuracy, others accept 1, 2, or 3 percent error. Regardless of the specific accuracy decided upon, the important point is that the level be dependable so that safety stocks may be provided as a cushion. Accuracy is important for a smooth production process so that customer orders can be processed as scheduled and not held up due to the unavailability of parts.

Inventory control in services

In order to demonstrate how inventory control is conducted in services, we have selected three areas to describe: a department store, an automobile service agency, and a savings and loan institution.

Department store inventory policy. The common term used to identify an inventory item in a department store is *SKU*, or stock-keeping unit. The SKU identifies each item, its manufacturer, and its cost. The number of SKUs becomes large even for small departments. For example, if towels carried in a domestic items department are obtained from three manufacturers in three quality levels, three sizes (hand towel, face towel, and bath towel), and four colors, there are 108 different items (3 × 3 × 3 × 4). Even if towels are sold only in sets of a hand towel, face towel, and bath towel, the number of SKUs needed to identify the towel sets is 3 × 3 × 1 × 4, or 36. Depending on the store, a housewares department may carry 3,000 to 4,000 SKUs, and a linen and domestic items department may carry 5,000 to 6,000.

Obviously, such large numbers mean that individual economic order quantities cannot be calculated for each item by hand. How, then, does a department keep tab on its stock and place orders for replenishment? We will answer this question in the context of an example dealing with a housewares department. But first, we will give some background on the operation of a typical department in a department store.

Operations of a department. Individual departments in a department store are generally autonomous units and are accountable for profit or loss. The staff consists of a buyer, who is also head of the department, an assistant buyer, a secretary, clerks, and stock personnel. Items are separated into categories, generally as staple items and fashion or promotional items. Staple items are standard stock items and have a fairly predictable demand pattern. Promotional and fashion items are special-purpose items. Such items and their promotion method are never precisely repeated, and usually, they are not regular stock.

The buyer's efforts are concentrated primarily on the second category, fashion and promotion items. He (or she) searches for special purchase opportunities from vendors, including product line closeouts. The objective with promotional and fashion items is to clear out the stock by the end of the season or by the final day of the promotional campaign. Determining what the selling price should be and what demand to expect is to a large extent based on the experience and market sensitivity of the buyer. If the demand is underestimated, the shortage may embarrass the department by creating unhappy customers, or more costly merchandise must be substituted. Too large a purchase or too high a selling price will leave unsold items at the end of the promotion. The problem, then, is how to clear out the stock. Extending its length defeats the idea of a promotion, indicating that perhaps the item has become standard stock.

To estimate demand for promotion and fashion items, advertising history results are useful, and the attempt is made to correlate the number of units sold at particular prices with their promotional advertising. Although promotions at different points of time are rarely identical, some indications can nevertheless be derived by comparing a planned promotion with previous ones.

More than half of the buyer's time is spent in finding new products, closing out old items, searching for factory specials, preparing advertising, and determining promotional strategies. The remaining time is devoted to overseeing the operation of the department.

Housewares department. A wide variety of ways is available to operate this type of department. Generally, housewares are divided into staple and promotional items, as previously described. Within these major divisions, further classifications are used, such as cookware and tableware. Also, items are frequently classified by price, as $5 items, $4, $3, and so forth.

The housewares department usually purchases from a distributor rather than directly from a vendor. The use of a distributor who handles products from many vendors has the advantage of fewer orders and faster shipping time (shorter lead time). Further, the distributor's sales personnel may visit the housewares department weekly and count all the items he supplies to this department. Then, in line with the replenishment level that has been established by the buyer, the distributor's salesman will place orders for the buyer. This saves the department time in counting inventory and placing orders. The typical lead time for receipt of stock from a housewares distributor is two or three days. The safety stock, therefore, is quite low, and the buyer establishes the replenishment level so as to supply only enough items for the two- to three-day lead time, plus expected demand during the period until the distributor's sales personnel's next visit.

It is interesting to note that a formal method of estimating stockout and establishing safety stock levels is usually not followed because the number of items is too great. Instead, the total value of items in the department is monitored. Thus, replenishment levels are set by dollar allocation.

Through planning, each department has an established monthly value for inventory. By tabulating inventory balance, monthly sales, and items on order, an "open-to-buy" figure is determined ("open-to-buy" is the yet unspent portion of the budget). This dollar amount is the sum available to the buyer for the following month. When an increase in demand is expected (Christmas, Mother's Day, and so forth), the allocation of funds to the department is increased, resulting in a larger open-to-buy position. Then the replenishment levels are raised in line with the class of goods responding to the demand increase, thereby creating a higher stock of goods on hand.

In practice, the open-to-buy funds are largely spent during the first days of the month. However, the buyer tries to reserve some of the funds for special purchases or to restock fast-moving items. (Promotional items in housewares are controlled individually [or by class] by the buyer.)

Maintaining auto replacement parts inventory. A firm in the automobile service business purchases the bulk of its parts supplies from a small number of distributors. Franchised new-car dealers purchase the great bulk of their supplies from the automobile manufacturer. A dealer's demand for auto parts originates primarily from the general public and other departments of the agency, such as the service department or body shop. The problem, in this case, is to determine the order quantities for the several thousand items carried.

A franchised automobile agency of medium size may carry a parts inventory valued in the area of $500,000. Because of the nature of this industry, alternate uses of funds are plentiful, and therefore, opportunity costs are high. For example, dealers may lease cars, carry their own contracts, stock a larger new-car inventory, or open sidelines such as tire shops, trailers, or recreational vehicles—all with potentially high returns. This creates pressure to try to carry a low inventory level of parts and supplies while still meeting an acceptable service level.

While many dealers still perform their inventory ordering by hand, there is a definite trend in the industry to using a computer for parts ordering. For both manual and computerized systems, an ABC-type classification works well. Expensive and high turnover supplies are counted and ordered frequently; low-cost items are ordered in large quantities at infrequent intervals. A common drawback of frequent order placement is the extensive amount of time needed to physically put the items on the shelves and log them in. (However, this restocking procedure does not greatly add to an auto agency's cost since parts department personnel generally do this during lulls or "slow" periods.)

A great variety of computerized systems is currently in use. One program gives a choice of using either a simple weighted average or exponential smoothing to forecast the next period's demand. In a monthly reordering system, for example, the items to be ordered are counted and the number on hand is entered into the computer. By subtracting the number on hand from the previous month's inventory and adding the orders received during the month, the usage rate is determined. The computer program stores the usage rate for, say, four previous months. Then, with the application of a set of weighting factors, a forecast is made in the same manner as described in Chapter 4. This works as follows. Suppose usage of a part during January, February, March, and April was 17, 19, 11, and 23, respectively, and the set of corresponding weights was 0.10, 0.20, 0.30 and 0.40. Thus, the forecast for May is $0.10(17) + 0.20(19) + 0.30(11) + 0.40(23)$, or 18 units. If the order policy including safety stock is based on a two-month demand, 36 units will be ordered, less whatever is on hand at the time of order placement. The simple two-month rule allows for forecasted usage during the lead time plus the review period, with the balance providing the safety stock.

The computer output provides a useful reference file since it identifies the item, lists the cost, states the order size, and gives the number of units on hand. The output itself constitutes the purchase order and is sent to the distributor or factory supply house. The simplicity in this is attractive since, once the forecast weighting is selected, all that must be done is to input the number of units of each item on hand. Thus, negligible computation is involved, and very little preparation is needed to send the order out.

Savings and loan institution construction loans. A large part of the funds of a savings and loan institution is invested in mortgages and construction loans. *Mortgage* loans are single-sum loans, effective on the transfer of existing property. *Construction* loans are made to contractors to cover their expenses incurred during the construction process. The latter are usually made in segments, and a loan terminates when the construction project is completed. At the start of a project, a contractor's financial needs are small, but as the project nears completion, the contractor has a sizable investment and, consequently, a greater need for funds. The ideal timing of the sequence of loans to a contractor to support a project would be such that it corresponds with the contractor's investment in that project. A contractor who is building individual residential homes, for example, might draw five equal cash sums on each home from a prearranged bank loan, totaling to the agreed upon loan. Large construction projects, such as commercial buildings or shopping centers, may draw cash in 20 to 30 unequal sums, as needed.

The problem for the loan institution is to predict the cash flow. The inventory in this case is cash, and the exogenous demand on this cash inventory is the cash draw on approved mortgages and construction loans. Whereas inventory shortages and averages are vague in department stores, they are specific and obvious in financial institutions. If the demand for mortgage and construction cash exceeds the inventory set aside by the loan institution, funds must be immediately obtained elsewhere to avoid violation of operating statutes. There is a strong desire, therefore, not to run short of funds. Conversely, excess cash inventory results in lost income to the institution because it has not invested this unused portion in interest-bearing loans or securities.[6]

Consider the following construction-loan example of an institution that, for illustration, is restricted solely to single-unit residential construction. In planning for a housing development, a contractor approaches the institution and obtains a construction loan on each home in his proposed development. A condition of the loan contract is that the contractor may draw cash from the total loan in five equal installments. (The size of draws may vary, but for most home-construction loans, five draws is common.) In theory, the construction loan is awarded to the contractor in increments rather than as a lump sum. The idea, as previously mentioned, is that as construction of the home progresses, it increases in value and, therefore, provides increased collateral for the mortgage. Further, the contractor's need for funds increases as his investment in the home increases. Thus on a $50,000 construction-loan arrangement, a contractor may go to the institution and make five withdrawals of $10,000 each against this loan (less the interest charges). Thus, if the contractor takes five months to complete this home and his investment in labor, materials, and equipment increases linearly, he would draw $10,000 against the loan in each of the five months of construction. When the home is sold, the buyer (or new mortgage holder) pays off the construction loan.

The difficulties for the loan institution in forecasting draws on construction loans arise because there are many contractors who have many homes under development. Progress and investment on the construction are *not* linear, and contractors do not draw sums of money against the loans at the *same* time intervals. Also, a contractor frequently skips a draw completing the home—for example, after having taken only 60 or 80 percent of his available loan. He then may draw the last two increments simultaneously. This variation in the time of draws, combined with the operating differences among contractors, makes the calculation of cash needs difficult.

This situation, however, lends itself to solution by computer simulation. As is discussed in the Chapter 12 Technical note, the procedure is to design a model of the real system and then simulate the behavior of that system over time. The model, in this case, consists of the approved loans, the contractors who are likely to draw against the loans, and the cash inventory. The simulation procedure requires that the history of each contractor and his draws be analyzed, and then a probability forecast is made for each contractor's likelihood of making specific cash draws. Then, based on these sets of probabilities, the model is run a number of times on

---

[6] The amount of lost revenue due to excess cash inventory can be significant. For a $2 million construction loan operation (a relatively small operation), a 5 percent excess in cash amounts to a surplus of $100,000, which if invested at 10 percent represents an annual loss of $10,000. Losses are actually larger than this since errors between forecasted and actual cash draws by contractors leave more in the order of 15 percent excess cash in inventory.

the computer in simulation of the planning period, and this gives a range of possible cash inventory needs. Confidence intervals are computed and printed out to allow the loan officer to select an inventory level with the degree of risk to suit his judgment.

For example, the simulation of cash draws by contractors in one simulation had a mean expected cash flow of $2 million. However, 90 percent of the loans ranged from $1.75 to $2.3 million, and 95 percent were included in the range $1.6 to $2.5 million.[7] In light of this, if the loan officer planned that $2.3 million in cash would be drawn during the month, there would be a 5 percent chance that more than $2.3 million would be drawn. By computing various confidence intervals, the loan officer has a good estimate of the range of cash demands and can plan on alternative ways to meet them.

INVENTORY MANAGEMENT PROGRAM AND CONTROL TECHNIQUES (IMPACT)

IBM's Inventory Management Program and Control Techniques software system (IMPACT) was designed for firms whose main concern is the distribution phase of a production/distribution system.[8] Wholesalers, for example, are prime users. In these applications, the basic decisions of order size, order points, and so forth become of paramount importance since they are an essential, rather than a peripheral, feature of the firm's mission as a supplier. In this section, the theoretical bases of the IMPACT system will be presented, along with discussion on various aspects of the computer program itself.

IMPACT is based on independent demand and, therefore, uses traditional or classical inventory analysis. These models apply to wholesalers, retailers, or suppliers of basic materials, where most items ordered are in their own right and not because of the simultaneous order for some other item. (Obviously, however, there is the desire to consolidate orders where possible to save handling and shipping charges.)

Functions and objectives of IMPACT

The goal of IMPACT is to provide operating rules to minimize cost. In order to do this, the following functions must be performed.

1. Forecast demand.
2. Determine the safety stock required for a specified level of service.
3. Determine the order quantity and time for reorder.
4. Consider the effects of freight rates and quantity discounts.
5. Estimate the expected results of the inventory plan.

---

[7] K. G. Brown and J. C. Heckman, "The Prediction of Construction Loan Cash Flow" (College of Business and Public Administration, University of Arizona, June 1971).

[8] This section is based on the following IBM publications: *Inventory Control*, 520–14491; *Introduction to IBM Wholesale IMPACT*, E20–0278–0; *Basic Principles of Wholesale IMPACT*, E20–8105–1; *Wholesale IMPACT—Advanced Principles and Implementations Manual*, E20–0174–0.

The IMPACT system does all this in two phases: a startup phase and an operating phase. The startup phase consists of the initializing and estimating segment, which sets up the system and is brought into play whenever conditions or objectives change. The basic functions in this phase are:

1. Select the forecasting model and ordering strategy.
2. Calculate starting values for factors used in forecasting and ordering.
3. Estimate the results.

The operating system on a day-to-day basis does the following.

1. Decides when and how much to order
2. Makes new forecasts of demand and forecast error
3. Keeps records of issues, receipts, inventory status, etc.
4. Collects data to measure performance of the system

Exhibit 15.20 shows the work flow of the IBM IMPACT system. In this diagram, the solid black line indicates that transactions are entered. They may occur at any time.

The solid color line indicates functions that are performed every review period. If a fixed-time period plan is used, items are reviewed each week, biweekly, or monthly. In a fixed-quantity system, the inventory status is reviewed after each transaction to see if the stock on hand has dropped to the reorder point, justifying placement of a new order.

The dashed color line indicates that new forecasts are made. Typically, demand forecasts are made for periods of one, two, or four weeks.

The dashed black line shows initialization or reinitialization. This occurs when the program is started and whenever the conditions or objectives are changed.

The flows in the figure are typical, although differences may appear in individual applications because of various program options.

To operate the system, the users provide their own program routines, which are to be used in combination with the IMPACT program. They write their own programs for record keeping, updating the master file, forecasting, performance measurement, order follow-up (preparing purchase orders, status listings, and so forth), and linkages between their programs and IMPACT library functions. (The IMPACT library programs for initializing, estimating, and ordering.)[9]

To get an idea of the detailed operations carried out by IMPACT, we have summarized (below) the way it treats forecasting and ordering.

Forecasting. The forecasting models used in IMPACT are horizontal, trend, and seasonal (or cyclical) models.

The *horizontal* model represents demand about the average value, which

---

[9] The IMPACT program gives very good, though not optimal, results. For more detailed comments and correction factors see: J. P. C. Kleijnen and P. J. Rens, "IMPACT Revisited: A Critical Analysis of IBM's Inventory Package 'IMPACT'," *Production and Inventory Management,* vol. 19, no 1. (First Quarter 1978), pp. 71–90.

EXHIBIT 15.20
Work flow and functions performed in a typical IMPACT system

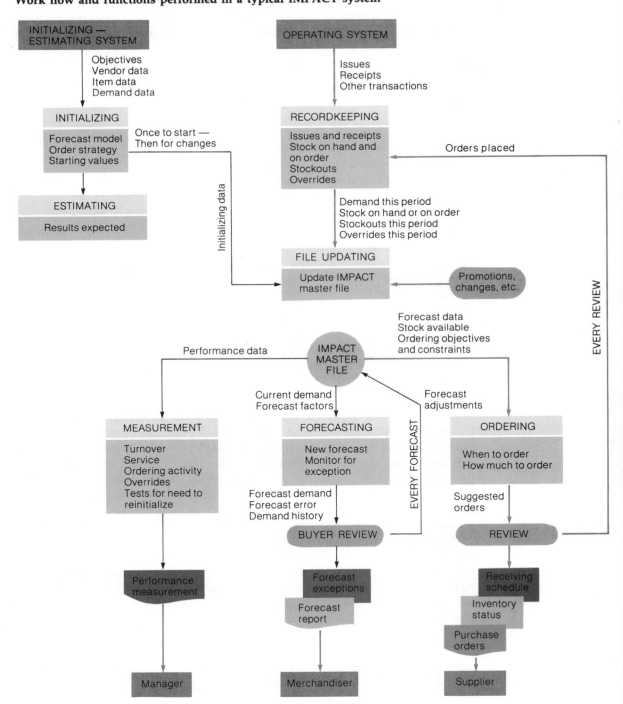

contains only random variation. Exponential smoothing is used to forecast demand, thereby placing more emphasis on recent history. The *trend* model looks for an increasing or decreasing demand over time. Trends may be determined in a variety of ways, although the IMPACT program itself uses double exponential smoothing.

The *seasonal* model can be used when there is some known reason for upswings and downswings. The model can be used for prediction only if the cause is identifiable or if it is repetitive over time. IBM suggests that the peaks and valleys should vary by at least 30 to 50 percent to justify the expense of using the seasonal model. Seasonal items are handled by applying a multiplier to each period of the year. For example, if the average monthly demand for the year is taken as a base value of one, each month is related to that base. If August demand is twice that of the average month, its index would be 2. If March is 60 percent of the average, its index is 0.6. A seasonal forecast is then derived by forecasting average demand by exponential smoothing and multiplying the resultant value by the index value for the period to be forecast.

Forecast error. Deviations are expected regardless of the forecasting model employed. In IMPACT, the assumption is that the deviations are normally distributed and can be represented by the mean absolute deviation (MAD).[10] The program recommends either the horizontal, trend, or seasonal model, based on its calculation of the minimum mean absolute error. When errors in forecasts are consistently above or below the forecast, a measurement is made to help correct this bias. This is called a *tracking signal* and algebraically is equal to the sum of errors divided by the mean absolute deviation.

Additional inputs to the forecast can be made at the option of the user. For example, if a promotion is planned for a particular time period, a straight historical analysis would be incomplete in this case, and the buyer who handles the promotion must therefore insert information about when the promotion is to start and how long it will last. The buyer may estimate demands or may utilize a program feature which will provide him with an estimate. Exhibit 15.21 shows the monthly forecasting results for a ball-point pen promotion. Note that MAD is exponentially smoothed and also that tracking signal limits of ±6 are quite wide.

Forecast monitoring. To guard against errors, exception reporting is provided. The program detects significant differences both for demands that differ from the forecast and for forecasts that consistently differ from demand. This monitoring will usually detect errors in data or in keypunching.

Ordering. This phase determines what, when, and how much to order. It is accomplished by establishing some service level and then considering the appropriate inventory costs.

---

[10] As stated in Chapter 4, MAD is the average of the differences between the forecast sales and the actual sales, disregarding the plus or minus signs.

EXHIBIT 15.21

Example of forecasting a ball-point pen promotion with machine computation of promotion estimates

α = 0.1
Tracking signal limits = ±6

Item #4364
Description: bargain ball-point pens

Period	Demand	Forecast (made previous period)	Error	MAD*	Error SUM†	Tracking signal‡	This period promotional effect	Error from old promotional forecast	New promotion index	Promotion forecast MAD	Next month forecast
Initial Values				(329)	(−125)				(900)	(500)	(Index) (2,750)
June	3,285	2,750	+535	350	+410	+1.17					2,804
July	3,047	2,804	+243	339	+653	+1.93					2,828 (+900)
August§	3,873	2,828 (+900)	=	=	=	=	+1045	+145	915	(464)	2,828#
September	2,661	2,828#	−167	322	+486	+1.51					2,811
October	2,806	2,811	−5	290	+481	+1.66					2,810
November	2,514	2,810	−296	291	+185	+.64					2,780
December	2,909	2,780	+129	275	+314	+1.10					2,793 (+915)
January§	3,889	2,793 (+915)	=	=	=	=	+1096	+181	933	(436)	2,793#
February	2,873	2,793#	+80	255	+391	+1.55					2,801
March	2,659	2,801	−142	244	+252	+1.03					2,787
April	3,133	2,787	+346	254	+598	+2.35					2,822
May	2,729	2,822	−93	238	+505	+2.12					2,813

* Calculated from equation as in Chapter 4. $MAD_t = \alpha|A_{t-1} - F_{t-1}| + (1 - \alpha)MAD_{t-1}$. For example $MAD_{June} = .1|3285 - 2750| + .9(329) = 350$.
† This is the Running Sum of Forecast Errors (RSFE) used in Chapter 4.
‡ The tracking signal is the error sum divided by MAD.
§ Promotion month.
‖ Not calculated; use value for former period.
Not calculated; use same forecast and MAD as for previous month but exclude promotional corrections.

Service level. The IMPACT program defines service level the same way as does common usage; that is, as the percentage of demand that is filled from stock on hand. A 98 percent service level means that 98 units can be offered directly from stock for each 100 demanded.

Order strategy. Items may be ordered independently (without regard for other items) or jointly (to take advantage of quantity discounts or transportation savings). The costs that are considered are (1) the cost of ordering (clerical and handling costs), (2) inventory carrying costs, and (3) opportunity costs (for example, savings or avoidable expenditures available but not taken, such as quantity discounts or lower freight rates).

When to order. The program decides the time for order placement, based on individual or joint order placement, and the forecasted demand, error, and lead time.

Order quantity. For individual items, the classic fixed-order quantity model is used:

$$Q = \sqrt{\frac{2DS}{H}}$$

where

Q = Economic order quantity
D = Annual demand
S = Cost for handling and processing an order
H = Inventory carrying costs, such as insurance, taxes, depreciation, and so forth

If discounts are available for larger-quantity purchases, the program computes the additional feasible order quantities and selects the lowest cost.

When several items are ordered at the same time (termed a *joint ordering strategy*), the total must meet some quantity range (such as a carload lot) while at the same time satisfying individual item service level requirements. This is accomplished by an "allocation" subroutine that adjusts the total order up or down, based on individual economic order quantities and desired service levels.

Overrides in order placement are always allowed. This may be purely a management decision, for whatever purpose, or may be aimed to correct such things as erroneous data.

Results from using the IMPACT system

Among the results claimed by users of IMPACT are:

1. Reduced inventory costs because
    a. Either inventory size has been reduced with no loss in service to customers or service levels have increased with no additional inventory stocking.
    b. Buyers can spend more time in problem areas or in developing new strategies since they have been relieved of routine purchasing decisions.

2. Improved management control because
    a. The specified rules and objectives are consistent.
    b. Rules and objectives can be easily revised.
    c. Effective measures of system effectiveness are available.
    d. Service is more stable.
    e. There is a smoother work load for personnel.
    f. Awareness of inventory concepts brought out by this program brings improvement in other areas.
    g. The process of data gathering needed to set up the program points out unprofitable product lines and abnormally slow-moving items.
    h. The costs output from the program are valuable for profit analysis and planning.
    i. A framework is created that can be expanded to include potentially valuable applications, such as automatic generation and placement of orders with the vendor and provision of forecasts and other information directly to the retailer.

CONCLUSION

To reiterate the focus of this chapter, demand for inventory items falls into two main classes: independent demand, for the most part referring to the external demand for a firm's end product, and dependent demand, usually referring—within the firm—to the demand for items created because of the demand for more complex items of which they are a part. Most industries, however, have items in both classes. In manufacturing, for example, independent demand is common for finished products, service and repair parts, and operating supplies; and dependent demand is common for those parts and materials needed to produce the end product. In wholesale and retail sales, most demand is independent since each item is an end item with no assembly or fabrication taking place, although there are some supply-type items for which the demand may be imputed from customer orders. That is, demand for wrapping paper and boxes for a wholesaler is a function of the size and number of shipments, demand for bagging material in the produce area of a market is derived from the volume of produce sold, and the demand for plastic trays and plastic wrap in the meat department is related to the volume of meat sold.

For independent demand, the subject of this chapter, analysis for inventory control is based on statistics. Several fixed-order quantity and fixed-time period models were described. Service level was defined, and its influence was shown on safety stock and reorder point determinations. Two special purpose models—price break and single-period models using marginal analysis—were also presented. ABC analysis was offered as a means for distinguishing among item categories for purposes of general inventory analysis and control and an ABC example of one company was shown.

Further, the importance of inventory accuracy was noted, and cycle counting was described. Brief descriptions of inventory procedures in a department store, an auto parts shop, and a savings and loan institution were intended to illustrate some of the simpler ways in which non-manufacturing firms carry out their inventory control function. Finally, IBM's IMPACT program was presented as one example of the many useful computer programs that enable managers to deal effectively with complex independent demand situations.

REVIEW AND DISCUSSION QUESTIONS

1. What are the various purposes of inventory.

2. Distinguish between in-process inventory, safety stock inventory, and seasonal inventory.

3. Discuss the nature of the costs that affect inventory size.

4. Under what conditions would one elect to use a fixed-order quantity model as opposed to a fixed-time period model? What are the disadvantages of using a fixed-time period ordering system?

5. The two main categories for inventory models are deterministic and probabilistic models. What are the distinguishing differences of these categories?

6. Define the term *service level* as used in this text. How does it differ from the concept of "probability of stockout?"

7. Describe what is happening (i.e., the sequence of calculations) in Exhibit 15.20, the IMPACT forecast for a ball-point pen promotion.

8. Discuss the general procedure for determining the order quantity when price breaks are involved. Would there be any differences in the procedure if holding cost were a fixed percentage of price rather than a constant amount?

9. What two basic questions must be answered by an inventory control decision rule?

10. Discuss the assumptions that are inherent in production setup cost, ordering cost, and carrying costs. How valid are they?

11. "The nice thing about inventory models is that you can pull one off the shelf and apply it so long as your cost estimates are accurate." Comment.

12. What type of inventory system do you use in the following situations?
    a. Supplying your kitchen with fresh food
    b. Obtaining a daily newspaper
    c. Buying gasoline for your car
    To which of the above items do you impute the highest stockout cost?

13. Why is it desirable to classify items into groups as does the ABC classification?

14. What kind of policy or procedure would you recommend to improve the inventory operation in a department store? What advantages and disadvantages does your system have vis-à-vis the department store inventory operation described in this chapter?

15. What types of firms might use IBM's IMPACT program? What functions does the program perform?

16. How does the IMPACT system forecast demand?

PROBLEMS

1. Items purchased from a vendor cost $20 each, and the forecast for next year's demand is 1,000 units. If it costs $5 every time an order is placed for more units and the storage cost is $4 per unit per year, what quantity should be ordered each time.
   a. What is the total ordering cost for a year?
   b. What is the total storage cost for a year?

2. Item X is a standard item stocked in a company's inventory of component parts. Each year, the firm, on a random basis, uses about 2,000 of item X. Item X costs $25 each. Storage costs which include insurance, cost of capital, and so forth amount to $5 per unit of average inventory. Every time an order is placed for more item X, it costs $10.
   a. Whenever item X is ordered, what should the order size be?
   b. What is the annual cost for ordering item X?
   c. What is the annual cost for storing item X?

3. Annual demand for an item is 2,500 units. The cost to place an order is $5, and holding cost is 20 percent of the cost of the item. Items have the following cost schedule:

1 to 99	$10 each
100 to 199	$ 9.80 each
over 200	$ 9.60 each

   What is the optimum number to order each time?

4. Demand for an item is 1,000 units per year. Each time an order is placed, there is a $10 cost involved. The cost to carry items in inventory is $2 each.
   a. In what quantities should the item be ordered?
   b. Supposing that an annual savings of $200 can be obtained if orders are placed in quantities of 500 or more ($100 discount on each order). Should orders be placed in quantities of 500, or should you stick to your decision in a above.

5. A particular raw material is available to a company at three different prices, depending on the size of the order as follows:

Less than 100 pounds	$20 per pound
100 pounds to 999 pounds	$19 per pound
more than 1,000 pounds	$18 per pound

   The cost to place an order is $40.
   Annual demand is 3,000 units.
   Holding (or carrying) cost is 25 percent of the material cost.

   Question: What is the economic order quantity to buy each time?

6. In the past, Taylor Industries has used a fixed-time period inventory system which involved taking a complete inventory count of all items each month. However, increasing labor costs are forcing Taylor Industries to examine alternate ways to reduce the amount of labor involved in inventory stock-rooms and yet without increasing their other costs, such as shortage costs, and so forth.

Following is a random sample of 20 of their items.

Item number	Annual usage	Item number	Annual usage
1......	$ 1,500	11	$13,000
2......	12,000	12	600
3......	2,200	13	42,000
4......	50,000	14	9,900
5......	9,600	15	1,200
6......	750	16	10,200
7......	2,000	17	4,000
8......	11,000	18	61,000
9......	800	19	3,500
10......	15,000	20	2,900

a. What would you recommend they do to cut back their labor cost? (Use an ABC plan.)
b. Item 15 is critical to continued operations. How would you recommend classifying number 15 under this condition?

7. Gentle Ben's Bar and Restaurant uses 5,000 quart bottles of an imported wine each year. The particular effervescent wine costs $3 per bottle and is served in whole bottles only since it looses its bubbles quickly. Ben figures that it costs $10 each time an order is placed, and holding costs are 20 percent of the purchase price.

It takes three weeks for an order to arrive. Weekly demand is 100 bottles (closed two weeks per year) with a standard deviation of 30 bottles.

Ben would like to use an inventory system which minimizes his inventory cost and will satisfy 95 percent of his customers who order this wine.
a. What is the economic order quantity for Ben to order?
b. At what inventory level should he place an order?
c. How many bottles of wine will be short during each order cycle?

8. University Drug Pharmaceuticals orders its antibiotics every two weeks (14 days) when a salesman visits from one of the pharmaceutical companies. Tetracycline is one of its most prescribed antibiotics with an average daily demand of 2,000 capsules. The standard deviation of daily demand was derived from examining prescriptions filled over the past three months and was found to be 800 capsules. It takes five days for the order to arrive. University Drug would like to satisfy 99 percent of the perscriptions. The salesman just arrived, and there are currently 25,000 capsules in stock.

How many capsules should be ordered?

9. According to the economic lot size formula, if the annual requirement for an item iś 8,000 units, setup costs are $20, and the cost of holding the item in inventory is $0.20 per year, what is the economic lot size to order?

Supposing the holding cost doubled to $0.40 per year, what is the percentage effect on the order size?

10. Magnetron, Inc., manufactures microwave ovens for the commercial market. Currently, Magnetron is producing part 2104 in its fabrication shop for use in the adjacent unit assembly area. Next year's requirement for part 2104 is estimated at 20,000 units. Part 2104 is valued at $50 per unit, and the combined storage and handling cost is $8 per unit per year. The cost of preparing the order and making the production setup is $200. The plant operates 250 days per year. The assembly area operates every working day, completing 80 units, and the fabrication shop produces 160 units per day when it is producing part 2104.

   a. Compute the economic order quantity.
   b. How many orders will be placed each year?
   c. If part 2104 could be purchased from another firm with the same costs as above, what would the order quantity be? (The order is received all at once.)
   d. If the average lead time to order from another firm is ten working days and a safety stock level is set at 500 units, what is the reorder point?

11. Garrett Corporation, a turbine manufacturer, works an 18-hour day, 300 days a year. Titanium blades can be produced on its turbine blade machine number 1, TBM1, at a rate of 500 per hour, and the average usage rate is 5,000 per day. The blades cost $15 apiece, and storage costs $0.10 per day per blade because of insurance, interest on investments, and space allocation. TBM1 costs $250 to set up for each run. Lead time requires production to begin after stock drops to 500 blades. What is the optimum production run for TBM1?

12. A popular item stocked by the Fair Deal Department Store has an expected demand for next year of 600 units. The cost to purchase these units from a supplier is $20 per unit and $12 to prepare the purchase order. The annual carrying cost is $4 per unit.

   a. Show graphically (cost versus order quantity) the various costs involved in this problem.
   b. Mathematically, determine the economic order quantity.
   c. If Fair Deal is currently ordering 100 units at a time, how much could it save by using the EOQ?

13. Sunrise Baking Company is trying to determine the number of doughnuts it should make each day. From an analysis of its past demands, Sunrise estimates the demand for doughnuts as

Demand	Probability of demand
1,800 dozen	0.05
2,000	0.10
2,200	0.20
2,400	0.30
2,600	0.20
2,800	0.10
3,000	0.05

Each dozen sells for $0.69 and costs $0.49, which includes handling and transportation, as well as the mix. Doughnuts that are not sold at the end of the day are reduced to $0.29 and sold the following day as day-old merchandise.

a. Construct a table showing the profit or losses for each possible quantity.

b. What is the optimum number of doughnuts to make?

c. Solve this problem by using marginal analysis.

14. Apples that are not sold during the season for immediate consumption by eating, canning, or freezing are used to make cider, and a food broker is trying to decide how many apples he should buy from the orchards in order to maximize his profit. He estimates his potential sales to be normally distributed with a mean of 10,000 bushels and a standard deviation of 1,000 bushels. He can buy the apples for $3 per bushel, and will receive $5 per bushel for those he sells. Unsold apples to be used for cider are worth $2 per bushel for that purpose.

Using marginal analysis and Appendix D at the end of the book, how many apples should the broker buy? Do the problem both by marginal analysis and in the tabular form for a range of purchase levels.

15. The text described how one department store conducted its inventory ordering for a housewares department. How could you apply the theory and models in this chapter to enhance the operation of the system?

SELECTED BIBLIOGRAPHY

Backes, Robert W. "Cycle Counting—A Better Way for Achieving Accurate Inventory Records," *Production and Inventory Management,* vol. 21, no. 2 (Second Quarter 1980), pp. 36–44.

Hadley, G., and Whitin, T. M. *Analysis of Inventory Systems.* Englewood Cliffs, N.J.: Prentice-Hall, 1963.

International Business Machines Corporation *Basic Principles of Wholesale IMPACT.* Publication E20–8105–1.

———— *Introduction to IBM Wholesale IMPACT.* Publication E20–0278–0.

———— *Inventory Control.* Publication 520–14491.

———— *Wholesale IMPACT—Advanced Principles and Implementations Manual.* Publication E20–0174–0.

Plossl, G. W., and Wight, O. W. *Production and Inventory Control.* Englewood Cliffs, N.J.: Prentice-Hall, 1967.

Plossl, George W., and Welch, W. Evert *The Role of Top Management in the Control of Inventory.* Reston, Va: Reston Publishing Co., Inc., 1979.

Wight, Oliver W. *Production and Inventory Management in the Computer Age.* Boston, Mass: Cahners Books, 1974.

Chapter

16

DESIGN OF INVENTORY SYSTEMS FOR DEPENDENT DEMAND: MATERIAL REQUIREMENTS PLANNING

When demand for materials, components, or subassemblies occurs because of the demand for a "higher level" item, then these materials, components, or subassemblies are referred to as dependent demand items. Their need depends on the demand for some product of which they are a part. In our introductory example in the previous chapter, the higher level item was cars, and the dependent items were wheels.

Dependent demand implies that the process of determining how many items are needed and when they are needed is simply computed from how the end product is designed and the production process which it goes through. This contrasts with independent demand items which must be forecast. The term independence implies that there is a distinct separate demand for the item. That is, it faces its own market, and determining the size of that market requires a forecasting technique or model such as those presented in Chapters 4 and 15.

Also discussed in Chapters 4 and 15 was that independent demand items are dispersed throughout some time period and may consist of time series components such as trend, seasonal cyclical, and random factors. This necessitates that we forecast demand and also provide safety stocks to achieve some specified service level.

Dependent demand, in contrast, is usually not dispersed throughout the time period but rather tends to occur at specific points. Thus, dependent demand is called *lumpy*. Lumpy demand is caused by the way the production process is operated. Most manufacturing occurs in lots, and all the items needed to produce the lot are usually withdrawn from inventory at the same time, not unit-by-unit.

In addition to the demand for units created through dependent demand, the timing of their need is also crucial. The main topic of this chapter, Material Requirements Planning,[1] deals also with this scheduling problem. After discussing the logic of Material Requirements Planning and presenting an example, we will comment on various aspects of the procedure and then follow this with a brief description of the Production Information and Control System (PICS), which incorporates the same logic, and the Communications Oriented Production Information and Control System (COPICS), which is still in the developmental stage.

BENEFITS OF A MATERIAL REQUIREMENTS PLANNING (MRP) SYSTEM

Most companies with over $20 million in annual sales either have a computerized Material Requirements Planning system or are planning to install one. A computerized system is necessary because of the sheer volume of materials, supplies, and components which are part of expanding product lines, and the speed which firms need to react to constant changes in the system. In past years, when firms switched from existing manual or computerized systems to an MRP system, they realized the following benefits.

Increased sales.

Reduced sales price.

Reduced inventory.

Better customer service.

Better response to market demands.

Ability to change the master schedule.

Reduced setup and tear-down costs.

Reduced idle time.

In addition, the MRP system:

Gives advance notice so managers can see the planned schedule before actual release of orders.

Tells when to de-expedite as well as expedite.

Delays or cancels orders.

Changes order quantities.

---

[1] The current popularity of Materials Requirements Planning is due in great part to the campaigning of Dr. Joseph Orlicky of IBM, the American Production and Inventory Control Society with its large number of publications and teaching aids, and the highly successful lectures, consulting assignments, and writings of men such as Oliver Wight and George Plossl. Much of the material in this chapter has been influenced by the authors' attendance at MRP workshops hosted by Dr. Orlicky and IBM.

Advances or delays order due dates.

Aids capacity planning.

Some users have claimed as much as a 40 percent reduction in inventory investment.

Today, firms that do convert still realize the same benefits. Moreover, it has become necessary for them to adopt the system because competitor firms are using it.

A SIMPLE MRP EXAMPLE

Before we develop the subject of material requirements planning systems in detail, let us give a very brief illustration of MRP calculations.

Suppose that we are to produce a product called T, which is made of two parts U and three parts V. Part U, in turn, is made of one part W and two parts X. Part V is made of two parts W and two parts Y. Exhibit 16.1 shows the product structure tree of product T. By simple computation, then, we can calculate that if 100 units of T are required, then we will need:

$$
\begin{aligned}
\text{Part U:} \quad & 2 \times \text{number of T's} = & 2 \times 100 & = 200 \\
\text{Part V:} \quad & 3 \times \text{number of T's} = & 3 \times 100 & = 300 \\
\text{Part W:} & \begin{cases} 1 \times \text{number of U's} \\ +2 \times \text{number of V's} \end{cases} = \begin{cases} 1 \times 200 \\ +2 \times 300 \end{cases} & = 800 \\
\text{Part X:} \quad & 2 \times \text{number of U's} = & 2 \times 200 & = 400 \\
\text{Part Y:} \quad & 2 \times \text{number of V's} = & 2 \times 300 & = 600
\end{aligned}
$$

Now, consider the time element to obtain these items. This time can pertain either to the time needed to produce the part internally or to the time needed to obtain the part from an outside vendor. Assume, now, that T takes one week to make; U, 2 weeks; V, 2 weeks; W, 3 weeks; X, 1 week; and Y, 1 week. If we know when product T is required, we can create a time schedule chart specifying when all materials must be ordered and received to meet the demand for T. Exhibit 16.2 shows which items are needed and when they are needed. We have thus created a materials requirements plan based on the demand for product T and the knowledge of how T is made and the time needed to obtain each part.

EXHIBIT 16.1
Product structure tree for product T

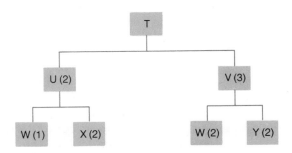

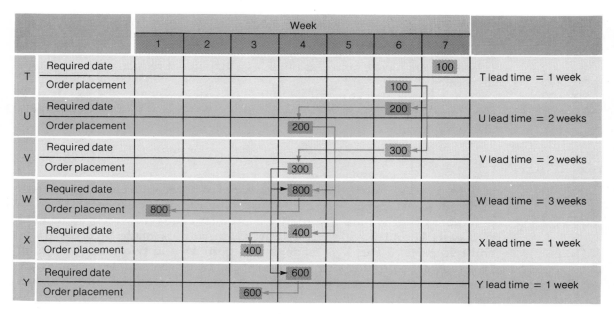

		Week							
		1	2	3	4	5	6	7	
T	Required date							100	T lead time = 1 week
	Order placement						100		
U	Required date						200		U lead time = 2 weeks
	Order placement				200				
V	Required date						300		V lead time = 2 weeks
	Order placement				300				
W	Required date				800				W lead time = 3 weeks
	Order placement	800							
X	Required date				400				X lead time = 1 week
	Order placement			400					
Y	Required date				600				Y lead time = 1 week
	Order placement			600					

EXHIBIT 16.2
Material requirements plan for completing 100 units of product T in period 7

From this simple illustration, it is apparent that developing a materials requirements plan manually for thousands or even hundreds of items would be impractical—a great deal of computation is needed, and a tremendous amount of data must be available about the inventory status (number of units on hand, on order, and so forth) and about the product structure (how the product is made and how many units of each material are required). Because of this, we are compelled to use a computer, and hence, our emphasis from here on in this chapter is to discuss the files that are needed for a computer program and the general make-up of the system. However, *the basic logic of the program is essentially the same as that which we have just gone through for our simple example.*

MATERIAL REQUIREMENTS PLANNING SYSTEMS

Based on the forecasted demand for an end item, a material requirements planning system generates a complete list of parts and subassemblies required to produce the end item along with the required amounts and the correct timing to release orders for these items. Thus, *Material Requirements Planning creates schedules identifying the specific parts and materials required to produce an end item, the exact numbers needed, and the dates when orders for these materials should be released and be received or completed within the production cycle.* Current use of the term *Material Requirements Planning,* or MRP, implies the use of a large computer program to carry out the foregoing operations.

While most firms have used computerized inventory systems for years, these systems were independent of the scheduling system.

Material Requirements Planning is not new in concept. Logic dictates that the Romans probably used it in their construction projects, the Venetians in their shipbuilding, and the Chinese in building the Great Wall. Building contractors have always been forced into planning for material to be delivered when needed and not before, because of space requirements. What is new is the larger scale and the more rapid changes that can be made by the use of high-capacity computers. This allows Material Requirements Planning to be used in firms that produce many products involving thousands of parts and materials.

PURPOSES, OBJECTIVES, AND PHILOSOPHY OF MRP

The main purposes of an MRP system are to control inventory levels, operating priorities for items, and capacity planning to load the production system. These may be briefly expanded as follows:[2]

Inventory
  Order the right part.
  Order in the right quantity.
  Order at the right time.
Priorities
  Order with the right due date.
  Keep the due date valid.
Capacity
  Plan for a complete load.
  Plan an accurate load.
  Plan for an adequate time to view future load.

We could state that the *theme* of MRP is "getting the right materials to the right place at the right time."

The *objectives* of inventory management under an MRP system are to improve customer service, to minimize inventory investment, and to maximize production operating efficiency.

The *philosophy* of Material Requirements Planning is that materials should be expedited (hurried) when their lack would delay the overall production schedule and de-expedited (delayed) when the schedule falls behind and postpones their need. It is preferable not to have inventory before the actual need since inventories tie up finances, take space, clutter up areas, prohibit design changes, and prevent the cancellation or delay of orders.

MATERIAL REQUIREMENTS PLANNING SYSTEM STRUCTURE

As mentioned earlier, the term *Material Requirements Planning* (MRP) refers to a computer program that generates schedules to meet material needs. Often, however, MRP is also used to imply the total system of materials

---

[2] Joseph Orlicky, *Material Requirements Planning* (New York: McGraw-Hill Book Company, 1975) p. 158.

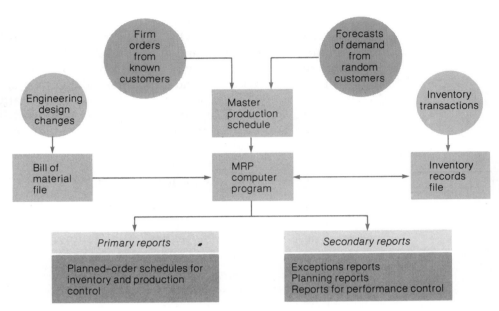

planning, which includes the inputs to the computer program as well, and is shown in Exhibit 16.3.

Each facet of Exhibit 16.3 will be explained in more detail in the following sections, but essentially the MRP system works as follows: Orders for products that arise both from known customers and from random sources are used to create a master production schedule, which states the number of items to be produced during specific time periods. A bill of materials file identifies the specific materials that are used to make each item and the correct quantities of each. The inventory records file contains data such as the number of units on hand and on order. These three sources—master production schedule, bill of materials file, and inventory records file—become the data sources for the Material Requirements program, which expands the production schedule into a detailed order schedule plan for the entire production sequence.

Demand for products

Product demand stems from two main categories: regular known customer orders and orders that occur randomly. In the normal course of operation, businesses usually receive orders from customers for specific items in specific amounts. These orders, usually generated by salesmen, include promised delivery dates. These constitute firm orders, and their sizes may need only slight adjustment based on experience (some percentage due to cancellation, for example).

In addition to these orders from known customers, there are random orders from other sources, which may be forecasted through traditional statistical analysis. This independent demand may then be subjected to further analytical procedures to determine safety stock levels, order points, and order quantities to satisfy a specific service level.

The regular customer demand and the independent demand for end products are combined to become the input for the master production schedule.

Demand for repair parts and supplies. In addition to their demand for end products, customers also order specific parts and components either as spares or for service and repair. These demands for items less complex than the end product are usually not part of a master schedule but are fed directly into the Material Requirements Planning (MRP) program at the appropriate levels. That is, they are added in as a gross requirement for that part or component.

Master production schedule

As stated in Chapter 14, the master production schedule states product needs by classes of items in specific time periods. Before it is adopted, the master schedule is used as a planning device. At this point in their development, MRP systems do not take into account resource limitations. The MRP program assumes that all master production schedules fed into it are feasible in that adequate capacity exists to meet the requirements. Therefore, trial master production schedules are run through the MRP program, and the resulting planned order releases (which are the detailed production schedules) are examined for availability of resources and reasonableness of times. What appears to be a feasible master schedule, when stated in end item classes, may turn out to require excessive resources when stated in terms of parts and components. The master production schedule is then modified to coincide more closely with available capacity, and the MRP program is run again. This procedure is repeated until the master production schedule that is input to the Material Requirements Planning system produces an acceptable production schedule.

Exhibit 16.4 shows a master schedule plan for product X for weekly time periods. (For clarity in this chapter, all figures are presented in ruled tables. Actual computer output is presented as columns or rows without lines, with some output extending to overlapping rows. Though not as neatly displayed, computer output is read almost as easily as the chapter exhibits.)

Once the master production schedule is produced, it must be broken down into demands for the parts and materials that go into making this end product. The file that contains the complete product description and the sequence in which it is created is called the bill of materials file. This bill of materials file (BOM) is one of the three main inputs to the MRP

EXHIBIT 16.4
Master production schedule for product X

Product X	Week number									
	1	2	3	4	5	6	7	8	9	10
Required quantity	200			400		200	100			900

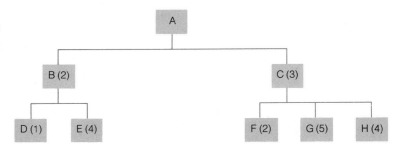

program, the other two being the master schedule and the inventory status file.

**Bill of
materials file**

The bill of materials file (BOM) is often called the product structure file or product tree since it shows how a product is put together. It contains the information to identify each item and the quantity used per unit of the item of which it is a part. To illustrate this, consider product A shown in Exhibit 16.5. Product A is made of two units of part B and three units of part C. Part B, in turn, is made of one unit of part D and four units of part E. Part C is made of two units of part F, five units of part G, and four units of part H.

In the past, bill of material files have often listed parts as an "indented" file. This clearly identifies each item and the manner in which it is assembled since each indentation signifies the components of the item. A comparison of the indented parts in Exhibit 16.6 with the item structure in Exhibit 16.5 shows the ease of relating the two displays. From a computer standpoint, however, storing items in indented parts lists is very inefficient. In order to compute the amount of each item needed at the lower levels, each item would need to be expanded ("exploded") and summed. A more efficient procedure is to store parts data in a single-level explosion. That is, each item and component is listed showing only its parent, and the number of units that are needed per unit of its parent. Exhibit 16.6 shows both the single level parts list and the indented parts list for product A. This avoids duplication by including each assembly only once.

A data element (called a "pointer" or "locator") is also contained in

EXHIBIT 16.6
**Parts list shown
both in an
indented format
and in a single
level list**

Indented parts list	Single level parts list
.A	.A
.B(2)	.B(2)
.D(1)	.C(3)
.E(4)	.B
.C(3)	.D(1)
.F(2)	.E(4)
.G(5)	.C
.H(4)	.F(2)
	.G(5)
	.H(4)

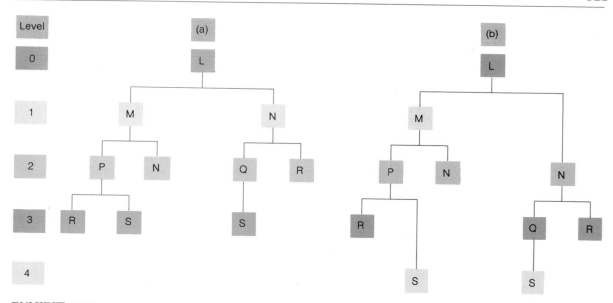

EXHIBIT 16.7
Product L hierarchy in (a) expanded to the lowest level of each item in (b)

each file to identify the parent of each part and allow a retracing upward through the process.

Low-level coding. The total number of parts and materials needed for a product can be computed easily when all identical parts occur at the same level for each end product. Consider product L shown in Exhibit 16.7 (a). Notice that item N, for example, occurs both as an input to L and as an input to M. Item N is lowered to level 2 (part b) to bring all Ns to the same level. By placing all identical items at the same level, it then becomes a simple matter for the computer to scan across each level and summarize the number of units of each item required.

Inventory records file

The inventory records file under a computerized system can be quite lengthy. Each item in inventory is carried as a separate file. Although records of each item are not usually kept in complete detail, it is possible for each item in the inventory record file to contain the data shown in Exhibit 16.8.

Items are carried in the *status* segment of the file according to specific time periods (termed time "buckets" in MRP slang). These files are accessed by the MRP program as needed during the program run. Exhibit 16.9 shows an illustration of an inventory record file with some of the optional data inputs.

The MRP program performs its analysis from the top of the product structure downward, exploding requirements level-by-level. There are times, however, when it is desirable to identify the parent item that caused the material requirement. The MRP program allows the creation of a *peg record* file either separately or as part of the inventory record file. The pegging of requirements allows one to retrace a material requirement up-

EXHIBIT 16.8
**Inventory record
file and the range
of possible data
elements**

1. Item master data segment
     Item identity
     Item characteristics
     Planning factors
     Safety stock
     Pointers to other files
2. Inventory status segment
     Gross requirements
        Control balance or past-due field
        Time-phased data fields
        Total
     Scheduled receipts
        Control balance or past-due field
        Time-phased data fields
        Total
     On hand
        Current on hand
        Allocated on hand
        Projected on-hand fields
        Total (ending inventory or net requirements)
     Planned-order releases
        Control balance or past-due field
        Time-phased data fields
        Total
3. Subsidiary data segment
     Order details
        External requirements
        Open (shop and purchase) orders
        Released portion of blanket orders
        Blanket order detail and history
        Other (user's choice)
     Records of pending action
        Purchase requisitions outstanding
        Purchase-order changes requested (quantity, due date)
        Material requisitions outstanding
        Shop order changes requested (rescheduled due dates)
        Planned (shop) orders held up, material shortage
        Shipment of item requested (requisition, etc.)
        Other (user's choice)
     Counters, accumulators
        Usage to date
        Scrap (or vendor rejects) to date
        Detail of demand history
        Forecast error, by period
        Other (user's choice)
     Keeping-track records
        Firm planned orders
        Unused scrap allowance, by open shop order
        Engineering change action taken
        Orders held up, pending engineering change
        Orders held up, raw material substitution
        Other interventions by inventory planner

Source: Joseph Orlicky, *Material Requirements Planning* (New York:
McGraw-Hill, 1975), pp. 181–83.

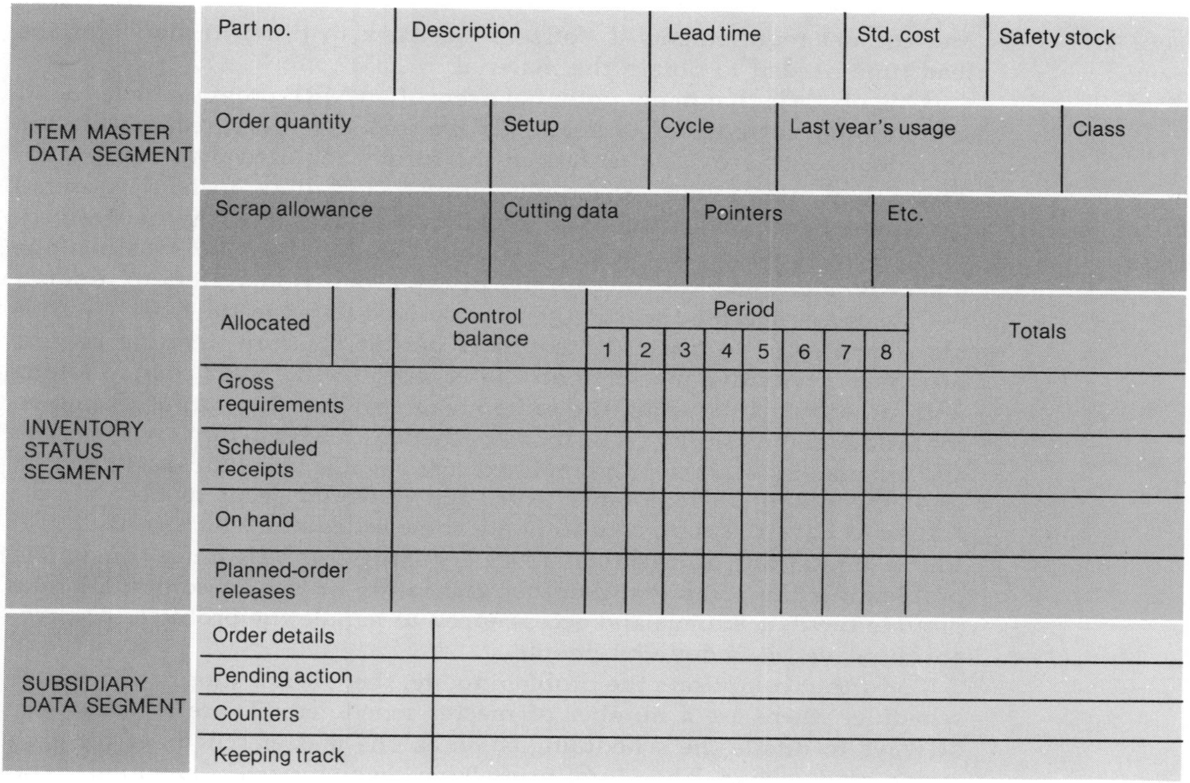
ITEM MASTER DATA SEGMENT
Part no.
Description
Lead time
Std. cost
Safety stock
Order quantity
Setup
Cycle
Last year's usage
Class
Scrap allowance
Cutting data
Pointers
Etc.
INVENTORY STATUS SEGMENT
Allocated
Control balance
Period
1 2 3 4 5 6 7 8
Totals
Gross requirements
Scheduled receipts
On hand
Planned-order releases
SUBSIDIARY DATA SEGMENT
Order details
Pending action
Counters
Keeping track

Source: Joseph Orlicky, *Materials Requirements Planning* (New York: McGraw-Hill Book Company, 1975), p. 182.

EXHIBIT 16.9
The inventory status record for an item in inventory

ward in the product structure through each level, identifying each parent item that created the demand.

Inventory transactions file. The inventory status file is kept up to date by posting inventory transactions as they occur. These changes occur because of stock receipts and disbursements, scrap losses, wrong parts, cancelled orders, and so forth.

MRP computer program

The Material Requirements Planning program operates on the inventory file, the master schedule, and the bill of materials file. It works in this way: a list of end items needed by time periods is specified by the master schedule. A description of the materials and parts needed to make each item is specified in the bill of materials file. The number of units of each item and material currently on hand and on order is contained in the inventory file. The MRP program "works" on the inventory file (which is segmented into time periods) while continually referring to the bill of materials file to compute the quantities of each item needed. The number of units of each item required is then corrected for on-hand amounts, and the net requirements is "offset" (set back in time) to allow for the lead time needed to obtain the material.

(One obstacle that many potential users of an MRP program have found is that their current bill of materials file and inventory records file are not adequate to provide the data in the format required by the program. Thus, they must modify these files prior to installing an MRP system.)

As noted previously, the MRP program presumes that any master production schedule fed into it is a feasible schedule. The MRP system alone makes no allowance for the capacity of the production system to produce the quantities specified within the time periods stated in the master schedule. Therefore, the master scheduler (a person) uses an iterative process in which a tentative master schedule is fed into the MRP system (along with other items requiring the same resources) and the output examined for production feasibility. The master schedule is adjusted to try to correct any imbalances, and the program is executed again. This process is repeated until the output is acceptable. Although it would seem to be a simple matter to have the computer simulate some schedules which consider resource limitations, in reality it is a very large and very time consuming problem for the computer. Another generation or two of computers may provide the data storage and access speed to handle the problem. At present, however, it is done by people.

To further complicate the problem today, there is not simply one master scheduler, there are a number of master schedulers. There are a variety of ways to divide the scheduling, such as one master scheduler for each major product line. Therefore, firms have several master schedulers who are each competing for limited resources while trying to balance resource usage and meeting due dates.

Output reports

Since the MRP program has access to the bill of materials file, the master production schedule, and the inventory records file, outputs can take on an almost unlimited range of format and content. These reports are usually classified as primary reports and secondary reports.

Primary reports. Primary reports are the main or "normal" reports used for inventory and production control. These reports consist of:

1. *Planned orders* to be released at a future time.
2. *Order release notices* to execute the planned orders.
3. *Changes in due dates* of open orders due to rescheduling.
4. *Cancellations or suspensions* of open orders due to cancellation or suspension of orders on the master production schedule.
5. *Inventory status data.*

Secondary reports. Additional reports, which are optional under the MRP system, fall into the following main categories:

1. *Planning reports* to be used, for example, in forecasting inventory and specifying requirements over some future time horizon.

2. *Performance reports* for purposes of pointing out inactive items, and determining the agreement between actual and programmed item lead times and between actual and programmed quantity usages and costs.

3. *Exceptions reports,* which point out serious discrepancies, such as errors, out-of-range situations, late or overdue orders, excessive scrap, or nonexistent parts.

Net change systems

Ordinarily an MRP system is operated every week or two. This results in the complete explosion of items and the generation of the normal and exception reports. Some MRP programs, however, offer the option of generating intermediate schedules that are called "net change" schedules. Under this option, rather than making a full-blown run, only updating quantities are entered, and the system accounts solely for those changes that occurred since the last complete program run. For example, the master production schedule may be updated by adding or subtracting only the differences from its previous amounts. Inventory files may be modified to take account of such factors as a lost shipment, scrap losses, or a counting error. Based on these changes, new reports are generated.

On the surface, it appears that a daily net change program run would be highly satisfactory. In practice, however, few companies are electing to use the net change option, and most are relying instead on their weekly or biweekly complete MRP schedule run. The reasons are not completely known as yet, but it seems that the more frequent net change runs may not be worth the added effort required to perform them, and too-frequent runs cause overreaction or "system nervousness."

We will now present a more elaborate example to show the operation of an MRP system.

EXAMPLE OF AN MRP SYSTEM

Ampere, Inc., produces a line of electric meters installed in residential buildings by electric utility companies to measure power consumption. Meters used on single family homes are of two basic types for different voltage and amperage ranges. In addition to complete meters, some parts and subassemblies are sold separately to be used for repair or to facilitate a changeover to a different voltage or power load. The problem for the MRP system, then, is to determine a production schedule that would identify each item, the period in which it is needed, and the appropriate quantities. This schedule is then checked for feasibility, and the schedule modified if necessary.

Forecasting demand

Demand for the meters and components originates from two sources: regular customers that place firm orders and unidentified customers that make the normal random demands for these items.

EXHIBIT 16.10
**Future
requirements for
meters A and B,
subassembly D,
and part E
stemming from
specific customer
orders and from
random sources**

Month	Meter A		Meter B		Subassembly D		Part E	
	Known	*Random*	*Known*	*Random*	*Known*	*Random*	*Known*	*Random*
3	1,000	250	400	60	200	70	300	80
4	600	250	300	60	180	70	350	80
5	300	250	500	60	250	70	300	80
6	700	250	400	60	200	70	250	80
7	600	250	300	60	150	70	200	80
8	700	250	700	60	160	70	200	80

Exhibit 16.10 shows the requirement for meters *A* and *B*, subassembly *D*, and Part *E* for a six-month period. The known requirements were firm customer orders, and the random requirements were forecasted using one of the usual classical techniques and past demand data.

**Developing a
master
production
schedule**

For the meter and component requirements specified in Exhibit 16.10 assume that the quantities to satisfy the known demands are to be delivered according to customers' delivery schedules throughout the month but that the items to satisfy random demands must be available during the first week of the month.

The first schedule that we will develop will assume that *all* items are to be available the first week of the month. This trial is reasonable since management prefers to produce meters in one single lot each month rather than a number of lots throughout the month.

Exhibit 16.11 shows the first trial master schedule under these conditions, with demands for months 3 and 4 shown as the first week of the month, or as weeks 9 and 13. For brevity, we will work only with these two demand periods.

EXHIBIT 16.11
**A master
schedule to
satisfy demand
requirements as
specified in
Exhibit 16.10**

	Week								
	9	10	11	12	13	14	15	16	17
Meter A	1,250				850				550
Meter B	460				360				560
Subassembly D	270				250				320
Part E	380				430				380

**Bill of
materials
(product
structure) file**

The product structure for meters A and B are shown in Exhibit 16.12 in the typical way using low-level coding, in which each item is placed at the lowest level at which it appears in the structure hierarchy. Meters A and B consist of two subassemblies, C and D, and two parts, E and

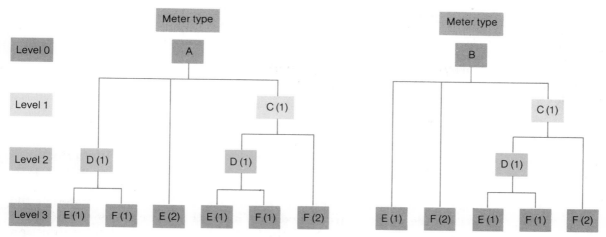

EXHIBIT 16.12
Product structure for meters A and B showing the subassemblies and parts that make up the meters and the numbers of units required per unit of parent shown in parentheses

F. Quantities in parentheses indicate the number of units required per unit of the parent item.

Exhibit 16.13 shows an indented parts list for the structure of meters A and B. As mentioned earlier in the chapter, the bill of materials file carries all items without indentation for computational ease, but the indented printout clearly shows the manner of product assembly.

EXHIBIT 16.13
Indented parts list for meter A and meter B, with the required number of items per unit of parent listed in parentheses

```
Meter A                                Meter B
.A                                     .B
    .D(1)                                  .E(1)
        .E(1)                              .F(2)
        .F(1)                              .C(1)
    .E(2)                                      .D(1)
    .C(1)                                          .E(1)
        .D(1)                                      .F(1)
            .E(1)                              .F(2)
            .F(1)
        .F(2)
```

Inventory records (item master) file

The inventory records file would be similar to the one that was shown in Exhibit 16.9. The differences, as stated earlier in this chapter, are that the inventory records file also contains much additional data, such as vendor identity, cost, lead times, and so forth. For this example, the pertinent data contained in the inventory records file are the on-hand inventory at the start of the program run and the lead times. These data are taken from the inventory records file and shown in Exhibit 16.14.

EXHIBIT 16.14
Number of units on hand and lead time data that would appear on the inventory record file

Item	On-hand inventory	Lead time (weeks)
A	50	2
B	60	2
C	40	1
D	30	1
E	30	1
F	40	1

Running the MRP program

The correct conditions are now set to run the MRP computer program—end-item requirements have been established through the master production schedule, the status of inventory and the order lead times are contained in the inventory item master file, and the bill of materials file contains the product structure data. The MRP program now explodes the item requirements according to the BOM file, level by level, in conjunction with the inventory records file. A release date for the net requirements order is offset to an earlier time period to account for the lead time. Orders for parts and subassemblies are added through the inventory file, bypassing the master production schedule, which, ordinarily, does not schedule at a low enough level to include spares and repair parts.

Exhibit 16.15 shows the planned order release dates for this particular run. The program logic can best be understood by following the analysis below. (We will confine our analysis to the problem of meeting the gross requirements for 1,250 units of meter A, 460 units of meter B, 270 units of subassembly D and 380 units of part E, all in week 9.)

The 50 units of A on hand results in a net requirement of 1,200 units of A. To receive meter A in week 9, the order must be placed in week 7 to account for the two-week lead time. The same procedure follows for item B, resulting in a planned 400-unit order released in period 7.

The rationale for these steps is that for an item to be released for processing, all of its components must be available. The planned order release date for the parent item therefore becomes the same gross requirement period for the sub-items.

Referring to Exhibit 16.12, level 1, one unit of C is required for each A and each B. Therefore, the gross requirements for C in week 7 are 1,600 units (1,200 for A and 400 for B). Taking into account the 40 units on hand and the one week lead time, 1,560 units of C must be ordered in week 6.

Level 2 of Exhibit 16.12 shows that one unit of D is required for each A and each C. The 1,200 units of D required for A are gross requirements in week 7, and the 1,560 units of D for item C are the gross requirements for week 6. Using the on-hand inventory first and the one-week lead time results in the planned order releases for 1,530 units in week 5 and 1,200 units in week 6.

Level 3 contains items E and F. Because E and F are each used in several

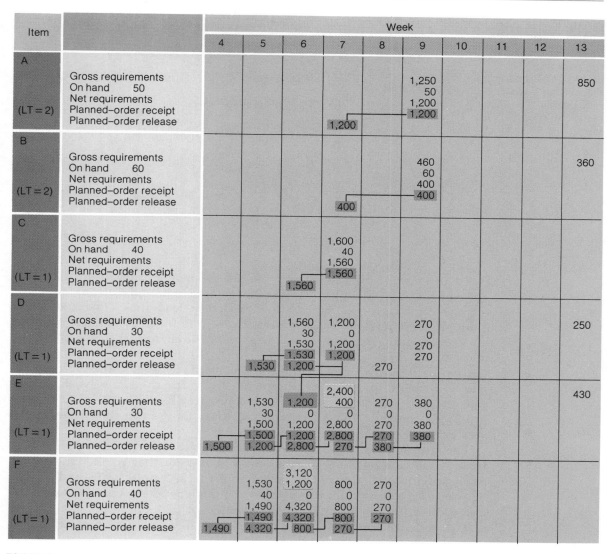

Item		Week										
		4	5	6	7	8	9	10	11	12	13
A	Gross requirements						1,250				850
	On hand 50						50				
	Net requirements						1,200				
(LT = 2)	Planned–order receipt						1,200				
	Planned–order release				1,200						
B	Gross requirements						460				360
	On hand 60						60				
	Net requirements						400				
(LT = 2)	Planned–order receipt						400				
	Planned–order release				400						
C	Gross requirements				1,600						
	On hand 40				40						
	Net requirements				1,560						
(LT = 1)	Planned–order receipt				1,560						
	Planned–order release			1,560							
D	Gross requirements			1,560	1,200		270				250
	On hand 30			30	0		0				
	Net requirements			1,530	1,200		270				
(LT = 1)	Planned–order receipt			1,530	1,200		270				
	Planned–order release		1,530	1,200		270					
E	Gross requirements		1,530	1,200	2,400	270	380				430
	On hand 30		30	0	400	0	0				
	Net requirements		1,500	1,200	0	270	380				
					2,800						
(LT = 1)	Planned–order receipt		1,500	1,200	2,800	270	380				
	Planned–order release	1,500	1,200	2,800	270	380					
F	Gross requirements		1,530	3,120	800	270					
				1,200							
	On hand 40		40	0	0	0					
	Net requirements		1,490	4,320	800	270					
(LT = 1)	Planned–order receipt		1,490	4,320	800	270					
	Planned–order release	1,490	4,320	800	270						

EXHIBIT 16.15

Material requirements planning schedule for meters A and B, subassemblies C and D, and parts E and F

places, Exhibit 16.16 is presented to identify more clearly the parent item, the number of units required for each parent item, and the week in which it is required. Two units of item E are used in each item A. The 1,200-unit planned order release for A in period 7 becomes the gross requirement for 2,400 units of E in the same period. One unit of E is used in each B, so the planned order release for 400 units of B in period 7 becomes the gross requirement for 400 units of E in week 7. Item E is also used in item D at the rate of one per unit. The 1,530-unit planned order release

EXHIBIT 16.16
The identification of the parent of items C, D, E, and F and item gross requirements stated by specific weeks

Item	Parent	Number of units per parent	Resultant gross requirement	Gross requirement week
C	A	1	1,200	7
C	B	1	400	7
D	A	1	1,200	7
D	C	1	1,560	6
E	A	2	2,400	7
E	B	1	400	7
E	D	1	1,530	5
E	D	1	1,200	6
F	B	2	800	7
F	C	2	3,120	6
F	D	1	1,200	6
F	D	1	1,530	5

for D in period 5 becomes the gross requirement for 1,530 units of E in period 5 and a 1,500-unit planned order release in period 4 after accounting for the 30 units on hand and the one-week lead time. The 1,200-unit planned order release for D in period 6 results in gross requirements for 1,200 units of E in week 6 and a planned order release for 1,200 units in week 5.

Item F is used in B, C, and D. The planned order releases for B, C, and D become the gross requirements for F for the same week, except that the planned order release for 400 units of B and 1,560 of C become gross requirements for 800 and 3,120 units of F since the usage rate is two per unit.

The independent order for 270 units of subassembly D in week 9 is handled as an input to D's gross requirements for that week. This is then exploded into the derived requirements for 270 units of E and F. The 380-unit requirement for part E to meet an independent repair part demand is fed directly into the gross requirements for part E.

The independent demands for week 13 have not been expanded as yet.

The bottom line of each item in Exhibit 16.15 is taken as a proposed load on the productive system. The final production schedule is developed manually or with the firm's computerized production package. If the schedule is infeasible or the loading severely unbalanced, the master production schedule is revised and the MRP package is run again with the new master schedule.

Where MRP can be used

MRP has been installed and is being used in a variety of industries. The products manufactured by companies can be classified as assembly, fabrication, and process. These will be defined with the benefits of MRP following:

Assemble-to-stock—Combines multiple component parts into a finished product which is then stocked in inventory to satisfy customer demand.

Examples: Watches, tools, appliances.

Fabricate-to-stock—Items are manufactured by machine rather than assembled from parts. These are standard stock items carried in anticipation of customer demand.

Examples: Piston rings, electrical switches.

Assemble-to-order—A final assembly is made from standard options which the customer chooses.

Examples: Trucks, generators, motors.

Fabricate-to-order—Items manufactured by machine to customer order. These are generally industrial orders.

Examples: Bearings, gears, fasteners.

Manufacture-to-order—Items fabricated or assembled completely to customer specification.

Examples: Turbine-generators, heavy machine tools.

Process—Industries, such as foundries, rubber and plastics, specialty paper, chemicals, paint, drug, food processors.

Benefits of Material Requirements Planning[3]

Fabricator—low benefit.

Assemble-to-stock—high.

Assemble-to-order—high.

Manufacture-to-order—high.

Process—medium

As noted above, MRP is most valuable to companies involved in assembly operations and least valuable to those in fabrication.

One more point is worthy of note. MRP does not work well in companies which have a low annual output in terms of the number of units produced. Especially for companies producing complex expensive products requiring advanced research and design, experience has shown that lead times tend to be too long and too uncertain, and the product configuration too complex for MRP to handle. Further, such companies need the control features that network scheduling techniques offer.

MRP IN SERVICES

It has been asserted that MRP cannot be used for services. The reasoning is that MRP is limited to systems having inventoriable items. Although little has been done on the issue to the present time, it appears quite

---

[3] IBM Manufacturing Implementation Guide, SH30–0211–0, vol. 1 (July 1977), pp. 3–6.

likely that MRP can be a very valuable asset in the production of services. It seems to us that one need only consider the producing elements as inventory (equipment, space, personnel) and the procedure would be valid. Consider, for example, an open heart surgery operation. The master schedule can establish a time for the surgery (or surgeries if there are several scheduled). The bill of materials could specify all required equipment and personnel—MD's, nurses, anesthesiologist, operating room, heart/lung machine, defibrillator, and so forth. The inventory status file would show the availability of the resources and commit them to the project. The MRP program could then produce a schedule showing when various parts of the operation are to be started, expected completion times, required materials, and so forth. Checking this schedule would allow "capacity planning" in answering such questions as: "Are all the materials and personnel available?" and "Does the system produce a feasible schedule?"

For more complicated service systems—that is, those that perform many and varied services simultaneously—the use of MRP seems worthy of consideration.

MISCELLANEOUS ISSUES ON MRP

MRP seems to have the logic to allow it to be used with other systems. Hershauer and Eck[4] have used it to tie into a higher-level planning system and provide a variety of reports such as projected cash requirements, expenses, flow of funds, and inventory levels, budget sheets, and income statements. Partly for this desire to broaden the range of application, some authors are using MRP to mean Manufacturing Resource Planning rather than Material Requirements Planning.

MRP has also been extended to look at the distributing and procurement portions of business.[5] In addition to savings in reduced inventory, there are also savings in improved warehouse and labor utilization and in scheduling and receiving inventories.

Problems in installing and using MRP systems

MRP is very well developed technically, and implementation of an MRP system should be pretty straightforward. Yet there are many problems with the MRP systems and many "failures" in trying to install them. Why do such problems and outright failures occur with a "proven" system?

The answer may lie with organizational and behavioral factors.

White has done an excellent job in stating the causes of the problem which stem from resistance to change:[6]

---

[4] James C. Hershauer, and Roger D. Eck, "Extended MRP Systems for Evaluating Master Schedules and Materials Requirements Plans," *Production and Inventory Management*, vol. 21, no. 2 (Spring 1980), pp. 53–66.

[5] Alan J. Strenger and Joseph L. Cavinato, "Adapting MRP to the Outbound Side—Distribution Requirements Planning," *Production and Inventory Management*, vol. 20, no. 4 (Fourth Quarter 1979), pp. 1–14.

[6] Edna M. White, "Implementing an MRP System Using the Lewin-Schein Theory of Change," *Production and Inventory Management*, vol. 21, no. 1 (First Quarter 1980), pp. 1–2.

Clearly, the problems of implementing an MRP system are behavioral problems. This paper argues that these behavioral problems stem from a natural resistance to change on the part of individuals. It is further argued that this resistance to change is particularly strong with MRP.

Massive changes must occur within an organization due to the nature of an MRP system. The need to constantly update the MRP data base will result in many procedures. New communication lines and methods must be established. Detailed auditing procedures for information must be developed. New inventory control methods and engineering change notice procedures are usually required.

Successful implementation of an MRP system, however, requires even more drastic changes. The rationale for an MRP system is the concept of dependent demand. To successfully implement an MRP system requires that individuals change not only their procedures but also their view of inventory management. In many cases, this will also require that individuals change their job definition.

An MRP system is driven by the master schedule. This implies that at the lower levels of management, those below the master schedule level, change must occur to accept the idea of dependent demand. At this level, the master schedule, through parts explosion, gives the kind, amount, and timing for required parts. Individuals must redefine their jobs to working within and for the master schedule.

A further implication is that change must also occur within individuals at the top management level, where the master schedule is developed. It is clear that since MRP allows control of inventory through the master schedule, top management must change their procedure and viewpoints to accept the responsibility for this control. If the master schedule is not used as a method for planning and control by top management, the concept of dependent demand will falter and successful implementation cannot occur.

To successfully implement an MRP system, then, change must occur in procedures, in job definitions, and in both upper and lower management levels.

White continues drawing on the work of Kurt Lewin who believed that, for attitudinal and behavioral changes to occur, a sequence of stages must be passed through. The stages are:[7]

1. Unfreezing: There must be a desire for change; a felt need, some dissatisfaction with the status quo; a belief that the old way is no longer desirable or acceptable.
2. Changing: The desired new set of behaviors and attitudes are introduced. Individuals should see the changes in other people and begin to change their own behavior.
3. Refreezing: Behavior should now be stable. Individuals should respond to the system. These responses should be integrated into the individual's personality. There needs to be sufficient reinforcement to prevent slipping back to the "old ways."

---

[7] For an easy reading introduction to problems in change see Chapter 16, "Managing Organizational Change" in *Management: A Life Cycle Approach* by D. Tansik; R. Chase; and N. Aquilano (Homewood, Ill.: Richard D. Irwin, Inc., 1980).

Finally, White offers some suggestions on how to overcome resistance, such as showing poor efficiency and declining customer service, to encourage the acceptance of the change.

In the many meetings which we have attended, both professional and industrial, we have heard similar installation and operational problems. It seems to distill down to the fact that an MRP system becomes the thread which weaves through and holds together the entire organization. All functional areas converse through the MRP schedule. The MRP essentially runs the firm with the main objective simply to meet the schedule. Entire attitudes must change. People become subservient to the MRP system. Even such simple decisions as determining a runlot size no longer is possible.

In short, MRP is a "formal system" which requires strict adherence to function properly. This is frequently alien to foreman and workers who have developed an "informal system" for getting the job done. MRP advocates would say this informal system arises because the existing formal system was inadequate to deal with real inventory scheduling problems. In any event, it appears that employees at all levels must change—from the company president down to the lowest-level employee. While MRP is good, will work, and currently does work in many installations, it should be thoroughly planned in installation. One of the most important requirements is that top management must understand the system and back it fully.[8] The White article cites some other sources to help all employees understand and accept the system and, most importantly, to have some say in its design.

Criticism of MRP as a concept

We have just discussed some behavioral problems in installing the system, but some authorities believe the problem is deeper and more serious.

Sandman, an authority on job shop scheduling, claims very limited success for MRP.[9] The difficulty, he claims, is that MRP is not the production control system people are led to believe it is. A production control system should provide:

1. A plan to achieve an objective.
2. Work assignments to meet the plan.
3. Feedback to improve the quality of the plan.

Rather than meet these requirements, Sandman accuses MRP of simply tracking orders which show where everything is or should be. It does not assign work or test the effects of different order sequences. In order

---

[8] Robert W. Hall, "Getting the Commitment of Top Management," *Production and Inventory Management,* vol. 18, no. 1 (First Quarter 1977), pp. 1–9. See also J. W. Rice and T. Yoshikawa, "MRP and Motivation—What Can We Learn from Japan?," *Production and Inventory Management,* vol. 21, no. 2 (Second Quarter 1980), pp. 45–52.

[9] William E. Sandman, *How to Win Productivity in Manufacturing* (Dresher, Pa.: Yellow Book of Pennsylvania, Inc., 1980), pp. 62–65.

to accomplish true production control, Sandman continues, there must be a simulation control system which provides:

1. A daily work schedule, sequenced job-by-job, work-center-by-work-center, hour-by-hour.
2. A look ahead at the jobs for the next few days (and, upon request, up to 12 months).

The simulation schedule is used to schedule jobs through the system and help achieve the profit goal. MRP systems ignore the congestion of orders waiting in queues at machines and work centers. MRP supporters, on the other hand, would say that this is a capacity requirements planning problem—MRP just gives need dates and status information. Capacity planning (and shop floor control) just execute the material plan.

Safety stock

Ordinarily, safety stock is not advised in an MRP system that is based on derived demand. There is some feeling, however, that when the availability of parts could suffer from a long and inflexible lead time or is subject to strikes or cancellation, a safety stock offers protection against production delays.[10] A safety stock is sometimes intentionally created by overplanning. One of the main arguments against using safety stock is that the MRP system considers it a fixed quantity, and the safety stock will never actually be used.

Production lot sizes

Utilizing lot sizes for convenience in production runs or in economic order quantities is practical only for lower-level items (basic parts or raw materials). The difficulty in using a lot size at a higher level is that the discrepancy between actual demand and the lot size becomes exaggerated for the sub-items. Consider the following illustration:

Item A is made of one unit of B, which is made of one unit of C, and the lot sizes of A, B, and C are equal to 100, 150, and 200 respectively. If there are no units currently in inventory, then a demand for 75 units of A will cause 200 units of C to be ordered—the 25-unit excess in A leads to a 125-unit excess of C.

$$.A \qquad\qquad\qquad \text{lot size of } A = 100$$
$$.B(1) \qquad\qquad \text{lot size of } B = 150$$
$$.C(1) \qquad\quad \text{lot size of } C = 200$$

The higher the product-structure level of lot sizing, the greater the potential exaggeration of demand at low levels.

A variety of lot sizing techniques have been studied which consider carrying costs, unit costs, total costs, and setup costs. No technique has been shown to be successful. Therefore, with the exception of the lower-

---

[10] See Naren Mehta, "How to Handle Safety Stock in an MRP System," *Production and Inventory Management*, vol. 21, no. 3 (Third Quarter 1980), pp. 16–22.

level items as previously mentioned, the best technique is simply lot-for-lot (L4L). In lot-for-lot, there is no standard lot size. The planned order is the quantity given as net requirements.

Accuracy of records

Maintaining accurate records is critical to the success of an MRP system. Some of the inaccuracies that find their way into the major files are discussed below.

Bill of materials file. Often, the bill of materials file does not accurately represent either the product or the manufacturing procedure. Original product designs are usually modified based on production and use experience, and operating personnel usually modify the process or assembly procedure. These changes may not have been entered into the BOM file.

Inventory records file. In Chapter 15, we commented upon some issues in inventory accuracy. To again point out some of these, many companies have made a practice of having an "open stockroom." Any person needing inventory supplies could simply walk in, take whatever he needed, make the appropriate entries if necessary, and leave. Periodic inventory counting and replenishment would bring stocks back to an acceptable level. In a Materials Requirement Planning system, however, open stockrooms cannot be tolerated. Inventory count must be accurate for MRP to function correctly, since in most cases, there is no safety stock and every unit must be accounted for. In order to maintain the integrity of the inventory stock firms using MRP restrict entry into the stockroom and keep the area locked. So important is inventory accuracy that some firms have even resorted to high fencing around every inventory stock area to prohibit unauthorized use of material.[11]

The inventory records file must also contain the true inventory status. There should be assurance that daily transactions are entered.

Master production schedule. The entire MRP system is founded on the objective of satisfying the master production schedule. Schedules change, however, because of increases in orders, delays, cancellation of orders, and so forth. It is critical, therefore, that the master production schedule be updated to reflect the true demands for products and realistic due dates. (See the master scheduling discussion in Chapter 14.)

ONE FIRM'S EXPERIENCE IN INSTALLING AN MRP SYSTEM

The following article reports the experience of a firm that introduced MRP into its operating system.[12] It was written by the vice president of Moog Automotive, Inc., and provides an interesting perspective of MRP in practice.

---

[11] Consider the Johnny Cash song about the Cadillac built from parts smuggled out of the car factory: "I got it one piece at a time, and it didn't cost me a dime. . . ."

[12] Robert A. Dennis, vice president, Moog Automotive, Inc., St. Louis, Mo. "Coping With the Materials Crunch," *Factory* (August 1974), pp. 50–51.

Coping with the Materials Crunch

MRP, in conjunction with a new computer, is making it possible for this company and, importantly, its suppliers, to outmaneuver today's critical materials crunch.

In a period of critical shortages, material and inventory control at Moog Automotive, Inc., has actually been improving. The situation has been caused by a new computer-managed Material Requirements Planning (MRP) system. It is run on an IBM System/370 Model 145 computer. Moog produces steering and suspension replacement parts totaling about 4,200. Its customers number about 450, ranging from wholesale distributors to tire store outlets.

Essentially, our material requirements planning system is based on time-phased scheduling and is a vast improvement over order-point systems of the past. MRP provides information which enables each Moog inventory analyst to closely follow the critical element or problem in his area of responsibility and take effective action.

As one example: each day we run a fillable/non-fillable report for planners, with full information on each order that can be filled and each order that cannot be filled. For the orders that cannot be filled, the report tells the planner what components are missing, in what quantity, and the planner who is responsible for the missing items. Similarly, the planners receive a daily component allocation analysis showing them the demands against their assigned parts.

If an order is listed as fillable, the planner merely releases it, and the computer generates the paperwork necessary for manufacturing or packaging. But if a ball joint, for instance, requires six components, we no longer schedule it onto the machines to later find out that only five components are available. Instead, based on the commonality of some of these components, we allocate them to another ball joint which can be assembled.

In 1972, we decided that MRP provided the facilities Moog needed because it is time-phased and permits us to plan farther into the future. We also decided to install the following companion computer-managed programs: forecasting, capacity planning, allocation, and shop floor control.

Under our system, the inventory control manager develops finished goods forecasts by part number and product group. He reviews them with a forecast committee, then enters the refined figures into the computer. Input are both the current and the following years' forecasts. He enters a base index percentage to divide the forecast into monthly increments. The monthly forecasts are based on seasonal demand, on inventory and production levels desired, and so forth.

This data, which is stored in the computer, then is the basis for MRP. The System/370 calculates weekly gross requirements for each item. It then produces a summary report, by product group, which is a "rough cut" monthly master schedule for the coming year. This is reviewed in detail to ensure we have a level master schedule. If it is not level, the basic assumptions are altered, and the master schedule is rerun.

The MRP system generates a weekly master requirements planning report—which develops requirements weekly for the quarter, then monthly for the rest of the year. It is regenerated weekly. The report shows production planners, for each part number, the weekly gross requirement for both the end item and all its components, all lead times, and ordering policy guidelines for each item. Such comprehensive data help the planner to avoid overplanning and underplanning. Also, when a part is needed, the system generates the order quantity and date needed.

A similar report is produced for purchasing, and includes sufficient data to alert the suppliers to our long-range needs. Each week, too, purchasing receives a list of parts that are scheduled for order release in the current month. This is an action report indicating what components and materials to order, the date the order is to be released, when it is due at Moog, and if we need it in less than the normal lead time. We also run an exception report for planners flagging problems with inventory, checking misscheduled orders and other problems.

On a daily basis, the firm-planned orders are analyzed by the allocation system that assigns inventory to manufacturing orders and packaging. Also produced daily are the fillable/non-fillable report and the component allocation analysis.

Expediting is much improved. Now, when the computer prints an expedite list for purchasing, they know it is 100 percent valid and can expedite the required items more effectively. Supplier performance has been improved too because suppliers know that when we give them our requirements, they are honest requirements. With MRP we know exactly what we need and when we have to have it.

Before installing MRP, members of the MRP project team visited key suppliers to brief them on the program, including projected benefits to each supplier. For example, we can now tell a supplier Moog's long-range requirements to let him better plan his own production procurement and capacity. We told our suppliers that we felt that this then entitled Moog to preferential treatment.

Generally, we have been able to convince our suppliers both of MRP's importance and the need for accurate information. They now provide more realistic lead times and updating as their situations change and also can better differentiate between procurement lead times and production lead times. Cooperation of suppliers is vital in the success of MRP, of course. Incidentally, one of our largest suppliers is now installing his own MRP system.

As an additional control factor, we established a central stores area where all raw materials are now received, except steel bars. Stores checks all materials and components for proper identity, makes counts, and issues to the manufacturing departments as scheduled.

Capacity planning system

Released orders and orders to be released are used to update the capacity planning system which generates a weekly report showing the load by work center, by hours available, machine load, and amount over or under capacity. It includes manpower figures. The first quarter workload is itemized by week and each subsequent quarter by month. The work center summary provides enough short-range data to enable us to determine whether additional production time needs to be scheduled on a weekly basis.

In contrast, our previous systems generally considered only each quarter, which was too gross a segment to provide the level of detail necessary for adequate priority scheduling. This resulted in numerous problems, such as the wrong mix of components and materials, excess inventory, and little or no time-phasing for lead times.

Looking into the near term: we expect to have shop floor control operational within a few months. We are now researching data collection and data transmission equipment to support the control aspects of our MRP plans and making appropriate cost justification studies.

Today, a Moog planner can quickly determine that on the third week of the month he should package, say, 1,000 specific ball joints based on the master schedule; and he can find out with equal speed if the order is fillable—and if not, why. Consequently, if he dispatches an order to the packaging department, personnel there can know its status immediately.

Similarly, if a component is missing and we have to contact a vendor for expedited service, most of the time we are able to do so in time to meet the schedule. The expedite is further supported by the vendor's realization that any request from Moog for rush service is based on genuine need.

PRODUCTION AND INFORMATION CONTROL SYSTEM (PICS)

Many of the topics that have been presented in this book thus far are integrated in the computer system described in this section.

The Production and Information Control System (PICS) is designed for fabrication and assembly types of manufacturing.[13] PICS was prompted by two necessities: (1) the recognized need for a central information system in a fabrication and assembly plant and (2) the desire for a framework to facilitate computerization of the information system. A major problem in any production system is that data and information about the system are dispersed throughout the entire operation. PICS would provide a central location for data files containing accurate current data easily accessible to a variety of users.

The PICS system is based on *dependent demand*. A forecast for product demand is fed into the system from some external source, usually an analysis made by the marketing department. The data contained in this forecast for specific time periods is then available to the PICS program.

The Material Requirements Program (MRP) is a significant part of the PICS program. Although MRP and PICS were developed separately, they are quite similar, and now parts of the MRP system have been incorporated in PICS, as some of the findings from experience in using PICS have been included in MRP. The major differences between PICS and MRP are first, that PICS can be installed as a complete system whereas MRP is a software program dependent on other files, and second, that PICS extends the inventory control system to include scheduling. In addition to computing the required materials in the right amounts according to time periods as needed, PICS also contains a job scheduling or shop loading routine. While MRP stops, leaving the actual scheduling and routing to human personnel, PICS routes each job to specific work centers. (It does this through a simulation procedure that tests alternative routings until a satisfactory load balance is achieved.) PICS is also able to provide information about machine and labor utilization and the exact location of jobs in the system at any point in time.

---

[13] IBM, *The Production Information and Control System*, GE20–0280–2.

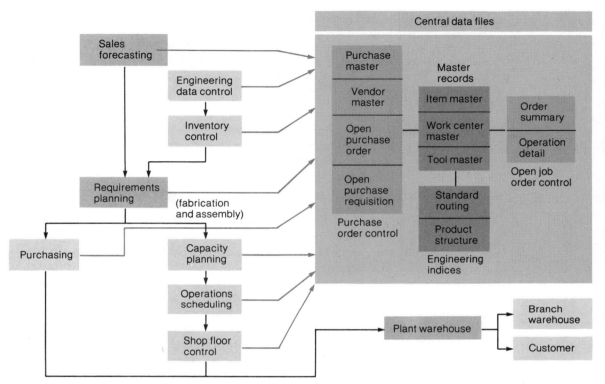

EXHIBIT 16.17

Integrated Production and Information Control System (PICS) with access to central data files

Exhibit 16.17 shows the basic structure and information flow of the PICS system. The entire system is linked together by immediate access to a common data file that contains the firm's operational records. With only a part number, for example, the product description, standard routing, purchase order status, job order summary, and even the work center in which the job is being performed may be identified.[14]

In PICS, each functional area has been developed as an independent subsystem. Not only is this more practical from a computer system development aspect, but it is highly beneficial for implementation into an ongoing production system. The user can, at his own discretion, decide which subsystems he would like to incorporate first and in what sequence. In practice, the user would not try to put all products and all functional areas into use at the same time; he gradually builds this up with a small number of products and develops one area at a time.

---

[14] Each file contains varied data of interest. The "item master" is the master file, and it contains 117 fields that tell all about the item: its description, cost, structure, routing, order policy, forecast, lead time, usage history, stock on hand, projected orders, committed units, items on order, and engineering change status. The master file directs further search to specific files for more detailed information.

Information flows from two sources: (1) sales forecasting and (2) engineering data control. Exhibit 16.18 lists the subsystems, along with some of the main features of each.

The sales forecasting subsystem analyzes historical data and employs a sales forecast as input to requirements planning. The mission of engineering data control is to organize and maintain the basic records: item master, product structure, standard routing, and work center master. The inventory control subsystem computes inventory on hand, on order, and usage rates. The inputs from inventory control and sales forecasting are combined to project future requirements of finished goods. Product structure records then break this requirement down into components to be directed to the purchasing, assembly, and fabrication departments.

EXHIBIT 16.18
**Features of
PICS
subsystems**

Sales forecasting	Model selection
	Forecast plans
	Evaluation and measurement
Engineering data control	Basic records file organization
	Engineering drawings
	Engineering changes
	Production structure and standard routing
	Records maintenance
Inventory control	Stock status report
	ABC inventory analysis
	Order policy
	Inventory maintenance and update
	Physical inventory
Requirements planning	Finished product requirements gross to net
	Component requirements gross to net
	Special features:
	Lot sizing
	Offset requirements
	Net change
	Pegged requirements
Purchasing	Requisition and purchase order preparation
	Purchase order followup
	Purchase evaluation
	Vendor evaluation and selection
Capacity planning	Projected work center load report
	Planned order load
	Order start date calculations
	Load leveling
Operations scheduling	Dispatching sequence
	Order estimator
	Load summary by work center
	Priority rules
	Queue time analysis
	Tool control
Shop floor control	Labor reporting
	Material movement
	Work-in-process feedback
	Creation of control forms
	Machine utilization

The flow continues as purchasing prepares purchase orders and receiving cards, based on item identification and the vendor master. An open purchase order is created so that the order will be followed up.

Assembly and fabrication order requirements are used in capacity planning for facility and manpower needs. Order start times are computed from the standard routing records and the available capacity as given by the work center master record. Operations scheduling takes the orders released by capacity planning and makes short-range schedules for work centers. An analysis of work loads and completion dates is then conducted, based on various dispatching sequences and priority rules. The tools needed in production are designated in this step.

Shop floor control is the last phase of this system. It prepares shop packets and other factory documentation, open job order summaries, and operation detail records for monitoring and reporting work progress. The output of purchasing, assembly, and fabrication converges at the plant warehouse.

COPICS—COMMUNICATIONS ORIENTED PRODUCTION INFORMATION AND CONTROL SYSTEM

PICS (Production and Information Control System) was developed by IBM on the basis of an idea or concept of how a manufacturing firm might function under a computer-processing software system. This concept finally came to realization as was described in the preceding section of this chapter.

COPICS is a similar case. The Communication Oriented Production Information and Control System is not now a working system. Exhibit 16.19, which shows the functional flow of COPICS, is hypothetical. Many individual parts of the proposed COPICS system, however, do currently exist. There are programs for forecasting, inventory control, engineering data management, and so forth. What remains to be done on this system is to link and integrate the various existing independent programs into an efficient operating system. This will entail modifying existing programs and writing some new programs. Overall, this is likely a decade-long project.

In concept, COPICS is intended to evolve into a dynamic on-line manufacturing control system. Its extensive and common data base is accessible for problem solving, planning, and control purposes through a network of computer terminals. It is concerned with the entire scope of the manufacturing system, from forecasting demand through materials and processing control on to plant maintenance. Additional features of COPICS include simulation capabilities to test alternative strategies.

The Material Requirements Planning program presented in this chapter, along with its required bill of materials file, master production schedule, and inventory status file, will eventually become integrated parts of the COPICS system. When completed, COPICS is expected to provide many

COPICS Manufacturing – Functional Flow

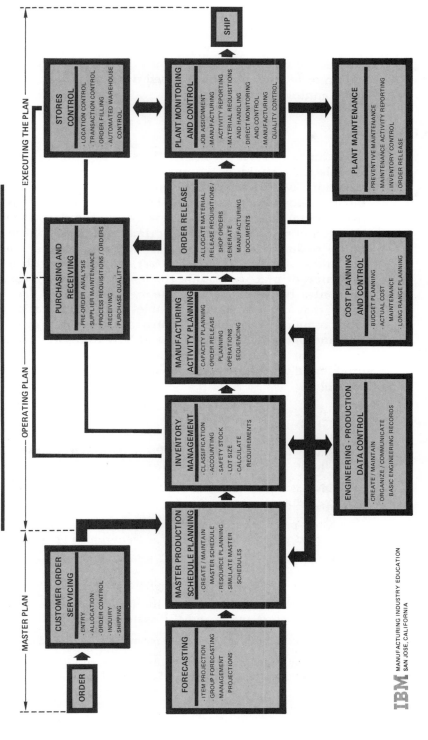

ORDER

CUSTOMER ORDER SERVICING
- ENTRY
- ALLOCATION
- ORDER CONTROL
- INQUIRY
- SHIPPING

FORECASTING
- ITEM PROJECTION
- GROUP FORECASTING
- MANAGEMENT PROJECTIONS

MASTER PRODUCTION SCHEDULE PLANNING
- CREATE / MAINTAIN MASTER SCHEDULE
- RESOURCE PLANNING
- SIMULATE MASTER SCHEDULES

INVENTORY MANAGEMENT
- CLASSIFICATION
- ACCOUNTING
- SAFETY STOCK
- LOT SIZE
- CALCULATE REQUIREMENTS

ENGINEERING - PRODUCTION DATA CONTROL
- CREATE / MAINTAIN
- ORGANIZE / COMMUNICATE BASIC ENGINEERING RECORDS

MANUFACTURING ACTIVITY PLANNING
- CAPACITY PLANNING
- ORDER RELEASE PLANNING
- OPERATIONS SEQUENCING

COST PLANNING AND CONTROL
- BUDGET PLANNING
- ACTUAL COST MAINTENANCE
- LONG RANGE PLANNING

ORDER RELEASE
- ALLOCATE MATERIAL
- RELEASE REQUISITIONS / SHOP ORDERS
- GENERATE MANUFACTURING DOCUMENTS

PURCHASING AND RECEIVING
- PRE-ORDER ANALYSIS
- SUPPLIER MAINTENANCE
- PROCESS REQUISITIONS / ORDERS
- RECEIVING
- PURCHASE QUALITY

STORES CONTROL
- LOCATION CONTROL
- TRANSACTION CONTROL
- ORDER FILLING
- AUTOMATED WAREHOUSE CONTROL

PLANT MONITORING AND CONTROL
- JOB ASSIGNMENT
- MANUFACTURING ACTIVITY REPORTING
- MATERIAL REQUISITIONS AND HANDLING
- DIRECT MONITORING AND CONTROL
- MANUFACTURING QUALITY CONTROL

PLANT MAINTENANCE
- PREVENTIVE MAINTENANCE
- MAINTENANCE ACTIVITY REPORTING
- INVENTORY CONTROL
- ORDER RELEASE

SHIP

MASTER PLAN

OPERATING PLAN

EXECUTING THE PLAN

IBM MANUFACTURING INDUSTRY EDUCATION
SAN JOSE, CALIFORNIA

benefits. Some of these are: reduced inventories, improved customer service, better utilization of production facilities, reduced work-in process, greater productivity, higher quality, fewer shortages, reduced costs, elimination of redundant data, reduced risks, and faster information processing for planning.

CONCLUSION

Historically, research and writings on inventory theory have emphasized models and techniques that were most appropriate in independent demand situations. Meanwhile, practitioners struggled with the conceptually simple but time-consuming common-sense methods to deal with dependent demand situations. In the past few years, however, inventory practice has changed in many organizations primarily because of the capability of computers to automate the heavy data-handling chores inherent in dependent demand cases. We are now, in fact, confronted with the interesting phenomenon of practice leading theory—MRP is a *fait accompli,* doing the job without a body of scientific theory to support it. Yet, practice seems to show that the job should be able to be done easier and better. Much work remains to be done in trying to find what, precisely, are the installation and operational problems, and how to resolve them. What also needs to be done is to better integrate MRP with the other critical tools of production control—the master schedule, capacity planning, and shop floor control.[15]

REVIEW AND DISCUSSION QUESTIONS

1. Since Material Requirements Planning appears so reasonable, discuss reasons why its popularity was delayed until the past several years.

2. Discuss the meaning of MRP terms such as "planned order release" and "scheduled order receipts."

3. Most practitioners currently run an MRP program weekly or biweekly. Would it be more valuable if it were run daily? Discuss.

4. What is the role of safety stock in an MRP system?

5. Discuss the concept of dependent and independent demand.

6. Contrast the significance of the term "lead time" both in the traditional EOQ context and in an MRP system.

7. Discuss the importance of the master production schedule in an MRP system.

8. MRP systems are difficult to install. Discuss these problems relating to the system requirements (ignore behavioral problems).

---

[15] For an interesting perspective on the current state of MRP by one of its developers, see George W. Plossl, "MRP Yesterday, Today, and Tomorrow," *Production and Inventory Management,* vol. 21, no. 3 (Third Quarter 1980), pp. 1–10.

9. "MRP just prepares shopping lists—it doesn't do the shopping or cook the dinner." Comment.

10. What are the sources of demand in an MRP system? Are these dependent or independent, and how are they used as inputs of the system?

11. State the types of data that would be carried in the bill of materials file and the inventory record file.

12. Distinguish between the intended uses of the IMPACT system presented in Chapter 15 and the Production and Information Control System (PICS).

13. What are the PICS subsystems, and what functions do they perform?

PROBLEMS

1. In the following material requirements plan for Item J, indicate the correct net requirements, planned order receipts and planned order releases to meet the gross requirements. Lead time is one week.

Week number

Item J	0	1	2	3	4	5
Gross requirements			75		50	70
On hand 40						
Net requirements						
Planned order receipt						
Planned order releases						

2. Product X is made of two units of Y and three of Z. Y is made of one unit of A and two units of B. Z is made of two units of A and four units of C.

   Lead time for X is one week, Y is two weeks, Z is three weeks, A is two weeks, B is one week, C is three weeks.
   a. Draw the product structure tree.
   b. If 100 units of X are needed in week ten, develop a Material Requirements Plan showing when each item should be ordered and in what quantity.

3. Repeat problem 2 except that there are currently on hand in stock 20 X, 40 Y, 30 Z, 50 A, 100 B, and 900 C.

4. Assume that product Z is made of two units of A and four units of B. A is made of three units of C and four of D. D is made of two units of E.

   The lead time for purchase and/or fabrication of each unit is: final assembly; Z takes two weeks, A, B, C, and D take one week each, and E takes three weeks.

   Fifty units are required in period ten. (Assume that there is currently no inventory on hand of any of these items).
   a. Draw a product structure tree.
   b. Develop an MRP schedule showing gross and net requirements, order release and order receipt dates.

5. Assume that a very simple product X is made of two units of Y and three units of Z. The lead time for X is one week, Y is two weeks, and Z is three weeks.

   Annual demand for X is 2,000 units. There is a $20 setup cost. Product X costs $30 each, and the inventory carrying cost is 20 percent of the product cost.
   a. Determine the economic order quantity (production run size).
   b. Draw the product structure tree.
   c. Create the complete MRP schedule for a two-month period. There are no units of X, nor Y, nor Z on hand.

6. Product A is an end item and is made from two of B and four of C. B is made of three units of D and two units of E. C is made of two units of F and two units of E.

   A has a lead time of one week. B, C, and E have lead times of two weeks, and D and F have lead times of three weeks.
   a. Draw the product structure tree.
   b. If 100 units of A are required in week ten, develop the MRP plan specifying when items are to be ordered and received. There are currently no units of inventory on hand.

7. Product M is made of two units of N and three of P. N is made of two units of R and four units of S. R is made of one unit of S and three units of T. P is made of two units of T and four units of U.
   a. Show the product structure tree.
   b. If 100 M are required, how many units of each component are needed?
   c. Show both a single level bill of materials and an indented bill of materials.

8. Product A consists of two units of subassembly B, three units of C, and one unit of D. B is composed of four units of E and three units of F. C is made of two units of H and three units of D. H is made of five units of E and two units of G.
   a. Construct a simple product structure tree.
   b. Construct a product structure tree using low-level coding.
   c. Construct an indented bill of materials.
   d. In order to produce 100 units of A, determine the numbers of units of B, C, D, E, F, G, and H required.

9. Old C.B. Radios, Inc., produces two automatic scanner citizens-band models for mobile installation, a standard model and a deluxe model of its "Good Buddy" line. The two radio models are internally identical, but the enclosures and finish trims differ.

   Old C.B. handles the production in the following way: The chassis (radio unit) is produced by Old C.B. to meet expected demand and has a manufacturing lead time of two weeks. The enclosures are purchased from a sheet steel company and have a three-week lead time. The trim is purchased from an electronics company as pre-packaged units consisting of knobs, trim pieces, and mounting hardware. Trim packages have a two-week lead time. Final assembly time may be disregarded since the addition of the trim package as well as the mounting are performed by the customer.

   Old C.B. supplies wholesalers and retailers who place specific orders for both models up to eight weeks in advance. These orders, together with enough additional units to satisfy the small number of individual sales, are summarized in the following demand schedule:

Week

	1	2	3	4	5	6	7	8
Deluxe model				300				400
Standard model					200			100

There are currently 50 radio unit chassis on hand but no trim packages or enclosures.

Prepare a material requirements plan to meet the demand schedule exactly. Specify the gross and net requirements, on-hand amounts, and the planned order release and receipt periods for the radio chassis, the deluxe trim, standard trim, deluxe enclosure, and standard enclosure.

10. Repeat the example in the section titled "Example of an MRP system" given in this chapter. However, assume that unexpected changes have caused the lead time for Item C to be two weeks instead of one week. Construct a new modified MRP schedule to account for the new lead time.

11. White and Peters, Inc., are manufacturers of electrical tools for the home handyman. One of the items in W & P's hand-drill line is a quarter-inch drill. Demand for this quarter-inch drill is randomly distributed with an annual amount estimated to be 100,000 units. The manufacturing cost of this drill is $7.50, and its suggested retail price is $19.95.

Each operating unit of White and Peters is operated as a separate cost center. The organizational structure assigns to the marketing and sales department the responsibility for finished goods inventory, which is stored in a factory warehouse. Marketing personnel have computed that the cost of holding units in inventory is 16⅔ percent of manufacturing cost. This amount is the total due to allocated warehouse space, the firm's pro-rated cost of capital, and miscellaneous costs. Marketing personnel have further estimated that the cost to place each order with manufacturing is $100 since they perform an inventory count and records check each time an order is placed.

Each quarter-inch drill consists of five subassemblies: the motor assembly, chuck assembly, switch and cord assembly, housing assembly (consisting of a left and a right half), and the packaging assembly (consisting of a styrofoam pack, operating instructions, warranty card, chuck key, and the enclosing carton). Manufacturing lead time of the motor assembly and chuck assembly is four weeks, and the lead times for the switch and cord assembly and the housing assembly are two weeks. Lead time for the packaging assembly is one week, and lead time for final assembly is also one week.

The drills are put together and packaged on an assembly line, so all subassembly units must be available at the same time. Assembly time is 15 seconds per drill, so the assembly line is used for other drill sizes and models when it is not assembling the quarter-inch drill. Scheduling the various products accounts for the one-week lead time for the assembly process. W & P closes down the entire manufacturing operation during a two-week vacation period each year.

a. In view of the costs involved, compute the order quantity that marketing should submit to manufacturing.

b. For manufacturing, determine a master schedule to meet the orders which can be met for the next eight weeks. Develop a material requirements plan for each subassembly, specifying gross and net requirements and planned order-release and order-receipt dates. Identify the soonest that a lot can be completed. Assume that there are no subassembly units currently in stock.

SELECTED BIBLIOGRAPHY

American Production and Inventory Control Society   *APICS Special Report: Materials Requirement Planning by Computer,* American Production and Inventory Control Society, 1971.

International Business Machines Corporation   *Communications Oriented Production Information and Control System.* Publications G320–1974 through G320–1981.

————   *The Production Information and Control System.* Publication GE20–0280–2.

————   *Manufacturing Implementation Guides.* Publication SH30–0211 to 30–0218.

Journal of American Production and Inventory Control Society   (Numerous articles on MRP appear. Most of these cite the difficulties and experiences of practitioners.)

Journal of American Institute of Decision Science   (Several articles on MRP that are more analytical, examining some foundations of MRP.)

Orlicky, Joseph   *Materials Requirements Planning.* New York: McGraw-Hill Book Company, 1975.

————, Plossl, G. W., and Wight, O. W.   *Materials Requirements Planning Systems,* IBM publication, G320–1170, 1971.

Proceedings of APICS and AIDS   (Many papers on all aspects of Materials Replenishment Planning Systems are usually presented at the annual society meetings and reprinted in the proceedings.)

Thurston, Phillip H.   "Requirements Planning for Inventory Control," *Harvard Business Review* (May–June 1972), pp. 67–71.

Wight, Oliver W.   *Production and Inventory Management in the Computer Age.* Boston: Cahners Books, 1974.

Startup of the system

Startup deals with the transitional period between the design of the system and its steady state operation. Because startup constitutes a project, the project management techniques of PERT and CPM are discussed in detail within this section (as well as our own technique, CPM/MRP). Also presented are different ways of going about startup and learning curves to predict and evaluate startup progress.

CRITICAL PATH SCHEDULING

Ninety Ninety Rule of Project Schedules: the first 90 percent of the task takes 90 percent of the time, the last 10 percent takes the other 90 percent.

Critical path scheduling refers to a set of graphical techniques used in planning and controlling projects. In any given project, there are three factors of concern: *time, cost,* and *resource availability,* and critical path techniques have been developed to deal with each of these, individually and in combination. The organization of this technical note follows the lines of these three factors, with major sections focusing on time-based models, time cost models, and limited resource models.

PERT *(Program Evaluation and Review Technique)* and CPM *(Critical Path Method),* the two best-known techniques, were both developed in the late 1950s. PERT was developed under the sponsorship of the U.S. Navy Special Projects Office in 1958 as a management tool for scheduling and controlling the Polaris missile project.[1] CPM was developed in 1957 by J. E. Kelly of Remington-Rand and M. R. Walker of du Pont to aid in scheduling maintenance shutdowns of chemical processing plants. Since their development, a number of variants have been devised, which, though little different on basic concept, have raised the invention of acronyms almost to an art form.[2]

In Chapter 14, we defined a project as a *series of related jobs usually directed toward some major output and requiring an extensive period of time to perform.* Critical path scheduling techniques display a project in graphical form and relate

---

[1] Which it did with notable success, being credited for reducing the project length by 18 months.

[2] Acronyms of some of the better-known techniques are SPERT, HEP, ICONS, PEP, LESS, GERT, and NASA PERT.

its component tasks in such a way as to focus attention on those which are crucial to the project's completion. For critical path scheduling techniques to be most applicable, a project must have the following characteristics:

1. It must have well-defined jobs or tasks whose completion marks the end of the project.
2. The jobs or tasks are independent in that they may be started, stopped, and conducted separately within a given sequence.
3. The jobs or tasks are ordered in that they must follow each other in a given sequence.
4. A job or task, once started, must continue without interruption until completion.

Construction, aerospace, and shipbuilding industries commonly meet these criteria, and hence, critical path techniques find wide application within them. "Big business," in general, made substantial use of PERT and CPM as far back as 1965, with 44 percent of a sample of 186 (from the *Fortune 500*) indicating such use.[3] A breakdown of specific applications derived from the same survey is given in Exhibit 17.1.[4]

EXHIBIT 17.1
Areas of application of PERT and CPM

Areas of application	Respondents using techniques
Construction	53.3%
Research and development	48.1
Product planning	37.0
Maintenance	29.6
Computer installation	25.9
Marketing	7.4
Other	29.6

Source: Modified from Peter B. Schoderbek, *A Study of the Applications of PERT,"* *Academy of Management Journal* (September 1965), p. 203.

TIME-ORIENTED TECHNIQUES

The basic forms of PERT and CPM focus on finding the longest time-consuming path through a network of tasks as a basis for planning and controlling a project. As will be observed in the ensuing discussion, there are some differences in the way the networks of the two techniques are structured and in their terminologies. However, the basic difference lies in the fact that PERT permits explicit treatment of probability in its time

---

[3] Peter B. Schoderbek, "A Study of the Applications of PERT," *Academy of Management Journal* (September 1965), pp. 199–206.

[4] A 1975 survey of manufacturing firms indicated that PERT and CPM were the most widely used operations research techniques, with over 65 percent of companies using any OR technique using PERT or CPM. (See N. Gaither, "The Adoption of Operations Research Techniques by Manufacturing Organizations," *Decision Sciences*, vol. 6, no. 4 [October 1975], pp. 794–814.)

estimates whereas CPM does not. This distinction reflects PERT's origin in scheduling advanced development projects that are characterized by uncertainty and CPM's origin in the scheduling of the fairly routine activity of plant maintenance.

In a sense, both techniques owe their development to their widely used predecessor, the Gantt chart.[5] While the Gantt chart is able to relate activities to time in a usable fashion for very small projects, the interrelationship of activities, when displayed in this form, becomes extremely difficult to visualize and to work with for projects greater than 25 or 30 activities. Moreover, the Gantt chart provides no direct procedure for ascertaining the *critical path*, which, despite its theoretical shortcomings, is of great practical value.[6]

PERT

The following steps are required in developing and solving a PERT network.

1. Identify each activity to be done in the project. Assuming that the PERT analyst has an understanding of the technical aspects of the program, the output from this step is simply a listing of activities. While it is important that all activities required to complete the project are included, care should be taken to ensure that they are presented at a constant level of detail. For example, in building a house, an activity such as *nail down front step* would not be shown on the same PERT chart as *lay foundation*. In network terminology, they are at different *levels* of *indenture*, and hence, such a mixture of major and minor activities would be inappropriate.

2. Determine the sequence of activities and construct a network reflecting the precedence relationships. This is a valuable step, even if a complete PERT analysis is not performed, since it forces the analyst to consider the interrelationships of activities and present them in visual form. PERT networking follows an *activity on arrow, event on node* structure; that is, arrows denote activities and nodes denote events. Activities consume time and resources, and events mark their start or completion. Thus, *write book* would be an activity and *book completed* would be an event.

In the network segment illustrated in Exhibit 17.2, we have specified three events and two activities, although each event node signifies two events: the end of one event and the beginning of another. That is, event 2 marks not only the completion of the book but the start of printing the book. Event 3 signifies the completion of printing, and perhaps the start of the distribution, and so on.

EXHIBIT 17.2

Start writing   Book completed   Printing completed

Write book   Print book

1   2   3

---

[5] A Gantt chart is illustrated in Chapter 14.

[6] See "Picking on PERT and CPM", page 576.

In the construction of a network, care must be taken to assure that the activities and events are in the proper order and that the logic of their relationships is maintained. For example, it would be illogical to have a situation where event A precedes event B, B precedes C, and C precedes A. Also, in many projects, problems arise in showing the precise form of dependencies, and the networking device termed a *dummy activity* must be employed. Dummy activities consume no resources and are typically depicted as dashed arrows. A summary of some of the situations in which dummies are used is provided in Exhibit 17.3.

   3. *Ascertain time estimates for each activity.*   The PERT algorithm requires that three estimates be obtained for each activity:

   a = optimistic time: the minimum reasonable period of time in which the activity can be completed. (There is only a small probability, typically assumed to be 1 percent, that the activity can be completed in a shorter period of time.)

   m = most likely time: the best guess of the time required. (This would be the only time estimate submitted if one is using CPM.) Since m would be the time thought most likely to appear, it is also the mode of the beta distribution discussed in step 4.

   b = pessimistic time: the maximum reasonable period of time the activity would take to be completed. (There is only a small probability, typically assumed to be 1 percent, that it would take longer to complete the activity.)

Typically, this information is gathered from those people who are to perform the activity.

   4. *Calculate the expected time (ET) for each activity.*   The formula for this calculation is as follows:

$$ET = \frac{a + 4m + b}{6}$$

This is based upon the beta statistical distribution and weights the most likely time *(m)* four times more than either the optimistic time *(a)* or the pessimistic time *(b)*. The beta distribution was selected by the PERT research team because it is extremely flexible; that is, it can take on the variety of forms that typically arise in project activity durations, it has finite end points, which limit the possible activity times to the area between a and b (see Exhibit 17.4), and in the simplified version used in PERT, it permits straightforward computation of the activity mean and standard deviation. Four "typical" beta curves are illustrated in Exhibit 17.4.

   5. *Calculate the variances (σ^2) of the activity times.* Specifically, this is the variance, σ^2, associated with each ET, and is computed as follows:

$$\sigma^2 = \left(\frac{b - a}{6}\right)^2$$

As can be seen, the variance is the square of one sixth the difference

EXHIBIT 17.3
The use of dummy activities in network construction

1. Partial dependence

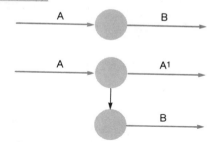

Implies A must be completely finished before B can start.

Indicates that B can start when A is partially completed.

2. Clarify precedence relationships

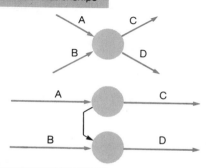

Implies that C and D are dependent on A and B.

Indicates that D depends on A and B; C depends only on A.

3. Existence of competing resource requirements

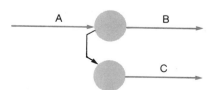

Indicates that C cannot start (in this case) until equipment becomes available from A.

4. Clarify event numbers for computer use

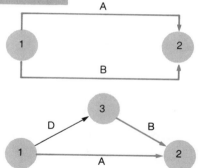

Conceptually correct but two activities have identical event numbers.

Enables separate activity designations that is, for activity D, 1-3; A, 1-2; and B, 3-2.

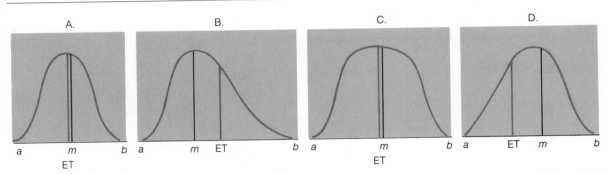

Curve A indicates very little uncertainty about the activity time, and since it is symmetrical, the expected time (ET) and the most likely or modal time *(m)* fall along the same point.

Curve B indicates a high probability of finishing the activity early, but if something goes wrong, the activity time could be greatly extended.

Curve C is almost a rectangular distribution, which suggests that the estimator sees the probability of finishing the activity early or late as equally likely, and $m \cong ET$.

Curve D indicates that there is a small chance of finishing the activity early, but it is more probable that it will take an extended period of time.

EXHIBIT 17.4
Typical beta curves

between the two extreme time estimates, and of course, the greater this difference, the larger the variance.

6. Determine the critical path.   The critical path is the longest sequence of connected activities through the network and is defined as the path with zero *slack* time. *Slack time (Ts),* in turn, is calculated for each event and is the difference between the earliest expected completion time and the latest expected completion time for an event. Slack may be thought of as the amount of time the start of a given event may be delayed without delaying the completion of the project.

7. Determine the probability of completing the project on a given date.   A unique feature of PERT is that it enables the analyst to assess the effect of uncertainty on project completion time. The mechanics of deriving this probability are as follows:

a.   Sum the variance values associated with each activity on the critical path.

b.   Substitute this figure, along with the project due date and the project expected completion time, into the Z transformation formula. This formula is as follows:

$$Z = \frac{D - T_E}{\sqrt{\Sigma \sigma_{cp}^2}}$$

where

D = Due date for project
T_E = Earliest expected completion time for last activity
$\Sigma \sigma_{cp}^2$ = Sum of the variances along critical path

c.   Calculate the value of Z, which is the number of standard deviations the project due date is from the expected completion time.

d. Using the value for Z, find the probability of meeting the project due date (using a table of normal probabilities—see Exhibit 17.5). The *earliest expected completion time* (T_E) for an event is found by starting at the beginning of the network and summing the expected times (ETs) for each event preceding the event of interest. If two or more arrows converge on an event node, use the *largest* computed figure. The *latest expected completion time* (T_L) for an event is found by starting at the end of the network and working toward the beginning, subtracting the expected completion time (ET) for each event from the value of the T_L for each successor event. To begin the process requires the establishment of some T_L for the last event. This value is typically set equal to T_E for that event, or to the desired project completion time (D). If two or more arrows converge on an event node, take the smallest computed figure as the T_L value.

EXHIBIT 17.5
Values of the standard normal distribution function

Z	Probability	Z	Probability	Z	Probability
−3.0	0.0013	−0.9	0.1841	1.1	0.8643
−2.9	0.0019	−0.8	0.2119	1.2	0.8849
−2.8	0.0026	−0.7	0.2420	1.3	0.9032
−2.7	0.0035	−0.6	0.2743	1.4	0.9192
−2.6	0.0047	−0.5	0.3085	1.5	0.9332
−2.5	0.0062	−0.4	0.3446	1.6	0.9452
−2.4	0.0082	−0.3	0.3821	1.7	0.9554
−2.3	0.0107	−0.2	0.4207	1.8	0.9641
−2.2	0.0139	−0.1	0.4602	1.9	0.9713
−2.1	0.0179	0	0.5000	2.0	0.9772
−2.0	0.0228	0.1	0.5398	2.1	0.9821
−1.9	0.0287	0.2	0.5793	2.2	0.9861
−1.8	0.0359	0.3	0.6179	2.3	0.9893
−1.7	0.0446	0.4	0.6554	2.4	0.9918
−1.6	0.0548	0.5	0.6915	2.5	0.9938
−1.5	0.0668	0.6	0.7257	2.6	0.9953
−1.4	0.0808	0.7	0.7580	2.7	0.9965
−1.3	0.0968	0.8	0.7881	2.8	0.9974
−1.2	0.1151	0.9	0.8159	2.9	0.9981
−1.1	0.1357	1.0	0.8413	3.0	0.9987
−1.0	0.1587				

Applying the PERT procedure: A sample problem. In order to meet the exhaust emissions standards, an automobile manufacturing company must modify the design of the antismog device on all its cars. In order to install the device on next year's models, the vice president of manufacturing can allow only 35 weeks' time to build a prototype, along with specifying the required changes in tooling and methods to produce it. The vice president assigns this project to the manager of development engineering and requests him to "PERT chart" the problem and to provide an estimate of the likelihood of completing the project in the time allowed. Let us follow the steps listed above and show how the manager might proceed.

1. Activity identification. The research manager decides that the following activities are the major components of the project: redesign of the antismog device, prototype construction, prototype testing, methods specification (summarized in a report), new tooling evaluation studies, a tooling report, and a final report summarizing all aspects of the design, tooling, and methods.

2. Activity sequencing and network construction. On the basis of discussion with his staff of engineers, the research manager develops the precedence table and sequence network shown in Exhibit 17.6. Note that he must add a "dummy" time line to permit unique activity designations for the writing of the tooling report and methods report. In this example, the table reflects this adjustment, even though it is presumed to be identified before the network was developed. In practice, the manager would be unlikely to recognize the need for dummy activities before at least a rough network is drawn.

3 and 4. Establish time estimates and calculate activity time variances. Once he decides on the activities to be performed, the manager would ask his staff to estimate the optimistic, most likely, and pessimistic times for those activities under their control. He would then calculate ET and σ^2 for each activity and list it in a form such as that shown in Exhibit 17.7.

5. Determine critical path. Exhibit 17.8 is a "working" PERT chart in that it is in the form an analyst would use to arrive at the critical path and expected completion time for the project. Each T_E is found first by summing from event 0 forward; each T_L is found next by setting T_L and T_E equal to 38 and subtracting, moving backward through the network. Slack times are calculated below the chart. Examining the slack values, we see that events 0, 1, 2, 3, 5, and 6 are critical and that part of the network shows two critical paths, since the events associated with parallel activities 1–3 and 1–2, 2–3 each has zero slack.

6. Probability of completion. Since there are two critical paths in the network, a decision must be made as to which variances to use in arriving

EXHIBIT 17.6
Precedence relationships

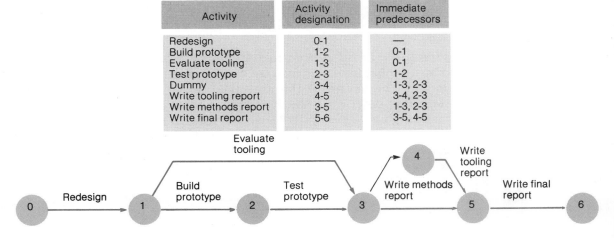

Activity	Activity designation	Immediate predecessors
Redesign	0-1	—
Build prototype	1-2	0-1
Evaluate tooling	1-3	0-1
Test prototype	2-3	1-2
Dummy	3-4	1-3, 2-3
Write tooling report	4-5	3-4, 2-3
Write methods report	3-5	1-3, 2-3
Write final report	5-6	3-5, 4-5

EXHIBIT 17.7
Activity expected times and variances

Activity	Activity designation	Time estimates a	m	b	Expected times (ET) $\frac{a + 4m + b}{6}$	Activity variances (σ^2) $\left(\frac{b - a}{6}\right)^2$
Redesign	0–1	10	22	28	21	9
Build prototype	1–2	4	4	10	5	1
Evaluate tooling	1–3	4	6	14	7	$2\frac{7}{9}$
Test prototype	2–3	1	2	3	2	$\frac{1}{9}$
Dummy	3–4	–	–	–	–	–
Write tooling report	4–5	1	5	9	5	$1\frac{7}{9}$
Write methods report	3–5	7	8	9	8	$\frac{1}{9}$
Write final report	5–6	2	2	2	2	0

at the probability of completion. A conservative approach dictates that the path with the largest total variance be used since this would focus mangement's attention on those activities that are most likely to exhibit broad variations. On this basis, the variances associated with activities 0–1, 1–3, 3–5, and 5–6 would be used to find the probability of completion. Thus $\Sigma\sigma_{cp}^2 = 9 + 2\frac{7}{9} + \frac{1}{9} + 0 = 11\frac{8}{9}$. (We will round this to 12.) The due date *(D)* was given as 35 weeks and the earliest expected completed time (*T_E* for the last event) was found to be 38. Substituting into the Z equation and solving, we obtain

$$Z = \frac{D - T_E}{\sqrt{\Sigma\sigma_{cp}^2}} = \frac{35 - 38}{\sqrt{12}} = \frac{-3}{3.46} \cong -0.9$$

EXHIBIT 17.8
Identification of critical path

Looking at Exhibit 17.5, we see that a Z value of −0.9 yields a probability of 0.18, which means that the research manager has only about an 18 percent chance of completing the project on time.

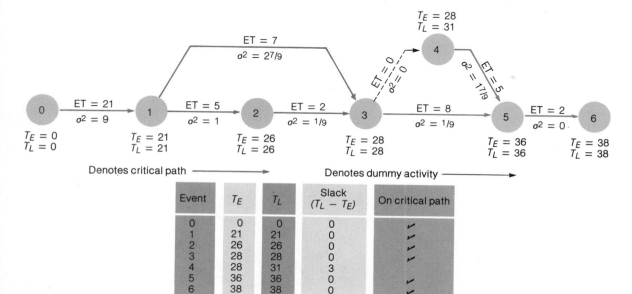

Event	T_E	T_L	Slack ($T_L - T_E$)	On critical path
0	0	0	0	✓
1	21	21	0	✓
2	26	26	0	✓
3	28	28	0	✓
4	28	31	3	
5	36	36	0	✓
6	38	38	0	✓

CPM

As mentioned earlier, the major distinction between CPM and PERT is the use of statistics in the latter. Otherwise, despite some differences in network construction and terminology, the approaches are similar.

The following steps are required in developing and solving a CPM network (Exhibit 17.9).

1. Identify each activity to be done in the project. In CPM, the term *job* is often used to refer to the task being performed, rather than separating out activities and events as in PERT. However, since current practice seems to be to treat the terms as synonymous, we will refer to the CPM tasks to be done as *activities.*

2. Determine the sequence of activities and construct a network reflecting precedence relationships. CPM is activity oriented with arrows denoting precedence only. A typical segment in using the book-writing example from PERT (step 2) would show the activity above the node rather than on the arrow. To restate, nodes in CPM represent activities in the PERT sense, not events.

3. Ascertain time estimates for each activity. This is the "best guess" time and can be thought of as equivalent to expected time (ET), which is derived statistically in PERT (step 4). While the CPM procedure has no provision for statistical estimation of this value, the individual who provides the

EXHIBIT 17.9
Steps to develop and solve a CPM network

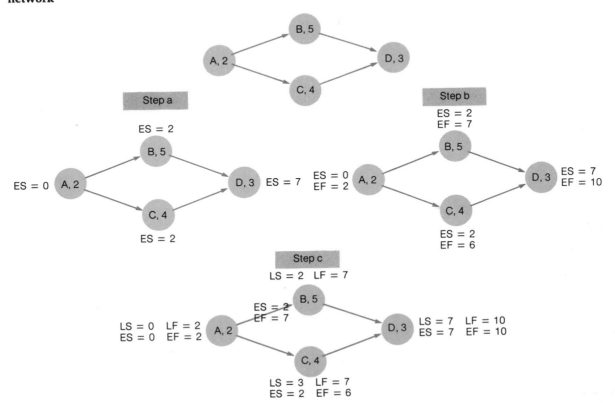

estimate may employ a simple statistical model in arriving at a figure. For example, he or she may feel that two times are equally likely and therefore take their average as his or her estimate.

4. Determine the critical path. As in PERT, this is the path with zero slack. To arrive at slack time requires the calculation of four time values for each activity:

Early start time (ES), which is the earliest possible time that the activity can begin.

Early finish time (EF), which is the early start time plus the time needed to complete the activity.

Late start time (LS), which is the latest time an activity can begin without delaying the project.

Late finish time (LF), which is the latest time an activity can end without delaying the project.

The procedure for arriving at these values and for determining slack and the critical path can best be explained by reference to the simple network shown (Exhibit 17.9). The letters denote the activities and the numbers the activity times.

a. Find ES time. Take zero as the start of the project and set this equal to ES for activity A. To find ES for B, we add the duration of A (which is 2) to zero and obtain 2. Likewise, ES for C would be 0 + 2, or 2. To find ES for D, we take the larger ES and duration time for the preceding activities: since B = 2 + 5 = 7 and C = 2 + 4 = 6, ES for D = 7. These values are entered on the diagram (Exhibit 17.9, step a). The largest value is selected since activity D cannot begin until the longest time-consuming activity preceding it is completed.

b. Find EF times. The EF for A is its ES time, 0, plus its duration of 2. B's EF is its ES of 2 plus its duration of 5, or 7. C's is 2 + 4, or 6, and D's is 7 + 3, or 10 (Exhibit 17.9, step b). In practice, one computes ES and EF together while proceeding through the network. Since ES plus activity time equals EF, the EF becomes the ES of the following event, and so forth.

c. Find late start and late finish times. While the procedure for making these calculations can be presented in mathematical form, the concept is much easier to explain and understand if it is presented in an "intuitive" way. The basic approach is to start at the end of the project with some desired or assumed completion time. Working back toward the beginning, one activity at a time, we determine how long the starting of this activity may be delayed without affecting the start of the one that follows it.

In reference to the sample network, let us assume that the late finish time for the project is equal to the early finish time for activity D, that is, 10. If this is the case, the latest possible starting time for

D will be 10 − 3, or 7. The latest time C can finish without delaying the LS of D is 7, which means that C's LS is 7 − 4, or 3. The latest time B can finish without delaying the LS of D is also 7, which means that B's LS is 7 − 5, or 2. Since A precedes two activities, the choice of LS and LF values depends upon which of those activities must be started first. Clearly, B determines the LF for A since its LS is 2, whereas C can be delayed one day without extending the project. Finally, since A must be finished by day 2, it cannot start any later than day 0, and hence, its LS is 0. These LS and LF values are entered in the network (Exhibit 17.9, step c).

d. Determine slack time for each activity. Slack for each activity is defined as either LS − ES or LF − EF. In this example, only activity C has slack (1 day); therefore the critical path is A, B, D.

EXHIBIT 17.10
CPM network for antismog device redesign project

Applying CPM to the design modification project. For the sake of brevity, we have summarized the results of the various steps of the CPM procedure in the form shown in Exhibit 17.10. Note that the CPM network appears

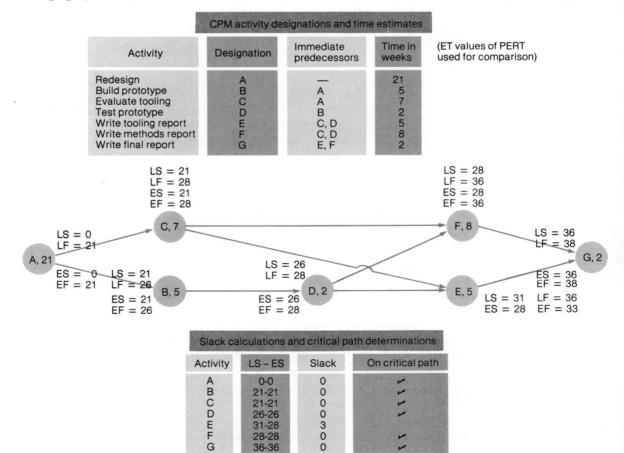

CPM activity designations and time estimates

Activity	Designation	Immediate predecessors	Time in weeks	(ET values of PERT used for comparison)
Redesign	A	—	21	
Build prototype	B	A	5	
Evaluate tooling	C	A	7	
Test prototype	D	B	2	
Write tooling report	E	C, D	5	
Write methods report	F	C, D	8	
Write final report	G	E, F	2	

Slack calculations and critical path determinations

Activity	LS − ES	Slack	On critical path
A	0-0	0	✓
B	21-21	0	✓
C	21-21	0	✓
D	26-26	0	✓
E	31-28	3	
F	28-28	0	✓
G	36-36	0	✓

greatly different from the PERT network even though the activities and the critical path(s) are the same. Also note that no dummy arrows are required for this problem. (In general, CPM uses fewer dummies than PERT because an activity is designated only by a node rather than by an arrow connecting two events.)

TIME-COST MODELS

In practice, project managers are as much concerned with the cost to complete a project as with the time to complete the project. For this reason, extensions of PERT and CPM have been devised that attempt to develop a minimum-cost schedule for an entire project and to control budgetary expenditures during the conduct of a project. Current usage indicates that the approaches that focus on minimum cost scheduling typically use CPM networks, while those that focus on budgetary control generally fall under the heading PERT–COST. However, it should be emphasized that minimum-cost scheduling has been employed as an option in PERT–COST systems, and budgetary control schemes have been employed in conjunction with CPM scheduling.

Minimum-cost scheduling (time-cost trade-off)

The basic assumption in minimum cost scheduling of a project is that there is a relationship between activity completion time and the cost of a project. On one hand, it costs money to expedite the completion of an activity, while on the other, it costs money to sustain (or lengthen) the project. The costs associated with expediting activities are termed *activity direct costs.* Some of these may be worker-related, such as overtime work, hiring more workers, and transferring workers from other jobs, while others are resource-related, such as buying or leasing additional or more efficient equipment and drawing upon additional support facilities.

The costs associated with sustaining the project are termed *project indirect costs* and consist of overhead, facilities, and resource opportunity costs, and—under certain contractual situations—penalty costs or lost incentive payments. Since these two categories of opposing costs are dependent upon time, the scheduling problem is essentially one of finding that project duration that minimizes their sum or, in other words, finding the optimum point in a time-cost trade-off.

The procedure for finding this point consists of six steps, and it will be explained by using the simple four-activity network employed in the previous section. Exhibit 17.11 shows the data.

1. Prepare a CPM-type network diagram. For each activity this diagram should list:
   a. Normal Cost (NC): The lowest expected activity cost (these are the lesser of the cost figures shown under each node below).
   b. Normal Time (NT): The time associated with each normal cost.
   c. Crash Time (CT): The shortest possible activity time.
   d. Crash Cost (CC): The cost associated with each crash time.

2. Determine the cost per unit of time (assume days) to expedite each activity. The relationship between activity time and cost may be shown graphically by plotting CC and CT coordinates and connecting them to the NC and NT coordinates by a concave, convex, or straight line—or some other form, depending upon the actual cost structure of activity performance. For activity A, we assume a linear relationship between time and cost. This assumption is common in practice and facilitates the derivation of the cost per day to expedite since this value may be found directly by taking the slope of the line using the formula Slope = (CC − NC) ÷ (NT − CT). (When the assumption of linearity cannot be made, the cost of expediting must be determined graphically for each of the days the activity may be shortened.)

The calculations needed to obtain the cost of expediting the remaining activities are shown in Exhibit 17.12.

3. Prepare a normal-time, normal-cost schedule. For the simple network we have been using, this schedule would take ten days and would cost $26. The critical path would be A, B, D. Arriving at the values used to derive the expediting costs and the total cost for the schedule is facilitated by using the tabular format shown in Exhibit 17.11, step 3.

4. Prepare a crash-time, crash-cost schedule. This schedule would take five days and would cost $45. It should be noted, however, that the same schedule time could be achieved at a lower cost since activity B could be delayed one more day without delaying the total project. Hence, the "rational" crash schedule would appear as shown in Exhibit 17.11, step 4, and, in this case, would yield two critical paths.

EXHIBIT 17.11
Example of time-cost trade-off procedure

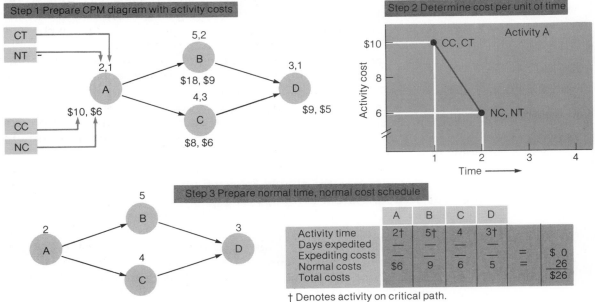

† Denotes activity on critical path.

EXHIBIT 17.11
(continued)

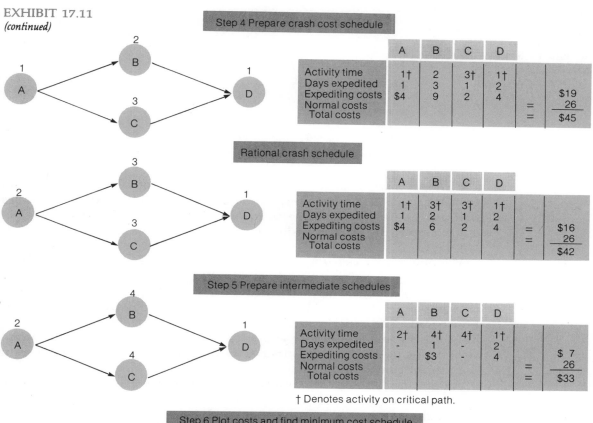

Step 4 Prepare crash cost schedule

	A	B	C	D		
Activity time	1†	2	3†	1†		
Days expedited	1	3	1	2		
Expediting costs	$4	9	2	4	=	$19
Normal costs						26
Total costs					=	$45

Rational crash schedule

	A	B	C	D		
Activity time	1†	3†	3†	1†		
Days expedited	1	2	1	2		
Expediting costs	$4	6	2	4	=	$16
Normal costs						26
Total costs					=	$42

Step 5 Prepare intermediate schedules

	A	B	C	D		
Activity time	2†	4†	4†	1†		
Days expedited	-	1	-	2		
Expediting costs	-	$3	-	4	=	$ 7
Normal costs						26
Total costs					=	$33

† Denotes activity on critical path.

Step 6 Plot costs and find minimum cost schedule

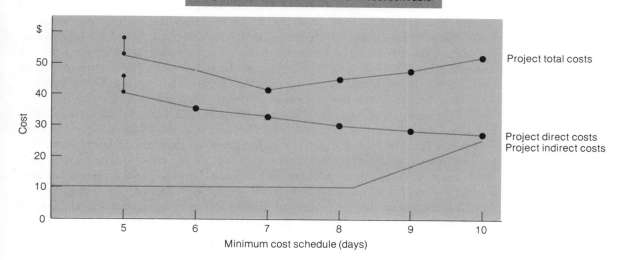

EXHIBIT 17.12
Calculation of cost per day to expedite each activity

Activity	$CC - NC$	$NT - CT$	$\dfrac{CC - NC}{NT - CT}$	Cost per day to expedite	Number of days activity may be shortened
A	$10 - $6	2 - 1	$\dfrac{\$10 - \$6}{2 - 1}$	$4	1
B	$18 - $9	5 - 2	$\dfrac{\$18 - \$9}{5 - 2}$	$3	3
C	$ 8 - $6	4 - 3	$\dfrac{\$8 - \$6}{4 - 3}$	$2	1
D	$ 9 - $5	3 - 1	$\dfrac{\$9 - \$5}{3 - 1}$	$2	2

5. Prepare intermediate schedules. Once the range of schedule times and costs is known, the next step is to find one or more intermediate schedules that can be used as coordinates to plot the project direct cost curve. In our example, the crash schedule is five days and the normal schedule is ten days.

We could approach the intermediate schedules from either direction: (1) by using the crash schedule and adding a day at a time to lengthen it, or (2) by using the normal schedule and shortening it a day at a time. It is important to proceed only one time period (day, in this case) at a time because the critical path might change. Also recognize that in shortening the schedule, only those activities on the critical path are shortened since reducing the time for other activities will not make a difference in the project completion date.

An arbitrarily selected intermediate schedule that might provide a clue to the slope of the curve is a seven-day schedule. To arrive at this schedule, we would start a crash schedule and add a total of two days to activity crash times of those activities on the critical path. Obviously, we would choose the activities that cost the most to expedite as the first ones to be "relaxed." Thus, we would add one day to the crash schedule of activity A, saving $4 (this is the maximum for A since this puts it back to its normal time of two days). Activity B has the next highest expediting cost, so we would add two days to its crash time, saving $6 (2 days × $3). This would yield the schedule shown in Exhibit 17.11, step 5.

6. Plot project-direct, indirect, and total-cost curves and find minimum-cost schedule. For the sake of comparison, all intermediate schedules have been derived for this example (see Exhibit 17.13). However, as can be seen from the project direct cost curve shown in Exhibit 17.11, step 6, connecting just the three cost coordinates associated with ten-, seven-, and 5-day schedules would provide a good estimate of the entire cost curve. To complete the example requires the inclusion of the indirect project cost curve, which in this case is a constant $10 per day for a five-, six-, or seven-day schedule, and increases at a rate of $5 per day for eight-, nine-, and ten-day project durations. (This type of curve would be typical of a situation where penalties are levied for exceeding a due date—or, conversely, where bonuses are awarded for meeting the schedule or for early completion.)

EXHIBIT 17.13
**Activity direct
cost calculations,
intermediate
schedules**

Schedule duration		Activity				Total expediting costs		Normal costs		Total direct costs per activity
		A	B	C	D					
6 days . . .	Activity time	1*	4*	4*	1*					
	Days expedited . .	1	1	—	2					
	Expediting costs .	$4	$3	—	$4	= $11	+	$26	=	$37
7 days . . .	Activity time	2*	4*	4	1*					
	Days expedited . .	—	1	—	2					
	Expediting costs .	—	$3	—	$4	= 7	+	26	=	33
8 days . . .	Activity time	2*	5*	4	1*					
	Days expedited . .	—	—	—	2					
	Expediting costs .	—	—	—	$4	= 4	+	26	=	30
9 days . . .	Activity time	2*	5*	4	2*					
	Days expedited . .	—	—	—	1					
	Expediting costs .	—	—	—	$2	= 2	+	26	=	28

*Denotes activity on critical path.

Summing the values for direct and indirect costs for each day yields the project total cost curve. As can be seen from the graph, this curve is at its minimum for a seven-day schedule, which costs $43. It should be noted that the black lines extending upward from the project total cost curve and the project direct cost curve at five days reflect the difference in cost between the all-crash and "rational" crash schedules.

PERT–COST

The basic objectives of PERT–COST are (1) to develop a realistic original project cost estimate and (2) to meet or better this cost estimate through detailed cost monitoring and control. The essential features of a PERT–COST system are:

1. A modified PERT–TIME network.
2. A work breakdown structure.
3. Work packages.
4. A series of reports.

Each of these will be discussed using the antismog device redesign project (introduced earlier).

1. Modified PERT–TIME network. The modification consists of adding cost estimates for the completion of each activity, based upon the expected completion time *(ET)* of each activity. (Hypothetical costs for three activities are shown in Exhibit 17.14.)

2. Work breakdown structure. The work breakdown structure specifies which organizational units are responsible for each activity required by the project. In our example, we might have a design group, a testing group, and a documentation group, each of which would be responsible for one of these three phases of the project. In addition, the work breakdown structure specifies different levels of project reporting. For example, the

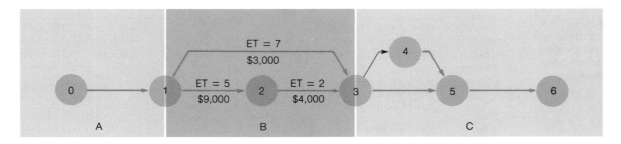

EXHIBIT 17.14
Work packages for three phases of the antismog device redesign project (data shown for work package *B* only)

president of the auto company would be on level 1, the research manager on level 2, and heads of the three groups on level 3. (Naturally, the work breakdown structure for a major project such as a missile system would be much more complex, would cut across organizational lines, and would be under the direction of a project manager who could command resources throughout the firm.)

3. *Work packages.*   A work package refers to a group of activities which are combined for purposes of budgetary control. Often termed *cost work packages,* they may be determined on the basis of activity duration time— for example, a work package equals three month's work—or on the basis of expenditure—for example, a work package equals $75,000 in cost. In our example, we have three work packages, A, B, and C, which relate directly to the three groups mentioned in the work breakdown structure. Work packages are commonly denoted by blocks around their activities. As can be seen in Exhibit 17.14, work package B consists of three activities and is budgeted at $16,000.

EXHIBIT 17.15
PERT–COST status report for antismog device redesign project [work package *B*], current date 1/3

4. *Reports.*   The more elaborate PERT–COST systems use a number of reports that go to different levels of the work breakdown structure as well as to certain functional areas of the firm, such as finance, accounting, and personnel. Information provided by these reports includes manpower availability and use, the general financial status of the project, and trends and prediction of deviations of cost and time from plan (the latter often

| Activity | Budget no. | Cost status | | | | | | Time status | | | | | | | |
| | | Work performed to date | | | Totals at completion | | | | | | | | | | |
		Value	Actual cost	(Over) or under	Planned cost	Latest revised estimate	Projected (over) or under	Expected time	Scheduled time	Scheduled completion date	Latest completion date	Activity slack	Percent completed	Scheduled percent	Percent ahead or (behind)
1-2	B-1	6	8	(2)	9	12	(3)	5	5	1/5	1/5	0	40	60	(20)
1-3	B-2	2	2	—	3	3	—	7	7	1/7	1/7	0	42.8	42.8	—
2-3	B-3	—	—	—	4	4	—	2	2	1/7	1/7	0	—	—	—

in graphical form). A key report, which goes to the project manager, is the *management summary report,* which summarizes both the cost and the well. In particular, the use of work packages generally requires new cost accounting codes, some adjustments in handling overhead, some means of determining allocation of indirect costs, and some way of pro-rating materials costs between work packages. Moreover, the sheer volume of accounting and budgetary data that are required to support an effective time status of the project as of a certain date. Exhibit 17.15, an example of such a report, shows this information for work package B on the antis-mog device redesign project as of January 3. Examination of this report indicates that the project is in trouble: activity 1–2 is $2,000 over its allotted cost for its stage of completion and is 20 percent behind schedule, or about a week and a half. The graphical report for a hypothetical company (Exhibit 17.16) shows time and cost data of this type for an extended period.

EXHIBIT 17.16
Budget and schedule status of a hypothetical project

Problems with PERT–COST. Although PERT–COST is subject to the same criticisms as PERT–TIME (which are considered later in the technical note), its emphasis on budgeting subjects it to additional problems as

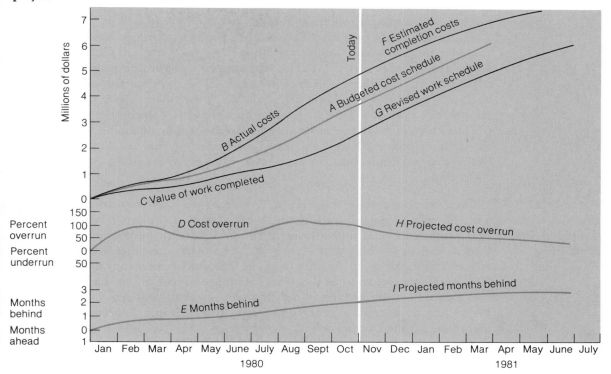

Source: Jerome D. Wiest and Ferdinand K. Levy, *A Management Guide to PERT/CPM,* © 1977. By permission of Prentice-Hall, Inc.

PERT–COST system can present a real information problem, even if the firm has good capability in data processing.

In summary, PERT–COST must be classified as an expensive technique, at least in comparison with the other techniques discussed in this technical note. And while it has been used with good success, it is not something that an organization should attempt without a good deal of prior research and planning.

Limited resource models

PERT and CPM implicitly assume that sufficient resources are always available to perform each activity. In practice, however, there is often competition for resources, especially manpower, between projects and between concurrently scheduled activities. Ideally, project managers would like to be able to incorporate into their network scheduling some mathematical way of assuring that resources will be optimally used and their availability never exceeded. Unfortunately, these goals are difficult to achieve, especially when other scheduling criteria, such as minimizing project duration or project cost, are also being considered. The complexity of the problem centers on the fact that for every possible starting time of an activity, there are generally several possible resource combinations, and therefore, for a project of even modest size, there is usually a vast number of combinations to evaluate.

To illustrate how we might schedule a project to manpower constraints, consider the following diagrams. Exhibit 17.17A is a small CPM-type network; the numbers in the circles denote both job number and crew size requirement, and the number above the circle denotes the activity time in days. In Exhibit 17.17B, a schedule graph of this project, the activities are plotted against a time scale. The number above each arrow represents the job number and daily crew size requirement. The dashed line represents slack time (defined here as a job's early start minus its late start time). If there is no limitation on crew size, this project can be completed in eight days.

Minimizing schedule time given limited manpower

Now suppose that there is a five-man-per-day resource limitation. Clearly, the project duration must be extended, and we would like to find a schedule that will minimize the additional time required. As mentioned above, problems of this type have many possible schedules, and while an optimizing technique (such as linear programming) might be used for a small project such as this one, it is more useful to consider a heuristic method, which more likely would be employed in practice. In this regard, Weist has developed a procedure using three simple heuristic rules that would be applied on a day-by-day basis.

1. Allocate resources serially in time. That is, start on the first day and schedule all jobs possible; then do the same for the second day; and so on.
2. When several jobs compete for the same resources, give preference to the jobs with the least slack.

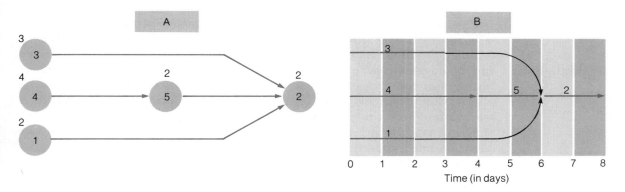

EXHIBIT 17.17
CPM network and schedule graph—no resource limitation

3. Reschedule noncritical jobs, if possible, in order to free resources for scheduling critical or nonslack jobs.[7]

Applying these rules yields the 11-day schedule shown in Exhibit 17.18. Note that the dashed lines no longer unequivocally denote slack since only job 1 can be delayed without extending the project. Is this the shortest schedule given the five-man resource limitation? The answer is yes—based upon comparing it to all possible schedules. However, while the heuristic rules "worked" in this case, recall from our discussion of layout techniques (in Chapter 8) that heuristic methods do not guarantee optimum solutions; they only increase the likelihood of a better one. Thus, following these rules for a different problem might result in a poor solution.

Other heuristic rules for deciding on job priority (subject to manpower limitations and technological ordering) are:

a. Schedule the job with the shortest duration first.
b. Schedule the job with the longest duration first.
c. Schedule the jobs for a particular organizational department first.
d. Schedule the job with the least technical uncertainty first.

EXHIBIT 17.18
Schedule graph—five-man resource limitation, 11-day schedule

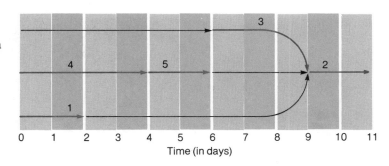

[7] J. Weist, "Heuristic Programs for Decision Making," *Harvard Business Review* (September–October 1966), pp. 129–43.

Manpower leveling given a fixed schedule date

The above example focused on the allocation of resources in order to minimize schedule time; however, a different sort of problem arises in resource leveling. In this situation, the project completion date is fixed and management wants to smooth out or balance resource requirements throughout the project so as to minimize the costs involved in acquiring or releasing resources. Consider the following example, in which four days are available for the project and the appropriate crew size (i.e., number of men per day) must be determined. For the sake of presentation, we have assumed that there are no sequence restrictions and no job 4. A schedule for this situation, in which all jobs are performed as soon as possible (termed *a left-justified schedule*), and the manpower loading chart for this solution appear in Exhibit 17.19. By inspection, it is obvious that the work load could be better balanced and the crew size reduced. One way to proceed would be to try pushing all slack jobs over to their late start time to derive a *right-justified schedule* (Exhibit 17.20).

This does not help the situation particularly other than to defer peak manpower requirements until the end of the project. (Such a schedule is

EXHIBIT 17.19
Schedule graph and manpower loading chart for left-justified schedule

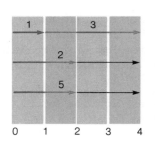

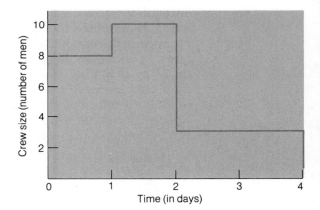

EXHIBIT 17.20
Schedule graph and manpower loading chart for right-justified schedule

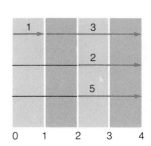

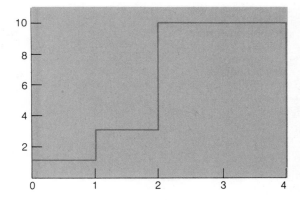

EXHIBIT 17.21
**Schedule graph
and manpower
loading chart for
trial and error
schedule**

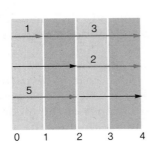

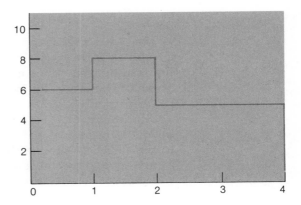

sometimes desirable for long projects where management is concerned with the time value of money and would prefer to forestall expenditures. Incidentally, right-justified schedules will always result in achieving peak loads toward the end of the project if slack exists.)

The third solution developed by trial and error (Exhibit 17.21) is the best one possible, and we note that the work load is better balanced and has a lower peak load than the other two. An ideal solution, in general, would be one yielding a rectangular manpower loading chart,[8] as the CPM/MRP appendix to this chapter illustrates.

CRITICAL PATH SCHEDULING AND THE COMPUTER

The rapid growth of critical path scheduling techniques has been accompanied by the development of computer programs to handle such tedious chores as calculating slack times, combining and updating networks, time-cost trade-offs, statistical estimates, and resource allocations. The decision whether or not to use a computer depends, in general, upon the number of activities, the number of performance reviews, and the amount of updating required for the project. A common rule of thumb is that when the number of arrows exceeds 100, a computer program should be seriously considered for the basic PERT and CPM models. Computers are generally considered a must for minimum-cost scheduling, PERT–COST, and limited resource problems. A listing of some of the available computer programs and their features is presented in the Davis and Phillips bibliographical references.

---

[8] Whether this is true in a given situation depends, of course, on the costs involved. The problem of minimizing the sum of all cost elements associated with a project, and a computer scheduling program designed to do it, is discussed in E. S. Buffa and J. G. Miller, *Production and Inventory Systems Planning and Control*, rev. ed. (Homewood, Ill.: Richard D. Irwin, Inc., 1980), pp. 635–61.

PICKING ON PERT AND CPM

The widespread application of critical path techniques has generated a number of theoretically oriented writings that challenge certain underlying assumptions of the models in general and PERT and CPM in particular. Some of the more significant assumptions and their criticisms are summarized in Exhibit 17.22.

In addition to theoretical questions, there are some practical problems in applying critical path techniques. One that is of particular relevance to the PERT method is the difficulty encountered by operating personnel in understanding the statistical underpinnings of the model. The beta distribution of activity times, the three time estimates, the activity variances,

---

EXHIBIT 17.22
Significant PERT/CPM assumptions and their criticisms

1. *Assumption:* Project activities can be identified as entities (that is, there is a clear beginning and ending point for each activity).

    Criticism: Projects, especially complex ones, change in content over time, and therefore a network made at the beginning may be highly inaccurate later on. Also, the very fact that activities are specified and a network formalized tends to limit the flexibility that is required to handle changing situations as the project progresses.

2. *Assumption:* Project activity sequence relationships can be specified and "networked."

    Criticism: Sequence relationships cannot always be specified beforehand. In some projects, in fact, the ordering of certain activities is conditional on previous activities. (PERT and CPM, in their basic form, have no provision for treating this problem, although some other techniques have been proposed that present the project manager with several contingency paths, given different outcomes from each activity.)

3. *Assumption:* Project control should focus on the critical path.

    Criticism: It is not necessarily true that the longest time-consuming path (or the path with zero slack) obtained from summing activity expected time values will ultimately determine project completion time. What often happens as the project progresses is that some activity not on the critical path becomes delayed to such a degree that it extends the entire project. For this reason it has been suggested that a critical activity concept replace the critical path concept as focus of managerial control. Under this approach, attention would center on those activities that have a high potential variation and lie on a "near-critical path." A near-critical path is one that does not share any activities with the critical path and, though it has slack, could become critical if one or a few activities along it become delayed. Obviously, the more parallelism in a network, the more likely that one or more near-critical paths will exist. Conversely, the more a network approximates a single series of activities, the less likely it is to have near-critical paths.

4. *Assumption:* The activity times in PERT follow the beta distribution, with the variance of the project assumed to be equal to the sum of the variances along the critical path.

    Criticism: As was mentioned in the discussion on PERT, the beta distribution was selected for a variety of good reasons. Nevertheless, each component of the statistical treatment in PERT has been brought into question. First, the formulas are in reality a modification of the beta distribution mean and variance, which, when compared to the basic formulas, could be expected to lead to absolute errors on the order of 10 percent for ET and 5 percent for the individual variances. Second, given that the activity time distributions have the properties of unimodality, continuity, and finite positive end points, other distributions with the same properties would yield different means and variances. Third, obtaining three "valid" time estimates to put into the PERT formulas presents operational problems—it is often difficult to arrive at one activity time estimate, let alone three, and the subjective definitions of a and b do not help the matter. (How optimistic and pessimistic should one be?)

and the use of normal distribution to arrive at project completion probabilities are all potential sources of misunderstandings, and with misunderstanding come distrust and obstruction. Thus if PERT is to be applied, management must be sure that the people charged with monitoring and controlling activity performance have a general understanding of the statistical features of PERT as well as the general nature of critical path scheduling. A trend in recent applications of PERT is to do away with the three time estimates in favor of one "best estimate." This modification removes some of the complexity from PERT and alleviates some of the theoretical problems in Exhibit 17.22. However, with this simplification comes a loss of the traits that set PERT apart and enable it to deal with statistical problems of project scheduling often in a better, though perhaps imperfect, way.

A second problem, investigated by Robert R. Britney,[9] relates to the cost of over- and underestimating activity duration times. "Underestimates precipitate reallocations of resources and, in many cases, cause costly project delays. Overestimates, on the other hand, result in inactivity and tend to misdirect management's attention to relatively unfruitful areas causing planning losses."[10] (Britney recommends a modification of PERT called BPERT (which employs concepts from Bayesian decision theory) to explicitly consider these two categories of cost in deriving a project network plan.)

Another problem that sometimes arises, especially when PERT is used by subcontractors working with the government, is the attempt to "beat" the network in order to get on or off the critical path. Many government contracts provide cost incentives for finishing a project early or on a "cost-plus-fixed-fee" basis. The contractor who is on the critical path generally has more leverage in obtaining additional funds from these contracts since he has a major influence in determining the duration of the project. On the other hand—for political reasons we will not go into here—some contractors deem it desirable to be less "visible" and therefore adjust their time estimates and activity descriptions in such a way as to ensure that they *won't* be on the critical path. This criticism, of course, reflects more on the use of the method than on the method itself, but PERT (and CPM, for that matter), by virtue of its focus on the critical path, enables such ploys to be used.

Finally, the cost of applying critical path methods to a project is sometimes used as a basis for criticism. However, the cost of applying PERT or CPM rarely exceeds 2 percent of total project cost, and PERT–COST rarely exceeds 5 percent of total project costs. Thus, this added cost is generally outweighed by the savings from improved scheduling and reduced project time.

---

[9] Robert R. Britney, "Bayesian Point Estimation and the PERT Scheduling of Stochastic Activities," *Management Science,* vol. 22, no. 9 (May 1976), pp. 938–48.

[10] Ibid., p. 939.

CONCLUSION

The critical path techniques of PERT and CPM have proven themselves in the past two decades and promise to be of continued value in the future. Certainly the fact that management has a tool that allows it to structure complex projects in an understandable way, to pick out possible sources of delay before they occur, to isolate areas of responsibility, and, of course, to save time in the performance of costly projects is sufficient to justify this assertion. It also seems likely that the various techniques employing cost features will become increasingly applied, especially in the construction industries, which are feeling a growing pressure to keep costs down. Finally, limited resource models that use heuristic methods will continue to be applied, abetted by practical observations as to which heuristic rules lead to better schedules. In this regard, Davis suggests that a likely mechanism for finding such heuristics is man-machine interactive procedures that can take advantage "of the full heuristic power of the computer much more imaginatively than has hitherto been realized."[11]

REVIEW AND DISCUSSION QUESTIONS

1. What characteristics must a project have in order for critical path scheduling to be applicable? What types of projects have been subjected to critical path analysis?

2. How does a PERT network differ from a CPM network?

3. Why was the beta distribution chosen by PERT developers to represent activity time variation?

4. What are the underlying assumptions of minimum cost scheduling? Are they equally realistic?

5. What is meant by a "rational" crash schedule?

6. Define or describe the following: work breakdown structure, work package, and management summary report.

7. What does the term *slack* refer to in limited resource scheduling? Compare it to the slack concept as used in CPM.

8. Compare the objectives of resource allocation models and manpower loading models.

9. "Project control should always focus on the critical path." Comment.

10. Why would subcontractors for a government project want their activities on the critical path? Under what conditions would they try to avoid being on the critical path?

PROBLEMS

1. Your spouse has decided that you will build a patio and barbecue grill during your vacation. Since your annual vacation starts next week, you

---

[11] E. W. Davis, "Project Scheduling under Resource Constraints—Historical Review," *AIIE Transactions*, vol. 5, no. 4 (December 1973), pp. 297–311. Quote on page 311.

must have a plan in order to complete the patio on time. And because your spouse wants an enclosed patio, you will have to hire some help. Listed below are the activities and events involved.

Prepare a PERT network for the patio project, including any additional events and activities you deem necessary to portray your plan adequately.[12]

Events	Activities
Spouse's approval of design	
Building permit applied for	Apply for building permit
Building materials ordered	Order building materials
Ground leveled	Level ground
Help hired	Hire help
Concrete forms laid out	Lay out concrete forms
Structure fabricated	Fabricate structure
Building inspection approved	Receive building permit
Lighting installed	Install lighting
Concrete work finished	Finish cement
Project completed	
Materials received	Receive materials
Help paid	Pay help
Ready-mix concrete ordered	Order concrete
Barbecue completed	Build barbecue
Painting completed	Paint
Building permit received	Building inspection
	Receive concrete

2. A wagon train of settlers is going to California and is due to leave Saint Joseph, Missouri, in the spring of 1849. According to Bart Whipwielder, the wagon boss, the trip will take the train through Fort Leavenworth, Kansas, and Reno, Nevada, en route to Sacramento. Competition for settlers is keen, so Bart is optimistic in his advertising. He says the first leg of the trip will take two weeks, the second leg three weeks, and the third leg two weeks. Harvey Weakwill, an irresolute settler, fears the worst. He says that the first leg will take four weeks, the second leg 11 weeks, and the third leg, ten weeks. However, Trotting Turkey, the trusty Indian guide who has made 12 trips and is considered the expert, indicates the most likely times for the trip are: first leg, three weeks; second leg, four weeks; and third leg, three weeks. How many weeks' provisions must be stocked so that the settlers can be 95 percent sure that they will arrive in Sacramento before their food is gone?

3. The following activities are part of a project to be scheduled using CPM.

Activity	Immediate predecessor	Time (weeks)
A	—	6
B	A	3
C	A	7
D	C	2
E	B,D	4
F	D	3
G	E,F	7

---

[12] Drawn from "PERT Exercise Manual," DOD 1.6/:P 94/6, PERT Orientation and Training Center, Washington, D.C. (1965).

    a. Draw the network.
    b. What is the critical path?
    c. How many weeks will it take to complete the project?
    d. How much slack does activity B have?

4. A project has been defined to contain the following list of activities, along with their required times for completion.

Activity	Time (days)	Immediate predecessors
A	1	—
B	4	A
C	3	A
D	7	A
E	6	B
F	2	C,D
G	7	E,F
H	9	D
I	4	G,H

    a. Draw the critical path diagram.
    b. Show the early start and early finish times.
    c. Show the critical path.
    d. What would happen if activity F was revised to take four days instead of two?

5. Given the following PERT network:

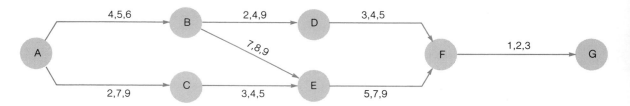

    a. Find the critical path.
    b. What is the standard deviation of the critical path?

6. Following is a CPM network with activity times in weeks.

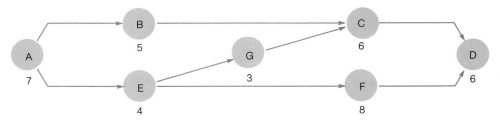

    a. Determine the critical path.
    b. How many weeks will the project take to complete?

      c. Supposing F could be shortened by two weeks and B by one week. What effect would this have on the completion date?

7. Following is a PERT network. The times shown are the three time estimates for the activities in weeks.

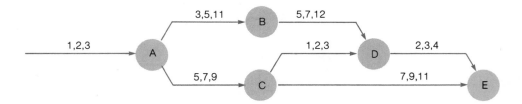

    a. What is the earliest the project can be completed?
    b. What is the critical path?
    c. What is the standard deviation of the critical path?
    d. What is the probability that the project will be completed in 20 weeks?

8. Following is a CPM network with the activity times shown under the nodes in days.

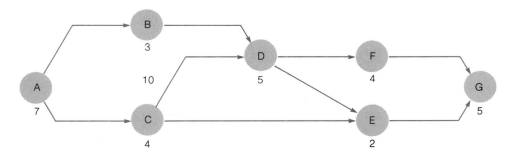

    a. Find the critical path.
    b. The following table shows the normal times and the crash times along with the associated costs for each of the activities.

Activity	Normal time	Crash time	Normal cost	Crash cost
A	7	6	$7,000	$8,000
B	3	2	5,000	7,000
C	4	3	9,000	10,200
D	5	4	3,000	4,500
E	2	1	2,000	3,000
F	4	2	4,000	7,000
G	5	4	5,000	8,000

      If the project is to be shortened by four days, show which activities in order of reduction would be shortened and the resulting cost.

9. The home office billing department of a chain of department stores prepares monthly inventory reports for use by the stores' purchasing agents. Given the information below, use the critical path method to determine

   a. how long the total process will take.
   b. which jobs can be delayed without delaying the early start of any subsequent activity.

Job and Description	Immediate predecessors	Time (in hours)
a Start	—	0
b Get computer printouts of customer purchases	a	10
c Get stock records for the month	a	20
d Reconcile purchase printouts and stock records	b,c	30
e Total stock records by department.....................	b,c	20
f Determine reorder quantities for coming period	e	40
g Prepare stock reports for purchasing agents	d,f	20
h Finish	g	0

10. You are planning a big party in honor of your birthday or whatever, and you are trying to coordinate all the things which must be done. Such things as sending out invitations, renting a nightclub, hiring a band and so forth are just a few of the activities which you must define and plan.

    Naturally you are sensible enough to use critical path scheduling to plan this big event since many of the activities are dependent on the completion of other activities, such as planning food catering and bar service depends on how many are coming.

    Following is a simplified set of activities as your first cut in planning the event.

Activity	Time (days)	Immediate predecessors
A	21	—
B	9	—
C	7	—
D	14	B,C
E	11	D
F	2	D
G	8	A,E
H	3	F,G

   a. Draw a diagram and show early start and early finish times.
   b. If this is May 1 and your birthday is June 10, will you make the date OK?
   c. Suppose the band you hired (Activity A) tells you after a week that they can't make it and you have to book another (requiring another 21 days). How will this affect your plan?
   d. How many days of slack exist for activity C?

11. Zapp, Inc., is nearly finished with a project to produce a small warning-signal generator. Because of a reduction in performance characteristics required, the remainder of the work is simpler than was originally planned, and a new estimate of time to completion must be made. The following is known:

Activity	Time (days)	Immediate predecessors	Description
a	1	—	Check total weight and approve
b	2	—	Check power consumption
c	2	—	Check temperature requirements
d	2	a,b	Choose connecting plug
e	4	b,c	Fix resistors' final values
f	1	c	Choose encapsulating foam
g	4	d	Ensure hermetic seal
h	8	g,e,f	Perform final test

a. Draw a critical path scheduling diagram and indicate the critical path.
b. What is the minimum time to completion?
c. If the starting day is day zero, what is the early start time for activity d?
d. What is the slack time for activity d?
e. During the second day of work (day 1), it is discovered that activity f (choose encapsulating foam) will take four days instead of one. Will this delay the project? If the activity takes six days, will the project be delayed?
f. Zapp, Inc., has a limited number of men available to work on the project, and only two activities can be under way at the same time. Will this delay the project beyond what the time would have been with unlimited resources (activity f takes six days to complete)? If you are interested, try creating a schedule with this limited resource restriction.

12. For the CPM network shown:
a. Determine the critical path and the early completion time for the project.

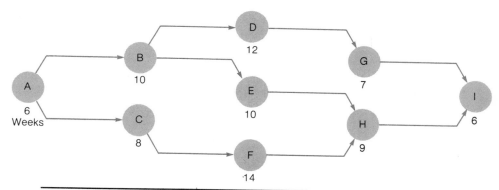

Activity*	Normal time (weeks)	Normal cost	Crash time (weeks)	Crash cost
A	6	$ 6,000	4	$12,000
B	10	10,000	9	11,000
C	8	8,000	7	10,000
D	12	12,000	10	14,000
E	10	10,000	7	12,000
F	14	14,000	12	19,000
G	7	7,000	5	10,000
H	9	9,000	6	15,000
I	6	6,000	5	8,000

* An activity cannot be shortened to less than its crash time.

    b. Using the data shown, reduce the project completion time by four weeks. Assume a linear cost per day shortened and show, step by step, how you arrived at your schedule. Also indicate the critical path.

13. The following network depicts the activity sequence required to complete a small project. The time to complete each activity is shown next to each activity designation, and for simplicity, it is assumed that the resource requirements for each job are the same as the job time; for example, activity *d* requires four days to complete using four men each day.

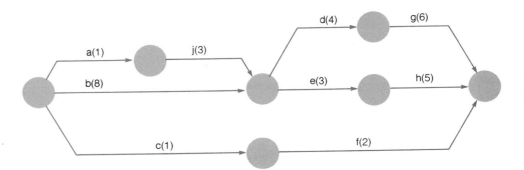

    a. Assuming a condition of unlimited resources, develop an early start (that is, left-justified) schedule using a schedule graph.

    b. Now, assuming that only ten men are available each day, develop a late start (that is, right-justified) schedule.

    c. Sketch the manpower loading charts for the solutions derived in *(a)* and *(b)*.

SELECTED BIBLIOGRAPHY

Britney, R. R. "Bayesian Point Estimation and the PERT Scheduling of Stochastic Activities," *Management Science*, vol. 22, no. 9 (May 1976), pp. 938–48.

Buffa, Elwood S., and Miller, Geoffery *Production-Inventory Systems: Planning and Control.* 3rd ed. Homewood, Ill.: Richard D. Irwin, Inc., 1980.

Davis, E. W. "Project Scheduling Under Resource Constraints—Historical Review," *AIIE Transactions,* vol. 5, no. 4 (December 1973), pp. 297–311.

Peterson, P. "Project Control Systems," *Datamation* (June 1979), pp. 147–63.

Weist, Jerome D., and Levy, Ferdinand K. *A Management Guide to PERT/CPM.* Englewood Cliffs, N.J.: Prentice-Hall, 1977.

Whitehouse, Gary E., and Washburn, Donald A. "Find Critical Path in an Arrow Diagram," *Industrial Engineering,* vol. 12, no. 12 (December 1980), pp. 18–21.

Supplement to Chapter 17

PROJECT SCHEDULING WITH CPM/MRP

The logic of Material Requirements Planning (MRP) can be applied to project scheduling. MRP is a data handling system of most value in assembly manufacturing and provides a schedule of order release dates for material requirements. Recall from Chapter 16 that MRP utilizes a master schedule, a bill of materials file, and an inventory records file to produce a schedule. This schedule shows the gross requirements, on-hand balances, and net requirements with the order release date offset to compensate for lead time. The lead times are those times required for either obtaining material or for the manufacturing time.

The critical path method of project scheduling utilizes a sequential computation to find start and completion times for a set of activities which comprise the project. The input to a CPM analysis is simply the set of activities and their sequence along with the expected duration time for each activity. CPM's shortcoming is that first, it concentrates on activity times, and second, it does not provide adequate storage files. MRP, on the other hand, provides storage files. Thus, it seemed reasonable to marry the two logics into a single combined system. *The result is a system which considers resource acquisition lead times, activity process times, and resource requirements with the built-in file of on-hand balances to provide a complete integrated project scheduling device.*

Thus far, we have only used the program on short projects of 300 activities and resources. However, computer processing times is short (ten seconds on a CYBER 175) so that larger projects should be no problem. Our continued research now is on adding features and improving efficiency rather than testing larger projects.

THE CPM/MRP MODEL

We will explain the CPM/MRP model with the aid of an example project, a simple patio bench. The CPM/MRP solution will be compared to the CPM schedule. The example project will be scheduled with the assumption that unlimited amounts of each resource are available.

The project network used for the CPM solution (Exhibit S.17.1) lists all of the project activities. The early and late times listed on the diagram were derived using the common CPM forward and backward pass techniques. Time measurement begins with the first day to be consistent with the shop calendar format used in MRP. Activities are started and finished at the beginning of the indicated periods.

EXHIBIT S.17.1
Activity-on-node diagram and schedule computed with critical path method

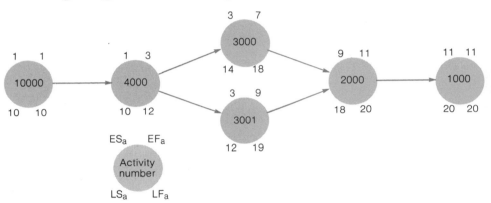

If the project is not due until day 20, then there is no critical path, since the project may be completed in 10 days. If the project was indeed due on day 11, then activities 1000, 2000, 3001, 4000, and 10000 would be critical, while activity 3001 would have two days of free slack.

This project in Exhibit S.17.1 can be also shown as an MRP product structure tree as in Exhibit S.17.2.

EXHIBIT S.17.2
MRP structure tree for the project shown in Exhibit S.17.1.

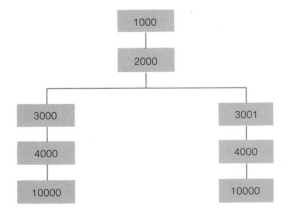

In order to make the bench, materials, labor, and equipment are required. Exhibit S.17.3 shows a single level bill of materials needed.

Exhibit S.17.4 shows the lead time required to order each resource and the performance time for each activity along with inventory records in the inventory record file.

EXHIBIT S.17.3
Bill of materials for the example project

Assembly (parent)	Part (child)	Quantity	Description
1000			Complete project
	2000	1	Assemble bench
2000			Assemble bench
	3000	1	Assemble back
	3001	1	Assemble seat
	9001	1	¼ lb., 10¢ nails
	9002	2	Carpenter hours
3000			Assemble back
	4000	1	Collect tools
	9000	2	2 × 4's
	9001	1	¼ lb., 10¢ nails
	9002	4	Carpenter hours
	9003	2	Handsaw hours
3001			Assemble seat
	4000	1	Collect tools
	9000	4	2 × 4's
	9001	1	¼ lb., 10¢ nails
	9002	12	Carpenter hours
	9003	4	Handsaw hours
	9004	2	Wrought iron legs
4000			Collect tools
	10000	1	Start project
9000			2 × 4's
	10000	1	Start project
9001			¼ lb., 10¢ nails
	10000.	1	Start project
9002			Carpenter hours
	10000	1	Start project
9003			Handsaw hours
	10000	1	Start project
9004			Wrought iron legs
	10000	1	Start project
10000			Start project

EXHIBIT S.17.4
Lead time, quantity on hand, and planned receipts for the activities and resources in the example project

Type	Number	On hand	Performance time	Lead time	On order
Activity	1000	0	0		0
Activity	2000	0	2		0
Activity	3000	0	4		0
Activity	3001	0	6		0
Activity	4000	0	2		0
Material	9000	0		6	0
Material	9001	0		3	0
Labor	9002	0		2	0
Facility and equipment	9003	0		5	0
Material	9004	0		8	0
Activity	10000	0	0		0

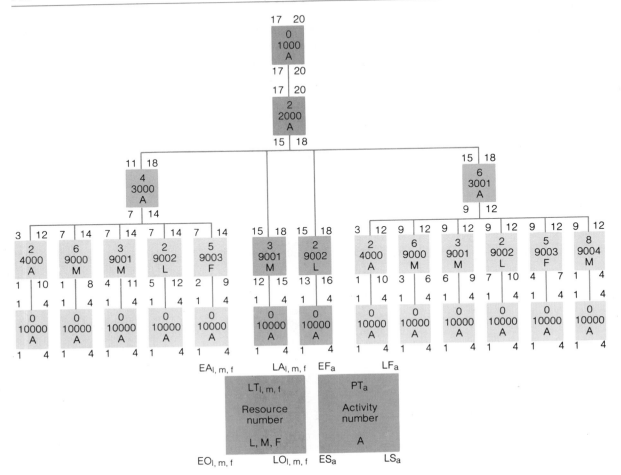

EXHIBIT S.17.5
Project structure tree with early and late schedules using CPM/MRP technique

It is possible to list this project, including resources, labor, and equipment in the form of the product structure tree used in MRP (Exhibit S.17.5). Note that due to the occurrences of multiple paths through most project networks, the project structure tree may list some activities more than once. As a consequence, resource inputs to these activities would be duplicated. To prevent this duplication, an activity is only permitted to occur once—at the time when it is first needed in the schedule. Later requirements are ignored.

THE LATE START SCHEDULE

As in MRP, the CPM/MRP technique branches out through the project structure tree (or, more properly, "explodes" the project bill of materials). All material requirement plans are late start schedules, since they schedule materials to arrive when they are needed in the due date completion schedule and not before. In the CPM/MRP program the project due date is established, and the project is exploded to find the late start schedule. All activity start times are subject to both the completion of previous activities and the acquisition of necessary resources.

The computation of net requirements for resources is essentially performed the same way as in MRP. Any amount of a nonstorable resource remaining at the end of a period, such as labor, may not be stored for future use. This means that while the order for a nonstorable resource used by an activity may be placed at one time, the resource will actually arrive in increments over the duration of the activity. The quantity of

EXHIBIT S.17.6
The CPM/MRP late start schedule

LATE START SCHEDULE

```
ACTIVITY COMPLETE PROJECT
  1000   LT = 0      1     2     3     4     5     6     7     8     9    10    11    12    13    14    15    16    17    18    19    20
RQMTS                0     0     0     0     0     0     0     0     0     0     0     0     0     0     0     0     0     0     0     1
PL'ED RECEIPTS       0     0     0     0     0     0     0     0     0     0     0     0     0     0     0     0     0     0     0     1
ENDING INV      0    0     0     0     0     0     0     0     0     0     0     0     0     0     0     0     0     0     0     0     1
ORDER RELEASE        0     0     0     0     0     0     0     0     0     0     0     0     0     0     0     0     0     0     0    -1
                                                                                                                                      1
ACTIVITY ASSEMBLE BENCH
  2000   LT = 2      1     2     3     4     5     6     7     8     9    10    11    12    13    14    15    16    17    18    19    20
RQMTS                0     0     0     0     0     0     0     0     0     0     0     0     0     0     0     0     0     1     0     0
PL'ED RECEIPTS       0     0     0     0     0     0     0     0     0     0     0     0     0     0     0     0     0     0     0     0
ENDING INV      0    0     0     0     0     0     0     0     0     0     0     0     0     0     0     0     0     0     0     0     0
ORDER RELEASE        0     0     0     0     0     0     0     0     0     0     0     0     0     0     0     0    -1     0     0     0
ACTIVITY ASSEMBLE BACK
  3000   LT = 4      1     2     3     4     5     6     7     8     9    10    11    12    13    14    15    16    17    18    19    20
RQMTS                0     0     0     0     0     0     0     0     0     0     0     0     0     0     0     0     0     0     0     0
PL'ED RECEIPTS       0     0     0     0     0     0     0     0     0     0     0     0     0     0     0     0     0     0     0     0
ENDING INV      0    0     0     0     0     0     0     0     0     0     0     0     0     0     0     0     0    -1    -1    -1
ORDER RELEASE        0     0     0     0     0     0     0     0     0     0     0     0     0     1     0     0     0    -1    -1    -1
ACTIVITY ASSEMBLE SEAT
  3001   LT = 6      1     2     3     4     5     6     7     8     9    10    11    12    13    14    15    16    17    18    19    20
RQMTS                0     0     0     0     0     0     0     0     0     0     0     0     0     0     0     0     0     1     0     0
PL'ED RECEIPTS       0     0     0     0     0     0     0     0     0     0     0     0     0     0     0     0     0     0     0     0
ENDING INV      0    0     0     0     0     0     0     0     0     0     0     0     0     0     0     0     0     0     0     0     0
ORDER RELEASE        0     0     0     0     0     0     0     0     0     0     0     0     1     0     0     0     0    -1    -1    -1
ACTIVITY COLLECT TOOLS
  4000   LT = 2      1     2     3     4     5     6     7     8     9    10    11    12    13    14    15    16    17    18    19    20
RQMTS                0     0     0     0     0     0     0     0     0     0     0     0     1     0     1     0     0     0     0     0
PL'ED RECEIPTS       0     0     0     0     0     0     0     0     0     0     0     0     0     1     0     1     0     0     0     0
ENDING INV      0    0     0     0     0     0     0     0     0     0     0     0    -1     0    -1     0     0     0     0     0
ORDER RELEASE        0     0     0     0     0     0     0     0     0     1     0     -1    0    -2    -2    -2    -2    -2    -2
MATERIAL START PROJECT
  9000   LT = 6      1     2     3     4     5     6     7     8     9    10    11    12    13    14    15    16    17    18    19    20
RQMTS                0     0     0     0     0     0     0     0     0     0     0     0     4     0     2     0     0     0     0     0
PL'ED RECEIPTS       0     0     0     0     0     0     0     0     0     0     0     0     0     0     0     0     0     0     0     0
ENDING INV      0    0     0     0     0     0     0     0     0     0     0     0    -4    -4    -6    -6    -6    -6    -6    -6
ORDER RELEASE        0     0     0     0     0     4     0     2     0     0     0    -4    -4    -6    -6    -6    -6    -6    -6
MATERIAL 10P. NAILS
  9001   LT = 3      1     2     3     4     5     6     7     8     9    10    11    12    13    14    15    16    17    18    19    20
RQMTS                0     0     0     0     0     0     0     0     0     0     0     1     0     1     0     0     0     1     0     0
PL'ED RECEIPTS       0     0     0     0     0     0     0     0     0     0     0     0     0     0     0     0     0     0     0     0
ENDING INV      0    0     0     0     0     0     0     0     0     0     0    -1     0    -2    -2    -2    -2    -3    -3    -3
ORDER RELEASE        0     0     0     0     0     0     0     0     1     0     0     1    0    -2    -2    -2    -2    -3    -3    -3
LABOR    CARPENTER HOURS
  9002   LT = 2      1     2     3     4     5     6     7     8     9    10    11    12    13    14    15    16    17    18    19    20
RQMTS              0.0   0.0   0.0   0.0   0.0   0.0   0.0   0.0   0.0   0.0   0.0   2.0   2.0   3.0   3.0   3.0   3.0   1.0   1.0   0.0
PL'ED RECEIPTS       0     0     0     0     0     0     0     0     0     0     0     0     0     0     0     0     0     0     0     0
ENDING INV      0    0     0     0     0     0     0     0     0     0     0   -12   -12   -16   -16   -16   -16   -18   -18   -18
ORDER RELEASE      0.0   0.0   0.0   0.0   0.0   0.0   0.0   0.0   0.0   2.0   2.0   3.0   3.0   3.0   3.0   1.0   1.0   0.0
FAC & EQ HANDSAW HOURS
  9003   LT = 5      1     2     3     4     5     6     7     8     9    10    11    12    13    14    15    16    17    18    19    20
RQMTS              0.0   0.0   0.0   0.0   0.0   0.0   0.0   0.0   0.0   0.0   0.0   0.7   0.7   1.2   1.2   1.2   1.2   0.0   0.0   0.0
PL'ED RECEIPTS       0     0     0     0     0     0     0     0     0     0     0     0     0     0     0     0     0     0     0     0
ENDING INV      0    0     0     0     0     0     0     0     0     0     0    -4    -4    -6    -6    -6    -6    -6    -6    -6
ORDER RELEASE      0.0   0.0   0.0   0.0   0.0   0.0   0.7   0.7   1.2   1.2   1.2   2.0   0.0   0.0   0.0   0.0   0.0   0.0   0.0
MATERIAL WROUGHT IRON LEGS
  9004   LT = 8      1     2     3     4     5     6     7     8     9    10    11    12    13    14    15    16    17    18    19    20
RQMTS                0     0     0     0     0     0     0     0     0     0     0     0     2     0     0     0     0     0     0     0
PL'ED RECEIPTS       0     0     0     0     0     0     0     0     0     0     0     0     0     0     0     0     0     0     0     0
ENDING INV      0    0     0     0     0     0     0     0     0     0     0     0    -2    -2    -2    -2    -2    -2    -2    -2
ORDER RELEASE        0     0     0     2     0     0     0     0     0     0     0    -2    -2    -2    -2    -2    -2    -2    -2
ACTIVITY START PROJECT
 10000   LT = 0      1     2     3     4     5     6     7     8     9    10    11    12    13    14    15    16    17    18    19    20
RQMTS                0     0     0     2     0     4     4     2     3    13     1     4     0     0     1     2     0     0     0     0
PL'ED RECEIPTS       0     0     0     0     0     0     0     0     0     0     0     0     0     0     0     0     0     0     0     0
ENDING INV      0    0     0     0    -2    -2    -6   -10   -12   -15   -28   -29   -33   -33   -33   -34   -36   -36   -36   -36
ORDER RELEASE        0     0     0     1     0     0     0     0     0     0     0     0     0     0     0     0     0     0    -36
```

this resource on hand at the end of a day is not saved for use the following day.

In an MRP fashion, then, a late start schedule can be developed as in Exhibit S.17.6. The negative numbers in the on-hand row follow the common procedure used by many firms. When a planned order is *actually* released, this amount is added to the on-hand and the negative disappears.

Activity 10,000 is the starting node of the entire project. Therefore, the first elements (those without predecessors) show requirements for 10,000 which means "start the project."

While the late start schedule is being computed, a set of records are constructed that list where each child is used in a parent assembly. A set of peg records are generated simultaneously with the late start schedule that are similar to the peg records in MRP. This set of records "pegs" the requirement for a child to each of its parents, as in Exhibit S.17.7.

EXHIBIT S.17.7
The peg record file

Child	Parent	Earliest REQ	This REQ	QTY
2000	1000	18	18	1
3000	2000	14	14	1
3001	2000	12	12	1
9001	2000	9	15	1
9002	2000	10	16	2
4000	3000	10	12	1
9000	3000	6	8	2
9001	3000	9	11	1
9002	3000	10	12	4
9003	3000	7	9	2
4000	3001	10	10	1
9000	3001	6	6	4
9001	3001	9	9	1
9002	3001	10	10	12
9003	3001	7	7	4
9004	3001	4	4	2
10000	4000	4	10	1
10000	9000	4	6	1
10000	9001	4	9	1
10000	9002	4	10	1
10000	9003	4	7	1
10000	9004	4	4	1

THE EARLY START SCHEDULE

The early start times in CPM/MRP are equivalent to those in CPM in that activities are scheduled to begin as early as possible, subject to technological and precedence constraints. Resource orders are timed so that resources arrive as they are required. Theoretically, they arrive as late as possible so that holding costs are not incurred. The order quantities are again computed, and the early start scheduled in Exhibit S.17.8 is created.

A final comparison between this schedule and the original CPM schedule will show that while CPM estimated projected duration as 10 days (ignor-

EARLY START SCHEDULE

ACTIVITY COMPLETE PROJECT — 1000 LT = 0

	1	2	3	4	5	6	7	8	9	10	11	12	13	14	15	16	17	18	19	20
RQMTS	0	0	0	0	0	0	0	0	0	0	0	0	0	0	0	0	1	0	0	0
PL'ED RECEIPTS	0	0	0	0	0	0	0	0	0	0	0	0	0	0	0	0	0	0	0	0
ENDING INV (0)	0	0	0	0	0	0	0	0	0	0	0	0	0	0	0	0	0	0	0	0
ORDER RELEASE	0	0	0	0	0	0	0	0	0	0	0	0	0	0	0	0	-1	-1	-1	-1

ACTIVITY ASSEMBLE BENCH — 2000 LT = 2

	1	2	3	4	5	6	7	8	9	10	11	12	13	14	15	16	17	18	19	20
RQMTS	0	0	0	0	0	0	0	0	0	0	0	0	0	0	0	0	0	0	0	0
PL'ED RECEIPTS	0	0	0	0	0	0	0	0	0	0	0	0	0	0	0	0	2	0	0	0
ENDING INV (0)	0	0	0	0	0	0	0	0	0	0	0	0	0	0	0	0	0	0	0	0
ORDER RELEASE	0	0	0	0	0	0	0	0	0	0	0	0	0	0	0	0	-2	-2	-2	-2

ACTIVITY ASSEMBLE BACK — 3000 LT = 4

	1	2	3	4	5	6	7	8	9	10	11	12	13	14	15	16	17	18	19	20
RQMTS	0	0	0	0	0	0	0	0	0	0	0	0	0	0	0	0	0	0	0	0
PL'ED RECEIPTS	0	0	0	0	0	0	0	0	0	0	0	0	0	0	1	0	0	0	0	0
ENDING INV (0)	0	0	0	0	0	0	0	0	0	0	0	0	0	0	1	0	0	0	0	0
ORDER RELEASE	0	0	0	0	0	0	1	0	0	0	-1	-1	-1	-1	-2	-2	-2	-2	-2	-2

ACTIVITY ASSEMBLE SEAT — 3001 LT = 6

	1	2	3	4	5	6	7	8	9	10	11	12	13	14	15	16	17	18	19	20
RQMTS	0	0	0	0	0	0	0	0	0	0	0	0	0	0	0	0	0	0	0	0
PL'ED RECEIPTS	0	0	0	0	0	0	0	0	0	0	0	0	0	0	2	0	0	0	0	0
ENDING INV (0)	0	0	0	0	0	0	0	0	0	0	0	0	0	0	0	0	0	0	0	0
ORDER RELEASE	0	0	0	0	0	0	0	0	1	0	0	0	0	0	-2	-2	-2	-2	-2	-2

ACTIVITY COLLECT TOOLS — 4000 LT = 2

	1	2	3	4	5	6	7	8	9	10	11	12	13	14	15	16	17	18	19	20
RQMTS	0	0	1	0	0	0	1	0	1	0	0	0	0	0	0	0	0	0	0	0
PL'ED RECEIPTS	0	0	0	0	0	0	0	0	0	0	0	0	0	0	0	0	0	0	0	0
ENDING INV (0)	0	0	-1	-1	-1	-1	-2	-2	-3	-3	-3	-3	-3	-3	-3	-3	-3	-3	-3	-3
ORDER RELEASE	1	0	-1	0	-1	0	-2	0	-3	-3	-3	-3	-3	-3	-3	-3	-3	-3	-3	-3

MATERIAL START PROJECT — 9000 LT = 6

	1	2	3	4	5	6	7	8	9	10	11	12	13	14	15	16	17	18	19	20
RQMTS	0	0	0	0	0	0	2	0	4	0	0	0	0	0	0	0	0	0	0	0
PL'ED RECEIPTS	0	0	0	0	0	0	0	0	0	0	0	0	0	0	0	0	0	0	0	0
ENDING INV (0)	0	0	0	0	0	0	-2	-2	-6	-6	-6	-6	-6	-6	-6	-6	-6	-6	-6	-6
ORDER RELEASE	2	0	4	0	0	0	-2	-2	-6	-6	-6	-6	-6	-6	-6	-6	-6	-6	-6	-6

MATERIAL 10P. NAILS — 9001 LT = 3

	1	2	3	4	5	6	7	8	9	10	11	12	13	14	15	16	17	18	19	20
RQMTS	0	0	0	0	0	0	1	0	1	0	0	0	0	0	0	0	0	0	0	0
PL'ED RECEIPTS	0	0	0	0	0	0	0	0	0	0	0	0	0	0	1	0	0	0	0	0
ENDING INV (0)	0	0	0	0	0	0	-1	-1	-2	-2	-2	-2	-2	-2	0	0	0	0	0	0
ORDER RELEASE	0	0	0	1	0	0	-1	-1	-2	-2	-2	-2	-3	-3	-3	-3	-3	-3	-3	-3

LABOR CARPENTER HOURS — 9002 LT = 2

	1	2	3	4	5	6	7	8	9	10	11	12	13	14	15	16	17	18	19	20
RQMTS	0.0	0.0	0.0	0.0	0.0	0.0	1.0	1.0	3.0	3.0	2.0	2.0	2.0	2.0	1.0	1.0	0.0	0.0	0.0	0.0
PL'ED RECEIPTS	0	0	0	0	0	0	0	0	0	0	0	0	0	0	0	0	0	0	0	0
ENDING INV (0)	0	0	0	0	0	0	-4	-4	-16	-16	-16	-16	-18	-18	-18	-18	-18	-18	-18	-18
ORDER RELEASE	0.0	0.0	0.0	0.0	1.0	1.0	3.0	3.0	2.0	2.0	2.0	2.0	1.0	1.0	0.0	0.0	0.0	0.0	0.0	0.0

FAC & EQ HANDSAW HOURS — 9003 LT = 5

	1	2	3	4	5	6	7	8	9	10	11	12	13	14	15	16	17	18	19	20
RQMTS	0.0	0.0	0.0	0.0	0.0	0.0	0.5	0.5	1.2	1.2	0.7	0.7	0.7	0.7	0.0	0.0	0.0	0.0	0.0	0.0
PL'ED RECEIPTS	0	0	0	0	0	0	0	0	0	0	0	0	0	0	0	0	0	0	0	0
ENDING INV (0)	0	0	0	0	0	0	-2	-2	-6	-6	-6	-6	-6	-6	0.0	0.0	0.0	0.0	0.0	0.0
ORDER RELEASE	0.0	0.5	0.5	1.2	1.2	0.7	0.7	0.7	0.0	0.0	0.0	0.0	0.0	0.0	0.0	0.0	0.0	0.0	0.0	0.0

MATERIAL WROUGHT IRON LEGS — 9004 LT = 8

	1	2	3	4	5	6	7	8	9	10	11	12	13	14	15	16	17	18	19	20
RQMTS	0	0	0	0	0	0	0	0	2	0	0	0	0	0	0	0	0	0	0	0
PL'ED RECEIPTS	0	0	0	0	0	0	0	0	0	0	0	0	0	0	0	0	0	0	0	0
ENDING INV (0)	0	0	0	0	0	0	0	0	-2	-2	-2	-2	-2	-2	-2	-2	-2	-2	-2	-2
ORDER RELEASE	0	0	0	0	0	0	0	0	-2	-2	-2	-2	-2	-2	-2	-2	-2	-2	-2	-2

ACTIVITY START PROJECT — 10000 LT = 0

	1	2	3	4	5	6	7	8	9	10	11	12	13	14	15	16	17	18	19	20
RQMTS	6	2	4	5	4	1	12	0	0	0	0	1	2	0	0	0	0	0	0	0
PL'ED RECEIPTS	0	0	0	0	0	0	0	0	0	0	0	0	0	0	0	0	0	0	0	0
ENDING INV (0)	-6	-8	-12	-17	-21	-22	-34	-34	-34	-34	-34	-35	-37	-37	-37	-37	-37	-37	-37	-37
ORDER RELEASE	1	0	0	0	0	0	0	0	0	0	0	0	0	0	0	0	0	0	0	0

EXHIBIT S.17.8

The CPM/MRP early start schedule

ing resources), the project duration would be 17 days if all resources must be ordered. This underestimation of project length may contribute to operational problems where CPM is used. Since amounts of activity slack are easily overestimated, Exhibit S.17.9 shows the slack which exists for the project.

EXHIBIT S.17.9

Slack on activities

Activity	Early start	Late start	Slack
1000	17	20	3
2000	15	18	3
3000	7	14	7
3001	9	12	3
4000	3	10	7
10000	1	4	3

Depending on the amount of resources on hand, the duration of the project should be somewhere between 11 and 17 days.

THE CRITICAL SEQUENCE

The critical sequence in CPM/MRP is defined as the connected path through the project structure tree that connects those activities and resource orders with zero slack. This is similar to the critical path in CPM.

To find the critical sequence:

1. Find the first activity in the project, and make this the first activity in the critical sequence.
2. Beginning with the first activity of the project, find the remaining members of the sequence:
    a. Consider the last element added to the sequence.
    b. Find all occurrences of this activity or resource where it occurs as a child in the peg records (Exhibit S.17.7).
    c. Find the parent activity or resource that generated the earliest requirement for the child in (b). Store this activity or resource as the next member of the sequence.
3. Continue until the last activity in the project has been added to the critical sequence.

This technique essentially branches through the network to find the longest connected path. The critical sequence for the example project (Exhibit S.17.10) was found using this technique.

EXHIBIT
S.17.10
**The critical
sequence for the
example project**

Type	Number
Activity	10000
Material	9004
Activity	3001
Activity	2000
Activity	1000

CONCLUSION

The CPM/MRP technique provides an integrated approach to project scheduling since it incorporates project activities and technological relationships with resource requirements and inventory records.

Further work is necessary in the area of development of a more efficient CPM/MRP computer program. The current program does not require excessive execution time, but the core requirements are rather large.

CPM/MRP provides the user with a technique for integrating resource acquisitions into the project schedule. It also allows the user to determine the effects of changes in resource lead times on the project schedule and the effects of changes in activity durations on resource order release dates.

SELECTED BIBLIOGRAPHY

Aquilano, Nicholas J. "Project Scheduling With MRP," (University of Arizona, College of Business and Public Administration, 1978).

Aquilano, Nicholas J., and Smith, Dwight E. "A Formal Set of Algorithms for Project Scheduling With Critical Path Scheduling—Material Requirements Planning," *Journal of Operations Management* (November 1980).

Davis, Edward W. "Project Scheduling Under Resource Constraints—Historical Review and Categorization of Procedures," *AIEE Transactions* (December 1973), pp. 297–313.

Orlicky, Joseph *Material Requirements Planning.* New York: McGraw-Hill Book Company, 1975.

Smith, O. C. "POWER—PERT Oriented Workshop Scheduling Evaluation Routine" (Proceedings of the Second International Congress on Product Planning by Network Analysis, North Holland Publishing Company, Amsterdam, 1969).

Wiest, Jerome D. "A Heuristic Model for Scheduling Large Projects With Limited Resources," *Management Science,* vol. 13, no. 6 (February 1967), pp. B359–77.

Wiest, Jerome D., and Levy, Ferdinand K. *A Management Guide to PERT/CPM.* Englewood Cliffs, N.J.: Prentice-Hall, 1977.

Zastera, Eugene P. "An Application of MRP to Engineering Management," (Master's Thesis, University of Arizona, 1978).

Chapter
18

SYSTEM STARTUP

"If we're ready, let's roll"

The startup period is that time which elapses from the manufacture of the first good unit in a new plant until the plant is producing regularly at full capacity. This period is often a "traumatic" time in the life cycle of a productive system since it is here that the separate elements considered in design must begin to function as a system. Indeed, not only must such technological components as processing equipment and material handling devices be integrated into an operational whole, but the management subsystems for planning and controlling production, inventory, quality, and so forth must be made to articulate properly as well.

In this chapter, we will discuss some of the factors that must be considered in achieving the integration of these subsystems, and we will present some concepts and techniques that have proved useful for this purpose in the past. In particular, we will consider some alternative organizational arrangements for managing startup, as well as the use of critical path techniques in planning it and learning curves for predicting and monitoring its progress.

STARTUP CONTRASTED WITH DESIGN AND STEADY STATE

Exhibit 18.1 illustrates the relationship of the startup period to design and steady state operations in terms of product output for a hypothetical productive system.

As a rule, the objective in managing the startup phase is to minimize the transition time; that is, to reach full-scale production as soon as possible. However, in certain instances it is desirable to go slowly—so as to permit more careful study of the performance of the system over different

EXHIBIT 18.1
**Relationship
between design,
startup, and
steady state and
system output for
a hypothetical
productive
system**

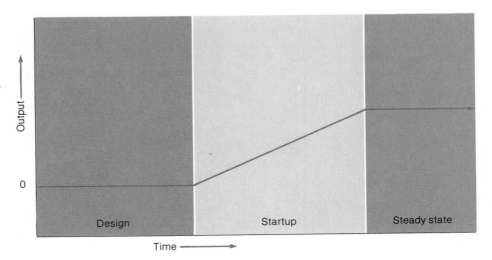

output ranges, to allow management and the work force to learn to cope
with operating problems when errors are less costly, or to achieve a particular production-inventory balance. In some cases, of course, the technology
is such that startup takes an exceptionally long time. Continuous casting
steel plants may take from one to six *years* before they produce at full
capacity.[1]

Exhibit 18.2 summarizes some of the key differences between design
and startup and steady state operations in terms of work force skills and
the focus of production subsystems. Looking first at the *work force* entries
in the exhibit, we see that management is generally concerned with planning during the design stage, coordinating the work flow and information
flow during startup, and monitoring operations during the steady state
period. The dashed line in the *labor* row means that operatives rarely participate in the formal design process. Later on, however, during startup, opera-
tive skill in handling unforeseen problems and debugging the system is
generally required, even though the worker generally is hired to meet
the more restricted demands of steady state production activities.

The entries under *focus of the production subsystems* are examples of the key
differences in managing design, startup, and steady state activities. As
far as startup is concerned, the general emphasis is on dealing with many
of the detailed decisions that are only implied by the system design. For
example, each machine will have its own peculiarities, and identifying
the tolerances that each can achieve and relating these tolerances to quality
control limits must be carried out on the basis of shop-floor experimentation. Likewise, establishing specific lot sizes, order points, and buffer stocks
for inventory control depend upon observation of actual demand, cost,

[1] See Ross Henderson, "Measuring Productivity Growth During Plant Startup," *I.E.E.E.
Transactions on Engineering Management* (February 1978), pp. 2–7.

		DESIGN	STARTUP	STEADY STATE
Work force		Primary skills of work force		
	Management	Planning	Coordinating	Monitoring
	Labor	—	Trouble shooting	Producing
Subsystems		Focus of production subsystems		
	Processes	Economic mix of equipment	Identification of tolerances	Equipment maintenance
	Facilities	Layout	Relocation of components	Smooth flow of goods
	Quality	Specification of quality measures	Identification of control limits	Economic sampling plans
	Production planning	Information requirements and procedures	Data gathering and information feedback	Testing alternative strategies
	Scheduling	Methods for scheduling	Sequence of operations	Determination of priorities
	Inventory	Procedures	Order rates, records, etc.	Optimal inventory level
	Tasks	Specification of jobs and workers	Selection and training	Increasing output

EXHIBIT 18.2
Key differences between design, startup, and steady state

and production figures. The concept of steady state production, of course, assumes that the bugs have been worked out of the design, and the emphasis shifts to keeping the system running smoothly.

STARTUP PLANNING

Organizing for implementation

Sometime during the design period, management must decide on the organizational arrangement whereby it will implement the startup. The broad strategies available to management for this purpose are:

1. Have the same personnel who are to run the system initiate it, following the steady state organization structure.
2. Organize a special startup team composed of representatives of various parts of the operating system and allow it to break the system in.
3. Obtain the services of outside specialists who would either direct operating personnel during the startup period or perform all startup activities with their own personnel.

We will now consider the pros and cons of each of these approaches.
Use of regular personnel. One advantage of having regular personnel handle startup activities is that they will be learning about the system as it takes shape and thereby will acquire insight into its particular foibles, which will be of great value later on. Of equal or even greater importance is the idea that since operating personnel are responsible for the success

of the system in the long run, they should be allowed to "bend and shape" the system during the transition period as well.

The main disadvantage in having operating personnel perform this function is that the skills required during startup may differ substantially from those required during steady state. In many instances the difference between startup and steady state is so vast that we might be viewing two distinct organizations rather than one at different points in time. From this observation, it may be argued that completely dissimilar organizational arrangements should be employed for each phase, depending, of course, upon the nature of the firm and industry being considered. For example, in the steady state operation of an oil refinery, the ability to cut costs and monitor technological processes is paramount, and operating management would likely be selected on the basis of these skills. In contrast, the startup period for a refinery entails a good deal of "fire fighting," demanding fast reactions on the part of management. Hence, dissimilar types of organization structures and managerial teams may very well be in order for a refinery, depending upon its stage in the life cycle.

Organizing specific startup teams. One difference between this approach and the strategy outlined above is that special attention is given to support activities, such as maintenance and quality control. This emphasis reflects the obvious truth that equipment problems and product defects are inevitable in any new undertaking. Another difference is that it is typical in certain industries, such as chemicals and petroleum, for the chief operating engineer to assume the directorship of the startup operation—rather than, say, the production manager, who will assume control during steady state operations. This organizational arrangement also reflects the significance of the technological aspects of the startup problem.

The exact composition of the startup team varies with the organization. In starting a chemical plant, for example, it has been suggested that the startup team should consist of the following four groups under the direction of the chief operating engineer.

1. A technical operating group, composed primarily of graduate engineers chosen especially for the startup.
2. A plant management group, which is expected to maintain supervisory and line control over the nontechnical operating personnel and which will assume technical control of the plant when the startup phase is over.
3. A maintenance group, which may be part of the normal plant staff but which may be supplemented with additional engineering members for the startup phase.
4. A laboratory group, which will be part of the normal plant staff but will be reinforced with additional technical advisers during the startup.[2]

---

[2] Manfred Gans and Frank A. Fitzgerald, "Plant Start-Up," Chap. 12 in *The Chemical Plant from Process Selection to Commercial Operation*, Ralph Landau and Alvin S. Cohan, eds. (New York: Reinhold Publishing Corp., 1966), pp. 270–89.

Use of outside specialists. A number of construction firms specialize in what are termed *turn-key operations,* in which they assume total responsibility for breaking in, as well as building, a new plant. Their services include hiring and training operating personnel and performing pilot runs in the completed facility. When they turn over the "key" to permanent management, the system—theoretically at least—is ready for full-scale production.

Another approach, also using outside specialists, involves development of mixed startup teams, in which certain skills not possessed by in-house personnel are provided by consulting firms. For example, systems engineering capability is generally required to initiate a computerized control system in a steel plant, but it might be unnecessary or too costly for a steel company to retain systems engineering specialists on a permanent basis.

Developing a startup schedule

Preparation for startup is usually begun during the later phases of design and consists of placing orders for productive resources, installing these resources, and testing the performance of key parts of the productive system. Regarding the order-placing aspects, requests for equipment, supplies, and raw materials must be placed with suppliers; orders for plant services, such as water, heat, and electricity, must be placed with local utilities; and manpower needs must be filled by transferring personnel from another company plant or recruiting new personnel. Each of these components, in turn, must be installed; or in the case of the labor force, it must be trained to operate the equipment and perform the necessary support functions. As far as testing is concerned, the equipment must be debugged, the labor force must be integrated into the work flow, and the production control system must undergo dry runs to check its capability to provide accurate and timely information and to take corrective action.

While it is easy to broadly define these activities, the actual scheduling of a startup is often an extremely complex task, if for no other reason than the sheer volume of order placing, installation, and testing that must be performed. To deal with its complexity, some formal mechanism of planning and control must be employed, and Gantt charts and simple precedence diagrams historically have been used for this purpose. In recent years, however, critical path networks of various types[3] have become increasingly popular and now are considered standard in administering startups of even modest complexity.

A number of examples of hypothetical critical path network applications, including three dealing with different plant startup situations, have been published by *Factory* magazine. One of these illustrated a network that might be used by a food processor in making a short-distance move from an urban to a suburban location; another illustrated a network that might be used by a machine tool manufacturer in consolidating several obsolete plants into one new plant; and a third (shown in Exhibit 18.3) illustrated

---

[3] See the previous chapter for an explanation of the theory and mechanics of these methods.

EXHIBIT 18.3
Startup PERT chart

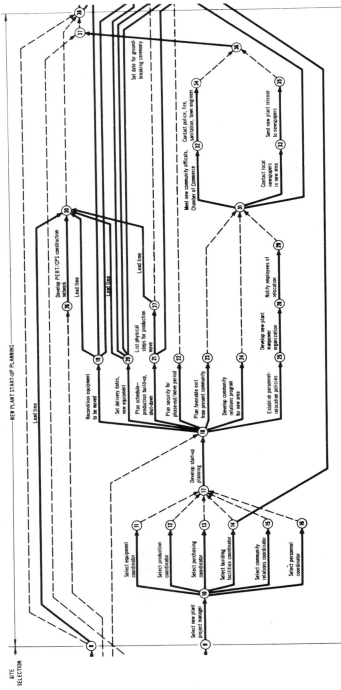

KEY TO TABLE

○ Event   S Start activity   C Complete activity

[Denotes site selection events   [Denotes building construction events

1   Plant relocation approved
2   C. Sign contract with architect
3   C. Issue site report
4   C. Preliminary layout and specifications
5   C. Revise drawings, specifications
6   C. Record property deed
7   C. Issue drawings, specifications for bids
8   C. Sign agreement with selected contractors
9   S. Propose new plant planning team

10 C. Appoint over-all project manager
11 C. Appoint equipment coordinator
12 C. Appoint production coordinator
13 C. Appoint purchasing coordinator
14 C. Appoint building facilities coordinator
15 C. Appoint community relations coordinator
16 C. Appoint personnel coordinator
17 C. Form new plant planning team
18 S. Detail plant start-up procedures

19 C. Approve equipment recondition/budget
20 C. Issue new equipment schedule
21 C. Approve production schedules
22 C. Approve security plans
23 C. Approve present community relations program
24 C. Approve new community relations program
25 C. Approve personnel policy manual
26 S. Develop PERT/CPS construction network
27 C. Issue production move plan

28 C. New plant manpower positions
29 C. Notify personnel asked to relocate
30 C. Initial network check-out report
31 S. Establish new community contacts
32 C. Community luncheon meetings
33 C. Approve publicity release
34 C. Visit community service departments
35 C. Issue relocation announcement
36 S. Plan ground-breaking program
37 C. Ground-breaking ceremony
38 S. Construction

SITE SELECTION

NEW PLANT START-UP PLANNING

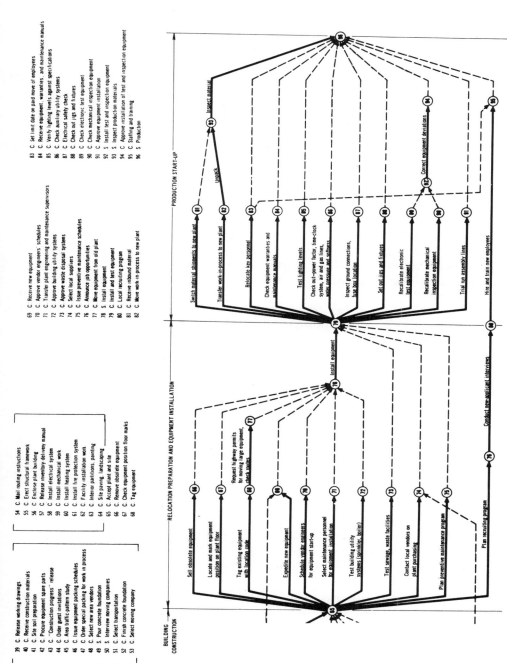

39 C: Release working drawings
40 C: Receive construction materials
41 C: Site soil preparation
42 C: Procure equipment spare parts
43 C: "Construction progress" release
44 C: Order guest invitations
45 C: Area traffic-pattern study
46 C: Issue equipment packing schedules
47 C: Order special packing for work in process
48 C: Select new area vendors
49 S: Pour concrete foundation
50 S: Interview moving companies
51 C: Select transportation
52 C: Finish concrete foundation
53 C: Select moving company

54 C: Mail routing instructions
55 C: Erect structural framework
56 C: Enclose plant building
57 C: Release inventory-delivery manual
58 C: Install electrical system
59 C: Install mechanical work
60 C: Install heating system
61 C: Install fire protection system
62 C: Facility installation work
63 C: Interior partitions, painting
64 C: Site paving, landscaping
65 S: Accept plant and site
66 C: Remove obsolete equipment
67 C: Check equipment position floor marks
68 C: Tag equipment

69 C: Receive new equipment
70 C: Approve vendor engineers' schedules
71 C: Transfer plant engineering and maintenance supervisors
72 C: Approve building utility systems
73 C: Approve waste disposal systems
74 C: Select local suppliers
75 C: Issue preventive maintenance schedules
76 C: Announce job opportunities
77 C: Move equipment from old plant
78 S: Install equipment
79 C: Install and test equipment
80 C: Local recruiting program
81 C: Receive inbound material
82 C: Move work-in-process to new plant

83 C: Set limit date on paid move of employees
84 C: Receive equipment, warranties, and maintenance manuals
85 C: Verify lighting levels against specifications
86 C: Check auxiliary utility systems
87 C: Electrical safety check
88 C: Check out jigs and fixtures
89 C: Check electronic, test equipment
90 C: Check mechanical inspection equipment
91 C: Approve equipment installation
92 S: Install test and inspection equipment
93 S: Inspect production materials
94 C: Approve installation of test and inspection equipment
95 C: Staffing and training
96 S: Production

Reprinted by special permission of *Factory* (February 1967). Copyright, Morgan-Grampian, Inc., February 1967.

a network that might be used by an electronics firm in making a cross-country relocation of an existing plant.

In looking at the network properties of this example, we see that it is a PERT-type network since the arrows denote activities and the nodes, events, and the start and completion of certain activities are explained separately.[4] (As mentioned in Chapter 17, this additional information is required because the PERT technique, unlike the critical path method, may not always indicate the relationship between the completion of one activity and the start of a subsequent one.) Further, a number of dummy time lines are used to preserve proper sequences when one activity does not depend directly on another. Finally, we note that the critical path is not depicted, although applying time estimates to this network should be a straightforward (though perhaps tedious) operation.

Turning to the startup aspects, we observe that this network displays layout, site selection, and building construction, in addition to new-plant startup planning and production startup. These phases reflect the special features of this startup situation and, of course, reflect its added complexity over a simple cross-country move or the construction of a new plant. Note that the startup planning phase is under the direction of a project manager who has several "coordinators" reporting to him; so it is essentially the same as the startup team strategy mentioned earlier in the chapter.

Also, the importance of lead time in placing orders for equipment, supplies, and internal and external services is reflected in the network by the number of lead-time activity arrows. Further, we can see that the developer of the network was careful to keep the various activities at the same level of abstraction, showing just the primary stages of the project. The development of subnetworks would probably be left to the various coordinators, with the exception of the construction network (activity 26–10), which would probably be developed by the architect with some member of management.

PREDICTING STARTUP PROGRESS: LEARNING CURVES

Determining when steady state and specific transient production levels will be achieved is of great importance in breaking in a productive system. Clearly, the ability to fill customers' orders, build inventory, coordinate transportation services, and perform a number of other vital production functions depends upon a realistic appraisal of production progress over time. A common approach to making this appraisal is the development and analysis of *learning curves*. A learning curve, in its basic form, is simply a line displaying the relationship between unit production time and the number of consecutive units of production.

Learning curves can be applied to individual learning or organizational learning. Individual learning is improvement which results from a person

---

[4] These starts and completions could be shown as individual nodes in the network, but they would increase its size substantially.

repeating a process and gaining skill or efficiency from his or her own experience. That is, "practice makes perfect." Organizational learning is improvement which results from practice as well but also comes from changes in administration, equipment, and product design. In organizational settings, we expect to see both kinds of learning occurring simultaneously and often describe the combined effect with a single learning curve.

Learning curve theory is based upon three assumptions:

1. The amount of time required to complete a given task or unit of a product will be less each time the task is undertaken.
2. The unit time will decrease at a decreasing rate.
3. The reduction in time will follow a specific and predictable pattern, such as an exponential function.[5]

Each of these assumptions was found to hold true in the airframe industry, where learning curves were first applied. Specifically, it was observed that, as output doubled, there was a 20 percent reduction in direct production man-hours per unit between doubled units. Thus, if it took 100,000 hours for plane 1, it would take 80,000 hours for plane 2, 64,000 hours for plane 4, and so forth. Since the 20 percent reduction meant that, say, unit 4 took only 80 percent of the production time required for unit 2, the line connecting the coordinates of output and time was referred to as an "80 percent learning curve." (By convention, the percentage learning rate is used to denote any given learning curve.)

A learning curve may be developed from an arithmetic tabulation or by logarithms, depending upon the amount and form of the available data.

Arithmetic tabulation

In following an arithmetic tabulation approach, the number of units produced (proposed or actual) is listed and the corresponding labor hours for each doubled unit level are calculated by multiplying the unit's direct labor hours by the selected learning percentage. Thus, if we are developing an 80 percent learning curve, we would arrive at the figures listed in column 2 of Exhibit 18.4. Since it is often desirable for planning purposes to know the cumulative average direct labor hours, column 4, which lists this information, is also provided. The calculation of these figures is straightforward; for example, for unit 4, cumulative average direct labor hours would be found by dividing cumulative direct labor hours by 4, yielding the figure given in column 4. These values are plotted in Exhibit 18.5.

In practice, learning curves are plotted on log-log paper, which results in the unit curves' becoming linear throughout their entire range and the cumulative curve's becoming linear after the first few units. The property of linearity is desirable because it facilitates extrapolation and permits a

---

[5] W. J. Fabrycky and P. E. Torgersen, *Operations Economy: Industrial Applications of Operations Research* (Englewood Cliffs, N.J.: Prentice-Hall, 1966), p. 100.

EXHIBIT 18.4
Unit, cumulative, and cumulative average direct labor man-hours required for an 80 percent learning curve

(1) Unit number	(2) Unit direct labor hours	(3) Cumulative direct labor hours	(4) Cumulative average direct labor hours
1	100,000	100,000	100,000
2	80,000	180,000	90,000
4	64,000	314,210	78,553
8	51,200	534,591	66,824
16	40,960	892,014	55,751
32	32,768	1,467,862	45,871
64	26,214	2,392,453	37,382
128	20,972	3,874,395	30,269
256	16,777	6,247,318	24,404

Source: W. J. Fabrycky and Paul E. Torgersen, *Operations Economy: Industrial Applications of Operations Research,* © 1966, Prentice-Hall, Inc., p. 100. Reprinted by permission of the publisher.

EXHIBIT 18.5
Arithmetic plot of an 80 percent learning curve

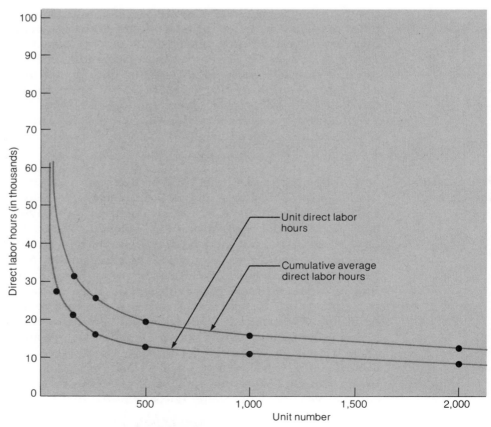

Source: W. J. Fabrycky and Paul E. Torgersen, *Operations Economy: Industrial Applications of Operations Research,* © 1966, Prentice-Hall, Inc., p. 101. Reprinted by permission of the publisher.

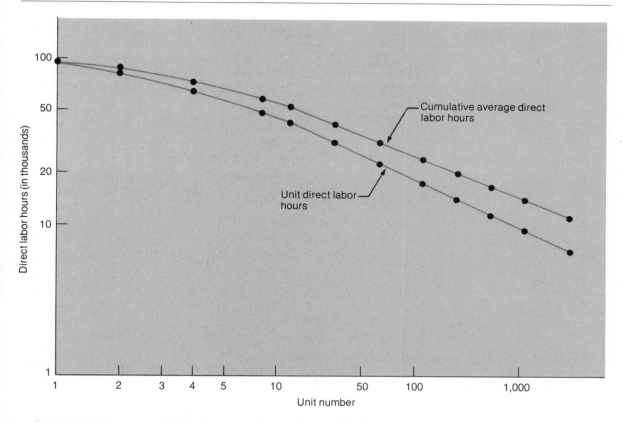

Direct labor hours (in thousands)

Cumulative average direct
labor hours

Unit direct labor
hours

Unit number

Source: W. J. Fabrycky and Paul E. Torgersen, *Operations Economy: Industrial Applications of Operations Research*, © 1966, Prentice-Hall, Inc., p. 101. Reprinted by permission of the publisher.

EXHIBIT 18.6
Logarithmic plot of an 80 percent learning curve

more accurate reading of the cumulative curve. Exhibit 18.6 shows the 80 percent curve on logarithmic paper.

While the arithmetic tabulation approach is useful, direct logarithmic analysis of learning curve problems is generally more efficient since it does not require a complete enumeration of successive time-output combinations. Moreover, where such data are not available, an analytical model that uses logarithms may be the most convenient way of obtaining output estimates.

Logarithmic analysis

It may be shown that the mathematical expression for the relationship between direct labor hour requirements and the number of units produced is[6]

$$Y_x = Kx^n$$

---

[6] This equation says that the number of direct labor hours required for any given unit is reduced exponentially as more units are produced.

where

x = Unit number
Y_x = Number of direct labor hours required to produce the xth unit
K = Number of direct labor hours required to produce the first unit
n = Log b/log 2
b = Learning factor

Thus to find the labor hour requirement for the eighth unit in our example (Exhibit 18.4), we would substitute as follows:

$$Y_8 = (100,000)\ (8)^n$$

This may be solved by using logarithms, as follows:

$$\begin{aligned}
Y_8 &= 100,000(8)^{\log 0.8/\log 2} \\
&= 100,000(8)^{-0.322} \\
&= \frac{100,000}{(8)^{0.322}} \\
&= \frac{100,000}{1.9535} \\
&= 51,200
\end{aligned}$$

Therefore it would take 51,200 hours to make the eighth unit.

Estimating the learning percentage

If production has been under way for some time, then the learning percentage is easily obtained from production records. Generally speaking, the longer the production history, the more accurate will be the estimate.

If production has not started, estimating the learning percentage becomes enlightened guesswork. In these cases the options open to the analyst are:

1. Assume that the learning percentage will be the same as it has been for previous applications within the same industry.
2. Assume that it will be the same as it has been for the same or similar products.
3. Analyze the similarities and differences between the proposed startup and previous startups and develop a revised learning percentage that appears best to fit the situation.

In selecting the option, the decision turns on how closely the startup under consideration approximates previous startups in the same industry or with the same or similar products. In any case, while a number of industries have used learning curves extensively, uncritical acceptance of the industry norm (such as the 80 percent figure for the airframe industry) is risky, and therefore, an analysis of the similarities and differences should be undertaken even though it may ultimately lead to the industry improvement percentage. The reasons for disparities between a firm's learning rate and that of its industry are two. First, there are the inevitable differences in operating characteristics between any two firms, stemming from the equipment, methods, product design, plant organization, and so forth. Second, procedural differences are manifested in the development of the learning percentage itself, such as whether the industry rate is based upon a single product or on a product line, and the manner in which the data were aggregated.

Learning curve tables

Where the learning percentage is known, Tables I and II in the chapter appendix can be easily used to calculate estimated labor hours for a specific unit or for cumulative groups of units. All that is required is that one multiply the initial unit labor hour figure by appropriate tabled value.

To illustrate, suppose we want to double check the figures in Exhibit 18.2 for unit and cumulative labor hours for unit 16. From Table I, the improvement factor for unit 16 at 80% is .4096. This multiplied by 100,000 (the hours for unit number 1) gives 40,960. From Table II, the improvement factor for cumulative hours for the first 16 units is .8920, which when multiplied by 100,000 gives 892,000 which is reasonably close to the exact value of 892,014 shown on Exhibit 18.2.

A more involved example of the application of learning curves to a production problem is given in Exhibit 18.7.

EXHIBIT 18.7
Example learning curve problem

1. Captain Nemo, owner of the Sub-optimum Underwater Boat Company (SUB), is puzzled. He has a contract for 11 boats and has completed four of them. He has observed that his production manager, young Mr. Overick, has been reassigning more and more men to torpedo assembly after the construction of the first four boats. The first boat, for example, required 225 men, each working a 40-hour week, while 45 fewer men were required for the second boat. Overick has told him that "this is just the beginning" and that he will complete the last boat in the current contract with only 100 men!

   Overick is banking on the learning curve, but has he gone overboard?

   Answer. Since the second boat required 180 men, then the learning percentage is 80% (180 ÷ 225). To find out how many men are required for the 11th boat, we look up unit 11 for and 80% improvement ratio in Table I in the Appendix and multiplying this value by the number required for the first sub. By interpolating between unit 10 and unit 12 we find the improvement ratio equal to 0.4629. This yields 104.15 men (.4629 interpolated from table × 225). Thus, Overick's assertion can't be substantiated.

2. SUB has produced the first unit of a new line of minisubs at a cost of $500,000; $200,000 of which was for materials and the remaining $300,000 was for labor. It has agreed to accept a 10 percent profit, based upon cost, and it is willing to contract on the basis of a 70 percent learning curve. What will be the contract price for three minisubs?

   Answer.

Cost of first sub		$ 500,000
Cost of second sub		
Materials	$200,000	
Labor: .70 × $300,000	210,000	410,000
Cost of third sub		
Materials	200,000	
Labor: .5682 × $300,000	170,460	370,460
(Table I)		
Total cost		1,280,460
Markup: .10 × $1,280,460		128,046
Selling price		$1,408,506

Managerial considerations in using the learning curve

Management should be aware of the following factors in using the learning curve.

1. Individual learning and incentives. A recent study by Globerson[7] indicates that subjects performing a manual task under controlled conditions showed significant improvement only when an incentive was applied. This is consistent with findings from an earlier study by Gershoni[8] (as well as others) in which the learning curve leveled off quickly in cases where incentives were absent. The implication of these findings is clear—if you want to enhance worker learning, there must be adequate incentives. (It should be noted, however, that the concept of incentives may be broadened to include any of the positive or negative administrative options available to managers.)

2. Learning on new jobs versus old jobs. The newer the job, the greater will be the improvement in labor hours and cost. Conversely, when production has been underway for a long time, improvement will be less discernable. For example, for an 80 percent learning curve situation, the improvement between the first and second units will be 20 percent. However, if the product has been manufactured for 50 years, it will take another 50 years to reduce labor hours by 20 percent.

3. Improvement comes from working smarter, not harder. While incentives must be included to motivate the individual worker, most improvement in output comes from better methods and effective support systems rather than simply increased worker effort.

4. Built-in production bias through suggesting any learning rate. If a manager expects an 80 percent improvement factor, he or she may treat this percentage as a goal rather than as an unbiased measure of actual learning. In short, it may be a "self-fulfilling prophecy." This, however, is not necessarily undesirable. What is wrong with setting a target improvement factor and then attempting to control production to achieve it?

5. Preproduction versus postproduction adjustments. The amount of learning shown by the learning curve depends both on the initial unit(s) of output and on the learning percentage. If there is much preproduction planning, experimentation, and adjustment, the early units will be produced more rapidly than if improvements are made after the first few units—other things being equal. In the first case, therefore, the apparent learning will be less than in the second case, even though subsequent "actual" learning may be the same in each instance.

6. Changes in indirect labor and supervision. Learning curves represent direct labor output, but if the mix of indirect labor and supervision changes, it is likely that the productivity of direct labor will be altered. We would

---

[7] Globerson, Shlomo, "The Influence of Job-Related Variables on the Predictability Power of Three Learning Curve Models," *AIIE Transactions,* vol. 12, no. 1 (March 1980), pp. 64–69.

[8] Gershoni, Haim, "Motivation and Micro-Method When Learning Manual Tasks," *Work Study and Management Services,* vol. 15, no. 9 (September 1971), pp. 585–95.

expect, for example, that more supervisors, repairmen, and material handlers would speed up production, whereas a reduction in their numbers would slow it down.

7. Changes in purchasing practices, methods, and organization structure. Obviously, significant adjustments in any of these factors will affect the production rate and, hence, the learning curve. Likewise, the institution of preventive maintenance programs, zero defect programs, and other schemes designed to improve efficiency or product quality generally would have some impact on the learning phenomenon.

8. Contract phaseout. Though not relevant to all contract situations, the point should be made that the learning curve may begin to turn upward as a contract nears completion. This may result from transferring trained workers to other projects, nonreplacement of worn tooling, and reduced attention to efficiency on the part of management.

Range of application. While the learning curve is most commonly thought to be appropriate for primarily manual work, such as assembly, it is generally applicable to any situation where deliberate efforts are made to improve a productive process. In airframe manufacture, the 80 percent learning factor is derived not only from increasing experience on the part of direct labor but also from various staff and service groups that contributed improvements in methods, tooling, material handling, and so forth. Thus, the general improvement phenomenon depicted by learning curves really reflects the results of the constellation of activities performed by organization personnel whose function is to enhance production.[9] This point is underscored when we note that learning curves have been successfully applied in a number of industries that exhibit highly dissimilar production processes, such as petroleum, construction, textiles, candy making and metal working.

Learning curves and corporate strategy. No discussion of learning curves is complete without commenting on their wide use by major firms in developing corporate strategy.

Learning curves reflect the cost-volume relationship which exists for a company's product line. This means that a firm has at its disposal a tool to predict its manufacturing costs and, hence, to set cost-based sales prices. For setting corporate strategy then, a firm with a good understanding of its own learning curve might choose the following approach for a new product: Price at a rock-bottom level to establish its market share and then sustain this share by reducing its price in relationship to its volume-based cost reduction experience. Alternatively, a firm facing an existing market may use the learning curve idea to see if it is logical to enter with a similar product. This company may examine its own facilities management and worker skills and conclude that it can take advantage of

---

[9] The terms *improvement curve, experience curve, manufacturing progress function, progress acceleration curve,* and *performance curve* are alternative designations used to emphasize the fact that the learning curve describes more than worker learning.

the learning which it has achieved from similar products and be competitive sooner (e.g., at a lower volume).

The pros and cons of these two strategies can be gleaned from the following quote taken from *Prespectives on Experience.*

> The lower the initial price is set by the first producer, the more rapidly he builds up volume and a differential cost advantage over succeeding competitors, and the faster the market develops. In a sense, this is a purchase of time advantage. However, the lower the initial price, the greater the investment required before the progressive reduction of cost will result in a profit. This in turn means that once again the comparative investment resources of the competitors involved can become a significant, or even the critical, determinant of competitive survival.[10]

Perhaps nowhere is the learning curve used more aggressively in corporate strategy than in the electronics industry. Companies such as Motorola, IBM, and General Electric are advocates of the technique, but Texas Instruments (TI) is usually given credit as being the major exponent of the concept:

> The learning curve certainly is chapter one in the TI "bible." The concept is fundamental to the success of TI's strategy in driving for the leadership position in a high-volume market because, the gospel goes, the company with the largest share of the sales has the best opportunity for profit.[11]

Further study of learning curves. It should be evident from this brief review that learning curves are of great value to the operations manager. To learn more about learning curves, we recommend the following article: "The Learning Curves: Historical Review and Comprehensive Survey" by Louie E. Yelle, *Decision Sciences,* vol. 10, no. 2 (April 1979), pp. 302–28.

STARTUP OF A CHEMICAL PLANT

In addition to such basic techniques as PERT and learning curve derivation in the implementation of the startup process, attention must be given to other pertinent considerations. *Maintenance, quality control, budgeting, information flow, personnel training,* and *testing* programs must also be regarded as major areas of concern in getting a new facility operational.

To explore these factors in context, we draw upon a comprehensive article by Gans and Fitzgerald[12] describing the startup activities required in commissioning a first-of-a-kind chemical plant.[13]

---

[10] *Perspectives on Experience* by the staff of the Boston Consulting Group (Boston, 1972) is the classic work on the subject of learning curves and corporate strategy.

[11] "Texas Instruments Shows U.S. Business How to Survive the 1980s," *Business Week* (September 18, 1978), pp. 66–92.

[12] Gans and Fitzgerald, "Plant Start-Up," pp. 270–89.

[13] In their introduction, the authors emphasize the difficulty of this startup situation and note that it "presents the most exciting and demanding challenge to the chemical engineer" (p. 270).

Maintenance. Maintenance programs are run on records; so early in the planning phase, department files should be set up for each process area. These files should include such information as construction and equipment specifications, spare parts and provisioning lists (including availability), and operating instructions. In addition, maintenance schedules specifying time intervals for inspection and parts replacement should be prepared and manuals detailing maintenance procedures and reliability features of the equipment should be developed. Further, maintenance personnel should become familiar with the equipment, perhaps through training at the manufacturers' facilities. Also, schedules should be developed to assure maintenance personnel availability during both production startup and preoperational testing.

Quality control. Steady state quality control in chemical plants is performed in a laboratory and generally by technicians. However, during startup, it is desirable to have trained chemists assist not only in the setting up of quality control methods but in the actual sampling of process output as well. (It bears mention that startup is a poor time to "shake down" a testing laboratory; hence, whenever possible, laboratory equipment and procedures should be debugged during the planning phase.)

Budgeting. Budgets for startup can be divided into three types: (1) budgets for "normal" expenditures for equipment, material, and personnel; (2) contingency budgets for changes and additions; and (3) contingency budgets for equipment breakdowns. The first type is developed from the startup schedule and can be calculated with good accuracy. The second type varies according to the amount and quality of engineering and research that has been invested in plant design. Previous experience in plant startup provides a good basis for this budget, assuming, of course, that adjustments are made for the technological differences between the new plant and the existing facilities upon which the budget is predicated. Gans and Fitzgerald note that it is not unusual to find provision in a startup budget for a sum of money equal to 5 to 10 percent of plant capital investment for alterations and additions.

Budgets for equipment breakdown (the third type) are the most difficult to derive because of uncertainty about their occurrence. Care in selecting manufacturers and thorough testing of equipment are the best steps to take to minimize the amount of funds allocated for this purpose.

Information systems. Since operating problems and questions are bound to arise during startup, it is essential that an information system be set up that can permit adjustments in real time. Gans and Fitzgerald urge the establishment of an information center, which may range from a simple filing system to a sophisticated computer-based information retrieval operation. They also recommend that the system be instigated at the beginning of the project and that it be readily accessible to all responsible personnel on a 24-hour basis.

The information center should have a wide range of source material. A partial listing would include data on the standards used in designing pipes, electrical equipment, and so forth; process flow characteristics in the form of process flowsheets, process descriptions, and so forth; an engineering data file containing information on equipment, vendors, and purchase order numbers; plant layout data, such as drawings and plot plans; operating instructions describing the plant, testing procedures, preparation and startup procedures, shutdown procedures, and steady state operating procedures; analytical procedures data detailing quality control methods from raw materials through finished goods; and calculation instructions for evaluating plant performance, production, and yield. In practice, the value of the information retrieval system increases tremendously with maturity of the overall facility.

Personnel training. Gans and Fitzgerald suggest that a three-phase training program be provided for chemical operators and maintenance and laboratory personnel. These phases consist of (1) general classroom training, (2) specific classroom training, coupled with work in pilot plants, on laboratory equipment, and special training devices, and (3) plant instructions and in-plant training during testing and pre-operational activities. Regarding the third phase, the special nature of chemical processing enables training to progress with the product; that is, by operating safety interlocks between different parts of the process, the early sections of the plant can operate as a training ground for subsequent sections as the latter are taken over.

Testing programs. The testing actions required before a chemical plant becomes operational are quite extensive. Among these are pressure tests on piping and equipment, dry runs on pumps, furnaces, and so forth, "hot tests" to ensure leak-tightness at high temperatures, and closed-loop dynamics testing with safe fluids to check the facility as a total flow system.

Some of the principles developed for planning testing procedures in the chemical industry are relevant to other technologies. One is that tests should be run for several days to give all shifts a chance to conduct the same test and to allow repetition of the test if the results are not as expected. A second is that critical instruments must be calibrated over their full range to enable accurate feedback under all output levels. A third is that equipment should be run at all levels to test its limits. If a valve is "destined" to burst, having it burst during a test period is usually far less costly than during actual production.

STARTUP IN NONMANUFACTURING ORGANIZATIONS

Retailing organizations   It is usually difficult to determine the length of the startup period in retailing operations. This is so because achievement of the steady state level of service is in large part dependent upon the amount of customer demand, which in turn can be only partially controlled by the system. Department stores, for instance, often experience their highest demand for service during their first few days of operation, and hence, the long-run steady state level of demand may be lower than it is during startup. (Manufacturing systems, in contrast, can negotiate order delivery dates and order quantities to permit a smooth break-in period.) Steady state achievement in retail outlets, therefore, must often be defined in subjective terms, such as "that point in time at which the store runs smoothly" or "when people know their jobs," rather than by achievement of a particular output goal. Further, when ancillary services, such as credit accounts and home delivery, are being developed, the determination of when steady state has been achieved may become even more difficult since each of these services also is subject to a break-in period.

Clerical operations

In insurance companies, brokerage houses, and other service systems that have a large volume of posting, typing, and filing, it is sometimes possible to describe the attainment of steady state in terms of output. In these situations, learning curves also may be derived for clerical personnel performing such tasks as filling out forms and sorting mail. On the other hand, when a clerical staff grows as a function of demand, total output may be inappropriate as a measure of steady state achievement. In these cases, management would have to examine the general performance level of the office to gauge whether or not the system has made the transition from startup to steady state.

Hospitals

Hospitals have startup characteristics that are common to both manufacturing and retailing operations. They are similar to manufacturing systems in that they build up to their steady state level in increments, rather than by permitting full use of their available physical capacity from the day they first open their doors. The University of Arizona Medical Center, for example, offered limited out-patient care and permitted the use of only 40 of its 300 beds in its first few months of operation. This enabled its staff to become familiar with the layout of the facility and refine its medical and support procedures. Hospitals, while they may refuse to meet demands for their services, are similar to retailing operations in that they cannot achieve a full-capacity steady state level without customer demand.

Hospital startups vary substantially in degree of difficulty. Convalescent hospitals, small private hospitals, and other hospitals offering a limited range of health services encounter far fewer startup problems than medical centers which also engage in teaching and research. Thus, planning for startup in the latter type of institutions must be more extensive, and implementation often requires special organizational arrangements. The University of Arizona Medical Center employed a startup team approach wherein a planning committee, consisting of the director of nursing, director of pharmacy and supplies, manager of systems engineering, and administrator of business and finance, reported to the hospital administrator, who acted as a program manager. During the planning phase, the planning committee developed an inventory of hospital functions that were translated into activities and assigned to members of the group. To keep track of the progress in each of these activities, a critical path network to this was employed. The administration was generally satisfied with this approach, and the six-month transition from startup to steady state went fairly smoothly.

Other types of startup situations

The issues discussed thus far relate mainly to the startup of a new facility. However, equivalent situations can arise after the plant has been established. Some of these may be plantwide in impact, such as those which occur after a drawn-out strike, a major technological change, or a shift in product line. Others may be limited in scope, such as reopening a department after the installation of a new piece of equipment or performing extensive maintenance or repair. Indeed, it could be argued that a startup situation arises after any production hiatus.

Startups after a plant shutdown present problems different from those that accompany new-plant startups. The main reason for such differences is that, in the latter situation, achieving design integrity of the plant is paramount while, in the former, reversing the procedures required to shut down operations is the central undertaking. In other words, new-plant startup inevitably entails tinkering with processes, equipment, management controls, and even the product itself in order to get the productive system on line. In contrast, the problems encountered in a startup after a shutdown derive primarily from the way in which production was terminated and the extensiveness of the "mothballing" process. The kinds of problems that occur in these types of startups initially revolve around the acquiring of resources: raw materials supply lines must be reestablished, plant utility services must be reactivated, and, most importantly, operating personnel must be regrouped.

In startups associated with product changes of intermittent production situations, such as batch production, worker relearning time is of great interest, and some research has been done on the topic. Citing empirical data, Nicholas Baloff observed "a definite relearning phenomenon taking place after the initial run of a new product," and hypothesized that "the amount of readaptation or relearning that is encountered during subsequent production runs is inversely and geometrically related to the length of the initial run; as the length of the initial run increases, the relearning required in subsequent runs decreases rapidly.[14] The rationale is that since relearning time is in effect a setup-type cost, it should tend to favor fewer production runs.[15]

PROBLEMS IN STARTUP

The problems that arise during startup are as varied as the systems. However, the following excerpts from *Plant Relocation: A Case History of a*

---

[14] Nicholas Baloff, "Start-up Management," *I.E.E.E. Transactions on Engineering Management,* vol. EM 17, no. 4 (November 1970), pp. 132–41.

[15] Economic batch-size models, incorporating learning functions, are currently being developed.

Move, describing some of the pitfalls encountered by General Foods in opening a new plant, are indicative of problems encountered by other firms.

> The startup of production lines did not always go smoothly. . . . For example, in some production areas, the dust collection system proved to be inadequate, and a consulting firm was retained to correct the problems. . . . Startup operations almost always revealed minor—but important—problems in electrical systems, drainage systems, pumps, valves, and so forth, which had to be corrected before full-scale production could begin.
>
> One major problem occurred in the startup of rice production. This was caused not by in-plant troubles but by a delay in completion of a secondary sewage-treatment plant being constructed for the city. Rice production was scheduled to begin in the summer of 1964. However, with the additional sewage treatment capacity not available, the starchy effluent of the rice would have been released into a nearby river where it would have created an odor problem, particularly during warm weather. Therefore, production of rice was delayed until late fall [with another plant producing rice inventory][16]

Some other problems encountered by General Foods included maintaining the required level of sanitation, the training and indoctrination of new employees, and coping with insufficient warehousing and shipping space.

In addition to the above types of problems, which for the most part are unavoidable even with the best planning, management may encounter problems arising from its own mistakes. In the previously cited article on startup management, Nicholas Baloff observed that such mistakes fall into four major categories: (1) changes in production design and production factors, (2) discontinuous manufacturing policies, (3) insufficient provision of technical supervision and assistance, and (4) ineffective motivation and compensation programs.

A product design change, such as a switch from hot rolled to cold rolled steel, may require substantial retraining of the work force and yield a minimal amount of learning transfer. A production factor change, such as the substitution of a plastic component for a metal one, may impede operation of the system by necessitating new quality control procedures, new tooling, and new suppliers. In a similar vein, Woods and Elgie, in a study of 106 Canadian manufacturing firms, found that startup problems were enhanced when a firm was an early adopter of a new manufacturing technology.[17]

Discontinuous manufacturing, in which the initial run of a new product is interrupted, can entail significant relearning costs during subsequent

---

[16] E. S. Whitman and W. J. Schmidt, *Plant Relocation: A Case History of a Move* (New York: American Management Association, 1966), p. 85.

[17] Albert R. Wood and Richard J. Elgie, "Problems in Early versus Late Adoption of Manufacturing Innovations," *Proceedings of 35th Annual Meeting, Academy of Management* (August 1975), pp. 92–94.

production runs. This point is illustrated by Baloff in an example in which the rate of output for a second production run of television tubes of six weeks averaged only about half that achieved at the end of an initial eight-week run. Of particular interest here is the fact that the break between the two runs was only one month, illustrating how rapidly a system "forgets."

Insufficient technical supervision may lead to delays in decision making and reduced production during startup or, even worse, to incorrect decisions that may stop production entirely. While necessary for all types of startup, good technical supervision is of key importance in industries where technological innovation is a natural concomitant of the startup operation. Steel mills, chemical plants, and oil refineries, for example, are often confronted with technical problems that require research and development personnel to design customized processes or oversee operation of advanced sensing and control devices. Unfortunately, management does not always recognize the fact that the startup of such advanced technological systems represents "the final stage of an engineering development effort—not merely a reduction to efficient operating practice—and, therefore, demands the involvement of design and development engineers."[18]

Motivation and compensation problems during startup often stem from improper design and administration of incentive systems. Indeed, incentives are tricky under the best of circumstances, and therefore, it is not surprising that they can be especially troublesome during startup, when there is uncertainty about the process and about what constitutes a fair productivity level. A very serious hazard is that labor may use the uncertainty about the true steady state production level to obtain loose output standards for an incentive plan. Again, Baloff provides a useful illustration.

> Exhibit 18.8 shows two curves: (1) an estimated startup curve made by the company (without reference to learning curve analysis), and (2) the actual production history of the startup. Compensation was . . . based upon the past average earnings in the early stage of the startup, and this period was marked by steady productivity increases at a level exceeding management expectations. When the permanent incentive was installed, however, the increases ceased and productivity remained essentially constant for approximately ten months at well below the projected level. Management needed production and, consequently, "bought out" the workers by loosening the production standard. The immediate and significant jump in productivity that followed indicates the degree to which the operating crew was able to bargain for a higher incentive rate.[19]
>
> Clearly, it is up to management to avoid falling into such situations as this by "designing compensation systems that motivate workers to perform—not bargain—during startup."[20]

---

[18] Ibid., p. 136.

[19] Ibid., p. 139.

[20] Ibid.

EXHIBIT 18.8
**Steel plant
startup**

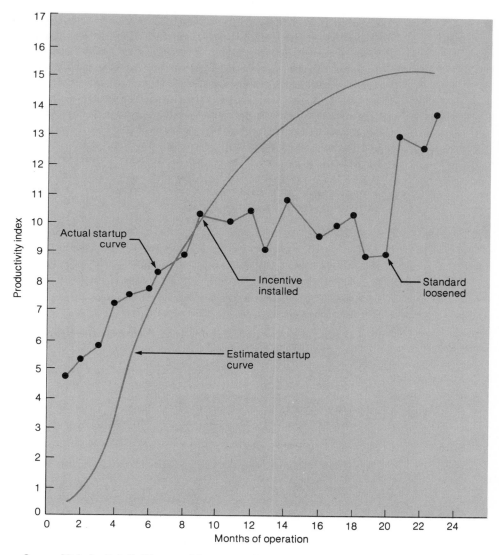

Source: Nicholas Baloff, "Start-up Management," *I.E.E.E. Transactions on Engineering Management*, vol.
EM 17, no. 4 (November 1970), p. 139.

CONCLUSION

Despite the fact that every productive system encounters some transition
period between design and steady state operation, there is nothing like
a complete body of literature on the topic. Indeed, management theory
and operations management—the disciplines from which we would expect
a good deal of research on startup—have yielded little in the way of

empirical findings and even less in the way of theoretical analysis.[21] Instead, it has been the technology-oriented disciplines, notably chemical and petroleum engineering, that—by necessity—have considered the managerial aspects of the problem. This is not to say that management researchers are not generally aware of the startup problem; rather, they have preferred to focus their efforts on design and steady state problems. Unfortunately, the effect of this emphasis is that startup is treated as a special case and its existence is noted simply as something that is *not* covered by the particular theory or model that is under discussion.

Learning curves, the major technique covered in this chapter, provide a practical yet powerful tool for management of startup and other projects. Despite the fact that they have been around for over 50 years, we are still discovering new applications for them.

REVIEW AND DISCUSSION QUESTIONS

1. What makes the management of startup different from steady state management? What characteristics would you look for in a startup manager?

2. What are three strategies for implementing a startup? What are the pros and cons of each?

3. It has been asserted that the best startup is the fastest startup. Do you agree? Explain.

4. By this point in your OM course, you have probably taken at least two exams. Use a learning curve to estimate your grade on the next exam.

5. How might the following business specialists use learning curves: accountants, marketers, financial analysts, personnel managers, computer programmers?

6. What types of management errors did Baloff observe in his study of startup?

7. Does labor generally have the upper hand during startup? Discuss.

8. As a manager, which learning percentage would you prefer (other things being equal), 110 percent or 60 percent? Explain.

PROBLEMS

1. After completing a total of ten minisubs, SUB (Exhibit 18.7) receives an order for two subs from a Loch Ness Monster search team. Given the fact that a 70 percent learning curve prevailed for the previous order, what price should they quote the search team assuming that they wish to make the same percentage profit as before?

2. Relative to problem 1 and Exhibit 18.7, what would be the cumulative numbers of labor hours required for the tenth sub assuming a 70 percent learning rate and six weeks of full-time work by the labor force?

---

[21] Even learning curves, which have been studied extensively, provide information only on the progress of a startup; they do not provide guidance on *how* the startup should be accomplished.

3. A time standard was set as .20 hours per unit after observing 50 cycles. If the task has a 90 percent learning curve, what would be the average time per unit after 100, 200, and 400 cycles? What percent of standard would be expected at each number if the worker performed at 100 percent capacity?

4. You have just received ten units of a special subassembly from an electronics manufacturer at a price of $250 per unit. A new order has also just come in for your company's product which uses these subassemblies, and you wish to purchase 40 more to be shipped in lots of ten units each. (The subassemblies are bulky, and you only need ten a month to fill your new order.)

   a. Assuming a 70 percent learning curve by your supplier on a similar product last year, how much should you pay for each lot? What would be your justification for your bid to the supplier? (Hint: Treat each lot of ten as your basis for pricing.)

   b. Suppose you are the supplier and can produce 20 units now but cannot start production on the second 20 units for two months. What price would you try to negotiate?

5. Jack Simpson, contract negotiator for Nebula Airframe Company, is currently involved in bidding on a follow-up government contract. In gathering cost data from the first three units which Nebula produced under a research and development contract, Jack found that the first unit took 2,000 labor hours, the second took 1,800 labor hours, and the third took 1,692 hours. In a contract for three more units, how many labor hours should Jack figure would be required?

6. Chrysler Corp. has discovered a problem in the exhaust system of one of its automobile lines. Chrysler has voluntarily agreed to make the necessary modifications to conform with government safety requirements. Standard procedure in making repairs is for an automobile firm to pay a flat fee to dealers for each modification completed.

   Chrysler is trying to establish a fair amount of compensation to pay dealers and has decided to observe a number of randomly selected mechanics and observe their performance and learning rate. Analysis demonstrated that the average learning rate was 90 percent, and Chrysler then decided to pay a $60 fee for each repair (3 hours × $20 per flat-rate hour).

   Southwest Chrysler, Inc., has complained to Chrysler Corp. that six of their mechanics have completed two modifications each. Working independently, they each took nine hours on the average to do the first unit and 6.3 hours to do the second. They have refused to do any more unless Chrysler allows them at least 4½ hours.

   What is your feeling about Chrysler's allowed rate and the mechanic's performance?

7. United Assembly Products has a personnel screening process for their job applicants which tests each applicant's ability to perform at the department's long-term average rate. UAP has asked you to modify their test by incorporating learning theory. From their data, you discovered that if a person can perform a given task in 30 minutes or less on the 20th unit, they do achieve the group long-run average. Obviously, all job applicants cannot be subjected

to 20 performances of such a task, so you are to determine whether they will likely achieve the desired rate based only on two performances.

  a. Suppose a person took 100 minutes on the first unit and 80 minutes on the second. Should this person be hired?

  b. What approximate learning rate would you establish as the employee selection criterion (i.e., what rate must the job applicant show for his or her two performances in order to be hired)?

8. A job applicant is being tested for an assembly line position. Management feels that steady state times have been approximately reached after 1,000 performances. Regular assembly line workers are expected to perform the task within four minutes.

  a. If the job applicant performed the first test operation in ten minutes and the second one in nine minutes, should he be hired?

  b. What is the expected time that the job applicant would be expected to finish the tenth unit?

9. A potentially large customer has promised to subcontract assembly work to you if you can perform the operations at an average time of less than 20 hours each. The contract is for 1,000 units.

     You run a test and do the first one in 50 hours and the second one in 40 hours.

  a. How long would you expect it to take to do the third one?

  b. Would you take the contract? Explain.

10. Western Turbine Inc., has just completed the production of the tenth unit of a new high-efficiency turbine/generator. Their analysis showed that a learning rate of 84 percent existed over the production of the ten units.

     If the tenth unit contained labor costs of $2.5 million, what price should they charge for labor on the 11th and 12th units in order to make a profit of ten percent of the selling price?

CASE: THE FAWCETT OPTICAL EQUIPMENT COMPANY* ────────────

On May 25, Mr. William Thomas, manager of manufacturing of the Fawcett Optical Equipment Company, was holding a meeting to discuss and evaluate plans for the assembly activities for the KD 780 photo-reconnaissance Air Force Camera contract. These plans (Exhibit A–3) had been developed during April and May by Mr. Robert Phillips, superintendent of the assembly of noncommercial products of the Fawcett factory at Cleveland, Ohio. Mr. Thomas and others at this meeting were not at all certain that Mr. Phillips' plans were feasible. The KD 780 camera job was Fawcett's first defense-product contract, and Mr. Thomas was anxious for the manufacturing division to look good on this job to enhance prospects for more business with the Air Force.

The Fawcett Optical Equipment Company of Cleveland, Ohio, designed, manufactured, and sold optical equipment used in laboratories, factories, and medical facilities. Two years earlier, the company purchased a factory building and some machine tools, which had been declared surplus property by the U.S. Department

───────────
* This case has been edited by the authors.

of Defense. These new facilities provided about 25 percent more space and machine capacity than was to be required by optical equipment manufacturing, according to a ten-year forecast of sales. However, the price and especially the location of this former government property were so attractive and Fawcett's former plant space had been so inadequate that the added investment in the surplus plant and machines was easily justified. During the ensuing nine months, the move to the new plant had been completed and operations were running smoothly.

The previous September, Mr. J. F. Pickering, president of the company, had decided to solicit government contracts to manufacture and assemble defense products in order to utilize the extra available plant space and machine tools more fully. No commitments were to be made for Fawcett to design or develop new products because Fawcett's engineers were fully occupied with optical equipment design work. Accordingly, a sales engineer and a production engineer had made a series of calls at various military equipment procurement offices. In December, Fawcett was awarded a prime contract to manufacture 840 model KD 780 night-photo reconnaissance cameras for the Air Force. Fawcett had been chosen among competitive bidders as the alternate prime source of supply of these cameras, which had previously been designed and produced by the Sedgewick Instrument Company.

To prepare Fawcett's quotation for this contract, a group comprised of a manufacturing engineer, a tool engineer, a cost estimator, and a purchasing agent had reviewed and analyzed over 600 Sedgewick Instrument Company drawings of detail and assembly parts of the KD 780 camera. After Fawcett was awarded the contract, these drawings were thoroughly checked to insure that Fawcett had drawings showing the latest Sedgewick engineering change information. Then, various make-buy decisions had been made and accordingly materials and tool orders placed with various vendors and/or with the machining and tool-making departments at the Fawcett plant. Air Force procurement officers had stated they desired these cameras as soon as possible. The contract stipulated that Fawcett was to ship the first KD 780 cameras in July, and by October, Fawcett was to build up its camera output rate to at least 120 units per month until the 840 cameras had been produced and shipped.

DEVELOPMENT OF MR. PHILLIPS' ASSEMBLY PLAN

By February, Mr. Phillips received copies of the parts lists, assembly drawings, and test specifications after the various procurement and parts manufacturing planning decisions had been made. Mr. Phillips turned these documents over to the assembly methods engineer on his staff, with instructions to plan the layout of the benches in assembly area, to design and order necessary tools and fixtures, and to provide estimates of the standard hours per unit required at each assembly work station deemed necessary. The standard hour estimates were prepared by using predetermined methods and time standard data and by presuming planned assembly work station layouts, methods, and carefully selected and fully trained assembly operators. Assisting the methods engineer were the project foreman and four "assembly-technicians" assigned as a "nucleus crew" to assembly the first, small production lot of cameras and to "debug" the assembly processing methods. The technicians were later to become working foremen and job leaders of new assembly personnel to be added to the assembly working force as the assembly output rate was boosted to the minimum rate of 120 units per month. On April 15, the assembly methods planning group advised Mr. Phillips that after the assembly work force were skilled in using the planned methods, each camera would require a total 85 standard man-hours to assemble completely. The 85 standard man-hours were the sum of the standard man-hours per unit for different jobs involved in assembling one camera.

While his assembly methods planning group were engaged in their work, Mr. Phillips concentrated on how to approach the problems of programming the build-up of the assembly work force and of controlling the rate of build-up in output of the cameras while new personnel were being hired and trained. He anticipated the possibilities of production delays and man-idleness during the entire period of assembling the 840 KD 780 cameras. He had heard of production delay problems in companies producing defense products, in which as much as 95 percent of the units ordered were delayed in shipment to the customer until the last month of a 12-month planned period devoted to producing a particular defense product. This was an experience Mr. Phillips had hoped to avoid. He realized that a desirable approach was one enabling him to anticipate a specific quantitative pattern of output during the entire period the cameras were being assembled.

While discussing the KD 780 job at lunch one day in March, Mr. Phillips heard the sales engineer, who had "landed" this contract, briefly describe "The Manufacturing Progress Function" (otherwise called the "learning curve"), which Air Force procurement officers frequently used as a guide in negotiating price and delivery terms of contracts with manufacturers. Mr. Phillips investigated the literature on this subject and, as a result, decided to adapt the manufacturing progress function as a means for solving his problem of programming and controlling the KD 780 assembly activities.

As his first step in adapting the manufacturing progress function to his assembly activities, Mr. Phillips listed pertinent conditions that would affect his assembly program.

1. After lengthy discussion with his methods engineer and technicians, Mr. Phillips decided that 90 KD cameras would have been assembled by the time the assembly personnel had developed sufficient skill and experience to meet the standard rate of 85 total man-hours per unit.

2. Starting with the nucleus crew of four assembly technicians, it was decided that additional assembly personnel could be selected, hired, and effectively trained at the maximum rate of 25 new employees per month. To attempt to train more than 25 new operators would overtax training facilities and personnel, Mr. Phillips believed. The personnel manager, Mr. P. D. Kenworthy, had advised that all additional assembly personnel required for the KD 780 job would have to be recruited from the Cleveland area and would require Fawcett company orientation training as well as job methods training. During their first month on the KD 780 job, new employees were presumed to be 70 percent efficient (100 percent efficient meant that an operator completed the job in exactly the standard labor hours set for the assembly tasks assigned for him to complete.) After the first month, all operators were presumed to be at least 100 percent efficient.

3. For purposes of developing these plans, Mr. Phillips assumed that there would be 160 assembly operating hours in any calendar month. Since a calendar month contained $4\frac{1}{3}$ weeks, this meant that every third month, a "margin of safety" of one week was available as a reserve for contingencies such as material shortages, quality problems, and other delays interfering with the flow of assembly work.

4. The KD 780 camera contained over 800 parts. Plans for the process specified assembly work to be done at 27 different work stations on four major subassemblies and 35 work stations in the final assembly area. Standard times at these work stations were not uniform, and to insure reasonable continuity of flow of work, buffer stocks were to be provided and certain operators were to be shifted among several work stations. From these plans, Mr. Phillips estimated that the elapsed time for assembling a camera would be four weeks, two weeks for final and test, and two weeks for subassembly work.

5. The initial production-lot quantity planned was two cameras—just enough for the methods engineer and the four assembly technicians to check on the assembly methods, tools and work place arrangements in the assembly area. The Air Force desired to make thorough acceptance tests of the performance of the first two units produced by Fawcett.

6. To use the manufacturing progress function, Mr. Phillips had to make an assumption of the measured rate of progress he could expect the growing labor force to achieve while assembling the 840 KD 780 cameras. He had noted in the literature that an 80 percent learning curve was rather widely used in the aircraft industry. An 80 percent learning rate meant that each time the cumulative number of units produced doubled, the labor hours per unit dropped to 80 percent of its former value. For example, the direct labor cost or time for assembling the 20th unit was 80 percent of the average direct labor time for assembling the 10th unit completed; and the direct labor hours for assembling the 40th unit was 80 percent of the direct labor hours for assembling the 20th unit completed; and so on.

Mr. Phillips had realized that to choose a progress rate parameter of 80 percent, 70 percent, or whatever, he would have to use good judgment in extrapolating from past experiences. He therefore examined blueprints, methods specifications, and labor time tickets for several optical equipment products assembled by Fawcett employees in the past. Each past experience had some degree of similarity with the KD 780 job with respect to such factors as: the numbers of different parts to be assembled; the clearances between parts; the fragility of the parts; the numbers of different assembly operations required and the total assembly hours required per unit. By plotting learning curves for several such similar assembly activities in the past, Mr. Phillips had determined that the assembly progress-rate parameters for these past jobs had ranged from 70 percent to 75 percent.

From this, Mr. Phillips had chosen 72 percent as the expected rate of progress that would be achieved on the KD 780 Air Force camera assembly job.

From these six presumed conditions, Mr. Phillips had developed his assembly production schedule and his manpower build-up schedule, shown in Exhibit A–3. The detailed, step-by-step procedure Mr. Phillips followed to determine these schedules is summarized in the Appendix. Mr. Phillips had completed the work of determining these schedules on May 20.

APPENDIX: FAWCETT OPTICAL EQUIPMENT COMPANY

General Technical Specifications of the Manufacturing Progress Function. When empirical data on direct-labor hours per unit are plotted against the production count of units produced, the resulting curve appears, for example, as shown on the following page for the KD 780 camera assembly operations (Exhibit A–1):

Graph of the 72 percent assembly progress curve

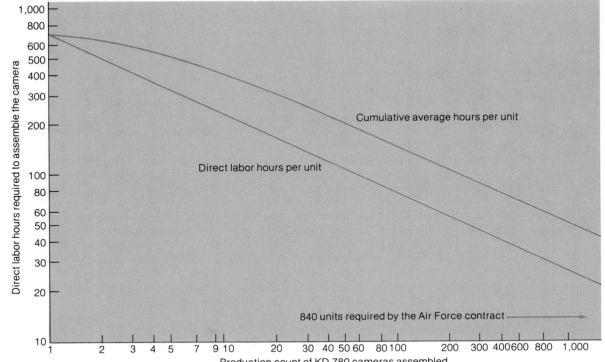

Production count of KD 780 cameras assembled

Note: Graphs are plotted on log-log graph paper.
Source: Mr. Robert Phillips KD 780 camera assembly project files.

EXHIBIT A–2

Table of cumulative production and labor hour data

Cumulative production	Hours this unit	Cumulative average hours per unit	Cumulative total hours (column 1 × column 3)
1...............	716	716	716
2...............	517	616	1,232
10...............	240	371	3,714
12...............	221	347	4,165
15...............	198	319	4,780
20...............	173	285	5,692
40...............	125	214	8,564
60...............	103	180	10,806
75...............	93	163	12,262
100...............	81	144	14,412
150...............	67	120	18,054
200...............	58	106	21,153
250...............	52	96	23,903
300...............	48	88	26,402
400...............	42	77	30,868
500...............	38	70	34,830
600...............	35	64	38,431
700...............	32	60	41,757
800...............	30	56	44,864
840...............	29	55	46,055

EXHIBIT A–3
Assembly schedule

	Assembly operators added	Total operators available	Effective man-hours available	Cameras assembled during month	Cumulative total cameras assembled
June and July......	0	4	1,280	2	2
August............	25	29	3,440*	12	14
September........	25	54	7,440*	59	73
October..........	0	54	8,640	120	193
November........	0	54	8,640	173	366
December........	0	54	8,640	223	589
January..........	0	54	8,640†	241†	840†

* Sample calculations:

August: 25 new workers × 160 hrs. × .70 eff. = 2,800 hrs
+ 4 available × 160 hrs.   =   640
                                                   3,440

September: 25 new workers × 160 hrs. × .70 eff. = 2,800
+ 29 available × 160 hrs.   = 4,640
                                                    7,440

† The 665 effective man-hours available in January will not be needed to achieve the total production of 840 units.

Source: Mr. Robert Phillips' KD 780 Camera Assembly Project File.

Assignment questions

1. Do you like the way Mr. Phillips went about preparing the plan? Should he have done anything differently?

2. What are the major sources of uncertainty in the plan?

3. As Mr. Thomas, would you accept Mr. Phillips' plan? If not, what alternative plan would you recommend? (Be specific.)

4. How will you implement the plan you choose? (Again be specific about the information you will use and the methods you would employ in controlling the project.)

APPENDIX: LEARNING CURVE TABLES

TABLE I
Improvement curves: Table of unit values

Unit	60%	65%	70%	75%	80%	85%	90%	95%
				Improvement ratios				
1	1.0000	1.0000	1.0000	1.0000	1.0000	1.0000	1.0000	1.0000
2	.6000	.6500	.7000	.7500	.8000	.8500	.9000	.9500
3	.4450	.5052	.5682	.6338	.7021	.7729	.8462	.9219
4	.3600	.4225	.4900	.5625	.6400	.7225	.8100	.9025
5	.3054	.3678	.4368	.5127	.5956	.6857	.7830	.8877
6	.2670	.3284	.3977	.4754	.5617	.6570	.7616	.8758
7	.2383	.2984	.3674	.4459	.5345	.6337	.7439	.8659
8	.2160	.2746	.3430	.4219	.5120	.6141	.7290	.8574
9	.1980	.2552	.3228	.4017	.4930	.5974	.7161	.8499
10	.1832	.2391	.3058	.3846	.4765	.5828	.7047	.8433
12	.1602	.2135	.2784	.3565	.4493	.5584	.6854	.8320
14	.1430	.1940	.2572	.3344	.4276	.5386	.6696	.8226
16	.1296	.1785	.2401	.3164	.4096	.5220	.6561	.8145
18	.1188	.1659	.2260	.3013	.3944	.5078	.6445	.8074
20	.1099	.1554	.2141	.2884	.3812	.4954	.6342	.8012
22	.1025	.1465	.2038	.2772	.3697	.4844	.6251	.7955
24	.0961	.1387	.1949	.2674	.3595	.4747	.6169	.7904
25	.0933	.1353	.1908	.2629	.3548	.4701	.6131	.7880
30	.0815	.1208	.1737	.2437	.3346	.4505	.5963	.7775
35	.0728	.1097	.1605	.2286	.3184	.4345	.5825	.7687
40	.0660	.1010	.1498	.2163	.3050	.4211	.5708	.7611
45	.0605	.0939	.1410	.2060	.2936	.4096	.5607	.7545
50	.0560	.0879	.1336	.1972	.2838	.3996	.5518	.7486
60	.0489	.0785	.1216	.1828	.2676	.3829	.5367	.7386
70	.0437	.0713	.1123	.1715	.2547	.3693	.5243	.7302
80	.0396	.0657	.1049	.1622	.2440	.3579	.5137	.7231
90	.0363	.0610	.0987	.1545	.2349	.3482	.5046	.7168
100	.0336	.0572	.0935	.1479	.2271	.3397	.4966	.7112
120	.0294	.0510	.0851	.1371	.2141	.3255	.4830	.7017
140	.0262	.0464	.0786	.1287	.2038	.3139	.4718	.6937
160	.0237	.0427	.0734	.1217	.1952	.3042	.4623	.6869
180	.0218	.0397	.0691	.1159	.1879	.2959	.4541	.6809
200	.0201	.0371	.0655	.1109	.1816	.2887	.4469	.6757
250	.0171	.0323	.0584	.1011	.1691	.2740	.4320	.6646
300	.0149	.0289	.0531	.0937	.1594	.2625	.4202	.6557
350	.0133	.0262	.0491	.0879	.1517	.2532	.4105	.6482
400	.0121	.0241	.0458	.0832	.1453	.2454	.4022	.6419
450	.0111	.0224	.0431	.0792	.1399	.2387	.3951	.6363
500	.0103	.0210	.0408	.0758	.1352	.2329	.3888	.6314
600	.0090	.0188	.0372	.0703	.1275	.2232	.3782	.6229
700	.0080	.0171	.0344	.0659	.1214	.2152	.3694	.6158
800	.0073	.0157	.0321	.0624	.1163	.2086	.3620	.6098
900	.0067	.0146	.0302	.0594	.1119	.2029	.3556	.6045
1,000	.0062	.0137	.0286	.0569	.1082	.1980	.3499	.5998
1,200	.0054	.0122	.0260	.0527	.1020	.1897	.3404	.5918
1,400	.0048	.0111	.0240	.0495	.0971	.1830	.3325	.5850
1,600	.0044	.0102	.0225	.0468	.0930	.1773	.3258	.5793
1,800	.0040	.0095	.0211	.0446	.0895	.1725	.3200	.5743
2,000	.0037	.0089	.0200	.0427	.0866	.1683	.3149	.5698
2,500	.0031	.0077	.0178	.0389	.0806	.1597	.3044	.5605
3,000	.0027	.0069	.0162	.0360	.0760	.1530	.2961	.5530

Source: A. L. Schrieber, et al., *Cases in Manufacturing Management* (New York: McGraw-Hill Book Company, 1965), pp. 464–65.

TABLE II
Improvement curves: Table of cumulative values

Units	Improvement ratios							
	60%	65%	70%	75%	80%	85%	90%	95%
1	1.000	1.000	1.000	1.000	1.000	1.000	1.000	1.000
2	1.600	1.650	1.700	1.750	1.800	1.850	1.900	1.950
3	2.045	2.155	2.268	2.384	2.502	2.623	2.746	2.872
4	2.405	2.578	2.758	2.946	3.142	3.345	3.556	3.774
5	2.710	2.946	3.195	3.459	3.738	4.031	4.339	4.662
6	2.977	3.274	3.593	3.934	4.299	4.688	5.101	5.538
7	3.216	3.572	3.960	4.380	4.834	5.322	5.845	6.404
8	3.432	3.847	4.303	4.802	5.346	5.936	6.574	7.261
9	3.630	4.102	4.626	5.204	5.839	6.533	7.290	8.111
10	3.813	4.341	4.931	5.589	6.315	7.116	7.994	8.955
12	4.144	4.780	5.501	6.315	7.227	8.244	9.374	10.62
14	4.438	5.177	6.026	6.994	8.092	9.331	10.72	12.27
16	4.704	5.541	6.514	7.635	8.920	10.38	12.04	13.91
18	4.946	5.879	6.972	8.245	9.716	11.41	13.33	15.52
20	5.171	6.195	7.407	8.828	10.48	12.40	14.61	17.13
22	5.379	6.492	7.819	9.388	11.23	13.38	15.86	18.72
24	5.574	6.773	8.213	9.928	11.95	14.33	17.10	20.31
25	5.668	6.909	8.404	10.19	12.31	14.80	17.71	21.10
30	6.097	7.540	9.305	11.45	14.02	17.09	20.73	25.00
35	6.478	8.109	10.13	12.72	15.64	19.29	23.67	28.86
40	6.821	8.631	10.90	13.72	17.19	21.43	26.54	32.68
45	7.134	9.114	11.62	14.77	18.68	23.50	29.37	36.47
50	7.422	9.565	12.31	15.78	20.12	25.51	32.14	40.22
60	7.941	10.39	13.57	17.67	22.87	29.41	37.57	47.65
70	8.401	11.13	14.74	19.43	25.47	33.17	42.87	54.99
80	8.814	11.82	15.82	21.09	27.96	36.80	48.05	62.25
90	9.191	12.45	16.83	22.67	30.35	40.32	53.14	69.45
100	9.539	13.03	17.79	24.18	32.65	43.75	58.14	76.59
120	10.16	14.11	19.57	27.02	37.05	50.39	67.93	90.71
140	10.72	15.08	21.20	29.67	41.22	56.78	77.46	104.7
160	11.21	15.97	22.72	32.17	45.20	62.95	86.80	118.5
180	11.67	16.79	24.14	34.54	49.03	68.95	95.96	132.1
200	12.09	17.55	25.48	36.80	52.72	74.79	105.0	145.7
250	13.01	19.28	28.56	42.08	61.47	88.83	126.9	179.2
300	13.81	20.81	31.34	46.94	69.66	102.2	148.2	212.2
350	14.51	22.18	33.89	51.48	77.43	115.1	169.0	244.8
400	15.14	23.44	36.26	55.75	84.85	127.6	189.3	277.0
450	15.72	24.60	38.48	59.80	91.97	139.7	209.2	309.0
500	16.26	25.68	40.58	63.68	98.85	151.5	228.8	340.6
600	17.21	27.67	44.47	70.97	112.0	174.2	267.1	403.3
700	18.06	29.45	48.04	77.77	124.4	196.1	304.5	465.3
800	18.82	31.09	51.36	84.18	136.3	217.3	341.0	526.5
900	19.51	32.60	54.46	90.26	147.7	237.9	376.9	587.2
1,000	20.15	34.01	57.40	96.07	158.7	257.9	412.2	647.4
1,200	21.30	36.59	62.85	107.0	179.7	296.6	481.2	766.6
1,400	22.32	38.92	67.85	117.2	199.6	333.9	548.4	884.2
1,600	23.23	41.04	72.49	126.8	218.6	369.9	614.2	1001.
1,800	24.06	43.00	76.85	135.9	236.8	404.9	678.8	1116.
2,000	24.83	44.84	80.96	144.7	254.4	438.9	742.3	1230.
2,500	26.53	48.97	90.39	165.0	296.1	520.8	897.0	1513.
3,000	27.99	52.62	98.90	183.7	335.2	598.9	1047.	1791.

SELECTED BIBLIOGRAPHY

Abernathy, William J., and Wayne, Kenneth   "Limits of the Learning Curve," *Harvard Business Review,* vol. 52, no. 5 (September-October 1974), pp. 109–19.

Baloff, Nicholas   "Start-up Management," *I.E.E.E. Transactions on Engineering Management,* vol. EM 17, no. 4 (November 1970), pp. 132–41.

Boston Consulting Group   *Perspectives on Experience.* (Boston, Mass., 1972).

Gans, Manfred, and Fitzgerald, Frank A.   "Plant Start-up," *The Chemical Plant,* ed. Ralph Landau, Chap. 12. New York: Reinhold Publishing Corp., 1966.

Globerson, Shlomo, "The Influence of Job-Related Variables on the Predictability Power of Three Learning Curve Models," *AIIE Transactions,* vol. 12, no. 1 (March 1980), pp. 64–69.

Henderson, Ross   *"Plant Start-Up Productivity."* Ph.D. dissertation, School of Business Administration, University of Western Ontario, London, Ontario, 1974.

Whitman, Edmund S., and Schmidt, W. James   *Plant Relocation: A Case History of a Move.* New York: American Management Association, 1966.

Wood, Albert R., and Elgie, Richard J.   "Problems in Early versus Later Adoption of Manufacturing Innovations," *Proceedings of 35th Annual Meeting, Academy of Management* (August 1975), pp. 92–94.

Yelle, Louie E.   "The Learning Curves: Historical Review and Comprehensive Survey," *Decision Sciences,* vol. 10, no. 2 (April 1979), pp. 302–28.

SECTION FOUR

The system in steady state

The steady state period constitutes the "long-run" operation of the production system. In addition to operating the system as designed, steady state management entails maintenance and improvement activities. It also entails periodic changes in production strategy in light of changes in goals of the overall organization of which the production system is a part.

Chapter

19

MAINTAINING AND IMPROVING THE SYSTEM

In this chapter, we address two major functions of the operations manager: system maintenance and system improvement. Our system maintenance discussion will focus on equipment maintenance policies and maintenance control systems. Our improvement discussion will focus on productivity improvement techniques.

MAINTENANCE

> The home of Thomas Edison will be closed to the public for maintenance on the lighting system.
>
> News release, August 16, 1968.

> Companies have spent almost as much on maintenance as they have earned in net profits.
>
> Sheldon Vernon, *Maintenance Engineering* (November 1975), p. 10.

The maintenance function as a second system

The maintenance function may be thought of as a second production system operating in parallel with the firm's product manufacturing system. That is, in maintenance, as in direct productive activities, work must be scheduled, inventories of spare parts maintained, prescribed quality standards met, and labor standards and wage payment systems established. On one hand, the significance of this similarity is that the quantitative techniques employed in direct production are generally applicable to maintenance, and therefore, it is theoretically possible to have a highly effective

633

maintenance operation. On the other hand, the fact that maintenance must have access to the physical components of the production system means that there is always a potential for conflict between the two systems.

To develop the latter point, it may be, for example, that the *most desirable maintenance policy* dictates that preventive maintenance be performed after the 2,000th hour of a machine's operation, while the *most efficient production rate* dictates that a production run consuming 2,500 hours be completed. Clearly, there are strong arguments on both sides—maintenance holding that extended operation will lead to more extensive repair and a less efficient work schedule, and production arguing that it has a deadline to meet and must "get the product out." The ideal way of resolving such a problem is to boil the issue down to relative costs and decide on the least expensive alternative. Unfortunately, attaching a price tag to late deliveries (if maintenance is permitted to delay production) or to the possible additional repairs and inefficiencies of a new maintenance schedule (if production is allowed to proceed) can be extremely difficult. Thus, the issue in many cases is decided by relative organizational power, organizational "log rolling," or an intuitively based managerial decree.

Another problem arising from this "second system" status of maintenance is crew-size determination. Maintenance skills can be expensive, and union restrictions often limit the type of work that can be performed by any one maintenance worker. Hence, we are faced with another trade-off—this time balancing the cost of retaining a given number of maintenance service personnel against the cost of equipment downtime. This problem has been analyzed by the use of queuing theory and simulation, but here too, the problem of costing intangibles often arises. One such intangible is maintenance-worker idle time. Ideally, management would like to have enough maintenance staff to enable immediate repair of any breakdown and to perform preventive maintenance at the exact time prescribed by its maintenance policy. In most companies, however, complete coverage would result in substantial nonmaintenance time and would become prohibitively expensive unless there is some interim job for the worker to do. Moreover, even if there is work to be done, it may not be suitable (e.g., skilled repairmen having to perform material handling work). Thus, even before a queuing or simulation analysis is undertaken, considerable investigation may be required to determine just how much idle time costs, and in some instances, it may even be necessary to develop an idle-time work schedule to evaluate the feasibility of a supplemental work routine.

Organizationally, the maintenance manager may report to the production manager, the plant manager, or, perhaps, the plant engineer. His or her responsibility typically includes machine and equipment maintenance and building and building service maintenance. (Building and building services would be the maintenance supervisor's only concerns in the vast majority of service systems). With regard to the physical location of the maintenance function in a plant, it may be centralized, with workers assigned to different parts of the facility as need arises, or it may be decentralized into particular areas of the plant. Whether it is decentralized depends on several factors: adequate demand for maintenance services, the time required to travel from a central shop, the degree of specialization required of maintenance personnel, and the seriousness of downtime to the operation of a particular plant activity.

Maintenance policy determination

Focusing on machine and equipment maintenance, the major operational question is whether to fix equipment before it malfunctions (preventive maintenance) or wait and fix it after it malfunctions (remedial maintenance). Again, we are confronted with a trade-off situation. In this case, the trade-off appears as shown in Exhibit 19.1, where preventive maintenance costs consist of those costs arising from inspecting and adjusting equipment, replacing or repairing parts, and the loss of production time engendered by these activities. Corrective maintenance costs are those that arise when the equipment fails or cannot be operated at a reasonable cost. These costs also include lost production time, the costs of performing the maintenance, and, in some instances, the part of the cost of replacement equipment which, with better maintenance, would have been deferred.

The objective in dealing with this cost trade-off is to find that point in time and that amount of maintenance that minimize the total cost of the maintenance operation, as well as those productive operations that are affected by maintenance activities. Finding the optimum time and level of maintenance activities is often a complex task because the probable breakdown times for various parts of pieces of equipment must be known, the repair times must be known, and—if maintenance personnel and resources are limited—maintenance priorities among machines and among departments must be determined.

Moreover, even if these factors are known, evaluating and choosing

EXHIBIT 19.1
Preventive versus corrective maintenance

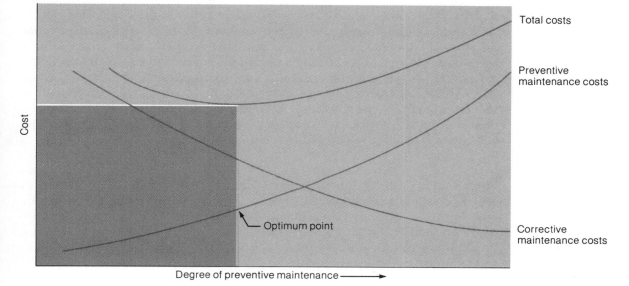

Total costs

Preventive maintenance costs

Cost

Optimum point

Corrective maintenance costs

Degree of preventive maintenance ⟶

EXHIBIT 19.2
**Maintenance
policies and
alternatives**

Maintenance policies	Maintenance alternatives			
	Repair, overhaul, or replace at the end of n hours of operation	Repair, overhaul, or replace at set time periods	Repair, overhaul, or replace after breakdown	Inspect and measure need for repair, overhaul, or replacement
Remedial maintenance			✓	
Preventive maintenance	✓	✓		
Conditional maintenance				✓

from the broad range of possible maintenance policies present a sticky decision problem. Exhibit 19.2 summarizes the possible policies available under three general approaches to maintenance: remedial maintenance, preventive maintenance, and conditional maintenance. The check marks denote various alternatives that can be used in each policy. *Remedial maintenance* refers to carrying out a complete overhaul, or replacement, or repair of a piece of equipment when it breaks down. Such work can be performed immediately after a breakdown occurs or be placed in a queue of work that is performed at set intervals, such as every week or month. The latter policy might be followed where there is standby equipment and maintenance crews follow a specified schedule of rounds. (By definition, remedial maintenance would not be performed at the end of *n* hours of equipment operation unless the equipment breaks down at exactly that time, and hence, no such possibility is provided in Exhibit 19.2.)

Preventive maintenance refers to maintenance performed prior to breakdown and may be either minor in nature, such as a simple repair, or major, such as a complete overhaul or replacement. A preventive maintenance *program* may include provision for immediate repair or overhaul after a breakdown as well as for repairs or overhaul at predetermined time periods. A *conditional maintenance* policy refers to overhaul or repair that is performed on the basis of inspecting and measuring the state of the equipment. If the equipment passes the test, it might be allowed to operate until it breaks down or until it has reached a certain number of operating hours, after which it is replaced, overhauled, or repaired.

**Policy
selection: An
example**

Suppose an electronics firm has 100 laser etching machines and management wants to determine whether it should follow a remedial policy, in which overhauls are performed only after a machine breaks down, or whether it should employ a preventive maintenance policy, in which overhauls are performed on all equipment at the end of specified periods and breakdowns are repaired as they occur.

To determine which policy to use, we must know the cost of preventive maintenance, the cost of breakdown repairs, and the probability of break-

EXHIBIT 19.3

Month after maintenance (j)	Probability of breakdown (p_j)
1	0.25
2	0.15
3	0.10
4	0.10
5	0.15
6	0.25

down after an overhaul or repair as a function of time since the previous repair. Assume that we have this information, and it is as follows:

Cost of providing preventive maintenance for one machine (C_1) = $20
Cost of servicing a breakdown (C_2) = $100

Probability distribution, as a function of time since previous repair or overhaul (we'll take months as our units of time), is shown in Exhibit 19.3.

The probabilities shown in this table are the results of "life testing." Data of this type are derived by subjecting a sample to a test and observing what happens to all the units over the passage of time. For example, if we subjected 100 machines to a test until they broke down and found the results as: 25 breakdowns in the first month, 15 in the second, 10 in the third, 10 in the fourth, 15 in the fifth, and 25 in the sixth, these data could be plotted as a histogram shown in Exhibit 19.4.

EXHIBIT 19.4
Life testing showing the number of machines that broke down period by period

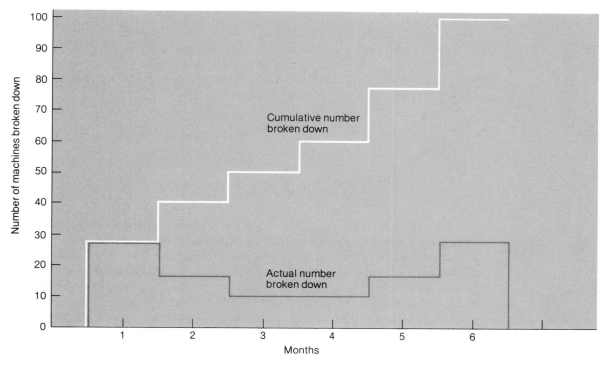

The average life of the machines, then, is derived by computing the total number of months all machines lasted divided by the number of machines, or:

Number of machines		Time (months) before breakdown		Number of months operated
25	×	1	=	25
15	×	2	=	30
10	×	3	=	30
10	×	4	=	40
15	×	5	=	75
25	×	6	=	150
Total months for 100 machines			=	350

Average life = 350/100 = 3.5 months before breakdown

The average number of breakdowns in one month, then, would be 100/3.5, or 28.57.

Life testing data are generally plotted as a probability distribution, and care should be taken to interpret the meaning correctly. For example, Exhibit 19.3 shows that within two months, 40 percent of the *original* machines will break down. There is a strong but erroneous tendency to express the number of breakdowns as $0.25N + 0.15(N - 0.25N)$, where N is the original number of units (100 machines in our example). The number of breakdowns calculated this way is only 36.25 instead of the correct number, 40.

We are now ready to evaluate and compare the remedial policy of repairing breakdowns and the preventive maintenance policy.

Remedial policy. The total monthly cost of this policy (TC_R) is determined simply by dividing the cost of repairing all machines (N) by the expected number of months between breakdowns, or

$$TC_R = \frac{NC_2}{\sum_{i=1}^{j} ip_i} = \frac{(100)(\$100)}{1(0.25) + 2(0.15) + 3(0.10) + 4(0.10) + 5(0.15) + 6(0.25)}$$

$$= \frac{\$10,000}{3.50} = \$2,857.14 \text{ per month}$$

Preventive policy. This policy should be viewed as consisting of six subpolicies, each corresponding to a given number of months between maintenance operations. That is, we must determine the cost of a preventive maintenance program involving maintenance every one month, every two months, every three months, and so on. To do this, we must first calculate the expected total number of breakdowns for each alternative.

The expected number of breakdowns, if preventive maintenance is performed on all machines each month, may be designated B_1 and is simply the number of machines times the probability of a breakdown within one month after maintenance (p_1), or

$$B_1 = Np_1 = (100)(0.25) = 25 \text{ machines}$$

The total number of breakdowns occurring by the end of period 2 is $N(p_1 + p_2)$ plus $B_1 p_1$ (to account for the machines that were repaired in the first period and will need repair in the second). Hence

$$\begin{aligned} B_2 &= N\,(p_1 + p_2) + B_1 p_1 \\ &= 100(0.25 + 0.15) + 25(0.25) \\ &= 46.25 \text{ machines} \end{aligned}$$

The expected number of breakdowns for maintenance every three months is:

$$\begin{aligned} B_3 &= N\,(p_1 + p_2 + p_3) + B_2 p_1 + B_1 p_2 \\ &= 100(0.25 + 0.15 + 0.10) + 46.25(0.25) + 25(0.15) \\ &= 65.31 \text{ machines} \end{aligned}$$

And for every four months:

$$\begin{aligned} B_4 &= N\,(p_1 + p_2 + p_3 + p_4) + B_3 p_1 + B_2 p_2 + B_1 p_3 \\ &= 100(0.25 + 0.15 + 0.10 + 0.10) + 64.31(0.25) + 46.25(0.15) + 25(0.10) \\ &= 85.77 \text{ machines} \end{aligned}$$

And for every n months:

$$B_n = N\,(p_1 + p_2 + p_3 + \cdots + p_n) + B_1 p_{n-1} + B_2 p_{n-2} + \cdots + B_{n-1} p_1$$

Proceeding this way, we obtain

$$B_5 = 113.36 \text{ machines}$$
$$B_6 = 156.12 \text{ machines}$$

Given these values, we may derive the total monthly cost of maintenance for each subpolicy as shown in Exhibit 19.5. Examination of the total cost column (f) indicates that the best subpolicy is to perform preventive maintenance every four months. Such an approach is also less costly than the remedial policy by \$213.14 (\$2,857.14 − \$2,644.00).

EXHIBIT 19.5
Calculation of preventive maintenance costs for six different maintenance periods

(a) Preventive maintenance every M months	(b) Total expected breakdowns in M months (B)	(c) Mean number of breakdowns per month (b ÷ a)	(d) Expected breakdown cost per month (c × \$100)	(e) Expected preventive maintenance cost per month $\left(\dfrac{1}{M} \times \$20 \times 100\right)$	(f) Expected total monthly cost of maintenance subpolicy (d + e)
1..........	25	25	\$2,500	\$2,000	\$4,500
2..........	46.25	23.12	2,312	1,000	3,312
3..........	65.81	21.77	2,177	667	2,844
4..........	85.77	21.44	2,144	500	2,644
5..........	113.36	22.67	2,267	400	2,667
6..........	156.12	26.02	2,602	333	2,935

In evaluating this problem, there are certain features worth noting. First, it may be surprising to discover that the expected breakdown cost for a one-month policy is greater than for any of the other policies considered. This point may be easily clarified, however, when we check back to the breakdown probabilities given at the beginning of the discussion and note the high failure rate in the first month after maintenance. In maintenance situations, this phenomenon is known as *infant mortality* and reflects the common occurrence of malfunctions associated with break-in operations. Such malfunctions may arise because new parts are coupled with worn parts, gaskets and fittings are slightly rearranged during repair, or the repair or overhaul was incorrectly performed. Incidentally, even though the breakdown percentage after six months is the same as after the first month (25 percent), the "tampering effect" has been watered down by the maintenance activities of the preceding five months.

Second, if the breakdown probabilities were graphed, they would yield a dish-shape curve depicting—in addition to an infant mortality period at the beginning—a normal operating period in the center and a wear-out period toward the end. This configuration reflects the fact that equipment breakdown is typically a function of age. That is, if a machine survives its break-in period, it will probably operate satisfactorily for a relatively extended period of time until it ultimately shows signs of wear and is again overhauled or replaced.

Maintenance as a system reliability problem

Hardy and Krajewski[1] suggest that the major purpose of maintenance is to maintain the reliability of the operating system at a reasonable level and still maximize profits or minimize costs. They point out that maintenance acts that tend to improve system reliability fall under two broad policy categories: (1) policies that tend to reduce the frequency of failures and (2) policies that tend to reduce the severity of failures. Their listing of such policies includes the following:

1. Policies tending to reduce the frequency of failures.
   a. Preventive maintenance (including conditional maintenance).
   b. Proper instruction of operators.
   c. Overbuilding-underutilization.
   d. Simplification of the operation.
   e. Early replacement.
   f. Designing reliability into the components of the system.
2. Policies tending to reduce the severity of failures.
   a. Speeding the repair service (e.g., increase size of repair crews).
   b. Easing the task of repair (e.g., modular design of equipment).
   c. Providing alternative output during repair time (e.g., redundant equipment).

[1] S. T. Hardy and L. J. Krajewski, "A Simulation of Interactive Maintenance Decisions," *Decision Sciences*, vol. 6, no. 1 (January 1975), pp. 92–105.

For purposes of maintenance planning, they suggest that different policies be tested via simulation to determine their effect on total annual cost. Their approach differs from the one shown in the previous example by explicitly including policies that reduce the *severity* of failures (as well as those that reduce the frequency of failures). Our example dealt with but a few frequency of failure policy alternatives and, hence, does not capture all of the policy considerations that affect most maintenance decisions.

Maintenance information systems

A large amount of data is required to support a comprehensive maintenance program even in a moderate-size plant. And not only must this information be accurate, but to be of real value, it must be timely as well. For these reasons, it is not surprising that many companies have turned to the computer as the nucleus of their maintenance information system. To get an idea of the type of information required for such a system and the way in which it is used, we have reproduced a comprehensive system developed by Efraim Turban.[2] As Turban points out, this is a hypothetical system, and most organizations use only various segments of it. Nevertheless, it is particularly useful for our purposes because it shows the full range of information options that could be employed for any maintenance situation.

The essential features of this system, as shown in Exhibit 19.6, will now be described.

Inputs. The input to the computer can be divided into routine and special data. The routine data include completed work orders, specifying the amount of labor, parts, and materials used, and a description of the maintenance activity. Special input data might consist of cost comparisons with other plants, breakdown distributions, time study data, and so forth, which would be the bases for special output reports shown in Exhibit 19.6 and discussed below.

Files. This diagram separates two types of files: master files for individual units and master files for resources.

The master files for equipment are usually kept on magnetic tape, and they contain such data as specifications, capacity, cost, economic age, setup costs, location, and floor space for all major pieces of equipment. The master files for resources contain information on workers (skills, wages, and so forth) and on such resources as spare parts, optimal order quantities for maintenance materials, preferred vendor, and the like.

Outputs. The *preventive maintenance routine (output I)* issues work orders for various machines on the basis of programmed priority rules that are based upon file data. It may also prepare a list of materials and parts to be reserved for a particular job, as well as a list of upcoming jobs, in order to notify production departments of planned maintenance. Likewise, it

---

[2] Efraim Turban, "The Complete Computerized Maintenance System," *Industrial Engineering* (March 1969), pp. 20–27.

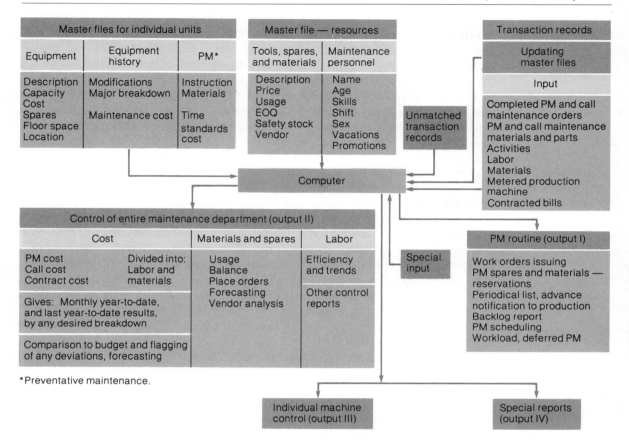

Source: Efraim Turban, "The Complete Computerized Maintenance System," *Industrial Engineering* (March 1969), p. 20.

EXHIBIT 19.6
The major parts of a completely computerized maintenance system

may provide backlog reports of jobs waiting to be completed and may generate a revised schedule in which, for example, overdue jobs are given first priority in the next period.

Maintenance control (output II) is a key control feature of this system, and it could be programmed to provide printouts of efficiency ratios, breakdown repair costs, preventive maintenance costs, budget overruns, and even trends in these factors in graphical form.

Individual machine control (output III), as used here, refers simply to developing the types of reports shown in output II for a specific machine rather than for all machines. This would enable detailed analysis of poorly functioning machines and provide valuable information on the effectiveness of the preventive maintenance policy.

Special reports (output IV) refers to the output from simulations, critical path studies, inventory models, and other output report tools that would be useful in carrying out the maintenance function. Also in the special report category would be completely automated maintenance activities, such as automatic sensing, analysis, and action (i.e., shutdown), of a malfunctioning machine. (In the future, it is possible that computerized trouble shooting and repair will be included as part of the complete maintenance system.)

FAME—A computer program for maintenance scheduling. The FAME (Facilities Maintenance Engineering) program is one of several commercial computer programs for maintenance scheduling that implements many of the elements of the generalized system proposed by Turban (described above). The FAME program provides maintenance managers with a preventive maintenance data base that in turn can be conveniently used to develop preventive maintenance schedules and labor requirements. The program, developed by General Electric, will:

Accept up to 10,000 equipment records.

Store up to 72,000 maintenance records, identifying, by craft, the required inspection procedures.

Generate upon request preventive maintenance schedules.

Accumulate and report craft labor hour requirements in support of maintenance schedules.

Automatically log preventive maintenance completions.

The data base used by FAME is composed of two record types—equipment records and maintenance records. A typical equipment record with two associated maintenance records is graphically illustrated as follows:

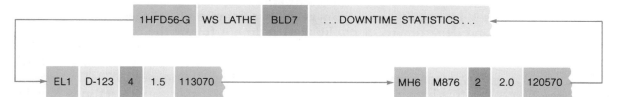

The computer, when reading the equipment record, notes that the equipment is a Warner Swasey Lathe with an equipment tag number of 1HFD56-G located in building 7. Upon inspecting the two associated maintenance records, the computer further recognizes that two types of preventive maintenance are performed on the equipment. The first is electrical maintenance (Craft Code EL1) performed every four weeks and requiring 1.5 hours. The specific procedure for this maintenance may be found in company instruction D-123. The next scheduled date for preventive maintenance is November 30, 1970. (Not shown in the illustration is the last inspection date.) The second type of maintenance performed on the equipment is mechanical maintenance (Craft Code MH6). It is performed every two weeks and requires 2.0 hours. The next scheduled date for this maintenance is December 5, 1970.

The actual preventive maintenance schedule is initiated in response to the user's keyboard request (FAME is an interactive program). A schedule

EXHIBIT 19.7
A sample FAME preventive maintenance schedule

```
LIST PMØFILE

PMØFILE      12:05

1000 MAINTENANCE SCHEDULE THRU 123170
1010    1 CATALØGUE#1   ANNEX     PMINST#1 MACH    3.3   52270 ......
1020    1 CATALØGUE#1   ANNEX     PMINST#1 MACH    3.3   52970 ......
1030    1 CATALØGUE#1   ANNEX     PMINST#1 MACH    3.3   60570 ......
1040    1 CATALØGUE#1   ANNEX     PMINST#1 MACH    3.3   61270 ......
1050    1 CATALØGUE#1   ANNEX     PMINST#1 MACH    3.3   61970 ......
1060    1 CATALØGUE#1   ANNEX     PMINST#1 MACH    3.3   62670 ......
1070    1 CATALØGUE#1   ANNEX     PMINST#1 MACH    3.3   70370 ......

1360    1 CATALØGUE#1   ANNEX     PMINST#1 MACH    3.3   122570 ......
1370    6 EQUIP NØ 17   DEPT-137  PM#1003  MASN    56.0   71470 ......
1380    5 EQUIP NØ 17   DEPT-137  PM#173   INST    24.0   92570 ......
1390    5 EQUIP NØ 17   DEPT-137  PM#173   INST    24.0  122570 ......
1400 99999
1410**TØTAL-HØURS**                                          DATE
1420 CRAFT   MAN/HRS                                         HOURS
1430  MACH     105.6                                         CRAFT CODE
1440  PLMR      10.0                                         PM INSTRU. NO.
1450  ELEC       4.9                                         EQUIP. LOCATION
1460  CPTR      16.0                                         EQUIPMENT NAME
1470  MASN      56.0                                         LINE NUMBER
1480  INST      48.0                                         CRAFT HOURS REQUIREMENTS

READY
```

Source: General Electric Company, *Preventive Maintenance Planning and Scheduling, FAME,* User's Guide (1973), p. 4.

such as the one shown in Exhibit 19.7 can be made for a week, a month, or a year.

Maintenance in services

Service organizations have equipment and buildings which must be maintained. However, a recent study by Fischer and Zmud suggests that service maintenance managers (in a sample of colleges, public utilities, and departments of public works) do not follow the cost-minimizing approach commonly found in manufacturing. "The maintenance managers were concerned with keeping costs aligned with predetermined budgets; they were not concerned with cost minimization per se."[3] The reasons for this behavior and its generalizability to other service settings remains to be determined.

PRODUCTIVITY IMPROVEMENT

Foreign competition, endemic inflation, and spiraling energy costs have combined to focus a great deal of attention on the topic of productivity. For the field of operations management, this interest is both welcomed and discomforting. It is welcomed because OM is the logical home of applied productivity studies, for after all, the value of OM concepts is measured by their effect on productivity. It is discomforting because operations management, like most other business functions, can exert little direct

---

[3] W. A. Fischer and R. W. Zmud, "Operating Objectives and Policies in Budget Based Maintenance Organizations," *American Institute for Decision Sciences Proceedings,* 10th Annual National Meeting (St. Louis, Mo., 1978), p. 256.

control over foreign competition, inflation, and energy costs. Thus, while the techniques and concepts of the field can indeed make productivity improvements, they generally come hard—there are no magic wands or productivity pills.

Is there a productivity crisis?

There is no doubt that the United States has experienced smaller productivity gains than its competition, notably Japan and West Germany. Some reasons for this include: (1) declining capital investment, (2) an increase in younger, less-skilled workers in the work force, (3) a reduction in research and development (R&D) spending, (4) a decline in mechanization, (5) a lack of worker motivation,[4] and (6) supply shortages.

With reference to Exhibit 19.8, we see that the United States is last in productivity growth in manufacturing as measured by output per labor hour (i.e., output ÷ labor hours). Exhibit 19.9 indicates similar bad news for most sectors of U.S. industry. Unfortunately (or fortunately for our economy), output per labor hour is only a partial measure and not a very good one at that. The problem is that labor is not the only factor which measures productivity. Capital investment and capacity utilization, for example, are input factors which would provide logical alternative denominators for productivity ratios. Likewise, output in units carries no indication of the value of those units, and thus, revenue or sales volume would constitute alternative and useful measures to be placed in the numerator of the productivity ratio. A clear evaluation of productivity is even more difficult for government and nonprofit institutions where there are no independent measures of output (except for government enterprises whose output is sold).

EXHIBIT 19.8
Growth in labor productivity since 1960 (United States and abroad)

	Average annual percent change	
	Manufacturing 1960–1978	All industries 1960–1976
United States	2.8%	1.7%
United Kingdom	2.9	2.2
Canada	4.0	2.1
Germany	5.4	4.2
France	5.5	4.3
Italy	5.9	4.9
Belgium	6.9	—
Netherlands	6.9	—
Sweden	5.2	—
Japan	8.2	7.5

Source: R. H. Hayes and W. J. Abernathy, "Managing Our Way to Economic Decline," *Harvard Business Review*, vol. 58, no. 4 (July–August 1980), p. 69.

[4] For an interesting discussion of this point, see Thomas H. Patten, Jr., "The Productivity of Human Resources in Government: Making Human Effort and Energy Count," *Human Resources Management*, vol. 19, no. 1 (Spring 1980), pp. 2–10.

EXHIBIT 19.9
**Growth of labor
productivity by
sector, 1948–1978**

Time sector	Growth of labor productivity (annual average percent)		
	1948–65	1965–73	1973–78
Private business	**3.2%**	**2.3%**	**1.1%**
Agriculture, forestry, and fisheries	5.5	5.3	2.9
Mining.............................	4.2	2.0	−4.0
Construction.......................	2.9	−2.2	−1.8
Manufacturing	3.1	2.4	1.7
Durable goods	2.8	1.9	1.2
Nondurable goods	3.4	3.2	2.4
Transportation	3.3	2.9	0.9
Communication	5.5	4.8	7.1
Electric, gas, and sanitary services	6.2	4.0	0.1
Trade	2.7	3.0	0.4
Wholesale	3.1	3.9	0.2
Retail	2.4	2.3	0.8
Finance, insurance, and real estate	1.0	−0.3	1.4
Services	1.5	1.9	0.5
Government enterprises	−0.8	0.9	−0.7

Source: R. H. Hayes and W. J. Abernathy, "Managing Our Way to Economic Decline," *Harvard Business Review*, vol. 58, no. 4 (July–August 1980), p. 69.

In summary, there is indeed a significant productivity problem, but the true extent of it will be impossible to determine until we develop sharper measuring instruments. In this regard, we are in agreement with the Bureau of Labor Statistics bulletins which explicitly warn their readers about the shortcomings of the output-per-worker-hour measure. We are also in agreement with the Panel to Review Productivity Statistics (funded by the National Center of Productivity and Quality of Working Life) who advocate the development of multifactor measurements for productivity analysis.[5] On the other hand, just because we can't measure it precisely doesn't mean we shouldn't do something about it!

A survey of improvement approaches

As mentioned, there are no productivity pills, but there are a variety of techniques and concepts which if properly applied can lead to productivity improvement for many organizations. We will now turn to a review of these looking first at product, process, and motivation improvement approaches whose primary application is in manufacturing. Then we will present our approach to improving productivity in service operations.

Improving the product

The design of a product commits the productive system to specific processing methods; therefore, the greatest opportunity for cost savings occurs during the initial design phase. Once the manufacturing process is under

---

[5] See Albert Rees, "Improving the Concepts and Techniques of Productivity Measurement," *Monthly Labor Review*, vol. 102, no. 79 (September 1979), pp. 23–27.

way, however, cost reduction may be possible through redesign, changes in the processing methods, and the selection of components and materials. Value engineering and value analysis are useful techniques in the investigation.

Value engineering and value analysis

Value engineering. The purpose of value engineering is to make certain that every element of cost (for example, labor, materials, supplies, styling, and service) contributes proportionately to the function of the item. This purpose may be stated in different ways, depending on the intent and audience. One way is to state that value engineering has two fundamental goals: (1) to provide better value in delivered products and (2) to improve the company's competitive position. Another way is to state that value engineering includes a trade-off decision—that is, to improve the product for a given cost or to provide the same or better performance at lower cost without reducing quality or reliability. In any situation, however, the approach of value engineering is the same; that is

1. Break down the product into separate parts and operations.
2. Determine the production cost for each part and operation.
3. Determine the relative value of each part or operation in the end product.
4. For the high-cost, low-value items, search for a new approach.

The concept of value is difficult to express. Value depends on the usefulness to the user, which is supposedly based on the value of the function performed by the product or service. But how does one go about determining the value of a bolt on the wing of an airplane, without which the plane cannot fly? Or how much quality and reliability does one build into an automobile tire to lessen the chances of a blowout and possible accident? Clearly, the idea of relative costs is part of the analysis procedure. Whether it is recognized directly or indirectly, automobile manufacturers, for example, establish the "cost" of human life through a trade-off between vehicle design and reliability and the amount of court settlements.

The methodology of the value engineering plan or program is demonstrated by the use of six elementary steps that were developed primarily for analyzing high-production consumer products.

1. Item selection. High-volume items are preferred for study because of their greater potential savings. The product or process should be in the earliest possible stage of production planning in order to reduce the implementation costs of design changes.

2. Information phases. Pertinent information and the relevant facts surrounding the product or process should be collected to estimate the possible cost savings. Then the item should be studied to determine its specific function. All aspects of the item should be challenged and simple tests for value should be made, as follows.

Questions	Tests for value
What is it?	Is cost proportionate to value?
What does it do?	Does the object need all these features?
Is it necessary?	Is there anything better for the same use?
What does it cost?	
What else can do the same job?	Can any component be made by a lower cost method?
	Can a standard part be used?
	Is the object made with the proper tooling and materials?

3. Development of alternatives. In the speculative or creative phase of the study, "brainstorming" sessions are held and "cloud 9" thinking is encouraged. The primary or basic functions of the product are listed in detail. The methods used to provide each function are examined, and alternative ways to provide the same functions are proposed. The emphasis in this phase is on creativity; criticism and evaluation of ideas are barred. The value engineer is simply seeking a large number of unique and unusual ideas as feasible alternatives. (See the Procter and Gamble approach, Exhibit 19.10.)

4. Cost analysis of alternatives. Cost comparisons and analyses are made of all alternatives that appear to be feasible. The lowest-cost methods are chosen for further scrutiny and analysis.

5. Testing and verification. All promising alternatives are evaluated to assure economic and technical feasibility.

6. Proposal submission and follow-up. The alternatives that have survived 4 and 5 (above) are formally submitted to the engineering staff for final evaluation. Also included are the assumptions, cost estimates of materials, labor, tooling, and design sketches, and any other relevant data that may be helpful in the evaluation.

In studies of firms that have been using value engineering for a number of years, it appears quite evident that the most popular method of measur-

---

EXHIBIT 19.10
Procter and Gamble's approach to value engineering

Procter and Gamble has been using value engineering concepts for many years under the title of "Deliberate Change." This approach takes the philosophy that

Perfection is no barrier to change. This implies that where further improvement to an existing work method is nearly impossible, there is probably a different and superior method that may be feasible.

Every dollar of cost should contribute its share of the profit. Because each dollar that is invested in anything is done so with the idea of making a profit, the investment should not be made if it does not have this result.

The savings potential is the full existing cost. This attitude does not consider any item of cost as necessary. An example is the procedure of using a liner and a carton to package shampoo. The liner was omitted first, and then the carton, and the shampoo sold better unpackaged. In another example, a storage-tank roof required high maintenance costs, but upon investigation, it was determined that neither evaporation into the air nor dilution through rainfall significantly affected the tank's contents. Thus, there was no need for the roof, and it was eliminated.

ing success is in net dollar savings (total cost reduction less cost of implementation). Also popular is the ratio of return—that is, the net savings divided by the cost. In one survey, the ratios ran between eight and ten to one; that is, a $10,000 investment in value analysis effort returned a net savings of $80,000 to $100,000!

Value analysis. "VA," as it is sometimes called, follows the general procedures as value engineering. The distinction between the two is that value analysis is typically used in conjunction with the cost analysis of purchased items, and thus, the VA program is often coordinated by the purchasing department.

Improving procedures and processes

Here we briefly review the traditional improvement procedures approaches of work simplification and methods engineering which are worker-oriented and generally low cost, and the increasingly popular Group Technology approach which is process-oriented and generally expensive.

Work simplification. The famous motto "Work smarter—not harder" was first proclaimed by Allan H. Morgensen, a pioneer in work simplification. He believes that every person in an organization should participate in the effort to magnify the returns from work simplification programs. As a consultant, he initiates formal classes on the subject which are open to all employees. The duration of classes is variable, but they usually meet once or twice a week for 10 or 12 weeks. The class instructor gives a lecture on work simplification concepts, including principles of motion economy, time study, procedures for flow, process and man-machine charting, and work place layout. These lectures are then supplemented with workshop projects and movies showing representative "successes" in applying work simplification. Participants are encouraged to bring their own projects to be worked on. Over the years, this type of program achieved a good deal of success, and many large manufacturing concerns have adopted Morgensen's approach and developed their own in-house staffs to administer their programs. Such programs have also spread into service industries, with numerous major hospitals, for example, routinely conducting such training programs.

Methods engineering. Methods engineering, the more technical approach to cost reduction, has been defined by Niebel as "the systematic procedure for subjecting all direct and indirect operations to close scrutiny in order to introduce improvements that will make work easier to perform and will allow work to be done in less time and with less investment per unit."[6]

One of the objectives of methods engineering is to eliminate unnecessary processing time. While every task has some technologically defined minimum time to perform, in practice a host of delays are added to this basic

[6] Benjamin W. Niebel, *Motion and Time Study*, 6th ed. (Homewood, Ill.: Richard D. Irwin, Inc., 1976), p. 6.

EXHIBIT 19.11
Opportunities for savings in a typical work task through application of methods engineering and time study

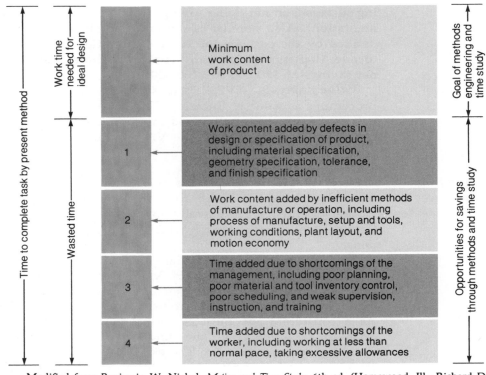

Modified from Benjamin W. Niebel, *Motion and Time Study*, 6th ed. (Homewood, Ill.: Richard D. Irwin, Inc., 1976), p. 4.

time requirement. These delays are attributable to flaws in product design, defective materials, shortages of materials, inefficient methods, poor management practice, and worker inefficiencies. Exhibit 19.11 shows that the time actually needed to perform a job task takes less than one-third of the total time used. Thus, a completely effective application of methods engineering and time study could save more than two-thirds of the time taken by the existing method.

When the intent of a methods study is to improve the current method of work, experience has shown that the best procedure is to use a systematic study similar to that used during the initial work center design. Westinghouse Electric Corporation advocates the following classic engineering steps to assure the most favorable results.

1. Make a preliminary survey.
2. Determine the extent of analysis justified.
3. Develop process charts.
4. Investigate the approaches to operations analysis.
5. Make a motion study when justified.
6. Compare the old and new method.

7. Present the new method.
8. Check the installation of the new method.
9. Correct time values.
10. Follow up the new method.

Group technology systems. Group Technology systems are designed to reduce manufacturing costs by grouping machinery according to common processes needed to make parts having similar production requirements. Their overall objective is to gain the benefits of product layout in job-shop-type production. Such benefits, in turn, arise not from reducing machine time required to produce the parts, but rather from improvements in the efficiency of material handling and production setup and design operations.[7]

The primary application of Group Technology is in metal working where 75 percent of the production consists of lot sizes containing fewer than 50 pieces. However, given the fact that new component designs increase rapidly with new technological innovations, it is estimated that in the next decade, 75 percent of *all* manufacturing will be on a small lot basis; thus, Group Technology concepts will certainly continue beyond metal working.

Features of a group technology system. The essential features of a Group Technology system are a plant layout based upon part "families" and a parts classification and coding system. The classification and coding system is used to identify the parts which are sufficiently homogeneous to be grouped into families and, in addition, to indicate what machines should be grouped into machine centers (or "cells") in light of product demand. Exhibit 19.12 illustrates the improvement in work flow from a Group Technology arrangement.

Far and away, the greatest cost of a Group Technology system is the development and maintenance of the classification and coding system. Such systems must have capability for handling as many as 19 different characteristics (e.g., threads, length, finish), which can be practically maintained and retrieved for companies which may have 30,000 or more parts. Thus, Group Technology is already a big-time computer application calling for a significant investment in data base development and management.

Nevertheless, for some companies, it is well worth the cost, as can be seen by Langston's experience summarized below. Certainly, Group Technology is something that manufacturing management should be aware of.

One of the most complete applications of Group Technology in the United States has occurred at the Langston Division of Harris-Intertype Corporation in Camden, New Jersey. The Langston plant produces semi-custom heavy machinery for the paper converting industries and paper mills. Langston firmly committed themselves to a program which they called Family of

---

[7] There is also a "job enlargement effect" because workers must develop skills in setting up and running a variety of machines.

A. Complicated material flow system (process layout)

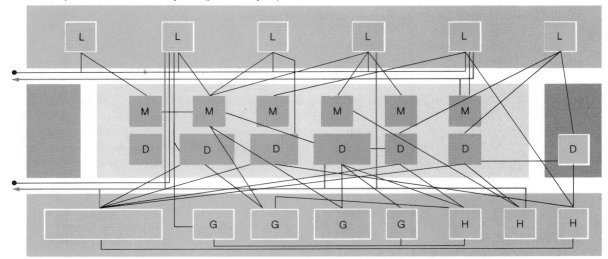

B. Simple material flow system (work cell layout)

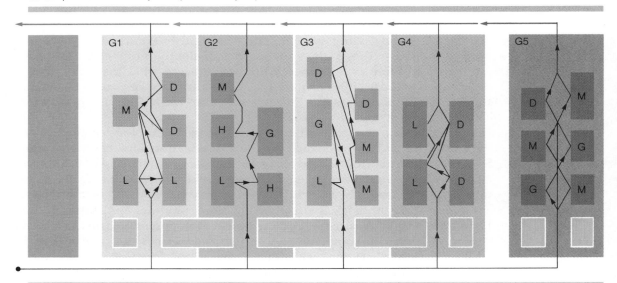

EXHIBIT 19.12
Simplification of material flow with work cell layout

Parts Line Manufacturing in 1969. The primary benefits of their program included a 50 percent increase in parts produced per man hour, a reduction in floor space of 20,000 square feet (22%) and a greatly reduced throughput time—from 30 to 45 days down to 2 to 5 days. Langston began their program by making a thorough analysis of the 21,000 different parts produced by their small-parts machine shop. Using a self-developed classification scheme which consisted of taking a Polaroid shot of every seventh part in stock lying on a grid of one-inch squares, it was revealed that some 93 percent of their parts fell into one of five families. Beginning on a small scale with a single family, they grouped machine tools and conveyors in such a way to form a line for producing the parts belonging to that family. The success of the first line led to the establishment of four additional lines or groups of machines that were dedicated to the production of the parts belonging to their respective families.

The results of Langston's program included a reduction in excess of 50 percent in the number of employees required for the traditional central dispatch and expediting activities. Tooling kits were prepared for each line which greatly reduced the number of trips to the tool crib. Productivity, a year after the program's inception, was up about 50 percent. This increase was attributed to many factors, including: reduced setup times caused by the use of similar setups for similar jobs, the ability to reduce lot sizes because of shorter cycle times, improved operator performance due to familiarity of working on all similar parts within a family, fewer trips to the tool crib, and more meaningful work assignments since each line manufactures a complete product, which the operator can observe and appreciate. Another tangible benefit was the ability to better determine required machine capacity.[8]

Improving worker motivation

In Chapter 11, we discussed two general approaches to increasing motivation—job enlargement and wage incentives. In this section, we will consider two motivation approaches of more recent origin: variable work schedules and zero defects programs.

Variable work schedules. Variable work schedules were first tried on a national scale in 1970 when many firms replaced their normal five-day, eight-hour work week with a four-day, ten-hour (or "4/40") schedule. The belief was that employees with three days off each week would perform better while on the job and show a reduction in absenteeism, turnover, and so forth. The results of such schedules have been mixed. While some firms have remained with them, others have reverted back to the traditional five-day week in the face of such worker objections as increased fatigue, family adjustment difficulties, and commuting problems.

A type of variable work schedule which is less restrictive for the worker is "flextime." Flextime started in West Germany in 1967 and is in wide use in Europe. The method allows workers to put in their required number of hours within a wider period of time. For example, an employee working an eight-hour day in a firm operating from 8 A.M. to 10 P.M. may choose his or her own time of day for the eight hours. The flexibility varies widely. Some firms require the presence of employees for some specific periods and then allow them to choose the remainder. Others even allow a wide latitude of variation by weeks, so long as at the end of each month, each employee fulfills his or her required number of working hours.

---

[8] Marvin F. DeVries, et al., *Group Technology, An Overview and Bibliography* (Watertown, Mass.: Army Materials and Mechanics Research Center, 1976), p. 13.

Flextime is now being tried by many firms in the United States, and the number of workers under such plans seems to be growing. Experience in Europe has shown that when a flexible work hour plan is installed in a compatible managerial environment, productivity improves, morale rises, labor turnover drops, absenteeism decreases, and overtime declines.[9] A recent review of flextime applications in the United States and Canada indicates that employees, first time supervisors, and managers favor it although there is a lack of objective data on its true effect on production.[10]

Zero defects programs. *Zero defects* has become a general term to describe companywide programs to achieve better product quality. Other programs include PRIDE (Personal Responsibility in Daily Effort), and "Accent on Quality." These types of programs have had a particularly strong push due to cost pressures from foreign competition and the Department of Defense requirement that they be included in their contractural agreements.

The zero defects philosophy creates an "attitude of defect prevention." It relies entirely on moral suasion since there are no direct monetary rewards. Zero defects is neither a production design goal nor a quality control design feature; that is, the selection and method of the production process were not chosen with the objective of zero or very low defective output. Nor are the sampling plans and inspection procedures designed to assure 100 percent acceptable output. Rather, the system is designed for, say, 95 to 98 percent good quality, and the workers seek to eliminate the normally expected 2 to 5 percent bad output. This improvement, in essence, is viewed as "all gravy" since a higher than designed output quality is drawn from the system without incurring additional costs.

For example, consider two machines that are available for purchase. The more expensive machine may produce at higher quality, though at a high cost. To hold the product cost down, however, the lower-cost machine may be bought. Now if, through "babying" this machine and frequently "tweaking it up" the output quality can be increased beyond what would be its normally expected output, we have the idea of the zero defects approach. The machine operator must be encouraged to get the best that he or she can out of the machine without significantly reducing output or increasing cost.

In order for a firm to benefit from zero defects–type motivational programs, there must be:

1. Intensive communication—constant reminders of the importance of the effort through signs, stickers, contests, posters, and so forth. This

---

[9] Alvar O. Elbing, Herman Gadon, and John R. M. Gordon, "Flexible Working Hours, It's About Time," *Harvard Business Review,* vol. 52, no. 1 (January–February 1974), p. 154.

[10] R. T. Golembiewski and C. W. Prochl, "Survey of the Empirical Literature on Flexible Working Hours: Character and Consequences of a Major Innovation," *Academy of Management Review,* vol. 3, no. 4 (October 1978), pp. 837–53.

is aimed at instilling pride in workmanship and extolling the importance of the job.

2. Plantwide recognition—publicly granting rewards, certificates, and plaques. ("Hero medals," if you will.)
3. Problem identification. Employees point out areas that in their opinion may be improved, but they need not suggest how the improvements might be achieved.
4. Employee goal setting. Employees participate in establishing their own goals because there is more motivation to achieve these goals if one has participated in their creation. Generally, employees set their goals higher than others might set them.

Obviously, zero defects programs have the same general aim as Japanese quality circles[11] but lack the heavy technical emphasis which the Japanese employ. Zero defects programs are therefore probably best viewed as an intermediate step leading to a quality circle program following the Japanese model.

Improving service systems

Throughout this book, we have distinguished among service systems according to the degree of contact they have with the customer in creating the service product. In Chapter 3, we pointed out that low-contact systems are potentially more efficient than high-contact systems because they do not have to account for the customer's physical presence in the production process. We also noted that high-contact systems must be located near the customer, be layed out to meet the customer's needs and expectations, be staffed by workers who are people-oriented, and be able to react to immediate variations in customer demand, to name but a few requirements.

These differences in system characteristics suggest to us that a logical improvement approach is, wherever possible, to substitute low-contact work for high-contact work; then, concentrate on making the remaining high-contact service more customer-oriented at one extreme and the low-contact work more efficiency-oriented at the other.

This approach is summarized in the following four steps.

1. Identify those points in the service system where decoupling is possible and desirable. (It will be necessary to trade off cost savings from operations improvement against marketing losses that result from changes in the nature of the services provided.)
2. Employ contact reduction strategies where appropriate.
3. Employ contact enhancement strategies where appropriate.
4. Employ traditional efficiency improvement techniques (production control, industrial engineering, and so forth) to improve low contact operations.

In carrying out these steps, we can employ the contact reduction and improvement strategies given in Exhibit 19.13.

---

[11] See quality control, Chapter 10.

EXHIBIT 19.13
Contact reduction and improvement strategies

Contact reduction strategies:
Handle only exceptions on a face-to-face basis; all other transactions by phone, or better yet, by mail.
Use reservations or appointments-only systems.
Decentralize using kiosks with one person for information handling (this takes pressure off the main facility.)
Use drop-off points such as "ugly tellers."
Bring service to customers through postal rounds or mobile offices.
Use a roving greeter or signs outside facility to act as buffers and information providers.

Contact improvement strategies:
Take-a-number systems.
Assign contact workers who are people-oriented and knowledgeable about service system processes and policies.
Maintain consistent work hours.
Partition back office from the public service counter; do not permit work breaks in front of the customer.
Provide queuing patterns and signs to indicate standardized and customized service channels.

Low-contact improvement strategies (for back office or home office):
Establish control points for items entering and leaving departments (log times and quantities to control work in process and provide a basis for capacity planning).
Process standard items in an assembly line mode; customized items as whole tasks.
Utilize such manufacturing-based concepts as standard times, cost centers, acceptance sampling techniques, and resource-oriented scheduling and dispatching criteria.

Some examples of how organizations have applied these kinds of strategies are as follows:

An international bank in Paris is in the process of physically relocating its back office (low-contact) operations outside the city to take advantage of lower office-space costs and to utilize a newly constructed building designed to handle paper work in a factory-like way.

Benihana of Tokyo restaurants have flamboyant chefs cook all meals on a hibachi at the customer's table (thereby providing a "show"), while simultaneously eliminating the need for a large kitchen at their expensive downtown locations.

A local car wash, in response to declining business, shifted its high seniority but less personable old-timers from customer contact points at the beginning and end of the process to low-contact points at intermediate stages. They were replaced by clean-cut college students who could relate well to the customers. (The sign on the car wash marquee subsequently read "Sudsiness with a smile.")

A branch bank reduced its customer contact time in the system by 27 percent by separating customers into teller lines according to complex and simple transactions. This permitted instantaneous matching of high-skilled tellers to complex transactions and low-skilled tellers to simple transactions. The procedure used entails arranging tellers windows according to skills: high skills at one end, low skills at the other, with windows in the middle opened up as needed. Balance is obtained by sensing devices in each line activating red or green lights above each window. When the red light is on, customers in the complex line move to the indicated window; when the green light is on, customers in the simple line move to the indicated window. In addition to increasing throughput, the system generally improves the quality of the service experience for the customer and enhances utilization of bank personnel.[12]

CONCLUSION

Maintenance is one of the least "glamourous" topics in operations management, yet as the opening quote by Sheldon Vernon points out, maintenance is a significant cost to the firm. Thus, for this reason alone, it should not be ignored. Of the topics within it, preventive maintenance is a most important concept, and Burt Lance's comment not withstanding,[13] one is well advised to have a grasp of the trade-off it emphasizes.

Productivity improvement *is* glamorous, and is attracting attention of federal agencies, the popular press, and even academics! In this chapter, we have only been able to scratch the surface of this vast and still ill-defined topic. In any case, how operations managers came to grips with the productivity question will have a great deal of impact on their own success, as well as the success of the organizations that employ them.

REVIEW AND DISCUSSION QUESTIONS

1. What problems does maintenance's second system status present to management?

2. What are the main features of the completely computerized maintenance system proposed by Turban? Does it have any similarity to an MRP system? Explain.

3. How could you apply simulation to developing a maintenance policy for the lazer etching machines given in the policy selection example in the chapter?

4. What are some of the shortcomings of measuring productivity as output divided by labor hours? What other factors might be considered in the productivity ratio?

5. What role does volume of output play in productivity?

6. Distinguish between value analysis and value engineering.

7. Suppose you are a purchasing agent for your family. What VA questions would you ask relative to your family's most recent major purchase? Would you recommend a different course of action based upon answers to these questions?

---

[12] Jon M. Ament, "Change A Queue System from Passive to Active," *Industrial Engineering,* vol. 12, no. 4 (April 1980), pp. 40–46.

[13] "If it ain't broke, don't fix it."

8. What does Exhibit 19.11 imply about how productivity might be improved?

9. What is Group Technology? What are its major objectives and costs?

10. What is your opinion about 4/40 schedules as a manager and as a worker?

PROBLEMS

1. For the maintenance policy selection example used in the chapter, assume that the probability of breakdown for the lazer etching machines has changed and is now as follows:

Month after maintenance (j)	Probability of breakdown (pⱼ)
1	.05
2	.10
3	.15
4	.20
5	.20
6	.30

What is the new optimum policy?

2. Same as one except probabilities have been inverted (i.e., month 1, probability = .30, month 2, probability = .20, and so forth).

3. A bank of 200 switching relays is used under very adverse conditions. In such an environment, the life cycle testing data shows the probabilities of breakdown as:

Weeks of use	Probability of breakdown
1	.30
2	.20
3	.10
4	.12
5	.14
6	.14

How many relays must be replaced at the end of the first week, second week, and third week?

4. A particular duplicating machine under constant use has the following life testing data:

Months of use	Probability of breakdown
1	.10
2	.15
3	.20
4	.25
5	.30

A company has the service contract to maintain 200 of the machines. How many machines will they service in the first month, second month, and third month if they have just started the contract with all new machines?

5. In an effort to upgrade its entire corporate image, Timely Watch Company has instituted a "quality in worksmanship" program. What methods or alternatives should it consider as feasible ways of improving labor performance?

6. A university accounting and billing office is located on the second floor of the administration building. It receives a great deal of walk-in business from students who have to pay various fees, who have questions about general billing practices, or who have questions about their own bills and fees.

   What are some specific actions that the university administration should take to improve operations following the four-step approach to service improvement?

7. Universal Insurance, Inc., is essentially a financial institution acting as a money broker for its subsidiary companies. Approximately 80 percent of the revenue of these subsidiaries comes from casualty insurance premiums. A Department of Productivity Improvement (DPI) has just been formed and is now staffed with several relatively young business school and engineering school graduates. Because of the large amount of clerical help, data processing analysts, policy writers, and claims adjusters involved, DPI is seeking ways to improve the labor force. There are several subsidiaries, and the results of their work improvement programs will be implemented at each of these companies.

   Question: What alternatives would you suggest they look at in their work improvement efforts?

CASE: THE BOYD MOTOR CAR COMPANY

COMMUNICATION AND CONTROL IN A SERVICE ORGANIZATION

The Boyd Motor Car Company combined a new car sales dealership and an automobile repair service. The service department handled between 65 and 75 cars per day for repair work of relatively minor character; that is, in and out of the shop within 24 hours. In addition, there were always some 20 to 30 cars in the shop from two days to several weeks for major repair work such as complete overhauls, repaint jobs, severe damage from wrecks.

The volume of service department work was subject to considerable daily variation and some seasonal fluctuation, the summer months being the most active. Charges to service customers on repair jobs were divided into labor, parts, and supplies such as gas, oil, and accessories. Monthly labor billings of the service department averaged between $30,000 and $35,000. The normal payroll consisted of: a service manager, three service salesmen, one parts stores man, 11 general mechanics, one engine tune-up man, one wheel alignment specialist, one electrical system mechanic, six body men, four painters, two grease-rack operators, one wash stand operator, one car jockey, and a control tower operator. One of the body men and one of the painters were designated as lead men in their respective shops.

With a view toward increasing shop performance and improving customer service, particularly in meeting delivery promises, the company installed a control tower. It was located in a central position in the shop area and elevated a few feet above the floor level to facilitate the vision of the tower operator. The control tower, enclosed on three sides with glass, was equipped with an electric intercommunication system to each repair stall in the main shop as well as to the body and paint shops which were housed in separate but adjacent buildings. A panel of control lights was installed on the outside of the tower; there was a red light, a green light, and a yellow light for each of the eight main departments in the shop: heavy repairs, light repairs, electrical, engine tune-up, wheel alignment, body work, paint, and lubrication.

The green light indicated that the department was not busy and could start work immediately on any job. The yellow light indicated that the department was temporarily busy and the salesman should call the control tower to find out when work ahead of the department would be completed. The red light indicated that the department was scheduled with work for the remainder of the day and the service salesman should check with the control tower to find out when the department could take on additional jobs.

Under the present procedure, one of the service salesmen met the customer at the drive-in entrance to the shop. The salesman discussed the customer's repair and service needs. Before he made a delivery promise, the salesman referred to the control tower light panel to determine when the shop would be able to start work on the various jobs needed on the customer's car. The salesman drew upon his own experience in estimating how long the customer's work would take once it was started. On the basis of this calculation, he made the delivery promise. If this date was satisfactory to the customer, the service salesman wrote up the job order (see Exhibit 19.14).

The job order, which also served as the ultimate invoice, was made out in triplicate, and the three copies followed the steps shown in Exhibit 19.15. As indicated by this chart, the first two copies of the job order were passed to the control tower operator while the stiff copy went along with the car to provide necessary information to the mechanics. The control tower operator entered pertinent data from the job order to the master daily service control sheet (Exhibit 19.16). In the columns listed under the various types of service or repair work, the tower operator listed the particular mechanic, by number, who was assigned the particular job.

The jobs to be done were entered on the control sheet in the order in which they were received at the control tower, and this sequence established the priority of the job orders. Once a job order was entered on the control sheet, it was the responsibility of the tower operator to meet the promised delivery time. He had complete authority for routing cars around the shop and for assigning mechanics to jobs. If the tower operator foresaw that it was going to be impossible to meet a promised completion time, it was his further responsibility to inform the customer and give a new delivery promise.

When a job had been booked, scheduled, and assigned on the control sheet, the tower operator passed the first two copies of the job order to the parts stores room. The two copies were held there until the work to be performed on a car was completed. Each mechanic informed the control tower by the intercommunication system when he completed work on any car. The last mechanic working on the car brought the stiff copy of the job order to the control tower when he completed his assignment. The tower operator, indicating on the control sheet that that particular job was finished, passed the third copy of the job order to the parts stores room. Upon receipt of this stiff copy, the parts man entered

EXHIBIT 19.14

Date _____

Name _____ Phone bus. _____

Address _____ Phone res. _____

City _____ Model _____ Type _____

Promised _____ Serial no. _____ Engine no. _____

Remarks _____ License no. _____ Mileage _____

	Operation no.	Description of work	Charge for		Amount
			Labor	Material	
Invoice					

Foreman's O.K.

Cash ▦

Credit ▦

Estimates for labor only-material additional
_____

It is understood that this company assumes no responsibility for loss or damage by theft or fire to vehicles placed with them for storage, sale or repair.

This work authorized by

_____

Total labor *only*
Total parts
Total accessories
Total gas-oil-grease
Total sub-let repairs

Total amount

EXHIBIT 19.15

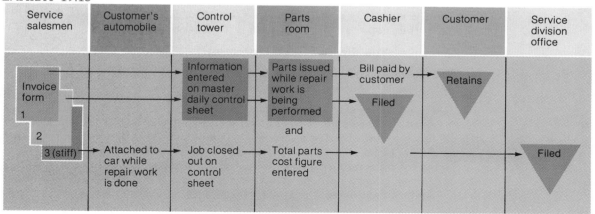

Owner	License no.	Model	Invoice order no.	Service salesmen initials	Promise date	Wash	Simonize	Gas	Hour promised	Lube	Seat covers	Tires	Air cleaner	Flush motor	Flush radiator	Motor					Straighten frame	Body	Paint	Radiator	Miscellaneous
																Tune choke	Tappets	Clean carbon	Valves grind	Motor supports / Heavy line					

EXHIBIT 19.16

the total list and cost of parts on all three copies of the job order and sent the full set of copies to the cashier. The customer was given the first copy of the job order when he paid the bill. The second copy was filed in the central office, and the third copy was sent to the service department for analysis and filing.

QUESTIONS

1. What is your opinion of the service control sheet (Exhibit 19.16)? How could it be improved?

2. Can the system as described handle the major repair jobs; that is, those that are in the shop for more than twenty-four hours? Explain.

3. Comment upon the signal light system.

4. Ordinarily, customer arrivals are at a peak during the first half hour of the work day. Will the system meet this situation effectively?

5. The Boyd Motor Car Company is located in an area where the union contract covering mechanics guarantees a 40-hour week; that is, if a mechanic shows up for work on Monday morning, he is guaranteed 40 hours of pay for that week. To avoid this penalty, the company must, before the close of work on Friday, inform those mechanics for whom work is not available on Monday not to report until notified. How can this production control system be used to handle this problem?

6. With a view toward improving its service department cost performance, the company considered introducing the following incentive plan. For each job, a mechanic would be paid his hourly rate for the time estimated by the service salesman regardless of how much time was consumed (e.g., if a job time were estimated at three hours, the mechanic would be paid his hourly rate for three hours even though he may actually have taken two hours or four hours for the job). Each service salesman, all of whom were on salaries, would receive a bonus of five per cent of the labor charges on all job orders he wrote up over $9,000 per month. Is this incentive program feasible? Discuss both its advantages and disadvantages.

SELECTED BIBLIOGRAPHY

Blanchard, B. B., and Lowery, Edward E. *Maintainability: Principles and Practice.* New York: McGraw-Hill Book Company, 1969.

Dearden, John "How to Make Incentive Plans Work," *Harvard Business Review* (July–August 1972), pp. 117–24.

Elbing, Alvar O.; Gadon, Herman; and Gordon, John R. M. "Flexible Working Hours, It's About Time," *Harvard Business Review*, vol. 52, no. 1 (January–February 1974), pp. 18–33.

Gradon, F. *Maintenance Engineering: Organization and Management.* New York: John Wiley & Sons, 1973.

Greve, J. W., and Wilson, F. W. (eds). *Value Engineering in Manufacturing.* Englewood Cliffs, N.J.: Prentice-Hall, 1967.

Hardy, S. T., and Krajewski, L. J. "A Simulation of Interactive Maintenance Decisions," *Decision Sciences*, vol. 6, no. 1 (January 1975), pp. 92–105.

Konz, S. "Quality Circles: Japanese Success Story," *Industrial Engineering*, vol. 11, no. 8 (October 1979), pp. 24–27.

Rice, J. W., and Yoshikawa, T. "MRP and Motivation: What Can We Learn from Japan?" *Production and Inventory Management* (Second Quarter 1980), pp. 45–52.

Chapter 20

MANUFACTURING AND SERVICE STRATEGY

Managers can no longer afford to view operations as a neutral apparatus for turning out goods. Every bit as much as, say, marketing, manufacturing has significant data to contribute to the broad process of strategic planning.

Alan M. Kantrow, "The Strategy-Technology Connection,"
Harvard Business Review (July–August 1980), p. 12.

The production system operates under an umbrella of corporate strategy which upper-level operations managers help to define and implement. In this chapter, we will discuss how production strategy is developed for manufacturing and service firms and then provide some short case studies for student analysis.

STRATEGY

Strategy is a set of plans and policies by which a company aims to gain advantages over its competition.[1] For the organization as a whole, strategy should be predicated on matching its "distinctive competence" (what it is good at) with its "primary task" (what it *must* do in light of competitive conditions). For the production function (represented at the strategy level by the vice president of manufacturing or operations), strategy should provide clear and consistent operating policies, and objectives which production can reasonably achieve.

---

[1] Wickham Skinner, "Manufacturing—Missing Link in Corporate Strategy," *Harvard Business Review*, vol. 47, no. 3 (May–June 1969), p. 139.

Production
capabilities as
a competitive
weapon

Some students and executives tend to view the production function as removed from "the action" of strategic decisions made by the firm. In most successful companies, however, nothing could be further from the truth. Indeed, numerous firms have prospered because they used their production capabilities as a strategic weapon while their competitors, ignoring this philosophy, have fallen by the wayside.

Some of the production capabilities we are referring to and some current concepts or tools used to enhance them or "make them go" are as follows:

Production capabilities	Illustrative supporting concepts or tools
High quality	Quality circles
Adaptive production system	MRP
Cost/volume pricing	Learning curves
Small lot manufacture	Group Technology

The way in which these capabilities are used as a part of the firm's arsenal of weapons varies. Sometimes the capabilities have a particular marketing benefit. For example, Zenith and GE have long pushed the quality features of their TV sets. In other instances, production capabilities will have significant implications for corporate management in deciding what types of markets to enter. For example, an adaptive production system may permit taking on a wide range of products and producing them quickly. Cost/volume pricing (a capability derived from a variety of other production proficiencies) helps the company in bidding on contracts or, as discussed in the startup chapter, to set optimal prices over range of output. Of course, each of these capabilities can be used in combination as will be developed in our subsequent discussion of the task of production.

PRODUCTION STRATEGY IN MANUFACTURING

The process of developing production strategy for manufacturing as manifested in specific *policies* (i.e., standing plans) and requirements of manufacturing management is depicted in Exhibit 20.1. Ignoring feedbacks for the moment, we see that it starts with an evaluation of the competitive situation ① and then taking account of the company's inventory of skills, resources, and so forth, ②, develops the company strategy ③. The company strategy, in turn, dictates the task of the manufacturing function ④, which, as we shall discuss shortly, is the central issue in production strategy.

Next we see company manufacturing policies which are a function of the manufacturing task ④, an evaluation of the company's inventory ⑦, and industry economics ⑤ and technology ⑥. Company manufacturing policies then specify requirements to be met by manufacturing management ⑨ which are implemented through manufacturing systems ⑩,

EXHIBIT 20.1: **The determination of manufacturing policy**

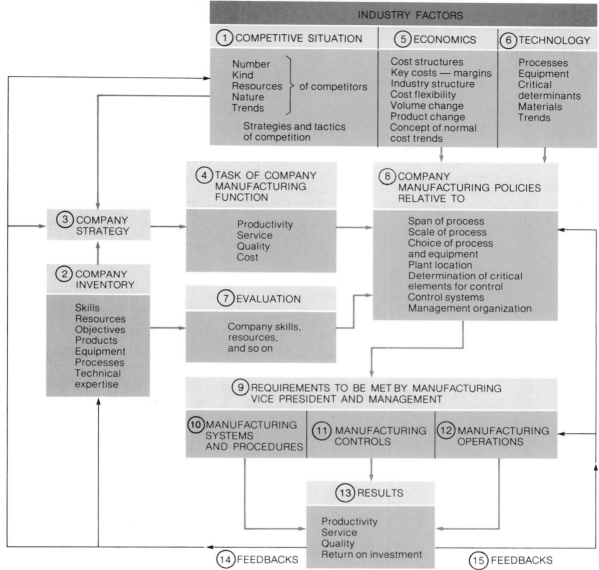

1. What the others are doing.
2. What we have got or can get to compete with.
3. How we can compete.
4. What we must accomplish in manufacturing in order to compete.
5. Economic constraints and opportunities common to the industry.
6. Constraints and opportunities common to the technology.
7. Our resources evaluated.
8. How we should set ourselves up to match resources, economics, and technology to meet the tasks required by our competitive strategy.
9. The implementation requirements of our manufacturing policies.
10. Basic systems in manufacturing (e.g., production planning, use of inventories, use of standards, and wage systems).
11. Controls of cost, quality, flows, inventory, and time.
12. Selection of operations or ingredients critical to success (e.g., labor skills, equipment utilization, and yields).
13. How we are performing.
14. Changes in what we have got, effects on competitive situation, and review of strategy.
15. Analysis and review of manufacturing operations and policies.

Source: Modified from Wickham Skinner "Manufacturing—Missing Link in Corporate Strategy," *Harvard Business Review*, vol. 47, no. 3 (May–June 1969), p. 143.

EXHIBIT 20.2
Manufacturing policy alternatives (by decision areas)

Decision area	Decision	Alternatives
Plant and equipment	Span of process	Make or buy
	Plant size	One big plant or several smaller ones
	Plant location	Locate near markets or locate near materials
	Investment decisions	Invest mainly in buildings or equipment or inventories or research
	Choice of equipment	General-purpose or special-purpose equipment
	Kind of tooling	Temporary, minimum tooling or "production tooling"
Production planning and control	Frequency of inventory taking	Few or many breaks in production for buffer stocks
	Inventory size	High inventory or a lower inventory
	Degree of inventory control	Control in great detail or in lesser detail (i.e., MRP vs. order point)
	What to control	Controls designed to minimize machine downtime or labor cost or time in process, or to maximize output of particular products or material usage
	Quality control	High reliability and quality or low costs
	Use of standards	Formal or informal or none at all
Labor and staffing	Job specialization	Highly specialized or not highly specialized
	Supervision	Technically trained first-line supervisors or nontechnically trained supervisors
	Wage system	Many job grades or few job grades; incentive wages or hourly wages
	Supervision	Close supervision or loose supervision
	Industrial engineers	Many or few such personnel
Product design/engineering	Size of product line	Many customer specials or few specials or none at all
	Design stability	Frozen design or many engineering change orders
	Technological risk	Use of new processes unproved by competitors or follow-the-leader policy
	Engineering	Complete packaged design or design-as-you-go approach
	Use of manufacturing engineering	Few or many manufacturing engineers
Organization and management	Kind of organization	Functional or product focus or geographical or other
	Executive use of time	High involvement in investment or production planning or cost control or quality control or other activities
	Degree of risk assumed	Decisions based on much or little information
	Use of staff	Large or small staff group
	Executive style	Much or little involvement in detail; authoritarian or nondirective style; much or little contact with organization

Source: Wickham Skinner "Manufacturing—Missing Link in Corporate Strategy," *Harvard Business Review,* vol. 47, no. 3 (May–June 1969), p. 141.

controls ⑪, and operations ⑫; and measured by results ⑬. The feed-backs indicate that policy determination is ongoing and takes into account past performance.

Some specific alternatives that would be considered in company manu-facturing policies ⑧ are listed in Exhibit 20.2.

The task of production

Those things that the production function must do well are collectively referred to as the *task of production*. In developing this task, management is confronted with an identification problem—What exactly are the task elements for our company?—and a trade-off problem—Which elements must we concentrate on and which ones are of lesser importance?

With respect to the identification problem, we can break out some finer task elements under the headings given in Exhibit 20.1 ④.

Productivity	*Service*
Output/labor hour	Delivery lead time
Goods shipped	Percentage of orders filled
Utilization of equipment	Dependable delivery promises
	Ability to produce new products quickly
	Volume changes
Quality	*Cost*
Product field failures	Long-run and short-run per unit
Meeting design requirements	

For some companies, especially those in a stable industry, the task ele-ments are easily identified and quickly ranked in order of importance. Thus, we are sometimes justified in using logical rules of thumb rankings such as given by Constable and New in Exhibit 20.3.

The plot thickens, however, when a company is in a tight competitive market, when product differentiation is important, when technology is undergoing change, or when resources are scarce. And since these factors are closer to the rule than the exception, this means that the "plot is thick" most of the time!

In this type of environment, management must make trade-offs among its task elements.

To do this effectively, management must, of course, have a grasp of the corporate task but, in addition, must recognize three basic concepts proposed by Skinner:[2]

1. *There are many ways to compete besides producing at low cost.* While this point is self-evident, some managers look upon noncost competition as sec-ond best or become uncomfortable when technological innovations result in early high-cost production.

---

[2] Wickham Skinner, "The Focused Factory," *Harvard Business Review* (May–June 1974), p. 115.

	Make-to-customer-order	Make-for-stock
Product characteristics	Customer specified Large range Expensive	Producer specified Small range Inexpensive
Production facilities	General purpose	Often special purpose
Key performance variables (or task elements and their ranking)	1) Delivery lead times 2) Delivery performance 3) Quality 4) Cost 5) Plant utilization	1) Cost 2) Quality 3) Utilization 4) Customer service
Main operating problem areas	Control of operations once started Commitment control	Planning production Forecasting Responsiveness

Source: Modified from C. J. Constable and C. C. New, *Operations Management: A Systems Approach Through Text and Cases* (London: John Wiley & Sons, 1976), p. 21.

EXHIBIT 20.3
Comparison of the make-to-order and make-for-stock situations

2. *A factory cannot perform well on every measure.* This, of course, is a major point of our discussion here and implicit in our treatment of production decisions throughout the book. Some examples of inherent conflicts between measures are low inventory investment versus short delivery cycles; high-production volume versus multiple product lines; and low training costs versus high product quality.

3. *Simplicity and repetition breed competence.* Concentration of effort on a limited set of activities is one of the keys to success for an individual or an organization. Thus, whenever possible—that is, competitive factors permitting, this concept should be the cornerstone of manufacturing task development.

These basic concepts, in turn, are central to the nature of *factory focus,* which is the most significant design concept in manufacturing strategy to date.[3] The focus idea is simple—it holds that a factory should focus on a limited, concise, manageable set of products, technologies, volumes, and markets. As Skinner notes (based upon a study of 50 plants):

> A factory that focuses on a narrow product mix for a particular market niche will out-perform the conventional plant, which attempts a broader mission. Because its equipment, supporting systems, and procedures can concentrate on a limited task for one set of customers, its costs and especially its overhead are likely to be lower than those of the conventional plant. But, more importantly, such a plant can become a competitive weapon because its entire apparatus is focused to accomplish the particular manufactur-

---

[3] We have mentioned focus earlier in the book, but its most important application is in strategy.

ing task demanded by the company's overall strategy and marketing objective.[4]

The focused factory concept can be applied not only to a single plant but to departments within a plant. This pertains when a company has a diversity of products, technologies, and market requirements which must be served by a single facility. Called the "plant within a plant" (PWP) concept, it divides the plant both organizationally and physically into separate units, each of which has its own manufacturing task, its own work force, production control system, and processing equipment. Engineering, materials handling, and so forth are specialized as needed.

> An example of separating a company's total manufacturing capability into specialized units is provided by the Lynchburg Foundry, a wholly owned subsidiary of the Mead Corporation. This foundry has five plants in Virginia. One plant is a job shop, making mostly one-of-a-kind products. Two plants use a decoupled batch process and make several major products. A fourth plant is a paced assembly line operation that makes only a few products, mainly for the automative market. The fifth plant is a highly automated pipe plant, making what is largely a commodity item.
>
> While the basic technology is somewhat different in each plant, there are many similarities. However, the production layout, the manufacturing processes, and the control systems are very different. This company chose to design its plants so that each would meet the needs of a specific segment of the market in the most competitive manner. Its success would suggest that this has been an effective way to match manufacturing capabilities with market demand.[5]

Making trade-offs in task determination

Unlike most of the subjects in operations management, strategy development is a highly subjective process and, hence, has not been approached through mathematical techniques. Rather, the approaches to date have focused on how manufacturing management and other corporate management can evaluate and reach consensus on factors of importance to the manufacturing strategy.

A systematic approach to evaluating the priority of specified task elements has been proposed by Wheelwright.[6] With reference to Exhibit 20.4, this approach starts by identifying strategic business units (SBUs) which are essentially homogenous product-market groupings within, say, a division of a company. (Such a grouping might be large home appliances for the consumer market, which is part of a general appliance division.) The next step is defining the task elements ("criteria and measurement"), which can be done through structured discussions or brainstorming. The third step is, through a series of conferences, identifying historical priorities and determining required priorities. The results of this step are shown

---

[4] Skinner, "The Focused Factory," p. 114.

[5] Robert H. Hayes and Steven C. Wheelwright, "Link Manufacturing Process and Product Life Cycles," *Harvard Business Review* (January–February 1979), pp. 133–40.

[6] Steven C. Wheelwright, "Reflecting Corporate Strategy in Manufacturing Decisions," *Business Horizons* (February 1978), pp. 57–66.

EXHIBIT 20.4
**Application of
manufacturing
criteria by
corporate
manufacturing
staff**

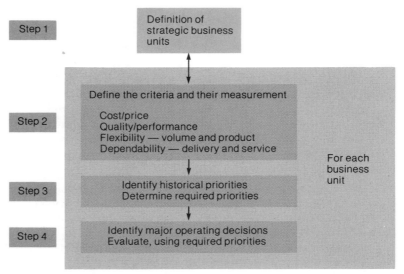

Source: Steven C. Wheelwright, "Reflecting Corporate Strategy in Manufacturing Decisions," *Business Horizons* (February 1978), p. 63.

in the table in Exhibit 20.5. This particular table was developed by a vice president of manufacturing to see how his peers (vice presidents) and subordinates (marketing managers) perceived current and required task element priorities. The task elements (cost, quality, dependability, and so forth) are given across the top of the table. The numerical entries in the table reflect the point totals (from 0 to 100) assigned by nonmanufacturing vice presidents (VP) and manufacturing managers (MM) to each product and task combination. "As is" refers to the current priority weighting for a task element relative to a given product; "should be" refers to what weighting should actually be applied in light of the mission of manufacturing in the corporate strategy; and "needs more (less)" refers to the numerical difference between "as is" and "should be."

The final step of the process is to make changes in operating decisions in light of the evaluation exercise.

Some of the actions indicated from an analysis of the table (Exhibit 20.5) were:

Product 1 should have modest increases in quality and dependability at the expense of manufacturing cost efficiencies.

Products 2 and 3 should have no significant changes in manufacturing.

Product 4 should have a significant improvement in manufacturing cost efficiencies at the expense of quality and flexibility.

Product 5 should have a significant increase in dependability at the expense of manufacturing cost efficiencies.

Developing the task statement. The following guidelines for specify-

EXHIBIT 20.5
Current and required priorities as assessed by vice presidents (VP)* and manufacturing managers (MM)*

	Cost		Quality		Dependability		Flexibility	
	VP	MM	VP	MM	VP	MM	VP	MM
Product 1:								
As is	42	44	17	15	25	26	16	15
Should be	28	46	24	16	31	26	17	12
Needs more (less)	(14)	2	7	1	6	0	1	(3)
Product 2:								
As is	26	20	37	43	24	22	13	15
Should be	26	30	36	38	26	20	12	12
Needs more (less)	0	10	(1)	(5)	2	(2)	(1)	(3)
Product 3:								
As is	34	36	27	28	23	19	16	17
Should be	34	38	29	24	24	20	13	18
Needs more (less)	0	2	2	(4)	1	1	(3)	1
Product 4:								
As is	24	34	30	22	19	17	27	27
Should be	39	44	20	25	23	15	18	16
Needs more (less)	15	10	(10)	3	4	(2)	(9)	(11)
Product 5:								
As is	45	37	21	14	18	31	16	18
Should be	22	31	24	13	35	35	19	21
Needs more (less)	(23)	(6)	3	(1)	17	4	3	3

* Criteria totals for VP and MM for each priority = 100.
Source: Steven C. Wheelwright, "Reflecting Corporate Strategy in Manufacturing Decisions," *Business Horizons* (February 1978), p. 65.

ing the production task have been recommended by Skinner.[7] An illustrative task statement is presented in Exhibit 20.6.

1. The task must be written in sentences and paragraphs, not merely outlined.
2. It must explicitly state the demands and constraints on manufacturing relative to corporate strategy, marketing policy, financial policy, industry and firm economics, and industry and firm technology.
3. It must state how production can be a competitive weapon and how performance can be judged.
4. It must identify what will be especially difficult ("the name of the game").
5. It must explicitly state priorities including what may have to suffer.
6. It must explicitly state the requirements on the production control system, quality control system, production work force, and production organization structure.
7. It should be boiled down to a symbol, slogan, cartoon, and so forth to communicate it to all members of the production organization and managers in other parts of the organization.

[7] Modified from Wickham Skinner, *Manufacturing in the Corporate Strategy* (New York: John Wiley & Sons, 1978), pp. 107–8.

EXHIBIT 20.6
Illustrative task statement for an automobile manufacturer

Our task is to be number one in the production of economy cars within the next five years. We recognize that our tooling may not be as efficient as we would like and we expect many engineering change orders (ECOs) in our new models. Nevertheless, we will scramble to meet this objective, understanding full well that competitive pressures force us off our historical production and development sequence. We will be judged by how quickly we can adapt our methods and technology to a competitive car design and by how our product performs under rigorous testing. The name of the game is quality output in a hurry. Cost reduction through productivity improvements will have to come later. We will structure our production organization as a project team with QC, PIC, and union representatives working closely with the project manager. Our slogan will be "40 MPG and quality."

PRODUCTION STRATEGY IN SERVICES

Production strategy development in a service organization is analogous to that followed in manufacturing. However, since most services are characterized by simultaneous production and marketing, the identification of a distinct production task is difficult. On the other hand, we can discern at least some of the *adjustments* required of the production system in light of corporate strategy changes. A sampling of these in several types of service organizations is given in Exhibit 20.7.[8]

EXHIBIT 20.7
Production system adjustments as a result of strategic change in several service systems

Service organization	Strategic change	Production system adjustments
Fast-food restaurant	Broaden product by addition of health foods and salad bar	Retraining, relayout, handle increased inventory
Bank	Adding services such as pay-by-phone accounts and automatic lines of credit	Additional workers, reprogramming of computers, paperflow adjustments
Hospital	Adding a burn center	Purchase specialized equipment, add specialized people
Accounting firm	Broadened to include management services	Add new division and personnel
Auto agency	Improve quality of repair service	Purchase new testing equipment, change procedures, quality based incentive programs
Emergency medical service (e.g., ambulance, fire department, reserve squad)	Broaden medical capabilities	Add equipment (e.g., cardiac defibrillator) on mobile units, upgrading paramedic skills

[8] For a discussion of the interactions between the design of services offered and the production system design relative to several types of services see Elwood S. Buffa, *Modern Production/Operations Management* (New York: John Wiley & Sons, 1980), pp. 60–61.

EXHIBIT 20.8
Production strategy determination for a banking operation

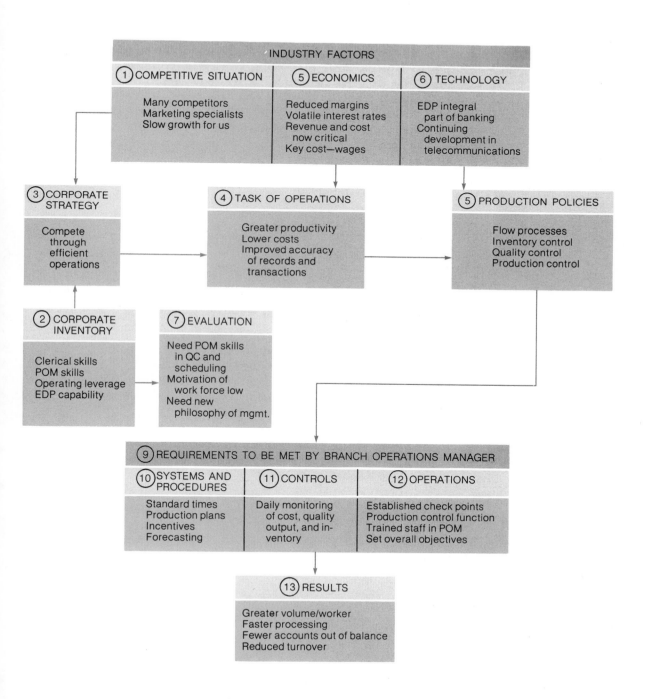

Production
strategy
determination
and
implemen-
tation by an
international
bank

Corporate management of a large international banking organization realized that it was being faced with a situation in which marketing of bank services, especially lending, was not sufficient to maintain the industry rate of return. Its foreign branches, in particular, were losing out on the revenue side with risk-asset growth reduced to 1 percent in 1979 compared with 25 percent for the previous five years. Thus, in addition to deciding to develop new marketing strategies, corporate management also decided that they would pursue a strategy of productivity and cost improvement on the operations side. The flow chart in Exhibit 20.8 (modeled on the one given in Exhibit 20.1) illustrates the process by which this strategy decision was integrated with production policy and ultimately implemented by the operations manager of the corporation's largest branch. Note that the branch was experiencing some severe production problems and that major changes were made in branch marketing and operations management prior to strategy development.

AUDITING PRODUCTION POLICY AND OPERATIONS

Policy and operations audits are desirable for strategy formulation and operations control.

Exhibits 20.9 and 20.10 present questionnaires which can be used for these purposes in manufacturing and services respectively. The ways they can be used are as follows:

1. To compare current and required policies ("as is" versus "should be"). In this application, one can derive a percentage score to obtain an estimate of the degree of alignment (see bottom of Exhibit 20.9).
2. As a checklist for examining major operations areas for purposes for problem solving or improvement.

In the following section the questionnaires are used for the purpose of policy evaluation. They can be employed for checklist purposes in analyzing the cases presented at the end of the chapter.

EXHIBIT 20.9
Manufacturing audit questionnaire

Product

A. *Design*
1. Breadth of product line (standardized/mixed/customized)   A B C
2. Allowable variability in component specifications (little/some/much)   A B C
3. Coordination among engineering, marketing, and manufacturing (little/some/much)   A B C
4. Design from scratch rather than around existing components (usually/sometimes/rarely)   A B C
5. Concern for producibility (little/some/much)   A B C

B. *Introduction*
6. Use of specialized startup procedures (little/some/much)   A B C
7. Stability of design after production release (little/some/much)   A B C

Technology of transformation
8. Degree of mechanization of product assembly (little/some/much)   A B C
9. Degree of automatic inspection and testing (little/some/much)   A B C
10. Degree of mechanization of materials handling (little/some/much)   A B C
11. Degree of equipment specialization (little/some/much)   A B C
12. Flexibility of equipment to meet changes in volume, run length, and product mix (little/some/much)   A B C
13. Number of plants (one/few/many)   A B C
14. Plants located to be near (suppliers/markets/labor pools)   A B C
15. Plants specialized by (product/both/process)   A B C
16. Extent of production-related R & D (little/some/much)   A B C
17. Extent of subcontracting (little/some/much)   A B C

Operating-control system
18. Investment in production and inventory control system (low/medium/high)   A B C
19. Use of inventory to decouple production stages (little/some/much)   A B C
20. Production to order vs. production for stock (order/mixed/stock)   A B C
21. Production strategy (level production/mixed/adjust with demand)   A B C
22. Emphasis on quality control (little/moderate/much)   A B C
23. Amount of inspection throughout the manufacturing process (little/some/much)   A B C
24. Organization of manufacturing (functional/project/product)   A B C
25. Number of supervisory levels in manufacturing (few/several/many)   A B C
26. Number of staff departments to support manufacturing (few/several/many)   A B C

Work force
27. Range of worker skills (narrow/medium/broad)   A B C
28. Job content of most jobs (short cycle/medium/long)   A B C
29. Extent of worker control over work pace (little/some/much)   A B C
30. Extent of worker or group discretion in work planning (little/some/much)   A B C
31. Wage payment system (salary/salary + output/output)   A B C

Instructions for scoring
1. Circle either A, B, or C to identify what you believe to be the *correct* policy alternative (A, B, and C correspond to the order of the descriptive terms in the parentheses.)
2. Place an X over either A, B, or C to identify what appears to be the policy *currently* being used.
3. Calculate the percentage of items in agreement out of the total items that you were able to score (i.e., the items that have both a circle and an X associated with them). This gives an alignment percentage.
   General scoring guide: 90–100% = excellent; 80–89% = good; 70–79% = fair; 60–69% = poor; below 60% = very poor.

This questionnaire is based upon a questionnaire entitled "Choices and Alternatives in Production System Design," developed by Wickham Skinner and his associates at the Harvard Graduate School of Business Administration.

EXHIBIT 20.10
**Service systems
audit
questionnaire**

Product
1. Ratio of customer direct contact time with system to service creation time (low/medium/high)   A B C
2. Extent of direct labor input in creating service product (small/medium/large)   A B C
3. Primary service is viewed as (professional/trade/artistic)   A B C
4. Breadth of service (standard/mixed/customized)   A B C
5. Variability of customer service demands (low/medium/high)   A B C
6. Number of major elements defining service product (few/some/many)   A B C
7. Range of supplementary services (narrow/medium/wide)   A B C
8. Uniqueness of service relative to regional competition (little/some/much)   A B C
9. Introduction of major new services (rare/occasional/frequent)   A B C
10. Concern with legal restrictions in performing service (little/some/much)   A B C

Technology of transformation
11. Capability to alter service capacity rapidly (little/some/much)   A B C
12. Degree of mechanization of service (little/some/much)   A B C
13. Amount of preparatory work prior to providing a unit of service (little/some/much)   A B C
14. Average number of processing stages customer goes through in obtaining service (few/several/many)   A B C
15. Emphasis on efficiency in layout of facility (little/moderate/major)   A B C
16. Emphasis on aesthetics in layout of facility (little/moderate/major)   A B C
17. Extent of equipment specialization (little/some/much)   A B C
18. Number of service centers (one/few/many)   A B C
19. Size of service center relative to direct competitors (small/medium/large)   A B C
20. Specific service centers located primarily for (convenience of customer/convenience of owner/other)   A B C
21. Reliance upon suppliers (little/some/much)   A B C

Operating-control system
22. Investment in inventory control system (low/medium/high)   A B C
23. Extent of use of supplies to produce service (little/some/much)   A B C
24. Primary inventory viewed as (space/people/supplies)   A B C
25. Service strategy (level/mixed/adjust with demand)   A B C
26. Allowed variability in service scheduling (little/some/much)   A B C
27. Ability to backlog service orders (little/some/much)   A B C
28. Number of supervisory levels (few/several/many)   A B C
29. Number of staff departments to support service (none/some/many)   A B C
30. Method of assignment of service personnel (customer selects/mixed/system selects)   A B C

Work force
31. Size of work force relative to competition (small/medium/large)   A B C
32. Required range of worker skills (narrow/medium/broad)   A B C
33. Use of certified professionals in creating service produce (none/some/much)   A B C
34. Job content of most jobs (short cycle/medium/long cycle)   A B C
35. Work pace controlled by (customer/worker/system)   A B C
36. Wage payment system based primarily on (fees/hourly/output or sales)   A B C

Instructions for scoring
1. Circle either A, B, or C to identify what you believe to be the *correct* policy alternative (A, B, and C correspond to the order of the descriptive terms in the parentheses).
2. Place an X over either A, B, or C to identify what appears to be the policy *currently* being used.
3. Calculate the percentage of items in agreement out of the total items that you were able to score (i.e., the items that have both a circle and an X associated with them). This gives an alignment percentage.
   General scoring guide: 90–100% = excellent; 80–89% = good; 70–79% = fair; 60–69% = poor; below 60% = very poor.

APPLICATION OF QUESTIONNAIRES TO POLICY EVALUATION

The Miami Toy Company and Big Jim's Gym cases are juxtaposed with audit questionnaires for manufacturing and service organizations, respectively. The reader is encouraged to analyze these cases using the questionnaires and answer the questions posed at the end of the cases.[9] The objectives of the exercise are first, to practice taking a systematic approach to analyzing the admittedly fuzzy but highly important issue of production policy; second, to develop a heightened awareness of the interaction between primary task and policy; and third, to deduce from limited data what policy alternatives are appropriate and inappropriate for a given productive system. Our ultimate goal is for the reader to gain "a new set of eyes" for viewing the subtle dynamics among the many factors that define production operations.

Miami Toy Company

The Miami Toy Company (MTC) views its primary task as making for stock a standardized line of high quality, unique toys that "last from pablum to puberty." As a rule, they introduce one or two new toys a year. In August of this year, the owner and manufacturing manager, Dwight Smith, has been informed by his toy inventors that they have designed a Darth Vader Doll." This doll will stand two feet high and is capable of swinging a "lightsaber" and of making heavy breathing sounds from an electronic voice synthesizer. One of the company's three manufacturing staff departments, design engineering, states that the product can be made primarily from molded plastic using the firm's new all-purpose molders (now used for making small attachments to the firm's wooden toys). MTC, in its previous initial production of new toys, has relied heavily on its skilled work force to "debug" the product design as they make the product and to perform quality inspections on the finished product. Production runs have been short runs to fill customer orders. If the Darth Vader doll is to go into production, however, the production run size will have to be large and assembly and testing procedures will have to be more refined. Currently, each toy maker performs almost all processing steps at his workbench. The production engineering department believes that the assembly of the new toy is well within the skill levels of the current work force but that the voice synthesizer and battery-operated movement mechanism will have to be subcontracted. MTC has always had good relations with subcontractors primarily because the firm has placed its orders with sufficient lead time so that its vendors could optimally sequence MTC's orders with those of some larger toy producers in Miami. Dwight Smith has always favored long range production planning so that he can keep his 50 toy makers busy all year. (One of the reasons he set up the factory in Miami was so that he could draw upon the large population of toy makers from the "old country" who lived

---

[9] Our scoring and interpretation of the Miami Toy Company is given in problem 4 at the end of the chapter.

there.) The supervisors of the firm's three production departments—castles, puppets, and novelties—have been perceived by Dwight Smith to be favorable to the new product. The novelty department supervisor, Fred Avide, has stated "my men can make any toy—you give us an output incentive, and we'll produce around the clock."

The marketing department has forecast a demand of 5,000 Darth Vader dolls for the Christmas rush. They should sell for $29.50. A preliminary cost analysis made by the process engineering department is that they will cost no more than $7.00 apiece to manufacture. The company is currently operating at 70 percent capacity. Financing is available and there is no problem with cash flow. Dwight Smith is wondering if he should go into production of Darth Vader dolls.

QUESTIONS FOR THE READER

a. Indicate the correct and current policy choices on the manufacturing policy questionnaire. Calculate the percentage of items that are in agreement.

b. Based upon your findings, should MTC introduce the Darth Vader doll? Explain.

CONCLUSION

To managers and students alike, identifying the primary task of the firm and selecting the appropriate production policy alternatives to support it seldom provide the feeling of satisfaction one obtains from a crisp, clean solution to a mathematical production problem. Nevertheless, a correct reading of the task of the firm (or production system) and then the identification of appropriate production policies can greatly enhance the performance of the organization and help assure that subsequent quantitative analyses will be "on target."

REVIEW AND DISCUSSION QUESTIONS

1. What production capabilities are included in the arsenals of the following automotive firms:
    a. Volkswagen.
    b. Rolls Royce.
    c. Chrysler.

2. Explain why most Swiss watch manufacturers' distinctive competence was not consistent with their primary task over the past five years. Explain why Rolex watches are an exception in this situation.

3. Explain the concept of factory focus. How could it be applied to a restaurant? An automobile agency?

4. Using your college or university as an example, refute or support the assertion that a production system cannot excel on every measure of performance.

5. Propose another method for scoring the policy questionnaires that would

permit a more extensive quantitative measurement of the difference between correct and current policy.

6. What additional policy choices might one wish to consider in dealing with a processing organization such as a chemical plant?

7. Give an example of how the strategy decision of automating through the use of robots would affect the personnel function and the finance function of an organization.

CASE PROBLEMS

1. BIG JIM'S GYM

Big Jim has been in the body building business for many years in Glendale, California. His gymnasium, originally for men, now consists of separate facilities for men and women located beneath a pizza parlor in downtown Glendale. Jim views the primary task of his business as "providing a full range of body building and weight reduction services for upper and middle class men, women and children in the Glendale area."

Currently, he has 20 employees who work with the customers in designing their health programs. At present, his gym has separate weight-lifting and exercise rooms for men and women, a pool, a sauna bath, and a small running track behind the building. While Jim states that every customer is different, he makes men go through his 23-step conditioning course and women follow the diet in "Big Jim's Energy Diet" pamphlet. (Customers are usually enrolled in a ten-week introductory course, and then left to advance at their own pace.)

The gym is modeled after the one Jim first managed on an army base in Pennsylvania "right down to the olive-drab walls." Jim maintains that the spartan atmosphere is necessary "to build mental and physical toughness." With some pride, Jim notes that he has all of the latest barbells and slant-board apparatus. Jim has always viewed his major inventory items as liniments and bandages, which are ordered periodically from a wholesaler or are purchased from a nearby drug store if stockouts occur. (Other items are purchased from a local sporting goods store.)

Jim is very concerned about keeping all of his staff busy and keeping the equipment in constant use, so he requires that customers follow a specific hour-by-hour schedule on equipment use. If the equipment is scheduled to capacity, he requests that his customers come at slow periods during the day or evening. (This procedure has met with some resistance on the part of customers, but Jim tells them that that is the price they must pay if he is to provide the most up-to-date health center services.)

Jim has done a survey of the prices charged by the other four health centers in the area and his fees are about average.* The other health centers have about the same number of employees, although two of them use licensed beauty consultants. Jim considers this an "unnecessary frill" and tells all of his customers that

---

* Within this market segment, Jim is competing with, among others, the Glendale Athletic Club. GAC's facilities include ten handball-racquetball courts, eight tennis courts, a 50-meter pool, sauna and steam rooms, a weight room with five $5,000 Nautilus weight lifting machines, and a fully equipped health bar. GAC's staff includes a trainer, five masseuses, five instructors, and ten other staff members.

anybody who works for him is an expert on all aspects of body maintenance. Jim has instituted a policy of job rotation whereby each member of the staff, with the exception of the clerk-typist, changes activities each hour. Employees are paid by the hour and are primarily college graduates who are interested in athletics. Turnover has not been a problem, even though Jim pays only slightly more than the minimum wage.

Although Jim's capacity is fully utilized, the number of memberships has dropped off from 500 to about 300 in the last six months, and profits have dropped proportionately. His accountant is looking into the possibility of raising membership fees.

ASSIGNMENT FOR THE READER:

a.   Develop a new primary task for Big Jim's Gym.

b.   Use the service audit questionnaire (Exhibit 20.10) to determine the alignment percentage between current policy and correct policy in light of the primary task you have proposed.

c.   Based upon your analysis, what steps do you recommend Jim take to reverse the trend in memberships?

2.   THE BARNSTAPLE COMPANY

The Barnstaple Company was a family owned long-established manufacturer of diaries. Up to the time of the death of Mr. James Barnstaple, Sr., the company had been prosperous. Thereafter, under the management of the company's treasurer, losses occurred. At the time of this case, Mrs. Barnstaple had just placed complete responsibility on her 24-year-old son. All the information in the case was provided by this young man.

"I'm James Barnstaple, Jr. I'm the newly appointed general manager of my mother's company, the Barnstaple Company. Ten days ago—that was the 17th of this month, January—I called a conference of the company's production manager, the sales manager, and the treasurer. The subject of our discussion was an inventory of diaries which we manufactured last year at a cost of $50,000. Today these diaries are obsolete because of their dates, and although we still carry them on our books as a $50,000 asset, actually they are valueless.

"This company is a nationally known manufacturer of diaries. For years the business has been profitable. Three years ago, my father died, and since then, profits have declined steadily. Last year and the year before, there were no profits; last year's loss was substantial. When Father died, Mother decided to keep on with the business. She asked Mr. Williams, the treasurer, who has been with the business for many years, to assume full responsibility for operations. He agreed, and the others who worked for my father stayed on.

"A year ago last June when I graduated from college I went right to work in the company office. I had worked in the factory and in the shipping room summers ever since my first year in high school; so I know a lot about our business, and a lot of our workers know me. I believe that during the past 18 months, I have become thoroughly familiar with all aspects of our operations, our policies, and our problems. Last Christmas Mother gave me half the company's stock—she has the other half—and announced that on the first of this January—I would be in full charge of the business with the title of general manager. That's how I got here.

"The line of diaries we make includes about 300 items. We sell single diaries direct to individuals by means of magazine advertising. We supply the retail trade through jobbers, most of whom have handled our line for years. Then our salesmen sell diaries in lots of 500 or more to banks, building and loan associations, and to other similar businesses that use them for advertising purposes. Of course, most of this business is very seasonal: wholesalers want delivery by August for diaries dated the following year; banks and similar commercial buyers want delivery before January 1, usually in late November and December. Our mail order sales are spread over a much longer period. They are highest early in the year, but we do get a few mail orders as late as June of the year for which the diary is dated.

"Our college business is different. College cooperative stores and student associations buy relatively large quantities of special designs, dated from August to the next August, for distribution to purchasers of memberships at the beginning of the school year in September. These diaries usually have a certificate of membership in the association printed in them and often contain quite an amount of advertising as well. When a student joins the association, the certificate is filled out, and upon payment of the membership fee, the diary is given to the member without extra charge.

"Sales of individual items in our line vary from 100 or 200 to as many as 30,000 units in a year. Last year four fifths of our sales were of 200 staple items, designs that have been in our line for several years. The remaining one fifth was about equally divided between a group of 100 novelty styles—items that are changed frequently—and a group of 12 exclusive styles made up on special order according to designs furnished by college cooperative stores and student associations. Our novelty items differ from the standard lines in binding, size, shape, inside layout, and accessories such as locks, zipper closures, attached pencils, and the like. They are sold through jobbers along with the standard lines for the retail trade.

"We sell the college lines during the summer for September and December delivery. Each order usually specifies the number to be delivered in September and indicates the probable number wanted in December. The number to be delivered in December is subject to adjustment up or down, final determination of the exact amount being delayed until late November or early December when college executives have a better indication of probable mid-year enrollment. In the past, such adjustments have been few and almost always have been increases above the original estimates. It has been our practice to make up each of these orders complete in time for the September delivery, stocking that portion of the order which is for future delivery. If an order is made up in two lots, the second lot usually is much smaller than the first, and therefore, the total unit cost of diaries made in the second lot runs from 5 to 7 percent more than the total unit cost of diaries made in the first lot.

"When we took our year-end inventory early this month, we found that we had on hand diaries that we manufactured last year at a cost of $50,000. These are shown on our books and balance sheet as assets valued at what it cost us to make them. Actually, they are worth nothing. About half of this inventory is of novelty items with last year's dates. No one is going to now buy diaries with last year's dating. Last fall's college enrollments turned out to be lower than expected, and for the first time, in recent years at least, substantial portions of the college orders were canceled. Actually, what has happened is that practically none of the special-order diaries which we made and stocked for spring-semester delivery to college organizations have been, or will be, shipped. They constitute a loss of about $25,000.

"At the conference I called ten days ago, Mr. Williams, our treasurer, presented the following figures of sales and costs of the novelty and the college lines.

	College lines	Novelty lines	College lines	Novelty lines
Sales			$120,000	$130,000
Manufacturing costs:				
Labor	$ 37,500	$ 62,500*		
Materials	37,500	37,500		
Factory overhead†	50,000	25,000		
Total cost of goods manufactured ..	$125,000	$125,000		
Cost of inventory on hand	25,000	25,000		
Manufacturing cost of goods sold			100,000	100,000
Gross margin			$ 20,000	$ 30,000
Selling and administrative expense			25,000	30,000
Net profit or loss			$ 5,000	$ 00,000

* Novelty items were made in small lots and, therefore, entailed a relatively high hand labor cost.

† Factory overhead consisted of such items of cost as heat, light, power, maintenance, supervision, depreciation, rent, and supplies. Some of these costs varied with the rate of production; others remained relatively fixed on an annual basis irrespective of the volume of output. The college lines were produced in relatively large volume which made possible utilization of the company's machines and equipment. They were, therefore, assigned a larger share of the overhead than were the novelty lines.

"Early in the conference, someone pointed out that had the inventory carryover from last year been no greater than the usual nominal amount (in the previous year it had been less than $3,000) a satisfactory profit would have resulted. This comment started a discussion of the college and novelty lines, but we made little progress in working out a solution. After three hours, all that had been accomplished was clarification of the positions of the executives present.

"The treasurer argued that both the college and novelty lines should be dropped on the basis that they were the cause of all the trouble. He said that there was no advantage in obtaining volume of output unless profit resulted therefrom. He urged that the activities of the company be somewhat curtailed. The sales manager agreed that the college lines should be discontinued but urged that the novelty lines be retained. He pointed out that the college lines had been substantially responsible for the loss, that the gross margin on those lines was relatively small, and that they in no way contributed to the sale of the company's standard lines. The production manager objected to the retention of the novelty lines. He pointed out that while the gross margin on those lines was high, the selling expense was likewise high. He also made the statement that up to two years ago the company had made few novelty items and had experienced no difficulty in selling its standard lines. He maintained that it was no fault of the production department that the company took a loss on the college lines, and he wanted to keep them.

"Two days ago, I called a second conference. We made no further progress. All that happened was that the treasurer, the production manager, and the sales manager just went over again what they had said earlier. When I saw that we were getting nowhere, I called the meeting off saying that I would think it over. Now it is clear that it is up to me. We can't afford losses such as we had this year. I'm new in the business, in a way, but I've been around here a lot for the past ten years, and everyone knows that. I have to decide what to do, and conferences such as we have been having are of no help to me."

BARNSTAPLE CASE QUESTIONS

a. Is there a conflict between the marketing task and the production task at Barnstaple?

b. What business is the Barnstaple Company really in?

c. How much confidence do you have in the financial statement prepared by the treasurer?

d. Can you clarify the inventory situation?

e. What should young Barnstaple do next? How should he do it?

3. BELL SUPERMARKET*

History of the business.   In 1948, W. J. Bell moved to a small city of 8,000 and bought out an independent food store. Previously, he had operated grocery stores in two other cities, having opened his first store ten years earlier at the age of 20. The purchased store was heavily involved in selling on credit, and Bell's first move was to go into a strict cash sales operation—the first of its kind in the city.

Bell's motto was "Low Prices Every Day," and he emphasized friendly, efficient service, high quality merchandise, and reasonable prices. His competitors were old-line stores who did not welcome the strong competition. Several innovations helped him to get established and increase sales volume. For example, Bell Supermarket was the first store in the city to feature advertised weekend specials. Bell was also one of the first stores in that area of the state to give trading stamps. By 1958, his store had become the number one food store in the city.

By 1958, the store had also outgrown the original downtown location. A modern, 10,000-square-foot store was erected at the east edge of the city—the direction of city growth. Shortly after this move, Gulfway, a regional food chain, opened the first real chain store in the city. This competition was of great concern to Bell, but he continued to follow his basic business philosophy and to operate even more efficiently. As a result, Bell Supermarket continued to show yearly progress in sales and profits.

---

* Source: N. H. Broom and J. G. Longenecker, *Small Business Management* (Cincinnati, Ohio: South-Western Publishing Company, 1975) pp. 525–26.

Recent developments in Bell Supermarket. In the late 1960s, Bell sold a 25 percent interest in the business to his brother and another 25 percent interest to his son David. David had recently been graduated from college, and he became an active partner in the business. For many years, the store had been recognized as one of the leading independent food-store operations in that section of the state.

As of 1970, the city's population had grown to 14,000, and Bell Supermarket was located in the newest section of the city. Residents in the area were predominantly in the middle to high income brackets. However, there was also a substantial amount of lower income trade.

Bell affiliated with one of the nation's largest independent wholesalers in 1970. This made possible the use of many private labels and permitted more effective competition. The wholesaler also provided advertising themes and promotions to member stores. Examples were promotions featuring china, art reproductions, record albums, and stainless steel mixing bowls. These promotions served as good stimulants for increasing sales volume. Customers were inclined to say, "There's always something going on at Bell's!"

Local market structure in 1970. The Gulfway chain store was located at the edge of the downtown section and catered primarily to customers in middle to lower income brackets. However, they also had some middle to upper income trade and were Bell's major competitor.

Bell's strongest independent competitor was Morgan Food Store—which was also the strongest independent when Bell came in 1948. Morgan Food Store had also moved to the east edge of the city but still had a problem of limited parking space. Its major appeal was the credit offered to customers and goodwill which had been built up through years of service. This business had dwindled in recent years, however.

The pricing structure could be described as very healthy. There was no excess of large food stores, and a "reasonable" markup was possible. There was competition, but it was not fierce.

Beginning of discount store competition. In 1971, a new type of competition entered the city with the opening of a discount store. Kelly Discount Center, a 20,000-square-foot operation, carried not only a complete line of nonfood items but also a wide line of grocery items—dry groceries as well as fresh meats, dairy products, produce, and frozen foods. The store was franchised, and the owner operated two other Kelly Discount Centers in a large city some 80 miles away.

When Kelly Discount Center opened for business, they dropped prices drastically, especially in staple items. They featured many "deep-cut" loss leaders, seemingly using the food operation as a drawing card for their more profitable lines.

Competitive developments. Gulfway made it apparent immediately that it did not intend to be undersold—even by a discount house that gave no stamps and provided no carryout service. Week-long specials, rather than weekend specials, became the rule. Competition became intense, and everyday shelf items were lowered to near cost or below.

J. A. Morgan, owner of Morgan Food Store, died in 1971, shortly after the opening of the discount store. A young man with chain store management experience purchased the store from the Morgan estate. He immediately eliminated both credit and stamps and tried to start a discount-type of operation himself.

Loss leaders became more prevalent. The Gulfway chain not only met the discount prices but even attempted to undersell. They also increased their advertising—more newspaper advertising, handbills, and some radio commercials. Morgan, likewise, stayed in the thick of the price competition.

Bell's dilemma. The arrival of the discounter marked the beginning of a disturbing period for Bell Supermarket. The relatively calm situation that had prevailed for several years was suddenly shattered. Their sales volume quickly declined about 20 percent.

The Bells reacted, as might be expected, by lowering prices. As they saw prices cut to profitless levels, however, they questioned the wisdom of such extreme competition. Part of the question was the type of store they should try to be. They wondered whether Bell Supermarket could continue to project an image that distinguished it from the discounter. At times, it seemed that the price war made price cutting the only effective weapon in attracting business.

QUESTIONS

a. What has been the basis of Bell's successful operation and growth in the past?

b. What are its greatest sources of strength in the current period of intense competition?

c. Which store would be likely to suffer the most from the opening of the discount store? Why?

d. What general course of action should be followed by Bell Supermarket during the next few months?

4. ANALYSIS OF MIAMI TOY COMPANY CASE

Scoring: Our application of the manufacturing policy questionnaire yielded only eight items in alignment (items 1, 3, 13, 19, 23, 24, 25, and 26). This gives an alignment percentage of 26.

Interpretation: The primary task of MTC has been to produce items that apparently are traditional toys, characterized by durability and simplicity. Little effort goes into standardization of design or into procedures, since the toy makers seemingly design as they produce. The Darth Vader doll, however, will require a good deal more in the way of planning and coordination because it is a radical departure for MTC in terms of toy technology. (The company's "distinctive competence" seems to be in wooden toys, whereas the Darth Vader doll is plastic, mechanical, and electronic.) The technology of transformation will have to be changed from a quasi-craft operation to a production line. This in turn implies mechanization to some degree for parts handling and inspection; and probably the use of special purpose equipment at various stages of the process. The company has done little in the way of process engineering, and the equipment is general-purpose. MTC will have to engage in more subcontracting than it currently does and will have to consider carefully the extent of inventory it will keep on hand. The firm currently does not use inventory to decouple production stages since the work is not specialized by department. (If a production-line-type operation is undertaken, such decoupling will still not be mandatory if care is taken to balance workloads across operations.) A major problem, if the Darth Vader doll is introduced, will be the change in work procedures required on the part of the work force. Currently, the workers have a great deal of freedom in performing their jobs, but a switch to a line technology will no doubt eliminate much of it. Fred Avide indicates, however, that the workers are anxious to make more money, but it remains to be seen how they would take to specialized jobs. In summary, the Darth Vader doll is ill-suited to MTC's current policies and primary task. Other, more compatible toys should be investigated.

SELECTED BIBLIOGRAPHY

Hayes, R. H., and Schmenner, R. W. "How Should you Organize Manufacturing," *Harvard Business Review* (January–February 1978), pp. 105–18.

Hayes, R. H., and Wheelwright, S. G. "Link Manufacturing Process and Product Life Cycles," *Harvard Business Review* (January–February 1979), pp. 133–40.

Hill, T. J. "Manufacturing Implications in Determining Corporate Policy," *International Journal of Operations & Production Management,* vol. 1, no. 1, 1980, pp. 3–11.

Kantrow, Alan M. "The Strategy-Technology Connection," *Harvard Business Review* (July–August 1980), pp. 6–8, 12.

Skinner, W. "Manufacturing-Missing Link in Corporate Strategy," *Harvard Business Review,* (May–June 1969), pp. 136–45.

———. "The Focused Factory," *Harvard Business Review* (May–June, 1974), pp. 113–21.

———. *Manufacturing in the Corporate Strategy* (New York: John Wiley & Sons, 1979).

Thomas, D. R. "Strategy is Different in A Service Business," *Harvard Business Review* (July–August 1978), pp. 158–65.

Van Dierdonck, R. and Miller, J. G. "Designing Production Planning and Control Systems," *Journal of Operations Management,* vol. 1, no. 1 (August 1980), pp. 37–46.

Wheelwright, S. "Reflecting Corporate Strategy in Manufacturing Decisions," *Business Horizons* (February 1978), pp. 57–66.

SECTION FIVE

Termination of the system

It is common for all or parts of a production system to be discontinued or merged with other systems. This section presents a classification scheme for termination and suggests some strategies for handling the various types. Also considered are some observations about future developments in the field of production and operations management.

Chapter 21

TERMINATION, REBIRTH, AND CONCLUSIONS

Few production systems remain constant over time. Some evolve into larger combinations of workers, material, and facilities, some decentralize into smaller units separated geographically from their starting point, and still others, for a variety of reasons, simply cease to exist. In this chapter, we will discuss evolutionary changes under the general topic of termination. Then we will engage in termination of the book—offering some conjecture about the future of production and operations management.

TERMINATION AND REBIRTH

The productive system is terminated when (1) production ceases permanently or (2) when a system is so greatly revised that the major portion of the original design is no longer relevant to its subsequent operations. The first view reflects the common conception of termination—that of a company and, hence, its productive system ceasing operations. The second reflects the orientation of the text—that the system design derives from a particular product objective and that this objective may change over time, rendering that system obsolete. This view conveys the idea that termination of the productive system can occur without termination of the firm of which it is a part, and it underscores the fact that a viable firm will normally phase out old systems and introduce new ones throughout the course of its existence.

**Product and
system life
cycles**

The distinction between the two views of termination, as well as the long-term relationship between a productive system and its product, can be developed by considering the interrelationship of system life cycles and product life cycles.

Product life cycles. This concept is widely used in marketing to describe the sales performance of a product over time. The basic idea is that products go through five stages:

1. *Introduction:* the product is put on the market and awareness and acceptance are minimal.
2. *Growth:* the product begins to make rapid sales gains because of the cumulative effects of introductory promotion, distribution, and word-of-mouth influence.
3. *Maturity:* sales growth continues but at a declining rate, because of the diminishing number of potential customers who remain unaware of the product or who have taken no action.
4. *Saturation:* sales reach and remain on a plateau (marked by the level of replacement demand).
5. *Decline:* sales begin to diminish absolutely as the product is gradually edged out by better products or substitutes.[1]

EXHIBIT 21.1
**Stages in the
product life cycle**

Exhibit 21.1 illustrates the general relationship between sales volume and these stages over time.

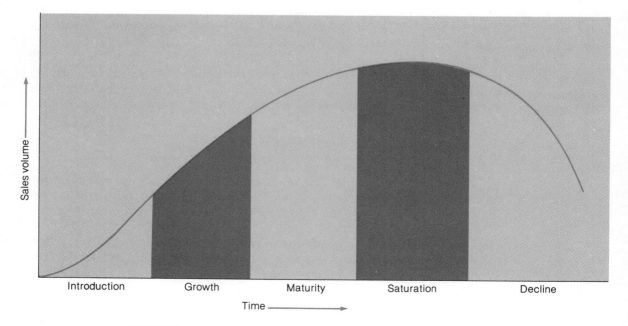

---

[1] Taken from Philip Kotler, *Marketing Management, Analysis, Planning, and Control* (Englewood Cliffs, N.J.: Prentice-Hall, 1967), p. 291.

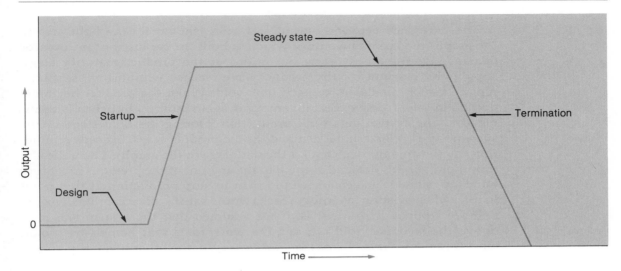

EXHIBIT 21.2
**Productive
system life cycle**

Productive system life cycles. As was described throughout the book, the productive system has four general phases: design, startup, steady state, and termination. The generalized relationship between these phases and system output is shown in Exhibit 21.2.

If we combine the product and the productive system life cycles and assume a hypothetical one-product firm, we get the graph shown in Exhibit 21.3. Examining these combined cycles, we see that the initial phases of the product life cycle continue past the point at which the productive system has achieved steady state output levels. What we have presumed here is that a typical system produces more than it sells during the product's growth phase since the system is usually designed to meet forecast maturity and saturation phase demands.

EXHIBIT 21.3
**Product and
productive
system life cycles**

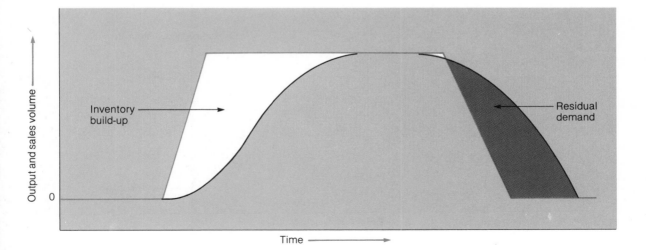

The difference between output and sales (shown by the light area in the graph) represents inventory which is built up because output exceeds demand. During steady state operations at the product maturity stage, supply and demand for the product have reached equilibrium, so that a replacement is available for each item sold. When the product begins to decline in sales, some excess inventory is again built up but then is eliminated as the system cuts back production. During the final stage of the system's life cycle, residual demand for the product at last exceeds production (by the amount depicted by the dark area in the graph). Theoretically, the amount of this demand is equal to the amount of the previous inventory build-up, since management would plan to stop production at that point in time when existing inventory stocks would satisfy all remaining demand.

If we stopped here—that is, if we assumed that the system was shut down, the resources sold off, and the work force sent home—we would label this an example of *permanent termination.* On the other hand, if management decides to produce a new product, stops production on existing products, and engages in a complete overhaul of the original system, we would consider it an example of *temporary termination,* and our product and system life cycles might take the form shown in Exhibit 21.4.

In this illustration, we have assumed that redesign of the system is undertaken during the steady state and termination phases of the initial system's life cycle. This might be a reasonable strategy in that it permits startup of the revised system to begin as soon as operations of the initial system are terminated. We have also assumed (for simplicity) that only one new product is to be produced by the redesigned system and that the life cycle curves for both product and system are roughly equivalent to those of their original counterparts. In actuality, of course, these assumptions are highly restrictive since most manufacturing firms produce several

EXHIBIT 21.4
Temporary termination with design and startup of revised system begun during latter phases of original system

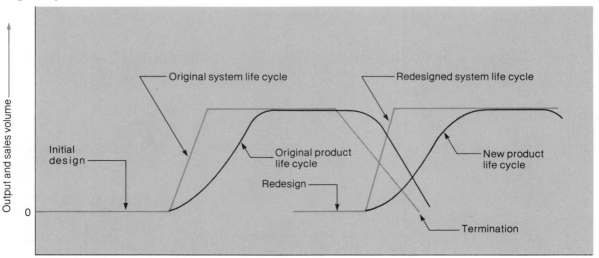

products rather than one, and we would not expect any two system life cycles or any two product life cycles to be identical.[2] With this as a background, we will consider both types of termination in more detail.

Temporary termination

To repeat, temporary termination refers to a situation in which a system is so greatly revised that the major portion of the original design is no longer relevant to its subsequent operations. Common reasons that the original design would no longer be relevant are: major technological changes, vertical integration, and major changes in output requirements.

Major technological changes. Shifting from nonautomated to automated processes in a factory, changing from table to cafeteria service in a restaurant, or converting from a clinic to a nursing home entail major redesign of the production system. The procedures for scheduling, maintaining inventories, controlling quality, and performing maintenance would have to be specified anew, and the tasks of direct labor and management adjusted accordingly. In terms of life cycle curves, if we take the introduction of automation as an example, it is quite probable that the change from the initial system to the revised system would appear as shown in Exhibit 21.5.

In this instance, product demand is seen as growing throughout the operation of the initial system and automation is chosen as a way of meeting long-run future demand. The termination of the initial system

EXHIBIT 21.5
Life cycles before and after a major technological change

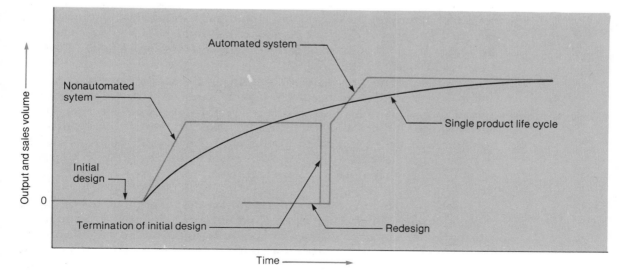

[2] For a discussion of product and production process life cycles as they pertain to multiple products, see R. H. Hayes and S. C. Wheelwright, "Link Manufacturing and Product Life Cycles," *Harvard Business Review,* vol. 57, no. 1 (January–February 1979), pp. 133–40; and "The Dynamics of Process–Product Life Cycles" by the same authors, *Harvard Business Review* (March–April 1979), pp. 127–36.

would be instantaneous, and there would be a short production hiatus until the redesigned system became operational. It would be reasonable to expect that the automated system would be redesigned during the latter stages of the initial system's operation, and familiarity with the product would allow rapid achievement of steady state operations for the redesigned system.

Vertical integration.   Vertical integration refers to the growth of a firm by its extension backward—so to speak—so as to incorporate its source of supply or by its extension forward so as to incorporate its distribution or retailing activities. Under certain conditions, therefore, vertical integration can lead to a major redesign of the productive system. For example, a small company might become integrated with a larger one and therefore be required to concentrate on producing only certain models of its existing line. This could compel a system redesign in order to take advantage of the potential production economies that derive from a narrowed product line. Similarly, a system redesign might be desirable when a firm, through integration, obtains a stable source of supply that permits a higher production rate.

Major changes in output requirements.   A common cause of temporary system termination is an increase in product output requirements that necessitates the expansion of existing facilities or the introduction of a new facility. In the latter case, especially, production may become "a brand new ballgame" since a new plant would undoubtedly tend to incorporate the latest advances in operating technology and management. Also, the desirable features of the old system would be included and the undesirable excluded, and even if the basic process is the same, the supporting activities are likely to be altered so greatly that the revised system would bear little resemblance to the original.

In contrast to meeting increased output requirements, temporary termination and redesign can occur because a manufacturing firm decides to reduce output at one of its facilities. In this situation, the firm might sell its equipment, or transfer it to another plant, and restructure its production process in such a way that a smaller work force could operate efficiently at a smaller-scale plant. It might also rent out the newly available space or (as often happens) use it as a warehouse.

System
blending

Closely related to the issue of temporary termination is the problem of *system blending,* which denotes the dovetailing of one system with another. This problem is most often encountered in business mergers and is probably more acute in mergers of the horizontal type. A *horizontal merger* combines companies whose products are virtually identical and that operate in the same geographic market.[3] Consider, for example, a merger of two local

---

[3] Other types are *vertical mergers* and *conglomerate mergers.* A vertical merger is one in which the firms involved have had a buyer-seller relationship. (In these cases, the comments made regarding vertical integration pertain.) A conglomerate merger covers all other cases and includes mergers to extend the product line or to enter new markets. (These types of mergers often have no effect on the production systems of the combining firms.)

newspapers that results in combining the two productive systems into one. Beyond the marketing, distribution, and financial issues involved, critical decisions must be made regarding the production system itself. Among these are:

Who will be in charge of production operations? Each newspaper presumably has a production manager, and now there is need for only one.

Which production employees will remain? Union regulations will apply to most direct labor—printers, stereotypers, linotype operators, and so forth—but what about clerical personnel and non-union supervisory people?

Which equipment is to be transferred from the vacated plant? Which is to be sold?

What new equipment is to be purchased? (The combining of operations is often an ideal situation in which to introduce new technologies.

What about maintenance policies? Introducing new equipment and transferring old equipment will undoubtedly alter maintenance operations and schedule.

What about the changeover period? Will production cease? If so, for how long?

As far as actually making these decisions is concerned, the methods covered in the literature on organizational change pertain.[4] Conventional economic analysis would most certainly be employed for the equipment-related decisions, and critical path methods would be highly useful in planning and controlling the activities of the changeover period.

From a broader standpoint, however, the key requirement is objectivity, which means that the management of the acquiring company should eschew some rather common misconceptions about management policies and procedures. Three of these misconceptions have been identified by Searby,[5] and the first one is the "halo assumption"—which holds that because the acquiring company was bigger and more successful before the merger, its people and policies should be retained and adopted after the merger. The flaw here, of course, is that no company is always correct in its handling of personnel and procedures, nor is any company completely lacking in these areas. Then there is the "small world assumption," which holds that one of the companies must be doing things the right way and so the decision should boil down to picking one approach from two alternatives. Clearly, this overlooks other alternatives that might be even better. Finally, there is the "compromise assumption," which holds that decisions can be made by choosing one company's approach one time, another's

---

[4] See, for example, "Managing Organizational Change," Chapter 16 in D. A. Tansik, R. B. Chase, and N. J. Aquilano, *Management: A Life Cycle Approach* (Homewood, Ill.: Richard D. Irwin, Inc., 1980).

[5] F. W. Searby, "Controlling Postmerger Change," *Harvard Business Review* (September–October 1969), pp. 154–55.

the next time, and a combination of approaches at other times.[6] Again, this overlooks new alternatives that may be superior.

Permanent termination

Permanent termination—the permanent closing of a production system—can be further broken down into general and local termination.

General termination.   *General termination* refers to the dissolution of a productive system as a result of a firm's going out of business.[7] The causes for this type of termination include product failures, marketing failures, misallocation of capital, governmental rulings, and production inefficiencies. Quite often, however, these causes are closely interrelated, and it is therefore difficult to isolate the production system's role in a firm's termination. Nevertheless, whether the production system remains healthy and contributes to the firm's stability or becomes weak and contributes to its demise depends on how well it responds to a variety of pressures. In this regard, Wickham Skinner has identified three classes of pressure that affect operations on the production side of the manufacturing firm. These are:[8]

1.   New pressures from outside the firm.
2.   New problems within the firm.
3.   The impact of accelerating technology.

Outside pressures.   According to Skinner, the primary sources of pressure from outside the firm are new trends in industry and in the marketplace. There is increasing competition not only because of the trend on the part of U.S. firms to diversify and enter new markets but because foreign firms have developed products that compete on the basis of quality as well as price. As noted throughout the book, the inroads made by Japan and West Germany in electronics, textiles, and automobiles are ample evidence of this.

In addition to competing in product quality and price, production systems have been forced to provide more rapid output and greater product variety in order to fulfill the marketing objectives necessitated by competition; this in the face of supply shortages and delays.

Internal pressures.   Cost control, staffing the operation, and handling paper work are three areas that create internal pressures. Cost control has become a greater problem than in the past primarily because mechanization, shorter production runs, and higher quality have increased the proportion of indirect workers to direct workers. Indirect jobs, such as maintenance and

---

[6] Searby gives this a more colorful title—"the Henry Clay assumption," because it reflects this famous legislator's approach to settling disputes.

[7] Permanent general termination is fairly common in American industry. Among small businesses, half fail to survive a year of operations; only one third survive past year four. Among large businesses, out of the 100 largest firms in 1900, only two (American Sugar and Exxon) survive today.

[8] Wickham Skinner, "Production under Pressure," *Harvard Business Review* (November–December 1966), pp. 137–46.

material handling, are generally harder to measure and consequently more difficult to improve than most direct labor activities. Direct jobs are often partly machine controlled and less repetitive, and therefore, determining their contribution to cost and output for purposes of enhancing efficiency is also a greater problem than ever before.

Staffing the operation also has become a bigger problem because the shift from direct to indirect work and from manual tasks to machine monitoring makes worker selection and training more complicated and more important. In the past, the dividing line between jobs requiring skilled workers and those suited to unskilled or semiskilled workers was fairly clear. Now, however, with the development of more sophisticated machinery (and a more sophisticated work force to operate it), the distinction has become blurred.

Handling paper work is a widely discussed problem of contemporary industry—and one that tends to grow as the productive system produces a wider range of products, increases its output, and speeds up its deliveries. Certainly the amount and kind of information and the way in which it is used tell much about the health of the production function and the enterprise as a whole.

Accelerating technology. Technological innovations in equipment, products, and materials have in some respects complicated production management decision making. The introduction of numerically controlled machinery, for example, not only entails a sizable investment of capital but may alter the operation and scheduling of every part of the production process. Innovations in product design and materials also can change the whole character of the transformation process and, if incorrectly handled, can be sources of trouble for the production system. Further complicating the issue of innovation is the fact that management has only imperfect knowledge of the technological possibilities in any of these areas. A company may select a state-of-the-art process one week and find it is out of date the next. Thus, a firm might find itself being forced out of business because it chose to increase capacity by adopting a new but less efficient process than the one that was adopted by its competitor only a week or a month later.

Local termination. In *local termination* a firm closes down one of two or more productive systems but otherwise continues in business. Unlike general termination, local termination may be undertaken by a healthy or even an expanding firm. An organization may initiate this type of termination for several reasons: (1) it wishes to combine productive facilities, (2) it desires to buy components it previously made, (3) it has exhausted the market or resource supply in a particular locale, or (4) a combination of factors has raised its costs too high to permit continued operation at its present location. Also, a number of terminations have been the direct result of firms' taking advantage of the special taxation and labor benefits offered by some states and foreign countries that are anxious to increase their industrial base.

The manner in which firms conduct local terminations has changed substantially in recent years and especially with regard to the handling of their employees. For example, it used to be common practice to keep employees in the dark as long as possible about an imminent plant closing. The presumption was that the workers would either curtail their production or, if they were on incentive, try to "overproduce" in order to make a killing on their last few paychecks. However, while these fears were sometimes borne out in situations where employees were forewarned, an even more chaotic state of affairs often developed in those situations where they were not forewarned. Moreover, management's "strategy of silence" commonly resulted in an abiding bitterness after the plant closed its doors.

But, as we said, things have changed. In the first place, there are restrictions on the conditions under which a plant may be closed down. By way of example, in 1965 textile workers at one of a company's plants organized a union, which was duly recognized as a legitimate bargaining agent by the National Labor Relations Board. As a result of this unionization, the company management elected to close down the plant and move elsewhere, and the union thereupon filed suit with the NLRB, which found in the union's favor and decreed that a plant could not shut down for anti-union reasons. This ruling was then appealed by the company to the U.S. Supreme Court, which concluded that a plant could be shut down for any reason provided the *entire firm* is terminated. However, in what was to become a landmark decision, it also ruled that the closing of a specific plant solely for purposes of "chilling the union" was illegal.

In the second place, management has become more sensitive to the loss of goodwill engendered by a cavalier attitude toward the welfare of its work force and the effects of the surrounding community when faced with a plant termination. This has led large organizations (especially) to give ample warning that a plant is to be closed down and to spend rather substantial sums in arranging personnel transfers and establishing retraining programs.

System phase-out

Despite the fact that the phase-out period is generally unpleasant for management, it is nonetheless amenable to planning. Indeed, the decisions made regarding output reduction can have a marked effect on the ultimate financial position of the firm.

To get an insight into the problem, consider four of the many possible patterns of output reduction shown in Exhibit 21.6.

Pattern *a* shows a two-stage decrease in production and would be typical of a system that requires large chunks of capacity to operate. An example would be a company that uses two identical assembly lines to make its product, so that the first drop in output would be associated with closing down one line and the second drop with closing down the other line.

Pattern *b* indicates a gradual linear termination and would be typical of a system that can reduce output in small increments. An example of this would be a job shop that can handle product orders on a variety of

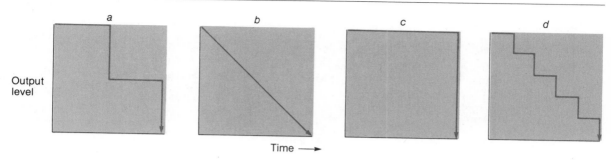

a   b   c   d

Output level

Time →

EXHIBIT 21.6
Four patterns of output reduction

different machines, and therefore, the elimination of one machine at a time would have relatively small influence on output.

Pattern *c* represents an instantaneous termination and would be typified by a small system that simply cannot operate at reduced capacity—or by a system of any size that cannot obtain enough revenue to cover its variable costs. An example of the first case would be a restaurant that closes due to lack of business; an example of the second would be an ocean liner's being sold for scrap because of its high operating costs.

Pattern *d*, exhibiting a stairstep decrease, is probably the most common phase-out pattern. Certainly most process industries would close down by incremental steps, as would certain service systems, such as hospitals and schools.

System phase-out: General termination. *Finding the optimum termination point.* Even when an entire firm is going out of business, the rational manager would like to choose that phase-out pattern that meets residual demand at the lowest cost. In most respects, this becomes an aggregate planning problem similar to those encountered during steady state operations. That is, demand must be forecast, production levels must be set in light of existing inventories, and the size of the work force must be established to meet output requirements. There are some differences, however, and—depending upon the system under consideration—they can make the problem more complex.

Consider a company that finds that its main product is no longer demanded in sufficient quantity for it to make a profit and whose facilities are so specialized that it cannot effect a changeover to some other product. In this situation, termination is probably not unexpected, and management would therefore have some discretion over the rate at which it phases out its operations. If we assume that demand from retailers will be gradually reduced to zero by some time period *(T)*, the problem would be to find the point *(t_i)* during that period when the system should be terminated. To see how this determination might be made, consider the modified break-even chart in Exhibit 21.7.

Here we see that fixed costs are reduced in steps, reflecting the fact that assets are being sold off piecemeal. This phasing of liquidation is also reflected in the curve labeled *income from asset selloff*. With each reduction

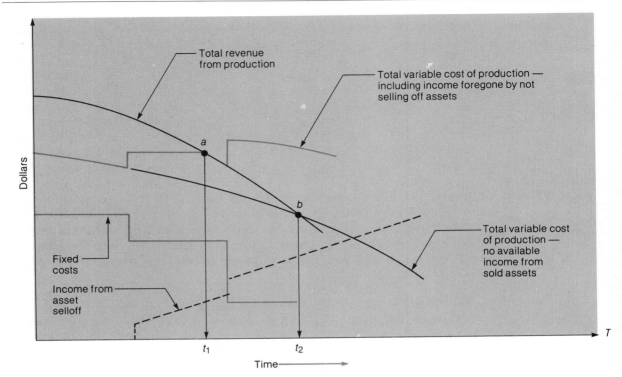

EXHIBIT 21.7
**Modified break-
even chart for
termination
analysis**

in assets comes a reduction in production capability, which we have considered by reducing the total variable cost of production. In this example,
the point of optimum termination would be at one of two times, depending
upon whether there is an income obtainable from asset selloff. If there
is, termination should take place where total revenue intersects total variable costs—at point *a* (time t_1). If there is none, the system should continue
in operation until total revenue intersects total variable cost—at point *b*
(time t_2). Obviously, if termination occurs at time t_1, the fixed-cost line
would no longer exist; also, the remaining assets would be immediately
sold, so the *income from asset selloff* line would no longer be relevant.

To generalize from this illustration is risky, but it seems fair to say
that the key problem in finding the optimum termination point is deciding
when to sell off resources. The factors that must be weighed in this decision
are the cost savings from asset liquidation (e.g., maintenance, obsolescence,
depreciation, and opportunity costs) versus the foregone revenue from a
loss of productive capacity. From an operational standpoint, obtaining
accurate projections of all these costs would pose a severe problem, which
would be compounded if management wished to consider alternative patterns of output reduction.

System phase-out: Local termination. The number of options available
to the branch plant production manager regarding output levels, disposition

of equipment, and work force levels varies according to the role of the phased-out system in the total organization. If the terminated facility is a supplier to other facilities in the organization, production might be expected to continue at the steady state level right up to the closing day. This would tend to eliminate some of the sticky timing decisions, such as those encountered in equipment selloff in phase-out under general termination.

On the other hand, if central management adopts a "total systems" viewpoint, these timing problems could increase during a local phase-out. For example, management might want to consider the desirability of transferring equipment to one of its other facilities versus selling it in the used-equipment market. To make this decision requires the consideration of a whole host of related factors, including the anticipated state of the used equipment over the phase-out period, the likely effect on output at both the terminating facility and the remaining plants, the forecast demand for the output, and the desired inventory position of the organization.[9]

Summary on termination

Termination is a relatively unexplored phase in the system life cycle, and in order to analyze it, we were forced to develop our own classification scheme. This scheme, along with some of the key considerations (in parentheses), is illustrated in Exhibit 21.8.

In addition, we have suggested that there is a good deal more to termination than sending the work force home and putting a "closed" sign on

EXHIBIT 21.8
Termination classification

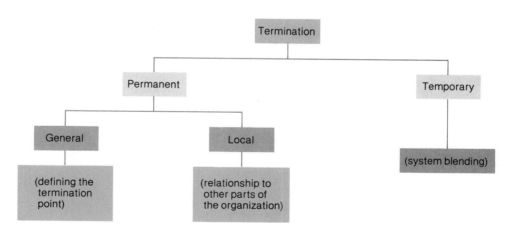

_____

[9] Roodman and Schwarz have developed a mathematical approach to minimizing discounted costs from phasing out facilities as demand shifts and declines over a specified planning horizon. The costs considered are the variable operating cost at each facility, the transportation costs between facilities and demand centers, and the costs to operate and close each facility. (See G. M. Roodman and L. B. Schwarz, "Optimal and Heuristic Facility Phase-out Strategies," *AIIE Transactions*, vol. 7, no. 2 [February 1975], pp. 177–84.)

the front door. We have also tried to convey the fact that there are good reasons why termination should be attended to as carefully as startup and steady state operations. What remains to be done, however, is to develop guidelines for managing this final phase of a system's life cycle.

CONCLUSION: FUTURE TRENDS IN PRODUCTION AND OPERATIONS MANAGEMENT

A major component of production and operations management is forecasting, and it seems only reasonable that forecasting can be applied to the field itself. Thus, relying on a general trend analysis, the following observations about the near future of production and operations management are offered.

1. Increased study of the nature of production and operations management in services

We have attempted throughout the book to illustrate the production management applications in service industries. And, as we also indicated, service systems differ among themselves (as well as from manufacturing) along several dimensions. The next questions which we believe will be investigated in the near future, are "What differences affect the actual design and operation of service systems?" and "How will the new service technologies—word processing, mini computers, paperless buying and selling, and so forth—affect production strategy and operations?"

2. Increased emphasis on productivity

There is really no option here for the production or operations manager. International competition is such that no major company can afford not to seek every means possible to enhance productivity. Thus, in addition to absorbing technological innovations and new production control systems, operations management will have to find means of increasing worker involvement. Increasing worker involvement, in turn, means understanding human behavior and carefully balancing the requirements of technology with the needs of the work force.[10]

3. Increased emphasis on quality

Quality competition will become a major feature of corporate strategy in the 1980s and, hence, will be a major concern for production management. Look to U.S. firms to adopt major portions of the Japanese quality philosophy and study carefully parallel developments in Sweden and West Germany.

4. Continued expansion of international production

Beyond the standard reasons for "going international" (lower labor costs, nearness to supply sources and markets), foreign manufacturers will continue to expand because of relaxed trade restrictions. For example, free trade zones established in several countries permit importing and exporting

---

[10] For further discussion of this point, see the following two articles: L. L. Cummings, "Needed Research in Production/Operations Management: A Behavioral Perspective," and L. G. Sprague, "Needed Research in Organizational Behavior: A Production/Operations Management Perspective," *Academy of Management Review* (July 1977), pp. 500–507.

with little or no tariffs. This changes the product mix and production emphasis. It also affects the location of production facilities since it becomes desirable to locate near or within free trade zones. We also anticipate that other countries will continue to move their operations to the U.S. and Canada.

5. Continuation of the computer (and electronics) revolution

Mini computers and extensive software packages will continue to grow in development and application. More products will be manufactured under computer control, and production decision making will be facilitated through the use of real time simulations and interactive computer terminals. Regarding other applications of electronics, it appears that any process that can be converted to semiconductor technology, will be converted to it.

6. Continued increases in energy costs

The energy problem will continue to affect day-to-day production operations but, in addition, will no doubt affect strategic decisions such as what type of capacity to add and where to locate facilities. The production manager will more and more become an "energy manager" faced with complicated trade-offs between energy costs on one hand and environmental concerns (clear air and water) on the other.

7. Continued increases in resource costs and lead times

In the past few years, energy problems and increasing national and international competition have combined to make the acquisition of production resources (capital equipment and certain raw materials) more expensive. They have also had the effect of extending delivery lead times. Components once available in weeks now take months. Thus, the supply process has become, and will probably remain, a real bottleneck for many plants.

8. Continued increasing recognition of the importance of OM as a field of study

Operations management has come into its own field of study in business administration. The corporate-wide impact of its newer tools (notably MRP) and the recognition of its major role in achieving higher levels of productivity are but two of the factors which make it central to the management of organizations.

REVIEW AND DISCUSSION QUESTIONS

1. Define general termination, local termination, system blending.

2. How does the decision problem of selling off equipment in the face of termination differ from equipment selloff during steady operations?

3. What managerial problems are encountered by merging two systems for the purpose of combining production operations?

4. What is involved in finding the optimum termination point? How might break-even analysis be used in this determination?

5. What are some of the pressures currently confronting the production side of a manufacturing firm? Do you see similar pressures confronting service firms in the next decade? Discuss.

6. Our forecast of future trends was made in 1980. What trends do you see emerging at the present time?

SELECTED BIBLIOGRAPHY

Chase, R. B. "A Classification and Evaluation of Research in Operations Management," *Journal of Operations Management,* vol. 1, no. 1 (August 1980), pp. 9–14.

Cummings, L. L. "Needed Research in Production/Operations Management: A Behavioral Perspective, *Academy of Management Review* (July 1977), pp. 500–507.

Hayes, R. H., and Wheelwright, S. C. "Link Manufacturing and Product Life Cycles," *Harvard Business Review,* vol. 57, no. 1 (January–February 1979), pp. 133–40.

————. "The Dynamics of Process–Product Life Cycles," *Harvard Business Review* (March-April 1979), pp. 127–36.

Smith, R. D., and Robey, D. "Research and Applications in Operations Management: Discussion of a Paradox, *Academy of Management Journal,* vol. 16, no. 4 (December 1973), pp. 647–57.

Sprague, L. G. "Needed Research in Organizational Behavior: A Production/Operations Management Perspective," *Academy of Management Review* (July 1977), pp. 500–507.

Tansik, D. A.; Chase, R. B.; and Aquilano, N. J. "Managing Organizational Change," Chapter 16 in *Management: A Life Cycle Approach* (Homewood, Ill.: Richard D. Irwin, Inc., 1980).

Appendixes

Appendix A

Uniformly distributed random digits

56970	10799	52098	04184	54967	72938	50834	23777	08392
83125	85077	60490	44369	66130	72936	69848	59973	08144
55503	21383	02464	26141	68779	66388	75242	82690	74099
47019	06683	33203	29603	54553	25971	69573	83854	24715
84828	61152	79526	29554	84580	37859	28504	61980	34997
08021	31331	79227	05748	51276	57143	31926	00915	45821
36458	28285	30424	98420	72925	40729	22337	48293	86847
05752	96065	36847	87729	81679	59126	59437	33225	31280
26768	02513	58454	56958	20575	76746	40878	06846	32828
42613	72456	43030	58085	06766	60227	96414	32671	45587
95457	12176	65482	25596	02678	54592	63607	82096	21913
95276	67524	63564	95958	39750	64379	46059	51666	10433
66954	53574	64776	92345	95110	59448	77249	54044	67942
17457	44151	14113	02462	02798	54977	48340	66738	60184
03704	23322	83214	59337	01695	60666	97410	55064	17427
21538	16997	33210	60337	27976	70661	08250	69509	60264
57178	16730	08310	70348	11317	71623	55510	64750	87759
31048	40058	94953	55866	96283	40620	52087	80817	74533
69799	83300	16498	80733	96422	58078	99643	39847	96884
90595	65017	59231	17772	67831	33317	00520	90401	41700
33570	34761	08039	78784	09977	29398	93896	78227	90110
15340	82760	57477	13898	48431	72936	78160	87240	52710
64079	07733	36512	56186	99098	48850	72527	08486	10951
63491	84886	67118	62063	74958	20946	28147	39338	32109
92003	76568	41034	28260	79708	00770	88643	21188	01850
52360	46658	66511	04172	73085	11795	52594	13287	82531
74622	12142	68355	65635	21828	39539	18988	53609	04001
04157	50070	61343	64315	70836	82857	35335	87900	36194
86003	60070	66241	32836	27573	11479	94114	81641	00496
41208	80187	20351	09630	84668	42486	71303	19512	50277
06433	80674	24520	18222	10610	05794	37515	48619	62866
39298	47829	72648	37414	75755	04717	29899	78817	03509
89884	59651	67533	68123	17730	95862	08034	19473	63971
61512	32155	51906	61662	64430	16688	37275	51262	11569
99653	47635	12506	88535	36553	23757	34209	55803	96275
95913	11085	13772	76638	48423	25018	99041	77529	81360
55804	44004	13122	44115	01601	50541	00147	77685	58788
35334	82410	91601	40617	72876	33967	73830	15405	96554
57729	88646	76487	11622	96297	24160	09903	14047	22917
86648	89317	63677	70119	94739	25875	38829	68377	43918
30574	06039	07967	32422	76791	30725	53711	93385	13421
81307	13114	83580	79974	45929	85113	72268	09858	52104
02410	96385	79067	54939	21410	86980	91772	93307	34116
18969	87444	52233	62319	08598	09066	95288	04794	01534
87863	80514	66860	62297	80198	19347	73234	86265	49096
08397	10538	15438	62311	72844	60203	46412	65943	79232
28520	45247	58729	10854	99058	18260	38765	90038	94209
44285	09452	15867	70418	57012	72122	36634	97283	95943
86299	22510	33571	23309	57040	29285	67870	21913	72958
84842	05748	90894	61658	15001	94005	36308	41161	37341

Appendix B

Normally distributed random digits.

An entry in the table is the value Z from a normal distribution with a mean of O and a standard deviation of 1.

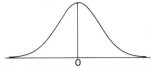

1.98677	1.23481	-.28360	.99427 / 1.08372	-.87919	-.21600
-.59341	1.54221	-.65806		1.68560	1.14899
.11340	.19126	-.65084	.12188	.02338	-.61545
.89783	-.54929	-.03663	-1.89506	.15158	-.20061
-.50790	1.14463	1.30917	1.26528	.09459	.16423
-1.63968	-.63248	.21482	-1.16241	-.60015	-.55233
1.14081	-.29988	-.48053	-1.21397	-.34391	-1.84881
-.43354	-.32855	.67115	.52289 / .01847	-1.42796	-.14181
.05707	.35331	.20470		1.71086	-1.44738
.77153	.72576	-.29833	.26139	1.25845	-.35468
-1.38286	.04406	-.75499	.61068	.61903	-.96845
1.60166	-1.66161	.70886	-.20302	-.28373	2.07219
-.48781	.02629	-.34306	2.00746	-1.12059	.07943
-1.10632	1.18250	-.60065	.09737	.63297	1.00659
.77000	-.87214	-.63584	-.39546	-.72776	.45594
-.56882	-.23153	-2.03852	-.28101	.30384	-.14246
.27721	-.04776	.11740	-.17211	1.63483	1.34221
-.40251	-.31052	-1.04834	-.23243	-1.52224	.85903
1.27086	-.93166	.03766	1.21016	.13451	.81941
1.14464	.56176	.89824	1.54670	1.48411	.14422
.04172	1.49673	-.15490	.77084	-.29064	2.87643
-.36795	1.22318	-1.05084	-1.05409	.82052	.09670
1.94110	1.00826	-.85411	-1.31341	-1.85921	.74578
.14946	-2.75470	-.10830	1.02845	.69291	-.78579
.32512	1.11241	.45138	.79940	-.91803	-1.35919
.66748	-.55806	.27694	.80928	-.18061	1.26569
-1.23681	-.49094	.34951	1.66404	.30419	-1.32670
-.57808	-.04187	2.01897	.92651	.10518	-.34227
1.24924	-.98726	-.24277	-.48852	1.14221	-.43447
.38640	-.26990	-.21369	.65047	.27436	-2.30590
.47191	.52304	-1.16670	1.11789	-.10954	1.17787
-1.12401	.24826	.03741	-.72132	-.44131	-1.10636
-.04997	-1.19941	-.63591	1.27889	.69289	-.27419
-.08265	1.08497	.12277	-.61647	-2.74235	1.10660
.28522	.04496	-1.53535	.42616	-.54092	-1.99089
-.60318	-.00926	-1.57852	-.68966	-1.07899	-2.26274
1.66247	-.94171	-1.84672	.14506	-1.79616	-.03350
-.06993	.82752	-1.79937	-.58224	.38834	1.17421
.22572	-.23812 / .15124	1.38760	.97453	-.48264	.42092
2.12500		.22034	1.06353	-.84988	-1.40673
-.51185	-1.35882	1.34636	-.03440	.31133	1.63670
.35724	-1.45402	.16793	1.16726	-.76094	-.38834
-1.29352	-.28185	-.86607	.68714	2.16262	1.82108
.34521	1.16515	-.11361	-1.35778	.16051	.93119
-1.33783	-.28278	-.09756	1.38268	-1.74537	.76566

Appendix C

Areas of the standard normal distribution

An entry in the table is the proportion under the entire curve which is between $z = 0$ and a positive value of z. Areas for negative values of z are obtained by symmetry.

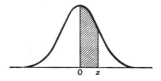

z	.00	.01	.02	.03	.04	.05	.06	.07	.08	.09
0.0	.0000	.0040	.0080	.0120	.0160	.0199	.0239	.0279	.0319	.0359
0.1	.0398	.0438	.0478	.0517	.0557	.0596	.0636	.0675	.0714	.0753
0.2	.0793	.0832	.0871	.0910	.0948	.0987	.1026	.1064	.1103	.1141
0.3	.1179	.1217	.1255	.1293	.1331	.1368	.1406	.1443	.1480	.1517
0.4	.1554	.1591	.1628	.1664	.1700	.1736	.1772	.1808	.1844	.1879
0.5	.1915	.1950	.1985	.2019	.2054	.2088	.2123	.2157	.2190	.2224
0.6	.2257	.2291	.2324	.2357	.2389	.2422	.2454	.2486	.2517	.2549
0.7	.2580	.2611	.2642	.2673	.2703	.2734	.2764	.2794	.2823	.2852
0.8	.2881	.2910	.2939	.2967	.2995	.3023	.3051	.3078	.3106	.3133
0.9	.3159	.3186	.3212	.3238	.3264	.3289	.3315	.3340	.3365	.3389
1.0	.3413	.3438	.3461	.3485	.3508	.3531	.3554	.3577	.3599	.3621
1.1	.3643	.3665	.3686	.3708	.3729	.3749	.3770	.3790	.3810	.3830
1.2	.3849	.3869	.3888	.3907	.3925	.3944	.3962	.3980	.3997	.4015
1.3	.4032	.4049	.4066	.4082	.4099	.4115	.4131	.4147	.4162	.4177
1.4	.4192	.4207	.4222	.4236	.4251	.4265	.4279	.4292	.4306	.4319
1.5	.4332	.4345	.4357	.4370	.4382	.4394	.4406	.4418	.4429	.4441
1.6	.4452	.4463	.4474	.4484	.4495	.4505	.4515	.4525	.4535	.4545
1.7	.4554	.4564	.4573	.4582	.4591	.4599	.4608	.4616	.4625	.4633
1.8	.4641	.4649	.4656	.4664	.4671	.4678	.4686	.4693	.4699	.4706
1.9	.4713	.4719	.4726	.4732	.4738	.4744	.4750	.4756	.4761	.4767
2.0	.4772	.4778	.4783	.4788	.4793	.4798	.4803	.4808	.4812	.4817
2.1	.4821	.4826	.4830	.4834	.4838	.4842	.4846	.4850	.4854	.4857
2.2	.4861	.4864	.4868	.4871	.4875	.4878	.4881	.4884	.4887	.4890
2.3	.4893	.4896	.4898	.4901	.4904	.4906	.4909	.4911	.4913	.4916
2.4	.4918	.4920	.4922	.4925	.4927	.4929	.4931	.4932	.4934	.4936
2.5	.4938	.4940	.4941	.4943	.4945	.4946	.4948	.4949	.4951	.4952
2.6	.4953	.4955	.4956	.4957	.4959	.4960	.4961	.4962	.4963	.4964
2.7	.4965	.4966	.4967	.4968	.4969	.4970	.4971	.4972	.4973	.4974
2.8	.4974	.4975	.4976	.4977	.4977	.4978	.4979	.4979	.4980	.4981
2.9	.4981	.4982	.4982	.4983	.4984	.4984	.4985	.4985	.4986	.4986
3.0	.4987	.4987	.4987	.4988	.4988	.4989	.4989	.4989	.4990	.4990

Source: Paul G. Hoel, *Elementary Statistics* (New York: John Wiley & Sons, 1960), p. 240.

Appendix D

Areas of the cumulative standard normal distribution

An entry in the table is the proportion under the curve cumulated from the negative tail.

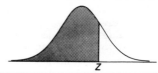

z	$G(z)$	z	$G(z)$	z	$G(z)$
−4.00	0.00003	−3.60	0.00016	−3.20	0.00069
−3.99	0.00003	−3.59	0.00017	−3.19	0.00071
−3.98	0.00003	−3.58	0.00017	−3.18	0.00074
−3.97	0.00004	−3.57	0.00018	−3.17	0.00076
−3.96	0.00004	−3.56	0.00019	−3.16	0.00079
−3.95	0.00004	−3.55	0.00019	−3.15	0.00082
−3.94	0.00004	−3.54	0.00020	−3.14	0.00084
−3.93	0.00004	−3.53	0.00021	−3.13	0.00087
−3.92	0.00004	−3.52	0.00022	−3.12	0.00090
−3.91	0.00005	−3.51	0.00022	−3.11	0.00094
−3.90	0.00005	−3.50	0.00023	−3.10	0.00097
−3.89	0.00005	−3.49	0.00024	−3.09	0.00100
−3.88	0.00005	−3.48	0.00025	−3.08	0.00104
−3.87	0.00005	−3.47	0.00026	−3.07	0.00107
−3.86	0.00006	−3.46	0.00027	−3.06	0.00111
−3.85	0.00006	−3.45	0.00028	−3.05	0.00114
−3.84	0.00006	−3.44	0.00029	−3.04	0.00118
−3.83	0.00006	−3.43	0.00030	−3.03	0.00122
−3.82	0.00007	−3.42	0.00031	−3.02	0.00126
−3.81	0.00007	−3.41	0.00032	−3.01	0.00131
−3.80	0.00007	−3.40	0.00034	−3.00	0.00135
−3.79	0.00008	−3.39	0.00035	−2.99	0.00139
−3.78	0.00008	−3.38	0.00036	−2.98	0.00144
−3.77	0.00008	−3.37	0.00038	−2.97	0.00149
−3.76	0.00008	−3.36	0.00039	−2.96	0.00154
−3.75	0.00009	−3.35	0.00040	−2.95	0.00159
−3.74	0.00009	−3.34	0.00042	−2.94	0.00164
−3.73	0.00010	−3.33	0.00043	−2.93	0.00169
−3.72	0.00010	−3.32	0.00045	−2.92	0.00175
−3.71	0.00010	−3.31	0.00047	−2.91	0.00181
−3.70	0.00011	−3.30	0.00048	−2.90	0.00187
−3.69	0.00011	−3.29	0.00050	−2.89	0.00193
−3.68	0.00012	−3.28	0.00052	−2.88	0.00199
−3.67	0.00012	−3.27	0.00054	−2.87	0.00205
−3.66	0.00013	−3.26	0.00056	−2.86	0.00212
−3.65	0.00013	−3.25	0.00058	−2.85	0.00219
−3.64	0.00014	−3.24	0.00060	−2.84	0.00226
−3.63	0.00014	−3.23	0.00062	−2.83	0.00233
−3.62	0.00015	−3.22	0.00064	−2.82	0.00240
−3.61	0.00015	−3.21	0.00066	−2.81	0.00248

Source: Bernard Ostle, *Statistics in Research*, 2nd ed. (Ames, Iowa: Iowa State University Press, 1967), pp. 517–22.

APPENDIX D
(continued)

z	G(z)	z	(Gz)	z	G(z)
−2.80	0.00256	−2.30	0.01072	−1.80	0.03593
−2.79	0.00264	−2.29	0.01101	−1.79	0.03673
−2.78	0.00272	−2.28	0.01130	−1.78	0.03754
−2.77	0.00280	−2.27	0.01160	−1.77	0.03836
−2.76	0.00289	−2.26	0.01191	−1.76	0.03920
−2.75	0.00298	−2.25	0.01222	−1.75	0.04006
−2.74	0.00307	−2.24	0.01255	−1.74	0.04093
−2.73	0.00317	−2.23	0.01287	−1.73	0.04182
−2.72	0.00326	−2.22	0.01321	−1.72	0.04272
−2.71	0.00336	−2.21	0.01355	−1.71	0.04363
−2.70	0.00347	−2.20	0.01390	−1.70	0.04457
−2.69	0.00357	−2.19	0.01426	−1.69	0.04551
−2.68	0.00368	−2.18	0.01463	−1.68	0.04648
−2.67	0.00379	−2.17	0.01500	−1.67	0.04746
−2.66	0.00391	−2.16	0.01539	−1.66	0.04846
−2.65	0.00402	−2.15	0.01578	−1.65	0.04947
−2.64	0.00415	−2.14	0.01618	−1.64	0.05050
−2.63	0.00427	−2.13	0.01659	−1.63	0.05155
−2.62	0.00440	−2.12	0.01700	−1.62	0.05262
−2.61	0.00453	−2.11	0.01743	−1.61	0.05370
−2.60	0.00466	−2.10	0.01786	−1.60	0.05480
−2.59	0.00480	−2.09	0.01831	−1.59	0.05592
−2.58	0.00494	−2.08	0.01876	−1.58	0.05705
−2.57	0.00508	−2.07	0.01923	−1.57	0.05821
−2.56	0.00523	−2.06	0.01970	−1.56	0.05938
−2.55	0.00539	−2.05	0.02018	−1.55	0.06057
−2.54	0.00554	−2.04	0.02068	−1.54	0.06178
−2.53	0.00570	−2.03	0.02118	−1.53	0.06301
−2.52	0.00587	−2.02	0.02169	−1.52	0.06426
−2.51	0.00604	−2.01	0.02222	−1.51	0.06552
−2.50	0.00621	−2.00	0.02275	−1.50	0.06681
−2.49	0.00639	−1.99	0.02330	−1.49	0.06811
−2.48	0.00657	−1.98	0.02385	−1.48	0.06944
−2.47	0.00676	−1.97	0.02442	−1.47	0.07078
−2.46	0.00695	−1.96	0.02500	−1.46	0.07215
−2.45	0.00714	−1.95	0.02559	−1.45	0.07353
−2.44	0.00734	−1.94	0.02619	−1.44	0.07493
−2.43	0.00755	−1.93	0.02680	−1.43	0.07636
−2.42	0.00776	−1.92	0.02743	−1.42	0.07780
−2.41	0.00798	−1.91	0.02807	−1.41	0.07927
−2.40	0.00820	−1.90	0.02872	−1.40	0.08076
−2.39	0.00842	−1.89	0.02938	−1.39	0.08226
−2.38	0.00866	−1.88	0.03005	−1.38	0.08379
−2.37	0.00889	−1.87	0.03074	−1.37	0.08534
−2.36	0.00914	−1.86	0.03144	−1.36	0.08691
−2.35	0.00939	−1.85	0.03216	−1.35	0.08851
−2.34	0.00964	−1.84	0.03288	−1.34	0.09012
−2.33	0.00990	−1.83	0.03362	−1.33	0.09176
−2.32	0.01017	−1.82	0.03438	−1.32	0.09342
−2.31	0.01044	−1.81	0.03515	−1.31	0.09510

z	$G(z)$	z	$G(z)$	z	$G(z)$
−1.30	0.09680	−0.85	0.19766	−0.40	0.34458
−1.29	0.09853	−0.84	0.20045	−0.39	0.34827
−1.28	0.10027	−0.83	0.20327	−0.38	0.35197
−1.27	0.10204	−0.82	0.20611	−0.37	0.35569
−1.26	0.10383	−0.81	0.20897	−0.36	0.35942
−1.25	0.10565	−0.80	0.21186	−0.35	0.36317
−1.24	0.10749	−0.79	0.21476	−0.34	0.36693
−1.23	0.10935	−0.78	0.21770	−0.33	0.37070
−1.22	0.11123	−0.77	0.22065	−0.32	0.37448
−1.21	0.11314	−0.76	0.22363	−0.31	0.37828
−1.20	0.11507	−0.75	0.22663	−0.30	0.38209
−1.19	0.11702	−0.74	0.22965	−0.29	0.38591
−1.18	0.11900	−0.73	0.23270	−0.28	0.38974
−1.17	0.12100	−0.72	0.23576	−0.27	0.39358
−1.16	0.12302	−0.71	0.23885	−0.26	0.39743
−1.15	0.12507	−0.70	0.24196	−0.25	0.40129
−1.14	0.12714	−0.69	0.24510	−0.24	0.40517
−1.13	0.12924	−0.68	0.24825	−0.23	0.40905
−1.12	0.13136	−0.67	0.25143	−0.22	0.41294
−1.11	0.13350	−0.66	0.25463	−0.21	0.41683
−1.10	0.13567	−0.65	0.25785	−0.20	0.42074
−1.09	0.13786	−0.64	0.26109	−0.19	0.42465
−1.08	0.14007	−0.63	0.26435	−0.18	0.42858
−1.07	0.14231	−0.62	0.26763	−0.17	0.43251
−1.06	0.14457	−0.61	0.27093	−0.16	0.43644
−1.05	0.14686	−0.60	0.27425	−0.15	0.44038
−1.04	0.14917	−0.59	0.27760	−0.14	0.44433
−1.03	0.15150	−0.58	0.28096	−0.13	0.44828
−1.02	0.15386	−0.57	0.28434	−0.12	0.45224
−1.01	0.15625	−0.56	0.28774	−0.11	0.45620
−1.00	0.15866	−0.55	0.29116	−0.10	0.46017
−0.99	0.16109	−0.54	0.29460	−0.09	0.46414
−0.98	0.16354	−0.53	0.29806	−0.08	0.46812
−0.97	0.16602	−0.52	0.30153	−0.07	0.47210
−0.96	0.16853	−0.51	0.30503	−0.06	0.47608
−0.95	0.17106	−0.50	0.30854	−0.05	0.48006
−0.94	0.17361	−0.49	0.31207	−0.04	0.48405
−0.93	0.17619	−0.48	0.31561	−0.03	0.48803
−0.92	0.17879	−0.47	0.31918	−0.02	0.49202
−0.91	0.18141	−0.46	0.32276	−0.01	0.49601
−0.90	0.18406	−0.45	0.32636	0.00	0.50000
−0.89	0.18673	−0.44	0.32997	0.01	0.50399
−0.88	0.18943	−0.43	0.33360	0.02	0.50798
−0.87	0.19215	−0.42	0.33724	0.03	0.51197
−0.86	0.19489	−0.41	0.34090	0.04	0.51595

z	$G(z)$	z	$G(z)$	z	$G(z)$
0.05	0.51994	0.50	0.69146	0.95	0.82894
0.06	0.52392	0.51	0.69497	0.96	0.83147
0.07	0.52790	0.52	0.69847	0.97	0.83398
0.08	0.53188	0.53	0.70194	0.98	0.83646
0.09	0.53586	0.54	0.70540	0.99	0.83891
0.10	0.53983	0.55	0.70884	1.00	0.84134
0.11	0.54380	0.56	0.71226	1.01	0.84375
0.12	0.54776	0.57	0.71566	1.02	0.84614
0.13	0.55172	0.58	0.71904	1.03	0.84850
0.14	0.55567	0.59	0.72240	1.04	0.85083
0.15	0.55962	0.60	0.72575	1.05	0.85314
0.16	0.56356	0.61	0.72907	1.06	0.85543
0.17	0.56749	0.62	0.73237	1.07	0.85769
0.18	0.57142	0.63	0.73565	1.08	0.85993
0.19	0.57535	0.64	0.73891	1.09	0.86214
0.20	0.57926	0.65	0.74215	1.10	0.86433
0.21	0.58317	0.66	0.74537	1.11	0.86650
0.22	0.58706	0.67	0.74857	1.12	0.86864
0.23	0.59095	0.68	0.75175	1.13	0.87076
0.24	0.59483	0.69	0.75490	1.14	0.87286
0.25	0.59871	0.70	0.75804	1.15	0.87493
0.26	0.60257	0.71	0.76115	1.16	0.87698
0.27	0.60642	0.72	0.76424	1.17	0.87900
0.28	0.61026	0.73	0.76730	1.18	0.88100
0.29	0.61409	0.74	0.77035	1.19	0.88298
0.30	0.61791	0.75	0.77337	1.20	0.88493
0.31	0.62172	0.76	0.77637	1.21	0.88686
0.32	0.62552	0.77	0.77935	1.22	0.88877
0.33	0.62930	0.78	0.78230	1.23	0.89065
0.34	0.63307	0.79	0.78524	1.24	0.89251
0.35	0.63683	0.80	0.78814	1.25	0.89435
0.36	0.64058	0.81	0.79103	1.26	0.89617
0.37	0.64431	0.82	0.79389	1.27	0.89796
0.38	0.64803	0.83	0.79673	1.28	0.89973
0.39	0.65173	0.84	0.79955	1.29	0.90147
0.40	0.65542	0.85	0.80234	1.30	0.90320
0.41	0.65910	0.86	0.80511	1.31	0.90490
0.42	0.66276	0.87	0.80785	1.32	0.90658
0.43	0.66640	0.88	0.81057	1.33	0.90824
0.44	0.67003	0.89	0.81327	1.34	0.90988
0.45	0.67364	0.90	0.81594	1.35	0.91149
0.46	0.67724	0.91	0.81859	1.36	0.91309
0.47	0.68082	0.92	0.82121	1.37	0.91466
0.48	0.68439	0.93	0.82381	1.38	0.91621
0.49	0.68793	0.94	0.82639	1.39	0.91774

z	$G(z)$	z	$G(z)$	z	$G(z)$
1.40	0.91924	1.85	0.96784	2.30	0.98928
1.41	0.92073	1.86	0.96856	2.31	0.98956
1.42	0.92220	1.87	0.96926	2.32	0.98983
1.43	0.92364	1.88	0.96995	2.33	0.99010
1.44	0.92507	1.89	0.97062	2.34	0.99036
1.45	0.92647	1.90	0.97128	2.35	0.99061
1.46	0.92785	1.91	0.97193	2.36	0.99086
1.47	0.92922	1.92	0.97257	2.37	0.99111
1.48	0.93056	1.93	0.97320	2.38	0.99134
1.49	0.93189	1.94	0.97381	2.39	0.99158
1.50	0.93319	1.95	0.97441	2.40	0.99180
1.51	0.93448	1.96	0.97500	2.41	0.99202
1.52	0.93574	1.97	0.97558	2.42	0.99224
1.53	0.93699	1.98	0.97615	2.43	0.99245
1.54	0.93822	1.99	0.97670	2.44	0.99266
1.55	0.93943	2.00	0.97725	2.45	0.99286
1.56	0.94062	2.01	0.97778	2.46	0.99305
1.57	0.94179	2.02	0.97831	2.47	0.99324
1.58	0.94295	2.03	0.97882	2.48	0.99343
1.59	0.94408	2.04	0.97932	2.49	0.99361
1.60	0.94520	2.05	0.97982	2.50	0.99379
1.61	0.94630	2.06	0.98030	2.51	0.99396
1.62	0.94738	2.07	0.98077	2.52	0.99413
1.63	0.94845	2.08	0.98124	2.53	0.99430
1.64	0.94950	2.09	0.98169	2.54	0.99446
1.65	0.95053	2.10	0.98214	2.55	0.99461
1.66	0.95154	2.11	0.98257	2.56	0.99477
1.67	0.95254	2.12	0.98300	2.57	0.99492
1.68	0.95352	2.13	0.98341	2.58	0.99506
1.69	0.95449	2.14	0.98382	2.59	0.99520
1.70	0.95543	2.15	0.98422	2.60	0.99534
1.71	0.95637	2.16	0.98461	2.61	0.99547
1.72	0.95728	2.17	0.98500	2.62	0.99560
1.73	0.95818	2.18	0.98537	2.63	0.99573
1.74	0.95907	2.19	0.98574	2.64	0.99585
1.75	0.95994	2.20	0.98610	2.65	0.99598
1.76	0.96080	2.21	0.98645	2.66	0.99609
1.77	0.96164	2.22	0.98679	2.67	0.99621
1.78	0.96246	2.23	0.98713	2.68	0.99632
1.79	0.96327	2.24	0.98745	2.69	0.99643
1.80	0.96407	2.25	0.98778	2.70	0.99653
1.81	0.96485	2.26	0.98809	2.71	0.99664
1.82	0.96562	2.27	0.98840	2.72	0.99674
1.83	0.96638	2.28	0.98870	2.73	0.99683
1.84	0.96712	2.29	0.98899	2.74	0.99693

z	G(z)	z	G(z)	z	G(z)
2.75	0.99702	3.20	0.99931	3.65	0.99987
2.76	0.99711	3.21	0.99934	3.66	0.99987
2.77	0.99720	3.22	0.99936	3.67	0.99988
2.78	0.99728	3.23	0.99938	3.68	0.99988
2.79	0.99736	3.24	0.99940	3.69	0.99989
2.80	0.99744	3.25	0.99942	3.70	0.99989
2.81	0.99752	3.26	0.99944	3.71	0.99990
2.82	0.99760	3.27	0.99946	3.72	0.99990
2.83	0.99767	3.28	0.99948	3.73	0.99990
2.84	0.99774	3.29	0.99950	3.74	0.99991
2.85	0.99781	3.30	0.99952	3.75	0.99991
2.86	0.99788	3.31	0.99953	3.76	0.99992
2.87	0.99795	3.32	0.99955	3.77	0.99992
2.88	0.99801	3.33	0.99957	3.78	0.99992
2.89	0.99807	3.34	0.99958	3.79	0.99992
2.90	0.99813	3.35	0.99960	3.80	0.99993
2.91	0.99819	3.36	0.99961	3.81	0.99993
2.92	0.99825	3.37	0.99962	3.82	0.99993
2.93	0.99831	3.38	0.99964	3.83	0.99994
2.94	0.99836	3.39	0.99965	3.84	0.99994
2.95	0.99841	3.40	0.99966	3.85	0.99994
2.96	0.99846	3.41	0.99968	3.86	0.99994
2.97	0.99851	3.42	0.99969	3.87	0.99995
2.98	0.99856	3.43	0.99970	3.88	0.99995
2.99	0.99861	3.44	0.99971	3.89	0.99995
3.00	0.99865	3.45	0.99972	3.90	0.99995
3.01	0.99869	3.46	0.99973	3.91	0.99995
3.02	0.99874	3.47	0.99974	3.92	0.99996
3.03	0.99878	3.48	0.99975	3.93	0.99996
3.04	0.99882	3.49	0.99976	3.94	0.99996
3.05	0.99886	3.50	0.99977	3.95	0.99996
3.06	0.99889	3.51	0.99978	3.96	0.99996
3.07	0.99893	3.52	0.99978	3.97	0.99996
3.08	0.99897	3.53	0.99979	3.98	0.99997
3.09	0.99900	3.54	0.99980	3.99	0.99997
3.10	0.99903	3.55	0.99981	4.00	0.99997
3.11	0.99906	3.56	0.99981		
3.12	0.99910	3.57	0.99982		
3.13	0.99913	3.58	0.99983		
3.14	0.99916	3.59	0.99983		
3.15	0.99918	3.60	0.99984		
3.16	0.99921	3.61	0.99985		
3.17	0.99924	3.62	0.99985		
3.18	0.99926	3.63	0.99986		
3.19	0.99929	3.64	0.99986		

Appendix E

Negative exponential distribution: Values of e^{-x}

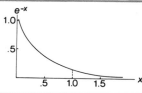

x	e^{-x} (value)	x	e^{-x} (value)	x	e^{-x} (value)	x	e^{-x} (value)
0.00	1.00000	0.50	0.60653	1.00	0.36788	1.50	0.22313
0.01	0.99005	0.51	.60050	1.01	.36422	1.51	.22091
0.02	.98020	0.52	.59452	1.02	.36060	1.52	.21871
0.03	.97045	0.53	.58860	1.03	.35701	1.53	.21654
0.04	.96079	0.54	.58275	1.04	.35345	1.54	.21438
0.05	.95123	0.55	.57695	1.05	.34994	1.55	.21225
0.06	.94176	0.56	.57121	1.06	.34646	1.56	.21014
0.07	.93239	0.57	.56553	1.07	.34301	1.57	.20805
0.08	.92312	0.58	.55990	1.08	.33960	1.58	.20598
0.09	.91393	0.59	.55433	1.09	.33622	1.59	.20393
0.10	.90484	0.60	.54881	1.10	.33287	1.60	.20190
0.11	.89583	0.61	.54335	1.11	.32956	1.61	.19989
0.12	.88692	0.62	.53794	1.12	.32628	1.62	.19790
0.13	.87809	0.63	.53259	1.13	.32303	1.63	.19593
0.14	.86936	0.64	.52729	1.14	.31982	1.64	.19398
0.15	.86071	0.65	.52205	1.15	.31664	1.65	.19205
0.16	.85214	0.66	.51685	1.16	.31349	1.66	.19014
0.17	.84366	0.67	.51171	1.17	.31037	1.67	.18825
0.18	.83527	0.68	.50662	1.18	.30728	1.68	.18637
0.19	.82696	0.69	.50158	1.19	.30422	1.69	.18452
0.20	.81873	0.70	.49659	1.20	.30119	1.70	.18268
0.21	.81058	0.71	.49164	1.21	.29820	1.71	.18087
0.22	.80252	0.72	.48675	1.22	.29523	1.72	.17907
0.23	.79453	0.73	.48191	1.23	.29229	1.73	.17728
0.24	.78663	0.74	.47711	1.24	.28938	1.74	.17552
0.25	.77880	0.75	.47237	1.25	.28650	1.75	.17377
0.26	.77105	0.76	.46767	1.26	.28365	1.76	.17204
0.27	.76338	0.77	.46301	1.27	.28083	1.77	.17033
0.28	.75578	0.78	.45841	1.28	.27804	1.78	.16864
0.29	.74826	0.79	.45384	1.29	.27527	1.79	.16696
0.30	.74082	0.80	.44933	1.30	.27253	1.80	.16530
0.31	.73345	0.81	.44486	1.31	.26982	1.81	.16365
0.32	.72615	0.82	.44043	1.32	.26714	1.82	.16203
0.33	.71892	0.83	.43605	1.33	.26448	1.83	.16041
0.34	.71177	0.84	.43171	1.34	.26185	1.84	.15882
0.35	.70469	0.85	.42741	1.35	.25924	1.85	.15724
0.36	.69768	0.86	.42316	1.36	.25666	1.86	.15567
0.37	.69073	0.87	.41895	1.37	.25411	1.87	.15412
0.38	.68386	0.88	.41478	1.38	.25158	1.88	.15259
0.39	.67706	0.89	.41066	1.39	.24908	1.89	.15107
0.40	.67032	0.90	.40657	1.40	.24660	1.90	.14957
0.41	.66365	0.91	.40252	1.41	.24414	1.91	.14808
0.42	.65705	0.92	.39852	1.42	.24171	1.92	.14661
0.43	.65051	0.93	.39455	1.43	.23931	1.93	.14515
0.44	.64404	0.94	.39063	1.44	.23693	1.94	.14370
0.45	.63763	0.95	.38674	1.45	.23457	1.95	.14227
0.46	.63128	0.96	.38289	1.46	.23224	1.96	.14086
0.47	.62500	0.97	.37908	1.47	.22993	1.97	.13946
0.48	.61878	0.98	.37531	1.48	.22764	1.98	.13807
0.49	.61263	0.99	.37158	1.49	.22537	1.99	.13670
0.50	.60653	1.00	.36788	1.50	.22313	2.00	.13534

Appendix F

Cumulative Poisson distribution

The table lists the probability of c or less. The probability of exactly c is obtained by subtraction (e.g., the probability of exactly $4 = P_4 - P_3$)

Example λ, μ, or $pn = 2.00$

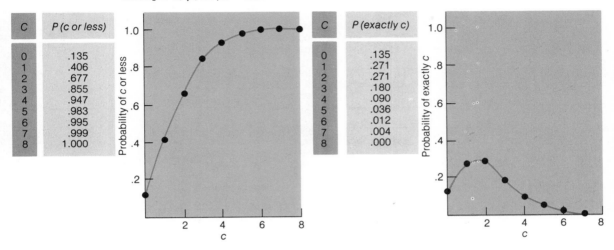

C	P (c or less)
0	.135
1	.406
2	.677
3	.855
4	.947
5	.983
6	.995
7	.999
8	1.000

C	P (exactly c)
0	.135
1	.271
2	.271
3	.180
4	.090
5	.036
6	.012
7	.004
8	.000

APPENDIX F *(continued)*

λ, μ, or *pn* \ *c*	0	1	2	3	4	5	6	7	8
0.02	.980	1.000							
0.04	.961	.999	1.000						
0.06	.942	.998	1.000						
0.08	.923	.997	1.000						
0.10	.905	.995	1.000						
0.15	.861	.990	.999	1.000					
0.20	.819	.982	.999	1.000					
0.25	.779	.974	.998	1.000					
0.30	.741	.963	.996	1.000					
0.35	.705	.951	.994	1.000					
0.40	.670	.938	.992	.999	1.000				
0.45	.638	.925	.989	.999	1.000				
0.50	.607	.910	.986	.998	1.000				
0.55	.577	.894	.982	.998	1.000				
0.60	.549	.878	.977	.997	1.000				
0.65	.522	.861	.972	.996	.999	1.000			
0.70	.497	.844	.966	.994	.999	1.000			
0.75	.472	.827	.959	.993	.999	1.000			
0.80	.449	.809	.953	.991	.999	1.000			
0.85	.427	.791	.945	.989	.998	1.000			
0.90	.407	.772	.937	.987	.998	1.000			
0.95	.387	.754	.929	.984	.997	1.000			
1.00	.368	.736	.920	.981	.996	.999	1.000		
1.1	.333	.699	.900	.974	.995	.999	1.000		
1.2	.301	.663	.879	.966	.992	.998	1.000		
1.3	.273	.627	.857	.957	.989	.998	1.000		
1.4	.247	.592	.833	.946	.986	.997	.999	1.000	
1.5	.223	.558	.809	.934	.981	.996	.999	1.000	
1.6	.202	.525	.783	.921	.976	994	.999	1.000	
1.7	.183	.493	.757	.907	.970	.992	.998	1.000	
1.8	.165	.463	.731	.891	.964	.990	.997	.999	1.000
1.9	.150	.434	.704	.875	.956	.987	.997	.999	1.000
2.0	.135	.406	.677	.857	.947	.983	.995	.999	1.000

APPENDIX F *(continued)*

c λ, μ or pn	0	1	2	3	4	5	6	7	8	9	10	11
2.2	.111	.355	.623	.819	.928	.975	.993	.998	1.000			
2.4	.091	.308	.570	.779	.904	.964	.988	.997	.999	1.000		
2.6	.074	.267	.518	.736	.877	.951	.983	.995	.999	1.000		
2.8	.061	.231	.469	.692	.848	.935	.976	.992	.998	.999	1.000	
3.0	.050	.199	.423	.647	.815	.916	.966	.988	.996	.999	1.000	
3.2	.041	.171	.380	.603	.781	.895	.955	.983	.994	.998	1.000	
3.4	.033	.147	.340	.558	.744	.871	.942	.977	.992	.997	.999	1.000
3.6	.027	.126	.303	.515	.706	.844	.927	.969	.988	.996	.999	1.000
3.8	.022	.107	.269	.473	.668	.816	.909	.960	.984	.994	.998	.999
4.0	.018	.092	.238	.433	.629	.785	.889	949	.979	.992	.997	.999
4.2	.015	.078	.210	.395	.590	.753	.867	.936	.972	.989	.996	.999
4.4	.012	.066	.185	.359	.551	.720	.844	.921	.964	.985	.994	.998
4.6	.010	.056	.163	.326	.513	.686	.818	.905	.955	.980	.992	.997
4.8	.008	.048	.143	.294	.476	.651	.791	.887	.944	.975	.990	.996
5.0	.007	.040	.125	.265	.440	.616	.762	.867	.932	.968	.986	.995
5.2	.006	.034	.109	.238	.406	.581	.732	.845	.918	.960	.982	.993
5.4	.005	.029	.095	.213	.373	.546	.702	.822	.903	.951	.977	.990
5.6	.004	.024	.082	.191	.342	.512	.670	.797	.886	.941	.972	.988
5.8	.003	.021	.072	.170	.313	.478	.638	.771	.867	.929	.965	.984
6.0	.002	.017	.062	.151	.285	.446	.606	.744	.847	.916	.957	.980

	12	13	14	15	16
3.8	1.000				
4.0	1.000				
4.2	1.000				
4.4	.999	1.000			
4.6	.999	1.000			
4.8	.999	1.000			
5.0	.998	.999	1.000		
5.2	.997	.999	1.000		
5.4	.996	.999	1.000		
5.6	.995	.998	.999	1.000	
5.8	.993	.997	.999	1.000	
6.0	.991	.996	.999	.999	1.000

APPENDIX F *(continued)*

λ, μ or p n \ c	0	1	2	3	4	5	6	7	8	9	10	11
6.2	.002	.015	.054	.134	.259	.414	.574	.716	.826	.902	.949	.975
6.4	.002	.012	.046	.119	.235	.384	.542	.687	.803	.886	.939	.969
6.6	.001	.010	.040	.105	.213	.355	.511	.658	.780	.869	.927	.963
6.8	.001	.009	.034	.093	.192	.327	.480	.628	.755	.850	.915	.955
7.0	.001	.007	.030	.082	.173	.301	.450	.599	.729	.830	.901	.947
7.2	.001	.006	.025	.072	.156	.276	.420	.569	.703	.810	.887	.937
7.4	.001	.005	.022	.063	.140	.253	.392	.539	.676	.788	.871	.926
7.6	.001	.004	.019	.055	.125	.231	.365	.510	.648	.765	.854	.915
7.8	.000	.004	.016	.048	.112	.210	.338	.481	.620	.741	.835	.902
8.0	.000	.003	.014	.042	.100	.191	.313	.453	.593	.717	.816	.888
8.5	.000	.002	.009	.030	.074	.150	.256	.386	.523	.653	.763	.849
9.0	.000	.001	.006	.021	.055	.116	.207	.324	.456	.587	.706	.803
9.5	.000	.001	.004	.015	.040	.089	.165	.269	.392	.522	.645	.752
10.0	.000	.000	.003	.010	.029	.067	.130	.220	.333	.458	.583	.697

	12	13	14	15	16	17	18	19	20	21	22
6.2	.989	.995	.998	.999	1.000						
6.4	.986	.994	.997	.999	1.000						
6.6	.982	.992	.997	.999	.999	1.000					
6.8	.978	.990	.996	.998	.999	1.000					
7.0	.973	.987	.994	.998	.999	1.000					
7.2	.967	.984	.993	.997	.999	.999	1.000				
7.4	.961	.980	.991	.996	.998	.999	1.000				
7.6	.954	.976	.989	.995	.998	.999	1.000				
7.8	.945	.971	.986	.993	.997	.999	1.000				
8.0	.936	.966	.983	.992	.996	.998	.999	1.000			
8.5	.909	.949	.973	.986	.993	.997	.999	.999	1.000		
9.0	.876	.926	.959	.978	.989	.995	.998	.999	1.000		
9.5	.836	.898	.940	.967	.982	.991	.996	.998	.999	1.000	
10.0	.792	.864	.917	.951	.973	.986	.993	.997	.998	.999	1.000

APPENDIX F *(continued)*

λ, μ, or $p\,n$ \ c	0	1	2	3	4	5	6	7	8	9	10	11
10.5	.000	.000	.002	.007	.021	.050	.102	.179	.279	.397	.521	.639
11.0	.000	.000	.001	.005	.015	.038	.079	.143	.232	.341	.460	.579
11.5	.000	.000	.001	.003	.011	.028	.060	.114	.191	.289	.402	.520
12.0	.000	.000	.001	.002	.008	.020	.046	.090	.155	.242	.347	.462
12.5	.000	.000	.000	.002	.005	.015	.035	.070	.125	.201	.297	.406
13.0	.000	.000	.000	.001	.004	.011	.026	.054	.100	.166	.252	.353
13.5	.000	.000	.000	.001	.003	.008	.019	.041	.079	.135	.211	.304
14.0	.000	.000	.000	.000	.002	.006	.014	.032	.062	.109	.176	.260
14.5	.000	.000	.000	.000	.001	.004	.010	.024	.048	.088	.145	.220
15.0	.000	.000	.000	.000	.001	.003	.008	.018	.037	.070	.118	.185

	12	13	14	15	16	17	18	19	20	21	22	23
10.5	.742	.825	.888	.932	.960	.978	.988	.994	.997	.999	.999	1.000
11.0	.689	.781	.854	.907	.944	.968	.982	.991	.995	.998	.999	1.000
11.5	.633	.733	.815	.878	.924	.954	.974	.986	.992	.996	.998	.999
12.0	.576	.682	.772	.844	.899	.937	.963	.979	.988	.994	.997	.999
12.5	.519	.628	.725	.806	.869	.916	.948	.969	.983	.991	.995	.998
13.0	.463	.573	.675	.764	.835	.890	.930	.957	.975	.986	.992	.996
13.5	.409	.518	.623	.718	.798	.861	.908	.942	.965	.980	.989	.994
14.0	.358	.464	.570	.669	.756	.827	.883	.923	.952	.971	.983	.991
14.5	.311	.413	.518	.619	.711	.790	.853	.901	.936	.960	.976	.986
15.0	.268	.363	.466	.568	.664	.749	.819	.875	.917	.947	.967	.981

	24	25	26	27	28	29
11.5	1.000					
12.0	.999	1.000				
12.5	.999	.999	1.000			
13.0	.998	.999	1.000			
13.5	.997	.998	.999	1.000		
14.0	.995	.997	.999	.999	1.000	
14.5	.992	.996	.998	.999	.999	1.000
15.0	.989	.994	.997	.998	.999	1.000

APPENDIX F *(continued)*

c λ, μ, or p n	5	6	7	8	9	10	11	12	13	14	15
16	.001	.004	.010	.022	.043	.077	.127	.193	.275	.368	.467
17	.001	.002	.005	.013	.026	.049	.085	.135	.201	.281	.371
18	.000	.001	.003	.007	.015	.030	.055	.092	.143	.208	.287
19	.000	.001	.002	.004	.009	.018	.035	.061	.098	.150	.215
20	.000	.000	.001	.002	.005	.011	.021	.039	.066	.105	.157
21	.000	.000	.000	.001	.003	.006	.013	.025	.043	.072	.111
22	.000	.000	.000	.001	.002	.004	.008	.015	.028	.048	.077
23	.000	.000	.000	.000	.001	.002	.004	.009	.017	.031	.052
24	.000	.000	.000	.000	.000	.001	.003	.005	.011	.020	.034
25	.000	.000	.000	.000	.000	.001	.001	.003	.006	.012	.022

	16	17	18	19	20	21	22	23	24	25	26
16	.566	.659	.742	.812	.868	.911	.942	.963	.978	.987	.993
17	.468	.564	.655	.736	.805	.861	.905	.937	.959	.975	.985
18	.375	.469	.562	.651	.731	.799	.855	.899	.932	.955	.972
19	.292	.378	.469	.561	.647	.725	.793	.849	.893	.927	.951
20	.221	.297	.381	.470	.559	.644	.721	.787	.843	.888	.922
21	.163	.227	.302	.384	.471	.558	.640	.716	.782	.838	.883
22	.117	.169	.232	.306	.387	.472	.556	.637	.712	.777	.832
23	.082	.123	.175	.238	.310	.389	.472	.555	.635	.708	.772
24	.056	.187	.128	.180	.243	.314	.392	.473	.554	.632	.704
25	.038	.060	.092	.134	.185	.247	.318	.394	.473	.553	.629

	27	28	29	30	31	32	33	34	35	36	37
16	.996	.998	.999	.999	1.000						
17	.991	.995	.997	.999	.999	1.000					
18	.983	.990	.994	.997	.998	.999	1.000				
19	.969	.980	.988	.993	.996	.998	.999	.999	1.000		
20	.948	.966	.978	.987	.992	.995	.997	.999	.999	1.000	
21	.917	.944	.963	.976	.985	.991	.994	.997	.998	.999	.999
22	.877	.913	.940	.959	.973	.983	.989	.994	.996	.998	.999
23	.827	.373	.908	.936	.956	.971	.981	.988	.993	.996	.997
24	.768	.823	.868	.904	.932	.953	.969	.979	.987	.992	.995
25	.700	.763	.818	.863	.900	.929	.950	.966	.978	.985	.991

	38	39	40	41	42	43
21	1.000					
22	.999	1.000				
23	.999	.999	1.000			
24	.997	.998	.999	.999	1.000	
25	.994	.997	.998	.999	.999	1.000

Indexes

AUTHOR INDEX

SUBJECT INDEX

733

*This book has been set VideoComp in 10 and 9
point Compano, leaded 2 points. Section numbers are
20 point Compano Semi-Bold Oblique and section
titles are 28 point Compano Oblique. Chapter numer-
als are 72 point Caslon Old Style #540 italic.
Chapter titles are 20 point Compano. The size of
the type area is 37 by 48 picas.*